Lyn Birkbeck is a professional astrologer
specializing in relationship issues.
He is author of the bestselling *Do It Yourself Astrology*.

by the same author
Do It Yourself Astrology

DO IT YOURSELF
RELATIONSHIP ASTROLOGY

Lyn Birkbeck

ELEMENT

Shaftesbury, Dorset • Boston, Massachusetts • Melbourne, Victoria

First published in the UK in 1999 by
Element Books Limited
Shaftesbury, Dorset SP7 8BP

Published in the USA in 1999 by
Element Books, Inc.
160 North Washington Street
Boston, MA 02114

Published in Australia in 1999 by
Element Books and distributed
by Penguin Australia Limited
487 Maroondah Highway, Ringwood,
Victoria 3134

Cover design and illustration Slatter-Anderson
Designed and typeset by PPG Design and Print Ltd.
Printed and bound in the USA

British Library Cataloguing in Publication
data available

Library of Congress Cataloging in Publication
data available

ISBN 1 86204 372 8

Eternal thanks to ...

My partner, Talia, for shadow-catching, ground-floor editing, and her love.

My mother for suffering to bring me here.

Michael, Florence, Matthew and all the other Elementals who helped make this book a reality.

CONTENTS

PART ONE

CHAPTER ONE – An Astrological View of Relationship 3

   Relating in the Aquarian Age 5

   Reunion 7

   Planets of Love – Love's Eleven 11

      The Sun 12

      The Moon 13

      Mercury 14

      Venus 15

      Mars 16

      Jupiter 17

      Saturn 18

      Uranus 19

      Neptune 20

      Pluto 21

      The Earth 22

CHAPTER TWO – The Individual 23

   The Relationship You have with Yourself 25

   How to Read the Tables 26

      The Chartwheel 27

      Entering the Planets on the Chartwheel 28

      The Tables for the Sun, Moon and Planet-Sign Positions 31

   The Planet-Sign Profiles 147

      The Sun 149

      The Moon 163

      Mercury 177

      Venus 185

      Mars 199

      Jupiter 213

      Saturn 227

      Uranus, Neptune and Pluto 241

   Rising Sign – Setting Sign 243

      Rising Sign Tables and how to use them 247

      Rising and Setting Sign Profiles 263

      Ruling Planets 276

      Your Underlying Attitude to Relationship 277

PART TWO

CHAPTER THREE – The Interaction 281

The Interaction 283

Sign-to-Sign Interaction 285

   Sign-to-Sign Interaction (and Relationship Theme) Chart 286

The Sign-to-Sign Profiles 289

Planet-to-Planet Interaction 303

How to use the Planet-to-Planet Profiles 306

The Planet-to-Planet Profiles Index 309

The Planet-to-Planet Profiles 315

   The Sun 317

   The Moon 343

   Mercury 365

   Venus 385

   Mars 403

   Jupiter 419

   Saturn 433

   Uranus 445

   Neptune 455

   Pluto 463

   Ascendant 469

The Final Focus 473

   Planet-to-Planet Interaction – Final Focus Chart 475

   Focal Planet Ready-Reckoner 478

Keyword Corner 483

The Mirror 485

CHAPTER FOUR – The Relationship 489

The Third Entity 491

The Relationship Theme 493

The 12 Laws or Themes of the Zodiac 497

The Relationship Dynamic 511

APPENDIX 515

Glossary 517

Blank charts 523

Resources 530

Only in relationship can you know yourself,
not in abstraction, and certainly not in isolation.
The movement of behaviour is the sure guide to yourself, it's the mirror of your consciousness;
the mirror will reveal its contents, its images, the attachments, the fears, the loneliness, the joy, and the sorrow.
Poverty lies in running away from this ...

J Krishnamurti

The difficulty lies in the terrible fact that individual relationships are based in
emotional investments ... In the everyday world, emotional investments are not normally examined,
and we live an entire lifetime waiting to be reciprocated.

Carlos Castaneda

Let the winds of the heavens dance between you.
from *The Prophet* by Kahlil Gibran

The greatest thing you can ever learn
is to love and be loved in return.
from *Nature Boy* by Eden Ahbez

HOW THIS BOOK WORKS

DO IT YOURSELF
RELATIONSHIP ASTROLOGY
is in two parts

PART ONE

Introduces you to how astrology sees and explores Relationship

•

Tells you what and how anyone attracts and relates as an Individual

•

Involves virtually *no calculations* – just look up and learn

PART TWO

Discovers the nature of the chemistry between one person and another

•

Looks at the Theme and Dynamics of the Relationship itself

•

Involves *simple calculation* and some *application*

PART ONE

How astrology sees and explores Relationship

●

What and how anyone attracts and relates as an Individual

●

No calculations – just look up and learn

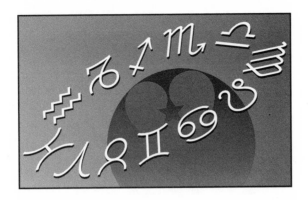

Chapter One

AN ASTROLOGICAL VIEW OF RELATIONSHIP

When first I saw Her Star
Rising over the fields of my longing –
At last! – there you are,
The dream of my wandering,
Coming to meet me now,
Coming to show me how …

from *VENUS – Planet of Attraction, Loving and Relating*

RELATING IN THE AQUARIAN AGE

A common misconception often occurs when using astrology to explore relationships. This is that one can somehow choose a certain astrological type who will be 'compatible', and with whom one will enjoy a harmonious relationship that has both security and excitement, with a minimum of conflict, instability or boredom. Unfortunately – or perhaps not – choosing partners, let alone family, is not like selecting a carpet that matches the rest of the room, or buying a car that gets you where you want to get to in comfort and style.

Significant others in your life are chosen in the Unconscious, or by Fate. This means that, at any given moment, what and where you are determines who or what you are going to attract, happen upon, collide with, meet again, or be born to and into. In other words, the real determinant of what and who you are involved with – or not! – is your mental, emotional, physical and spiritual states. Astrology will tell you about these states.

A cursory look at relationship through history shows us that at first the male simply sought and secured a mate who possessed certain qualities, whether physically attractive or practical ones. In time, the rituals of courting and the customs of family-raising and society-building became more firmly established and, from culture to culture, more sophisticated.

For quite some time now – around 800 years – Western culture has been under the sway of something called Romantic Love. This began, more or less, with the courtly love of knights and the ladies (not their wives) whom they championed and pledged themselves to in a pure and chaste way. Over the centuries this practice of the upper classes filtered through to the lower ones – and became intermixed with sex and family-raising in the process. If this wasn't getting confusing enough, at the beginning of the twentieth century along came Hollywood. The idea that a certain someone was the ideal partner and the perfect human being got firmly ensconced in our collective consciousness – or unconsciousness, more like. With such a rosy screen cast over what is actually going on between two human beings, it was only a matter of time before some kind of reappraisal and readjustment was deemed necessary – by the Unconscious.

In astrological terms, this readjustment is part and parcel of what is called the Age of Aquarius, a 2160-year period of which we are now on the brink. Astrological Ages all last this amount of time, and they mark periods when new values are first introduced, then installed and stabilized, and finally phased out as they become less and less appropriate to the Evolution of the Species. While the tail end of the Age before Aquarius, Pisces, witnesses the emotional and religious illusions of over 2,000 years going critical, incipient Aquarius is already refreshing and disrupting the masses with new views, ideas and values.

Aquarius is the Water Bearer, and Picture 1 graphically and symbolically shows how this process of refreshment operates in two ways. On a personal level, we can now view the nature of relating as the make-up of one person being mingled together with the make-up of another. On a collective level, we see each individual's new or previously unexpressed thoughts and feelings being pooled and contained as the new culture. Initially, this is rather experimental, and as this in-pouring proceeds, it naturally disturbs what has been lying there for some time – the somewhat stagnant waters of the

Piscean Age. This is one way of seeing the current social and emotional confusion: an utterly necessary part of clearing out the old and bringing in the new. Humanity is being reminded, and reminding itself, of its true and spiritual nature, through each person honestly sharing their inner selves with whoever resonates with them, wherever the opportunity presents itself. At the very time of writing this, the world is mourning the tragic death of Princess Diana. One of the main things that she seems to be remembered for is her 'giving people permission to be human', as one lady so aptly put it. This was the great contribution made to the Aquarian Age by the 'People's Princess' – who was a Cancerian with her Moon in Aquarius.

Many of us are aware, like Princess Diana obviously was, of how spiritually starved – and therefore physically damaged and emotionally needy – most of society is. This means many things, but most significantly – at least in the context of this book – that this lack of awareness can cause us to feel alone and separate from one another. But just because we may have forgotten what Spirit is and means – or that it even exists – does not mean that Spirit has forgotten us!

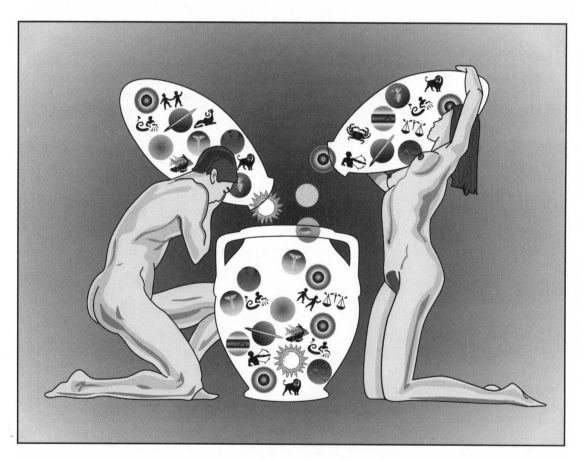

Picture 1: **Relating in the Aquarian Age**

Each INDIVIDUAL commits varying amounts of themselves to other people. Here the Planets and Zodiacal Signs represent parts of their personalities and lives. These parts or energies interact with one another. This INTERACTION progressively forms a third entity, which is the RELATIONSHIP itself. This picture also symbolizes the process during the Aquarian Age whereby individuals of all races, classes and creeds – and both sexes – share and pool previously unexpressed thoughts and feelings, thus creating a new society and culture. Inevitably, the old order of the waning Piscean Age is disrupted as it is replaced by Aquarian energies and ethics.

REUNION

All relationships are spiritual in that they are all in aid of Reunion, Reunion being the Force and Process through which Humanity seeks to become once again conscious of its great Oneness. This is a powerful force and a very long process.

Following upon this, relationships fall into two main types: family-raising and consciousness-raising. Bearing in mind that the two types are not mutually exclusive – quite the opposite in fact – here is a brief description of each type.

Family-raising

In order for Humanity to pursue the ages-long process of Reunion, a constant supply of human beings is necessary. So that these young humans become loving, caring and able to relate, their mothers and fathers themselves need to set a good example of seeking Reunion.

Consciousness-raising

In order that Humanity might eventually reach Reunion, each individual has to learn to love and know him/herself enough for the ego boundaries of fear that keep us divided to be dissolved and surrendered. Consciousness-raising relationships can take place within the light and dark of an individual's own being. However, a relationship with another has the advantage of keeping one mindful of one's own Shadow process. The Shadow process is the unconscious way in which a person expresses and projects on to others sides of their own nature of which they are unconscious; these are usually negative, but not always. It is possibly more accurate to say that one regards a certain trait as negative and, by keeping it in the dark, it actually becomes negative. A partner will, consciously or unconsciously, act as a Mirror that reflects this process. THE 'VENOUS BLOOD SYNDROME' is the name I give to this process. Venous blood is the deoxygenated blood in your body that is returning to the lungs for re-oxygenation. It is purplish in colour, but people are often surprised to discover this, saying that they have never bled any purple blood. This is because if you cut a vein, the blood immediately hits the air and is re-oxygenated, turning bright red. The metaphor here is that what we regard as negative in ourselves (the deoxygenated blood in need of regeneration) we are inclined to keep to ourselves until we are attacked or wounded. If we then let the 'blood' out, it changes into something (more) positive because we have 'aired' it.

This process of Shadow Projection could be regarded as the true Original Sin. In terms of the Christian Myth of the Garden of Eden, when after eating the fruit of the Tree of the Knowledge of Good and Evil, Adam and Eve were ashamed of their nakedness when God discovered them. God then cast them out of the Garden – *not* because they had eaten of the Fruit and discovered their nakedness, but because they *felt* they had done wrong. In other words, if you judge yourself to be guilty (for being vulnerable and merely human), you will be treated as such and lose what you value above all else.

Spirit most definitely wants us to all get back together again as a divinely functioning whole that will grace this Planet rather than be a disgrace to Her. And so Spirit conspires to reunite us through that channel we find so irresistible or unavoidable: the one-to-one relationship.

But for this spiritual process of Reunion to be successful, we have to co-operate with it. This can be difficult, because we have either grown neurotically attached to being separate and responsible only to ourselves, or at the other extreme, our attempts to get more intimately involved with another are confused and obscured by romantic and mass media driven notions of what relating is all about. Or simply by a sheer ignorance of our own human nature. Astrology is the mirror to human nature.

So what is relating all about? Astrology responds to this question as it responds to everything – by reflecting back at us what we already know just beneath the surface of our consciousness. The most important part of this response is based upon something that is absolutely fundamental to astrology, and life as we perceive it – Duality.

DUALITY = ONE and OTHER

When there is One then there will always be Other – a point which is totally relevant to the subject of relating.

So throughout this book we'll return again and again to the theme of Duality, of One and Other – for these long to be reunited (*see* below and Picture 2, The Divine Ellipse, on the page opposite). I will often use the word 'Other' rather than 'partner' because this book is aimed at all forms of personal relationship, not just sexual/romantic ones. Because the latter attracts the most interest and presents the most problems, I have placed the greater emphasis upon these relationships. At the same time I have done my best to cater to the issues that arise from interactions with family members, friends, colleagues, pets, and even inanimate objects. And Other can also refer to someone you have not yet met! They are all Other – that is someone or something that is perceived as being separate to One. With regard to homosexual relationships, I have not made specific allowances for them as it would just make the text too complicated – but adapting it to fit such relationships should not be too difficult.

The magnificent point that astrology makes is that ONE IS NOT SEPARATE FROM OTHER. ONE IS SEPARATE FROM THE PART OF ONESELF THAT IS NOT RECOGNIZED AS BELONGING TO ONESELF – either by oneself or others. And so Spirit, Fate or the Unconscious will ceaselessly endeavour to reunite us with that part through what appears to be Other – another human being, animal or thing.

THE DIVINE ELLIPSE

This is an ancient image of the process whereby Humanity loses itself and eventually finds itself again. Being 'banished from the Garden' is a theme in more than just the Bible myth. Man comes to Earth, innocent and free, to dwell in the Garden of Eden. He then becomes self-conscious and loses his natural innocence, which is replaced by guilt – the Fall. We have been playing out our guilt for millennia, projecting it upon one another until a great rift has been created. This is the Vale of Sorrow or Vale of Tears – or in more modern parlance, the Battle of the Sexes – that we all are travelling through as part of our Process of Evolution (represented by ———▶). Some say we are now at the point of maximum separation, and can now only get closer again, and ultimately reach Reunion. It is also mooted that homo- and bisexuality are vague echoes of Eden or even before that when the human type was androgynous (the Divine Androgyne), as well as being confused pre-echoes of Reunion. Whether any of this is true or not, who's to say, but it certainly has a ring about it.

'EDEN'
PARADISE
LOST –
BEFORE
THE FALL

THE DIVINE ELLIPSE
OR
VALE OF SORROW

'REUNION'
PARADISE
REGAINED –
CREATION AS
ONE THING

Astrology, as a map and mapper of the Unconscious, is therefore a highly important aid towards Reunion.

So to be 'compatible' with anyone is entirely a reflection of how compatible you are with yourself – *all* of yourself, not just the part you think of as yourself, your ego. The ego is a false or, at least, incomplete sense of self.

And as for the actual meaning of the word, 'compatible' means *to be able to suffer with*. In this book, I will try to show you, through astrology, how relating is worth the suffering, and that relating is life's lessons in the learning – and that these lessons are worth studying.

Picture 2: **The Vale of Sorrow or Divine Ellipse**

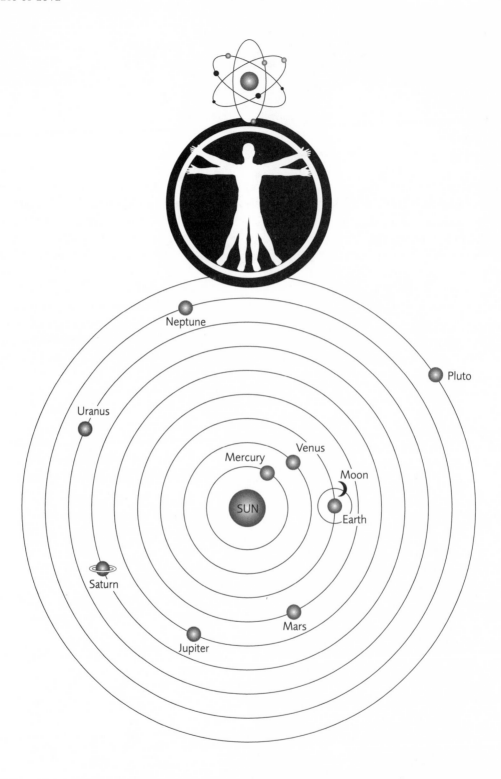

Picture 3: **Word magic: PLANETS = TEN LAPS = SET PLAN**

PLANETS OF LOVE
LOVE'S ELEVEN

The Sun, Moon and Planets work and play together like a team. They relate perfectly. The Solar System is like a family or society that is living, moving and changing in dynamic equilibrium – constantly. Astrology can show us how to do the same by modelling ourselves on this greater whole, for each Planet represents and reflects a part of us as individual human beings. 'As above, so below' – the Greater is mirrored in the Smaller. This is plainly seen in the fact that the structure and movement of the Solar System is identical to that of an atom – a nucleus or central body orbited by electrons or other bodies – and that, between the two, a human being is exactly midway in size. Picture 3 on page 10 illustrates this; the Planets orbit the central Sun in an anti-clockwise direction, as does the Moon around the Earth.

In order that you may identify with these perfectly relating entities, the Planets of Love, they are described in this section both as they stand alone and in Relationship. Words in *italics* are keywords for that planet. Remember that all of these Planetary Laws apply to ALL Sun Signs as universal guidelines to living and loving. However, you may well identify more with the Planet which rules your Sun Sign or Rising Sign (*see* page 243). If you do not know the Ruling Planet of each Sign, here they are:

SIGN	RULING PLANET		SIGN	RULING PLANET
Aries	Mars		**Libra**	Venus
Taurus	Venus		**Scorpio**	Pluto
Gemini	Mercury		**Sagittarius**	Jupiter
Cancer	Moon		**Capricorn**	Saturn
Leo	Sun		**Aquarius**	Uranus
Virgo	Mercury		**Pisces**	Neptune

> You will discover the meaning of the Planets of Love for you as an individual in Chapter 2 by finding out their Sign positions at your time of birth

THE SUN • *Love of Life*

The Sun is the Creator of everything – 'Life-Truth blazed in the sky'. The dying words of the celebrated painter William Turner were 'The Sun is God'. Astrologically, the Sun therefore represents your *life* itself, and what is *generating it* – your *heart* and *spirit* – which is more than you know. The 12 Signs of the Zodiac are rather like the 12 chapters in a year of the Sun's life as experienced here on Earth. So your Sun Sign is a general indication of what kind of life you have to lead and *play* out. As the Sun touches every planet in its system with its rays, so too does the Sun in your chart affect every part of your being which the planets represent.

IN RELATIONSHIP the Sun can be the *warm light* of your heart that shows the way, or it can be the harsh light of your *ego* which obscures it. Being true to the Sun – that is, following the deepest dictates of your heart – will enable you to manage not only your relationships strongly and successfully, but all other areas of your life too. Following the path that is *illuminated* by your Sun Sign (*see* Sun Profiles on pages 149 – 61) will help you do just this. Regard this as a directive from the highest *command*.

Merely following your ego – that is, a false sense of what you are – will blind you to who you truly are. If you are blind to who you really are, then you will also be blind to who Other is and what they are doing in your life. The ego is a false god who has usurped the real thing. It is the author of most, if not all, of Humanity's problems. Humanity is, after all, a gigantic set of relationships. Any relationship of yours is therefore contributing to the state of Humanity, in the same way that the Sun shines on all, *vitalizing* or *dominating, warming* or *burning*.

Your Sun is the light which sheds itself upon Other. It is powerful and effective, whether you know it or not. Someone with a weak *will* and little *confidence* may not have such an obvious effect as someone who is a stronger *individual,* but they do have a significant influence because they elicit a response from the *'strong'*. The 'strong' can dominate the 'weak' or protect them, overwhelm them or strengthen them. If you feel you are the weaker half of a relationship it is probably because you have not yet noticed the effect that you have on Other. The more you observe this, then the more conscious you become of your life in terms of its significance and *importance*. You may not like some of what you see – but that is probably why you never felt like looking! But persist and you will progressively see how you can be more positive and *creative* in the way that you relate, and be someone in your own right. The Sun for many people is rather like a torch they do not realize that they are holding. This is very likely owing to some authority in your life – often your *father* – that has given a negative impression and/or suppressed your own self-expression.

Good examples of the Sun in the form of *generosity* and *dignity, respect* and *strength,* go a long way to giving Other a better idea of life and people generally. Your own father will have probably given you a mixture of both the bad and the good examples, but this would be entirely in accord with your own Sun Profile. For instance, a tyrannical father would indicate that your *inner core* was in need of strengthening or purifying itself. A kind father would be someone to look up to – but he may have been weak too, indicating that you would need to be more sure of yourself. Your relationship with your father strongly affects how you manage your relationships, or whether Other does that, or whether you do it together like two equal Suns shining as One.

PLANETS OF LOVE

THE MOON • *Love of Feeling*

The Moon is your *soul* – the realm of *feelings, dreams* and *memories*. It is your *personal unconscious,* your *past,* your *eternal and inner child.* It is also the *care* of such tender things in yourself and others, and also meeting the *need* for *security, familiarity* and *comfort.* The Moon is the *Mother* – whether you are male or female, an actual mother or not. The Moon can also be looked at as being the Sun in the chart from your previous lifetime. So, if I have my Moon in Aries now, that means I had Sun in Aries then. Whether you believe in reincarnation or not, this gives a good feel of what the Moon is – a memory of how and who you once were filtering through as a *predisposition* to the present.

IN RELATIONSHIP how your Moon *behaves, responds* and *reacts* is vitally important. Love of Feeling means recognizing and *nurturing* these Lunar qualities in yourself and Other – but without becoming a victim or slave to unmet *childhood needs* in yourself or Other. True Love of Feeling cannot exist without an awareness of the state of the soul – be it of an adult (which means his or her inner child) or of an actual child. Without this awareness, which unfortunately is poor in most cases, relationships become a battleground where your hurt and unrecognized *feelings* from the past vie in vain for attention and concern from Other, who is doing exactly the same thing with you. Needless to say, negative childhood feelings surfacing in this manner turn into *resentment, defensiveness* and *alienation.* When functioning positively in a relationship, our Moons can, like children, spontaneously play together – hence the 'baby-talk' of people in love.

The child, inner or actual, is the fragile *membrane* between the person and their soul. Love of Feeling is to be aware of and sympathetically in touch with this membrane. If the membrane has been damaged, feelings will either be denied and hardened (like a blocked *waterway*), or become *over-sensitive* (like an unchecked *flood*). As a result, relationships become unstable, or *dependent* upon one person doing most or all of the *caring.* To halt this negative pattern of behaviour, recourse to therapy or counselling may well be necessary.

Love of Feeling needs to exist for a healthy relationship to do so too. To create it – or simply maintain the feeling of care and *tenderness* that is felt upon most initial encounters that are *emotionally* significant, like falling in love or having a *baby* – we must consciously focus upon what we and Other are feeling, with *tenderness* in our hearts.

Women are usually far more in touch with the Moon than men are, if only for the simple reason that their bodies are attuned to the Moon by the *menstrual cycle.* It is highly important at this time in human evolution for men to recognize and attune to the Moon – their feelings – but without falling into a dependency upon the woman as Mother. The male obsession with *breasts* is symptomatic of a need for emotional nurturance that is being denied and displaced into sexuality. If you think how large breasts appear to a suckling baby then you get some idea of why our preoccupation with them being big rather than small came into being. The reason why it is more so of late is possibly because we are more insecure than we have been for a long, long time. This would account for there also being a female obsession here, but in addition this would be owing to the need to be attractive towards men, or to be too caring by way of compensation.

PLANETS OF LOVE

MERCURY • *Love of Words*

Mercury is how you *communicate* – which would include how you *listen* and *interpret* the *words* being said to you. We learn to communicate from very early on in life, particularly with *brothers and sisters*, and of course at *school*. Mercury is the *mental* way in which you *perceive, map out, identify* and *categorize* your thoughts, feelings, sensations and intuitions. In myth, Mercury is the Messenger of the Gods – not a god in himself. This means to say that what we make of life, ourselves and others, is only that – what we make of them – not necessarily the thing itself. What they actually are is usually far more complex and indeterminate than our faculties of perception and *reason* are able to appreciate.

IN RELATIONSHIP saying the wrong thing or the right thing can at times be utterly critical. It may only be one inappropriate word being used at a crucial moment that will make the difference between accord and discord, success or failure. On the other hand, we can sweet-talk or be sweet-talked, and be totally seduced purely by what someone is saying. Words are like fingers pushing buttons. Get the right combination and 'Open sesame!' – you have talked your way into someone's emotional and/or mental interior. Whether your actions and style can live up to this is another matter – so too can be whether or not you want to stay in the place you so cleverly talked your way into. In the end then, it is your inner state rather than what you say that matters – or rather it is how much in touch you are with that inner state that determines how you verbally express it. If there is little or no *connection* of this kind, someone with the 'gift of the gab' can make an impression on another but, like a single coat of paint, it won't last very long. All of this is only too apparent when we consider that if a bond of trust is broken, nothing you say, however well-informed or well-put, will make much difference towards re-establishing contact.

Ultimately, the trick with Mercury is being able to listen to yourself – before expecting anyone to understand what you are trying to communicate to them. Often the trouble is that our sense of our real inner selves and feelings is perceived a bit like over-hearing one end of a *telephone* conversation. This is reminiscent of the scientific finding that we say 60 per cent of what we mean, and of this, 60 per cent is understood by Other. This means that most communications are only 36 per cent (60 per cent of 60 per cent) effective. The most Mercurial way of increasing this rate is to improve that first 60 per cent by *writing* down what you think you feel. In the process, you will invariably find that what you thought was one thing is really another, and what you thought was clear-cut resembles *reading* a newspaper at the bottom of a well.

A disinclination to take the trouble to make *contact* with yourself, in this or some other way, would indicate a reluctance to know yourself. This amounts to a reluctance to know Other. This is how people lose touch with one another – through losing touch with themselves.

In myth, Mercury is a *mischievous* sort of guy. He would sometimes edit what one god was saying to another for his own reasons, or just for laughs. In our reality, this is equivalent to *rationalizing* our feelings to the point of not recognizing what or how we feel. We also sometimes make fun or light of how we feel or how Other feels – because we cannot emotionally accommodate it. It is well worth remembering to 'clip Mercury's wings' regularly by resisting the impulse to label how we feel. Let the feeling have its head – but without letting it run away with you – then you will know how to express it, verbally or otherwise.

VENUS • *Love of Harmony*

Venus is *beauty* and *pleasure* – which can be merely skin-deep, but often has more to do with an inner *quality* of being. In both cases, *harmony* is what creates the beauty or the pleasure. In the first case it is a harmony that is merely *superficial,* like room-spray masking a bad smell, or pretty wallpaper covering cracks – or more to the point, *good looks* hiding a weak personality. In the second case, it has more to do with *grace.* Grace is a state of being that is *socially* and/or *artistically* attuned to what truly constitutes harmony, whether it is between two people or in a musical composition. The pleasure side of Venus can also become perverted into sheer *indulgence* and *affectation,* or be something which has been bought for a *price,* rather than done out of love. Positively, it is *appreciativeness, generosity* and *affection.* In the end, Venus is all about *value* and *values,* and whether or not they are sound or questionable.

IN RELATIONSHIP Venus is the planet which is actually running the show, for Venus represents harmony, and harmony is what relating and *relationships* are mostly about. Having said this though, it is always important to bear in mind that sooner or later one has to go though conflict in order to reach or establish true harmony, or grace as described above. Falling in *love* with love, just being *nice* and wanting to *please* and *be pleased,* or to have peace at any price – these are some of the expressions of Venus which are not harmony of the true and tried variety. This version of Venus could be called *fancy,* for such notions of love and harmony are fanciful and not based upon sincere feelings or real values. Unfortunately, Western culture is currently infected with these superficial values – that anything can be bought for a price, or obtained immediately like fast-food – and the difficulties that most relationships find themselves in bear witness to this state of affairs.

And so it is very much an issue of 'false' Venus/values or 'true' Venus/values – something which is only too commonly the case with relationships. A lover, friend or family member can be false, or they can be true. Everything depends upon the *worth* you are ascribing to another person, a relationship or, most of all, yourself. Venus is about *attracting* and being *attracted,* so if you feel worthwhile as a person, then to the same degree you will attract a worthwhile partner and relationship. If you have little or no sense of your emotional or physical worth, then all too often you will attract someone who under-values and fails to appreciate you.

Venus is also symbolic of *female sexuality,* the hallmarks of which are *sensuous appeal* and *mysterious allure.* This stresses that femininity is something which draws things to it, as distinct from masculinity (Mars) which goes and gets things. This is not to say that Venus is exclusive to females, any more than Mars is exclusive to males. The presence of what Jung called the 'anima', or the feminine nature within a male, is something that the position of Venus (along with the Moon) indicates the nature of. The anima is what determines for a man the kind of female he is attracted to. Conversely, the 'animus' or the masculine within a woman, and the kind of male to whom she is attracted, is revealed by her Sun and Mars position (*see* pages 149 – 61 and 199 – 211).

Developing one's artistic, *aesthetic* and *social* talents, is a sound way of increasing your sense of self-esteem and being worthy of love. Above all, the best way to find harmony with Other is through *sharing* both one's Light and Shadow.

MARS • *Love of Action*

Mars is the *impulse* to *act* and *get*. Mars is *raw energy, desire, decisiveness* and *self-assertion*. Before anything can happen in life, something has to *move* in the direction of making it happen. There are people who make very little happen of their own volition, depending upon others to make things happen. But even they would have to *want* something before long. Even moving their hand or just saying something would entail the *desire* to do so, then the *decision* to do so, and finally the *energy* and *muscles* to do so. Such people are very possibly lacking in the *courage* to accept the consequences of their own *actions*. There is probably a good reason for this in their personal history, like doing too much, or *violence* or *abuse* – given or received. Nature has a way of putting on hold anything that has got out of control. Unfortunately, such thwarting of desire eventually leads to *anger* – for anger is simply the troublesome residue of unexpressed or frustrated desires. And so ...

IN RELATIONSHIP the expression of Mars, possibly more than any other planetary energy, determines whether there is going to be *strife* or *satisfaction*. It is not that it creates these states all on its own – it is just that the wrong move, or the lack of any move at all, can lead to *offence* or misunderstanding. And the moves we make, or do not make, are determined by our thoughts and feelings – which are represented by every planet and astrological influence in the book. But it is Mars that makes that move – or again, doesn't make it.

Mars is the planet of *masculinity,* which obviously does not mean to say that it only exists in *men*. Everyone has a Mars in their chart. Masculinity is simply another word for all these Martian attributes, and because of this, the male of the species is traditionally or biologically expected to act first, or to 'be a man'. As someone once said 'Men do, woman are'. Traditionally, the male makes the move towards the female, taking the risk of being accepted or rejected. But then there is many a woman who is 'twice the man', being far more decisive and effective than many men. But whatever the gender, there is always a *doer* and a *done to*. In any relationship, deciding or being instinctively aware of who should be active and who should be passive, and when, is a critical issue. I refer to this time and time again, in one context or another, throughout this book. Because Mars is so important in relating, a good general rule is: whoever acts or reacts, or does not act at all, should take full responsibility or credit for it.

Sex. It would be wrong to say that Mars is entirely representative of sex, for the whole personality (that is, all astrological influences) has some bearing on it. However, it is again a case of it being the actual act, and not necessarily the thoughts and feelings that are behind it. There may be little or no thought or feeling behind it at all – just *lust,* the physical desire to gratify the senses, or the *primal urge* to procreate. Then again, there are very few people who are so *primitive* as to have no premeditation at all concerning sex. On the contrary, today this would be impossible considering that we are bombarded constantly with sexual words, sounds and images that *inflame* the senses – or *offend* them.

When another human being affects us sexually in some way, it ultimately means that they are reaching more than just our Mars, that is unless one is a mindless sex machine! Sex, like Mars, is the first or decisive move that sets in motion a whole lot else; the fire that ignites. Sex is Cupid's bow and arrow; the hearts and flowers are delivered later – or not, as the case may be.

JUPITER • *Love of God*

Jupiter is the Law-Giver. In life there are *laws* which are quite obvious, like, for example, the Law of Gravity. But there are laws that govern everything, some of which are not so provable as the one which states that if you fall you hit the ground. Science has taken over much of our sense of there being laws other than scientifically provable ones. But these laws still exist, and without an awareness of them we are like falling aeroplanes, and we will hit the ground!

These less obvious laws were traditionally ascribed to 'God'. I put this word in inverted commas because it needs its meaning clarifying. For many people, 'God' is associated with the stuffy world of *churches* and Bible-bashers or whatever might be the name of the place of worship and its *priests*. Such things are the result of 'God's' Laws being interpreted by people who did so with their own little laws – that is, their ambitions and egos – getting in the way. In other words, they used our natural sense of there being a *deity* or *Higher Power*, to hoodwink and frighten us into believing something that had more to do with their own intent rather than 'God's'. This, combined with science's upstaging of 'God', has rendered 'God' dead, unacceptable or unbelievable to many people. What's really happening here though is that it is not so much 'God' that so many are no longer accepting or believing in, but that perversion of 'God' that got stuffed down their throats. The trouble is that those 'false priests' will have succeeded if we throw the baby out with the bath-water. And now we need that baby, that something that is *divine* and beyond what mere science has told us and sold us. Fortunately it appears we are beginning to return to 'God' – but a new and more intuitively and personally defined version.

IN RELATIONSHIP Jupiter takes on a particularly subtle importance which is owing to the above-described demise of 'God'. Because human beings have an innate need to find 'God' – that is, a sense of *greater meaning*, a sense that there is some *greater being or plan* that is ultimately managing our lives – we will still unconsciously look for it even when science has told us that it never existed. And so we will look for 'God' in our mate. This is why we expect far too much of them, attach the wrong sort of importance to them, and feel the world has ended if we lose them.

Jupiter is also important in relationships because it represents qualities that are often omitted from relationship, or at least fall by the wayside with our romantic or idealistic intentions – or marriage *vows*. These qualities go beyond immediate physical desires and emotional needs, and include *virtue, pledges, morality* and a *belief* in and *reverence* for some *Higher Good*. All in all, Jupiter is about *growth* – in terms of the *development* of a better character and relationship.

Jupiter is the *bigger picture*. There are *far-reaching* reasons for relationships that have to do with such things as having inner connections with certain people that must be *explored* and *experienced* for reasons that often escape a more limited viewpoint that is defined by some romantic or average expectation. For instance, a relationship's *path* could entail great suffering and endurance, the experience of which took the couple to a level of *understanding* they could not have reached without taking that *journey*.

Each person's respective *opinions* and *religious and cultural beliefs* (or lack of them) – and how they are shared or accepted, rejected or imposed – can be critical to the relationship's stability and harmony.

PLANETS OF LOVE

SATURN • *Love of Duty*

Saturn teaches us our *lessons* and confronts us with what we cannot get away with doing, or leaving undone, any longer. Saturn puts us on notice that the *time* has come or is coming when we must get ourselves together, grow up, and generally be more *objective* and *mature* about whatever the issue might be. Saturn is not interested in or impressed by our emotional reactions, so whenever we are under the Saturnian *pressure* to learn and *take stock* of a situation, no amount of wheedling, complaining, blaming or evading will pass its *test* or excuse us from it. A good example of Saturn is the force of gravity, for it imposes *limitations,* puts the *weight* on us, and is what we have to rise and grow against. (The Law of Gravity referred to on the previous page under Jupiter, appertains to just that, the 'law' of gravity, not gravity itself).

IN RELATIONSHIP Saturn is particularly important because it governs what many people feel either *denied* or *afraid* of where relationships are concerned: *commitment.* Commitment could be described as an equal blend of Love and Duty – but these two things often seem to be poles apart. If we say to someone we do such-and-such for them out of a sense of duty, they may well feel 'unloved' by this. But the word 'duty' simply comes from the word *'due'.* To be dutiful to someone or something is to render what is due to them. This can be done purely because you know in your own mind what must be done and that you must do it, or, because some external pressure or *condition* forces you to discover your duty and perform it. It may also be a mixture of the two. In either case, time and *circumstances* will be the elements that *restrict* or pressurize you until you realize what is 'due'.

And so, the primary objective with Saturnian, that is, *difficult* or *onerous* relationship situations, is to recognize and *establish* what your duty is to Other. The ultimate objective is to perform that duty with love. If when we reluctantly recognize and grudgingly accept what our duty is, we are not doing it with love. The reason for this is that the *inadequate* or *irresponsible* part of us is still looking for an easy way out of or through the relationship. Of course, there is also the case when one does not recognize or fulfil one's duty at all. If this is the case, you can be sure that in the fullness of time Saturn will re-present one with the bill, so to speak. And it being 'overdue', the pressure will be all the greater. On the other hand, gladly committing yourself to the *tasks* and *obligations* that relationship *imposes* will progressively establish a *foundation* upon which a *real* and *lasting* love can be built. This is not easy; it is rather like the alchemist who through hard *work* and *trial and error* transmutes lead (called 'Butter of Saturn', the weight of basic reality) into gold (heart-love, spiritual enlightenment, the Sun).

However, because Saturn is, by its very nature, to do with setting limits and allotting *responsibilities,* it poses the *necessity* of knowing your own ground if you are to know where your duties end and some-one else's begin. In other words, having a *purpose* or *position* all your very own is essential if you are to prevent impossible demands being made of you by those to whom you are responsible. Drawing such lines of *demarcation* is made difficult because we may feel that we will not be liked or loved for doing so. In truth, we are loved all the more – given time – because Other then knows where they *stand.* Then again, one may draw one's lines too far out, allowing few or no people into one's increasingly *cold, lonely* and *overly controlled* space. Saturn says 'Render what is due – no more and no less'.

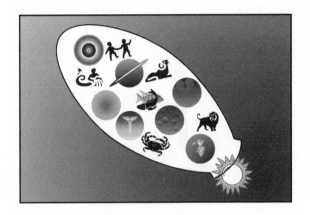

Chapter 2

THE INDIVIDUAL

I set out once into this world –
A man alone with spear and shaft –
To simply hunt and make a mate,
To catch the scent
Of wild estate.
But now my loins they linger – pause,
The hunter now he hunts his Cause ...

from *MARS – Planet of Independent Action, Pursuit and Effect*

THE RELATIONSHIP YOU HAVE
WITH YOURSELF

The most important relationship you ever have is the one you have with yourself. All relationships that you have with Other – be it a person or a thing – are something to do with you. This sounds obvious, 'it takes two to tango', but when we look at ourselves astrologically, we can see just how much what we are as individuals determines the kind of people, relationships and situations we attract. The way we see and treat ourselves, and how well we know ourselves, are all reflected in how Other sees and treats us, and how well they relate to us. And this reflection usually comes in the form of one of two extremes: the *same* or the *opposite* of whatever the trait of character in question happens to be.

For instance, if I see myself as not deserving time and space of my own, I will then attract one of two extremes. I will either find myself in a relationship where Other imposes upon my time and space, or in one where Other leaves me on my own more than I think I like. Alternatively, the second extreme could take the form of not being in any particular relationship so that I have all the time in the world to myself, but I do not really enjoy it. This would be because I am avoiding the confrontation with myself that relationship so effectively imposes. In all cases though, life is trying to tell me something through its most significant medium – relationship, with myself or Other. And it is trying to tell me about me as an individual. In more general terms, inner discord or harmony will be played out externally.

So by knowing more about myself, or Other, as an individual in terms of how we relate and what we attract, relationships will become more manageable and appropriate, and thereby more positive. In order to accomplish this through astrology, we will look at the Sun, Moon and Planets as they were positioned in the various Signs of the Zodiac at birth.* After that, we will then look at a profoundly informative astrological feature with regard to relationship – the RISING SIGN.

On the next page, I show you how to look up your Sun, Moon and Planet-Sign positions in the easy-to-use TABLES (no calculations necessary). Having accomplished this, or if you are aware of them already (you probably know your Sun Sign), you can then plot those Planet-Sign positions on the CHARTWHEEL, in the way that I show you on page 28. After that I refer you to the interpretations, THE PLANET-SIGN PROFILES. How to ascertain RISING SIGNS (and Setting Signs) follows upon these Profiles, along with interpretations for them.

In addition to Sign positions, there are other astrological features in an individual Birthchart, like Houses (as previously mentioned) and Aspects, but they are outside the scope of this book. If you wish to obtain such information and what it means, I refer you to the very last page of the book where you will find a list of addresses for astrological resources.

HOW TO READ THE TABLES

SIGN-NAME ABBREVIATIONS

Aries	ARI	**Leo**	LEO	**Sagittarius**	SAG
Taurus	TAU	**Virgo**	VIR	**Capricorn**	CAP
Gemini	GEM	**Libra**	LIB	**Aquarius**	AQU
Cancer	CAN	**Scorpio**	SCO	**Pisces**	PIS

EXAMPLE BIRTH TIME AND DATE:
5 AUGUST 1955 at 4.30pm British Summer Time (BST) in OXFORD, ENGLAND

1 All the Tables, beginning on page 31, are in Greenwich Mean Time (GMT), so convert Birth Time to that, if necessary. *In our example, then, we subtract one hour to give 3.30pm (BST is one hour ahead of GMT).*

2 All times given in the Tables are in 24-hour clock time, *so our example becomes 15.30 GMT.*

3 Turn to the page of the year in question. *For our example (1955) this will be page 88.*

4 First of all we find the Sign positions for SUN, MERCURY, VENUS, MARS, JUPITER and SATURN, which are given in the panels on the top half of the page. Each of the Tables for these planets gives the MONTH (mth), DAY (dy) and TIME (time) when the relevant Planet changed or entered a Sign. *Using our example 5 AUGUST 1955 at 15.30 GMT, we look at the SUN table and see that this time and day fell between 23 JULY 15.25 when the SUN entered the Sign of LEO, and 23 AUGUST 22.20, when the SUN left LEO and entered VIRgo. At our example time and day, then, the SUN was in LEO.* If, however, our example was for the same time but on 5 SEPTEMBER, then the SUN would have been in VIRgo.

   NOTE: If you were born at the exact time that a Planet entered a new Sign, then that would be that Planet's Sign position.

   Using the Tables for MERCURY, VENUS, MARS, JUPITER and SATURN in the same way as for the SUN will give *for our example (5 AUGUST 1955 at 15.30 GMT) the following Sign positions: MERCURY in LEO, VENUS in LEO, MARS in LEO, JUPITER in LEO, and SATURN in SCOrpio.*

5 Now we will find the Sign position for the MOON which is given in the panel on the bottom half of the page. This is set out differently because, compared to the other Planets, the MOON moves a lot more quickly through the Signs.

   First go to the MONTH column. *Example: AUGUST (aug).* Then go to the row for the DAY (dy) of the month in question *(example: 5th)* and there where column and row intersect will be given the MOON's Sign position, or for a day when the MOON entered a new Sign, a time is given in GMT/24-hour clock-time for when that Sign change occurred. If you were born *before* that changeover time, then the Sign position of the MOON will be given immediately *above* that changeover time *(ie the previous day)* or at the bottom of the previous column. If you were born *after* or *exactly on* that changeover time, then the position of the MOON will be given immediately *below* that changeover time *(ie the following day)* or at the top of the next column.

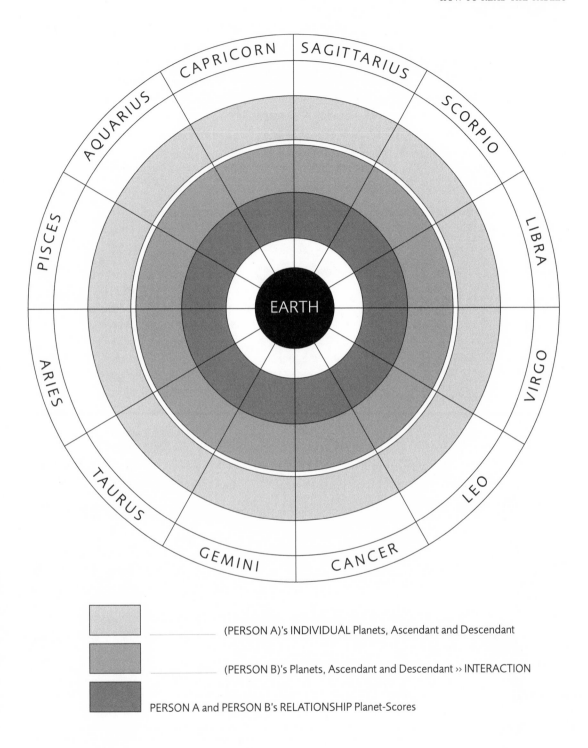

(PERSON A)'s INDIVIDUAL Planets, Ascendant and Descendant

(PERSON B)'s Planets, Ascendant and Descendant ›› INTERACTION

PERSON A and PERSON B's RELATIONSHIP Planet-Scores

The Chartwheel

In our example, then, the MOON was placed in PISces. If, however, he was born the day before on 4 August, we would see the time 08.05, the time that the MOON left AQUarius and entered PISces. But as he was born after that time, he'd still have his MOON in PISces.

Note: In a few cases, when the MOON has changed Signs twice within 48 hours, because of the space available, both the time of the changeover and the new Sign that the MOON has just entered are given on the same line. An example of this is 13 February 1957, where it is written: 00.19 > LEO – meaning that the MOON moved from CANcer to LEO at 00.19 GMT. On the following day the time given for the Sign change is read in the usual way, *ie* looking to the Sign name above or below the line. In this example of 13 Feb 1957, then, on the following day of 14 Feb the time given is 23.17, meaning that the MOON moved from LEO to VIRgo at 23.17 GMT.

6 With all the above concerning MOON Sign positions, for 1 January birthdays, you may have to refer to 31 December of the previous year for the Sign position. Likewise, for 31 December birthdays, you may have to refer to 1 January of the following year.

7 Finally we will look up the Sign positions for URANUS, NEPTUNE and PLUTO. Refer to page 146 where you will find a single page of Tables with a column for each one of these Outer Planets, as they are called. These give the YEAR (year), MONTH (mth), DAY (dy) and TIME (time) when the relevant Planet changed or entered a Sign. *Using our example then, we look to the URANUS column and see that this time and day fell between 1949 on 10 JUNE at 04.04 when URANUS entered the Sign of CANcer, and 1955 on 24 AUG at 17.57 when URANUS left CANcer and entered LEO. So at our example time and day, URANUS was in CANcer.*

Using the columns of Tables for NEPTUNE and PLUTO in the same way as for URANUS will give *for our example: NEPTUNE in LIBra, and PLUTO in LEO.*

ENTERING THE PLANETS ON THE CHARTWHEEL

After you have looked up the Planet-Sign positions for the birth date in question (or as you do so, if you feel up to it), you can enter them on the CHARTWHEEL which you can see on page 27. You can use this one to pencil in the Planets' positions. There is also a copy at the back of the book which can be photocopied. Also, a photocopied sheet is easier to fill in.

Looking at the blank CHARTWHEEL we see the Zodiac surrounding the Earth. The shaded rings in between are where we will plot in the Planets, etc.

First we enter the Planet-Sign positions we have just looked up in the Tables. Throughout this book, the first person we look up and enter is always called PERSON A. So just below the CHARTWHEEL itself, to the right of ▓▓▓▓, enter the name of PERSON A. *In our example, PERSON A will from hereon be called JACK.*

Then we enter all those Planet-Sign positions we have just looked up into the ring shaded ▓▓▓▓, in the appropriate Sign segments. As we do so, we abbreviate each Planet to its first three letters, for reasons of space and speed.

So eventually our CHARTWHEEL would, with all of JACK's Planet-Sign positions entered, look as shown opposite, THE CHARTWHEEL – EXAMPLE 1. NOTE: I have also entered the ASCendant and DEScendant which you will be shown–how to look up and enter on page 247. For JACK they are ASCendant in SAGittarius, and DEScendant in GEMini.

We will actually use the CHARTWHEEL later on, but for now you may just like to ponder the image of the CHARTWHEEL (with your Planet-Sign positions entered) in order to absorb for a moment the impression that is given of the Sun, Moon and Planets travelling through the Zodiac in relation to the Earth. As you do so, bear in mind that the Sun, Moon and Planets are travelling at different speeds, progressively through the Zodiac in an *anti-clockwise* direction (although every so often the Planets appear to wander backwards: the word 'Planet' means 'wanderer')*. However, the Earth's own *faster* anti-clockwise rotation creates the illusion of the Sun, Moon and Planets revolving around us in a *clockwise* direction. So at any given moment, the Sun, Moon and each Planet will be positioned in a certain Zodiacal Sign. These are the positions given in the Planet-Sign Tables. The positions of the ASCendant and DEScendant are determined by the Earth's own rotation, as you will soon discover.

* The SUN is of course what the EARTH orbits, rather than the other way around, but it appears to go around it, along with the Planets. The same applies to the MOON, which is orbiting the EARTH rather than the SUN. For these reasons, the SUN and MOON never appear to wander backwards.

Now to turn to the beginning of the PLANET-SIGN PROFILES on page 147 for Important Tips on how to use them, and then turn to the PLANET-SIGN PROFILES INDEX on page 148 to find the relevant pages for the meanings of these Planet-Sign positions. These PLANET-SIGN PROFILES do not include the Outer Planets, but you will still need to know them, as shall become evident later.

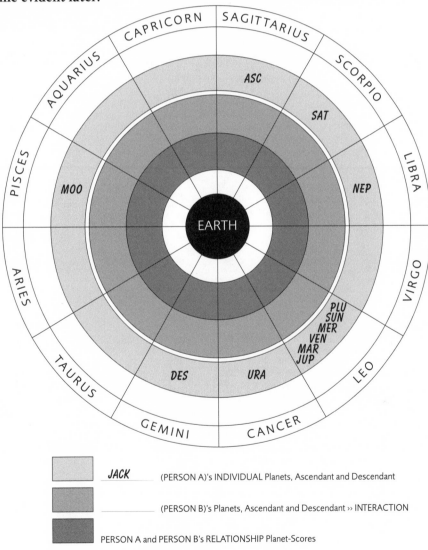

JACK _____ (PERSON A)'s INDIVIDUAL Planets, Ascendant and Descendant

_____ (PERSON B)'s Planets, Ascendant and Descendant ›› INTERACTION

PERSON A and PERSON B's RELATIONSHIP Planet-Scores

Chartwheel – Example 1

THE TABLES
FOR THE SUN, MOON, AND
PLANET-SIGN POSITIONS

SUN

mth	dy	time → sign
JAN	1	00.00 → CAP
JAN	20	11.35 → AQU
FEB	19	02.01 → PIS
MAR	21	01.38 → ARI
APR	20	13.27 → TAU
MAY	21	13.18 → GEM
JUN	21	21.41 → CAN
JUL	23	08.36 → LEO
AUG	23	15.20 → VIR
SEP	23	12.21 → LIB
OCT	23	20.55 → SCO
NOV	22	17.49 → SAG
DEC	22	06.42 → CAP

MERCURY

mth	dy	time → sign
JAN	1	00.00 → SAG
JAN	9	02.13 → CAP
JAN	28	17.11 → AQU
FEB	15	00.05 → PIS
MAR	3	21.23 → ARI
MAR	29	23.09 → PIS
APR	17	01.05 → ARI
MAY	11	00.16 → TAU
MAY	26	10.51 → GEM
JUN	9	09.23 → CAN
JUN	27	09.14 → LEO
SEP	3	00.39 → VIR
SEP	18	23.19 → LIB
OCT	7	08.22 → SCO
OCT	30	06.27 → SAG
NOV	18	20.38 → SCO
DEC	12	15.04 → SAG

VENUS

mth	dy	time → sign
JAN	1	00.00 → AQU
JAN	20	01.40 → PIS
FEB	13	14.08 → ARI
MAR	10	18.09 → TAU
APR	6	04.15 → GEM
MAY	5	15.47 → CAN
SEP	8	20.55 → LEO
OCT	8	13.37 → VIR
NOV	3	21.34 → LIB
NOV	28	21.56 → SCO
DEC	23	07.48 → SAG

MARS

mth	dy	time → sign
JAN	1	00.00 → CAP
JAN	21	18.56 → AQU
FEB	28	22.15 → PIS
APR	8	03.54 → ARI
MAY	17	09.09 → TAU
JUN	27	09.21 → GEM
AUG	10	01.13 → CAN
SEP	26	18.04 → LEO
NOV	23	08.46 → VIR

SATURN

mth	dy	time → sign
JAN	1	00.00 → SAG
JAN	21	08.21 → CAP
JUL	18	17.43 → SAG
OCT	17	05.20 → CAP

JUPITER

mth	dy	time → sign
JAN	1	00.00 → SAG

MOON

dy	jan	feb	mar	apr	may	jun	jul	aug	sep	oct	nov	dec	dy
1	CAP	07.46	PIS	05.02	GEM	15.44	10.42	LIB	13.49	05.57	23.07	08.22	1
2	21.26	PIS	18.02	TAU	22.24	LEO	VIR	19.10	SAG	CAP	PIS	ARI	2
3	AQU	07.37	ARI	07.14	CAN	LEO	22.59	SCO	22.27	12.04	PIS	10.01	3
4	22.08	ARI	18.25	GEM	CAN	02.35	LIB	SCO	CAP	AQU	00.27	TAU	4
5	PIS	09.49	TAU	13.18	07.01	VIR	LIB	06.02	CAP	14.22	ARI	11.27	5
6	23.44	TAU	22.05	CAN	LEO	15.00	11.13	SAG	02.53	PIS	00.25	GEM	6
7	ARI	15.08	GEM	23.11	18.36	LIB	SCO	13.15	AQU	14.06	TAU	14.04	7
8	ARI	GEM	GEM	LEO	VIR	LIB	21.05	CAP	03.47	ARI	00.50	CAN	8
9	03.26	23.51	05.46	LEO	VIR	02.45	SAG	16.33	PIS	13.16	GEM	19.19	9
10	TAU	CAN	CAN	11.27	07.10	SCO	SAG	AQU	03.00	TAU	03.22	LEO	10
11	09.36	CAN	16.39	VIR	LIB	12.06	03.28	17.11	ARI	14.02	CAN	LEO	11
12	GEM	10.48	LEO	VIR	18.42	SAG	CAP	PIS	02.45	GEM	09.49	04.03	12
13	18.07	LEO	LEO	00.01	SCO	18.31	06.41	17.09	TAU	18.02	LEO	VIR	13
14	CAN	23.00	05.04	LIB	SCO	CAP	AQU	ARI	04.58	CAN	09.48	15.49	14
15	CAN	VIR	VIR	11.37	04.08	22.37	08.13	18.25	GEM	CAN	VIR	LIB	15
16	04.31	VIR	17.39	SCO	SAG	AQU	PIS	TAU	10.40	01.53	VIR	LIB	16
17	LEO	11.37	LIB	21.39	11.20	AQU	09.38	22.14	CAN	LEO	08.09	04.34	17
18	16.27	LIB	LIB	SAG	CAP	01.27	ARI	GEM	19.39	12.52	LIB	SCO	18
19	VIR	23.45	05.35	SAG	16.31	PIS	12.17	GEM	LEO	20.48	15.56	SAG	19
20	VIR	SCO	SCO	05.37	AQU	03.57	TAU	04.56	LEO	VIR	SCO	SAG	20
21	05.07	SCO	16.03	CAP	20.02	ARI	16.49	CAN	06.53	01.25	SCO	SAG	21
22	LIB	09.54	SAG	11.06	PIS	06.54	GEM	14.03	VIR	LIB	08.09	00.33	22
23	16.55	SAG	23.57	AQU	22.22	TAU	23.20	LEO	19.19	14.05	SAG	CAP	23
24	SCO	16.33	CAP	14.00	ARI	10.52	CAN	LEO	LIB	SCO	17.27	06.35	24
25	SCO	CAP	CAP	PIS	ARI	GEM	CAN	00.57	LIB	SCO	CAP	AQU	25
26	01.50	19.16	04.26	15.00	00.21	16.28	07.49	VIR	08.06	01.50	CAP	10.47	26
27	SAG	AQU	AQU	ARI	TAU	CAN	LEO	13.13	SCO	SAG	00.30	PIS	27
28	06.48	19.05	05.42	15.34	03.06	CAN	18.18	LIB	20.10	11.47	AQU	14.02	28
29	CAP		PIS	TAU	GEM	00.19	VIR	LIB	SAG	CAP	05.24	ARI	29
30	08.13		05.13	17.30	07.55	LEO	VIR	02.03	SAG	19.02	PIS	16.55	30
31	AQU		ARI		CAN		06.30	SCO		AQU		TAU	31

SUN

mth	dy	time → sign
JAN	1	00.00 → CAP
JAN	20	17.18 → AQU
FEB	19	07.47 → PIS
MAR	21	07.25 → ARI
APR	20	19.16 → TAU
MAY	21	19.06 → GEM
JUN	22	03.28 → CAN
JUL	23	14.25 → LEO
AUG	23	21.09 → VIR
SEP	23	18.10 → LIB
OCT	24	02.46 → SCO
NOV	22	23.41 → SAG
DEC	22	12.37 → CAP

MERCURY

mth	dy	time → sign
JAN	1	00.00 → SAG
JAN	2	12.28 → CAP
JAN	21	06.30 → AQU
FEB	7	10.36 → PIS
APR	15	17.11 → ARI
MAY	3	13.58 → TAU
MAY	17	20.09 → GEM
JUN	1	23.35 → CAN
AUG	10	04.46 → LEO
AUG	25	22.24 → VIR
SEP	11	06.22 → LIB
OCT	1	04.35 → SCO
DEC	6	23.39 → SAG
DEC	26	09.32 → CAP

VENUS

mth	dy	time → sign
JAN	1	00.00 → SAG
JAN	16	11.27 → CAP
FEB	9	13.07 → AQU
MAR	5	14.52 → PIS
MAR	29	18.03 → ARI
APR	22	23.33 → TAU
MAY	17	07.34 → GEM
JUN	10	17.37 → CAN
JUL	5	05.21 → LEO
JUL	29	19.13 → VIR
AUG	23	12.34 → LIB
SEP	17	11.29 → SCO
OCT	12	19.14 → SAG
NOV	7	19.26 → CAP
DEC	5	13.32 → AQU

MARS

mth	dy	time → sign
JAN	1	00.00 → VIR
MAR	1	19.21 → LEO
MAY	11	06.12 → VIR
JUL	13	19.55 → LIB
AUG	31	18.18 → SCO
OCT	14	12.39 → SAG
NOV	24	04.48 → CAP

SATURN

mth	dy	time → sign
JAN	1	00.00 → CAP

JUPITER

mth	dy	time → sign
JAN	1	00.00 → SAG
JAN	19	08.26 → CAP

MOON

dy	jan	feb	mar	apr	may	jun	jul	aug	sep	oct	nov	dec	dy
1	19.54	CAN	19.31	VIR	LIB	11.46	05.32	AQU	ARI	23.29	CAN	LEO	1
2	GEM	13.12	LEO	21.58	16.45	SAG	CAP	01.58	14.17	GEM	13.10	03.12	2
3	23.35	LEO	LEO	LIB	SCO	22.43	13.34	PIS	TAU	GEM	LEO	VIR	3
4	CAN	21.34	04.39	LIB	SCO	CAP	AQU	05.17	16.33	01.55	20.06	12.25	4
5	CAN	VIR	VIR	10.37	05.27	CAP	19.23	ARI	GEM	CAN	VIR	LIB	5
6	04.58	VIR	15.37	SCO	SAG	07.31	PIS	08.08	20.11	06.52	VIR	LIB	6
7	LEO	08.19	LIB	23.31	16.55	AQU	23.37	TAU	CAN	LEO	06.16	00.38	7
8	13.03	LIB	LIB	SAG	CAP	13.55	ARI	11.08	CAN	14.27	LIB	SCO	8
9	VIR	22.57	04.12	SAG	CAP	PIS	ARI	GEM	01.27	VIR	18.30	13.45	9
10	VIR	SCO	SCO	11.03	01.59	18.03	02.46	14.38	LEO	VIR	SCO	SAG	10
11	00.06	SCO	17.04	CAP	AQU	ARI	TAU	CAN	08.33	00.26	SCO	SAG	11
12	LIB	09.26	SAG	19.27	07.55	20.10	05.10	19.05	VIR	LIB	07.33	02.05	12
13	12.54	SAG	SAG	AQU	PIS	TAU	GEM	LEO	17.53	12.18	SAG	CAP	13
14	SCO	19.10	03.56	23.57	10.44	21.11	07.32	LEO	LIB	SCO	20.10	12.42	14
15	SCO	CAP	CAP	PIS	ARI	GEM	CAN	01.18	LIB	SCO	CAP	AQU	15
16	00.42	CAP	10.56	PIS	11.16	22.23	10.54	VIR	05.31	01.23	CAP	21.13	16
17	SAG	00.51	AQU	01.06	TAU	CAN	LEO	10.14	SCO	SAG	07.04	PIS	17
18	09.30	AQU	13.52	ARI	11.07	CAN	16.44	LIB	18.33	14.01	AQU	PIS	18
19	CAP	03.06	PIS	00.35	GEM	01.24	VIR	21.58	SAG	CAP	15.04	03.10	19
20	14.47	PIS	14.06	TAU	12.03	LEO	VIR	SCO	SAG	CAP	PIS	ARI	20
21	AQU	03.44	ARI	00.18	CAN	07.40	01.55	SCO	06.44	00.18	19.32	06.23	21
22	17.41	ARI	13.41	GEM	15.49	VIR	LIB	10.54	CAP	AQU	ARI	TAU	22
23	PIS	04.42	TAU	02.12	LEO	17.42	14.00	SAG	15.45	06.46	20.52	07.23	23
24	19.45	TAU	14.37	CAN	23.18	LIB	SCO	22.18	AQU	PIS	TAU	GEM	24
25	ARI	07.22	GEM	07.28	VIR	LIB	SCO	CAP	20.43	09.26	20.24	07.23	25
26	22.16	GEM	18.15	LEO	VIR	06.14	02.45	CAP	PIS	ARI	GEM	CAN	26
27	TAU	12.22	CAN	16.20	10.18	SCO	SAG	06.13	22.29	09.34	20.02	08.19	27
28	TAU	CAN	CAN	VIR	LIB	18.51	13.33	AQU	ARI	TAU	CAN	LEO	28
29	01.53		01.00	VIR	23.07	SAG	CAP	10.36	22.47	09.01	21.43	12.04	29
30	GEM		LEO	03.54	SCO	SAG	21.09	PIS	TAU	GEM	LEO	VIR	30
31	06.51		10.29		SCO		AQU	12.44		GEM		19.57	31

SUN

mth	dy	time → sign
JAN	1	00.00 → CAP
JAN	20	23.14 → AQU
FEB	19	13.40 → PIS
MAR	21	13.16 → ARI
APR	21	01.05 → TAU
MAY	22	00.54 → GEM
JUN	22	09.17 → CAN
JUL	23	20.13 → LEO
AUG	24	02.53 → VIR
SEP	23	23.58 → LIB
OCT	24	08.36 → SCO
NOV	23	05.37 → SAG
DEC	22	18.39 → CAP

MERCURY

mth	dy	time → sign
JAN	1	00.00 → CAP
JAN	13	19.38 → AQU
FEB	1	15.58 → PIS
FEB	18	07.12 → AQU
MAR	19	03.04 → PIS
APR	9	12.09 → ARI
APR	25	08.41 → TAU
MAY	9	12.11 → GEM
MAY	29	08.28 → CAN
JUN	26	06.28 → GEM
JUL	13	09.31 → CAN
AUG	2	21.23 → LEO
AUG	17	16.34 → VIR
SEP	4	02.33 → LIB
SEP	28	07.22 → SCO
OCT	15	23.36 → LIB
NOV	10	15.08 → SCO
NOV	30	01.33 → SAG
DEC	19	03.01 → CAP

VENUS

mth	dy	time → sign
JAN	1	00.00 → AQU
JAN	11	17.49 → PIS
FEB	6	22.56 → AQU
APR	4	19.34 → PIS
MAY	7	07.05 → ARI
JUN	3	23.57 → TAU
JUN	30	06.28 → GEM
JUL	25	18.58 → CAN
AUG	19	18.25 → LEO
SEP	13	07.18 → VIR
OCT	7	12.04 → LIB
OCT	31	11.55 → SCO
NOV	24	09.06 → SAG
DEC	18	05.35 → CAP

MARS

mth	dy	time → sign
JAN	1	00.00 → CAP
JAN	1	23.49 → AQU
FEB	8	23.48 → PIS
MAR	19	04.34 → ARI
APR	27	10.47 → TAU
JUN	7	11.26 → GEM
JUL	20	17.38 → CAN
SEP	4	14.48 → LEO
OCT	23	22.55 → VIR
DEC	20	03.36 → LIB

SATURN

mth	dy	time → sign
JAN	1	00.00 → CAP

JUPITER

mth	dy	time → sign
JAN	1	00.00 → CAP
FEB	6	19.22 → AQU

MOON

dy	jan	feb	mar	apr	may	jun	jul	aug	sep	oct	nov	dec	dy
1	LIB	SCO	12.27	CAP	AQU	03.35	TAU	02.34	14.12	03.19	SCO	SAG	1
2	LIB	04.17	SAG	20.20	13.16	ARI	17.14	CAN	VIR	LIB	05.26	00.33	2
3	07.30	SAG	SAG	AQU	PIS	06.46	GEM	03.06	18.42	11.07	SAG	CAP	3
4	SCO	16.38	01.04	AQU	18.30	TAU	17.07	LEO	LIB	SCO	17.44	13.16	4
5	20.36	CAP	CAP	04.03	ARI	07.10	CAN	04.43	LIB	21.40	CAP	AQU	5
6	SAG	CAP	11.22	PIS	20.23	GEM	16.54	VIR	02.25	SAG	CAP	AQU	6
7	SAG	02.27	AQU	08.11	TAU	06.26	LEO	09.15	SCO	SAG	06.22	01.01	7
8	08.47	AQU	18.16	ARI	20.21	CAN	18.43	LIB	13.25	10.06	AQU	PIS	8
9	CAP	09.29	PIS	09.50	GEM	06.39	VIR	17.43	SAG	CAP	17.16	10.03	9
10	18.48	PIS	22.21	TAU	20.15	LEO	VIR	SCO	SAG	22.19	PIS	ARI	10
11	AQU	14.30	ARI	10.37	CAN	09.44	00.16	SCO	02.01	AQU	PIS	15.11	11
12	AQU	ARI	ARI	GEM	21.54	VIR	LIB	05.26	CAP	AQU	00.44	TAU	12
13	02.40	18.26	00.55	12.04	LEO	16.45	09.56	SAG	13.44	08.07	ARI	16.38	13
14	PIS	TAU	TAU	CAN	LEO	LIB	SCO	18.10	AQU	PIS	04.24	GEM	14
15	08.44	21.43	03.13	15.18	02.36	LIB	22.17	CAP	22.53	14.30	TAU	15.55	15
16	ARI	GEM	GEM	LEO	VIR	03.22	SAG	CAP	PIS	ARI	05.19	CAN	16
17	13.06	GEM	06.04	20.57	10.42	SCO	SAG	05.38	PIS	17.56	GEM	15.13	17
18	TAU	00.37	CAN	VIR	LIB	15.58	11.04	AQU	05.14	TAU	05.14	LEO	18
19	15.49	CAN	09.54	VIR	21.33	SAG	CAP	14.51	ARI	19.40	CAN	16.40	19
20	GEM	03.37	LEO	05.05	SCO	SAG	22.38	PIS	09.31	GEM	06.05	VIR	20
21	17.21	LEO	15.12	LIB	SCO	04.46	AQU	21.57	TAU	21.10	LEO	21.46	21
22	CAN	07.44	VIR	15.28	09.58	CAP	AQU	ARI	12.39	CAN	09.24	LIB	22
23	18.56	VIR	22.31	SCO	SAG	16.37	08.24	ARI	GEM	23.39	VIR	LIB	23
24	LEO	14.18	LIB	SCO	22.47	AQU	PIS	03.20	15.23	LEO	15.49	06.39	24
25	22.16	LIB	LIB	03.36	CAP	AQU	16.15	TAU	CAN	LEO	LIB	SCO	25
26	VIR	LIB	08.20	SAG	CAP	02.50	ARI	07.13	18.16	03.53	LIB	18.09	26
27	VIR	00.05	SCO	16.26	10.50	PIS	21.57	GEM	LEO	VIR	01.01	SAG	27
28	04.57	SCO	20.24	CAP	AQU	10.39	TAU	09.50	21.58	10.14	SCO	SAG	28
29	LIB		SAG	CAP	20.50	ARI	TAU	CAN	VIR	LIB	12.12	06.44	29
30	15.28		SAG	04.16	PIS	15.26	01.16	11.45	VIR	18.46	SAG	CAP	30
31	SCO		09.12		PIS		GEM	LEO		SCO		19.20	31

SUN

mth	dy	time → sign
JAN	1	00.00 → CAP
JAN	21	05.12 → AQU
FEB	19	19.44 → PIS
MAR	21	19.15 → ARI
APR	21	06.56 → TAU
MAY	22	06.45 → GEM
JUN	22	15.07 → CAN
JUL	24	01.58 → LEO
AUG	24	08.42 → VIR
SEP	24	05.45 → LIB
OCT	24	14.24 → SCO
NOV	23	11.22 → SAG
DEC	23	00.24 → CAP

MERCURY

mth	dy	time → sign
JAN	1	00.00 → CAP
JAN	6	19.34 → AQU
MAR	14	21.53 → PIS
APR	2	00.26 → ARI
APR	16	21.51 → TAU
MAY	2	13.39 → GEM
JUL	10	13.08 → CAN
JUL	25	12.13 → LEO
AUG	9	17.51 → VIR
AUG	29	05.35 → LIB
NOV	4	04.54 → SCO
NOV	22	19.22 → SAG
DEC	12	00.11 → CAP

VENUS

mth	dy	time → sign
JAN	1	00.00 → CAP
JAN	11	02.20 → AQU
FEB	4	00.49 → PIS
FEB	28	03.03 → ARI
MAR	24	11.54 → TAU
APR	18	06.43 → GEM
MAY	13	16.23 → CAN
JUN	9	03.07 → LEO
JUL	7	20.37 → VIR
AUG	17	21.53 → LIB
SEP	6	02.33 → VIR
NOV	8	14.41 → LIB
DEC	9	14.42 → SCO

MARS

mth	dy	time → sign
JAN	1	00.00 → LIB
APR	19	20.48 → VIR
MAY	30	17.23 → LIB
AUG	6	16.34 → SCO
SEP	22	13.54 → SAG
NOV	3	05.35 → CAP
DEC	12	09.49 → AQU

SATURN

mth	dy	time → sign
JAN	1	00.00 → CAP
JAN	19	22.01 → AQU

JUPITER

mth	dy	time → sign
JAN	1	00.00 → AQU
FEB	20	08.48 → PIS

MOON

dy	jan	feb	mar	apr	may	jun	jul	aug	sep	oct	nov	dec	dy
1	AQU	22.52	04.45	22.50	08.02	18.45	05.19	SCO	CAP	AQU	PIS	18.14	1
2	AQU	ARI	ARI	GEM	CAN	VIR	LIB	03.21	CAP	AQU	00.36	TAU	2
3	07.12	ARI	12.00	GEM	10.02	23.18	11.58	SAG	09.45	05.24	ARI	22.56	3
4	PIS	06.36	TAU	02.00	LEO	LIB	SCO	14.49	AQU	PIS	08.36	GEM	4
5	17.14	TAU	17.16	CAN	13.08	LIB	21.31	CAP	22.07	16.11	TAU	GEM	5
6	ARI	11.27	GEM	04.39	VIR	06.28	SAG	CAP	PIS	ARI	13.39	00.55	6
7	ARI	GEM	20.34	LEO	17.52	SCO	SAG	03.21	PIS	ARI	GEM	CAN	7
8	00.09	13.25	CAN	07.27	LIB	15.46	08.56	AQU	09.12	00.34	16.50	01.58	8
9	TAU	CAN	22.23	VIR	LIB	SAG	CAP	15.50	ARI	TAU	CAN	LEO	9
10	03.19	13.33	LEO	11.11	00.26	SAG	21.21	PIS	18.22	06.41	19.24	03.47	10
11	GEM	LEO	23.47	LIB	SCO	02.47	AQU	PIS	TAU	GEM	LEO	VIR	11
12	03.28	13.41	VIR	16.45	09.02	CAP	AQU	03.23	TAU	11.00	22.16	07.21	12
13	CAN	VIR	VIR	SCO	SAG	15.06	09.59	ARI	CAN	14.03	VIR	LIB	13
14	02.27	15.53	02.18	SCO	19.46	AQU	PIS	12.52	GEM	14.03	VIR	12.56	14
15	LEO	LIB	LIB	00.56	CAP	AQU	21.36	TAU	05.27	LEO	01.55	SCO	15
16	02.32	21.43	07.26	SAG	CAP	03.42	ARI	19.15	CAN	16.24	LIB	20.19	16
17	VIR	SCO	SCO	11.49	08.05	PIS	ARI	GEM	07.30	VIR	06.41	SAG	17
18	05.47	SCO	16.01	CAP	AQU	14.43	06.28	22.12	LEO	18.49	SCO	SAG	18
19	LIB	07.29	SAG	CAP	20.21	ARI	TAU	CAN	08.20	LIB	13.06	05.34	19
20	13.14	SAG	SAG	00.15	PIS	22.17	11.26	22.37	VIR	22.23	SAG	CAP	20
21	SCO	19.46	03.33	AQU	PIS	TAU	GEM	LEO	09.28	SCO	21.50	16.48	21
22	SCO	CAP	CAP	12.01	06.22	TAU	12.47	22.13	LIB	SCO	CAP	AQU	22
23	00.15	CAP	16.06	PIS	ARI	01.46	CAN	VIR	12.33	04.15	CAP	AQU	23
24	SAG	08.20	AQU	21.07	12.40	GEM	12.06	23.00	SCO	SAG	09.09	05.35	24
25	12.55	AQU	AQU	ARI	TAU	02.12	LEO	LIB	18.53	13.14	AQU	PIS	25
26	CAP	19.31	03.24	ARI	15.27	CAN	11.33	SAG	SAG	CAP	21.55	18.08	26
27	CAP	PIS	PIS	02.55	GEM	01.35	VIR	02.46	SAG	CAP	PIS	ARI	27
28	01.27	PIS	12.13	TAU	16.10	LEO	13.13	SCO	04.45	00.58	PIS	ARI	28
29	AQU		ARI	06.07	CAN	02.04	LIB	10.21	CAP	AQU	09.42	03.57	29
30	12.55		18.29	GEM	16.42	VIR	18.27	16.59	SAG	13.35	ARI	TAU	30
31	PIS		TAU		LEO		SCO	21.14		PIS		09.33	31

SUN

mth	dy	time → sign
JAN	1	00.00 → CAP
JAN	21	10.56 → AQU
FEB	20	01.23 → PIS
MAR	21	00.56 → ARI
APR	20	12.42 → TAU
MAY	21	12.29 → GEM
JUN	21	20.54 → CAN
JUL	23	07.52 → LEO
AUG	23	14.37 → VIR
SEP	23	11.43 → LIB
OCT	23	20.19 → SCO
NOV	22	17.18 → SAG
DEC	22	06.17 → CAP

SATURN

mth	dy	time → sign
JAN	1	00.00 → AQU

MERCURY

mth	dy	time → sign
JAN	1	00.00 → CAP
JAN	2	09.22 → AQU
JAN	14	03.48 → CAP
FEB	15	10.59 → AQU
MAR	7	08.07 → PIS
MAR	23	23.34 → ARI
APR	7	19.16 → TAU
JUN	14	06.23 → GEM
JUL	1	22.12 → CAN
JUL	16	00.26 → LEO
AUG	1	13.22 → VIR
AUG	28	08.17 → LIB
SEP	7	20.25 → VIR
OCT	9	01.54 → LIB
OCT	26	20.16 → SCO
NOV	14	13.48 → SAG
DEC	4	14.14 → CAP

VENUS

mth	dy	time → sign
JAN	1	00.00 → SCO
JAN	5	03.45 → SAG
JAN	30	09.28 → CAP
FEB	24	03.05 → AQU
MAR	19	16.03 → PIS
APR	13	03.27 → ARI
MAY	7	14.54 → TAU
JUN	1	02.28 → GEM
JUN	25	13.26 → CAN
JUL	19	23.03 → LEO
AUG	13	06.54 → VIR
SEP	6	13.55 → LIB
SEP	30	21.01 → SCO
OCT	25	05.38 → SAG
NOV	18	16.40 → CAP
DEC	13	09.05 → AQU

MARS

mth	dy	time → sign
JAN	1	00.00 → AQU
JAN	19	15.38 → PIS
FEB	27	03.04 → ARI
APR	6	18.19 → TAU
MAY	18	03.33 → GEM
JUN	30	14.51 → CAN
AUG	15	03.31 → LEO
OCT	1	13.51 → VIR
NOV	20	06.20 → LIB

JUPITER

mth	dy	time → sign
JAN	1	00.00 → PIS
MAR	1	03.15 → ARI
AUG	8	20.26 → TAU
AUG	31	13.52 → ARI

MOON

dy	jan	feb	mar	apr	may	jun	jul	aug	sep	oct	nov	dec	dy
1	GEM	LEO	09.16	21.04	10.36	CAP	AQU	02.59	TAU	21.50	LEO	21.33	1
2	11.25	21.45	VIR	SCO	SAG	11.13	06.58	ARI	07.59	CAN	12.40	LIB	2
3	CAN	VIR	08.53	SCO	16.58	AQU	PIS	15.13	GEM	CAN	VIR	LIB	3
4	11.18	22.01	LIB	00.41	CAP	23.15	19.55	TAU	14.47	02.38	14.27	00.01	4
5	LEO	LIB	10.24	SAG	CAP	PIS	ARI	TAU	CAN	LEO	LIB	SCO	5
6	11.22	LIB	SCO	07.57	02.50	PIS	ARI	00.30	17.53	04.36	15.20	02.38	6
7	VIR	01.08	15.18	CAP	AQU	12.02	07.29	GEM	LEO	VIR	SCO	SAG	7
8	13.25	SCO	SAG	18.49	15.17	ARI	TAU	05.44	18.18	04.45	16.54	06.46	8
9	LIB	07.49	SAG	AQU	PIS	22.50	15.32	CAN	VIR	LIB	SAG	CAP	9
10	18.20	SAG	00.03	AQU	PIS	TAU	07.30	GEM	17.44	04.43	20.56	13.53	10
11	SCO	17.41	CAP	07.38	03.51	TAU	19.41	LEO	LIB	SCO	CAP	AQU	11
12	SCO	CAP	11.47	PIS	ARI	06.06	21.10	VIR	18.05	06.25	CAP	AQU	12
13	02.03	CAP	AQU	20.04	14.12	GEM	07.25	SCO	SAG	11.31	04.47	00.30	13
14	SAG	05.36	AQU	ARI	TAU	10.10	07.25	SAG	21.05	11.31	AQU	PIS	14
15	11.58	AQU	00.43	ARI	21.30	CAN	21.48	SAG	CAP	CAP	16.14	13.19	15
16	CAP	18.27	PIS	06.31	GEM	12.26	VIR	09.12	SAG	20.39	PIS	ARI	16
17	23.32	PIS	13.13	TAU	GEM	LEO	23.14	SCO	03.45	AQU	PIS	ARI	17
18	AQU	PIS	ARI	14.31	02.21	14.26	LIB	13.50	CAP	AQU	05.14	01.33	18
19	AQU	07.10	ARI	GEM	CAN	VIR	LIB	SAG	13.55	08.50	ARI	TAU	19
20	12.18	ARI	00.09	20.22	05.50	17.11	02.34	21.37	AQU	PIS	17.06	10.57	20
21	PIS	18.31	TAU	CAN	LEO	LIB	SCO	CAP	AQU	21.51	TAU	GEM	21
22	PIS	TAU	08.52	CAN	08.49	21.09	08.10	CAP	02.20	ARI	TAU	17.08	22
23	01.10	TAU	GEM	00.27	VIR	SCO	SAG	08.02	PIS	ARI	02.25	CAN	23
24	ARI	03.05	14.55	LEO	11.48	SCO	16.01	AQU	15.20	09.44	GEM	21.04	24
25	12.09	GEM	CAN	03.10	LIB	02.31	CAP	20.16	ARI	TAU	09.17	LEO	25
26	TAU	08.00	18.16	VIR	15.08	SAG	CAP	PIS	ARI	19.38	CAN	LEO	26
27	19.26	CAN	LEO	05.05	SCO	09.39	02.01	PIS	03.33	GEM	14.26	00.01	27
28	GEM	09.36	19.31	LIB	19.29	CAP	AQU	09.17	TAU	GEM	LEO	VIR	28
29	22.32	LEO	VIR	07.06	SAG	19.07	13.58	ARI	13.59	03.24	18.27	02.56	29
30	CAN		19.54	SCO	SAG	AQU	PIS	GEM	CAN	CAN	VIR	LIB	30
31	22.38		LIB		01.53		PIS	TAU		09.04		06.12	31

SUN

mth	dy	time → sign
JAN	1	00.00 → CAP
JAN	20	16.55 → AQU
FEB	19	07.23 → PIS
MAR	21	06.56 → ARI
APR	20	18.47 → TAU
MAY	21	18.33 → GEM
JUN	22	02.53 → CAN
JUL	23	13.45 → LEO
AUG	23	20.27 → VIR
SEP	23	17.32 → LIB
OCT	24	02.08 → SCO
NOV	22	23.07 → SAG
DEC	22	12.04 → CAP

MERCURY

mth	dy	time → sign
JAN	1	00.00 → CAP
FEB	9	05.38 → AQU
FEB	27	22.08 → PIS
MAR	15	19.36 → ARI
APR	1	18.19 → TAU
APR	28	12.45 → ARI
MAY	15	20.06 → TAU
JUN	8	18.01 → GEM
JUN	23	09.54 → CAN
JUL	7	22.09 → LEO
JUL	27	06.51 → VIR
OCT	1	23.19 → LIB
OCT	19	07.45 → SCO
NOV	7	16.24 → SAG
DEC	2	04.44 → CAP
DEC	10	00.57 → SAG

VENUS

mth	dy	time → sign
JAN	1	00.00 → AQU
JAN	7	14.42 → PIS
FEB	3	04.43 → ARI
MAR	6	05.26 → TAU
MAY	9	10.37 → ARI
MAY	28	11.18 → TAU
JUL	8	12.02 → GEM
AUG	6	08.18 → CAN
SEP	1	20.16 → LEO
SEP	27	04.02 → VIR
OCT	21	18.34 → LIB
NOV	14	22.43 → SCO
DEC	8	21.33 → SAG

MARS

mth	dy	time → sign
JAN	1	00.00 → LIB
JAN	13	19.35 → SCO
AUG	21	19.46 → SAG
OCT	8	00.12 → CAP
NOV	18	04.12 → AQU
DEC	27	13.44 → PIS

SATURN

mth	dy	time → sign
JAN	1	00.00 → AQU
APR	13	08.23 → PIS
AUG	17	00.22 → AQU

JUPITER

mth	dy	time → sign
JAN	1	00.00 → ARI
MAR	7	18.11 → TAU
JUL	21	00.12 → GEM
DEC	4	22.20 → TAU

MOON

dy	jan	feb	mar	apr	may	jun	jul	aug	sep	oct	nov	dec	dy
1	SCO	CAP	CAP	05.03	00.03	TAU	23.17	LEO	03.32	SCO	00.37	AQU	1
2	10.08	CAP	12.05	PIS	ARI	06.55	CAN	17.09	LIB	13.35	21.26	PIS	2
3	SAG	06.08	AQU	17.52	12.52	GEM	CAN	VIR	04.12	SAG	05.19	PIS	3
4	15.20	AQU	23.12	ARI	TAU	15.57	05.27	19.20	SCO	16.20	AQU	PIS	4
5	CAP	16.39	PIS	ARI	TAU	CAN	LEO	LIB	06.04	CAP	14.05	08.24	5
6	22.43	PIS	PIS	06.44	00.21	22.59	09.53	21.28	SAG	22.36	PIS	ARI	6
7	AQU	PIS	11.46	TAU	GEM	LEO	VIR	SCO	10.13	AQU	PIS	21.06	7
8	AQU	05.03	ARI	18.35	10.01	LEO	13.16	SCO	CAP	AQU	01.48	TAU	8
9	08.57	ARI	ARI	GEM	CAN	04.17	LIB	00.24	17.02	08.09	ARI	TAU	9
10	PIS	18.00	00.42	GEM	17.34	VIR	16.04	SAG	AQU	PIS	14.32	09.24	10
11	21.29	TAU	TAU	04.28	LEO	07.53	SCO	04.45	AQU	19.49	TAU	GEM	11
12	ARI	TAU	12.35	CAN	22.40	LIB	18.46	CAP	02.20	ARI	TAU	20.14	12
13	ARI	05.17	GEM	11.30	VIR	10.01	SAG	11.00	PIS	ARI	02.54	CAN	13
14	10.11	GEM	21.48	LEO	VIR	SCO	22.12	AQU	13.35	08.25	GEM	CAN	14
15	TAU	13.05	CAN	15.13	01.12	11.29	CAP	19.34	ARI	TAU	14.14	05.19	15
16	20.25	CAN	CAN	VIR	LIB	SAG	CAP	PIS	ARI	20.59	CAN	LEO	16
17	GEM	17.00	03.19	16.04	01.50	13.46	03.29	PIS	02.05	GEM	23.50	12.30	17
18	GEM	LEO	LEO	LIB	SCO	CAP	AQU	06.30	TAU	GEM	LEO	VIR	18
19	02.56	18.05	05.18	15.30	02.05	18.33	11.36	ARI	14.40	08.29	LEO	17.25	19
20	CAN	VIR	VIR	SCO	SAG	AQU	PIS	19.02	GEM	CAN	06.47	LIB	20
21	06.13	18.03	05.03	15.28	03.56	AQU	22.39	TAU	GEM	17.33	VIR	20.01	21
22	LEO	LIB	LIB	SAG	CAP	02.57	ARI	TAU	01.37	LEO	10.29	SCO	22
23	07.46	18.42	04.26	18.03	09.12	PIS	ARI	07.18	CAN	23.03	LIB	21.00	23
24	VIR	SCO	SCO	CAP	AQU	14.33	11.16	GEM	09.17	VIR	11.19	SAG	24
25	09.09	21.31	05.25	CAP	18.34	ARI	TAU	17.12	LEO	VIR	SCO	21.53	25
26	LIB	SAG	SAG	00.41	PIS	ARI	23.01	CAN	13.07	00.55	10.47	CAP	26
27	11.35	SAG	09.40	AQU	PIS	03.16	GEM	23.31	VIR	LIB	SAG	CAP	27
28	SCO	03.19	CAP	11.15	06.53	TAU	GEM	LEO	13.54	00.24SCO	11.03	00.31	28
29	15.44		17.47	PIS	ARI	14.37	08.00	LIB	23.33	CAP	CAP	AQU	29
30	SAG		AQU	PIS	19.41	GEM	CAN	02.32	13.22	SAG	14.11	06.30	30
31	21.51		AQU		TAU		13.47	VIR		SAG		PIS	31

SUN

mth	dy	time → sign
JAN	1	00.00 → CAP
JAN	20	22.40 → AQU
FEB	19	13.18 → PIS
MAR	21	12.52 → ARI
APR	21	00.39 → TAU
MAY	22	00.25 → GEM
JUN	22	08.42 → CAN
JUL	23	19.36 → LEO
AUG	24	02.14 → VIR
SEP	23	23.16 → LIB
OCT	24	07.55 → SCO
NOV	23	04.51 → SAG
DEC	22	17.51 → CAP

MERCURY

mth	dy	time → sign
JAN	1	00.00 → SAG
JAN	12	20.59 → CAP
FEB	12	12.04 → AQU
FEB	20	03.33 → PIS
MAR	8	02.10 → ARI
MAY	15	03.08 → TAU
MAY	31	22.49 → GEM
JUN	14	19.23 → CAN
JUN	30	21.27 → LEO
SEP	7	21.52 → VIR
SEP	24	03.26 → LIB
OCT	11	23.32 → SCO
NOV	1	19.33 → SAG
DEC	6	22.07 → SCO
DEC	12	23.47 → SAG

VENUS

mth	dy	time → sign
JAN	1	00.00 → SAG
JAN	1	18.20 → CAP
JAN	25	15.10 → AQU
FEB	18	13.17 → PIS
MAR	14	13.43 → ARI
APR	7	17.59 → TAU
MAY	2	03.13 → GEM
MAY	26	18.19 → CAN
JUN	20	16.32 → LEO
JUL	16	01.19 → VIR
AUG	11	03.21 → LIB
SEP	7	15.35 → SCO
OCT	9	10.34 → SAG
DEC	15	11.40 → SCO
DEC	25	23.59 → SAG

MARS

mth	dy	time → sign
JAN	1	00.00 → PIS
FEB	4	23.39 → ARI
MAR	17	11.44 → TAU
APR	28	17.16 → GEM
JUN	11	19.31 → CAN
JUL	27	14.02 → LEO
SEP	12	12.41 → VIR
OCT	30	04.29 → LIB
DEC	17	12.17 → SCO

SATURN

mth	dy	time → sign
JAN	1	00.00 → AQU
JAN	8	12.38 → PIS

JUPITER

mth	dy	time → sign
JAN	1	00.00 → TAU
MAR	9	21.32 → GEM
JUL	30	23.27 → CAN

MOON

dy	jan	feb	mar	apr	may	jun	jul	aug	sep	oct	nov	dec	dy
1	16.16	TAU	TAU	05.20	LEO	19.38	05.43	15.58	AQU	20.56	TAU	GEM	1
2	ARI	TAU	09.31	CAN	LEO	LIB	SCO	CAP	06.28	ARI	TAU	20.01	2
3	ARI	01.17	GEM	15.31	07.03	21.35	06.53	17.57	PIS	ARI	00.56	CAN	3
4	04.33	GEM	21.19	LEO	VIR	SCO	SAG	AQU	13.04	06.20	GEM	CAN	4
5	TAU	12.21	CAN	21.53	10.53	21.15	07.06	21.36	ARI	TAU	13.43	08.37	5
6	16.58	CAN	CAN	VIR	LIB	SAG	CAP	PIS	22.21	17.52	CAN	LEO	6
7	GEM	20.32	06.16	VIR	11.23	20.40	08.11	PIS	TAU	GEM	CAN	19.30	7
8	GEM	LEO	LEO	00.25	SCO	CAP	AQU	04.07	TAU	GEM	02.13	VIR	8
9	03.38	LEO	11.34	LIB	10.24	21.55	11.52	ARI	10.05	06.38	LEO	VIR	9
10	CAN	01.50	VIR	00.29	SAG	AQU	PIS	13.55	GEM	CAN	12.10	03.00	10
11	11.57	VIR	13.53	SCO	10.12	AQU	19.12	TAU	22.39	18.27	VIR	LIB	11
12	LEO	05.07	LIB	00.08	CAP	02.40	ARI	TAU	CAN	LEO	18.00	06.31	12
13	18.11	LIB	14.48	SAG	12.45	PIS	ARI	02.03	CAN	LEO	LIB	SCO	13
14	VIR	07.34	SCO	01.23	AQU	11.20	05.55	GEM	09.37	03.02	19.54	06.55	14
15	22.48	SCO	16.01	CAP	19.06	ARI	TAU	14.23	LEO	VIR	SCO	SAG	15
16	LIB	10.08	SAG	05.39	PIS	22.55	18.25	CAN	17.18	07.34	19.29	06.02	16
17	LIB	SAG	18.54	AQU	PIS	TAU	GEM	CAN	VIR	LIB	SAG	CAP	17
18	02.08	13.32	CAP	13.10	04.54	TAU	GEM	00.50	21.39	09.00	18.58	06.03	18
19	SCO	CAP	CAP	PIS	ARI	11.35	06.37	LEO	LIB	SCO	CAP	AQU	19
20	04.36	18.17	00.06	23.15	16.49	GEM	CAN	08.31	23.53	09.14	20.23	08.48	20
21	SAG	AQU	AQU	ARI	TAU	23.51	17.09	VIR	SCO	SAG	AQU	PIS	21
22	06.59	AQU	07.38	ARI	TAU	CAN	LEO	13.40	SCO	10.14	AQU	15.17	22
23	CAP	00.52	PIS	10.56	05.27	CAN	LEO	LIB	01.35	CAP	00.59	ARI	23
24	10.26	PIS	17.10	TAU	GEM	10.49	01.29	17.10	SAG	13.24	PIS	ARI	24
25	AQU	09.45	ARI	23.28	17.54	LEO	VIR	SCO	04.02	AQU	08.53	01.15	25
26	16.12	ARI	ARI	GEM	CAN	19.50	07.38	19.55	CAP	19.11	ARI	TAU	26
27	PIS	20.58	04.27	GEM	CAN	VIR	LIB	SAG	07.58	PIS	19.17	13.23	27
28	PIS	TAU	TAU	12.02	05.14	VIR	11.46	22.38	AQU	PIS	TAU	GEM	28
29	01.06		16.58	CAN	LEO	02.13	SCO	CAP	13.34	03.18	TAU	GEM	29
30	ARI		GEM	23.09	14.10	LIB	14.17	CAP	PIS	ARI	07.15	02.11	30
31	12.45		GEM		VIR		SAG	01.56		13.18		CAN	31

SUN

mth	dy	time → sign
JAN	1	00.00 → CAP
JAN	21	04.33 → AQU
FEB	19	18.56 → PIS
MAR	21	18.35 → ARI
APR	21	06.14 → TAU
MAY	22	06.04 → GEM
JUN	22	14.23 → CAN
JUL	24	01.17 → LEO
AUG	24	08.04 → VIR
SEP	24	05.07 → LIB
OCT	24	13.52 → SCO
NOV	23	10.53 → SAG
DEC	22	23.53 → CAP

MERCURY

mth	dy	time → sign
JAN	1	00.00 → SAG
JAN	7	00.57 → CAP
JAN	26	05.00 → AQU
FEB	12	08.39 → PIS
MAR	3	20.52 → ARI
MAR	14	05.02 → PIS
APR	18	10.44 → ARI
MAY	8	15.23 → TAU
MAY	23	10.38 → GEM
JUN	6	16.43 → CAN
JUN	27	08.07 → LEO
JUL	26	14.36 → CAN
AUG	12	16.22 → LEO
AUG	31	06.54 → VIR
SEP	16	06.52 → LIB
OCT	5	04.36 → SCO
DEC	11	03.37 → SAG
DEC	31	03.58 → CAP

VENUS

mth	dy	time → sign
JAN	1	00.00 → SAG
FEB	6	16.27 → CAP
MAR	6	20.44 → AQU
APR	2	01.25 → PIS
APR	27	12.27 → ARI
MAY	22	15.14 → TAU
JUN	16	13.16 → GEM
JUL	11	06.43 → CAN
AUG	4	19.08 → LEO
AUG	29	02.31 → VIR
SEP	22	05.52 → LIB
OCT	16	06.58 → SCO
NOV	9	07.07 → SAG
DEC	3	07.25 → CAP
DEC	27	08.52 → AQU

MARS

mth	dy	time → sign
JAN	1	00.00 → SCO
FEB	5	09.38 → SAG
APR	1	18.21 → CAP
OCT	13	14.22 → AQU
NOV	29	04.43 → PIS

SATURN

mth	dy	time → sign
JAN	1	00.00 → PIS

JUPITER

mth	dy	time → sign
JAN	1	00.00 → CAN
AUG	18	23.01 → LEO

MOON

dy	jan	feb	mar	apr	may	jun	jul	aug	sep	oct	nov	dec	dy
1	14.29	VIR	21.31	SCO	20.59	AQU	21.14	TAU	17.22	14.05	VIR	LIB	1
2	LEO	15.10	LIB	11.59	CAP	09.10	ARI	21.56	CAN	LEO	19.43	11.35	2
3	LEO	LIB	LIB	SAG	23.07	PIS	ARI	GEM	CAN	LEO	LIB	SCO	3
4	01.18	20.55	02.26	14.24	AQU	14.46	04.56	GEM	06.20	01.49	LIB	14.28	4
5	VIR	SCO	SCO	CAP	AQU	ARI	TAU	10.27	LEO	VIR	01.23	SAG	5
6	09.41	SCO	06.04	17.35	03.12	23.12	15.41	CAN	17.56	10.39	SCO	15.18	6
7	LIB	00.34	SAG	AQU	PIS	TAU	GEM	23.26	VIR	LIB	04.25	CAP	7
8	14.55	SAG	09.03	21.47	09.20	TAU	GEM	LEO	VIR	16.38	SAG	15.53	8
9	SCO	02.35	CAP	PIS	ARI	09.55	04.16	LEO	03.07	SCO	06.24	AQU	9
10	17.07	CAP	11.50	PIS	17.29	GEM	CAN	11.16	LIB	20.47	CAP	17.44	10
11	SAG	03.50	AQU	03.16	TAU	22.16	17.18	VIR	10.01	SAG	08.38	PIS	11
12	17.21	AQU	14.56	ARI	TAU	CAN	LEO	21.07	SCO	SAG	AQU	21.48	12
13	CAP	05.41	PIS	10.35	03.41	CAN	LEO	15.07	00.07	11.52	ARI	13
14	17.20	PIS	19.20	TAU	GEM	11.21	05.29	LIB	SAG	CAP	PIS	ARI	14
15	AQU	09.38	ARI	20.24	15.50	LEO	VIR	04.35	18.46	03.13	16.24	04.24	15
16	18.55	ARI	ARI	GEM	CAN	23.35	15.34	SCO	CAP	AQU	ARI	TAU	16
17	PIS	16.58	02.10	GEM	CAN	VIR	LIB	09.31	21.12	06.20	22.31	13.25	17
18	23.42	TAU	TAU	08.34	04.52	VIR	22.34	SAG	AQU	PIS	TAU	GEM	18
19	ARI	TAU	12.10	CAN	LEO	09.05	SCO	12.05	23.02	09.57	TAU	GEM	19
20	ARI	03.46	GEM	21.25	16.37	LIB	SCO	CAP	PIS	ARI	06.43	00.31	20
21	08.21	GEM	GEM	LEO	VIR	14.43	02.11	13.00	PIS	15.00	GEM	CAN	21
22	TAU	16.30	00.36	LEO	VIR	SCO	SAG	AQU	01.25	TAU	17.24	13.09	22
23	20.04	CAN	CAN	08.17	00.54	16.42	03.06	13.33	ARI	22.38	CAN	LEO	23
24	GEM	CAN	13.07	VIR	LIB	SAG	CAP	PIS	05.55	GEM	CAN	LEO	24
25	GEM	04.41	LEO	15.22	05.03	16.30	02.46	15.28	TAU	GEM	06.04	02.06	25
26	08.56	LEO	23.10	LIB	SCO	CAP	AQU	ARI	13.49	09.25	LEO	VIR	26
27	CAN	14.28	VIR	18.47	06.05	16.00	03.00	20.26	GEM	CAN	18.50	13.27	27
28	21.00	VIR	VIR	SCO	SAG	AQU	PIS	TAU	GEM	22.14	VIR	LIB	28
29	LEO		05.46	20.02	05.54	17.07	05.37	TAU	01.09	LEO	VIR	21.26	29
30	LEO		LIB	SAG	CAP	PIS	ARI	05.19	CAN	LEO	05.09	SCO	30
31	07.12		09.33		06.26		11.53	GEM		10.28		SCO	31

SUN

mth	dy	time → sign
JAN	1	00.00 → CAP
JAN	21	10.26 → AQU
FEB	20	00.54 → PIS
MAR	21	00.28 → ARI
APR	20	12.13 → TAU
MAY	21	11.59 → GEM
JUN	21	20.19 → CAN
JUL	23	07.16 → LEO
AUG	23	13.58 → VIR
SEP	23	10.58 → LIB
OCT	23	19.39 → SCO
NOV	22	16.35 → SAG
DEC	22	05.34 → CAP

MERCURY

mth	dy	time → sign
JAN	1	00.00 → CAP
JAN	18	17.25 → AQU
FEB	5	04.24 → PIS
APR	12	22.46 → ARI
APR	29	19.03 → TAU
MAY	13	20.52 → GEM
MAY	30	04.35 → CAN
AUG	6	23.47 → LEO
AUG	22	01.34 → VIR
SEP	7	18.14 → LIB
SEP	28	19.38 → SCO
NOV	1	22.44 → LIB
NOV	11	17.55 → SCO
DEC	3	17.54 → SAG
DEC	22	22.31 → CAP

VENUS

mth	dy	time → sign
JAN	1	00.00 → AQU
JAN	20	13.52 → PIS
FEB	14	02.55 → ARI
MAR	10	08.07 → TAU
APR	5	20.58 → GEM
MAY	5	17.42 → CAN
SEP	8	22.32 → LEO
OCT	8	06.15 → VIR
NOV	3	11.28 → LIB
NOV	28	10.43 → SCO
DEC	22	20.03 → SAG

MARS

mth	dy	time → sign
JAN	1	00.00 → PIS
JAN	11	04.47 → ARI
FEB	23	03.22 → TAU
APR	7	04.12 → GEM
MAY	22	14.14 → CAN
JUL	8	03.48 → LEO
AUG	24	06.53 → VIR
OCT	10	06.14 → LIB
NOV	25	14.15 → SCO

SATURN

mth	dy	time → sign
JAN	1	00.00 → PIS
MAR	19	14.10 → ARI

JUPITER

mth	dy	time → sign
JAN	1	00.00 → LEO
SEP	12	10.19 → VIR

MOON

dy	jan	feb	mar	apr	may	jun	jul	aug	sep	oct	nov	dec	dy
1	01.28	13.32	AQU	ARI	TAU	CAN	LEO	22.56	SCO	SAG	AQU	PIS	1
2	SAG	AQU	00.05	13.04	03.44	CAN	LEO	LIB	SCO	13.12	AQU	10.26	2
3	02.25	12.50	PIS	TAU	GEM	07.59	03.58	LIB	00.52	CAP	02.10	ARI	3
4	CAP	PIS	00.20	18.26	12.23	LEO	VIR	09.53	SAG	17.16	PIS	13.37	4
5	01.58	13.31	ARI	GEM	CAN	20.42	16.19	SCO	06.40	AQU	03.58	TAU	5
6	AQU	ARI	02.50	GEM	CAN	VIR	LIB	17.47	CAP	18.49	ARI	18.01	6
7	02.03	17.24	TAU	03.43	00.01	VIR	LIB	SAG	09.06	PIS	05.43	GEM	7
8	PIS	TAU	09.13	CAN	08.33	SCO	02.23	21.57	AQU	19.01	TAU	GEM	8
9	04.24	TAU	GEM	15.58	12.46	LIB	SCO	CAP	09.04	ARI	09.00	00.33	9
10	ARI	01.23	19.39	LEO	VIR	17.30	08.49	22.53	PIS	19.42	GEM	CAN	10
11	10.05	GEM	CAN	LEO	VIR	SCO	SAG	AQU	08.21	TAU	15.18	09.52	11
12	TAU	12.48	CAN	04.41	00.01	22.52	11.40	22.09	ARI	22.54	CAN	LEO	12
13	19.10	CAN	08.28	VIR	LIB	SAG	CAP	PIS	09.11	GEM	CAN	21.38	13
14	GEM	CAN	LEO	15.33	08.12	SAG	12.07	21.49	TAU	GEM	01.07	VIR	14
15	GEM	01.46	21.09	LIB	SCO	01.25	AQU	ARI	13.27	06.00	LEO	VIR	15
16	06.45	LEO	VIR	23.44	13.26	CAP	11.58	23.55	GEM	CAN	13.23	10.12	16
17	CAN	14.28	VIR	SCO	SAG	02.35	PIS	TAU	16.51	VIR	LIB	LIB	17
18	19.33	VIR	08.04	SCO	16.44	AQU	13.02	TAU	CAN	LEO	VIR	21.12	18
19	LEO	VIR	LIB	05.41	CAP	03.51	ARI	05.48	CAN	LEO	01.44	SCO	19
20	LEO	01.48	16.52	SAG	19.14	PIS	16.46	GEM	09.42	05.32	LIB	SCO	20
21	08.23	LIB	SCO	10.10	AQU	06.27	TAU	15.26	LEO	VIR	12.04	05.02	21
22	VIR	11.14	23.45	CAP	21.49	ARI	23.48	CAN	22.34	17.43	SCO	SAG	22
23	20.03	SCO	SAG	13.40	PIS	11.09	GEM	CAN	VIR	LIB	19.39	09.38	23
24	LIB	18.15	SAG	AQU	PIS	TAU	GEM	03.32	VIR	LIB	SAG	CAP	24
25	LIB	SAG	04.48	16.25	01.03	18.16	09.44	LEO	10.46	03.59	SAG	12.01	25
26	05.17	22.28	CAP	PIS	ARI	GEM	CAN	16.23	LIB	SCO	00.54	AQU	26
27	SCO	CAP	07.57	18.57	05.30	GEM	21.38	VIR	21.30	12.12	CAP	13.38	27
28	11.08	CAP	AQU	ARI	TAU	03.44	LEO	VIR	SCO	SAG	04.40	PIS	28
29	SAG	00.04	09.33	22.16	11.48	CAN	LEO	04.47	SCO	18.34	AQU	15.48	29
30	13.33		PIS	TAU	GEM	15.14	10.24	LIB	06.28	CAP	07.39	ARI	30
31	CAP		10.41		20.37		VIR	15.55		23.12		19.24	31

SUN

mth	dy	time → sign
JAN	1	00.00 → CAP
JAN	20	16.13 → AQU
FEB	19	06.38 → PIS
MAR	21	06.12 → ARI
APR	20	17.58 → TAU
MAY	21	17.47 → GEM
JUN	22	02.06 → CAN
JUL	23	13.03 → LEO
AUG	23	19.44 → VIR
SEP	23	16.46 → LIB
OCT	24	01.23 → SCO
NOV	22	22.22 → SAG
DEC	22	11.23 → CAP

MERCURY

mth	dy	time → sign
JAN	1	00.00 → CAP
JAN	10	09.01 → AQU
MAR	17	11.32 → PIS
APR	6	01.25 → ARI
APR	21	10.00 → TAU
MAY	5	21.47 → GEM
JUL	13	06.04 → CAN
JUL	30	00.36 → LEO
AUG	13	21.32 → VIR
SEP	1	00.07 → LIB
NOV	7	18.06 → SCO
NOV	26	14.57 → SAG
DEC	15	16.32 → CAP

VENUS

mth	dy	time → sign
JAN	1	00.00 → SAG
JAN	15	23.22 → CAP
FEB	9	00.41 → AQU
MAR	5	02.12 → PIS
MAR	29	05.14 → ARI
APR	22	10.37 → TAU
MAY	16	18.31 → GEM
JUN	10	04.36 → CAN
JUL	4	16.32 → LEO
JUL	29	06.40 → VIR
AUG	23	00.37 → LIB
SEP	17	00.23 → SCO
OCT	12	09.29 → SAG
NOV	7	12.11 → CAP
DEC	5	13.03 → AQU

MARS

mth	dy	time → sign
JAN	1	00.00 → SCO
JAN	10	03.49 → SAG
FEB	24	02.01 → CAP
APR	9	20.34 → AQU
MAY	25	22.47 → PIS
JUL	21	08.26 → ARI
SEP	26	21.29 → PIS
NOV	20	20.37 → ARI

SATURN

mth	dy	time → sign
JAN	1	00.00 → ARI

JUPITER

mth	dy	time → sign
JAN	1	00.00 → VIR
OCT	11	23.50 → LIB

MOON

dy	jan	feb	mar	apr	may	jun	jul	aug	sep	oct	nov	dec	dy
1	TAU	14.32	CAN	LEO	20.11	SCO	SAG	06.22	17.18	03.14	16.57	08.17	1
2	TAU	CAN	CAN	00.51	LIB	SCO	17.04	AQU	ARI	TAU	CAN	LEO	2
3	00.54	CAN	06.41	VIR	LIB	01.32	CAP	07.42	17.26	04.04	23.10	16.50	3
4	GEM	00.50	LEO	13.31	08.04	SAG	21.14	PIS	TAU	GEM	LEO	VIR	4
5	08.24	LEO	18.48	LIB	SCO	08.54	AQU	08.22	19.55	08.09	LEO	VIR	5
6	CAN	12.35	VIR	LIB	18.16	CAP	23.41	ARI	GEM	CAN	09.04	04.30	6
7	18.01	VIR	VIR	01.33	SAG	14.04	PIS	10.05	GEM	15.58	VIR	LIB	7
8	LEO	VIR	07.23	SCO	SAG	AQU	PIS	TAU	01.35	LEO	21.19	17.17	8
9	LEO	01.10	LIB	12.17	02.26	17.40	01.45	13.55	CAN	LEO	LIB	SCO	9
10	05.33	LIB	19.40	SAG	CAP	PIS	ARI	GEM	10.11	02.42	LIB	SCO	10
11	VIR	13.30	SCO	20.57	08.26	20.21	04.29	20.08	LEO	VIR	10.04	05.01	11
12	18.11	SCO	SCO	CAP	AQU	ARI	TAU	CAN	20.54	15.01	SCO	SAG	12
13	LIB	23.48	06.37	CAP	12.14	22.50	08.30	CAN	VIR	LIB	21.57	14.31	13
14	LIB	SAG	SAG	02.44	PIS	TAU	GEM	04.29	VIR	LIB	SAG	CAP	14
15	06.02	SAG	14.46	AQU	14.13	TAU	14.07	LEO	09.00	03.46	SAG	21.39	15
16	SCO	06.27	CAP	05.26	ARI	01.53	CAN	14.42	LIB	SCO	08.09	AQU	16
17	15.01	CAP	19.09	PIS	15.24	GEM	21.41	VIR	16.02	CAP	AQU	17
18	SAG	09.08	AQU	05.51	TAU	06.28	LEO	VIR	SCO	SAG	16.05	02.48	18
19	20.09	AQU	20.08	ARI	17.13	CAN	LEO	02.36	SCO	SAG	AQU	PIS	19
20	CAP	09.00	PIS	05.43	GEM	13.32	07.32	LIB	10.11	02.37	21.20	06.25	20
21	22.00	PIS	19.17	TAU	21.15	LEO	VIR	15.24	SAG	CAP	PIS	ARI	21
22	AQU	08.08	ARI	07.02	CAN	23.29	19.26	SCO	20.13	10.13	PIS	08.57	22
23	22.09	ARI	18.50	GEM	CAN	VIR	LIB	SCO	CAP	AQU	00.02	TAU	23
24	PIS	08.44	TAU	11.34	04.36	VIR	LIB	03.16	CAP	14.09	ARI	11.04	24
25	22.36	TAU	20.55	CAN	LEO	11.36	08.01	SAG	02.22	PIS	00.57	GEM	25
26	ARI	12.33	GEM	20.02	15.14	LIB	SCO	12.01	AQU	15.02	TAU	13.45	26
27	ARI	GEM	GEM	LEO	VIR	23.51	19.00	CAP	04.32	ARI	01.31	CAN	27
28	01.02	20.08	02.55	LEO	VIR	SCO	SAG	16.37	PIS	14.27	GEM	18.17	28
29	TAU		CAN	07.33	03.39	SCO	SAG	AQU	04.07	TAU	03.26	LEO	29
30	06.22		12.43	VIR	LIB	10.03	02.32	17.45	ARI	14.27	CAN	LEO	30
31	GEM		LEO		15.37		CAP	PIS		GEM		01.49	31

SUN

mth	dy	time → sign
JAN	1	00.00 → CAP
JAN	20	21.57 → AQU
FEB	19	12.26 → PIS
MAR	21	12.05 → ARI
APR	20	23.46 → TAU
MAY	21	23.32 → GEM
JUN	22	07.49 → CAN
JUL	23	18.45 → LEO
AUG	24	01.29 → VIR
SEP	23	22.32 → LIB
OCT	24	07.11 → SCO
NOV	23	04.12 → SAG
DEC	22	17.14 → CAP

MERCURY

mth	dy	time → sign
JAN	1	00.00 → CAP
JAN	3	21.29 → AQU
JAN	31	02.44 → CAP
FEB	15	13.13 → AQU
MAR	11	21.34 → PIS
MAR	29	06.54 → ARI
APR	13	00.28 → TAU
APR	30	14.55 → GEM
JUN	1	23.39 → TAU
JUN	12	00.16 → GEM
JUL	7	03.28 → CAN
JUL	21	12.39 → LEO
AUG	6	04.37 → VIR
AUG	27	06.44 → LIB
SEP	28	13.21 → VIR
OCT	12	04.36 → LIB
OCT	31	18.11 → SCO
NOV	19	08.12 → SAG
DEC	8	18.24 → CAP

VENUS

mth	dy	time → sign
JAN	1	00.00 → AQU
JAN	15	20.54 → PIS
JAN	29	09.13 → AQU
APR	5	09.53 → PIS
MAY	7	02.29 → ARI
JUN	3	14.56 → TAU
JUN	29	19.33 → GEM
JUL	25	07.04 → CAN
AUG	19	05.56 → LEO
SEP	12	18.27 → VIR
OCT	6	23.11 → LIB
OCT	30	22.51 → SCO
NOV	23	20.13 → SAG
DEC	17	16.39 → CAP

MARS

mth	dy	time → sign
JAN	1	00.00 → ARI
JAN	23	01.45 → TAU
MAR	14	07.26 → GEM
MAY	1	20.34 → CAN
JUN	19	03.33 → LEO
AUG	6	00.49 → VIR
SEP	22	00.11 → LIB
NOV	6	13.28 → SCO
DEC	20	12.23 → SAG

SATURN

mth	dy	time → sign
JAN	1	00.00 → ARI
MAY	17	07.13 → TAU
DEC	14	23.02 → ARI

JUPITER

mth	dy	time → sign
JAN	1	00.00 → LIB
NOV	11	17.24 → SCO

MOON

dy	jan	feb	mar	apr	may	jun	jul	aug	sep	oct	nov	dec	dy
1	VIR	09.33	SCO	SAG	16.46	PIS	18.48	GEM	LEO	VIR	08.12	03.15	1
2	12.37	SCO	SCO	00.56	AQU	09.37	TAU	06.11	22.56	14.28	SCO	SAG	2
3	LIB	22.05	06.10	CAP	22.50	ARI	20.38	CAN	VIR	LIB	21.06	15.57	3
4	LIB	SAG	SAG	09.32	PIS	11.19	GEM	09.40	VIR	LIB	SAG	CAP	4
5	01.19	SAG	17.12	AQU	PIS	TAU	22.09	LEO	07.22	01.45	SAG	CAP	5
6	SCO	08.03	CAP	14.01	01.24	11.40	CAN	14.58	LIB	SCO	10.01	03.17	6
7	13.20	CAP	CAP	PIS	ARI	GEM	CAN	VIR	18.29	14.37	CAP	AQU	7
8	SAG	14.14	00.23	15.05	01.33	12.16	00.43	23.13	SCO	SAG	21.19	12.20	8
9	22.40	AQU	AQU	ARI	TAU	CAN	LEO	LIB	SCO	SAG	AQU	PIS	9
10	CAP	17.13	03.33	14.32	01.03	14.51	05.54	LIB	07.22	03.25	AQU	18.22	10
11	CAP	PIS	PIS	TAU	GEM	LEO	VIR	10.34	SAG	CAP	05.26	ARI	11
12	04.53	18.40	04.10	14.26	01.50	20.52	14.41	SCO	19.39	13.51	PIS	21.13	12
13	AQU	ARI	ARI	GEM	CAN	VIR	LIB	23.27	CAP	AQU	09.43	TAU	13
14	08.50	20.19	04.15	16.33	05.32	VIR	LIB	SAG	CAP	20.22	ARI	21.39	14
15	PIS	TAU	TAU	CAN	LEO	06.42	02.35	SAG	04.53	PIS	10.47	GEM	15
16	11.46	23.19	05.39	21.56	12.58	LIB	SCO	11.05	AQU	23.06	TAU	21.11	16
17	ARI	GEM	GEM	LEO	VIR	19.08	15.25	CAP	10.12	ARI	10.12	CAN	17
18	14.38	GEM	09.31	LEO	23.46	SCO	SAG	19.31	PIS	23.27	GEM	21.48	18
19	TAU	04.03	CAN	06.35	LIB	SCO	SAG	AQU	12.30	TAU	09.53	LEO	19
20	17.58	CAN	16.03	VIR	LIB	07.56	02.41	AQU	ARI	23.18	CAN	LEO	20
21	GEM	10.28	LEO	17.44	12.27	SAG	CAP	00.40	13.29	GEM	11.45	01.25	21
22	22.02	LEO	LEO	LIB	SCO	19.14	11.06	PIS	TAU	GEM	LEO	VIR	22
23	CAN	18.41	00.57	LIB	SCO	CAP	AQU	03.42	14.49	00.26	17.08	09.10	23
24	CAN	VIR	VIR	06.19	01.17	CAP	16.57	ARI	GEM	CAN	VIR	LIB	24
25	03.24	VIR	11.46	SCO	SAG	04.15	PIS	06.02	17.37	04.08	VIR	20.36	25
26	LEO	04.58	LIB	19.14	12.57	AQU	21.08	TAU	CAN	LEO	02.17	SCO	26
27	10.52	LIB	LIB	SAG	CAP	10.59	ARI	08.43	22.26	10.54	LIB	SCO	27
28	VIR	17.16	00.07	SAG	22.33	PIS	ARI	GEM	LEO	VIR	14.12	09.41	28
29	21.05		SCO	07.12	AQU	15.44	00.27	12.14	LEO	20.30	SCO	SAG	29
30	LIB		13.06	CAP	AQU	ARI	TAU	CAN	05.22	LIB	SCO	22.14	30
31	LIB		SAG		05.31		03.20	16.48		LIB		CAP	31

SUN

mth	dy	time → sign
JAN	1	00.00 → CAP
JAN	21	03.54 → AQU
FEB	19	18.22 → PIS
MAR	21	17.54 → ARI
APR	21	05.37 → TAU
MAY	22	05.19 → GEM
JUN	22	13.35 → CAN
JUL	24	00.29 → LEO
AUG	24	07.15 → VIR
SEP	24	04.19 → LIB
OCT	24	12.56 → SCO
NOV	23	09.56 → SAG
DEC	22	22.55 → CAP

MERCURY

mth	dy	time → sign
JAN	1	00.00 → CAP
FEB	13	04.05 → AQU
MAR	4	21.12 → PIS
MAR	21	03.30 → ARI
APR	5	09.00 → TAU
JUN	13	01.27 → GEM
JUN	28	23.57 → CAN
JUL	13	03.20 → LEO
JUL	30	13.43 → VIR
OCT	6	20.49 → LIB
OCT	24	06.34 → SCO
NOV	12	04.58 → SAG
DEC	3	01.44 → CAP
DEC	27	16.35 → SAG

VENUS

mth	dy	time → sign
JAN	1	00.00 → CAP
JAN	10	13.26 → AQU
FEB	3	12.05 → PIS
FEB	27	14.27 → ARI
MAR	23	23.25 → TAU
APR	17	18.53 → GEM
MAY	13	05.44 → CAN
JUN	8	18.46 → LEO
JUL	7	19.05 → VIR
NOV	9	00.55 → LIB
DEC	9	09.24 → SCO

MARS

mth	dy	time → sign
JAN	1	00.00 → SAG
JAN	31	21.23 → CAP
MAR	14	00.14 → AQU
APR	23	08.20 → PIS
JUN	2	21.37 → ARI
JUL	15	16.21 → TAU
SEP	5	15.28 → GEM
NOV	30	04.01 → TAU

SATURN

mth	dy	time → sign
JAN	1	00.00 → ARI
JAN	20	09.02 → TAU

JUPITER

mth	dy	time → sign
JAN	1	00.00 → SCO
DEC	10	11.48 → SAG

MOON

dy	jan	feb	mar	apr	may	jun	jul	aug	sep	oct	nov	dec	dy
1	CAP	PIS	PIS	00.14	GEM	LEO	VIR	06.44	SAG	CAP	06.12	ARI	1
2	09.02	PIS	12.49	TAU	11.06	LEO	13.59	SCO	14.37	10.56	PIS	ARI	2
3	AQU	05.57	ARI	01.49	CAN	00.14	LIB	18.21	CAP	AQU	13.49	04.43	3
4	17.50	ARI	16.21	GEM	13.09	VIR	23.27	SAG	CAP	20.59	ARI	TAU	4
5	PIS	10.36	TAU	03.53	LEO	07.07	SCO	SAG	02.35	PIS	17.54	06.18	5
6	PIS	TAU	19.23	CAN	17.49	LIB	SCO	07.10	AQU	PIS	TAU	GEM	6
7	00.33	14.03	GEM	07.15	VIR	17.21	11.39	CAP	12.17	03.56	19.29	05.55	7
8	ARI	GEM	22.24	LEO	VIR	SCO	SAG	19.02	PIS	ARI	GEM	CAN	8
9	05.01	16.28	CAN	12.23	01.26	SCO	SAG	AQU	19.31	08.12	20.11	05.39	9
10	TAU	CAN	CAN	VIR	LIB	05.37	00.32	AQU	ARI	TAU	CAN	LEO	10
11	07.17	18.33	01.45	19.36	11.35	SAG	CAP	05.00	ARI	10.55	21.38	07.27	11
12	GEM	LEO	LEO	LIB	SCO	18.27	12.34	PIS	00.49	GEM	LEO	VIR	12
13	08.03	21.39	06.04	LIB	23.33	CAP	AQU	13.02	TAU	13.12	LEO	12.35	13
14	CAN	VIR	VIR	05.06	CAP	23.04	ARI	04.47	CAN	01.05	LIB	14
15	08.48	VIR	12.19	SCO	SAG	06.44	PIS	19.12	GEM	15.54	VIR	21.09	15
16	LEO	03.22	LIB	16.46	12.20	AQU	PIS	TAU	07.47	LEO	07.04	SCO	16
17	11.30	LIB	21.21	SAG	CAP	17.27	07.35	23.23	CAN	19.41	LIB	SCO	17
18	VIR	12.39	SCO	SAG	CAP	PIS	ARI	GEM	10.18	VIR	15.28	08.08	18
19	17.47	SCO	SCO	05.34	00.40	PIS	13.34	GEM	LEO	VIR	SCO	SAG	19
20	LIB	SCO	09.05	CAP	AQU	01.32	TAU	01.42	13.05	01.05	SCO	20.24	20
21	LIB	00.53	SAG	17.33	10.53	ARI	16.42	CAN	VIR	LIB	01.54	CAP	21
22	04.06	SAG	21.53	AQU	PIS	06.14	GEM	02.54	17.21	08.36	SAG	CAP	22
23	SCO	13.37	CAP	AQU	17.41	TAU	17.30	LEO	LIB	SCO	13.55	09.05	23
24	16.54	CAP	CAP	02.41	ARI	07.46	CAN	04.26	LIB	18.34	CAP	AQU	24
25	SAG	CAP	09.13	PIS	20.48	GEM	17.24	VIR	00.17	SAG	CAP	21.18	25
26	SAG	00.17	AQU	08.03	TAU	07.20	LEO	08.06	SCO	SAG	02.40	PIS	26
27	05.30	AQU	17.14	ARI	21.12	CAN	18.26	LIB	10.21	06.37	AQU	PIS	27
28	CAP	07.51	PIS	10.13	GEM	06.54	VIR	15.16	SAG	CAP	14.32	07.36	28
29	15.57		21.52	TAU	20.37	LEO	22.32	SCO	22.39	19.14	PIS	ARI	29
30	AQU		ARI	10.39	CAN	08.34	LIB	SCO	CAP	AQU	23.35	14.31	30
31	23.55		ARI		21.03		LIB	02.01		AQU		TAU	31

SUN

mth	dy	time → sign
JAN	1	00.00 → CAP
JAN	21	09.27 → AQU
FEB	19	23.54 → PIS
MAR	20	23.28 → ARI
APR	20	11.12 → TAU
MAY	21	10.56 → GEM
JUN	21	19.17 → CAN
JUL	23	06.16 → LEO
AUG	23	13.03 → VIR
SEP	23	10.09 → LIB
OCT	23	18.52 → SCO
NOV	22	15.48 → SAG
DEC	22	04.46 → CAP

MERCURY

mth	dy	time → sign
JAN	1	00.00 → SAG
JAN	15	07.16 → CAP
FEB	7	02.24 → AQU
FEB	25	06.35 → PIS
MAR	12	01.26 → ARI
MAY	16	19.52 → TAU
JUN	5	05.14 → GEM
JUN	19	09.00 → CAN
JUL	4	09.04 → LEO
JUL	26	08.13 → VIR
AUG	21	03.21 → LEO
SEP	10	17.09 → VIR
SEP	28	07.27 → LIB
OCT	15	18.56 → SCO
NOV	4	14.48 → SAG

VENUS

mth	dy	time → sign
JAN	1	00.00 → SCO
JAN	4	18.36 → SAG
JAN	29	22.47 → CAP
FEB	23	15.29 → AQU
MAR	19	03.47 → PIS
APR	12	14.50 → ARI
MAY	7	01.54 → TAU
MAY	31	13.19 → GEM
JUN	25	00.14 → CAN
JUL	19	09.47 → LEO
AUG	12	17.42 → VIR
SEP	6	00.53 → LIB
SEP	30	08.24 → SCO
OCT	24	17.27 → SAG
NOV	18	05.03 → CAP
DEC	12	22.25 → AQU

MARS

mth	dy	time → sign
JAN	1	00.00 → TAU
JAN	30	21.13 → GEM
APR	5	11.43 → CAN
MAY	28	08.03 → LEO
JUL	17	02.34 → VIR
SEP	2	17.15 → LIB
OCT	18	02.43 → SCO
NOV	30	07.50 → SAG

SATURN

mth	dy	time → sign
JAN	1	00.00 → TAU
JUL	7	06.23 → GEM
NOV	30	18.26 → TAU

JUPITER

mth	dy	time → sign
JAN	1	00.00 → SAG

MOON

dy	jan	feb	mar	apr	may	jun	jul	aug	sep	oct	nov	dec	dy
1	17.28	CAN	LEO	01.40	SCO	16.17	10.57	PIS	09.20	GEM	11.46	VIR	1
2	GEM	03.47	14.14	LIB	22.30	CAP	AQU	17.40	TAU	GEM	LEO	23.26	2
3	17.25	LEO	VIR	06.15	SAG	CAP	23.40	ARI	16.45	03.09	14.34	LIB	3
4	CAN	03.23	15.53	SCO	SAG	04.19	PIS	ARI	GEM	CAN	VIR	LIB	4
5	16.17	VIR	LIB	13.47	08.42	AQU	PIS	03.37	21.06	06.11	17.32	04.22	5
6	LEO	05.12	20.25	SAG	CAP	16.55	11.30	TAU	CAN	LEO	LIB	SCO	6
7	16.23	LIB	SCO	SAG	20.50	PIS	ARI	10.10	22.43	07.55	21.17	10.48	7
8	VIR	10.53	SCO	00.24	AQU	PIS	20.33	GEM	LEO	VIR	SCO	SAG	8
9	19.42	SCO	04.43	CAP	AQU	04.03	TAU	12.57	22.51	09.24	SCO	19.10	9
10	LIB	20.35	SAG	12.47	09.08	ARI	TAU	CAN	VIR	LIB	02.44	CAP	10
11	LIB	SAG	16.12	AQU	PIS	11.46	01.34	13.00	23.18	12.04	SAG	CAP	11
12	03.07	SAG	CAP	AQU	19.20	TAU	GEM	LEO	LIB	SCO	10.48	05.51	12
13	SCO	08.52	CAP	00.42	ARI	15.33	02.55	12.14	LIB	17.18	CAP	AQU	13
14	13.57	CAP	04.50	PIS	ARI	GEM	CAN	VIR	01.54	SAG	21.45	18.26	14
15	SAG	21.33	AQU	10.15	02.04	16.24	02.16	12.48	SCO	SAG	AQU	PIS	15
16	SAG	AQU	16.28	ARI	TAU	CAN	LEO	LIB	07.58	01.56	AQU	PIS	16
17	02.28	AQU	PIS	16.51	05.33	16.16	01.49	16.28	SAG	CAP	10.24	07.00	17
18	CAP	09.13	PIS	TAU	GEM	LEO	VIR	SCO	17.42	13.30	PIS	ARI	18
19	15.07	PIS	01.59	21.03	07.04	17.09	03.37	23.59	CAP	AQU	22.17	16.57	19
20	AQU	19.17	ARI	GEM	CAN	VIR	LIB	SAG	CAP	AQU	ARI	TAU	20
21	AQU	ARI	09.16	23.53	08.18	20.33	08.52	SAG	05.51	02.08	ARI	22.51	21
22	03.06	ARI	TAU	CAN	LEO	LIB	SCO	10.43	AQU	PIS	07.13	GEM	22
23	PIS	03.26	14.37	CAN	10.40	LIB	17.34	CAP	18.25	13.29	TAU	GEM	23
24	13.41	TAU	GEM	02.22	VIR	02.58	SAG	23.07	PIS	ARI	12.40	01.11	24
25	ARI	09.15	18.22	LEO	15.00	SCO	SAG	AQU	PIS	22.15	GEM	CAN	25
26	21.52	GEM	CAN	05.17	LIB	11.58	04.41	AQU	05.44	TAU	15.36	01.43	26
27	TAU	12.30	20.54	VIR	21.27	SAG	CAP	11.40	ARI	TAU	CAN	LEO	27
28	TAU	CAN	LEO	09.15	SCO	22.49	17.01	PIS	15.04	04.22	17.34	02.27	28
29	02.42	13.42	22.58	LIB	SCO	CAP	AQU	23.21	TAU	GEM	LEO	VIR	29
30	GEM		VIR	14.47	05.54	CAP	AQU	ARI	22.12	08.36	19.55	04.55	30
31	04.15		VIR		SAG		05.40	ARI		CAN		LIB	31

SUN

mth	dy	time → sign
JAN	1	00.00 → CAP
JAN	20	15.21 → AQU
FEB	19	05.45 → PIS
MAR	21	05.18 → ARI
APR	20	17.05 → TAU
MAY	21	16.52 → GEM
JUN	22	01.11 → CAN
JUL	23	12.04 → LEO
AUG	23	18.47 → VIR
SEP	23	15.51 → LIB
OCT	24	00.36 → SCO
NOV	22	21.37 → SAG
DEC	22	10.35 → CAP

MERCURY

mth	dy	time → sign
JAN	1	00.00 → SAG
JAN	10	05.22 → CAP
JAN	30	01.47 → AQU
FEB	16	10.44 → PIS
MAR	4	22.35 → ARI
APR	7	15.04 → PIS
APR	14	02.48 → ARI
MAY	12	06.16 → TAU
MAY	28	00.30 → GEM
JUN	10	21.33 → CAN
JUN	28	05.37 → LEO
SEP	4	10.55 → VIR
SEP	20	10.03 → LIB
OCT	8	14.54 → SCO
OCT	30	18.09 → SAG
NOV	23	12.26 → SCO
DEC	13	08.52 → SAG

VENUS

mth	dy	time → sign
JAN	1	00.00 → AQU
JAN	7	05.29 → PIS
FEB	2	23.24 → ARI
MAR	6	17.09 → TAU
MAY	2	05.15 → ARI
MAY	31	09.47 → TAU
JUL	8	09.16 → GEM
AUG	5	23.32 → CAN
SEP	1	09.22 → LEO
SEP	26	16.05 → VIR
OCT	21	06.04 → LIB
NOV	14	09.57 → SCO
DEC	8	08.37 → SAG

MARS

mth	dy	time → sign
JAN	1	00.00 → SAG
JAN	10	13.36 → CAP
FEB	19	08.09 → AQU
MAR	30	05.45 → PIS
MAY	8	03.13 → ARI
JUN	17	00.36 → TAU
JUL	29	10.41 → GEM
SEP	15	17.27 → CAN

SATURN

mth	dy	time → sign
JAN	1	00.00 → TAU
MAR	26	13.18 → GEM

JUPITER

mth	dy	time → sign
JAN	1	00.00 → SAG
JAN	2	19.59 → CAP

MOON

dy	jan	feb	mar	apr	may	jun	jul	aug	sep	oct	nov	dec	dy
1	09.49	SAG	13.52	AQU	PIS	11.45	04.47	21.25	VIR	18.31	SAG	CAP	1
2	SCO	07.59	CAP	20.39	16.39	TAU	GEM	LEO	07.47	SCO	10.08	02.42	2
3	17.01	CAP	CAP	PIS	ARI	19.42	09.29	21.44	LIB	20.08	CAP	AQU	3
4	SAG	19.25	01.21	PIS	ARI	GEM	CAN	VIR	08.21	SAG	17.44	13.00	4
5	SAG	AQU	AQU	09.22	03.35	GEM	11.40	22.13	SCO	SAG	AQU	PIS	5
6	02.10	AQU	14.10	ARI	TAU	00.40	LEO	LIB	11.32	01.10	AQU	PIS	6
7	CAP	08.03	PIS	20.32	11.49	CAN	13.00	LIB	SAG	CAP	05.01	01.45	7
8	13.07	PIS	PIS	TAU	GEM	03.51	VIR	00.22	18.07	10.09	PIS	ARI	8
9	AQU	20.59	02.57	TAU	17.43	LEO	14.59	SCO	CAP	AQU	18.02	14.12	9
10	AQU	ARI	ARI	05.31	CAN	06.31	LIB	05.03	CAP	22.07	ARI	TAU	10
11	01.38	ARI	14.35	GEM	21.57	VIR	18.26	SAG	03.56	PIS	ARI	TAU	11
12	PIS	08.47	TAU	12.09	LEO	09.27	SCO	12.24	AQU	PIS	06.17	00.09	12
13	14.36	TAU	TAU	CAN	LEO	LIB	23.37	CAP	15.57	11.08	TAU	GEM	13
14	ARI	17.38	00.01	16.30	01.10	13.00	SAG	22.09	PIS	ARI	16.24	07.12	14
15	ARI	GEM	GEM	LEO	VIR	SCO	SAG	AQU	PIS	23.30	GEM	CAN	15
16	01.46	22.29	06.21	18.53	03.44	17.31	06.39	AQU	04.55	TAU	GEM	12.09	16
17	TAU	CAN	CAN	VIR	LIB	SAG	CAP	09.52	ARI	TAU	00.17	LEO	17
18	09.07	23.47	09.27	20.02	06.14	23.41	15.48	PIS	17.34	10.13	CAN	16.00	18
19	GEM	LEO	LEO	LIB	SCO	CAP	AQU	22.46	TAU	GEM	06.18	VIR	19
20	12.14	23.08	10.08	21.14	09.38	CAP	AQU	ARI	TAU	18.45	LEO	19.19	20
21	CAN	VIR	VIR	SCO	SAG	08.21	03.12	ARI	04.35	CAN	10.40	LIB	21
22	12.26	22.37	09.54	SCO	15.13	AQU	PIS	11.30	GEM	CAN	VIR	22.21	22
23	LEO	LIB	LIB	00.03	CAP	19.45	16.07	TAU	12.45	00.45	13.30	SCO	23
24	11.48	LIB	10.37	SAG	CAP	PIS	ARI	22.03	CAN	LEO	LIB	SCO	24
25	VIR	00.11	SCO	05.56	00.01	PIS	ARI	GEM	17.26	04.06	15.13	01.28	25
26	12.26	SCO	13.59	CAP	AQU	08.38	04.29	GEM	LEO	VIR	SCO	SAG	26
27	LIB	05.11	SAG	15.33	11.47	ARI	TAU	04.54	19.02	05.17	16.54	05.36	27
28	15.50	SAG	21.09	AQU	PIS	20.22	13.57	CAN	VIR	LIB	SAG	CAP	28
29	SCO		CAP	AQU	PIS	TAU	GEM	07.55	18.47	05.30	20.12	12.01	29
30	22.30		CAP	3.54	00.36	TAU	19.23	LEO	LIB	SCO	CAP	AQU	30
31	SAG		07.53		ARI		CAN	08.16		06.29		21.38	31

SUN

mth	dy	time → sign
JAN	1	00.00 → CAP
JAN	20	21.14 → AQU
FEB	19	11.39 → PIS
MAR	21	11.11 → ARI
APR	20	22.55 → TAU
MAY	21	22.38 → GEM
JUN	22	06.57 → CAN
JUL	23	17.47 → LEO
AUG	24	00.33 → VIR
SEP	23	21.35 → LIB
OCT	24	06.17 → SCO
NOV	23	03.22 → SAG
DEC	22	16.25 → CAP

MERCURY

mth	dy	time → sign
JAN	1	00.00 → SAG
JAN	3	19.22 → CAP
JAN	22	15.53 → AQU
FEB	8	19.11 → PIS
APR	16	16.04 → ARI
MAY	5	00.58 → TAU
MAY	19	10.06 → GEM
JUN	3	05.53 → CAN
AUG	11	06.33 → LEO
AUG	27	10.48 → VIR
SEP	12	15.47 → LIB
OCT	2	05.52 → SCO
DEC	8	04.53 → SAG
DEC	27	17.42 → CAP

VENUS

mth	dy	time → sign
JAN	1	00.00 → SAG
JAN	1	05.26 → CAP
JAN	25	02.12 → AQU
FEB	18	00.05 → PIS
MAR	14	00.33 → ARI
APR	7	04.48 → TAU
MAY	1	14.12 → GEM
MAY	26	05.36 → CAN
JUN	20	04.26 → LEO
JUL	15	14.11 → VIR
AUG	10	18.13 → LIB
SEP	7	10.59 → SCO
OCT	10	01.50 → SAG
DEC	5	23.23 → SCO
DEC	30	23.16 → SAG

MARS

mth	dy	time → sign
JAN	1	00.00 → CAN
MAY	1	20.25 → LEO
JUN	26	04.40 → VIR
AUG	14	14.00 → LIB
SEP	29	10.25 → SCO
NOV	11	10.38 → SAG
DEC	22	03.54 → CAP

SATURN

mth	dy	time → sign
JAN	1	00.00 → GEM
AUG	24	17.38 → CAN
DEC	7	06.34 → GEM

JUPITER

mth	dy	time → sign
JAN	1	00.00 → CAP
JAN	21	15.26 → AQU

MOON

dy	jan	feb	mar	apr	may	jun	jul	aug	sep	oct	nov	dec	dy
1	PIS	ARI	14.07	GEM	CAN	VIR	LIB	SAG	08.03	PIS	ARI	22.53	1
2	PIS	06.54	TAU	18.59	08.53	23.51	08.19	20.14	AQU	PIS	04.08	GEM	2
3	09.58	TAU	CAN	CAN	LEO	LIB	SCO	CAP	16.26	09.38	TAU	GEM	3
4	ARI	18.20	02.14	CAN	14.02	01.30	10.25	CAP	PIS	ARI	16.44	10.19	4
5	22.43	GEM	GEM	02.06	VIR	01.30	SAG	01.27	PIS	21.58	GEM	CAN	5
6	TAU	GEM	11.34	LEO	16.13	SCO	12.53	AQU	03.00	TAU	GEM	20.13	6
7	TAU	02.16	CAN	05.37	LIB	02.12	CAP	09.03	ARI	TAU	04.33	LEO	7
8	09.13	CAN	17.03	VIR	16.20	SAG	17.10	PIS	15.15	CAN	LEO	LEO	8
9	GEM	06.26	LEO	06.12	SCO	03.40	AQU	19.25	TAU	GEM	14.36	04.03	9
10	16.12	LEO	19.02	LIB	16.04	CAP	AQU	ARI	TAU	22.26	LEO	VIR	10
11	CAN	08.00	VIR	05.27	SAG	07.46	00.33	ARI	03.55	CAN	21.42	09.09	11
12	20.13	VIR	18.57	SCO	17.30	AQU	PIS	07.46	GEM	CAN	VIR	LIB	12
13	LEO	08.37	LIB	05.23	CAP	15.44	11.14	TAU	14.56	07.36	VIR	11.23	13
14	22.40	LIB	18.39	SAG	22.29	PIS	ARI	20.06	CAN	LEO	01.10	SCO	14
15	VIR	09.55	SCO	07.58	AQU	PIS	23.49	GEM	22.41	13.02	LIB	11.40	15
16	VIR	SCO	20.01	CAP	AQU	03.11	TAU	GEM	LEO	VIR	01.36	SAG	16
17	00.53	13.03	SAG	14.31	07.40	ARI	TAU	06.11	LEO	14.49	SCO	11.46	17
18	LIB	SAG	SAG	AQU	PIS	16.01	11.47	CAN	02.42	LIB	00.42	CAP	18
19	03.44	18.38	00.23	AQU	19.54	TAU	GEM	12.52	VIR	14.21	SAG	13.47	19
20	SCO	CAP	CAP	00.52	ARI	TAU	21.12	LEO	03.52	SCO	00.42	AQU	20
21	07.40	CAP	08.15	PIS	ARI	03.44	CAN	16.30	LIB	13.40	CAP	19.25	21
22	SAG	02.41	AQU	13.30	08.51	GEM	CAN	VIR	03.53	SAG	03.42	PIS	22
23	12.59	AQU	19.01	ARI	TAU	13.07	03.42	18.18	SCO	14.55	AQU	PIS	23
24	CAP	13.01	PIS	ARI	20.37	CAN	LEO	LIB	04.36	CAP	10.53	05.02	24
25	20.13	PIS	PIS	02.28	GEM	20.14	08.00	19.43	SAG	19.39	PIS	ARI	25
26	AQU	PIS	07.30	TAU	GEM	LEO	VIR	SCO	07.34	AQU	21.44	17.19	26
27	AQU	01.09	ARI	14.29	06.28	LEO	11.05	21.59	CAP	AQU	ARI	TAU	27
28	05.54	ARI	20.27	GEM	CAN	01.35	LIB	SAG	13.36	04.13	ARI	TAU	28
29	PIS		TAU	GEM	14.22	VIR	13.45	SAG	AQU	PIS	10.22	05.53	29
30	17.57		TAU	00.50	LEO	05.32	SCO	01.57	22.33	15.35	TAU	GEM	30
31	ARI		08.42		20.13		16.35	CAP		ARI		17.01	31

SUN

mth	dy	time → sign
JAN	1	00.00 → CAP
JAN	21	03.02 → AQU
FEB	19	17.25 → PIS
MAR	21	16.53 → ARI
APR	21	04.29 → TAU
MAY	22	04.11 → GEM
JUN	22	12.29 → CAN
JUL	23	23.28 → LEO
AUG	24	06.14 → VIR
SEP	24	03.24 → LIB
OCT	24	12.11 → SCO
NOV	23	09.17 → SAG
DEC	22	22.18 → CAP

MERCURY

mth	dy	time → sign
JAN	1	00.00 → CAP
JAN	15	04.26 → AQU
FEB	2	10.35 → PIS
FEB	23	15.04 → AQU
MAR	19	08.44 → PIS
APR	10	19.22 → ARI
APR	26	21.43 → TAU
MAY	10	23.49 → GEM
MAY	29	10.34 → CAN
AUG	4	09.04 → LEO
AUG	19	04.38 → VIR
SEP	5	09.04 → LIB
SEP	28	08.11 → SCO
OCT	21	01.15 → LIB
NOV	11	14.09 → SCO
DEC	1	09.18 → SAG
DEC	20	11.16 → CAP

VENUS

mth	dy	time → sign
JAN	1	00.00 → SAG
FEB	6	15.56 → CAP
MAR	6	13.14 → AQU
APR	1	15.17 → PIS
APR	27	00.56 → ARI
MAY	22	02.54 → TAU
JUN	16	00.22 → GEM
JUL	10	17.33 → CAN
AUG	4	05.47 → LEO
AUG	28	13.07 → VIR
SEP	21	16.31 → LIB
OCT	15	17.42 → SCO
NOV	8	18.07 → SAG
DEC	2	18.35 → CAP
DEC	26	20.23 → AQU

MARS

mth	dy	time → sign
JAN	1	00.00 → CAP
JAN	30	06.14 → AQU
MAR	9	12.48 → PIS
APR	16	20.35 → ARI
MAY	26	03.19 → TAU
JUL	6	06.12 → GEM
AUG	19	09.19 → CAN
OCT	7	20.37 → LEO

SATURN

mth	dy	time → sign
JAN	1	00.00 → GEM
MAY	11	21.36 → CAN

JUPITER

mth	dy	time → sign
JAN	1	00.00 → AQU
FEB	4	00.33 → PIS

MOON

dy	jan	feb	mar	apr	may	jun	jul	aug	sep	oct	nov	dec	dy
1	CAN	16.10	01.03	14.49	00.37	11.49	01.14	ARI	GEM	CAN	LEO	17.09	1
2	CAN	VIR	VIR	SCO	SAG	AQU	PIS	02.40	GEM	CAN	01.30	LIB	2
3	02.12	20.32	04.15	15.05	00.39	16.32	08.24	TAU	11.12	07.13	VIR	20.33	3
4	LEO	LIB	LIB	SAG	CAP	PIS	ARI	14.43	CAN	LEO	07.29	SCO	4
5	09.28	23.48	06.05	16.47	03.23	PIS	19.01	GEM	22.24	16.05	LIB	20.47	5
6	VIR	SCO	SCO	CAP	AQU	01.06	TAU	GEM	LEO	VIR	09.37	SAG	6
7	14.53	SCO	07.58	21.03	09.41	ARI	TAU	03.11	21.09	SCO	19.52	7
8	LIB	02.33	SAG	AQU	PIS	12.30	07.30	CAN	06.42	LIB	09.36	CAP	8
9	18.25	SAG	10.59	AQU	19.10	TAU	GEM	14.08	VIR	23.20	SAG	20.01	9
10	SCO	05.25	CAP	04.08	ARI	TAU	19.56	LEO	12.00	SCO	09.33	AQU	10
11	20.25	CAP	15.40	PIS	ARI	01.06	CAN	22.42	LIB	SCO	CAP	22.57	11
12	SAG	09.09	AQU	13.31	06.40	GEM	CAN	VIR	15.14	00.21	11.22	PIS	12
13	21.52	AQU	22.16	ARI	TAU	13.38	07.06	VIR	SCO	SAG	AQU	PIS	13
14	CAP	14.40	PIS	ARI	19.09	CAN	LEO	04.55	17.41	01.56	16.05	05.30	14
15	CAP	PIS	PIS	00.38	GEM	CAN	16.22	LIB	SAG	CAP	PIS	ARI	15
16	00.17	22.46	06.55	TAU	GEM	01.12	VIR	09.17	20.20	05.15	23.40	15.14	16
17	AQU	ARI	ARI	12.57	07.47	LEO	23.21	SCO	CAP	AQU	ARI	TAU	17
18	05.14	ARI	17.38	GEM	CAN	10.53	LIB	12.18	23.49	10.38	ARI	TAU	18
19	PIS	09.37	TAU	GEM	19.31	VIR	LIB	SAG	AQU	PIS	09.29	03.02	19
20	13.42	TAU	TAU	01.36	LEO	17.39	03.50	14.38	AQU	17.57	TAU	GEM	20
21	ARI	22.05	05.58	CAN	LEO	LIB	SCO	CAP	04.32	ARI	20.56	15.44	21
22	ARI	GEM	GEM	12.53	04.47	21.03	06.06	17.03	PIS	ARI	GEM	CAN	22
23	01.13	GEM	18.22	LEO	VIR	SCO	SAG	AQU	10.55	03.08	GEM	CAN	23
24	TAU	09.57	CAN	20.53	10.16	21.45	07.03	20.35	ARI	TAU	09.34	04.23	24
25	13.48	CAN	CAN	VIR	LIB	SAG	CAP	PIS	19.35	14.15	CAN	LEO	25
26	GEM	19.11	04.38	VIR	12.02	21.22	08.10	PIS	TAU	GEM	22.23	15.51	26
27	GEM	LEO	LEO	00.47	SCO	CAP	AQU	02.21	TAU	GEM	LEO	VIR	27
28	01.08	LEO	11.13	LIB	11.27	21.54	11.04	ARI	06.42	02.53	LEO	VIR	28
29	CAN		VIR	01.23	SAG	AQU	PIS	11.08	GEM	CAN	09.33	00.41	29
30	09.55		14.10	SCO	10.39	AQU	17.06	TAU	19.20	15.26	VIR	LIB	30
31	LEO		LIB		CAP		ARI	22.38		LEO		05.55	31

SUN

mth	dy	time → sign
JAN	1	00.00 → CAP
JAN	21	08.57 → AQU
FEB	19	23.19 → PIS
MAR	20	22.44 → ARI
APR	20	10.25 → TAU
MAY	21	10.04 → GEM
JUN	21	18.22 → CAN
JUL	23	05.24 → LEO
AUG	23	12.09 → VIR
SEP	23	09.15 → LIB
OCT	23	17.58 → SCO
NOV	22	14.56 → SAG
DEC	22	03.57 → CAP

MERCURY

mth	dy	time → sign
JAN	1	00.00 → CAP
JAN	8	01.25 → AQU
MAR	15	00.05 → PIS
APR	2	10.57 → ARI
APR	17	11.02 → TAU
MAY	2	16.14 → GEM
JUL	10	18.19 → CAN
JUL	26	01.43 → LEO
AUG	10	04.04 → VIR
AUG	29	04.53 → LIB
NOV	4	12.26 → SCO
NOV	23	03.40 → SAG
DEC	12	07.14 → CAP

VENUS

mth	dy	time → sign
JAN	1	00.00 → AQU
JAN	20	01.44 → PIS
FEB	13	15.26 → ARI
MAR	9	21.49 → TAU
APR	5	13.32 → GEM
MAY	5	20.37 → CAN
SEP	8	22.29 → LEO
OCT	7	22.11 → VIR
NOV	3	00.57 → LIB
NOV	27	23.03 → SCO
DEC	22	07.53 → SAG

MARS

mth	dy	time → sign
JAN	1	00.00 → LEO
MAY	28	18.34 → VIR
JUL	23	05.12 → LIB
SEP	8	17.55 → SCO
OCT	22	02.51 → SAG
DEC	1	17.23 → CAP

SATURN

mth	dy	time → sign
JAN	1	00.00 → CAN
OCT	17	15.26 → LEO
DEC	7	19.03 → CAN

JUPITER

mth	dy	time → sign
JAN	1	00.00 → PIS
FEB	12	07.01 → ARI
JUN	26	01.24 → TAU
OCT	26	14.41 → ARI

MOON

dy	jan	feb	mar	apr	may	jun	jul	aug	sep	oct	nov	dec	dy
1	SCO	CAP	03.18	17.48	07.49	GEM	CAN	01.18	LIB	12.28	CAP	09.29	1
2	07.43	18.09	AQU	ARI	TAU	11.46	06.57	VIR	01.24	SAG	00.50	PIS	2
3	SAG	AQU	05.27	ARI	17.12	CAN	LEO	11.54	SCO	16.23	AQU	13.34	3
4	07.25	19.16	PIS	00.11	GEM	CAN	19.32	LIB	07.05	CAP	04.04	ARI	4
5	CAP	PIS	08.56	TAU	GEM	00.47	VIR	19.56	SAG	19.28	PIS	19.35	5
6	06.58	22.45	ARI	09.19	04.53	LEO	VIR	SCO	10.44	AQU	07.59	TAU	6
7	AQU	ARI	15.08	GEM	CAN	13.15	06.06	SCO	CAP	22.00	ARI	TAU	7
8	08.21	ARI	TAU	21.11	17.51	VIR	LIB	00.56	12.39	PIS	13.07	03.40	8
9	PIS	05.50	TAU	CAN	LEO	22.59	13.16	SAG	AQU	PIS	TAU	GEM	9
10	13.07	TAU	00.46	CAN	LEO	LIB	SCO	03.08	13.42	00.40	20.19	14.00	10
11	ARI	16.30	GEM	10.01	05.45	LIB	16.43	CAP	PIS	ARI	GEM	CAN	11
12	21.43	GEM	13.03	LEO	VIR	04.40	SAG	03.28	15.17	04.45	GEM	CAN	12
13	TAU	GEM	CAN	21.07	14.15	SCO	17.20	AQU	ARI	TAU	06.19	02.18	13
14	TAU	05.13	CAN	VIR	LIB	06.40	CAP	03.29	19.09	11.38	CAN	LEO	14
15	09.18	CAN	01.41	VIR	18.42	SAG	16.46	PIS	TAU	GEM	18.44	15.19	15
16	GEM	17.38	LEO	04.40	SCO	06.33	AQU	05.02	TAU	21.58	LEO	VIR	16
17	22.07	LEO	12.12	LIB	20.09	CAP	16.55	ARI	02.38	CAN	LEO	VIR	17
18	CAN	LEO	VIR	08.48	SAG	06.16	PIS	09.45	GEM	07.33	CAN	02.50	18
19	CAN	04.08	19.37	SCO	20.30	AQU	19.32	TAU	13.45	VIR	10.40	LIB	19
20	10.33	VIR	LIB	10.52	CAP	07.39	ARI	18.27	CAN	LEO	18.03	10.52	20
21	LEO	12.13	LIB	SAG	21.33	PIS	ARI	GEM	CAN	23.04	LIB	SCO	21
22	21.32	LIB	00.26	12.34	AQU	11.55	01.46	GEM	02.41	VIR	LIB	14.58	22
23	VIR	18.09	SCO	CAP	AQU	ARI	TAU	06.21	LEO	VIR	0.48	SAG	23
24	VIR	SCO	03.48	15.07	00.35	19.26	11.36	CAN	14.47	08.45	SCO	16.07	24
25	06.26	22.20	SAG	AQU	PIS	TAU	GEM	19.24	VIR	LIB	04.12	CAP	25
26	LIB	SAG	06.43	19.05	06.03	TAU	23.53	LEO	VIR	15.09	SAG	16.05	26
27	12.43	SAG	CAP	PIS	ARI	05.43	CAN	LEO	00.22	SCO	05.45	AQU	27
28	SCO	01.13	09.47	PIS	13.54	GEM	CAN	07.30	LIB	19.07	CAP	16.41	28
29	16.18	CAP	AQU	00.35	TAU	17.55	12.56	VIR	07.21	SAG	PIS	07.06	29
30	SAG		13.18	ARI	23.53	CAN	LEO	17.34	SCO	22.00	AQU	19.25	30
31	17.43		PIS		GEM		LEO	LIB		CAP		ARI	31

SUN

mth	dy	time → sign
JAN	1	00.00 → CAP
JAN	20	14.39 → AQU
FEB	19	05.04 → PIS
MAR	21	04.37 → ARI
APR	20	16.14 → TAU
MAY	21	16.02 → GEM
JUN	22	00.11 → CAN
JUL	23	11.08 → LEO
AUG	23	17.52 → VIR
SEP	23	15.01 → LIB
OCT	23	23.44 → SCO
NOV	22	20.47 → SAG
DEC	22	09.48 → CAP

SATURN

mth	dy	time → sign
JAN	1	00.00 → CAN
JUN	24	13.38 → LEO

MERCURY

mth	dy	time → sign
JAN	1	00.00 → CAP
JAN	1	17.05 → AQU
JAN	18	04.28 → CAP
FEB	15	03.21 → AQU
MAR	8	15.36 → PIS
MAR	25	11.35 → ARI
APR	9	05.45 → TAU
JUN	14	18.11 → GEM
JUL	3	10.27 → CAN
JUL	17	13.28 → LEO
AUG	2	19.31 → VIR
AUG	26	22.52 → LIB
SEP	14	12.12 → VIR
OCT	10	04.45 → LIB
OCT	28	05.23 → SCO
NOV	15	21.26 → SAG
DEC	5	16.56 → CAP

VENUS

mth	dy	time → sign
JAN	1	00.00 → SAG
JAN	15	10.44 → CAP
FEB	8	11.51 → AQU
MAR	4	13.12 → PIS
MAR	28	16.01 → ARI
APR	21	21.15 → TAU
MAY	16	05.08 → GEM
JUN	9	15.13 → CAN
JUL	4	03.20 → LEO
JUL	28	17.50 → VIR
AUG	22	12.19 → LIB
SEP	16	13.03 → SCO
OCT	11	23.35 → SAG
NOV	7	05.04 → CAP
DEC	5	13.12 → AQU

MARS

mth	dy	time → sign
JAN	1	00.00 → CAP
JAN	9	12.46 → AQU
FEB	16	13.24 → PIS
MAR	26	17.49 → ARI
MAY	4	22.23 → TAU
JUN	14	20.45 → GEM
JUL	28	04.07 → CAN
SEP	12	10.45 → LEO
NOV	2	11.11 → VIR

JUPITER

mth	dy	time → sign
JAN	1	00.00 → ARI
FEB	12	15.44 → TAU
JUN	29	23.39 → GEM

MOON

dy	jan	feb	mar	apr	may	jun	jul	aug	sep	oct	nov	dec	dy
1	ARI	GEM	GEM	04.39	01.19	LIB	22.14	CAP	PIS	ARI	GEM	CAN	1
2	01.04	GEM	08.52	LEO	VIR	06.34	SAG	12.50	22.20	09.25	GEM	22.32	2
3	TAU	02.31	CAN	17.32	12.52	SCO	SAG	AQU	ARI	TAU	04.09	LEO	3
4	09.39	CAN	21.36	VIR	LIB	12.27	01.25	12.20	23.06	12.14	CAN	LEO	4
5	GEM	15.16	LEO	VIR	21.39	SAG	CAP	PIS	TAU	GEM	13.42	10.07	5
6	20.35	LEO	LEO	04.54	SCO	15.45	02.25	12.18	TAU	19.06	LEO	VIR	6
7	CAN	LEO	10.29	LIB	SCO	CAP	AQU	ARI	03.19	CAN	LEO	22.42	7
8	CAN	04.09	VIR	13.54	03.44	17.45	02.53	14.36	GEM	CAN	01.56	LIB	8
9	09.03	VIR	22.01	SCO	SAG	AQU	PIS	TAU	11.40	05.50	VIR	LIB	9
10	LEO	16.04	LIB	20.50	08.00	19.42	04.25	20.24	CAN	LEO	14.26	09.52	10
11	22.01	LIB	LIB	SAG	CAP	PIS	ARI	GEM	23.13	18.32	LIB	SCO	11
12	VIR	LIB	07.40	SAG	11.18	22.31	08.13	GEM	LEO	VIR	LIB	18.10	12
13	VIR	02.06	SCO	02.08	AQU	ARI	TAU	05.39	LEO	VIR	01.13	SAG	13
14	10.04	SCO	15.18	CAP	14.11	ARI	14.47	12.02	VIR	06.58	SCO	23.35	14
15	LIB	09.23	SAG	05.56	PIS	02.48	GEM	17.19	VIR	LIB	09.36	CAP	15
16	19.32	SAG	20.38	AQU	17.04	TAU	GEM	LEO	VIR	17.53	SAG	CAP	16
17	SCO	13.24	CAP	08.25	ARI	09.02	00.01	LEO	00.33	SCO	15.55	02.59	17
18	SCO	CAP	23.33	PIS	20.38	GEM	CAN	06.02	LIB	SCO	CAP	AQU	18
19	01.17	14.32	AQU	10.10	TAU	17.33	11.17	VIR	11.55	03.00	20.38	05.31	19
20	SAG	AQU	AQU	ARI	TAU	CAN	LEO	18.42	SCO	SAG	AQU	PIS	20
21	03.28	14.06	00.31	12.30	01.53	CAN	23.51	LIB	21.32	10.14	AQU	08.06	21
22	CAP	PIS	PIS	TAU	GEM	04.27	VIR	LIB	SAG	CAP	00.04	ARI	22
23	03.19	14.00	00.53	17.04	09.49	LEO	VIR	06.16	SAG	15.17	PIS	11.26	23
24	AQU	ARI	ARI	GEM	CAN	16.59	12.33	SCO	04.37	AQU	02.35	TAU	24
25	02.41	16.19	02.35	GEM	20.42	VIR	LIB	15.28	CAP	18.03	ARI	16.03	25
26	PIS	TAU	TAU	01.07	LEO	VIR	23.40	SAG	08.33	PIS	04.55	GEM	26
27	03.33	22.34	07.28	CAN	LEO	05.26	SCO	21.15	AQU	19.08	TAU	22.29	27
28	ARI	GEM	GEM	12.31	09.21	LIB	SCO	CAP	09.39	ARI	08.13	CAN	28
29	07.34		16.28	LEO	VIR	15.37	07.38	23.27	PIS	19.59	GEM	CAN	29
30	TAU		CAN	LEO	21.20	SCO	SAG	AQU	09.15	TAU	13.48	07.15	30
31	15.26		CAN		LIB		11.48	23.11		22.26		LEO	31

SUN

mth	dy	time → sign
JAN	1	00.00 → CAP
JAN	20	20.26 → AQU
FEB	19	10.55 → PIS
MAR	21	10.27 → ARI
APR	20	22.05 → TAU
MAY	21	21.44 → GEM
JUN	22	06.02 → CAN
JUL	23	16.51 → LEO
AUG	23	23.35 → VIR
SEP	23	20.46 → LIB
OCT	24	05.35 → SCO
NOV	23	02.36 → SAG
DEC	22	15.44 → CAP

MERCURY

mth	dy	time → sign
JAN	1	00.00 → CAP
FEB	10	09.26 → AQU
MAR	1	07.54 → PIS
MAR	17	07.24 → ARI
APR	2	13.16 → TAU
JUN	10	01.22 → GEM
JUN	24	23.52 → CAN
JUL	9	08.39 → LEO
JUL	28	01.28 → VIR
OCT	3	08.59 → LIB
OCT	20	16.49 → SCO
NOV	8	22.03 → SAG
DEC	1	16.19 → CAP
DEC	15	13.04 → SAG

VENUS

mth	dy	time → sign
JAN	1	00.00 → AQU
APR	5	20.14 → PIS
MAY	6	20.56 → ARI
JUN	3	05.26 → TAU
JUN	29	08.15 → GEM
JUL	24	18.44 → CAN
AUG	18	17.06 → LEO
SEP	12	05.23 → VIR
OCT	6	10.04 → LIB
OCT	30	09.45 → SCO
NOV	23	07.04 → SAG
DEC	17	03.30 → CAP

MARS

mth	dy	time → sign
JAN	1	00.00 → VIR
JAN	11	08.48 → LIB
FEB	25	19.13 → VIR
JUN	23	19.10 → LIB
AUG	17	04.27 → SCO
OCT	1	07.42 → SAG
NOV	11	10.22 → CAP
DEC	20	09.00 → AQU

SATURN

mth	dy	time → sign
JAN	1	00.00 → LEO

JUPITER

mth	dy	time → sign
JAN	1	00.00 → GEM
JUL	13	06.07 → CAN

MOON

dy	jan	feb	mar	apr	may	jun	jul	aug	sep	oct	nov	dec	dy
1	18.23	LIB	LIB	02.47	CAP	09.53	ARI	05.48	CAN	16.46	LIB	SCO	1
2	VIR	LIB	09.32	SAG	CAP	PIS	20.44	GEM	00.53	VIR	23.31	18.20	2
3	VIR	02.52	SCO	11.59	00.12	12.37	TAU	11.21	LEO	VIR	SCO	SAG	3
4	06.56	SCO	20.47	CAP	AQU	ARI	TAU	CAN	10.56	04.43	SCO	SAG	4
5	LIB	13.15	SAG	17.56	04.07	14.30	00.04	18.49	VIR	LIB	11.52	04.41	5
6	18.50	SAG	SAG	AQU	PIS	TAU	GEM	LEO	22.35	17.28	SAG	CAP	6
7	SCO	19.57	05.05	20.22	05.41	16.36	04.42	LEO	LIB	SCO	22.50	12.52	7
8	SCO	CAP	CAP	PIS	ARI	GEM	CAN	04.17	LIB	SCO	CAP	AQU	8
9	03.58	22.46	09.23	20.19	06.05	20.14	11.20	VIR	11.19	06.04	CAP	18.47	9
10	SAG	AQU	AQU	ARI	TAU	CAN	LEO	15.45	SCO	SAG	07.25	PIS	10
11	09.27	22.57	10.12	19.40	07.06	CAN	20.33	LIB	23.50	17.06	AQU	22.33	11
12	CAP	PIS	PIS	TAU	GEM	02.35	VIR	LIB	SAG	CAP	12.52	ARI	12
13	11.55	22.31	09.15	20.37	10.31	LEO	VIR	04.27	SAG	CAP	PIS	ARI	13
14	AQU	ARI	ARI	GEM	CAN	12.10	08.09	SCO	10.02	00.54	15.11	00.35	14
15	12.53	23.31	08.48	GEM	17.31	VIR	LIB	16.22	CAP	AQU	ARI	TAU	15
16	PIS	TAU	TAU	00.57	LEO	VIR	20.41	SAG	16.15	04.42	15.26	01.49	16
17	14.03	TAU	10.57	CAN	LEO	00.10	SCO	SAG	AQU	PIS	TAU	GEM	17
18	ARI	03.29	GEM	19.19	04.00	LIB	SCO	01.17	18.27	05.14	15.20	03.35	18
19	16.48	GEM	16.58	LEO	VIR	12.30	07.49	CAP	PIS	ARI	GEM	CAN	19
20	TAU	10.50	CAN	20.46	16.25	SCO	SAG	06.11	18.07	04.20	16.46	07.25	20
21	21.52	CAN	CAN	VIR	LIB	23.04	15.46	AQU	ARI	TAU	CAN	LEO	21
22	GEM	20.53	02.37	VIR	LIB	SAG	CAP	07.48	17.27	04.10	21.23	14.33	22
23	GEM	LEO	LEO	09.25	04.38	SAG	20.19	PIS	TAU	GEM	LEO	VIR	23
24	05.17	LEO	14.30	LIB	SCO	06.51	AQU	07.56	18.31	06.40	LEO	VIR	24
25	CAN	08.33	VIR	21.37	15.08	CAP	22.32	ARI	GEM	CAN	05.50	01.10	25
26	14.45	VIR	VIR	SCO	SAG	12.01	PIS	08.35	22.45	12.54	VIR	LIB	26
27	LEO	21.01	03.07	SCO	23.27	AQU	23.59	TAU	CAN	LEO	17.25	13.49	27
28	LEO	LIB	LIB	08.30	CAP	15.26	ARI	11.19	CAN	22.42	LIB	SCO	28
29	01.59		15.28	SAG	CAP	PIS	ARI	GEM	06.25	LIB	SCO	SCO	29
30	VIR		SCO	17.33	05.38	18.04	02.06	16.50	LEO	VIR	06.13	02.03	30
31	14.26		SCO		AQU		TAU	CAN		10.45		SAG	31

SUN

mth	dy	time → sign
JAN	1	00.00 → CAP
JAN	21	02.23 → AQU
FEB	19	16.46 → PIS
MAR	21	16.19 → ARI
APR	21	03.57 → TAU
MAY	22	03.39 → GEM
JUN	22	11.55 → CAN
JUL	23	22.46 → LEO
AUG	24	05.26 → VIR
SEP	24	02.37 → LIB
OCT	24	11.22 → SCO
NOV	23	08.25 → SAG
DEC	22	21.26 → CAP

MERCURY

mth	dy	time → sign
JAN	1	00.00 → SAG
JAN	13	18.15 → CAP
FEB	3	19.29 → AQU
FEB	21	14.11 → PIS
MAR	9	10.42 → ARI
MAY	16	02.27 → TAU
JUN	2	11.08 → GEM
JUN	16	08.44 → CAN
JUL	2	02.04 → LEO
SEP	9	03.43 → VIR
SEP	25	14.17 → LIB
OCT	13	07.26 → SCO
NOV	2	19.09 → SAG

VENUS

mth	dy	time → sign
JAN	1	00.00 → CAP
JAN	10	00.26 → AQU
FEB	2	23.05 → PIS
FEB	27	01.43 → ARI
MAR	23	11.06 → TAU
APR	17	07.03 → GEM
MAY	12	19.02 → CAN
JUN	8	10.33 → LEO
JUL	7	18.16 → VIR
NOV	9	08.05 → LIB
DEC	9	03.26 → SCO

MARS

mth	dy	time → sign
JAN	1	00.00 → AQU
JAN	27	11.11 → PIS
MAR	6	18.34 → ARI
APR	15	05.19 → TAU
MAY	26	09.29 → GEM
JUL	8	17.13 → CAN
AUG	23	06.26 → LEO
OCT	10	03.48 → VIR
NOV	30	12.00 → LIB

SATURN

mth	dy	time → sign
JAN	1	00.00 → LEO
AUG	12	13.43 → VIR

JUPITER

mth	dy	time → sign
JAN	1	00.00 → CAN
AUG	2	08.49 → LEO

MOON

dy	jan	feb	mar	apr	may	jun	jul	aug	sep	oct	nov	dec	dy
1	12.01	AQU	17.14	ARI	15.00	CAN	19.06	LIB	19.58	16.28	AQU	PIS	1
2	CAP	07.38	PIS	04.40	GEM	04.26	VIR	23.08	SAG	CAP	19.19	09.02	2
3	19.15	PIS	18.28	TAU	15.50	LEO	VIR	SCO	SAG	CAP	PIS	ARI	3
4	AQU	10.02	ARI	04.56	CAN	10.18	03.34	SCO	08.21	03.05	23.30	11.33	4
5	AQU	ARI	19.14	GEM	19.38	VIR	LIB	11.57	CAP	AQU	ARI	TAU	5
6	00.18	12.22	TAU	07.22	LEO	19.58	15.18	SAG	17.54	09.44	ARI	11.36	6
7	PIS	TAU	21.00	CAN	LEO	LIB	SCO	23.52	AQU	PIS	00.31	GEM	7
8	04.00	15.31	GEM	12.48	03.01	LIB	SCO	CAP	23.45	12.44	TAU	10.54	8
9	ARI	GEM	GEM	LEO	VIR	08.15	04.13	CAP	PIS	ARI	00.03	CAN	9
10	07.01	19.46	01.09	21.07	13.32	SCO	SAG	08.56	PIS	13.32	GEM	11.28	10
11	TAU	CAN	CAN	VIR	LIB	21.12	15.56	AQU	02.48	TAU	00.03	LEO	11
12	09.49	CAN	07.18	VIR	LIB	SAG	CAP	14.59	ARI	13.59	CAN	15.06	12
13	GEM	01.17	LEO	07.43	01.57	SAG	CAP	PIS	04.35	GEM	02.14	VIR	13
14	12.56	LEO	15.26	LIB	SCO	09.04	01.14	18.59	TAU	15.39	LEO	22.47	14
15	CAN	08.32	VIR	19.54	14.54	CAP	AQU	ARI	06.35	CAN	07.41	LIB	15
16	17.16	VIR	VIR	SCO	SAG	18.58	08.06	22.05	GEM	19.32	VIR	LIB	16
17	LEO	18.06	01.29	SCO	SAG	AQU	PIS	TAU	09.39	LEO	16.32	10.01	17
18	23.57	LIB	LIB	08.52	03.06	AQU	13.06	TAU	CAN	LEO	LIB	SCO	18
19	VIR	LIB	13.24	SAG	CAP	02.31	ARI	01.03	14.08	01.58	LIB	22.59	19
20	VIR	06.04	SCO	21.14	13.23	PIS	16.43	GEM	LEO	VIR	03.58	SAG	20
21	09.43	SCO	SCO	CAP	AQU	07.38	TAU	04.14	20.15	10.51	SCO	SAG	21
22	LIB	18.57	02.23	CAP	20.45	ARI	19.19	CAN	VIR	LIB	16.47	11.49	22
23	22.00	SAG	SAG	07.08	PIS	10.29	GEM	08.00	VIR	21.52	SAG	CAP	23
24	SCO	SAG	14.25	AQU	PIS	TAU	21.25	LEO	04.24	SCO	SAG	23.20	24
25	SCO	06.08	CAP	13.17	00.47	11.42	CAN	13.08	LIB	SCO	05.45	AQU	25
26	10.35	CAP	23.11	PIS	ARI	GEM	CAN	14.59	10.30	CAP	AQU	26
27	SAG	13.36	AQU	15.40	02.02	12.28	00.01	20.41	SCO	SAG	17.37	08.55	27
28	20.54	AQU	AQU	ARI	TAU	CAN	LEO	LIB	SCO	23.34	AQU	PIS	28
29	CAP		03.45	15.36	01.53	14.24	04.28	LIB	03.36	CAP	AQU	16.06	29
30	03.44		PIS	TAU	GEM	LEO	07.15	SAG	CAP	03.03	ARI	30
31	AQU		04.57		02.05		12.06	SCO		11.08		20.28	31

SUN

mth	dy	time → sign
JAN	1	00.00 → CAP
JAN	21	08.05 → AQU
FEB	19	22.31 → PIS
MAR	20	21.59 → ARI
APR	20	09.36 → TAU
MAY	21	09.22 → GEM
JUN	21	17.42 → CAN
JUL	23	04.35 → LEO
AUG	23	11.23 → VIR
SEP	23	08.28 → LIB
OCT	23	17.15 → SCO
NOV	22	14.12 → SAG
DEC	22	03.15 → CAP

MERCURY

mth	dy	time → sign
JAN	1	00.00 → SAG
JAN	8	05.52 → CAP
JAN	27	13.52 → AQU
FEB	13	18.42 → PIS
MAR	2	19.27 → ARI
MAR	19	16.26 → PIS
APR	17	18.07 → ARI
MAY	8	23.56 → TAU
MAY	24	00.35 → GEM
JUN	7	03.02 → CAN
JUN	26	12.32 → LEO
AUG	2	22.11 → CAN
AUG	10	09.15 → LEO
AUG	31	18.29 → VIR
SEP	16	17.15 → LIB
OCT	5	09.27 → SCO
OCT	30	12.42 → SAG
NOV	10	19.45 → SCO
DEC	11	04.36 → SAG
DEC	31	11.24 → CAP

VENUS

mth	dy	time → sign
JAN	1	00.00 → SCO
JAN	4	09.19 → SAG
JAN	29	11.55 → CAP
FEB	23	03.44 → AQU
MAR	18	15.31 → PIS
APR	12	02.11 → ARI
MAY	6	12.56 → TAU
MAY	31	00.05 → GEM
JUN	24	10.53 → CAN
JUL	18	20.28 → LEO
AUG	12	04.31 → VIR
SEP	5	11.54 → LIB
SEP	29	19.47 → SCO
OCT	24	05.13 → SAG
NOV	17	17.26 → CAP
DEC	12	11.43 → AQU

MARS

mth	dy	time → sign
JAN	1	00.00 → LIB
JAN	31	23.28 → SCO
APR	23	20.17 → LIB
JUL	10	18.11 → SCO
SEP	4	20.18 → SAG
OCT	18	13.33 → CAP
NOV	27	13.48 → AQU

SATURN

mth	dy	time → sign
JAN	1	00.00 → VIR

JUPITER

mth	dy	time → sign
JAN	1	00.00 → LEO
AUG	27	05.38 → VIR

MOON

dy	jan	feb	mar	apr	may	jun	jul	aug	sep	oct	nov	dec	dy
1	TAU	07.54	17.22	VIR	LIB	SAG	CAP	19.18	ARI	TAU	CAN	22.45	1
2	22.13	CAN	LEO	09.59	01.37	SAG	CAP	PIS	16.19	02.32	13.37	VIR	2
3	GEM	09.05	20.40	LIB	SCO	08.05	02.30	PIS	TAU	GEM	LEO	VIR	3
4	22.19	LEO	VIR	18.33	12.59	CAP	AQU	04.10	20.58	05.29	17.03	03.50	4
5	CAN	11.18	VIR	SCO	SAG	20.38	13.37	ARI	GEM	CAN	VIR	LIB	5
6	22.30	VIR	01.53	SCO	SAG	AQU	PIS	10.56	GEM	08.14	22.23	11.51	6
7	LEO	16.19	LIB	05.42	01.39	AQU	22.38	TAU	00.04	LEO	LIB	SCO	7
8	LEO	LIB	10.10	SAG	CAP	07.43	ARI	15.15	CAN	11.23	LIB	22.09	8
9	00.46	LIB	SCO	18.25	14.09	PIS	ARI	GEM	02.02	VIR	05.49	SAG	9
10	VIR	01.13	21.35	CAP	AQU	15.57	04.45	17.11	LEO	15.44	SCO	SAG	10
11	06.47	SCO	SAG	CAP	AQU	ARI	TAU	CAN	03.54	LIB	15.26	09.59	11
12	LIB	13.21	SAG	06.32	00.32	20.35	07.40	17.41	VIR	22.14	SAG	CAP	12
13	16.57	SAG	10.25	AQU	PIS	TAU	GEM	LEO	07.10	SCO	SAG	22.39	13
14	SCO	SAG	CAP	15.50	07.23	21.57	08.03	18.27	LIB	SCO	03.03	AQU	14
15	SCO	02.14	21.58	PIS	ARI	GEM	CAN	VIR	13.19	07.30	CAP	AQU	15
16	05.43	CAP	AQU	21.29	10.35	21.26	07.32	21.28	SCO	SAG	15.44	11.03	16
17	SAG	13.20	AQU	ARI	TAU	CAN	LEO	LIB	22.58	19.16	AQU	PIS	17
18	18.34	AQU	06.25	ARI	11.13	21.01	08.12	LIB	SAG	CAP	AQU	21.30	18
19	CAP	21.39	PIS	00.08	GEM	LEO	VIR	04.12	SAG	CAP	03.39	ARI	19
20	CAP	PIS	11.43	TAU	11.01	22.44	12.02	SCO	11.09	07.52	PIS	ARI	20
21	05.39	PIS	ARI	01.14	CAN	VIR	LIB	14.45	CAP	AQU	12.45	04.22	21
22	AQU	03.36	14.58	GEM	11.49	VIR	20.03	SAG	23.33	18.57	ARI	TAU	22
23	14.34	ARI	TAU	02.22	LEO	04.05	SCO	SAG	AQU	PIS	18.02	07.15	23
24	PIS	08.05	17.25	CAN	15.10	LIB	SCO	03.22	AQU	PIS	TAU	GEM	24
25	21.32	TAU	GEM	04.48	VIR	13.19	07.31	CAP	09.57	02.52	20.00	07.13	25
26	ARI	11.42	20.02	LEO	21.50	SCO	SAG	PIS	ARI	GEM	CAN	26	
27	ARI	GEM	CAN	09.21	LIB	SCO	20.22	AQU	17.35	07.33	20.12	06.16	27
28	02.43	CAN	23.20	VIR	LIB	01.15	CAP	AQU	ARI	TAU	CAN	LEO	28
29	TAU		LEO	16.18	07.32	SAG	CAP	01.55	ARI	09.59	20.32	06.37	29
30	06.05		LEO	LIB	SCO	14.06	08.37	PIS	TAU	GEM	LEO	VIR	30
31	GEM		03.48		19.20		AQU	10.03		11.34		10.06	31

SUN

mth	dy	time → sign
JAN	1	00.00 → CAP
JAN	20	13.57 → AQU
FEB	19	04.22 → PIS
MAR	21	03.51 → ARI
APR	20	15.34 → TAU
MAY	21	15.17 → GEM
JUN	21	23.38 → CAN
JUL	23	10.30 → LEO
AUG	23	17.17 → VIR
SEP	23	14.23 → LIB
OCT	23	23.01 → SCO
NOV	22	20.04 → SAG
DEC	22	09.07 → CAP

MERCURY

mth	dy	time → sign
JAN	1	00.00 → CAP
JAN	19	02.26 → AQU
FEB	5	10.14 → PIS
APR	14	02.14 → ARI
MAY	1	07.03 → TAU
MAY	15	10.07 → GEM
MAY	31	05.12 → CAN
AUG	8	07.41 → LEO
AUG	23	13.54 → VIR
SEP	9	02.35 → LIB
SEP	29	16.01 → SCO
DEC	5	00.25 → SAG
DEC	24	06.44 → CAP

VENUS

mth	dy	time → sign
JAN	1	00.00 → AQU
JAN	6	20.33 → PIS
FEB	2	18.34 → ARI
MAR	7	09.16 → TAU
APR	25	23.44 → ARI
JUN	2	04.21 → TAU
JUL	8	05.55 → GEM
AUG	5	14.42 → CAN
AUG	31	22.25 → LEO
SEP	26	04.08 → VIR
OCT	20	17.33 → LIB
NOV	13	21.12 → SCO
DEC	7	19.49 → SAG
DEC	31	16.31 → CAP

MARS

mth	dy	time → sign
JAN	1	00.00 → AQU
JAN	5	07.42 → PIS
FEB	13	05.23 → ARI
MAR	25	06.16 → TAU
MAY	6	01.36 → GEM
JUN	18	20.48 → CAN
AUG	3	11.14 → LEO
SEP	19	11.49 → VIR
NOV	6	16.22 → LIB
DEC	26	11.36 → SCO

SATURN

mth	dy	time → sign
JAN	1	00.00 → VIR
OCT	7	17.35 → LIB

JUPITER

mth	dy	time → sign
JAN	1	00.00 → VIR
SEP	25	23.28 → LIB

MOON

dy	jan	feb	mar	apr	may	jun	jul	aug	sep	oct	nov	dec	dy
1	LIB	10.04	SAG	CAP	21.46	ARI	TAU	03.18	13.06	LIB	16.08	08.32	1
2	17.27	SAG	SAG	01.22	PIS	ARI	15.23	CAN	VIR	LIB	SAG	CAP	2
3	SCO	22.14	05.03	AQU	PIS	01.03	GEM	03.11	13.05	01.37	23.38	18.41	3
4	SCO	CAP	CAP	13.28	08.14	TAU	16.55	LEO	LIB	SCO	CAP	AQU	4
5	03.58	CAP	17.46	PIS	ARI	05.17	CAN	02.18	15.24	06.22	CAP	AQU	5
6	SAG	10.59	AQU	23.31	15.32	GEM	16.33	VIR	SCO	SAG	10.17	07.03	6
7	16.10	AQU	AQU	ARI	TAU	06.46	LEO	02.51	21.20	14.45	AQU	PIS	7
8	CAP	23.03	05.44	ARI	19.51	CAN	16.26	LIB	SAG	22.51	PIS	19.37	8
9	CAP	PIS	PIS	07.00	GEM	07.18	VIR	06.33	SAG	CAP	PIS	ARI	9
10	04.50	PIS	15.58	TAU	22.19	LEO	18.28	SCO	06.58	02.12	PIS	ARI	10
11	AQU	09.51	ARI	12.16	CAN	08.41	LIB	13.59	CAP	AQU	10.52	05.46	11
12	17.10	ARI	ARI	GEM	CAN	VIR	23.43	SAG	19.01	14.51	ARI	TAU	12
13	PIS	18.45	00.14	15.58	00.16	12.10	SCO	SAG	AQU	PIS	20.19	12.07	13
14	PIS	TAU	TAU	CAN	LEO	LIB	SCO	00.30	AQU	PIS	TAU	GEM	14
15	04.15	TAU	06.29	18.47	02.51	18.10	08.05	CAP	07.39	02.34	TAU	15.12	15
16	ARI	00.54	GEM	LEO	VIR	SCO	SAG	12.42	PIS	ARI	02.41	CAN	16
17	12.40	GEM	10.36	21.21	06.46	SCO	18.43	AQU	19.29	12.08	GEM	16.34	17
18	TAU	03.58	CAN	VIR	LIB	02.28	CAP	AQU	ARI	TAU	06.41	LEO	18
19	17.23	CAN	12.52	VIR	12.21	SAG	CAP	01.20	ARI	19.21	CAN	18.02	19
20	GEM	04.34	LEO	00.24	SCO	12.39	06.43	PIS	05.41	GEM	09.32	VIR	20
21	18.35	LEO	14.07	LIB	19.53	CAP	AQU	13.30	TAU	GEM	LEO	20.52	21
22	CAN	04.20	VIR	04.54	SAG	CAP	19.23	ARI	13.41	00.32	12.17	LIB	22
23	17.45	VIR	15.49	SCO	SAG	00.24	PIS	ARI	GEM	CAN	VIR	LIB	23
24	LEO	05.21	LIB	11.45	05.34	AQU	PIS	00.07	19.06	04.08	15.31	01.33	24
25	17.04	LIB	19.33	SAG	CAP	13.04	07.42	TAU	CAN	LEO	LIB	SCO	25
26	VIR	09.28	SCO	21.27	17.17	PIS	ARI	07.58	21.57	06.40	19.37	08.02	26
27	18.46	SCO	SCO	CAP	AQU	PIS	17.58	GEM	LEO	VIR	SCO	SAG	27
28	LIB	17.36	02.34	CAP	AQU	01.02	TAU	12.17	23.01	08.49	SCO	16.16	28
29	LIB		SAG	09.26	05.50	ARI	TAU	CAN	VIR	LIB	01.03	CAP	29
30	00.25		12.58	AQU	PIS	10.14	00.37	13.31	23.41	11.33	SAG	CAP	30
31	SCO		CAP		17.05		GEM	LEO		SCO		02.31	31

SUN

mth	dy	time → sign
JAN	1	00.00 → CAP
JAN	20	19.46 → AQU
FEB	19	10.17 → PIS
MAR	21	09.47 → ARI
APR	20	21.29 → TAU
MAY	21	21.13 → GEM
JUN	22	05.27 → CAN
JUL	23	16.23 → LEO
AUG	23	23.04 → VIR
SEP	23	20.12 → LIB
OCT	24	04.54 → SCO
NOV	23	01.59 → SAG
DEC	22	14.57 → CAP

MERCURY

mth	dy	time → sign
JAN	1	00.00 → CAP
JAN	11	16.56 → AQU
FEB	1	17.44 → PIS
FEB	9	04.25 → AQU
MAR	18	06.33 → PIS
APR	7	10.22 → ARI
APR	22	23.17 → TAU
MAY	7	07.03 → GEM
JUN	1	03.06 → CAN
JUN	10	22.13 → GEM
JUL	13	20.02 → CAN
JUL	31	13.27 → LEO
AUG	15	08.58 → VIR
SEP	2	04.23 → LIB
OCT	1	09.14 → SCO
OCT	5	01.48 → LIB
NOV	8	22.32 → SCO
NOV	27	23.07 → SAG
DEC	17	00.28 → CAP

VENUS

mth	dy	time → sign
JAN	1	00.00 → CAP
JAN	24	13.13 → AQU
FEB	17	11.08 → PIS
MAR	13	11.32 → ARI
APR	6	15.51 → TAU
MAY	1	01.25 → GEM
MAY	25	17.04 → CAN
JUN	19	16.33 → LEO
JUL	15	03.22 → VIR
AUG	10	09.33 → LIB
SEP	7	07.14 → SCO
OCT	10	22.33 → SAG
NOV	28	21.49 → SCO

MARS

mth	dy	time → sign
JAN	1	00.00 → SCO
FEB	18	16.28 → SAG
SEP	13	13.13 → CAP
OCT	30	18.55 → AQU
DEC	11	13.23 → PIS

SATURN

mth	dy	time → sign
JAN	1	00.00 → LIB

JUPITER

mth	dy	time → sign
JAN	1	00.00 → LIB
OCT	26	19.28 → SCO

MOON

dy	jan	feb	mar	apr	may	jun	jul	aug	sep	oct	nov	dec	dy
1	AQU	10.35	ARI	20.29	09.12	22.48	07.04	20.35	CAP	AQU	07.04	03.00	1
2	14.44	ARI	ARI	GEM	CAN	VIR	LIB	SAG	18.12	ARI	11.40	TAU	2
3	PIS	22.41	04.52	GEM	14.05	VIR	10.29	SAG	AQU	PIS	19.40	13.34	3
4	PIS	TAU	TAU	03.46	LEO	01.43	SCO	03.22	AQU	PIS	TAU	GEM	4
5	03.42	TAU	14.49	CAN	17.19	LIB	15.05	CAP	05.41	00.36	TAU	21.34	5
6	ARI	07.42	GEM	08.13	VIR	04.42	SAG	12.19	PIS	ARI	06.33	CAN	6
7	14.58	GEM	21.19	LEO	19.21	SCO	21.12	AQU	18.29	13.20	GEM	CAN	7
8	TAU	12.30	CAN	10.09	LIB	08.18	CAP	23.23	ARI	15.23	03.33	8
9	22.27	CAN	CAN	VIR	21.00	SAG	CAP	PIS	ARI	TAU	CAN	LEO	9
10	GEM	13.39	00.09	10.36	SCO	13.30	05.27	PIS	07.24	00.44	22.05	08.09	10
11	GEM	LEO	LEO	LIB	23.32	CAP	AQU	12.05	TAU	GEM	LEO	VIR	11
12	01.47	12.58	00.22>VIR	11.07	SAG	21.25	16.16	ARI	18.50	09.52	LEO	11.39	12
13	CAN	VIR	23.44	SCO	SAG	AQU	PIS	ARI	GEM	CAN	02.36	LIB	13
14	02.21	12.34	LIB	13.25	04.25	AQU	PIS	00.57	GEM	16.01	VIR	14.14	14
15	LEO	LIB	LIB	SAG	CAP	08.25	04.59	TAU	03.13	LEO	05.01	SCO	15
16	02.13	14.23	00.13	19.01	12.46	PIS	ARI	11.42	CAN	19.04	LIB	16.28	16
17	VIR	SCO	SCO	CAP	AQU	21.12	17.28	GEM	07.48	VIR	05.59	SAG	17
18	03.21	19.31	03.33	CAP	AQU	ARI	TAU	18.40	LEO	19.43	SCO	19.34	18
19	LIB	SAG	SAG	04.28	00.21	ARI	TAU	CAN	09.08	LIB	06.52	CAP	19
20	07.02	SAG	10.41	AQU	PIS	09.09	03.10	21.45	VIR	19.26	SAG	CAP	20
21	SCO	04.05	CAP	16.44	13.13	TAU	GEM	LEO	08.43	SCO	09.31	01.08	21
22	13.33	CAP	21.18	PIS	ARI	18.02	08.56	22.16	LIB	20.05	CAP	AQU	22
23	SAG	15.12	AQU	PIS	ARI	GEM	CAN	VIR	08.27	SAG	15.36	10.14	23
24	22.28	AQU	AQU	05.37	00.46	23.27	11.26	22.05	SCO	23.33	AQU	PIS	24
25	CAP	AQU	09.56	ARI	TAU	CAN	LEO	LIB	10.11	CAP	AQU	22.22	25
26	CAP	03.45	PIS	17.08	09.29	CAN	12.21	23.02	SAG	CAP	01.39	ARI	26
27	09.16	PIS	22.49	TAU	GEM	02.28	VIR	SCO	15.15	07.00	PIS	ARI	27
28	AQU	16.41	ARI	TAU	15.26	LEO	13.26	SCO	CAP	AQU	14.20	11.13	28
29	21.34		ARI	02.19	CAN	04.36	LIB	02.26	CAP	18.07	ARI	TAU	29
30	PIS		10.38	GEM	19.34	VIR	15.59	SAG	00.02	PIS	ARI	22.02	30
31	PIS		TAU		LEO		SCO	08.53		PIS		GEM	31

SUN

mth	dy	time → sign
JAN	1	00.00 → CAP
JAN	21	01.33 → AQU
FEB	19	16.02 → PIS
MAR	21	15.29 → ARI
APR	21	03.03 → TAU
MAY	22	02.45 → GEM
JUN	22	11.05 → CAN
JUL	23	22.02 → LEO
AUG	24	04.52 → VIR
SEP	24	02.04 → LIB
OCT	24	10.54 → SCO
NOV	23	07.51 → SAG
DEC	22	20.52 → CAP

MERCURY

mth	dy	time → sign
JAN	1	00.00 → CAP
JAN	4	23.42 → AQU
FEB	6	15.34 → CAP
FEB	13	23.23 → AQU
MAR	13	02.38 → PIS
MAR	30	18.11 → ARI
APR	14	12.56 → TAU
MAY	1	05.18 → GEM
JUL	8	12.44 → CAN
JUL	23	02.07 → LEO
AUG	7	13.34 → VIR
AUG	27	22.27 → LIB
OCT	4	11.53 → VIR
OCT	11	22.24 → LIB
NOV	2	02.47 → SCO
NOV	20	16.24 → SAG
DEC	10	00.17 → CAP

VENUS

mth	dy	time → sign
JAN	1	00.00 → SCO
JAN	2	07.28 → SAG
FEB	6	14.33 → CAP
MAR	6	05.38 → AQU
APR	1	05.13 → PIS
APR	26	13.36 → ARI
MAY	21	14.52 → TAU
JUN	15	11.46 → GEM
JUL	10	04.38 → CAN
AUG	3	16.42 → LEO
AUG	27	23.56 → VIR
SEP	21	03.29 → LIB
OCT	15	04.46 → SCO
NOV	8	05.24 → SAG
DEC	2	06.05 → CAP
DEC	26	08.05 → AQU

MARS

mth	dy	time → sign
JAN	1	00.00 → PIS
JAN	21	10.23 → ARI
MAR	4	00.42 → TAU
APR	16	02.43 → GEM
MAY	30	21.28 → CAN
JUL	16	01.12 → LEO
SEP	1	00.50 → VIR
OCT	18	04.12 → LIB
DEC	4	02.22 → SCO

SATURN

mth	dy	time → sign
JAN	1	00.00 → LIB
DEC	20	04.09 → SCO

JUPITER

mth	dy	time → sign
JAN	1	00.00 → SCO
NOV	24	17.20 → SAG

MOON

dy	jan	feb	mar	apr	may	jun	jul	aug	sep	oct	nov	dec	dy
1	GEM	LEO	LEO	LIB	SCO	CAP	AQU	08.11	TAU	GEM	05.00	VIR	1
2	05.39	22.12	08.41	19.26	05.59	21.04	13.28	ARI	16.50	12.00	LEO	VIR	2
3	CAN	VIR	VIR	SCO	SAG	AQU	PIS	20.22	GEM	CAN	12.07	00.24	3
4	10.34	23.38	09.00	19.33	07.14	AQU	23.51	TAU	GEM	21.14	VIR	LIB	4
5	LEO	LIB	LIB	SAG	CAP	04.43	ARI	TAU	03.59	LEO	15.24	02.14	5
6	13.59	LIB	09.16	22.19	12.05	PIS	ARI	08.47	CAN	LEO	LIB	SCO	6
7	VIR	01.37	SCO	CAP	AQU	16.02	12.25	GEM	11.54	02.41	15.37	01.57	7
8	16.59	SCO	11.05	CAP	21.06	ARI	TAU	19.08	LEO	VIR	SCO	SAG	8
9	LIB	04.59	SAG	04.48	PIS	ARI	TAU	CAN	16.16	04.35	14.37	01.31	9
10	20.04	SAG	15.34	AQU	PIS	04.56	00.37	CAN	VIR	LIB	SAG	CAP	10
11	SCO	10.08	CAP	14.51	09.12	TAU	GEM	02.19	18.03	04.25	14.37	03.10	11
12	23.34	CAP	23.02	PIS	ARI	17.03	10.34	LEO	LIB	SCO	CAP	AQU	12
13	SAG	17.18	AQU	PIS	22.14	GEM	CAN	06.44	18.47	04.08	17.39	08.35	13
14	SAG	AQU	AQU	03.08	TAU	GEM	07.53	VIR	SCO	SAG	AQU	PIS	14
15	03.56	AQU	09.08	ARI	TAU	03.10	LEO	09.27	20.05	05.43	AQU	18.08	15
16	CAP	02.43	PIS	16.07	10.27	CAN	23.10	LIB	SAG	CAP	00.46	ARI	16
17	10.05	PIS	21.06	TAU	GEM	11.11	VIR	11.38	23.14	10.29	PIS	ARI	17
18	AQU	14.20	ARI	TAU	21.03	LEO	VIR	SCO	CAP	AQU	11.25	06.21	18
19	18.57	ARI	ARI	04.33	CAN	17.22	03.05	14.12	CAP	18.43	ARI	TAU	19
20	PIS	ARI	10.00	GEM	CAN	VIR	LIB	SAG	04.53	PIS	23.53	19.03	20
21	PIS	03.15	TAU	15.28	05.40	21.44	06.08	17.49	AQU	PIS	TAU	GEM	21
22	06.37	TAU	22.33	CAN	LEO	LIB	SCO	CAP	13.03	05.33	TAU	GEM	22
23	ARI	15.31	GEM	23.50	11.54	LIB	08.43	23.03	PIS	ARI	12.32	06.40	23
24	19.34	GEM	GEM	LEO	VIR	00.20	SAG	AQU	23.23	17.48	GEM	CAN	24
25	TAU	GEM	09.05	LEO	15.25	SCO	11.32	AQU	ARI	TAU	GEM	16.40	25
26	TAU	00.57	CAN	04.56	LIB	01.46	CAP	06.25	ARI	TAU	00.28	LEO	26
27	07.07	CAN	16.13	VIR	16.35	SAG	15.42	PIS	11.22	06.29	CAN	LEO	27
28	GEM	06.30	LEO	06.48	SCO	03.20	AQU	16.15	TAU	GEM	11.01	00.51	28
29	15.19		19.36	LIB	16.37	CAP	22.23	ARI	TAU	18.39	LEO	VIR	29
30	CAN		VIR	06.32	SAG	06.44	PIS	ARI	00.06	CAN	19.19	06.51	30
31	19.57		20.06		17.27		PIS	04.12		CAN		LIB	31

SUN

mth	dy	time → sign
JAN	1	00.00 → CAP
JAN	21	07.29 → AQU
FEB	19	21.53 → PIS
MAR	20	21.20 → ARI
APR	20	08.56 → TAU
MAY	21	08.40 → GEM
JUN	21	16.57 → CAN
JUL	23	03.56 → LEO
AUG	23	10.49 → VIR
SEP	23	07.59 → LIB
OCT	23	16.44 → SCO
NOV	22	13.44 → SAG
DEC	22	02.47 → CAP

MERCURY

mth	dy	time → sign
JAN	1	00.00 → CAP
FEB	14	03.16 → AQU
MAR	5	05.51 → PIS
MAR	21	15.39 → ARI
APR	5	16.23 → TAU
JUN	13	01.44 → GEM
JUN	29	13.22 → CAN
JUL	13	15.35 → LEO
JUL	30	16.48 → VIR
OCT	7	04.14 → LIB
OCT	24	15.59 → SCO
NOV	12	12.05 → SAG
DEC	2	23.41 → CAP
DEC	31	15.55 → SAG

VENUS

mth	dy	time → sign
JAN	1	00.00 → AQU
JAN	19	13.43 → PIS
FEB	13	04.13 → ARI
MAR	9	11.52 → TAU
APR	5	06.48 → GEM
MAY	6	01.49 → CAN
SEP	8	21.45 → LEO
OCT	7	14.17 → VIR
NOV	2	14.46 → LIB
NOV	27	11.46 → SCO
DEC	21	19.57 → SAG

MARS

mth	dy	time → sign
JAN	1	00.00 → SCO
JAN	19	19.20 → SAG
MAR	6	19.13 → CAP
APR	24	15.50 → AQU
JUN	24	16.21 → PIS
AUG	24	15.44 → AQU
OCT	19	18.49 → PIS
DEC	19	11.18 → ARI

SATURN

mth	dy	time → sign
JAN	1	00.00 → SCO
APR	6	08.33 → LIB
SEP	13	22.19 → SCO

JUPITER

mth	dy	time → sign
JAN	1	00.00 → SAG
DEC	18	06.13 → CAP

MOON

dy	jan	feb	mar	apr	may	jun	jul	aug	sep	oct	nov	dec	dy
1	10.23	21.03	CAP	PIS	ARI	14.47	09.28	LEO	02.38	SCO	00.39	AQU	1
2	SCO	CAP	07.11	PIS	20.37	GEM	CAN	13.05	LIB	15.54	CAP	13.38	2
3	11.48	23.43	AQU	03.45	TAU	GEM	21.11	VIR	06.54	SAG	02.53	PIS	3
4	SAG	AQU	12.44	ARI	TAU	03.27	LEO	20.20	SCO	18.02	AQU	20.10	4
5	12.22	AQU	PIS	14.11	08.48	CAN	LEO	LIB	10.00	CAP	07.34	ARI	5
6	CAP	04.12	20.26	TAU	GEM	15.29	07.15	LIB	SAG	21.19	PIS	ARI	6
7	13.54	PIS	ARI	TAU	21.30	LEO	VIR	01.24	12.41	AQU	14.39	05.33	7
8	AQU	11.36	ARI	02.13	CAN	LEO	14.55	SCO	CAP	AQU	ARI	TAU	8
9	18.13	ARI	06.35	GEM	CAN	01.41	LIB	04.32	15.33	02.06	23.44	16.52	9
10	PIS	22.09	TAU	14.53	09.30	VIR	19.36	SAG	AQU	PIS	TAU	GEM	10
11	PIS	TAU	18.43	CAN	LEO	08.41	SCO	06.20	19.17	08.31	TAU	GEM	11
12	02.22	TAU	GEM	CAN	18.57	LIB	21.32	CAP	PIS	ARI	10.34	05.21	12
13	ARI	10.35	GEM	02.15	VIR	11.57	SAG	07.52	PIS	16.50	GEM	CAN	13
14	13.48	GEM	07.08	LEO	VIR	SCO	21.49	AQU	00.42	TAU	22.57	18.13	14
15	TAU	22.34	CAN	10.21	00.28	12.17	CAP	10.28	ARI	TAU	CAN	LEO	15
16	TAU	CAN	17.31	VIR	LIB	SAG	22.11	PIS	08.39	03.23	CAN	LEO	16
17	02.28	CAN	LEO	14.27	02.10	11.28	AQU	15.32	TAU	GEM	11.51	06.07	17
18	GEM	08.09	LEO	LIB	SCO	CAP	AQU	ARI	19.24	15.48	LEO	VIR	18
19	14.05	LEO	00.27	15.24	01.33	11.42	00.30	23.54	GEM	CAN	23.11	15.15	19
20	CAN	14.45	VIR	SCO	SAG	AQU	PIS	TAU	GEM	CAN	VIR	LIB	20
21	23.33	VIR	04.00	15.04	00.48	14.52	06.12	TAU	07.54	04.21	VIR	20.26	21
22	LEO	18.57	LIB	SAG	CAP	PIS	ARI	11.14	CAN	LEO	06.51	SCO	22
23	LEO	LIB	05.27	15.33	02.04	21.56	15.36	GEM	19.52	14.33	LIB	21.55	23
24	06.49	21.47	SCO	CAP	AQU	ARI	TAU	23.48	LEO	VIR	10.17	SAG	24
25	VIR	SCO	06.29	18.30	06.49	ARI	TAU	CAN	LEO	20.49	SCO	21.18	25
26	12.14	SCO	SAG	AQU	PIS	08.27	03.36	CAN	05.06	LIB	10.38	CAP	26
27	LIB	00.16	08.37	AQU	15.16	TAU	GEM	11.19	VIR	23.26	SAG	20.41	27
28	16.09	SAG	CAP	00.39	ARI	20.51	16.11	LEO	10.53	SCO	09.57	AQU	28
29	SCO	03.12	12.47	ARI	ARI	GEM	CAN	20.19	LIB	SCO	CAP	22.06	29
30	18.52		AQU	09.39	02.23	GEM	CAN	VIR	14.00	00.03	10.25	PIS	30
31	SAG		19.13		TAU		03.38	VIR		SAG		PIS	31

SUN

mth	dy	time → sign
JAN	1	00.00 → CAP
JAN	20	13.22 → AQU
FEB	19	03.43 → PIS
MAR	21	03.13 → ARI
APR	20	14.51 → TAU
MAY	21	14.35 → GEM
JUN	21	22.52 → CAN
JUL	23	09.47 → LEO
AUG	23	16.33 → VIR
SEP	23	13.44 → LIB
OCT	23	22.31 → SCO
NOV	22	19.37 → SAG
DEC	22	08.36 → CAP

SATURN

mth	dy	time → sign
JAN	1	00.00 → SCO

MERCURY

mth	dy	time → sign
JAN	1	00.00 → SAG
JAN	14	07.12 → CAP
FEB	7	08.12 → AQU
FEB	25	16.53 → PIS
MAR	13	12.36 → ARI
APR	1	15.24 → TAU
APR	15	23.15 → ARI
MAY	17	01.32 → TAU
JUN	6	15.25 → GEM
JUN	20	23.07 → CAN
JUL	5	17.55 → LEO
JUL	26	11.46 → VIR
AUG	27	06.26 → LEO
SEP	11	05.09 → VIR
SEP	29	18.05 → LIB
OCT	17	03.52 → SCO
NOV	5	18.55 → SAG

VENUS

mth	dy	time → sign
JAN	1	00.00 → SAG
JAN	14	22.26 → CAP
FEB	7	23.13 → AQU
MAR	4	00.21 → PIS
MAR	28	03.03 → ARI
APR	21	08.17 → TAU
MAY	15	16.04 → GEM
JUN	9	02.16 → CAN
JUL	3	14.33 → LEO
JUL	28	05.25 → VIR
AUG	22	00.29 → LIB
SEP	16	02.07 → SCO
OCT	11	14.10 → SAG
NOV	6	22.35 → CAP
DEC	5	15.11 → AQU

MARS

mth	dy	time → sign
JAN	1	00.00 → ARI
FEB	5	10.02 → TAU
MAR	24	00.33 → GEM
MAY	9	22.52 → CAN
JUN	26	09.19 → LEO
AUG	12	21.12 → VIR
SEP	28	19.18 → LIB
NOV	13	14.16 → SCO
DEC	28	00.23 → SAG

JUPITER

mth	dy	time → sign
JAN	1	00.00 → CAP

MOON

dy	jan	feb	mar	apr	may	jun	jul	aug	sep	oct	nov	dec	dy
1	02.57	TAU	13.26	CAN	LEO	12.30	03.33	17.46	AQU	15.06	TAU	GEM	1
2	ARI	05.32	GEM	22.32	18.38	LIB	SCO	CAP	04.02	ARI	09.44	03.19	2
3	11.31	GEM	GEM	LEO	VIR	18.21	06.55	17.40	PIS	18.20	GEM	CAN	3
4	TAU	18.11	01.38	LEO	VIR	SCO	SAG	AQU	05.02	TAU	19.06	15.13	4
5	22.52	CAN	CAN	09.55	03.26	20.33	07.24	17.23	ARI	TAU	CAN	LEO	5
6	GEM	CAN	14.22	VIR	LIB	SAG	CAP	PIS	08.27	00.35	CAN	LEO	6
7	GEM	06.50	LEO	18.05	08.22	20.45	06.49	18.46	TAU	GEM	07.16	04.14	7
8	11.32	LEO	LEO	LIB	SCO	CAP	AQU	ARI	15.39	10.33	LEO	VIR	8
9	CAN	18.01	01.24	23.04	10.27	20.54	07.06	23.24	GEM	CAN	20.07	15.52	9
10	CAN	VIR	VIR	SCO	SAG	AQU	PIS	TAU	GEM	23.09	VIR	LIB	10
11	00.14	VIR	09.44	SCO	11.30	22.40	09.53	TAU	02.35	LEO	VIR	LIB	11
12	LEO	03.06	LIB	02.05	CAP	PIS	ARI	07.57	CAN	LEO	06.52	00.03	12
13	11.55	LIB	15.37	SAG	13.08	PIS	16.05	GEM	15.30	11.43	LIB	SCO	13
14	VIR	09.54	SCO	04.32	AQU	03.03	TAU	19.39	LEO	VIR	14.05	04.23	14
15	21.33	SCO	19.51	CAP	16.23	ARI	TAU	CAN	LEO	21.57	SCO	SAG	15
16	LIB	14.28	SAG	07.23	PIS	10.15	01.37	CAN	03.56	LIB	18.13	05.59	16
17	LIB	SAG	23.07	AQU	21.34	TAU	GEM	08.41	VIR	LIB	SAG	CAP	17
18	04.11	17.02	CAP	11.02	ARI	19.57	13.33	LEO	14.18	05.12	20.38	06.35	18
19	SCO	CAP	CAP	PIS	ARI	GEM	CAN	21.13	LIB	SCO	CAP	AQU	19
20	07.34	18.21	01.51	15.45	04.41	GEM	CAN	VIR	22.18	10.11	22.48	07.51	20
21	SAG	AQU	AQU	ARI	TAU	07.36	02.32	VIR	SCO	SAG	AQU	PIS	21
22	08.22	19.36	04.33	22.00	13.50	CAN	LEO	08.05	SCO	13.57	AQU	10.57	22
23	CAP	PIS	PIS	TAU	GEM	20.30	15.17	LIB	04.18	CAP	01.37	ARI	23
24	08.09	22.21	08.04	TAU	GEM	LEO	VIR	16.44	SAG	17.12	PIS	16.25	24
25	AQU	ARI	ARI	06.33	01.07	LEO	VIR	SCO	08.37	AQU	05.31	TAU	25
26	08.45	ARI	13.34	GEM	CAN	09.21	02.30	22.50	CAP	20.14	ARI	TAU	26
27	PIS	04.04	TAU	17.45	13.59	VIR	LIB	SAG	11.29	PIS	10.46	00.18	27
28	11.59	TAU	22.08	CAN	LEO	20.16	10.56	SAG	AQU	23.24	TAU	GEM	28
29	ARI		GEM	CAN	LEO	LIB	SCO	02.19	13.19	ARI	17.50	10.26	29
30	18.58		GEM	06.36	02.35	LIB	15.56	CAP	PIS	ARI	GEM	CAN	30
31	TAU		09.42		VIR		SAG	03.41		03.29		22.26	31

SUN

mth	dy	time	→ sign
JAN	1	00.00	→ CAP
JAN	20	19.11	→ AQU
FEB	19	09.35	→ PIS
MAR	21	09.03	→ ARI
APR	20	20.36	→ TAU
MAY	21	20.13	→ GEM
JUN	22	04.30	→ CAN
JUL	23	15.27	→ LEO
AUG	23	22.14	→ VIR
SEP	23	19.26	→ LIB
OCT	24	04.19	→ SCO
NOV	23	01.26	→ SAG
DEC	22	14.35	→ CAP

MERCURY

mth	dy	time	→ sign
JAN	1	00.00	→ SAG
JAN	11	07.29	→ CAP
JAN	31	10.03	→ AQU
FEB	17	21.33	→ PIS
MAR	6	02.57	→ ARI
MAY	13	10.55	→ TAU
MAY	29	13.51	→ GEM
JUN	12	10.06	→ CAN
JUN	29	05.01	→ LEO
SEP	5	20.35	→ VIR
SEP	21	20.57	→ LIB
OCT	9	21.55	→ SCO
OCT	31	11.01	→ SAG
NOV	28	05.06	→ SCO
DEC	13	20.36	→ SAG

VENUS

mth	dy	time	→ sign
JAN	1	00.00	→ AQU
APR	6	03.56	→ PIS
MAY	6	15.11	→ ARI
JUN	2	19.59	→ TAU
JUN	28	21.09	→ GEM
JUL	24	06.42	→ CAN
AUG	18	04.34	→ LEO
SEP	11	16.36	→ VIR
OCT	5	21.08	→ LIB
OCT	29	20.50	→ SCO
NOV	22	18.13	→ SAG
DEC	16	14.46	→ CAP

MARS

mth	dy	time	→ sign
JAN	1	00.00	→ SAG
FEB	9	03.23	→ CAP
MAR	23	04.26	→ AQU
MAY	3	17.20	→ PIS
JUN	15	00.36	→ ARI
AUG	1	09.19	→ TAU

SATURN

mth	dy	time	→ sign
JAN	1	00.00	→ SCO
DEC	2	22.49	→ SAG

JUPITER

mth	dy	time	→ sign
JAN	1	00.00	→ CAP
JAN	6	01.19	→ AQU

MOON

dy	jan	feb	mar	apr	may	jun	jul	aug	sep	oct	nov	dec	dy
1	LEO	VIR	12.03	SCO	23.32	AQU	20.14	TAU	01.48	LEO	VIR	22.39	1
2	LEO	06.11	LIB	12.08	CAP	11.53	ARI	11.24	CAN	LEO	03.22	SCO	2
3	11.26	LIB	22.28	SAG	CAP	PIS	23.59	GEM	13.01	07.49	LIB	SCO	3
4	VIR	16.39	SCO	18.04	03.31	14.45	TAU	20.08	LEO	VIR	14.37	07.32	4
5	23.44	SCO	SCO	CAP	AQU	ARI	TAU	CAN	LEO	20.28	SCO	SAG	5
6	LIB	SCO	06.40	22.01	06.32	18.28	05.57	CAN	LIB	23.51	SAG	13.52	6
7	LIB	00.02	SAG	AQU	PIS	TAU	GEM	07.12	VIR	LIB	CAP	CAP	7
8	09.19	SAG	12.06	AQU	08.55	23.43	14.16	LEO	14.23	07.59	SAG	18.22	8
9	SCO	03.49	CAP	00.03	ARI	GEM	CAN	19.39	LIB	SCO	07.11	AQU	9
10	15.02	CAP	14.40	PIS	11.33	GEM	CAN	VIR	LIB	17.54	CAP	21.44	10
11	SAG	04.37	AQU	01.02	TAU	07.16	00.50	VIR	02.15	SAG	12.42	PIS	11
12	17.09	AQU	15.03	ARI	15.46	CAN	LEO	08.26	SCO	SAG	AQU	PIS	12
13	CAP	03.57	PIS	02.31	GEM	17.28	13.07	LIB	12.22	01.47	16.22	00.33	13
14	17.07	PIS	14.52	TAU	22.52	LEO	VIR	20.18	SAG	CAP	PIS	ARI	14
15	AQU	03.47	ARI	06.20	CAN	LEO	VIR	SCO	19.37	07.02	18.28	03.23	15
16	16.48	ARI	16.06	GEM	CAN	05.48	01.52	SCO	CAP	ARI	TAU	16	
16	16.48	ARI	16.06	GEM	CAN	05.48	01.52	SCO	CAP	ARI	TAU		16
17	PIS	06.08	TAU	13.55	09.20	VIR	LIB	05.39	23.23	09.30	19.54	06.59	17
18	18.03	TAU	20.42	CAN	LEO	18.18	13.08	SAG	AQU	PIS	TAU	GEM	18
19	ARI	12.22	GEM	CAN	21.54	LIB	SCO	11.24	AQU	09.56	22.10	12.20	19
20	22.16	GEM	GEM	01.07	VIR	LIB	21.10	CAP	00.06 PIS	ARI	GEM	CAN	20
21	TAU	22.28	05.30	LEO	VIR	04.41	SAG	13.31	23.20	10.01	GEM	20.17	21
22	TAU	CAN	CAN	13.59	10.04	SCO	SAG	AQU	ARI	TAU	02.54	LEO	22
23	05.55	CAN	17.35	VIR	LIB	11.34	01.28	13.14	23.12	11.50	CAN	LEO	23
24	GEM	11.00	LEO	VIR	19.42	SAG	CAP	PIS	TAU	GEM	11.10	07.02	24
25	16.30	LEO	LEO	01.52	SCO	15.18	02.48	12.30	TAU	17.08	LEO	VIR	25
26	CAN	23.59	06.36	LIB	SCO	CAP	AQU	ARI	01.50	CAN	22.36	19.31	26
27	CAN	VIR	VIR	11.19	02.14	17.02	02.46	13.24	GEM	CAN	VIR	LIB	27
28	04.52	VIR	18.27	SCO	SAG	AQU	PIS	TAU	08.35	02.31	VIR	LIB	28
29	LEO		LIB	18.19	06.24	18.14	03.13	17.39	CAN	LEO	11.14	07.28	29
30	17.49		LIB	SAG	CAP	PIS	ARI	GEM	19.10	14.43	LIB	SCO	30
31	VIR		04.17		09.19		05.46	GEM		VIR		16.50	31

SUN

mth	dy	time → sign
JAN	1	00.00 → CAP
JAN	21	01.11 → AQU
FEB	19	15.34 → PIS
MAR	21	14.57 → ARI
APR	21	02.32 → TAU
MAY	22	02.06 → GEM
JUN	22	10.22 → CAN
JUL	23	21.15 → LEO
AUG	24	04.05 → VIR
SEP	24	01.15 → LIB
OCT	24	10.07 → SCO
NOV	23	07.11 → SAG
DEC	22	20.20 → CAP

MERCURY

mth	dy	time → sign
JAN	1	00.00 → SAG
JAN	5	01.55 → CAP
JAN	24	01.11 → AQU
FEB	10	04.27 → PIS
APR	17	12.24 → ARI
MAY	6	11.28 → TAU
MAY	21	00.07 → GEM
JUN	4	13.38 → CAN
JUN	28	19.34 → LEO
JUL	14	04.08 → CAN
AUG	12	03.46 → LEO
AUG	28	23.07 → VIR
SEP	14	01.34 → LIB
OCT	3	08.38 → SCO
DEC	9	09.24 → SAG
DEC	29	01.46 → CAP

VENUS

mth	dy	time → sign
JAN	1	00.00 → CAP
JAN	9	11.44 → AQU
FEB	2	10.36 → PIS
FEB	26	13.18 → ARI
MAR	22	22.57 → TAU
APR	16	19.23 → GEM
MAY	12	08.34 → CAN
JUN	8	02.52 → LEO
JUL	7	18.55 → VIR
NOV	9	13.28 → LIB
DEC	8	21.28 → SCO

MARS

mth	dy	time → sign
JAN	1	00.00 → TAU
FEB	22	00.32 → GEM
APR	17	01.20 → CAN
JUN	6	11.21 → LEO
JUL	25	07.33 → VIR
SEP	10	14.07 → LIB
OCT	26	00.01 → SCO
DEC	8	11.13 → SAG

SATURN

mth	dy	time → sign
JAN	1	00.00 → SAG

JUPITER

mth	dy	time → sign
JAN	1	00.00 → AQU
JAN	18	11.59 → PIS
JUN	6	10.01 → ARI
SEP	11	03.55 → PIS

MOON

dy	jan	feb	mar	apr	may	jun	jul	aug	sep	oct	nov	dec	dy
1	SAG	12.22	AQU	10.30	TAU	09.50	00.48	VIR	00.36	SAG	22.26	10.37	1
2	22.51	AQU	AQU	ARI	20.52	CAN	LEO	04.44	SCO	SAG	AQU	PIS	2
3	CAP	13.07	00.05>PIS	09.36	GEM	15.37	09.27	LIB	13.10	07.13	AQU	14.20	3
4	CAP	PIS	23.19	TAU	23.51	LEO	VIR	17.16	SAG	CAP	03.56	ARI	4
5	02.10	13.19	ARI	10.25	CAN	LEO	20.47	SCO	23.28	15.07	PIS	15.47	5
6	AQU	ARI	23.07	GEM	CAN	00.54	LIB	SCO	CAP	AQU	05.53	TAU	6
7	04.05	14.50	TAU	14.42	06.39	VIR	LIB	05.14	CAP	18.50	ARI	16.10	7
8	PIS	TAU	TAU	CAN	LEO	12.48	09.17	SAG	05.50	PIS	05.37	GEM	8
9	05.59	18.54	01.29	23.00	17.03	LIB	SCO	14.23	AQU	19.15	TAU	17.11	9
10	ARI	GEM	GEM	LEO	VIR	LIB	20.37	CAP	08.16	ARI	05.03	CAN	10
11	08.56	GEM	07.29	LEO	VIR	01.16	SAG	19.46	PIS	18.17	GEM	20.31	11
12	TAU	01.51	CAN	10.19	05.27	SCO	SAG	AQU	08.18	TAU	06.15	LEO	12
13	13.30	CAN	16.52	VIR	LIB	12.16	05.06	22.04	ARI	18.12	CAN	LEO	13
14	GEM	11.11	LEO	22.53	17.52	SAG	CAP	PIS	08.03	GEM	10.48	03.25	14
15	19.59	LEO	LEO	LIB	SCO	20.51	10.31	22.57	TAU	20.50	LEO	VIR	15
16	CAN	22.15	04.22	LIB	SCO	CAP	AQU	ARI	09.29	CAN	19.14	13.55	16
17	CAN	VIR	VIR	11.20	04.58	CAP	13.43	ARI	GEM	CAN	VIR	LIB	17
18	04.31	VIR	16.48	SCO	SAG	03.05	PIS	00.12	13.49	03.07	VIR	LIB	18
19	LEO	10.31	LIB	22.49	14.11	AQU	15.58	TAU	CAN	LEO	06.41	02.31	19
20	15.10	LIB	LIB	SAG	CAP	07.25	ARI	03.08	21.13	12.43	LIB	SCO	20
21	VIR	23.08	05.21	SAG	21.16	PIS	18.24	GEM	LEO	VIR	19.26	14.59	21
22	VIR	SCO	SCO	08.35	AQU	10.29	TAU	08.19	LEO	VIR	SCO	SAG	22
23	03.27	SCO	17.06	CAP	AQU	ARI	21.46	CAN	07.01	00.28	SCO	SAG	23
24	LIB	10.35	SAG	15.43	02.01	12.54	GEM	15.39	VIR	LIB	07.53	01.38	24
25	15.54	SAG	SAG	AQU	PIS	TAU	GEM	LEO	18.30	13.08	SAG	CAP	25
26	SCO	18.56	02.39	19.37	04.37	15.26	02.31	LEO	LIB	SCO	19.01	09.54	26
27	SCO	CAP	CAP	PIS	ARI	GEM	CAN	00.55	LIB	SCO	CAP	AQU	27
28	02.21	23.14	08.39	20.43	05.50	19.04	09.00	VIR	07.05	01.48	CAP	16.00	28
29	SAG		AQU	ARI	TAU	CAN	LEO	12.02	SCO	SAG	04.06	PIS	29
30	09.12		10.53	20.28	07.02	CAN	17.42	LIB	19.54	13.22	AQU	20.19	30
31	CAP		PIS		GEM		VIR	LIB		CAP		ARI	31

SUN

mth	dy	time → sign
JAN	1	00.00 → CAP
JAN	21	06.58 → AQU
FEB	19	21.17 → PIS
MAR	20	20.44 → ARI
APR	20	08.18 → TAU
MAY	21	07.52 → GEM
JUN	21	16.07 → CAN
JUL	23	03.02 → LEO
AUG	23	09.54 → VIR
SEP	23	07.09 → LIB
OCT	23	15.55 → SCO
NOV	22	13.02 → SAG
DEC	22	02.05 → CAP

MERCURY

mth	dy	time → sign
JAN	1	00.00 → CAP
JAN	16	13.33 → AQU
FEB	3	10.20 → PIS
FEB	29	06.00 → AQU
MAR	18	02.46 → PIS
APR	11	01.55 → ARI
APR	27	10.38 → TAU
MAY	11	12.08 → GEM
MAY	28	23.05 → CAN
AUG	4	20.02 → LEO
AUG	19	16.59 → VIR
SEP	5	16.22 → LIB
SEP	27	18.13 → SCO
OCT	24	21.46 → LIB
NOV	11	09.05 → SCO
DEC	1	16.58 → SAG
DEC	20	19.35 → CAP

VENUS

mth	dy	time → sign
JAN	1	00.00 → SCO
JAN	4	00.02 → SAG
JAN	29	01.11 → CAP
FEB	22	16.15 → AQU
MAR	18	03.26 → PIS
APR	11	13.35 → ARI
MAY	6	00.01 → TAU
MAY	30	11.00 → GEM
JUN	23	21.44 → CAN
JUL	18	07.16 → LEO
AUG	11	15.27 → VIR
SEP	4	23.03 → LIB
SEP	29	07.28 → SCO
OCT	23	17.13 → SAG
NOV	17	06.06 → CAP
DEC	12	01.22 → AQU

MARS

mth	dy	time → sign
JAN	1	00.00 → SAG
JAN	19	02.22 → CAP
FEB	28	06.21 → AQU
APR	7	14.39 → PIS
MAY	16	21.35 → ARI
JUN	26	09.15 → TAU
AUG	9	04.01 → GEM
OCT	3	03.40 → CAN
DEC	20	05.35 → GEM

SATURN

mth	dy	time → sign
JAN	1	00.00 → SAG

JUPITER

mth	dy	time → sign
JAN	1	00.00 → PIS
JAN	23	02.43 → ARI
JUN	4	04.38 → TAU

MOON

dy	jan	feb	mar	apr	may	jun	jul	aug	sep	oct	nov	dec	dy
1	23.15	GEM	CAN	11.53	03.36	SCO	SAG	AQU	17.26	03.59	14.40	01.28	1
2	TAU	11.21	22.38	VIR	LIB	10.38	05.23	AQU	ARI	TAU	CAN	LEO	2
3	TAU	CAN	LEO	21.47	15.38	SAG	CAP	05.34	20.07	05.09	17.14	05.16	3
4	01.20	15.53	LEO	LIB	SCO	23.00	15.32	PIS	TAU	GEM	LEO	VIR	4
5	GEM	LEO	05.51	LIB	SCO	CAP	AQU	10.33	22.43	07.21	22.41	12.52	5
6	03.28	22.09	VIR	09.27	04.32	CAP	23.23	ARI	GEM	CAN	VIR	LIB	6
7	CAN	VIR	15.04	SCO	SAG	09.42	PIS	14.18	GEM	11.18	VIR	23.46	7
8	06.52	VIR	LIB	22.20	17.09	AQU	PIS	TAU	01.51	VIR	07.05	SCO	8
9	LEO	07.03	LIB	SAG	CAP	17.55	05.04	17.22	CAN	17.13	LIB	SCO	9
10	12.53	LIB	02.31	SAG	CAP	PIS	ARI	GEM	05.49	VIR	17.53	12.29	10
11	VIR	18.41	SCO	10.56	03.58	23.14	08.49	20.03	LEO	VIR	SCO	SAG	11
12	22.18	SCO	15.24	CAP	AQU	ARI	TAU	CAN	11.01	01.14	SCO	SAG	12
13	LIB	SCO	SAG	21.07	11.35	ARI	11.00	22.57	VIR	LIB	06.20	01.29	13
14	LIB	07.32	SAG	AQU	PIS	01.45	GEM	LEO	18.12	11.29	SAG	CAP	14
15	10.26	SAG	03.33	AQU	15.30	TAU	12.20	LEO	LIB	SCO	19.25	13.36	15
16	SCO	18.54	CAP	03.19	ARI	02.25	CAN	03.07	LIB	23.44	CAP	AQU	16
17	23.06	CAP	12.31	PIS	16.25	GEM	14.06	VIR	04.04	SAG	CAP	23.49	17
18	SAG	CAP	AQU	05.40	TAU	02.34	LEO	09.53	SCO	SAG	07.40	PIS	18
19	SAG	02.47	17.20	ARI	15.56	CAN	17.53	LIB	16.23	12.50	AQU	PIS	19
20	09.49	AQU	PIS	05.36	GEM	04.02	VIR	19.57	SAG	CAP	17.19	07.15	20
21	CAP	07.05	18.54	TAU	15.57	LEO	VIR	SCO	SAG	CAP	PIS	ARI	21
22	17.27	PIS	ARI	05.09	CAN	08.27	01.02	SCO	05.16	00.33	23.14	11.25	22
23	AQU	09.09	19.06	GEM	18.17	VIR	LIB	08.29	CAP	AQU	ARI	TAU	23
24	22.24	ARI	TAU	06.14	LEO	16.43	11.46	SAG	16.01	08.50	ARI	12.40	24
25	PIS	10.42	19.53	CAN	LEO	LIB	SCO	20.59	AQU	PIS	01.30	GEM	25
26	PIS	TAU	GEM	10.11	00.07	LIB	SCO	CAP	23.01	13.04	TAU	12.17	26
27	01.48	13.07	22.42	LEO	VIR	04.15	00.34	CAP	PIS	ARI	01.23	CAN	27
28	ARI	GEM	CAN	17.28	09.36	SCO	CAP	06.57	PIS	14.16	GEM	12.07	28
29	04.42	17.04	CAN	VIR	LIB	17.13	12.47	AQU	02.31	TAU	00.43	LEO	29
30	TAU		04.04	VIR	21.40	SAG	CAP	13.31	ARI	14.11	CAN	14.12	30
31	07.47		LEO		SCO		22.33	PIS		GEM		VIR	31

SUN

mth	dy	time → sign
JAN	1	00.00 → CAP
JAN	20	12.44 → AQU
FEB	19	03.09 → PIS
MAR	21	02.33 → ARI
APR	20	14.11 → TAU
MAY	21	13.49 → GEM
JUN	21	22.03 → CAN
JUL	23	08.54 → LEO
AUG	23	15.43 → VIR
SEP	23	12.53 → LIB
OCT	23	21.42 → SCO
NOV	22	18.47 → SAG
DEC	22	07.54 → CAP

MERCURY

mth	dy	time → sign
JAN	1	00.00 → CAP
JAN	8	08.06 → AQU
MAR	16	01.07 → PIS
APR	3	21.22 → ARI
APR	19	00.22 → TAU
MAY	3	21.33 → GEM
JUL	11	21.06 → CAN
JUL	27	15.13 → LEO
AUG	11	14.45 → VIR
AUG	30	06.03 → LIB
NOV	5	19.28 → SCO
NOV	24	12.04 → SAG
DEC	13	14.44 → CAP

VENUS

mth	dy	time → sign
JAN	1	00.00 → AQU
JAN	6	12.02 → PIS
FEB	2	14.36 → ARI
MAR	8	07.33 → TAU
APR	20	02.05 → ARI
JUN	3	09.44 → TAU
JUL	8	02.02 → GEM
AUG	5	05.39 → CAN
AUG	31	11.22 → LEO
SEP	25	16.15 → VIR
OCT	20	05.12 → LIB
NOV	13	08.36 → SCO
DEC	7	07.05 → SAG
DEC	31	03.46 → CAP

MARS

mth	dy	time → sign
JAN	1	00.00 → GEM
MAR	10	23.29 → CAN
MAY	13	02.33 → LEO
JUL	4	10.20 → VIR
AUG	21	21.41 → LIB
OCT	6	12.17 → SCO
NOV	18	13.13 → SAG
DEC	29	10.40 → CAP

SATURN

mth	dy	time → sign
JAN	1	00.00 → SAG
MAR	15	13.59 → CAP
MAY	5	04.28 → SAG
NOV	30	04.03 → CAP

JUPITER

mth	dy	time → sign
JAN	1	00.00 → TAU
JUN	12	12.12 → GEM

MOON

dy	jan	feb	mar	apr	may	jun	jul	aug	sep	oct	nov	dec	dy
1	20.08	SCO	SCO	07.03	03.19	PIS	19.31	GEM	LEO	VIR	SCO	SAG	1
2	LIB	SCO	10.03	CAP	AQU	05.58	TAU	08.15	18.27	06.09	SCO	23.25	2
3	LIB	01.59	SAG	19.18	13.51	ARI	22.14	CAN	VIR	LIB	04.47	CAP	3
4	06.10	SAG	22.55	AQU	PIS	10.34	GEM	08.11	20.51	11.40	SAG	CAP	4
5	SCO	15.00	CAP	AQU	20.51	TAU	22.21	LEO	LIB	SCO	15.57	11.57	5
6	18.50	CAP	CAP	04.52	ARI	11.57	CAN	08.22	LIB	20.18	CAP	AQU	6
7	SAG	CAP	10.44	PIS	ARI	GEM	21.37	VIR	02.20	SAG	CAP	AQU	7
8	SAG	02.34	AQU	10.58	00.18	11.35	LEO	10.56	SCO	SAG	04.33	0.27	8
9	07.51	AQU	19.44	ARI	TAU	CAN	22.10	LIB	11.38	07.49	AQU	PIS	9
10	CAP	11.43	PIS	14.17	01.22	11.24	VIR	17.22	SAG	CAP	16.30	10.57	10
11	19.33	PIS	PIS	TAU	GEM	LEO	VIR	SCO	23.45	20.25	PIS	ARI	11
12	AQU	18.41	01.51	16.12	01.44	13.20	01.54	SCO	CAP	AQU	PIS	17.50	12
13	AQU	ARI	ARI	GEM	CAN	VIR	LIB	03.44	CAP	AQU	01.43	TAU	13
14	05.21	ARI	06.05	18.04	03.03	18.38	09.44	SAG	12.17	07.40	ARI	20.49	14
15	PIS	00.02	TAU	CAN	LEO	LIB	SCO	16.21	AQU	PIS	07.19	GEM	15
16	13.07	TAU	09.23	20.50	06.33	LIB	21.00	CAP	23.07	16.02	TAU	21.05	16
17	ARI	04.01	GEM	LEO	VIR	03.32	SAG	CAP	PIS	ARI	09.53	CAN	17
18	18.37	GEM	12.24	LEO	12.52	SCO	SAG	04.50	PIS	21.29	GEM	20.34	18
19	TAU	06.45	CAN	01.05	LIB	15.02	09.48	AQU	07.30	TAU	10.53	LEO	19
20	21.43	CAN	15.27	VIR	21.54	SAG	CAP	15.46	ARI	TAU	CAN	21.22	20
21	GEM	08.41	LEO	07.13	SCO	SAG	22.20	PIS	13.45	00.54	11.58	VIR	21
22	22.52	LEO	19.05	LIB	SCO	03.45	AQU	PIS	TAU	GEM	LEO	VIR	22
23	CAN	10.58	VIR	15.34	09.04	CAP	AQU	00.47	18.25	03.24	14.32	01.03	23
24	23.16	VIR	VIR	SCO	SAG	16.24	09.39	ARI	GEM	CAN	VIR	LIB	24
25	LEO	15.15	00.11	SCO	21.34	AQU	PIS	07.55	21.52	05.55	19.23	08.12	25
26	LEO	LIB	LIB	02.16	CAP	AQU	19.13	TAU	CAN	LEO	LIB	SCO	26
27	00.47	22.54	07.49	SAG	CAP	03.58	ARI	13.03	CAN	09.08	LIB	18.12	27
28	VIR	SCO	SCO	14.43	10.17	PIS	ARI	GEM	00.28	VIR	02.40	SAG	28
29	05.19		18.26	CAP	AQU	13.20	02.25	16.04	LEO	13.39	SCO	SAG	29
30	LIB		SAG	CAP	21.37	ARI	TAU	CAN	02.52	LIB	12.08	05.56	30
31	13.57		SAG		PIS		06.43	17.26		20.02		CAP	31

SUN

mth	dy	time → sign
JAN	1	00.00 → CAP
JAN	20	18.31 → AQU
FEB	19	09.00 → PIS
MAR	21	08.30 → ARI
APR	20	20.03 → TAU
MAY	21	19.42 → GEM
JUN	22	03.53 → CAN
JUL	23	14.48 → LEO
AUG	23	21.26 → VIR
SEP	23	18.36 → LIB
OCT	24	03.22 → SCO
NOV	23	00.35 → SAG
DEC	22	13.37 → CAP

MERCURY

mth	dy	time → sign
JAN	1	00.00 → CAP
JAN	2	10.25 → AQU
JAN	23	00.32 → CAP
FEB	15	15.09 → AQU
MAR	9	22.37 → PIS
MAR	26	23.36 → ARI
APR	10	17.05 → TAU
MAY	1	05.33 → GEM
MAY	17	11.06 → TAU
JUN	14	20.09 → GEM
JUL	4	22.11 → CAN
JUL	19	02.44 → LEO
AUG	4	02.36 → VIR
AUG	26	18.04 → LIB
SEP	20	02.13 → VIR
OCT	11	04.42 → LIB
OCT	29	14.35 → SCO
NOV	17	05.35 → SAG
DEC	6	20.57 → CAP

VENUS

mth	dy	time → sign
JAN	1	00.00 → CAP
JAN	24	00.24 → AQU
FEB	16	22.14 → PIS
MAR	12	22.33 → ARI
APR	6	02.57 → TAU
APR	30	12.37 → GEM
MAY	25	04.36 → CAN
JUN	19	04.39 → LEO
JUL	14	16.32 → VIR
AUG	10	00.54 → LIB
SEP	7	04.06 → SCO
OCT	12	02.45 → SAG
NOV	22	07.43 → SCO

MARS

mth	dy	time → sign
JAN	1	00.00 → CAP
FEB	6	18.26 → AQU
MAR	17	05.57 → PIS
APR	24	17.22 → ARI
JUN	3	03.14 → TAU
JUL	14	12.54 → GEM
AUG	28	11.28 → CAN
OCT	20	14.45 → LEO

SATURN

mth	dy	time → sign
JAN	1	00.00 → CAP

JUPITER

mth	dy	time → sign
JAN	1	00.00 → GEM
JUN	26	22.33 → CAN

MOON

dy	jan	feb	mar	apr	may	jun	jul	aug	sep	oct	nov	dec	dy
1	18.25	PIS	PIS	TAU	GEM	LEO	VIR	SCO	20.33	15.09	PIS	ARI	1
2	AQU	PIS	06.07	TAU	13.55	LEO	09.47	SCO	CAP	AQU	23.36	18.33	2
3	AQU	00.23	ARI	03.42	CAN	00.37	LIB	04.22	CAP	AQU	ARI	TAU	3
4	07.03	ARI	15.19	GEM	16.32	VIR	14.53	SAG	08.27	03.48	ARI	TAU	4
5	PIS	09.49	TAU	08.11	LEO	04.04	SCO	14.34	AQU	PIS	09.33	01.32	5
6	18.27	TAU	22.16	CAN	19.13	LIB	22.49	CAP	21.05	15.52	TAU	GEM	6
7	ARI	16.08	GEM	11.09	VIR	09.30	SAG	CAP	PIS	ARI	16.58	05.31	7
8	ARI	GEM	GEM	LEO	22.30	SCO	SAG	02.24	PIS	ARI	GEM	CAN	8
9	02.55	18.55	02.34	13.11	LIB	16.56	08.47	AQU	09.21	02.14	22.05	07.55	9
10	TAU	CAN	CAN	VIR	LIB	SAG	CAP	15.03	ARI	TAU	CAN	LEO	10
11	07.34	19.00	04.25	15.17	03.07	SAG	20.23	PIS	20.19	10.29	CAN	10.04	11
12	GEM	LEO	LEO	LIB	SCO	02.20	AQU	PIS	TAU	GEM	01.47	VIR	12
13	08.35	18.14	04.54	18.45	09.39	CAP	AQU	03.33	TAU	16.29	LEO	13.05	13
14	CAN	VIR	VIR	SCO	SAG	13.39	08.57	ARI	05.01	CAN	04.42	LIB	14
15	07.37	18.50	05.43	SCO	18.41	AQU	PIS	14.38	GEM	20.19	VIR	17.19	15
16	LEO	LIB	LIB	00.49	CAP	AQU	21.25	TAU	10.43	LEO	07.25	SCO	16
17	06.57	22.45	08.46	SAG	CAP	02.12	ARI	22.44	CAN	22.26	LIB	22.55	17
18	VIR	SCO	SCO	10.07	06.03	PIS	ARI	GEM	13.18	VIR	10.36	SAG	18
19	08.44	SCO	15.24	CAP	AQU	14.15	07.54	GEM	LEO	23.43	SCO	SAG	19
20	LIB	06.49	SAG	21.58	18.33	ARI	TAU	03.02	13.45	LIB	15.00	06.11	20
21	14.25	SAG	SAG	AQU	PIS	23.25	14.38	CAN	VIR	LIB	SAG	CAP	21
22	SCO	18.13	01.40	AQU	PIS	TAU	GEM	03.58	13.43	01.32	21.42	15.43	22
23	23.56	CAP	CAP	10.23	05.55	TAU	17.22	LEO	LIB	SCO	CAP	AQU	23
24	SAG	CAP	14.05	PIS	ARI	05.00	CAN	03.13	15.07	05.23	CAP	AQU	24
25	SAG	06.57	AQU	21.10	14.15	GEM	17.16	VIR	SCO	SAG	07.23	03.35	25
26	11.53	AQU	AQU	ARI	TAU	06.57	LEO	02.58	19.34	12.27	AQU	PIS	26
27	CAP	19.13	02.24	ARI	19.09	CAN	16.34	LIB	SAG	CAP	19.32	16.29	27
28	CAP	PIS	PIS	05.08	GEM	07.06	VIR	05.11	SAG	22.54	PIS	ARI	28
29	00.35		13.00	TAU	21.26	LEO	17.18	SCO	03.48	AQU	PIS	ARI	29
30	AQU		ARI	10.26	CAN	07.28	LIB	11.04	CAP	AQU	08.06	03.51	30
31	12.59		21.24		22.47		21.06	SAG		11.23		TAU	31

SUN

mth	dy	time → sign
JAN	1	00.00 → CAP
JAN	21	00.18 → AQU
FEB	19	14.40 → PIS
MAR	21	14.06 → ARI
APR	21	01.40 → TAU
MAY	22	01.15 → GEM
JUN	22	09.28 → CAN
JUL	23	20.21 → LEO
AUG	24	03.10 → VIR
SEP	24	00.23 → LIB
OCT	24	09.15 → SCO
NOV	23	06.25 → SAG
DEC	22	19.30 → CAP

MERCURY

mth	dy	time → sign
JAN	1	00.00 → CAP
FEB	11	12.27 → AQU
MAR	2	17.28 → PIS
MAR	18	19.31 → ARI
APR	3	13.38 → TAU
JUN	11	07.26 → GEM
JUN	26	13.49 → CAN
JUL	10	19.56 → LEO
JUL	28	23.24 → VIR
OCT	4	18.27 → LIB
OCT	22	02.08 → SCO
NOV	10	04.27 → SAG
DEC	2	00.00 → CAP
DEC	20	07.59 → SAG

VENUS

mth	dy	time → sign
JAN	1	00.00 → SCO
JAN	3	20.02 → SAG
FEB	6	12.25 → CAP
MAR	5	21.45 → AQU
MAR	31	19.04 → PIS
APR	26	02.10 → ARI
MAY	21	02.38 → TAU
JUN	14	23.04 → GEM
JUL	9	15.35 → CAN
AUG	3	03.29 → LEO
AUG	27	10.42 → VIR
SEP	20	14.15 → LIB
OCT	14	15.45 → SCO
NOV	7	16.32 → SAG
DEC	1	17.29 → CAP
DEC	25	19.44 → AQU

MARS

mth	dy	time → sign
JAN	1	00.00 → LEO
FEB	16	14.21 → CAN
MAR	30	03.43 → LEO
JUN	10	14.55 → VIR
AUG	1	16.32 → LIB
SEP	17	08.51 → SCO
OCT	30	12.41 → SAG
DEC	10	03.11 → CAP

SATURN

mth	dy	time → sign
JAN	1	00.00 → CAP

JUPITER

mth	dy	time → sign
JAN	1	00.00 → CAN
JUL	17	07.46 → LEO

MOON

dy	jan	feb	mar	apr	may	jun	jul	aug	sep	oct	nov	dec	dy
1	11.34	CAN	14.25	VIR	11.26	SAG	18.56	PIS	20.59	15.03	CAN	LEO	1
2	GEM	03.24	LEO	00.49	SCO	03.07	AQU	PIS	TAU	GEM	13.39	00.16	2
3	15.21	LEO	14.21	LIB	13.14	CAP	AQU	01.10	TAU	GEM	LEO	VIR	3
4	CAN	02.56	VIR	00.50	SAG	10.23	05.10	ARI	08.43	00.38	18.08	03.44	4
5	16.32	VIR	13.32	SCO	17.35	AQU	PIS	14.05	GEM	CAN	VIR	LIB	5
6	LEO	02.54	LIB	02.52	CAP	21.01	17.40	TAU	17.15	06.49	20.03	05.43	6
7	17.06	LIB	14.03	SAG	CAP	PIS	ARI	TAU	CAN	LEO	LIB	SCO	7
8	VIR	05.04	SCO	08.20	01.37	PIS	ARI	01.01	21.47	09.34	20.21	07.04	8
9	18.48	SCO	17.30	CAP	AQU	09.44	06.14	GEM	LEO	VIR	SCO	SAG	9
10	LIB	10.21	SAG	17.40	13.02	ARI	TAU	08.10	23.04	09.50	20.39	09.18	10
11	22.40	SAG	SAG	AQU	PIS	21.54	16.14	CAN	VIR	LIB	SAG	CAP	11
12	SCO	18.39	00.39	AQU	PIS	TAU	GEM	11.31	22.43	09.17	22.52	14.10	12
13	SCO	CAP	CAP	05.49	01.57	TAU	22.30	LEO	LIB	SCO	CAP	AQU	13
14	04.50	CAP	11.03	PIS	ARI	07.21	CAN	12.25	22.40	09.51	CAP	22.50	14
15	SAG	05.14	AQU	18.48	13.54	GEM	CAN	VIR	SCO	SAG	04.40	PIS	15
16	13.02	AQU	23.26	ARI	TAU	13.38	01.41	12.45	SCO	13.18	AQU	PIS	16
17	CAP	17.23	PIS	ARI	23.26	CAN	LEO	LIB	00.39	CAP	14.32	10.49	17
18	23.04	PIS	PIS	06.50	GEM	17.36	03.21	14.10	SAG	20.39	PIS	ARI	18
19	AQU	PIS	12.24	TAU	GEM	LEO	VIR	SCO	05.48	AQU	PIS	23.45	19
20	AQU	06.21	ARI	16.56	06.26	20.32	05.06	17.47	CAP	AQU	03.08	TAU	20
21	10.55	ARI	ARI	GEM	CAN	VIR	LIB	SAG	14.18	07.32	ARI	TAU	21
22	PIS	18.54	00.44	GEM	11.27	23.23	07.56	23.58	AQU	PIS	16.00	10.59	22
23	23.55	TAU	TAU	00.42	LEO	LIB	SCO	CAP	AQU	20.21	TAU	GEM	23
24	ARI	TAU	11.19	CAN	15.07	LIB	12.18	CAP	01.28	ARI	TAU	19.21	24
25	ARI	05.13	GEM	06.04	VIR	02.34	SAG	08.38	PIS	ARI	03.12	CAN	25
26	12.10	GEM	19.04	LEO	17.51	SCO	18.21	AQU	14.09	09.12	GEM	CAN	26
27	TAU	11.47	CAN	09.10	LIB	06.26	CAP	19.27	ARI	TAU	12.09	01.16	27
28	21.18	CAN	23.29	VIR	20.08	SAG	CAP	PIS	ARI	20.48	CAN	LEO	28
29	GEM		LEO	10.35	SCO	11.35	02.24	PIS	03.07	GEM	19.06	05.41	29
30	GEM		LEO	LIB	22.48	CAP	AQU	07.56	TAU	GEM	LEO	VIR	30
31	02.09		00.58		SAG		12.45	ARI		06.26		09.17	31

SUN

mth	dy	time → sign
JAN	1	00.00 → CAP
JAN	21	06.05 → AQU
FEB	19	20.28 → PIS
MAR	20	19.54 → ARI
APR	20	07.27 → TAU
MAY	21	07.06 → GEM
JUN	21	15.21 → CAN
JUL	23	02.18 → LEO
AUG	23	09.06 → VIR
SEP	23	06.16 → LIB
OCT	23	15.02 → SCO
NOV	22	12.10 → SAG
DEC	22	01.17 → CAP

MERCURY

mth	dy	time → sign
JAN	1	00.00 → SAG
JAN	14	12.45 → CAP
FEB	5	02.36 → AQU
FEB	23	00.52 → PIS
MAR	9	20.21 → ARI
MAY	15	22.47 → TAU
JUN	2	23.02 → GEM
JUN	16	22.30 → CAN
JUL	2	08.16 → LEO
JUL	27	20.38 → VIR
AUG	10	07.31 → LEO
SEP	9	07.18 → VIR
SEP	26	01.15 → LIB
OCT	13	15.42 → SCO
NOV	2	20.28 → SAG

VENUS

mth	dy	time → sign
JAN	1	00.00 → AQU
JAN	19	01.54 → PIS
FEB	12	16.58 → ARI
MAR	9	02.07 → TAU
APR	5	00.18 → GEM
MAY	6	09.04 → CAN
JUL	13	10.32 → GEM
JUL	28	12.36 → CAN
SEP	8	19.42 → LEO
OCT	7	05.46 → VIR
NOV	2	04.04 → LIB
NOV	27	00.06 → SCO
DEC	21	07.45 → SAG

MARS

mth	dy	time → sign
JAN	1	00.00 → CAP
JAN	18	00.37 → AQU
FEB	25	02.36 → PIS
APR	3	07.02 → ARI
MAY	12	10.51 → TAU
JUN	22	09.11 → GEM
AUG	4	19.52 → CAN
SEP	20	19.48 → LEO
NOV	13	21.22 → VIR

SATURN

mth	dy	time → sign
JAN	1	00.00 → CAP
FEB	24	02.22 → AQU
AUG	13	11.12 → CAP
NOV	20	02.25 → AQU

JUPITER

mth	dy	time → sign
JAN	1	00.00 → LEO
AUG	11	07.36 → VIR

MOON

dy	jan	feb	mar	apr	may	jun	jul	aug	sep	oct	nov	dec	dy
1	LIB	SAG	07.05	AQU	22.46	TAU	GEM	15.57	VIR	18.44	SAG	16.47	1
2	12.23	SAG	CAP	05.05	ARI	TAU	GEM	LEO	08.32	SCO	04.54	AQU	2
3	SCO	01.39	14.00	PIS	ARI	06.32	00.07	21.15	LIB	19.05	CAP	22.08	3
4	15.15	CAP	AQU	16.54	11.46	GEM	CAN	VIR	10.08	SAG	08.06	PIS	4
5	SAG	07.49	23.14	ARI	TAU	17.21	08.18	VIR	SCO	21.00	AQU	PIS	5
6	18.37	AQU	PIS	ARI	TAU	CAN	LEO	00.56	12.00	CAP	15.06	07.35	6
7	CAP	16.15	PIS	05.47	00.20	CAN	14.33	LIB	SAG	CAP	PIS	ARI	7
8	23.45	PIS	10.35	TAU	GEM	02.14	VIR	03.49	15.11	01.44	PIS	19.41	8
9	AQU	PIS	ARI	18.27	11.34	LEO	19.12	SCO	CAP	AQU	01.24	TAU	9
10	AQU	03.15	23.17	GEM	CAN	09.06	LIB	06.32	20.17	09.27	ARI	TAU	10
11	07.47	ARI	TAU	GEM	20.48	VIR	22.29	SAG	AQU	PIS	13.33	08.24	11
12	PIS	16.06	TAU	05.46	LEO	13.41	SCO	09.38	AQU	19.36	TAU	GEM	12
13	19.07	TAU	12.03	CAN	LEO	LIB	SCO	CAP	03.31	ARI	TAU	20.28	13
14	ARI	TAU	GEM	14.23	03.13	16.00	00.38	13.54	PIS	ARI	02.13	CAN	14
15	ARI	04.27	22.46	LEO	VIR	SCO	SAG	AQU	13.01	07.24	GEM	CAN	15
16	08.05	GEM	CAN	19.24	06.32	16.45	02.37	20.13	ARI	TAU	14.32	07.12	16
17	TAU	14.02	CAN	VIR	LIB	SAG	CAP	PIS	ARI	20.04	CAN	LEO	17
18	19.47	CAN	05.54	21.01	07.16	17.31	05.44	PIS	00.34	GEM	CAN	16.09	18
19	GEM	19.47	LEO	LIB	SCO	CAP	AQU	05.18	TAU	GEM	01.35	VIR	19
20	GEM	LEO	09.18	20.34	06.48	20.12	11.34	ARI	13.14	08.26	LEO	22.33	20
21	04.22	22.25	VIR	SCO	SAG	AQU	PIS	16.56	GEM	CAN	10.08	LIB	21
22	CAN	VIR	09.55	19.57	07.12	AQU	20.53	TAU	GEM	18.56	VIR	LIB	22
23	09.40	23.23	LIB	SAG	CAP	02.25	ARI	TAU	01.13	LEO	15.08	01.53	23
24	LEO	LIB	09.35	21.15	10.31	PIS	ARI	05.33	CAN	LEO	LIB	SCO	24
25	12.47	LIB	SCO	CAP	AQU	12.34	08.54	GEM	10.32	02.02	16.38	02.42	25
26	VIR	00.21	10.06	CAP	17.58	ARI	TAU	16.50	LEO	VIR	SCO	SAG	26
27	15.02	SCO	SAG	02.04	PIS	ARI	21.27	CAN	16.08	05.15	15.58	02.31	27
28	LIB	02.38	13.06	AQU	PIS	01.08	GEM	CAN	VIR	LIB	SAG	CAP	28
29	17.43	SAG	CAP	10.56	05.09	TAU	GEM	01.03	18.22	05.30	15.16	03.23	29
30	SCO		19.30	PIS	ARI	13.35	08.07	LEO	LIB	SCO	CAP	AQU	30
31	21.08		AQU		18.05		CAN	05.58		04.40		07.16	31

65

SUN

mth	dy	time → sign
JAN	1	00.00 → CAP
JAN	20	11.53 → AQU
FEB	19	02.17 → PIS
MAR	21	01.42 → ARI
APR	20	13.18 → TAU
MAY	21	12.59 → GEM
JUN	21	21.12 → CAN
JUL	23	08.05 → LEO
AUG	23	14.52 → VIR
SEP	23	12.01 → LIB
OCT	23	20.48 → SCO
NOV	22	17.57 → SAG
DEC	22	0f ˜8 → CAP

SATURN

mth	dy	time → sign
JAN	1	00.00 → AQU

MERCURY

mth	dy	time → sign
JAN	1	00.00 → SAG
JAN	8	10.26 → CAP
JAN	27	22.39 → AQU
FEB	14	05.06 → PIS
MAR	3	10.49 → ARI
MAR	25	21.52 → PIS
APR	17	15.27 → ARI
MAY	10	07.42 → TAU
MAY	25	14.26 → GEM
JUN	8	14.12 → CAN
JUN	27	01.11 → LEO
SEP	2	05.44 → VIR
SEP	18	03.48 → LIB
OCT	6	15.04 → SCO
OCT	30	04.28 → SAG
NOV	16	02.07 → SCO
DEC	12	03.43 → SAG

VENUS

mth	dy	time → sign
JAN	1	00.00 → SAG
JAN	14	09.54 → CAP
FEB	7	10.30 → AQU
MAR	3	11.22 → PIS
MAR	27	13.58 → ARI
APR	20	19.03 → TAU
MAY	15	02.47 → GEM
JUN	8	13.01 → CAN
JUL	3	01.29 → LEO
JUL	27	16.47 → VIR
AUG	21	12.23 → LIB
SEP	15	14.58 → SCO
OCT	11	04.32 → SAG
NOV	6	16.05 → CAP
DEC	5	18.00 → AQU

MARS

mth	dy	time → sign
JAN	1	00.00 → VIR
JUL	6	22.07 → LIB
AUG	26	06.30 → SCO
OCT	9	11.38 → SAG
NOV	19	07.12 → CAP
DEC	28	03.48 → AQU

JUPITER

mth	dy	time → sign
JAN	1	00.00 → VIR
SEP	10	05.23 → LIB

MOON

dy	jan	feb	mar	apr	may	jun	jul	aug	sep	oct	nov	dec	dy
1	PIS	10.40	TAU	GEM	23.06	VIR	LIB	SAG	07.00	PIS	13.53	06.45	1
2	15.13	TAU	TAU	03.50	LEO	23.15	10.57	21.40	AQU	22.51	TAU	GEM	2
3	ARI	23.06	07.18	CAN	LEO	LIB	SCO	CAP	09.46	ARI	TAU	18.53	3
4	ARI	GEM	GEM	15.17	08.41	LIB	12.32	22.22	PIS	ARI	00.05	CAN	4
5	02.32	GEM	19.43	LEO	VIR	02.25	SAG	AQU	14.15	06.18	GEM	CAN	5
6	TAU	11.13	CAN	23.33	14.17	SCO	12.18	AQU	ARI	TAU	12.05	07.49	6
7	15.19	CAN	CAN	VIR	LIB	02.32	CAP	00.11	21.35	16.18	CAN	LEO	7
8	GEM	21.18	06.14	VIR	16.08	SAG	12.05	PIS	TAU	GEM	CAN	20.00	8
9	GEM	LEO	LEO	04.00	SCO	01.33	AQU	04.40	TAU	GEM	00.59	VIR	9
10	03.15	LEO	13.42	LIB	15.43	CAP	14.01	ARI	08.00	04.29	LEO	VIR	10
11	CAN	04.33	VIR	05.32	SAG	01.41	PIS	12.45	GEM	CAN	12.24	05.18	11
12	13.26	VIR	18.03	SCO	15.15	AQU	19.33	TAU	20.26	17.02	VIR	LIB	12
13	LEO	09.59	LIB	05.52	CAP	04.49	ARI	23.57	CAN	LEO	20.13	10.27	13
14	21.43	LIB	20.28	SAG	16.47	PIS	ARI	GEM	CAN	LEO	LIB	SCO	14
15	VIR	13.46	SCO	06.53	AQU	11.50	04.49	GEM	08.30	03.24	23.52	11.48	15
16	VIR	SCO	22.18	CAP	21.34	ARI	TAU	12.35	LEO	VIR	SCO	SAG	16
17	04.03	16.42	SAG	10.02	PIS	22.12	16.46	CAN	18.16	10.07	SCO	11.08	17
18	LIB	SAG	SAG	AQU	PIS	TAU	GEM	CAN	VIR	LIB	00.36	CAP	18
19	08.26	19.24	00.47	15.54	05.45	TAU	GEM	00.22	VIR	13.27	SAG	10.37	19
20	SCO	CAP	CAP	PIS	ARI	10.25	05.25	LEO	00.51	SCO	00.23	AQU	20
21	10.54	22.29	04.39	PIS	16.26	GEM	CAN	10.07	LIB	14.54	CAP	12.15	21
22	SAG	AQU	AQU	00.14	TAU	23.06	17.19	VIR	05.01	SAG	01.21	PIS	22
23	12.17	AQU	10.16	ARI	TAU	CAN	17.29	LIB	16.13	AQU	17.15	ARI	23
24	CAP	02.57	PIS	10.31	04.31	CAN	LEO	07.49	CAP	04.52	ARI		24
25	13.56	PIS	17.49	TAU	GEM	11.17	03.35	22.44	SAG	18.48	PIS	ARI	25
26	AQU	09.42	ARI	22.18	17.12	LEO	VIR	SCO	10.23	AQU	11.13	01.42	26
27	17.33	ARI	ARI	GEM	CAN	22.01	11.44	SCO	CAP	23.17	ARI	TAU	27
28	PIS	19.20	03.32	GEM	CAN	VIR	LIB	02.21	13.29	PIS	20.04	12.43	28
29	PIS		TAU	10.58	05.33	VIR	17.21	SAG	AQU	PIS	TAU	GEM	29
30	00.23		15.13	CAN	LEO	06.11	SCO	04.52	17.27	05.40	TAU	GEM	30
31	ARI		GEM		16.06		20.27	CAP		ARI		01.07	31

SUN

mth	dy	time → sign
JAN	1	00.00 → CAP
JAN	20	17.37 → AQU
FEB	19	08.02 → PIS
MAR	21	07.27 → ARI
APR	20	19.00 → TAU
MAY	21	18.35 → GEM
JUN	22	02.48 → CAN
JUL	23	13.42 → LEO
AUG	23	20.32 → VIR
SEP	23	17.45 → LIB
OCT	24	02.36 → SCO
NOV	22	23.44 → SAG
DEC	22	12.49 → CAP

MERCURY

mth	dy	time → sign
JAN	1	18.40 → CAP
JAN	20	11.44 → AQU
FEB	6	17.24 → PIS
APR	15	04.13 → ARI
MAY	2	18.45 → TAU
MAY	16	23.43 → GEM
JUN	1	08.22 → CAN
AUG	9	13.49 → LEO
AUG	25	02.18 → VIR
SEP	10	11.29 → LIB
SEP	30	14.46 → SCO
DEC	6	06.42 → SAG
DEC	25	14.59 → CAP

VENUS

mth	dy	time → sign
JAN	1	00.00 → AQU
APR	6	09.22 → PIS
MAY	6	08.54 → ARI
JUN	2	10.11 → TAU
JUN	28	09.38 → GEM
JUL	23	18.22 → CAN
AUG	17	15.45 → LEO
SEP	11	03.32 → VIR
OCT	5	07.56 → LIB
OCT	29	07.37 → SCO
NOV	22	04.59 → SAG
DEC	16	01.39 → CAP

MARS

mth	dy	time → sign
JAN	1	00.00 → AQU
FEB	4	04.13 → PIS
MAR	14	09.09 → ARI
APR	22	15.40 → TAU
JUN	2	16.28 → GEM
JUL	15	21.36 → CAN
AUG	30	13.38 → LEO
OCT	18	04.52 → VIR
DEC	11	09.38 → LIB

SATURN

mth	dy	time → sign
JAN	1	00.00 → AQU

JUPITER

mth	dy	time → sign
JAN	1	00.00 → LIB
OCT	11	04.45 → SCO

MOON

dy	jan	feb	mar	apr	may	jun	jul	aug	sep	oct	nov	dec	dy
1	CAN	08.00	VIR	13.35	01.02	11.55	PIS	13.25	GEM	CAN	08.36	04.39	1
2	13.56	VIR	VIR	SCO	SAG	AQU	PIS	TAU	15.40	11.44	VIR	LIB	2
3	LEO	17.59	00.02	17.37	02.53	14.06	00.39	21.48	CAN	LEO	19.41	13.06	3
4	LEO	LIB	LIB	SAG	CAP	PIS	ARI	GEM	CAN	LEO	LIB	SCO	4
5	02.09	LIB	06.59	20.45	05.06	18.31	06.47	GEM	04.32	00.31	LIB	17.52	5
6	VIR	01.31	SCO	CAP	AQU	ARI	TAU	09.13	LEO	VIR	03.32	SAG	6
7	12.21	SCO	11.58	23.43	08.26	ARI	15.55	CAN	11.21	SCO	20.09		7
8	LIB	06.14	SAG	AQU	PIS	01.17	GEM	22.08	VIR	LIB	08.34	CAP	8
9	19.11	SAG	15.22	AQU	13.09	TAU	GEM	LEO	19.31	SAG	21.34	9
10	SCO	08.23	CAP	02.52	ARI	10.14	03.21	LEO	04.23	SCO	11.57	AQU	10
11	22.18	CAP	17.36	PIS	19.24	GEM	CAN	10.59	LIB	SCO	CAP	23.31	11
12	SAG	08.57	AQU	06.40	TAU	21.14	16.07	VIR	13.19	01.32	14.52	PIS	12
13	22.37	AQU	19.25	ARI	TAU	CAN	LEO	22.34	SCO	SAG	AQU	PIS	13
14	CAP	09.27	PIS	11.55	03.38	CAN	LEO	LIB	20.03	06.04	17.56	02.51	14
15	21.56	PIS	22.00	TAU	GEM	09.53	05.07	LIB	SAG	CAP	PIS	ARI	15
16	AQU	11.39	ARI	19.41	14.17	LEO	VIR	07.51	SAG	09.32	21.26	07.56	16
17	22.17	ARI	ARI	GEM	CAN	22.51	16.47	SCO	00.36	AQU	ARI	TAU	17
18	PIS	17.03	02.46	GEM	CAN	VIR	LIB	14.12	CAP	12.10	ARI	14.58	18
19	PIS	TAU	TAU	06.26	02.55	VIR	LIB	SAG	03.06	PIS	01.46	GEM	19
20	01.28	TAU	10.51	CAN	LEO	09.59	01.31	17.27	AQU	14.28	TAU	GEM	20
21	ARI	02.16	GEM	19.10	15.35	LIB	SCO	CAP	04.14	ARI	07.47	00.11	21
22	08.26	GEM	22.13	LEO	VIR	17.25	06.28	18.18	PIS	17.34	GEM	CAN	22
23	TAU	14.22	CAN	LEO	VIR	SCO	SAG	AQU	05.13	TAU	16.25	11.37	23
24	18.54	CAN	CAN	07.21	01.43	20.49	08.03	18.08	ARI	22.58	CAN	LEO	24
25	GEM	CAN	11.03	VIR	LIB	SAG	CAP	PIS	07.47	GEM	CAN	LEO	25
26	GEM	03.13	LEO	16.32	07.52	21.24	07.43	18.44	TAU	GEM	03.54	00.32	26
27	07.24	LEO	22.44	LIB	SCO	CAP	AQU	ARI	13.34	07.46	LEO	VIR	27
28	CAN	14.46	VIR	22.07	10.28	21.02	07.21	21.55	GEM	CAN	16.52	12.59	28
29	20.12		VIR	SCO	SAG	AQU	PIS	TAU	23.14	19.42	VIR	LIB	29
30	LEO		07.37	SCO	11.12	21.38	08.45	TAU	CAN	LEO	VIR	22.41	30
31	LEO		LIB		CAP		ARI	04.55		LEO		SCO	31

67

SUN

mth	dy	time → sign
JAN	1	00.00 → CAP
JAN	20	23.25 → AQU
FEB	19	13.52 → PIS
MAR	21	13.17 → ARI
APR	21	00.50 → TAU
MAY	22	00.24 → GEM
JUN	22	08.38 → CAN
JUL	23	19.32 → LEO
AUG	24	02.24 → VIR
SEP	23	23.38 → LIB
OCT	24	08.28 → SCO
NOV	23	05.35 → SAG
DEC	22	18.34 → CAP

MERCURY

mth	dy	time → sign
JAN	1	00.00 → CAP
JAN	13	01.17 → AQU
FEB	1	11.17 → PIS
FEB	15	03.04 → AQU
MAR	18	21.53 → PIS
APR	8	18.37 → ARI
APR	24	12.29 → TAU
MAY	8	17.22 → GEM
MAY	29	19.26 → CAN
JUN	20	17.56 → GEM
JUL	13	22.21 → CAN
AUG	2	01.45 → LEO
AUG	16	20.38 → VIR
SEP	3	09.34 → LIB
SEP	28	15.56 → SCO
OCT	12	18.03 → LIB
NOV	10	01.24 → SCO
NOV	29	07.05 → SAG
DEC	18	08.29 → CAP

VENUS

mth	dy	time → sign
JAN	1	00.00 → CAP
JAN	8	22.42 → AQU
FEB	1	21.37 → PIS
FEB	26	00.31 → ARI
MAR	22	10.29 → TAU
APR	16	07.38 → GEM
MAY	11	22.02 → CAN
JUN	7	19.12 → LEO
JUL	7	20.34 → VIR
NOV	9	16.34 → LIB
DEC	8	14.37 → SCO

MARS

mth	dy	time → sign
JAN	1	00.00 → LIB
JUL	29	17.33 → SCO
SEP	16	12.56 → SAG
OCT	28	18.21 → CAP
DEC	7	04.32 → AQU

SATURN

mth	dy	time → sign
JAN	1	00.00 → AQU
FEB	14	14.24 → PIS

JUPITER

mth	dy	time → sign
JAN	1	00.00 → SCO
NOV	9	02.49 → SAG

MOON

dy	jan	feb	mar	apr	may	jun	jul	aug	sep	oct	nov	dec	dy
1	SCO	CAP	CAP	PIS	ARI	GEM	CAN	09.07	LIB	SCO	CAP	AQU	1
2	04.24	18.28	05.17	15.34	02.03	20.44	14.13	VIR	16.22	08.41	CAP	14.03	2
3	SAG	AQU	AQU	ARI	TAU	CAN	LEO	21.55	SCO	SAG	04.38	PIS	3
4	06.44	17.47	05.13	16.18	05.26	CAN	LEO	LIB	SCO	17.02	AQU	16.55	4
5	CAP	PIS	PIS	TAU	GEM	06.19	02.08	LIB	02.48	CAP	08.20	ARI	5
6	07.03	17.49	04.40	19.35	11.50	LEO	VIR	09.57	SAG	22.20	PIS	19.03	6
7	AQU	ARI	ARI	GEM	CAN	18.25	14.52	SCO	10.08	AQU	09.56	TAU	7
8	07.17	20.24	05.43	GEM	21.56	VIR	LIB	19.25	CAP	AQU	ARI	21.38	8
9	PIS	TAU	TAU	02.49	LEO	VIR	LIB	SAG	13.44	00.27	10.29	GEM	9
10	09.02	TAU	10.14	CAN	LEO	06.57	02.17	SAG	AQU	PIS	TAU	GEM	10
11	ARI	02.35	GEM	13.55	10.26	LIB	SCO	01.10	14.15	00.20›ARI 11.52		01.54	11
12	13.24	GEM	18.52	LEO	VIR	17.35	10.27	CAP	PIS	23.54	GEM	CAN	12
13	TAU	12.24	CAN	LEO	22.48	SCO	SAG	03.20	13.21	TAU	15.55	09.08	13
14	20.43	CAN	CAN	02.47	LIB	SCO	15.03	AQU	ARI	TAU	CAN	LEO	14
15	GEM	CAN	06.48	VIR	LIB	00.58	CAP	03.20	13.11	01.17	23.51	19.33	15
16	GEM	00.35	LEO	15.01	08.55	SAG	16.54	PIS	TAU	GEM	LEO	VIR	16
17	06.37	LEO	19.51	LIB	SCO	05.21	AQU	02.55	15.48	06.21	LEO	VIR	17
18	CAN	13.36	VIR	LIB	16.13	CAP	17.30	ARI	GEM	CAN	11.10	07.58	18
19	18.28	VIR	VIR	01.09	SAG	07.56	PIS	04.08	22.27	15.35	VIR	LIB	19
20	LEO	VIR	08.08	SCO	21.20	AQU	18.36	TAU	CAN	LEO	23.53	20.03	20
21	LEO	02.02	LIB	09.06	CAP	09.56	ARI	08.25	CAN	LEO	LIB	SCO	21
22	07.19	LIB	18.44	SAG	CAP	PIS	21.21	GEM	08.51	03.44	LIB	SCO	22
23	VIR	13.04	SCO	15.13	01.09	12.23	TAU	16.17	LEO	VIR	11.36	05.44	23
24	19.59	SCO	SCO	CAP	AQU	ARI	TAU	CAN	21.18	16.31	SCO	SAG	24
25	LIB	21.40	03.24	19.43	04.13	15.54	02.42	CAN	VIR	LIB	21.08	12.27	25
26	LIB	SAG	SAG	AQU	PIS	TAU	GEM	03.00	VIR	LIB	SAG	CAP	26
27	06.46	SAG	09.49	22.40	06.59	21.06	10.43	LEO	10.05	04.15	SAG	16.46	27
28	SCO	03.04	CAP	PIS	ARI	GEM	CAN	15.20	LIB	SCO	04.28	AQU	28
29	14.11		13.41	PIS	09.59	GEM	21.04	VIR	22.06	14.17	CAP	19.42	29
30	SAG		AQU	00.26	TAU	04.26	LEO	VIR	SCO	SAG	10.00	PIS	30
31	17.47		15.14		14.11		LEO	04.08		22.31		22.15	31

SUN

mth	dy	time → sign
JAN	1	00.00 → CAP
JAN	21	05.14 → AQU
FEB	19	19.33 → PIS
MAR	20	18.56 → ARI
APR	20	06.31 → TAU
MAY	21	06.06 → GEM
JUN	21	14.21 → CAN
JUL	23	01.18 → LEO
AUG	23	08.13 → VIR
SEP	23	05.26 → LIB
OCT	23	14.19 → SCO
NOV	22	11.26 → SAG
DEC	22	00.27 → CAP

MERCURY

mth	dy	time → sign
JAN	1	00.00 → CAP
JAN	6	03.32 → AQU
MAR	13	06.40 → PIS
MAR	31	05.07 → ARI
APR	15	01.45 → TAU
MAY	1	01.30 → GEM
JUL	8	20.49 → CAN
JUL	23	15.39 → LEO
AUG	7	22.59 → VIR
AUG	27	17.42 → LIB
NOV	2	11.00 → SCO
NOV	21	00.39 → SAG
DEC	10	06.43 → CAP

VENUS

mth	dy	time → sign
JAN	1	00.00 → SCO
JAN	3	14.15 → SAG
JAN	28	14.00 → CAP
FEB	22	04.15 → AQU
MAR	17	14.53 → PIS
APR	11	00.43 → ARI
MAY	5	10.56 → TAU
MAY	29	21.39 → GEM
JUN	23	08.17 → CAN
JUL	17	17.51 → LEO
AUG	11	02.11 → VIR
SEP	4	10.03 → LIB
SEP	28	18.36 → SCO
OCT	23	05.01 → SAG
NOV	16	18.36 → CAP
DEC	11	14.53 → AQU

MARS

mth	dy	time → sign
JAN	1	00.00 → AQU
JAN	14	13.57 → PIS
FEB	22	04.02 → ARI
APR	1	21.38 → TAU
MAY	13	09.14 → GEM
JUN	25	21.53 → CAN
AUG	10	09.41 → LEO
SEP	26	14.51 → VIR
NOV	14	14.55 → LIB

SATURN

mth	dy	time → sign
JAN	1	00.00 → PIS

JUPITER

mth	dy	time → sign
JAN	1	00.00 → SAG
DEC	2	08.26 → CAP

MOON

dy	jan	feb	mar	apr	may	jun	jul	aug	sep	oct	nov	dec	dy
1	ARI	10.38	22.25	LEO	VIR	14.13	09.28	CAP	PIS	ARI	GEM	CAN	1
2	ARI	GEM	CAN	LEO	18.43	SCO	SAG	09.25	22.43	08.26	20.00	09.44	2
3	01.12	16.58	CAN	00.07	LIB	SCO	18.34	AQU	ARI	TAU	CAN	LEO	3
4	TAU	CAN	07.21	VIR	LIB	01.37	CAP	12.36	23.04	08.37	CAN	16.31	4
5	05.04	CAN	LEO	12.33	07.16	SAG	CAP	PIS	TAU	GEM	00.37	VIR	5
6	GEM	01.24	18.18	LIB	SCO	11.07	00.56	14.21	TAU	11.27	LEO	VIR	6
7	10.27	LEO	VIR	LIB	18.55	CAP	AQU	ARI	00.55	CAN	09.01	02.55	7
8	CAN	11.48	VIR	01.06	SAG	18.17	05.10	16.11	GEM	17.45	VIR	LIB	8
9	18.03	VIR	06.26	SCO	SAG	AQU	PIS	TAU	05.16	LEO	20.15	15.28	9
10	LEO	23.44	LIB	13.03	04.56	23.27	08.10	19.12	CAN	LEO	LIB	SCO	10
11	LEO	LIB	19.06	SAG	CAP	PIS	ARI	GEM	12.13	03.01	LIB	SCO	11
12	04.04	LIB	SCO	23.27	12.47	PIS	10.46	23.52	LEO	VIR	08.52	04.07	12
13	VIR	12.24	SCO	CAP	AQU	02.47	TAU	CAN	21.21	14.19	SCO	SAG	13
14	16.10	SCO	07.06	CAP	17.52	ARI	13.39	CAN	VIR	LIB	21.36	15.26	14
15	LIB	23.57	SAG	06.49	PIS	04.48	GEM	06.20	VIR	LIB	SAG	CAP	15
16	LIB	SAG	16.51	AQU	20.14	TAU	17.28	LEO	08.12	02.47	SAG	CAP	16
17	04.38	SAG	CAP	10.38	ARI	06.29	CAN	14.44	LIB	SCO	09.20	00.42	17
18	SCO	08.21	22.52	PIS	20.47	GEM	22.58	VIR	20.33	15.38	CAP	AQU	18
19	15.11	CAP	AQU	11.20	TAU	09.08	LEO	VIR	SCO	19.13	AQU	07.43	19
20	SAG	12.49	AQU	ARI	21.12	CAN	LEO	01.18	SCO	SAG	AQU	PIS	20
21	22.17	AQU	00.59	10.37	GEM	14.06	06.56	LIB	03.37	AQU	12.26	21
22	CAP	13.55	PIS	TAU	23.20	LEO	VIR	13.36	SAG	CAP	02.04	ARI	22
23	CAP	PIS	00.31ᐳARI	10.37	CAN	22.15	17.30	SCO	20.53	13.00	PIS	15.07	23
24	02.02	13.35	23.37	GEM	CAN	VIR	LIB	SCO	CAP	AQU	05.38	TAU	24
25	AQU	ARI	TAU	13.22	04.43	VIR	LIB	02.09	CAP	18.29	ARI	16.24	25
26	03.33	13.51	TAU	CAN	LEO	09.25	05.54	SAG	04.53	PIS	06.29	GEM	26
27	PIS	TAU	00.31	20.03	13.48	LIB	SCO	12.35	AQU	20.09	TAU	17.36	27
28	04.36	16.32	GEM	LEO	VIR	21.53	17.57	CAP	08.39	ARI	06.11	CAN	28
29	ARI	GEM	04.52	LEO	VIR	SCO	SAG	19.13	PIS	19.34	GEM	20.15	29
30	06.35		CAN	06.22	01.39	SCO	SAG	AQU	09.10	TAU	06.40	LEO	30
31	TAU		13.04		LIB		03.24	22.06		18.49		LEO	31

SUN

mth	dy	time → sign
JAN	1	00.00 → CAP
JAN	20	11.04 → AQU
FEB	19	01.21 → PIS
MAR	21	00.45 → ARI
APR	20	12.17 → TAU
MAY	21	11.57 → GEM
JUN	21	20.12 → CAN
JUL	23	07.09 → LEO
AUG	23	13.58 → VIR
SEP	23	11.13 → LIB
OCT	23	20.07 → SCO
NOV	22	17.18 → SAG
DEC	22	06.23 → CAP

MERCURY

mth	dy	time → sign
JAN	1	16.43 → AQU
JAN	9	21.28 → CAP
FEB	14	00.26 → AQU
MAR	6	14.07 → PIS
MAR	23	03.41 → ARI
APR	7	01.09 → TAU
JUN	13	22.28 → GEM
JUL	1	02.25 → CAN
JUL	15	04.11 → LEO
JUL	31	21.07 → VIR
OCT	8	10.13 → LIB
OCT	26	01.14 → SCO
NOV	13	19.25 → SAG
DEC	3	23.55 → CAP

VENUS

mth	dy	time → sign
JAN	1	00.00 → AQU
JAN	6	03.19 → PIS
FEB	2	10.39 → ARI
MAR	9	13.19 → TAU
APR	14	04.17 → ARI
JUN	4	06.41 → TAU
JUL	7	21.13 → GEM
AUG	4	20.15 → CAN
AUG	31	00.08 → LEO
SEP	25	04.03 → VIR
OCT	19	16.34 → LIB
NOV	12	19.43 → SCO
DEC	6	18.08 → SAG
DEC	30	14.43 → CAP

MARS

mth	dy	time → sign
JAN	1	00.00 → LIB
JAN	5	20.29 → SCO
MAR	13	03.06 → SAG
MAY	14	22.59 → SCO
AUG	8	22.18 → SAG
SEP	30	09.08 → CAP
NOV	11	18.39 → AQU
DEC	21	17.46 → PIS

SATURN

mth	dy	time → sign
JAN	1	00.00 → PIS
APR	25	06.45 → ARI
OCT	18	03.53 → PIS

JUPITER

mth	dy	time → sign
JAN	1	00.00 → CAP
DEC	20	04.24 → AQU

MOON

dy	jan	feb	mar	apr	may	jun	jul	aug	sep	oct	nov	dec	dy
1	01.45	LIB	15.23 SAG	CAP	08.58	ARI	09.29	21.22	08.27	LIB	SCO		1
2	VIR	07.10	SCO	SAG	18.08	PIS	ARI	GEM	LEO	VIR	07.48	02.05	2
3	10.54	SCO	19.57	00.16	AQU	14.22	00.34	11.34	LEO	15.31	SCO	SAG	3
4	LIB	19.57	04.08	CAP	AQU	ARI	TAU	CAN	01.34	LIB	19.46	15.06	4
5	22.58	SAG	SAG	10.37	01.57	16.37	02.16	13.35	VIR	LIB	SAG	CAP	5
6	SCO	SAG	16.23	AQU	PIS	TAU	GEM	LEO	07.47	00.54	SAG	CAP	6
7	SCO	07.34	CAP	16.59	05.47	16.46	02.53	16.54	LIB	SCO	08.50	03.40	7
8	11.44	CAP	CAP	PIS	ARI	GEM	CAN	VIR	16.59	12.44	CAP	AQU	8
9	SAG	16.02	01.36	19.26	06.34	16.32	03.59	22.58	SCO	SAG	21.19	14.21	9
10	22.53	AQU	AQU	ARI	TAU	CAN	LEO	LIB	SCO	SAG	AQU	PIS	10
11	CAP	21.10	06.50	19.39	05.56	17.44	07.16	LIB	04.57	01.46	AQU	21.56	11
12	CAP	PIS	PIS	TAU	GEM	LEO	VIR	08.37	SAG	CAP	07.07	ARI	12
13	07.25	PIS	09.00	19.34	06.01	22.01	14.04	SCO	17.52	13.37	PIS	ARI	13
14	AQU	00.18	ARI	GEM	CAN	VIR	LIB	20.59	CAP	AQU	12.59	01.50	14
15	13.29	ARI	09.54	21.05	08.27	VIR	LIB	SAG	CAP	22.03	ARI	TAU	15
16	PIS	02.34	TAU	CAN	LEO	06.08	00.36	SAG	04.51	PIS	15.12	02.42	16
17	17.48	TAU	11.19	CAN	14.19	LIB	SCO	09.37	AQU	PIS	TAU	GEM	17
18	ARI	05.22	GEM	01.11	VIR	17.31	13.20	CAP	12.19	02.33	15.10	02.04	18
19	21.07	GEM	14.25	LEO	23.35	SCO	SAG	20.05	PIS	ARI	GEM	CAN	19
20	TAU	09.05	CAN	08.17	LIB	SCO	SAG	AQU	16.31	04.09	14.47	01.48	20
21	23.55	CAN	19.35	VIR	LIB	06.25	01.50	AQU	ARI	TAU	CAN	LEO	21
22	GEM	13.51	LEO	17.51	11.18	SAG	CAP	03.28	18.49	04.40	15.55	03.57	22
23	GEM	LEO	LEO	LIB	SCO	18.58	12.20	PIS	TAU	GEM	LEO	VIR	23
24	02.39	20.05	02.44	LIB	SCO	CAP	AQU	08.23	20.46	05.47	19.55	09.53	24
25	CAN	VIR	VIR	05.21	00.11	CAP	20.21	ARI	GEM	CAN	VIR	LIB	25
26	06.08	VIR	11.47	SCO	SAG	05.54	PIS	11.57	23.24	08.42	VIR	19.45	26
27	LEO	04.26	LIB	18.06	12.53	AQU	PIS	TAU	CAN	LEO	03.22	SCO	27
28	11.30	LIB	22.51	SAG	CAP	14.37	02.15	15.01	CAN	14.01	LIB	SCO	28
29	VIR		SCO	SAG	CAP	PIS	ARI	GEM	03.14	VIR	13.46	08.12	29
30	19.49		SCO	06.54	00.15	20.50	06.31	18.03	LEO	21.47	SCO	SAG	30
31	LIB		11.32		AQU		TAU	CAN		LIB		21.17	31

SUN

mth	dy	time → sign
JAN	1	00.00 → CAP
JAN	20	16.57 → AQU
FEB	19	07.20 → PIS
MAR	21	06.43 → ARI
APR	20	18.17 → TAU
MAY	21	17.50 → GEM
JUN	22	02.04 → CAN
JUL	23	12.56 → LEO
AUG	23	19.46 → VIR
SEP	23	17.00 → LIB
OCT	24	01.56 → SCO
NOV	22	23.06 → SAG
DEC	22	12.14 → CAP

MERCURY

mth	dy	time → sign
JAN	1	00.00 → CAP
JAN	6	21.39 → SAG
JAN	12	22.30 → CAP
FEB	8	13.18 → AQU
FEB	27	03.01 → PIS
MAR	15	00.03 → ARI
APR	1	13.26 → TAU
APR	23	13.56 → ARI
MAY	16	17.46 → TAU
JUN	8	00.32 → GEM
JUN	22	13.09 → CAN
JUL	7	03.21 → LEO
JUL	26	22.56 → VIR
SEP	3	02.59 → LEO
SEP	10	15.38 → VIR
OCT	1	04.19 → LIB
OCT	18	12.43 → SCO
NOV	6	23.33 → SAG

VENUS

mth	dy	time → sign
JAN	1	00.00 → CAP
JAN	23	11.17 → AQU
FEB	16	09.01 → PIS
MAR	12	09.20 → ARI
APR	5	13.48 → TAU
APR	29	23.35 → GEM
MAY	24	15.58 → CAN
JUN	18	16.37 → LEO
JUL	14	05.45 → VIR
AUG	9	16.29 → LIB
SEP	7	01.36 → SCO
OCT	13	18.48 → SAG
NOV	15	16.07 → SCO

MARS

mth	dy	time → sign
JAN	1	00.00 → PIS
JAN	30	12.50 → ARI
MAR	12	07.48 → TAU
APR	23	18.45 → GEM
JUN	7	01.28 → CAN
JUL	22	22.23 → LEO
SEP	7	20.23 → VIR
OCT	25	06.20 → LIB
DEC	11	23.13 → SCO

SATURN

mth	dy	time → sign
JAN	1	00.00 → PIS
JAN	14	10.22 → ARI

JUPITER

mth	dy	time → sign
JAN	1	00.00 → AQU
MAY	14	07.23 → PIS
JUL	30	03.13 → AQU
DEC	29	18.25 → PIS

MOON

dy	jan	feb	mar	apr	may	jun	jul	aug	sep	oct	nov	dec	dy
1	CAP	AQU	09.13	ARI	15.45	CAN	12.24	LIB	00.28	CAP	AQU	PIS	1
2	CAP	01.59	PIS	04.44	GEM	02.09	VIR	06.49	SAG	CAP	05.09	00.02	2
3	09.32	PIS	16.16	TAU	16.50	LEO	16.09	SCO	12.30	AQU	PIS	ARI	3
4	AQU	09.54	ARI	07.33	CAN	04.21	LIB	17.02	CAP	AQU	14.35	07.01	4
5	20.07	ARI	21.29	GEM	18.42	VIR	23.47	SAG	CAP	20.27	ARI	TAU	5
6	PIS	15.58	TAU	10.07	LEO	09.35	SCO	SAG	01.11	PIS	20.42	10.19	6
7	PIS	TAU	TAU	CAN	22.19	LIB	SCO	05.33	AQU	PIS	TAU	GEM	7
8	04.30	20.08	01.33	13.07	VIR	18.03	10.45	CAP	12.28	05.22	TAU	11.08	8
9	ARI	GEM	GEM	LEO	VIR	SCO	SAG	18.15	PIS	ARI	00.03	CAN	9
10	10.06	22.22	04.46	16.51	04.06	SCO	23.25	AQU	21.40	11.43	GEM	11.17	10
11	TAU	CAN	CAN	VIR	LIB	04.57	CAP	AQU	ARI	TAU	01.57	LEO	11
12	12.51	23.33	07.23	22.02	12.16	SAG	CAP	05.45	ARI	16.10	CAN	12.38	12
13	GEM	LEO	LEO	LIB	SCO	17.21	12.05	PIS	04.55	GEM	03.50	VIR	13
14	13.21	LEO	10.05	LIB	22.40	CAP	AQU	15.34	TAU	19.31	LEO	16.27	14
15	CAN	00.57	VIR	05.23	SAG	CAP	23.53	ARI	10.23	CAN	06.38	LIB	15
16	13.09	VIR	14.08	SCO	SAG	06.07	PIS	23.25	GEM	22.19	VIR	23.13	16
17	LEO	04.28	LIB	15.19	10.51	AQU	PIS	TAU	14.09	LEO	11.03	SCO	17
18	14.12	LIB	20.53	SAG	CAP	18.02	10.02	TAU	CAN	LEO	LIB	SCO	18
19	VIR	11.37	SCO	SAG	23.37	PIS	ARI	04.51	16.26	01.09	17.25	08.32	19
20	18.27	SCO	SCO	03.31	AQU	PIS	17.31	GEM	LEO	VIR	SCO	SAG	20
21	LIB	22.33	07.01	CAP	AQU	03.42	TAU	07.40	18.02	04.43	SCO	19.39	21
22	LIB	SAG	SAG	16.11	11.06	ARI	21.44	CAN	VIR	LIB	01.56	CAP	22
23	02.56	SAG	19.32	AQU	PIS	09.50	GEM	08.27	20.19	10.00	SAG	CAP	23
24	SCO	11.28	CAP	AQU	19.35	TAU	22.55	LEO	LIB	SCO	12.37	07.59	24
25	14.51	CAP	CAP	02.54	ARI	12.25	CAN	08.43	LIB	17.54	CAP	AQU	25
26	SAG	23.36	07.56	PIS	ARI	GEM	22.26	VIR	00.57	SAG	CAP	20.41	26
27	SAG	AQU	AQU	10.08	00.17	12.27	LEO	10.26	SCO	SAG	00.58	PIS	27
28	03.58	AQU	17.52	ARI	TAU	CAN	22.18	LIB	09.03	04.39	AQU	PIS	28
29	CAP		PIS	14.02	01.52	11.45	VIR	15.26	SAG	CAP	13.30	08.14	29
30	16.00		PIS	TAU	GEM	LEO	VIR	SCO	20.20	17.08	PIS	ARI	30
31	AQU		00.33		01.55		00.35	SCO		AQU		16.48	31

SUN

mth	dy	time → sign
JAN	1	00.00 → CAP
JAN	20	22.51 → AQU
FEB	19	13.09 → PIS
MAR	21	12.28 → ARI
APR	20	23.55 → TAU
MAY	21	23.27 → GEM
JUN	22	07.39 → CAN
JUL	23	18.37 → LEO
AUG	24	01.31 → VIR
SEP	23	22.49 → LIB
OCT	24	07.44 → SCO
NOV	23	04.59 → SAG
DEC	22	18.06 → CAP

MERCURY

mth	dy	time → sign
JAN	1	00.00 → SAG
JAN	12	07.57 → CAP
FEB	1	17.57 → AQU
FEB	19	08.10 → PIS
MAR	7	09.14 → ARI
MAY	14	13.43 → TAU
MAY	31	02.44 → GEM
JUN	13	23.01 → CAN
JUN	30	06.41 → LEO
SEP	7	04.58 → VIR
SEP	23	07.48 → LIB
OCT	11	05.20 → SCO
NOV	1	07.03 → SAG
DEC	3	07.22 → SCO
DEC	13	19.16 → SAG

VENUS

mth	dy	time → sign
JAN	1	00.00 → SCO
JAN	4	21.48 → SAG
FEB	6	09.20 → CAP
MAR	5	13.29 → AQU
MAR	31	08.34 → PIS
APR	25	14.28 → ARI
MAY	20	14.13 → TAU
JUN	14	10.11 → GEM
JUL	9	02.25 → CAN
AUG	2	14.11 → LEO
AUG	26	21.24 → VIR
SEP	20	01.02 → LIB
OCT	14	02.41 → SCO
NOV	7	03.41 → SAG
DEC	1	04.52 → CAP
DEC	25	07.25 → AQU

MARS

mth	dy	time → sign
JAN	1	00.00 → SCO
JAN	29	09.52 → SAG
MAR	21	07.25 → CAP
MAY	25	00.23 → AQU
JUL	21	19.31 → CAP
SEP	24	01.17 → AQU
NOV	19	15.56 → PIS

SATURN

mth	dy	time → sign
JAN	1	00.00 → ARI
JUL	6	05.39 → TAU
SEP	22	05.11 → ARI

JUPITER

mth	dy	time → sign
JAN	1	00.00 → PIS
MAY	11	14.16 → ARI
OCT	30	00.49 → PIS
DEC	20	17.10 → ARI

MOON

dy	jan	feb	mar	apr	may	jun	jul	aug	sep	oct	nov	dec	dy
1	TAU	09.22	CAN	04.39	LIB	07.15	CAP	AQU	ARI	TAU	13.41	LEO	1
2	21.19	CAN	19.31	VIR	17.36	SAG	CAP	04.41	ARI	TAU	CAN	LEO	2
3	GEM	09.06	LEO	05.48	SCO	15.50	09.54	PIS	10.47	01.38	18.01	02.23	3
4	22.20	LEO	19.17	LIB	23.11	CAP	AQU	17.22	TAU	GEM	LEO	VIR	4
5	CAN	08.02	VIR	08.20	SAG	CAP	22.17	ARI	20.02	08.16	20.57	05.22	5
6	21.32	VIR	19.25	SCO	SAG	02.40	PIS	ARI	GEM	CAN	VIR	LIB	6
7	LEO	08.29	LIB	13.47	07.34	AQU	PIS	04.47	GEM	12.10	23.03	08.57	7
8	21.08	LIB	21.59	SAG	CAP	15.04	10.50	TAU	01.52	LEO	LIB	SCO	8
9	VIR	12.22	SCO	22.47	18.41	PIS	ARI	13.06	CAN	13.44	LIB	13.32	9
10	23.10	SCO	SCO	CAP	AQU	PIS	21.27	GEM	04.12	VIR	01.14	SAG	10
11	LIB	20.24	04.23	CAP	AQU	03.10	TAU	17.20	LEO	14.15	SCO	19.51	11
12	LIB	SAG	SAG	10.33	07.09	ARI	TAU	CAN	04.09	LIB	04.41	CAP	12
13	04.54	SAG	14.35	AQU	PIS	12.43	04.20	18.09	VIR	15.18	SAG	CAP	13
14	SCO	07.41	CAP	23.04	18.41	TAU	GEM	LEO	03.39	SCO	10.42	04.42	14
15	14.10	CAP	CAP	PIS	ARI	18.32	07.16	17.19	LIB	18.36	CAP	AQU	15
16	SAG	20.22	03.01	PIS	ARI	GEM	CAN	04.43	SAG	20.00	16.14	16
17	SAG	AQU	AQU	10.13	03.28	21.06	07.31	17.03	SCO	SAG	AQU	PIS	17
18	01.44	AQU	15.31	ARI	TAU	CAN	LEO	LIB	09.02	01.22	AQU	PIS	18
19	CAP	08.52	PIS	18.57	09.06	21.58	07.07	19.20	SAG	CAP	08.00	05.03	19
20	14.15	PIS	PIS	TAU	GEM	LEO	VIR	SCO	17.11	11.40	PIS	ARI	20
21	AQU	20.23	02.41	TAU	12.23	22.56	08.10	SCO	CAP	AQU	20.36	16.32	21
22	AQU	ARI	ARI	01.16	CAN	VIR	LIB	01.14	CAP	AQU	ARI	TAU	22
23	02.51	ARI	11.58	GEM	14.33	VIR	12.04	SAG	04.24	00.05	ARI	TAU	23
24	PIS	06.19	TAU	05.43	LEO	01.31	SCO	10.33	AQU	PIS	07.23	00.37	24
25	14.42	TAU	19.15	CAN	16.51	LIB	19.10	CAP	17.00	12.28	TAU	GEM	25
26	ARI	13.47	GEM	08.55	VIR	06.25	SAG	22.09	PIS	ARI	15.09	05.03	26
27	ARI	GEM	GEM	LEO	20.06	SCO	SAG	AQU	PIS	23.09	GEM	CAN	27
28	00.29	18.07	00.19	11.26	LIB	13.39	04.51	AQU	05.22	TAU	20.11	07.05	28
29	TAU		CAN	VIR	LIB	SAG	CAP	10.42	ARI	TAU	CAN	LEO	29
30	06.50		03.15	14.02	00.47	22.53	16.15	PIS	16.29	07.31	23.34	08.29	30
31	GEM		LEO		SCO		AQU	23.15		GEM		VIR	31

SUN

mth	dy	time → sign
JAN	1	00.00 → CAP
JAN	21	04.42 → AQU
FEB	19	19.04 → PIS
MAR	20	18.25 → ARI
APR	20	05.51 → TAU
MAY	21	05.23 → GEM
JUN	21	13.37 → CAN
JUL	23	00.34 → LEO
AUG	23	07.28 → VIR
SEP	23	04.46 → LIB
OCT	23	13.39 → SCO
NOV	22	10.48 → SAG
DEC	21	23.54 → CAP

MERCURY

mth	dy	time → sign
JAN	1	00.00 → SAG
JAN	6	07.57 → CAP
JAN	25	10.15 → AQU
FEB	11	14.01 → PIS
MAR	4	10.11 → ARI
MAR	8	01.26 → PIS
APR	17	04.56 → ARI
MAY	6	21.15 → TAU
MAY	21	13.58 → GEM
JUN	4	22.29 → CAN
JUN	26	14.32 → LEO
JUL	21	01.39 → CAN
AUG	11	17.06 → LEO
AUG	29	11.11 → VIR
SEP	14	11.34 → LIB
OCT	3	12.16 → SCO
DEC	9	12.45 → SAG
DEC	29	09.37 → CAP

VENUS

mth	dy	time → sign
JAN	1	00.00 → AQU
JAN	18	14.02 → PIS
FEB	12	05.51 → ARI
MAR	8	16.25 → TAU
APR	4	18.11 → GEM
MAY	6	18.46 → CAN
JUL	5	16.17 → GEM
AUG	1	02.20 → CAN
SEP	8	16.59 → LEO
OCT	6	21.14 → VIR
NOV	1	17.23 → LIB
NOV	26	12.33 → SCO
DEC	20	19.36 → SAG

MARS

mth	dy	time → sign
JAN	1	00.00 → PIS
JAN	4	00.25 → ARI
FEB	17	01.59 → TAU
APR	1	18.41 → GEM
MAY	17	14.45 → CAN
JUL	3	10.35 → LEO
AUG	19	15.58 → VIR
OCT	5	14.31 → LIB
NOV	20	17.22 → SCO

SATURN

mth	dy	time → sign
JAN	1	00.00 → ARI
MAR	20	09.35 → TAU

JUPITER

mth	dy	time → sign
JAN	1	00.00 → ARI
MAY	16	07.37 → TAU

MOON

dy	jan	feb	mar	apr	may	jun	jul	aug	sep	oct	nov	dec	dy
1	10.44	SCO	SAG	07.13	01.56	ARI	TAU	CAN	12.57	LIB	10.21	CAP	1
2	LIB	01.37	15.02	AQU	PIS	10.46	05.15	VIR	23.12	SAG	CAP	CAP	2
3	14.36	SAG	CAP	19.16	14.52	TAU	GEM	01.21	12.55	SCO	12.23	03.12	3
4	SCO	09.27	CAP	PIS	ARI	20.49	12.10	LEO	LIB	23.54	CAP	AQU	4
5	20.12	CAP	01.07	PIS	ARI	GEM	CAN	02.50	13.16	SAG	18.03	11.35	5
6	SAG	19.23	AQU	08.10	03.12	GEM	16.12	VIR	SCO	SAG	AQU	PIS	6
7	SAG	AQU	13.07	ARI	TAU	04.05	LEO	03.52	15.36	03.28	AQU	23.26	7
8	03.33	AQU	PIS	20.38	13.34	CAN	18.44	LIB	SAG	03.45	PIS	ARI	8
9	CAP	06.58	PIS	TAU	GEM	09.00	VIR	05.46	20.46	10.45	PIS	ARI	9
10	12.42	PIS	02.01	TAU	21.33	LEO	21.07	SCO	CAP	AQU	16.13	12.27	10
11	AQU	19.49	ARI	07.32	CAN	12.41	LIB	09.27	CAP	21.18	ARI	TAU	11
12	AQU	ARI	14.44	GEM	CAN	VIR	LIB	SAG	04.51	PIS	ARI	TAU	12
13	00.05	ARI	TAU	16.05	03.22	15.43	00.07	15.15	AQU	PIS	05.13	00.08	13
14	PIS	08.38	TAU	CAN	LEO	LIB	SCO	CAP	15.25	09.50	TAU	GEM	14
15	12.57	TAU	01.53	21.44	07.17	18.32	04.05	23.08	PIS	ARI	17.00	09.21	15
16	ARI	19.10	GEM	LEO	VIR	SCO	SAG	AQU	PIS	22.47	GEM	CAN	16
17	ARI	GEM	09.57	LEO	09.40	21.34	09.17	AQU	03.43	TAU	GEM	16.16	17
18	01.15	GEM	CAN	00.35	LIB	SAG	CAP	09.11	ARI	TAU	02.52	LEO	18
19	TAU	01.46	14.15	VIR	11.12	SAG	16.22	PIS	16.44	10.59	CAN	21.35	19
20	10.32	CAN	LEO	01.23	SCO	01.44	AQU	21.15	TAU	GEM	10.38	VIR	20
21	GEM	04.19	15.20	LIB	13.00	CAP	AQU	ARI	TAU	21.18	LEO	VIR	21
22	15.35	LEO	VIR	01.33	SAG	08.15	01.58	ARI	05.05	CAN	16.11	01.37	22
23	CAN	04.11	14.47	SCO	16.35	AQU	PIS	10.17	GEM	CAN	VIR	LIB	23
24	17.10	VIR	LIB	02.47	CAP	17.56	14.01	TAU	14.57	04.51	19.25	04.30	24
25	LEO	03.29	14.33	SAG	23.19	PIS	ARI	22.13	CAN	LEO	LIB	SCO	25
26	17.12	LIB	SCO	06.50	AQU	PIS	ARI	GEM	21.09	09.09	20.44	06.36	26
27	VIR	04.13	16.31	CAP	AQU	06.13	02.56	GEM	LEO	VIR	SCO	SAG	27
28	17.43	SCO	SAG	14.39	09.39	ARI	TAU	06.53	23.41	10.37	21.18	08.58	28
29	LIB	07.54	21.59	AQU	PIS	18.52	14.04	CAN	VIR	LIB	SAG	CAP	29
30	20.17		CAP	AQU	22.18	TAU	GEM	11.31	23.46	10.25	22.50	13.09	30
31	SCO		CAP		ARI		21.32	LEO		SCO		AQU	31

SUN

mth	dy	time → sign
JAN	1	00.00 → CAP
JAN	20	10.33 → AQU
FEB	19	00.56 → PIS
MAR	21	00.23 → ARI
APR	20	11.50 → TAU
MAY	21	11.23 → GEM
JUN	21	19.35 → CAN
JUL	23	06.26 → LEO
AUG	23	13.17 → VIR
SEP	23	10.33 → LIB
OCT	23	19.28 → SCO
NOV	22	16.38 → SAG
DEC	22	05.42 → CAP

SATURN

mth	dy	time → sign
JAN	1	00.00 → TAU

MERCURY

mth	dy	time → sign
JAN	1	00.00 → CAP
JAN	16	22.37 → AQU
FEB	3	13.08 → PIS
MAR	7	02.22 → AQU
MAR	16	12.28 → PIS
APR	12	07.19 → ARI
APR	28	23.09 → TAU
MAY	13	00.51 → GEM
MAY	29	17.33 → CAN
AUG	6	05.57 → LEO
AUG	21	05.18 → VIR
SEP	6	23.58 → LIB
SEP	28	09.22 → SCO
OCT	29	20.34 → LIB
NOV	11	20.11 → SCO
DEC	3	00.11 → SAG
DEC	22	03.54 → CAP

VENUS

mth	dy	time → sign
JAN	1	00.00 → SAG
JAN	13	21.32 → CAP
FEB	6	21.49 → AQU
MAR	2	22.33 → PIS
MAR	27	00.58 → ARI
APR	20	05.53 → TAU
MAY	14	13.37 → GEM
JUN	7	23.53 → CAN
JUL	2	12.35 → LEO
JUL	27	04.12 → VIR
AUG	21	00.29 → LIB
SEP	15	04.01 → SCO
OCT	10	19.23 → SAG
NOV	6	10.17 → CAP
DEC	5	23.05 → AQU

MARS

mth	dy	time → sign
JAN	1	00.00 → SCO
JAN	4	19.38 → SAG
FEB	17	23.34 → CAP
APR	2	11.32 → AQU
MAY	16	05.15 → PIS
JUL	2	05.24 → ARI

JUPITER

mth	dy	time → sign
JAN	1	00.00 → TAU
MAY	26	12.14 → GEM

MOON

dy	jan	feb	mar	apr	may	jun	jul	aug	sep	oct	nov	dec	dy
1	20.35	ARI	ARI	08.06	01.56	LEO	11.17	22.49	CAP	AQU	ARI	TAU	1
2	PIS	ARI	12.23	GEM	CAN	00.38	LIB	SAG	11.39	00.18	ARI	22.01	2
3	PIS	04.41	TAU	19.45	11.34	VIR	14.33	SAG	AQU	PIS	03.18	GEM	3
4	07.35	TAU	TAU	CAN	LEO	05.17	SCO	01.17	17.52	09.37	TAU	GEM	4
5	ARI	17.09	01.12	CAN	18.06	LIB	16.13	CAP	PIS	ARI	15.54	10.23	5
6	20.28	GEM	GEM	04.26	VIR	07.14	SAG	04.33	PIS	20.52	GEM	CAN	6
7	TAU	GEM	12.04	LEO	21.12	SCO	17.21	AQU	02.29	TAU	GEM	21.43	7
8	TAU	02.58	CAN	09.22	LIB	07.23	CAP	09.51	ARI	TAU	04.26	LEO	8
9	O8.27	CAN	19.19	VIR	21.34	SAG	19.36	PIS	13.32	09.23	CAN	LEO	9
10	GEM	09.07	LEO	10.54	SCO	07.31	AQU	18.14	TAU	GEM	15.46	07.12	10
11	17.34	LEO	22.51	LIB	20.47	CAP	AQU	ARI	TAU	21.54	LEO	VIR	11
12	CAN	12.22	VIR	10.31	SAG	09.42	00.43	ARI	02.04	CAN	LEO	13.46	12
13	23.39	VIR	23.51	SCO	21.03	AQU	PIS	05.32	GEM	CAN	00.29	LIB	13
14	LEO	14.07	LIB	10.07	CAP	15.33	09.34	TAU	14.09	08.29	VIR	16.53	14
15	LEO	LIB	LIB	SAG	CAP	PIS	ARI	18.09	CAN	LEO	05.23	SCO	15
16	O3.46	15.52	00.03	11.38	00.15	PIS	21.30	GEM	23.36	15.36	LIB	17.10	16
17	VIR	SCO	SCO	CAP	AQU	01.32	TAU	GEM	LEO	VIR	06.40	SAG	17
18	07.00	18.37	01.08	16.32	07.36	ARI	TAU	05.37	LEO	18.54	SCO	16.26	18
19	LIB	SAG	SAG	AQU	PIS	14.09	10.08	CAN	05.29	LIB	05.53	CAP	19
20	10.04	22.55	04.25	AQU	18.34	TAU	GEM	14.15	VIR	19.25	SAG	16.53	20
21	SCO	CAP	CAP	01.07	ARI	TAU	21.15	LEO	08.17	SCO	05.11	AQU	21
22	13.18	CAP	10.34	PIS	ARI	02.44	CAN	19.53	LIB	19.00	CAP	20.33	22
23	SAG	05.01	AQU	12.36	07.26	GEM	CAN	VIR	09.23	SAG	06.46	PIS	23
24	17.01	AQU	19.30	ARI	TAU	13.51	05.48	23.21	SCO	19.40	AQU	PIS	24
25	CAP	13.18	PIS	ARI	20.11	CAN	LEO	LIB	10.24	CAP	12.09	04.24	25
26	22.06	PIS	PIS	01.22	GEM	22.55	12.03	LIB	SAG	23.02	PIS	ARI	26
27	AQU	23.54	06.39	TAU	GEM	LEO	VIR	01.48	12.44	AQU	21.26	15.43	27
28	AQU	ARI	ARI	14.13	07.36	LEO	16.41	SCO	CAP	AQU	ARI	TAU	28
29	05.34		19.13	GEM	CAN	06.03	LIB	04.13	17.17	05.51	ARI	TAU	29
30	PIS		TAU	GEM	17.16	VIR	20.09	SAG	AQU	PIS	09.18	04.27	30
31	16.02		TAU		LEO		SCO	07.18		15.38		GEM	31

SUN

mth	dy	time → sign
JAN	1	00.00 → CAP
JAN	20	16.25 → AQU
FEB	19	06.46 → PIS
MAR	21	06.12 → ARI
APR	20	17.39 → TAU
MAY	21	17.08 → GEM
JUN	22	01.17 → CAN
JUL	23	12.07 → LEO
AUG	23	18.59 → VIR
SEP	23	16.16 → LIB
OCT	24	01.15 → SCO
NOV	22	22.32 → SAG
DEC	22	11.39 → CAP

MERCURY

mth	dy	time → sign
JAN	1	00.00 → CAP
JAN	9	15.26 → AQU
MAR	17	00.10 → PIS
APR	5	07.06 → ARI
APR	20	13.42 → TAU
MAY	5	04.38 → GEM
JUL	12	20.24 → CAN
JUL	29	04.24 → LEO
AUG	13	01.46 → VIR
AUG	31	08.27 → LIB
NOV	7	01.44 → SCO
NOV	25	20.27 → SAG
DEC	14	22.22 → CAP

VENUS

mth	dy	time → sign
JAN	1	00.00 → AQU
APR	6	13.13 → PIS
MAY	6	02.25 → ARI
JUN	2	00.26 → TAU
JUN	27	22.19 → GEM
JUL	23	06.10 → CAN
AUG	17	03.05 → LEO
SEP	10	14.38 → VIR
OCT	4	18.57 → LIB
OCT	28	18.41 → SCO
NOV	21	16.09 → SAG
DEC	15	12.53 → CAP

MARS

mth	dy	time → sign
JAN	1	00.00 → ARI
JAN	11	22.27 → TAU
MAR	7	08.03 → GEM
APR	26	06.18 → CAN
JUN	14	03.54 → LEO
AUG	1	08.24 → VIR
SEP	17	10.13 → LIB
NOV	1	22.36 → SCO
DEC	15	16.52 → SAG

SATURN

mth	dy	time → sign
JAN	1	00.00 → TAU
MAY	8	19.32 → GEM

JUPITER

mth	dy	time → sign
JAN	1	00.00 → GEM
JUN	10	10.31 → CAN

MOON

dy	jan	feb	mar	apr	may	jun	jul	aug	sep	oct	nov	dec	dy
1	16.41	LEO	LEO	LIB	SCO	CAP	AQU	ARI	20.40	17.03	LEO	VIR	1
2	CAN	18.57	03.07	19.55	06.04	15.58	03.46	ARI	GEM	CAN	LEO	18.55	2
3	CAN	VIR	VIR	SCO	SAG	AQU	PIS	01.48	GEM	CAN	01.19	LIB	3
4	03.31	VIR	08.23	21.04	06.04	19.14	09.12	TAU	09.01	05.36	VIR	LIB	4
5	LEO	01.19	LIB	SAG	CAP	PIS	ARI	12.54	CAN	LEO	09.22	00.07	5
6	12.42	LIB	11.51	22.42	07.57	PIS	18.22	GEM	21.15	16.13	LIB	SCO	6
7	VIR	05.56	SCO	CAP	AQU	02.12	TAU	GEM	LEO	13.27	13.27	01.34	7
8	19.48	SCO	14.28	CAP	12.44	ARI	TAU	01.31	LEO	23.34	SCO	SAG	8
9	LIB	09.07	SAG	01.56	PIS	12.16	06.11	CAN	07.32	LIB	14.48	01.06	9
10	LIB	SAG	17.09	AQU	20.32	TAU	GEM	13.39	VIR	LIB	SAG	CAP	10
11	00.25	11.19	CAP	07.18	ARI	TAU	18.51	LEO	15.05	03.46	15.18	00.57	11
12	SCO	CAP	20.30	PIS	ARI	00.13	CAN	LEO	LIB	SCO	CAP	AQU	12
13	02.33	13.28	AQU	14.49	06.37	GEM	CAN	00.10	20.18	06.11	16.49	02.57	13
14	SAG	AQU	AQU	ARI	TAU	12.50	07.08	VIR	SCO	SAG	AQU	PIS	14
15	03.07	16.51	01.09	ARI	18.15	CAN	LEO	08.31	23.57	08.14	20.29	08.04	15
16	CAP	PIS	PIS	00.19	GEM	CAN	18.08	LIB	SAG	CAP	PIS	ARI	16
17	03.52	22.47	07.42	TAU	GEM	01.18	VIR	14.38	SAG	11.01	PIS	16.18	17
18	AQU	ARI	ARI	11.37	06.49	LEO	VIR	SCO	02.49	AQU	02.30	TAU	18
19	06.44	ARI	16.39	GEM	CAN	12.34	03.02	18.36	CAP	15.05	ARI	TAU	19
20	PIS	07.57	TAU	GEM	19.21	VIR	LIB	SAG	05.27	PIS	10.37	02.48	20
21	13.08	TAU	TAU	00.11	LEO	21.04	09.02	20.46	AQU	20.36	TAU	GEM	21
22	ARI	19.48	04.02	CAN	LEO	LIB	SCO	CAP	08.34	ARI	20.35	14.47	22
23	23.18	GEM	GEM	12.21	06.07	LIB	11.58	22.08	PIS	ARI	GEM	CAN	23
24	TAU	GEM	16.33	LEO	VIR	01.51	SAG	AQU	12.57	03.52	GEM	CAN	24
25	TAU	08.15	CAN	22.03	13.22	SCO	12.38	23.55	ARI	TAU	08.18	03.35	25
26	11.43	CAN	CAN	VIR	LIB	03.09	CAP	PIS	19.35	13.19	CAN	LEO	26
27	GEM	19.07	04.06	VIR	16.32	SAG	12.37	PIS	TAU	GEM	21.09	16.10	27
28	GEM	LEO	LEO	03.50	SCO	02.32	AQU	03.38	TAU	GEM	LEO	VIR	28
29	00.03		12.36	LIB	16.39	CAP	13.49	ARI	05.05	LEO	LEO	VIR	29
30	CAN		VIR	05.59	SAG	02.00	PIS	10.29	GEM	CAN	09.30	02.45	30
31	10.38		17.36		15.43		17.55	TAU		13.48		LIB	31

SUN

mth	dy	time → sign
JAN	1	00.00 → CAP
JAN	20	22.19 → AQU
FEB	19	12.40 → PIS
MAR	21	12.03 → ARI
APR	20	23.31 → TAU
MAY	21	23.03 → GEM
JUN	22	07.12 → CAN
JUL	23	18.04 → LEO
AUG	24	00.55 → VIR
SEP	23	22.12 → LIB
OCT	24	07.08 → SCO
NOV	23	04.21 → SAG
DEC	22	17.29 → CAP

MERCURY

mth	dy	time → sign
JAN	1	00.00 → CAP
JAN	3	08.27 → AQU
JAN	27	23.43 → CAP
FEB	15	19.00 → AQU
MAR	11	04.59 → PIS
MAR	28	11.19 → ARI
APR	12	04.57 → TAU
APR	30	15.56 → GEM
MAY	26	10.22 → TAU
JUN	14	00.46 → GEM
JUL	6	09.05 → CAN
JUL	20	16.08 → LEO
AUG	5	10.33 → VIR
AUG	27	00.36 → LIB
SEP	25	09.56 → VIR
OCT	11	23.26 → LIB
OCT	30	23.37 → SCO
NOV	18	13.39 → SAG
DEC	8	01.47 → CAP

VENUS

mth	dy	time → sign
JAN	1	00.00 → CAP
JAN	8	10.03 → AQU
FEB	1	09.02 → PIS
FEB	25	12.04 → ARI
MAR	21	22.25 → TAU
APR	15	20.12 → GEM
MAY	11	11.56 → CAN
JUN	7	12.09 → LEO
JUL	7	23.56 → VIR
NOV	9	18.25 → LIB
DEC	8	07.44 → SCO

MARS

mth	dy	time → sign
JAN	1	00.00 → SAG
JAN	26	19.18 → CAP
MAR	8	12.44 → AQU
APR	17	10.25 → PIS
MAY	27	09.29 → ARI
JUL	7	23.08 → TAU
AUG	23	23.51 → GEM

SATURN

mth	dy	time → sign
JAN	1	00.00 → GEM

JUPITER

mth	dy	time → sign
JAN	1	00.00 → CAN
JUN	30	21.33 → LEO

MOON

dy	jan	feb	mar	apr	may	jun	jul	aug	sep	oct	nov	dec	dy
1	09.39	23.15	07.19	18.27	04.39	TAU	17.13	LEO	18.33	10.04	SAG	13.01	1
2	SCO	CAP	CAP	PIS	ARI	00.29	CAN	LEO	LIB	SCO	03.37	AQU	2
3	12.33	23.10	08.56	21.17	09.57	GEM	CAN	00.45	LIB	17.03	CAP	15.36	3
4	SAG	AQU	AQU	ARI	TAU	10.45	05.39	VIR	04.20	SAG	07.09	PIS	4
5	12.35	23.07	09.54	ARI	17.16	CAN	LEO	12.51	SCO	22.11	AQU	19.00	5
6	CAP	PIS	PIS	01.37	GEM	23.03	18.45	LIB	11.38	CAP	10.16	ARI	6
7	11.42	PIS	11.41	TAU	GEM	LEO	VIR	22.40	SAG	CAP	PIS	23.30	7
8	AQU	01.00	ARI	08.41	03.17	LEO	VIR	SCO	16.13	01.39	13.10	TAU	8
9	12.03	ARI	15.53	GEM	CAN	12.03	06.44	SCO	CAP	AQU	ARI	TAU	9
10	PIS	06.17	TAU	19.03	15.39	VIR	05.08	18.18		03.44	16.32	05.32	10
11	15.21	TAU	23.39	CAN	LEO	23.22	15.40	SAG	AQU	PIS	TAU	GEM	11
12	ARI	15.25	GEM	CAN	LEO	LIB	SCO	08.09	18.46	05.12	21.31	13.46	12
13	22.22	GEM	GEM	07.39	04.21	LIB	20.37	CAP	PIS	ARI	GEM	CAN	13
14	TAU	GEM	10.51	LEO	VIR	06.59	SAG	08.36	19.09	07.26	GEM	CAN	14
15	TAU	03.25	CAN	19.59	14.44	SCO	22.07	AQU	ARI	TAU	05.22	00.37	15
16	08.39	CAN	23.41	VIR	LIB	10.36	CAP	08.06	21.14	12.07	CAN	LEO	16
17	GEM	16.18	LEO	VIR	21.19	SAG	21.46	PIS	TAU	16.27	LEO	13.22	17
18	20.53	LEO	LEO	05.41	SCO	11.29	AQU	08.32	TAU	20.28	LEO	VIR	18
19	CAN	LEO	11.43	LIB	SCO	CAP	21.30	ARI	02.42	CAN	LEO	VIR	19
20	CAN	04.20	VIR	12.04	00.33	11.33	PIS	11.39	GEM	CAN	05.21	01.55	20
21	09.44	VIR	21.21	SCO	SAG	AQU	23.08	TAU	12.10	08.12	VIR	LIB	21
22	LEO	14.30	LIB	15.56	02.00	12.36	ARI	18.34	CAN	LEO	17.19	11.46	22
23	22.03	LIB	LIB	SAG	CAP	PIS	ARI	GEM	CAN	21.10	LIB	SCO	23
24	VIR	22.25	04.23	18.39	03.23	15.52	03.53	GEM	00.34	VIR	LIB	17.44	24
25	VIR	SCO	SCO	CAP	AQU	ARI	TAU	05.07	LEO	VIR	02.09	SAG	25
26	08.47	SCO	09.23	21.21	05.58	21.52	12.04	CAN	13.30	08.38	SCO	20.25	26
27	LIB	03.59	SAG	AQU	PIS	TAU	GEM	17.49	VIR	LIB	07.35	CAP	27
28	16.51	SAG	13.05	AQU	10.16	TAU	23.04	LEO	VIR	17.14	SAG	21.21	28
29	SCO		CAP	00.36	ARI	06.27	CAN	LEO	00.56	SCO	10.43	AQU	29
30	21.34		15.57	PIS	16.25	GEM	CAN	06.47	LIB	23.14	CAP	22.17	30
31	SAG		AQU		TAU		11.43	VIR		SAG		PIS	31

SUN

mth	dy	time → sign
JAN	1	00.00 → CAP
JAN	21	04.07 → AQU
FEB	19	18.27 → PIS
MAR	20	17.49 → ARI
APR	20	05.18 → TAU
MAY	21	04.51 → GEM
JUN	21	13.02 → CAN
JUL	22	23.56 → LEO
AUG	23	06.46 → VIR
SEP	23	04.02 → LIB
OCT	23	12.56 → SCO
NOV	22	10.08 → SAG
DEC	21	23.15 → CAP

MERCURY

mth	dy	time → sign
JAN	1	00.00 → CAP
FEB	12	14.17 → AQU
MAR	3	02.45 → PIS
MAR	19	07.43 → ARI
APR	3	17.29 → TAU
JUN	11	11.46 → GEM
JUN	27	03.39 → CAN
JUL	11	07.41 → LEO
JUL	28	23.44 → VIR
OCT	5	03.17 → LIB
OCT	22	11.33 → SCO
NOV	10	11.09 → SAG
DEC	1	15.31 → CAP
DEC	23	23.21 → SAG

VENUS

mth	dy	time → sign
JAN	1	00.00 → SCO
JAN	3	04.43 → SAG
JAN	28	03.11 → CAP
FEB	21	16.40 → AQU
MAR	17	02.46 → PIS
APR	10	12.09 → ARI
MAY	4	22.04 → TAU
MAY	29	08.39 → GEM
JUN	22	19.12 → CAN
JUL	17	04.47 → LEO
AUG	10	13.13 → VIR
SEP	3	21.17 → LIB
SEP	28	06.12 → SCO
OCT	22	17.07 → SAG
NOV	16	07.26 → CAP
DEC	11	04.47 → AQU

MARS

mth	dy	time → sign
JAN	1	00.00 → GEM
MAR	28	09.44 → CAN
MAY	22	14.16 → LEO
JUL	12	02.57 → VIR
AUG	29	00.27 → LIB
OCT	13	12.15 → SCO
NOV	25	16.10 → SAG

SATURN

mth	dy	time → sign
JAN	1	00.00 → GEM
JUN	20	07.55 → CAN

JUPITER

mth	dy	time → sign
JAN	1	00.00 → LEO
JUL	26	01.12 → VIR

MOON

dy	jan	feb	mar	apr	may	jun	jul	aug	sep	oct	nov	dec	dy
1	PIS	TAU	00.06	CAN	23.04	LIB	SCO	14.42	AQU	14.30	TAU	15.17	1
2	00.34	17.17	GEM	02.54	VIR	LIB	23.38	CAP	04.14	ARI	01.28	CAN	2
3	ARI	GEM	08.38	LEO	VIR	06.32	SAG	17.10	PIS	13.46	GEM	21.53	3
4	04.58	GEM	CAN	15.49	11.39	SCO	SAG	AQU	03.27	TAU	05.04	LEO	4
5	TAU	02.40	20.19	VIR	LIB	14.27	04.42	17.35	ARI	14.59	CAN	LEO	5
6	11.44	CAN	LEO	VIR	22.18	SAG	CAP	PIS	03.28	GEM	12.44	08.04	6
7	GEM	14.20	LEO	04.22	SCO	19.41	07.14	17.43	TAU	19.56	LEO	VIR	7
8	20.48	LEO	09.18	LIB	SCO	CAP	AQU	ARI	06.13	CAN	23.59	20.28	8
9	CAN	LEO	VIR	15.12	06.27	23.12	08.39	19.19	GEM	CAN	VIR	LIB	9
10	CAN	03.08	21.55	SCO	SAG	AQU	PIS	TAU	12.47	05.03	VIR	LIB	10
11	07.57	VIR	LIB	SCO	12.33	AQU	10.18	23.38	CAN	LEO	12.45	08.42	11
12	LEO	15.54	LIB	00.02	CAP	01.58	ARI	GEM	22.50	17.04	LIB	SCO	12
13	20.38	LIB	09.12	SAG	17.10	PIS	13.16	GEM	LEO	VIR	LIB	18.50	13
14	VIR	LIB	SCO	06.56	AQU	04.41	TAU	07.03	LEO	VIR	00.48	SAG	14
15	VIR	03.24	18.31	CAP	20.35	ARI	18.11	CAN	11.00	05.55	SCO	SAG	15
16	09.29	SCO	SAG	11.46	PIS	07.52	GEM	17.08	VIR	LIB	11.02	02.22	16
17	LIB	12.15	SAG	AQU	23.03	TAU	GEM	LEO	23.48	18.03	SAG	CAP	17
18	20.27	SAG	01.13	14.28	ARI	12.11	01.21	LEO	LIB	SCO	19.20	07.44	18
19	SCO	17.33	CAP	PIS	ARI	GEM	CAN	05.00	LIB	SCO	CAP	AQU	19
20	SCO	CAP	04.55	15.35	01.15	18.28	10.51	VIR	12.11	04.50	CAP	11.39	20
21	03.53	19.27	AQU	ARI	TAU	CAN	LEO	17.45	SCO	SAG	01.47	PIS	21
22	SAG	AQU	05.59	16.29	04.26	CAN	22.24	LIB	23.16	13.48	AQU	14.42	22
23	07.26	19.09	PIS	TAU	GEM	03.24	VIR	LIB	SAG	CAP	06.18	ARI	23
24	CAP	PIS	05.42	18.59	10.04	LEO	VIR	06.13	SAG	20.19	PIS	17.24	24
25	08.09	18.31	ARI	GEM	CAN	14.58	11.08	SCO	07.55	AQU	08.57	TAU	25
26	AQU	ARI	06.01	GEM	19.04	VIR	LIB	16.52	CAP	23.53	ARI	20.26	26
27	07.48	19.36	TAU	00.49	LEO	VIR	23.16	SAG	13.10	PIS	10.22	GEM	27
28	PIS	TAU	08.58	CAN	LEO	03.40	SCO	SAG	AQU	PIS	TAU	GEM	28
29	08.15	TAU	GEM	10.36	06.58	LIB	SCO	00.12	14.58	00.54	11.55	00.44	29
30	ARI		15.59	LEO	VIR	15.10	08.50	CAP	PIS	ARI	GEM	CAN	30
31	11.07		CAN		19.37		SAG	03.44		00.45		07.19	31

SUN

mth	dy	time → sign
JAN	1	00.00 → CAP
JAN	20	09.54 → AQU
FEB	19	00.14 → PIS
MAR	20	23.37 → ARI
APR	20	11.07 → TAU
MAY	21	10.40 → GEM
JUN	21	18.52 → CAN
JUL	23	05.45 → LEO
AUG	23	12.35 → VIR
SEP	23	09.50 → LIB
OCT	23	18.44 → SCO
NOV	22	15.55 → SAG
DEC	22	05.03 → CAP

MERCURY

mth	dy	time → sign
JAN	1	00.00 → SAG
JAN	14	03.04 → CAP
FEB	5	09.20 → AQU
FEB	23	11.26 → PIS
MAR	11	06.45 → ARI
MAY	16	15.21 → TAU
JUN	4	10.30 → GEM
JUN	18	12.27 → CAN
JUL	3	15.39 → LEO
JUL	26	14.48 → VIR
AUG	17	08.35 → LEO
SEP	10	07.20 → VIR
SEP	27	12.08 → LIB
OCT	15	00.13 → SCO
NOV	3	23.06 → SAG

VENUS

mth	dy	time → sign
JAN	1	00.00 → AQU
JAN	5	19.18 → PIS
FEB	2	08.07 → ARI
MAR	11	11.17 → TAU
APR	7	19.15 → ARI
JUN	4	22.57 → TAU
JUL	7	16.20 → GEM
AUG	4	10.59 → CAN
AUG	30	13.05 → LEO
SEP	24	16.06 → VIR
OCT	19	04.09 → LIB
NOV	12	07.05 → SCO
DEC	6	05.22 → SAG
DEC	30	01.56 → CAP

MARS

mth	dy	time → sign
JAN	1	00.00 → SAG
JAN	5	19.34 → CAP
FEB	14	09.53 → AQU
MAR	25	03.41 → PIS
MAY	2	20.28 → ARI
JUN	11	11.57 → TAU
JUL	23	08.48 → GEM
SEP	7	20.54 → CAN
NOV	11	21.03 → LEO
DEC	26	15.14 → CAN

SATURN

mth	dy	time → sign
JAN	1	00.00 → CAN

JUPITER

mth	dy	time → sign
JAN	1	00.00 → VIR
AUG	25	06.26 → LIB

MOON

dy	jan	feb	mar	apr	may	jun	jul	aug	sep	oct	nov	dec	dy
1	LEO	12.46	LIB	SCO	19.40	AQU	PIS	TAU	CAN	LEO	10.08	04.43	1
2	16.49	LIB	LIB	03.08	CAP	15.25	00.28	11.23	CAN	17.34	LIB	SCO	2
3	VIR	LIB	08.32	SAG	CAP	PIS	ARI	GEM	03.19	VIR	22.28	17.30	3
4	VIR	01.22	SCO	13.51	04.06	18.51	03.04	15.23	LEO	VIR	SCO	SAG	4
5	04.44	SCO	20.45	CAP	AQU	ARI	TAU	CAN	11.36	04.16	SCO	SAG	5
6	LIB	12.57	SAG	21.28	09.21	20.23	05.20	20.52	VIR	LIB	11.18	05.23	6
7	17.13	SAG	SAG	AQU	PIS	TAU	GEM	LEO	21.48	16.24	SAG	CAP	7
8	SCO	21.28	06.37	AQU	11.25	21.15	08.10	LEO	LIB	SCO	23.35	15.34	8
9	SCO	CAP	CAP	01.10	ARI	GEM	CAN	04.24	LIB	SCO	CAP	AQU	9
10	03.55	CAP	12.40	PIS	11.24	23.02	12.43	VIR	09.48	05.17	CAP	23.20	10
11	SAG	02.12	AQU	01.38	TAU	CAN	LEO	14.21	SCO	SAG	09.59	PIS	11
12	11.28	AQU	14.50	ARI	11.12	CAN	19.58	LIB	22.37	17.33	AQU	PIS	12
13	CAP	03.52	PIS	00.40	GEM	03.20	VIR	LIB	SAG	CAP	17.05	04.15	13
14	15.57	PIS	14.32	TAU	12.51	LEO	VIR	02.24	SAG	CAP	PIS	ARI	14
15	AQU	04.12	ARI	00.31	CAN	11.07	06.13	SCO	10.11	03.07	20.24	06.30	15
16	18.27	ARI	13.54	GEM	17.57	VIR	LIB	14.56	CAP	AQU	ARI	TAU	16
17	PIS	05.05	TAU	03.13	LEO	22.06	18.28	SAG	18.19	08.34	20.48	07.03	17
18	20.21	TAU	15.04	CAN	LEO	LIB	SCO	SAG	AQU	PIS	TAU	GEM	18
19	ARI	08.01	GEM	09.52	02.56	LIB	SCO	01.31	22.19	10.09	20.02	07.27	19
20	22.48	GEM	19.31	LEO	VIR	10.36	06.36	CAP	PIS	ARI	GEM	CAN	20
21	TAU	13.42	CAN	20.03	14.43	SCO	SAG	08.32	09.30	TAU	20.14	09.30	21
22	TAU	CAN	CAN	VIR	LIB	22.27	16.28	AQU	ARI	TAU	CAN	LEO	22
23	02.35	21.58	03.32	VIR	LIB	SAG	CAP	12.05	22.53	08.49	23.12	14.44	23
24	GEM	LEO	LEO	08.15	03.21	SAG	23.16	PIS	TAU	GEM	LEO	VIR	24
25	08.05	LEO	14.11	LIB	SCO	08.14	AQU	13.30	23.32	10.11	LEO	23.45	25
26	CAN	08.13	VIR	20.52	15.11	CAP	AQU	ARI	GEM	CAN	05.59	LIB	26
27	15.33	VIR	VIR	SCO	SAG	15.36	03.26	14.34	GEM	14.55	VIR	LIB	27
28	LEO	19.57	02.15	SCO	SAG	AQU	PIS	TAU	02.38	LEO	16.18	11.43	28
29	LEO		LIB	08.56	01.24	20.51	06.07	16.47	CAN	23.12	LIB	SCO	29
30	01.09		14.50	SAG	CAP	PIS	ARI	GEM	08.47	VIR	LIB	SCO	30
31	VIR		SCO		09.35		08.28	21.00		VIR		00.32	31

SUN

mth	dy	time → sign
JAN	1	00.00 → CAP
JAN	20	15.45 → AQU
FEB	19	06.08 → PIS
MAR	21	05.32 → ARI
APR	20	17.02 → TAU
MAY	21	16.34 → GEM
JUN	22	00.44 → CAN
JUL	23	11.37 → LEO
AUG	23	18.26 → VIR
SEP	23	15.41 → LIB
OCT	24	00.35 → SCO
NOV	22	21.46 → SAG
DEC	22	10.54 → CAP

MERCURY

mth	dy	time → sign
JAN	1	00.00 → SAG
JAN	9	14.10 → CAP
JAN	29	07.22 → AQU
FEB	15	15.43 → PIS
MAR	4	09.27 → ARI
APR	1	18.16 → PIS
APR	16	14.54 → ARI
MAY	11	14.29 → TAU
MAY	27	04.13 → GEM
JUN	10	02.00 → CAN
JUN	27	19.07 → LEO
SEP	3	16.29 → VIR
SEP	19	14.34 → LIB
OCT	7	21.21 → SCO
OCT	30	11.23 → SAG
NOV	20	20.16 → SCO
DEC	13	00.03 → SAG

VENUS

mth	dy	time → sign
JAN	1	00.00 → CAP
JAN	22	22.29 → AQU
FEB	15	20.12 → PIS
MAR	11	20.32 → ARI
APR	5	01.01 → TAU
APR	29	10.59 → GEM
MAY	24	03.40 → CAN
JUN	18	05.00 → LEO
JUL	13	19.22 → VIR
AUG	9	08.35 → LIB
SEP	7	00.16 → SCO
OCT	16	10.45 → SAG
NOV	8	08.56 → SCO

MARS

mth	dy	time → sign
JAN	1	00.00 → CAN
APR	22	19.40 → LEO
JUN	20	08.38 → VIR
AUG	9	13.17 → LIB
SEP	24	16.31 → SCO
NOV	6	18.18 → SAG
DEC	17	10.52 → CAP

SATURN

mth	dy	time → sign
JAN	1	00.00 → CAN
AUG	2	14.31 → LEO

JUPITER

mth	dy	time → sign
JAN	1	00.00 → LIB
SEP	25	10.28 → SCO

MOON

dy	jan	feb	mar	apr	may	jun	jul	aug	sep	oct	nov	dec	dy
1	SAG	05.23	AQU	09.16	TAU	06.29	LEO	12.05	SCO	SAG	10.36	04.30	1
2	12.11	AQU	20.25	ARI	20.03	CAN	20.45	LIB	17.31	14.29	AQU	PIS	2
3	CAP	11.32	PIS	09.56	GEM	07.39	VIR	21.23	SAG	CAP	20.32	12.05	3
4	21.38	PIS	23.23	TAU	20.23	LEO	VIR	SCO	SAG	CAP	PIS	ARI	4
5	AQU	15.38	ARI	10.25	CAN	11.57	03.21	SCO	06.24	02.27	PIS	15.48	5
6	AQU	ARI	ARI	GEM	23.04	VIR	LIB	09.36	CAP	AQU	03.29	TAU	6
7	04.47	18.47	01.08	12.21	LEO	19.57	13.41	SAG	17.41	ARI	11.09	16.30	7
8	PIS	TAU	TAU	CAN	LEO	LIB	SCO	22.23	AQU	PIS	04.49	GEM	8
9	09.56	21.45	03.12	16.37	04.57	LIB	SCO	CAP	AQU	16.05	TAU	15.50	9
10	ARI	GEM	GEM	LEO	VIR	07.04	02.20	CAP	01.46	ARI	O5.07	CAN	10
11	13.25	GEM	06.29	23.20	13.53	SCO	SAG	09.23	PIS	18.20	GEM	15.46	11
12	TAU	00.59	CAN	VIR	LIB	19.50	15.05	AQU	06.49	TAU	05.15	LEO	12
13	15.42	CAN	11.14	VIR	LIB	SAG	CAP	17.41	ARI	19.37	CAN	18.09	13
14	GEM	04.50	LEO	08.13	01.08	SAG	PIS	PIS	10.03	GEM	06.53	VIR	14
15	17.32	LEO	17.32	LIB	SCO	08.39	02.17	23.37	TAU	21.23	LEO	VIR	15
16	CAN	10.03	VIR	19.03	13.46	CAP	AQU	ARI	12.45	CAN	11.05	00.07	16
17	20.04	VIR	VIR	SCO	SAG	20.16	11.15	ARI	GEM	CAN	VIR	LIB	17
18	LEO	17.36	01.40	SCO	SAG	AQU	PIS	03.59	15.42	00.35	18.12	09.43	18
19	LEO	LIB	LIB	07.30	02.42	AQU	17.59	TAU	CAN	LEO	LIB	SCO	19
20	00.40	LIB	12.04	SAG	CAP	05.43	ARI	07.22	19.13	05.35	LIB	21.48	20
21	VIR	04.05	SCO	20.29	14.31	PIS	22.35	GEM	LEO	VIR	03.58	SAG	21
22	08.31	SCO	SCO	CAP	AQU	12.19	TAU	10.06	23.38	12.33	SCO	SAG	22
23	LIB	16.41	00.30	CAP	23.39	ARI	TAU	CAN	VIR	LIB	15.44	10.50	23
24	19.40	SAG	SAG	07.56	PIS	15.56	01.18	12.38	VIR	21.41	SAG	CAP	24
25	SCO	SAG	13.18	AQU	PIS	TAU	GEM	LEO	O5.40	SCO	SAG	23.29	25
26	SCO	05.01	CAP	15.54	05.05	17.07	02.44	15.54	LIB	SCO	04.40	AQU	26
27	08.27	CAP	23.51	PIS	ARI	GEM	CAN	VIR	14.12	09.03	CAP	AQU	27
28	SAG	14.34	AQU	19.45	07.03	17.10	03.57	21.15	SCO	SAG	17.30	10.43	28
29	20.18		AQU	ARI	TAU	CAN	LEO	LIB	SCO	21.59	AQU	PIS	29
30	CAP		06.26	20.31	06.54	17.47	06.32	LIB	01.32	CAP	AQU	19.31	30
31	CAP		PIS		GEM		VIR	05.49		CAP		ARI	31

SUN

mth	dy	time → sign
JAN	1	00.00 → CAP
JAN	20	21.31 → AQU
FEB	19	11.52 → PIS
MAR	21	11.13 → ARI
APR	20	22.39 → TAU
MAY	21	22.09 → GEM
JUN	22	06.19 → CAN
JUL	23	17.14 → LEO
AUG	24	00.09 → VIR
SEP	23	21.29 → LIB
OCT	24	06.26 → SCO
NOV	23	03.38 → SAG
DEC	22	16.43 → CAP

MERCURY

mth	dy	time → sign
JAN	1	00.00 → SAG
JAN	3	01.46 → CAP
JAN	21	21.06 → AQU
FEB	8	01.32 → PIS
APR	16	04.31 → ARI
MAY	4	06.03 → TAU
MAY	18	13.33 → GEM
JUN	2	13.40 → CAN
AUG	10	17.40 → LEO
AUG	26	14.50 → VIR
SEP	11	20.54 → LIB
OCT	1	15.26 → SCO
DEC	7	12.32 → SAG
DEC	26	23.18 → CAP

VENUS

mth	dy	time → sign
JAN	1	00.00 → SCO
JAN	5	16.45 → SAG
FEB	6	05.41 → CAP
MAR	5	05.09 → AQU
MAR	30	22.15 → PIS
APR	25	03.03 → ARI
MAY	20	02.06 → TAU
JUN	13	21.35 → GEM
JUL	8	13.30 → CAN
AUG	2	01.06 → LEO
AUG	26	08.17 → VIR
SEP	19	12.01 → LIB
OCT	13	13.49 → SCO
NOV	6	14.59 → SAG
NOV	30	16.23 → CAP
DEC	24	19.13 → AQU

MARS

mth	dy	time → sign
JAN	1	00.00 → CAP
JAN	25	11.41 → AQU
MAR	4	16.47 → PIS
APR	11	23.19 → ARI
MAY	21	03.44 → TAU
JUL	1	03.34 → GEM
AUG	13	21.21 → CAN
OCT	1	02.38 → LEO
DEC	1	11.41 → VIR

SATURN

mth	dy	time → sign
JAN	1	00.00 → LEO

JUPITER

mth	dy	time → sign
JAN	1	00.00 → SCO
OCT	24	03.10 → SAG

MOON

dy	jan	feb	mar	apr	may	jun	jul	aug	sep	oct	nov	dec	dy
1	ARI	GEM	20.59	LEO	19.24	SCO	SAG	07.50	PIS	ARI	GEM	CAN	1
2	01.06	13.38	CAN	08.30	LIB	18.54	13.03	AQU	12.02	02.15	17.32	02.30	2
3	TAU	CAN	23.00	VIR	LIB	SAG	CAP	19.49	ARI	TAU	CAN	LEO	3
4	03.26	14.01	LEO	12.39	02.35	SAG	CAP	PIS	20.10	07.44	20.03	04.23	4
5	GEM	LEO	LEO	LIB	SCO	06.51	01.50	PIS	TAU	GEM	LEO	VIR	5
6	03.28	14.42	00.46	18.56	12.09	CAP	AQU	06.20	TAU	11.47	22.55	08.14	6
7	CAN	VIR	VIR	SCO	SAG	19.38	14.03	ARI	02.18	CAN	VIR	LIB	7
8	02.53	17.39	03.51	SCO	23.55	AQU	PIS	14.43	GEM	14.41	VIR	14.24	8
9	LEO	LIB	LIB	04.12	CAP	AQU	PIS	TAU	06.12	LEO	02.42	SCO	9
10	03.45	LIB	09.51	SAG	CAP	07.47	00.34	20.17	CAN	16.57	LIB	22.49	10
11	VIR	00.28	SCO	16.08	12.41	PIS	ARI	GEM	08.03	VIR	08.02	SAG	11
12	07.54	SCO	19.34	CAP	AQU	17.34	08.12	22.49	LEO	19.31	SCO	SAG	12
13	LIB	11.15	SAG	CAP	AQU	ARI	TAU	CAN	08.51	LIB	15.33	09.14	13
14	16.15	SAG	SAG	04.51	00.20	23.45	12.16	23.06	VIR	23.45	SAG	CAP	14
15	SCO	SAG	08.00	AQU	PIS	TAU	GEM	LEO	10.16	SCO	SAG	21.16	15
16	SCO	00.12	CAP	15.47	08.56	TAU	13.14	22.49	LIB	SCO	01.37	AQU	16
17	04.03	CAP	20.35	PIS	ARI	02.23	CAN	VIR	14.11	06.53	CAP	AQU	17
18	SAG	12.38	AQU	23.25	13.51	GEM	12.34	VIR	SCO	13.45	09.59	18
19	17.10	AQU	AQU	ARI	TAU	02.32	LEO	00.04	21.49	17.14	AQU	PIS	19
20	CAP	22.57	06.57	ARI	15.51	CAN	12.19	LIB	SAG	CAP	AQU	21.37	20
21	CAP	PIS	PIS	03.56	GEM	02.06	VIR	04.44	SAG	CAP	02.16	ARI	21
22	05.37	PIS	14.23	TAU	16.27	LEO	14.33	SCO	08.58	05.39	PIS	ARI	22
23	AQU	06.57	ARI	06.27	CAN	03.01	LIB	13.34	CAP	AQU	12.53	06.11	23
24	16.23	ARI	19.29	GEM	17.18	VIR	20.41	SAG	21.38	17.45	ARI	TAU	24
25	PIS	13.08	TAU	08.22	LEO	06.51	SCO	SAG	AQU	PIS	20.06	10.47	25
26	PIS	TAU	23.16	CAN	19.50	LIB	SCO	01.31	AQU	PIS	TAU	GEM	26
27	01.10	17.47	GEM	10.44	VIR	14.17	06.40	CAP	09.24	03.31	23.55	12.03	27
28	ARI	GEM	GEM	LEO	VIR	SCO	SAG	14.18	PIS	ARI	GEM	CAN	28
29	07.45		02.26	14.15	00.54	SCO	19.01	AQU	18.58	10.16	GEM	11.41	29
30	TAU		CAN	VIR	LIB	00.46	CAP	AQU	ARI	TAU	01.31	LEO	30
31	11.52		05.22		08.42		CAP	02.03		14.36		11.47	31

SUN

mth	dy	time → sign
JAN	1	00.00 → CAP
JAN	21	03.17 → AQU
FEB	19	17.36 → PIS
MAR	20	16.57 → ARI
APR	20	04.25 → TAU
MAY	21	03.57 → GEM
JUN	21	12.11 → CAN
JUL	22	23.08 → LEO
AUG	23	06.03 → VIR
SEP	23	03.22 → LIB
OCT	23	12.17 → SCO
NOV	22	09.29 → SAG
DEC	21	22.33 → CAP

MERCURY

mth	dy	time → sign
JAN	1	00.00 → CAP
JAN	14	10.06 → AQU
FEB	2	00.47 → PIS
FEB	20	11.05 → AQU
MAR	18	08.14 → PIS
APR	9	02.26 → ARI
APR	25	01.38 → TAU
MAY	9	04.38 → GEM
MAY	28	10.50 → CAN
JUN	28	17.57 → GEM
JUL	11	20.56 → CAN
AUG	2	13.54 → LEO
AUG	17	08.44 → VIR
SEP	3	15.47 → LIB
SEP	27	07.19 → SCO
OCT	17	03.33 → LIB
NOV	10	02.19 → SCO
NOV	29	15.09 → SAG
DEC	18	16.47 → CAP

VENUS

mth	dy	time → sign
JAN	1	00.00 → AQU
JAN	18	02.14 → PIS
FEB	11	18.51 → ARI
MAR	8	07.00 → TAU
APR	4	12.40 → GEM
MAY	7	08.26 → CAN
JUN	29	07.58 → GEM
AUG	3	02.14 → CAN
SEP	8	13.40 → LEO
OCT	6	12.25 → VIR
NOV	1	06.42 → LIB
NOV	26	00.55 → SCO
DEC	20	07.28 → SAG

MARS

mth	dy	time → sign
JAN	1	00.00 → VIR
FEB	12	10.19 → LEO
MAY	18	20.51 → VIR
JUL	17	05.38 → LIB
SEP	3	13.52 → SCO
OCT	17	05.39 → SAG
NOV	26	21.57 → CAP

SATURN

mth	dy	time → sign
JAN	1	00.00 → LEO
SEP	19	04.23 → VIR

JUPITER

mth	dy	time → sign
JAN	1	00.00 → SAG
NOV	15	10.27 → CAP

MOON

dy	jan	feb	mar	apr	may	jun	jul	aug	sep	oct	nov	dec	dy
1	VIR	02.26	17.41	CAP	AQU	15.55	10.40	GEM	LEO	VIR	SCO	SAG	1
2	14.10	SCO	SAG	23.17	19.44	ARI	TAU	07.20	18.20	04.30	18.10	09.16	2
3	LIB	10.26	SAG	AQU	PIS	ARI	17.48	CAN	VIR	LIB	SAG	CAP	3
4	19.51	SAG	03.50	AQU	PIS	01.43	GEM	08.13	17.35	04.58	23.39	17.32	4
5	SCO	21.30	CAP	11.56	07.28	TAU	21.07	LEO	LIB	SCO	CAP	AQU	5
6	SCO	CAP	16.14	PIS	ARI	08.06	CAN	18.34	07.55	CAP	AQU		6
7	04.40	CAP	AQU	23.28	16.48	GEM	21.53	VIR	SCO	SAG	08.41	04.46	7
8	SAG	09.59	AQU	ARI	TAU	11.28	LEO	07.30	22.52	14.31	AQU	PIS	8
9	15.41	AQU	04.53	ARI	23.20	CAN	22.03	LIB	SAG	CAP	20.34	17.30	9
10	CAP	22.36	PIS	08.58	GEM	13.11	VIR	09.56	SAG	CAP	PIS	ARI	10
11	CAP	PIS	16.33	TAU	GEM	LEO	23.31	SCO	06.56	00.42	PIS	ARI	11
12	03.54	PIS	ARI	16.20	03.38	14.49	LIB	15.49	CAP	AQU	09.12	05.09	12
13	AQU	10.36	ARI	GEM	CAN	VIR	LIB	SAG	17.58	13.03	ARI	TAU	13
14	16.35	ARI	02.40	21.41	06.39	17.33	03.28	SAG	AQU	PIS	20.24	13.44	14
15	PIS	21.08	TAU	CAN	LEO	LIB	SCO	00.51	AQU	PIS	TAU	GEM	15
16	PIS	TAU	10.45	CAN	09.14	22.03	10.11	CAP	06.26	01.36	TAU	19.01	16
17	04.44	TAU	GEM	01.16	VIR	SCO	SAG	12.02	PIS	ARI	05.02	CAN	17
18	ARI	04.56	16.14	LEO	12.07	SCO	19.13	AQU	19.02	12.54	GEM	22.03	18
19	14.42	GEM	CAN	03.30	LIB	04.28	CAP	AQU	ARI	TAU	11.11	LEO	19
20	TAU	09.09	18.58	VIR	15.56	SAG	CAP	00.23	ARI	22.15	CAN	LEO	20
21	21.01	CAN	LEO	05.16	SCO	12.51	06.02	PIS	06.45	GEM	15.32	00.19	21
22	GEM	10.07	19.42	LIB	21.22	CAP	AQU	13.05	TAU	GEM	LEO	VIR	22
23	23.23	LEO	VIR	07.49	SAG	23.15	18.13	ARI	16.40	05.21	18.48	02.59	23
24	CAN	09.22	20.01	SCO	SAG	AQU	PIS	ARI	GEM	CAN	VIR	LIB	24
25	23.00	VIR	LIB	12.31	05.08	AQU	PIS	01.03	23.46	10.10	21.33	06.39	25
26	LEO	09.05	21.49	SAG	CAP	11.23	06.57	TAU	CAN	LEO	LIB	SCO	26
27	21.56	LIB	SCO	20.21	15.31	PIS	ARI	10.40	CAN	12.53	LIB	11.29	27
28	VIR	11.24	SCO	CAP	AQU	23.56	18.34	GEM	03.35	VIR	00.19	SAG	28
29	22.29	SCO	02.46	CAP	AQU	ARI	TAU	16.34	LEO	14.16	SCO	17.47	29
30	LIB		SAG	07.16	03.46	ARI	TAU	CAN	LEO	LIB	03.52	CAP	30
31	LIB		11.34		PIS		03.01	18.41		15.31		CAP	31

SUN

mth	dy	time → sign
JAN	1	00.00 → CAP
JAN	20	09.09 → AQU
FEB	18	23.27 → PIS
MAR	20	22.48 → ARI
APR	20	10.18 → TAU
MAY	21	09.50 → GEM
JUN	21	18.03 → CAN
JUL	23	04.57 → LEO
AUG	23	11.48 → VIR
SEP	23	09.06 → LIB
OCT	23	18.03 → SCO
NOV	22	15.16 → SAG
DEC	22	04.23 → CAP

MERCURY

mth	dy	time → sign
JAN	1	00.00 → CAP
JAN	6	08.53 → AQU
MAR	14	09.52 → PIS
APR	1	16.02 → ARI
APR	16	14.55 → TAU
MAY	2	02.19 → GEM
JUL	10	03.19 → CAN
JUL	25	05.20 → LEO
AUG	9	09.04 → VIR
AUG	28	15.48 → LIB
NOV	3	18.58 → SCO
NOV	22	09.07 → SAG
DEC	11	13.37 → CAP

VENUS

mth	dy	time → sign
JAN	1	00.00 → SAG
JAN	13	09.01 → CAP
FEB	6	09.06 → AQU
MAR	2	09.38 → PIS
MAR	26	11.54 → ARI
APR	19	16.44 → TAU
MAY	14	00.26 → GEM
JUN	7	10.47 → CAN
JUL	1	23.41 → LEO
JUL	26	15.44 → VIR
AUG	20	12.39 → LIB
SEP	14	17.12 → SCO
OCT	10	10.18 → SAG
NOV	6	04.53 → CAP
DEC	6	06.06 → AQU

MARS

mth	dy	time → sign
JAN	1	00.00 → CAP
JAN	4	17.50 → AQU
FEB	11	18.16 → PIS
MAR	21	22.02 → ARI
APR	30	02.33 → TAU
JUN	10	00.49 → GEM
JUL	23	05.54 → CAN
SEP	7	04.55 → LEO
OCT	27	00.58 → VIR
DEC	26	05.20 → LIB

SATURN

mth	dy	time → sign
JAN	1	00.00 → VIR
APR	3	03.44 → LEO
MAY	29	12.49 → VIR

JUPITER

mth	dy	time → sign
JAN	1	00.00 → CAP
APR	12	19.24 → AQU
JUN	27	18.37 → CAP
NOV	30	20.18 → AQU

MOON

dy	jan	feb	mar	apr	may	jun	jul	aug	sep	oct	nov	dec	dy
1	02.07	PIS	15.35	TAU	GEM	00.35	VIR	SCO	12.05	01.13	PIS	ARI	1
2	AQU	09.04	ARI	22.03	12.43	LEO	13.22	SCO	CAP	AQU	05.34	01.22	2
3	12.58	ARI	ARI	GEM	CAN	04.53	LIB	01.25	19.37	11.19	ARI	TAU	3
4	PIS	21.57	04.33	GEM	19.11	VIR	16.22	SAG	AQU	PIS	18.37	13.28	4
5	PIS	TAU	TAU	07.10	LEO	07.57	SCO	06.35	AQU	23.27	TAU	GEM	5
6	01.40	TAU	16.05	CAN	23.11	LIB	19.45	CAP	05.26	ARI	TAU	23.31	6
7	ARI	08.40	GEM	12.59	VIR	10.13	SAG	13.34	PIS	ARI	06.55	CAN	7
8	14.03	GEM	GEM	LEO	VIR	SCO	SAG	AQU	17.13	12.26	GEM	CAN	8
9	TAU	15.22	00.21	15.32	01.07	12.23	00.02	22.45	ARI	TAU	17.35	07.27	9
10	23.31	CAN	CAN	VIR	LIB	SAG	CAP	PIS	ARI	TAU	CAN	LEO	10
11	GEM	18.00	04.33	15.48	01.54	15.40	06.09	PIS	06.12	01.02	CAN	13.31	11
12	GEM	LEO	LEO	LIB	SCO	CAP	AQU	10.20	TAU	GEM	02.00	VIR	12
13	04.57	18.05	05.24	15.27	02.57	21.26	15.01	ARI	18.47	11.51	LEO	17.45	13
14	CAN	VIR	VIR	SCO	SAG	AQU	PIS	23.18	GEM	CAN	07.42	LIB	14
15	07.08	17.44	04.40	16.23	05.57	AQU	PIS	TAU	GEM	19.35	VIR	20.13	15
16	LEO	LIB	LIB	SAG	CAP	06.38	02.43	TAU	04.51	LEO	10.35	SCO	16
17	07.52	18.53	04.25	20.16	12.19	PIS	ARI	11.23	CAN	23.42	LIB	21.32	17
18	VIR	SCO	SCO	CAP	AQU	18.45	15.35	GEM	11.04	LIB	11.18	SAG	18
19	09.03	22.49	06.30	CAP	22.26	ARI	TAU	20.15	LEO	VIR	SCO	23.00	19
20	LIB	SAG	SAG	03.59	PIS	ARI	TAU	CAN	13.34	00.48	11.15	CAP	20
21	11.59	SAG	12.04	AQU	PIS	07.30	02.57	CAN	VIR	LIB	SAG	CAP	21
22	SCO	05.50	CAP	15.08	11.02	TAU	GEM	01.07	13.41	00.18	12.19	02.24	22
23	17.09	CAP	21.10	PIS	ARI	18.20	10.52	LEO	LIB	SCO	CAP	AQU	23
24	SAG	15.26	AQU	PIS	23.42	GEM	CAN	02.55	13.20	00.08	16.24	09.20	24
25	SAG	AQU	AQU	04.01	TAU	GEM	15.19	VIR	SCO	SAG	AQU	PIS	25
26	00.21	AQU	08.50	ARI	TAU	02.01	LEO	03.24	14.21	02.10	AQU	20.05	26
27	CAP	02.54	PIS	16.41	10.27	CAN	17.35	LIB	SAG	CAP	00.35	ARI	27
28	09.26	PIS	21.41	TAU	GEM	07.00	VIR	04.19	18.07	07.50	PIS	ARI	28
29	AQU		ARI	TAU	18.38	LEO	19.20	SCO	CAP	AQU	12.18	08.58	29
30	20.26		ARI	03.48	CAN	10.27	LIB	07.00	CAP	17.21	ARI	TAU	30
31	PIS		10.29		CAN		21.44	SAG		PIS		21.13	31

SUN

mth	dy	time → sign
JAN	1	00.00 → CAP
JAN	20	15.00 → AQU
FEB	19	05.17 → PIS
MAR	21	04.34 → ARI
APR	20	15.59 → TAU
MAY	21	15.27 → GEM
JUN	21	23.36 → CAN
JUL	23	10.30 → LEO
AUG	23	17.20 → VIR
SEP	23	14.44 → LIB
OCT	23	23.45 → SCO
NOV	22	21.02 → SAG
DEC	22	10.14 → CAP

MERCURY

mth	dy	time → sign
JAN	1	12.40 → AQU
JAN	15	07.34 → CAP
FEB	14	19.12 → AQU
MAR	7	22.05 → PIS
MAR	24	15.52 → ARI
APR	8	11.13 → TAU
JUN	14	14.33 → GEM
JUL	2	14.57 → CAN
JUL	16	17.08 → LEO
AUG	2	02.44 → VIR
AUG	27	14.17 → LIB
SEP	10	19.15 → VIR
OCT	9	14.40 → LIB
OCT	27	10.36 → SCO
NOV	15	03.10 → SAG
DEC	5	01.57 → CAP

VENUS

mth	dy	time → sign
JAN	1	00.00 → AQU
APR	6	15.13 → PIS
MAY	5	19.19 → ARI
JUN	1	14.19 → TAU
JUN	27	10.45 → GEM
JUL	22	17.50 → CAN
AUG	16	14.18 → LEO
SEP	10	01.37 → VIR
OCT	4	05.51 → LIB
OCT	28	05.33 → SCO
NOV	21	03.03 → SAG
DEC	14	23.54 → CAP

MARS

mth	dy	time → sign
JAN	1	00.00 → LIB
MAR	28	11.09 → VIR
JUN	11	20.18 → LIB
AUG	10	16.42 → SCO
SEP	25	19.45 → SAG
NOV	6	06.40 → CAP
DEC	15	08.47 → AQU

SATURN

mth	dy	time → sign
JAN	1	00.00 → VIR
NOV	20	15.45 → LIB

JUPITER

mth	dy	time → sign
JAN	1	00.00 → AQU
APR	15	08.51 → PIS
SEP	15	02.25 → AQU
DEC	1	19.48 → PIS

MOON

dy	jan	feb	mar	apr	may	jun	jul	aug	sep	oct	nov	dec	dy
1	GEM	22.34	08.30	VIR	11.37	21.27	09.19	PIS	02.19	GEM	CAN	21.53	1
2	GEM	LEO	LEO	00.40	SCO	CAP	AQU	07.03	TAU	GEM	05.38	VIR	2
3	06.56	LEO	12.25	LIB	10.50	23.18	13.51	ARI	14.45	LEO	10.59	VIR	3
4	CAN	02.37	VIR	00.34	SAG	AQU	PIS	18.06	GEM	CAN	14.21	04.29	4
5	13.58	VIR	14.00	SCO	11.08	AQU	22.25	TAU	GEM	21.40	VIR	LIB	5
6	LEO	05.19	LIB	00.37	CAP	04.57	ARI	TAU	LEO	19.10	SCO	07.19	6
7	19.06	LIB	14.55	SAG	14.22	PIS	ARI	06.44	CAN	LEO	LIB	SCO	7
8	VIR	07.50	SCO	02.29	AQU	14.44	10.13	GEM	12.34	04.54	20.29	07.17	8
9	23.08	SCO	16.37	CAP	21.34	ARI	TAU	18.27	LEO	VIR	SCO	SAG	9
10	LIB	10.51	SAG	07.25	PIS	ARI	23.02	CAN	18.55	08.29	19.51	06.16	10
11	LIB	SAG	20.07	AQU	PIS	03.12	GEM	CAN	VIR	LIB	SAG	CAP	11
12	02.28	14.45	CAP	15.38	08.18	TAU	GEM	03.36	22.28	09.31	19.25	06.34	12
13	SCO	CAP	CAP	PIS	ARI	16.05	10.33	LEO	LIB	SCO	CAP	AQU	13
14	05.16	19.57	01.52	PIS	20.59	GEM	CAN	10.03	LIB	09.44	21.14	10.10	14
15	SAG	AQU	AQU	02.32	TAU	GEM	19.52	VIR	00.27	SAG	AQU	PIS	15
16	08.06	AQU	09.59	ARI	TAU	03.45	LEO	14.31	SCO	10.55	AQU	17.58	16
17	CAP	03.11	PIS	15.00	09.52	CAN	LEO	LIB	02.12	CAP	02.38	ARI	17
18	12.07	PIS	20.21	TAU	GEM	13.37	03.05	17.49	SAG	14.27	PIS	ARI	18
19	AQU	13.01	ARI	TAU	21.50	LEO	VIR	SCO	04.49	AQU	11.39	05.09	19
20	18.41	ARI	ARI	03.54	CAN	21.31	08.34	20.36	CAP	20.53	ARI	TAU	20
21	PIS	ARI	08.32	GEM	CAN	VIR	LIB	SAG	08.59	PIS	23.08	17.49	21
22	PIS	01.12	TAU	16.02	08.06	VIR	12.27	23.23	AQU	PIS	TAU	GEM	22
23	04.37	TAU	21.28	CAN	LEO	03.09	SCO	CAP	15.09	05.59	TAU	GEM	23
24	ARI	14.03	GEM	CAN	15.50	LIB	14.55	CAP	PIS	ARI	11.38	06.18	24
25	17.08	GEM	GEM	01.51	VIR	06.19	SAG	02.53	23.32	17.03	GEM	CAN	25
26	TAU	GEM	09.17	LEO	20.26	SCO	16.39	AQU	ARI	TAU	GEM	17.45	26
27	TAU	01.03	CAN	08.30	LIB	07.26	CAP	08.02	ARI	TAU	00.13	LEO	27
28	05.43	CAN	18.04	VIR	22.01	SAG	18.55	PIS	10.08	CAN	05.22	LEO	28
29	GEM		LEO	11.25	SCO	07.48	AQU	15.44	TAU	GEM	12.02	03.41	29
30	15.50		23.01	LIB	21.43	CAP	23.19	ARI	22.26	18.03	LEO	VIR	30
31	CAN		VIR		SAG		PIS	ARI		CAN		11.20	31

SUN

mth	dy	time → sign
JAN	1	00.00 → CAP
JAN	20	20.52 → AQU
FEB	19	11.11 → PIS
MAR	21	10.26 → ARI
APR	20	20.48 → TAU
MAY	21	21.15 → GEM
JUN	22	05.25 → CAN
JUL	23	16.21 → LEO
AUG	23	23.16 → VIR
SEP	23	20.37 → LIB
OCT	24	05.36 → SCO
NOV	23	02.51 → SAG
DEC	22	16.00 → CAP

MERCURY

mth	dy	time → sign
JAN	1	00.00 → CAP
FEB	9	17.50 → AQU
FEB	28	13.04 → PIS
MAR	16	11.53 → ARI
APR	2	03.27 → TAU
MAY	1	21.25 → ARI
MAY	15	01.40 → TAU
JUN	9	08.43 → GEM
JUN	24	03.13 → CAN
JUL	8	13.40 → LEO
JUL	27	15.24 → VIR
OCT	2	14.25 → LIB
OCT	19	21.53 → SCO
NOV	8	04.59 → SAG
DEC	1	20.41 → CAP
DEC	12	12.40 → SAG

VENUS

mth	dy	time → sign
JAN	1	00.00 → CAP
JAN	7	21.11 → AQU
JAN	31	20.14 → PIS
FEB	24	23.27 → ARI
MAR	21	10.06 → TAU
APR	15	08.33 → GEM
MAY	11	01.42 → CAN
JUN	7	05.11 → LEO
JUL	8	04.54 → VIR
NOV	9	18.48 → LIB
DEC	8	00.20 → SCO

MARS

mth	dy	time → sign
JAN	1	00.00 → AQU
JAN	22	13.08 → PIS
MAR	1	22.13 → ARI
APR	10	09.37 → TAU
MAY	21	15.23 → GEM
JUL	3	23.42 → CAN
AUG	18	10.48 → LEO
OCT	5	00.20 → VIR
NOV	24	06.14 → LIB

SATURN

mth	dy	time → sign
JAN	1	00.00 → LIB
MAR	7	12.13 → VIR
AUG	13	16.36 → LIB

JUPITER

mth	dy	time → sign
JAN	1	00.00 → PIS
APR	21	14.42 → ARI

MOON

dy	jan	feb	mar	apr	may	jun	jul	aug	sep	oct	nov	dec	dy
1	LIB	01.16	SAG	AQU	PIS	02.33	GEM	CAN	VIR	LIB	05.20	CAP	1
2	15.58	SAG	09.29	22.44	11.26	TAU	GEM	03.07	VIR	18.23	SAG	15.45	2
3	SCO	02.52	CAP	PIS	ARI	14.03	GEM	LEO	05.32	SCO	06.40	AQU	3
4	17.38	CAP	12.11	PIS	20.46	GEM	CAN	14.18	LIB	21.48	CAP	18.08	4
5	SAG	04.04	AQU	05.16	TAU	GEM	21.00	VIR	11.49	SAG	08.43	PIS	5
6	17.32	AQU	15.45	ARI	TAU	02.31	LEO	23.34	SCO	SAG	AQU	23.18	6
7	CAP	06.29	PIS	13.52	07.51	CAN	LEO	LIB	16.11	00.30	12.23	ARI	7
8	17.35	PIS	21.16	TAU	GEM	15.12	08.36	LIB	SAG	CAP	PIS	ARI	8
9	AQU	11.43	ARI	TAU	20.13	LEO	VIR	06.24	19.06	03.20	17.52	07.04	9
10	19.56	ARI	ARI	00.41	CAN	LEO	18.04	SCO	CAP	AQU	ARI	TAU	10
11	PIS	20.33	05.33	GEM	CAN	02.46	LIB	10.31	21.11	06.46	ARI	16.54	11
12	PIS	TAU	TAU	13.04	08.49	VIR	LIB	SAG	AQU	PIS	01.07	GEM	12
13	02.05	TAU	16.36	CAN	LEO	11.31	00.20	12.18	23.21	11.20	TAU	GEM	13
14	ARI	08.18	GEM	CAN	19.44	LIB	SCO	CAP	PIS	ARI	10.15	04.22	14
15	12.11	GEM	GEM	01.18	VIR	16.17	03.03	12.53	PIS	17.37	GEM	CAN	15
16	TAU	20.51	05.06	LEO	VIR	SCO	SAG	AQU	02.47	TAU	21.27	17.05	16
17	TAU	CAN	CAN	11.07	03.05	17.26	03.14	13.52	ARI	TAU	CAN	LEO	17
18	00.36	CAN	16.44	VIR	LIB	SAG	CAP	PIS	08.41	02.22	CAN	LEO	18
19	GEM	08.01	LEO	17.13	06.23	16.38	02.41	16.58	TAU	GEM	10.12	05.52	19
20	13.06	LEO	LEO	LIB	SCO	CAP	AQU	ARI	17.47	13.42	LEO	VIR	20
21	CAN	16.43	01.40	19.56	06.44	16.04	03.29	23.26	GEM	CAN	22.35	16.41	21
22	CAN	VIR	VIR	SCO	SAG	AQU	PIS	TAU	GEM	CAN	VIR	LIB	22
23	00.12	23.01	07.21	20.40	06.07	17.49	07.21	TAU	05.34	02.25	VIR	23.38	23
24	LEO	LIB	LIB	SAG	CAP	PIS	ARI	09.27	CAN	LEO	08.09	SCO	24
25	09.26	LIB	10.36	21.20	06.41	23.13	15.07	GEM	18.08	14.01	LIB	SCO	25
26	VIR	03.31	SCO	CAP	AQU	ARI	TAU	21.44	LEO	VIR	13.32	02.27	26
27	16.46	SCO	12.40	23.32	10.05	ARI	TAU	CAN	LEO	22.25	SCO	SAG	27
28	LIB	06.49	SAG	AQU	PIS	08.17	02.07	CAN	05.05	LIB	15.20	02.24	28
29	22.04		14.51	AQU	16.53	TAU	GEM	10.11	VIR	LIB	SAG	CAP	29
30	SCO		CAP	04.13	ARI	19.51	14.42	LEO	13.08	03.09	15.22	01.36	30
31	SCO		18.02		ARI		CAN	21.00		SCO		AQU	31

SUN

mth	dy	time → sign
JAN	1	00.00 → CAP
JAN	21	02.38 → AQU
FEB	19	16.57 → PIS
MAR	20	16.13 → ARI
APR	20	03.37 → TAU
MAY	21	03.04 → GEM
JUN	21	11.12 → CAN
JUL	22	22.07 → LEO
AUG	23	05.03 → VIR
SEP	23	02.24 → LIB
OCT	23	11.23 → SCO
NOV	22	08.36 → SAG
DEC	21	21.43 → CAP

MERCURY

mth	dy	time → sign
JAN	1	00.00 → SAG
JAN	13	06.44 → CAP
FEB	3	01.38 → AQU
FEB	20	18.54 → PIS
MAR	7	17.11 → ARI
MAY	14	14.43 → TAU
MAY	31	15.26 → GEM
JUN	14	12.23 → CAN
JUN	30	10.27 → LEO
SEP	7	12.02 → VIR
SEP	23	18.45 → LIB
OCT	11	13.05 → SCO
NOV	1	05.34 → SAG

VENUS

mth	dy	time → sign
JAN	1	00.00 → SCO
JAN	2	18.44 → SAG
JAN	27	15.58 → CAP
FEB	21	04.42 → AQU
MAR	16	14.18 → PIS
APR	9	23.17 → ARI
MAY	4	08.55 → TAU
MAY	28	19.19 → GEM
JUN	22	05.46 → CAN
JUL	16	15.23 → LEO
AUG	9	23.58 → VIR
SEP	3	08.17 → LIB
SEP	27	17.36 → SCO
OCT	22	05.02 → SAG
NOV	15	20.03 → CAP
DEC	10	18.31 → AQU

MARS

mth	dy	time → sign
JAN	1	00.00 → LIB
JAN	20	01.41 → SCO
AUG	27	18.51 → SAG
OCT	12	04.38 → CAP
NOV	21	19.42 → AQU
DEC	30	21.27 → PIS

SATURN

mth	dy	time → sign
JAN	1	00.00 → LIB

JUPITER

mth	dy	time → sign
JAN	1	00.00 → ARI
APR	28	20.52 → TAU

MOON

dy	jan	feb	mar	apr	may	jun	jul	aug	sep	oct	nov	dec	dy
1	02.11	19.51	TAU	07.39	04.12	VIR	LIB	SAG	09.03	PIS	06.58	GEM	1
2	PIS	TAU	12.36	CAN	LEO	12.26	05.25	22.27	AQU	19.34	TAU	GEM	2
3	05.42	TAU	GEM	20.11	16.57	LIB	SCO	CAP	09.00	ARI	11.02	03.08	3
4	ARI	04.55	23.40	LEO	VIR	20.19	10.27	22.41	PIS	21.05	GEM	CAN	4
5	12.43	GEM	CAN	LEO	VIR	SCO	SAG	AQU	08.57	TAU	18.12	13.23	5
6	TAU	16.44	CAN	08.40	03.39	SCO	12.02	22.05	ARI	TAU	CAN	LEO	6
7	22.42	CAN	12.30	VIR	LIB	00.21	CAP	PIS	10.48	01.15	CAN	LEO	7
8	GEM	CAN	LEO	18.56	10.49	SAG	11.54	22.33	TAU	GEM	04.56	01.57	8
9	GEM	05.36	LEO	LIB	SCO	01.46	AQU	ARI	16.06	09.16	LEO	VIR	9
10	10.34	LEO	00.51	LIB	14.50	CAP	11.59	ARI	GEM	CAN	17.47	14.35	10
11	CAN	18.02	VIR	02.13	SAG	02.26	PIS	01.46	GEM	20.50	VIR	LIB	11
12	23.19	VIR	11.16	SCO	17.09	AQU	13.56	TAU	01.24	LEO	VIR	LIB	12
13	LEO	VIR	LIB	07.08	CAP	04.00	ARI	08.36	CAN	LEO	05.57	00.39	13
14	LEO	05.00	19.20	SAG	19.14	PIS	18.45	GEM	13.38	09.51	LIB	SCO	14
15	12.00	LIB	SCO	10.41	AQU	07.29	TAU	18.52	LEO	VIR	15.18	07.00	15
16	VIR	13.45	SCO	CAP	22.05	ARI	TAU	CAN	LEO	21.44	SCO	SAG	16
17	23.19	SCO	01.15	13.43	PIS	13.11	02.37	CAN	02.41	LIB	21.33	10.17	17
18	LIB	19.42	SAG	AQU	PIS	TAU	GEM	07.19	VIR	LIB	SAG	CAP	18
19	LIB	SAG	05.19	16.40	02.07	21.03	13.05	LEO	14.41	07.11	SAG	12.02	19
20	07.44	22.49	CAP	PIS	ARI	GEM	CAN	20.23	LIB	SCO	01.40	AQU	20
21	SCO	CAP	07.55	19.56	07.29	GEM	CAN	VIR	LIB	14.12	CAP	13.45	21
22	12.23	23.48	AQU	ARI	TAU	07.04	01.20	VIR	00.43	SAG	04.52	PIS	22
23	SAG	AQU	09.39	ARI	14.37	CAN	LEO	08.42	SCO	19.28	AQU	16.30	23
24	13.39	AQU	PIS	00.15	GEM	19.02	14.24	LIB	08.33	CAP	07.55	ARI	24
25	CAP	00.01	11.34	TAU	GEM	LEO	VIR	19.11	SAG	23.28	PIS	20.46	25
26	13.06	PIS	ARI	06.40	00.06	LEO	VIR	SCO	14.06	AQU	11.09	TAU	26
27	AQU	01.11	15.05	GEM	CAN	08.06	02.54	SCO	CAP	AQU	ARI	TAU	27
28	12.45	ARI	TAU	16.06	11.59	VIR	LIB	02.53	17.24	02.23	14.54	02.48	28
29	PIS	05.02	21.36	CAN	LEO	20.18	13.04	SAG	AQU	PIS	TAU	GEM	29
30	14.33		GEM	CAN	LEO	LIB	SCO	07.24	18.52	04.34	19.53	10.53	30
31	ARI		GEM		00.57		19.37	CAP		ARI		CAN	31

SUN

mth	dy	time → sign
JAN	1	00.00 → CAP
JAN	20	08.21 → AQU
FEB	18	22.42 → PIS
MAR	20	22.00 → ARI
APR	20	09.25 → TAU
MAY	21	08.53 → GEM
JUN	21	17.00 → CAN
JUL	23	03.52 → LEO
AUG	23	10.44 → VIR
SEP	23	08.06 → LIB
OCT	23	17.06 → SCO
NOV	22	14.22 → SAG
DEC	22	03.32 → CAP

MERCURY

mth	dy	time → sign
JAN	1	00.00 → SAG
JAN	6	13.24 → CAP
JAN	25	19.11 → AQU
FEB	11	23.57 → PIS
MAR	2	19.22 → ARI
MAR	15	21.01 → PIS
APR	17	16.47 → ARI
MAY	8	06.22 → TAU
MAY	23	03.58 → GEM
JUN	6	08.22 → CAN
JUN	26	11.00 → LEO
JUL	28	13.40 → CAN
AUG	11	14.04 → LEO
AUG	30	22.59 → VIR
SEP	15	21.44 → LIB
OCT	4	16.40 → SCO
OCT	31	15.51 → SAG
NOV	6	22.18 → SCO
DEC	10	14.48 → SAG
DEC	30	17.14 → CAP

VENUS

mth	dy	time → sign
JAN	1	00.00 → AQU
JAN	5	11.11 → PIS
FEB	2	05.54 → ARI
MAR	14	18.58 → TAU
MAR	31	04.50 → ARI
JUN	5	10.33 → TAU
JUL	7	10.29 → GEM
AUG	4	01.08 → CAN
AUG	30	01.35 → LEO
SEP	24	03.48 → VIR
OCT	18	15.29 → LIB
NOV	11	18.12 → SCO
DEC	5	16.24 → SAG
DEC	29	12.54 → CAP

MARS

mth	dy	time → sign
JAN	1	00.00 → PIS
FEB	8	01.12 → ARI
MAR	20	06.51 → TAU
MAY	1	06.12 → GEM
JUN	14	03.46 → CAN
JUL	29	19.25 → LEO
SEP	14	17.58 → VIR
NOV	1	14.14 → LIB
DEC	20	11.23 → SCO

SATURN

mth	dy	time → sign
JAN	1	00.00 → LIB
OCT	22	15.26 → SCO

JUPITER

mth	dy	time → sign
JAN	1	00.00 → TAU
MAY	9	15.24 → GEM

MOON

dy	jan	feb	mar	apr	may	jun	jul	aug	sep	oct	nov	dec	dy
1	21.17	VIR	VIR	05.19	SAG	14.44	00.08	10.57	GEM	18.53	VIR	LIB	1
2	LEO	VIR	11.41	SCO	SAG	AQU	PIS	TAU	03.30	LEO	VIR	21.30	2
3	LEO	05.31	LIB	14.58	03.55	18.12	02.22	15.10	CAN	LEO	01.51	SCO	3
4	09.41	LIB	23.31	SAG	CAP	PIS	ARI	GEM	13.05	06.40	LIB	SCO	4
5	VIR	17.21	SCO	22.29	09.12	21.01	05.22	21.59	LEO	VIR	14.12	08.09	5
6	22.36	SCO	SCO	CAP	AQU	ARI	TAU	CAN	LEO	19.28	SCO	SAG	6
7	LIB	SCO	09.20	CAP	12.46	23.41	09.42	CAN	00.47	LIB	SCO	16.33	7
8	LIB	02.20	SAG	03.29	PIS	TAU	GEM	07.16	VIR	LIB	01.06	CAP	8
9	09.44	SAG	16.10	AQU	14.49	TAU	15.54	13.29	07.56	SCO	SAG	22.59	9
10	SCO	07.32	CAP	05.49	ARI	03.03	CAN	18.33	LIB	SCO	10.18	AQU	10
11	17.14	CAP	19.37	PIS	16.12	GEM	CAN	VIR	LIB	19.19	CAP	AQU	11
12	SAG	09.16	AQU	06.19	TAU	08.17	00.28	VIR	02.05	SAG	17.31	03.46	12
13	20.55	AQU	20.17	ARI	18.29	CAN	LEO	07.08	SCO	SAG	AQU	PIS	13
14	CAP	08.58	PIS	06.31	GEM	16.29	11.28	LIB	13.32	04.51	22.17	07.06	14
15	21.57	PIS	19.39	TAU	23.16	LEO	VIR	19.43	SAG	CAP	PIS	ARI	15
16	AQU	08.30	ARI	08.29	CAN	LEO	VIR	SCO	22.21	11.34	PIS	09.22	16
17	22.07	ARI	19.44	GEM	CAN	03.36	00.04	SCO	CAP	AQU	00.35	TAU	17
18	PIS	09.51	TAU	13.53	07.47	VIR	LIB	06.30	CAP	14.55	ARI	11.29	18
19	23.08	TAU	22.35	CAN	LEO	16.16	12.17	SAG	03.30	PIS	01.15	GEM	19
20	ARI	14.29	GEM	23.29	19.31	LIB	SCO	13.53	AQU	15.29	TAU	14.40	20
21	ARI	GEM	GEM	LEO	VIR	LIB	21.59	CAP	05.06	ARI	01.54	CAN	21
22	02.20	22.47	05.29	LEO	VIR	03.57	SAG	17.29	PIS	14.47	GEM	20.22	22
23	TAU	CAN	CAN	11.53	08.16	SCO	SAG	AQU	04.30	TAU	04.31	LEO	23
24	08.21	CAN	16.14	VIR	LIB	12.47	04.06	18.12	ARI	15.04	CAN	LEO	24
25	GEM	10.05	LEO	VIR	19.32	SAG	CAP	PIS	03.44	GEM	10.40	05.24	25
26	17.07	LEO	LEO	00.40	SCO	18.29	07.03	17.46	TAU	18.24	LEO	VIR	26
27	CAN	22.51	LIB	LIB	SCO	CAP	AQU	ARI	05.01	CAN	20.41	17.11	27
28	CAN	VIR	VIR	11.52	04.08	21.51	08.07	18.10	GEM	CAN	VIR	LIB	28
29	04.06		17.51	SCO	SAG	AQU	PIS	TAU	09.56	01.55	VIR	LIB	29
30	LEO		LIB	20.52	10.17	AQU	08.56	21.07	CAN	LEO	09.06	05.43	30
31	16.35		LIB		CAP		ARI	GEM		13.04		SCO	31

SUN

mth	dy	time → sign
JAN	1	00.00 → CAP
JAN	20	14.11 → AQU
FEB	19	04.32 → PIS
MAR	21	03.53 → ARI
APR	20	15.19 → TAU
MAY	21	14.47 → GEM
JUN	21	22.54 → CAN
JUL	23	09.45 → LEO
AUG	23	16.36 → VIR
SEP	23	13.55 → LIB
OCT	23	22.56 → SCO
NOV	22	20.14 → SAG
DEC	22	09.25 → CAP

MERCURY

mth	dy	time → sign
JAN	1	00.00 → CAP
JAN	18	07.43 → AQU
FEB	4	18.03 → PIS
APR	13	11.34 → ARI
APR	30	11.26 → TAU
MAY	14	13.57 → GEM
MAY	30	16.13 → CAN
AUG	7	14.43 → LEO
AUG	22	17.42 → VIR
SEP	8	08.05 → LIB
SEP	29	04.06 → SCO
NOV	4	12.37 → LIB
NOV	11	10.23 → SCO
DEC	4	07.03 → SAG
DEC	23	12.10 → CAP

VENUS

mth	dy	time → sign
JAN	1	00.00 → CAP
JAN	22	09.22 → AQU
FEB	15	07.01 → PIS
MAR	11	07.22 → ARI
APR	4	11.55 → TAU
APR	28	22.03 → GEM
MAY	23	15.04 → CAN
JUN	17	17.04 → LEO
JUL	13	08.43 → VIR
AUG	9	00.34 → LIB
SEP	6	23.28 → SCO
OCT	23	22.07 → SAG
OCT	27	10.42 → SCO

MARS

mth	dy	time → sign
JAN	1	00.00 → SCO
FEB	9	19.11 → SAG
APR	12	16.24 → CAP
JUL	3	07.25 → SAG
AUG	24	13.27 → CAP
OCT	21	12.03 → AQU
DEC	4	07.42 → PIS

SATURN

mth	dy	time → sign
JAN	1	00.00 → SCO

JUPITER

mth	dy	time → sign
JAN	1	00.00 → GEM
MAY	24	04.36 → CAN

MOON

dy	jan	feb	mar	apr	may	jun	jul	aug	sep	oct	nov	dec	dy
1	16.39	CAP	CAP	PIS	ARI	GEM	CAN	VIR	22.48	18.41	CAP	AQU	1
2	SAG	15.38	02.07	15.40	01.42	12.46	02.16	VIR	SCO	SAG	CAP	14.38	2
3	SAG	AQU	AQU	ARI	TAU	CAN	LEO	03.14	SCO	SAG	00.22	PIS	3
4	00.45	18.03	04.32	14.43	01.06	16.34	08.56	LIB	11.32	07.04	AQU	19.34	4
5	CAP	PIS	PIS	TAU	GEM	LEO	VIR	15.03	SAG	CAP	07.34	ARI	5
6	06.09	19.14	04.40	14.40	02.30	LEO	18.53	SCO	23.10	16.45	PIS	21.23	6
7	AQU	ARI	ARI	GEM	CAN	00.06	LIB	SCO	CAP	AQU	10.42	TAU	7
8	09.43	20.47	04.32	17.29	07.29	VIR	LIB	03.32	CAP	22.17	ARI	21.16	8
9	PIS	TAU	TAU	CAN	LEO	10.59	07.04	SAG	07.31	PIS	10.48	GEM	9
10	12.27	23.54	06.06	CAN	16.23	LIB	SCO	14.20	AQU	23.58	TAU	21.06	10
11	ARI	GEM	GEM	00.05	VIR	23.30	19.19	CAP	11.55	ARI	09.50	CAN	11
12	15.10	GEM	10.37	LEO	VIR	SCO	SAG	21.54	PIS	23.32	GEM	22.48	12
13	TAU	05.10	CAN	10.03	04.03	SCO	SAG	AQU	13.22	TAU	09.59	LEO	13
14	18.29	CAN	18.17	VIR	LIB	11.37	05.40	AQU	ARI	23.10	CAN	LEO	14
15	GEM	12.34	LEO	21.57	16.42	SAG	CAP	02.17	13.45	GEM	13.03	03.54	15
16	23.01	LEO	LEO	LIB	SCO	22.05	13.19	PIS	TAU	GEM	LEO	VIR	16
17	CAN	22.00	04.22	LIB	SCO	CAP	AQU	04.37	14.55	00.50	19.52	12.51	17
18	CAN	VIR	VIR	10.32	04.53	CAP	18.33	ARI	GEM	CAN	VIR	LIB	18
19	05.24	VIR	15.57	SCO	SAG	06.26	PIS	06.26	18.13	05.41	VIR	LIB	19
20	LEO	09.14	LIB	22.55	15.49	AQU	22.07	TAU	CAN	LEO	06.02	00.43	20
21	14.14	LIB	LIB	SAG	CAP	12.37	ARI	08.56	CAN	13.45	LIB	SCO	21
22	VIR	21.43	04.26	SAG	CAP	PIS	ARI	GEM	00.04	VIR	18.13	13.34	22
23	VIR	SCO	SCO	10.11	00.48	16.43	00.52	12.50	LEO	VIR	SCO	SAG	23
24	01.30	SCO	16.56	CAP	AQU	ARI	TAU	CAN	08.11	00.12	SCO	SAG	24
25	LIB	10.00	SAG	19.02	07.08	19.09	03.30	18.22	VIR	LIB	07.01	01.40	25
26	14.03	SAG	SAG	AQU	PIS	TAU	GEM	LEO	18.11	12.11	SAG	CAP	26
27	SCO	19.58	03.55	AQU	10.31	20.41	06.41	LEO	LIB	SCO	19.24	12.00	27
28	SCO	CAP	CAP	00.22	ARI	GEM	CAN	01.45	LIB	SCO	CAP	AQU	28
29	01.42		11.37	PIS	11.33	22.34	11.10	VIR	05.52	00.59	CAP	20.09	29
30	SAG		AQU	02.08	TAU	CAN	LEO	11.12	SCO	SAG	06.19	PIS	30
31	10.26		15.16		11.41		17.50	LIB		13.36		PIS	31

SUN

mth	dy	time → sign
JAN	1	00.00 → CAP
JAN	20	20.02 → AQU
FEB	19	10.19 → PIS
MAR	21	09.35 → ARI
APR	20	20.58 → TAU
MAY	21	20.24 → GEM
JUN	22	04.31 → CAN
JUL	23	15.25 → LEO
AUG	23	22.19 → VIR
SEP	23	19.41 → LIB
OCT	24	04.43 → SCO
NOV	23	02.01 → SAG
DEC	22	15.11 → CAP

MERCURY

mth	dy	time → sign
JAN	1	00.00 → CAP
JAN	10	23.05 → AQU
MAR	17	20.49 → PIS
APR	6	16.14 → ARI
APR	22	02.57 → TAU
MAY	6	13.05 → GEM
JUL	13	14.44 → CAN
JUL	30	17.21 → LEO
AUG	14	13.08 → VIR
SEP	1	12.06 → LIB
NOV	8	06.57 → SCO
NOV	27	04.33 → SAG
DEC	16	06.07 → CAP

VENUS

mth	dy	time → sign
JAN	1	00.00 → SCO
JAN	6	06.48 → SAG
FEB	6	01.15 → CAP
MAR	4	20.21 → AQU
MAR	30	11.30 → PIS
APR	24	15.13 → ARI
MAY	19	13.35 → TAU
JUN	13	08.38 → GEM
JUL	8	00.15 → CAN
AUG	1	11.43 → LEO
AUG	25	18.52 → VIR
SEP	18	22.41 → LIB
OCT	13	00.39 → SCO
NOV	6	02.02 → SAG
NOV	30	03.42 → CAP
DEC	24	06.53 → AQU

MARS

mth	dy	time → sign
JAN	1	00.00 → PIS
JAN	15	04.26 → ARI
FEB	26	10.21 → TAU
APR	10	23.12 → GEM
MAY	26	00.50 → CAN
JUL	11	09.28 → LEO
AUG	27	10.13 → VIR
OCT	13	11.17 → LIB
NOV	29	01.30 → SCO

SATURN

mth	dy	time → sign
JAN	1	00.00 → SCO

JUPITER

mth	dy	time → sign
JAN	1	00.00 → CAN
JUN	13	00.07 → LEO
NOV	17	03.45 → VIR

MOON

dy	jan	feb	mar	apr	may	jun	jul	aug	sep	oct	nov	dec	dy
1	01.56	14.02	GEM	08.20	VIR	20.54	15.33	CAP	15.23	05.46	19.23	05.46	1
2	ARI	GEM	22.40	LEO	VIR	SCO	SAG	22.52	PIS	ARI	GEM	CAN	2
3	05.24	16.36	CAN	14.31	04.26	SCO	SAG	AQU	21.24	08.52	20.11	06.07	3
4	TAU	CAN	CAN	VIR	LIB	09.23	04.29	AQU	ARI	TAU	CAN	LEO	4
5	07.04	19.28	02.48	22.33	15.04	SAG	CAP	08.04	ARI	10.59	22.20	08.50	5
6	GEM	LEO	LEO	LIB	SCO	22.21	16.18	PIS	01.36	GEM	LEO	VIR	6
7	08.00	23.43	08.09	LIB	SCO	CAP	15.00	AQU	TAU	13.23	LEO	14.48	7
8	CAN	VIR	VIR	08.38	03.19	CAP	AQU	ARI	04.58	CAN	02.36	LIB	8
9	09.41	VIR	15.20	SCO	SAG	10.30	02.08	20.03	GEM	16.41	VIR	23.59	9
10	LEO	06.33	LIB	20.41	16.19	AQU	PIS	TAU	08.01	LEO	09.15	SCO	10
11	13.43	LIB	LIB	SAG	CAP	20.32	09.33	23.33	CAN	21.11	LIB	SCO	11
12	VIR	16.38	01.04	SAG	CAP	PIS	ARI	GEM	11.02	VIR	18.12	11.33	12
13	21.15	SCO	SCO	09.40	04.29	PIS	14.20	GEM	LEO	VIR	SCO	SAG	13
14	LIB	SCO	13.13	CAP	AQU	03.24	TAU	01.50	14.33	03.13	SCO	SAG	14
15	LIB	05.07	SAG	21.20	13.53	ARI	16.43	CAN	VIR	LIB	05.17	00.23	15
16	08.14	SAG	SAG	AQU	PIS	06.50	GEM	03.33	19.35	11.23	SAG	CAP	16
17	SCO	17.33	02.01	AQU	19.21	TAU	17.30	LEO	LIB	SCO	17.59	13.19	17
18	21.01	CAP	CAP	05.28	ARI	07.36	CAN	05.57	LIB	22.07	CAP	AQU	18
19	SAG	CAP	12.47	PIS	21.12	GEM	18.03	VIR	03.18	SAG	CAP	AQU	19
20	SAG	03.33	AQU	09.29	TAU	07.15	LEO	10.33	SCO	SAG	06.58	01.02	20
21	09.09	AQU	19.45	ARI	20.56	CAN	20.06	LIB	14.11	10.52	AQU	PIS	21
22	CAP	10.09	PIS	10.29	GEM	07.36	VIR	18.37	SAG	CAP	18.10	10.05	22
23	18.58	PIS	23.09	TAU	20.33	LEO	VIR	SCO	SAG	23.33	PIS	ARI	23
24	AQU	14.06	ARI	10.24	CAN	10.26	01.16	SCO	03.01	AQU	PIS	15.33	24
25	AQU	ARI	ARI	GEM	21.52	VIR	LIB	06.03	CAP	AQU	01.47	TAU	25
26	02.11	16.46	00.31	11.09	LEO	16.55	10.19	SAG	15.07	09.37	ARI	17.33	26
27	PIS	TAU	TAU	CAN	LEO	LIB	SCO	18.57	AQU	PIS	05.27	GEM	27
28	07.19	19.24	01.42	14.09	02.16	LIB	22.24	CAP	AQU	15.46	TAU	17.17	28
29	ARI		GEM	LEO	VIR	03.04	SAG	CAP	00.12	ARI	06.11	CAN	29
30	11.06		04.05	19.58	VIR	SCO	SAG	06.35	PIS	18.30	GEM	16.36	30
31	TAU		CAN		LIB		11.18	AQU		TAU		LEO	31

SUN

mth	dy	time → sign
JAN	1	00.00 → CAP
JAN	21	01.48 → AQU
FEB	19	16.05 → PIS
MAR	20	15.20 → ARI
APR	20	02.43 → TAU
MAY	21	02.12 → GEM
JUN	21	10.24 → CAN
JUL	22	21.20 → LEO
AUG	23	04.15 → VIR
SEP	23	01.35 → LIB
OCT	23	10.34 → SCO
NOV	22	07.50 → SAG
DEC	21	20.59 → CAP

MERCURY

mth	dy	time → sign
JAN	1	00.00 → CAP
JAN	4	09.15 → AQU
FEB	2	12.18 → CAP
FEB	15	06.34 → AQU
MAR	11	10.28 → PIS
MAR	28	22.41 → ARI
APR	12	17.10 → TAU
APR	29	22.42 → GEM
JUL	6	19.02 → CAN
JUL	21	05.35 → LEO
AUG	5	19.06 → VIR
AUG	26	13.29 → LIB
SEP	29	21.25 → VIR
OCT	11	07.28 → LIB
OCT	31	08.19 → SCO
NOV	18	21.42 → SAG
DEC	8	07.11 → CAP

VENUS

mth	dy	time → sign
JAN	1	00.00 → AQU
JAN	17	14.22 → PIS
FEB	11	07.47 → ARI
MAR	7	21.32 → TAU
APR	4	07.23 → GEM
MAY	8	02.17 → CAN
JUN	23	12.10 → GEM
AUG	4	09.48 → CAN
SEP	8	09.23 → LEO
OCT	6	03.12 → VIR
OCT	31	19.40 → LIB
NOV	25	13.01 → SCO
DEC	19	19.07 → SAG

MARS

mth	dy	time → sign
JAN	1	00.00 → SCO
JAN	14	02.26 → SAG
FEB	28	20.12 → CAP
APR	14	23.32 → AQU
JUN	3	07.53 → PIS
DEC	6	11.24 → ARI

SATURN

mth	dy	time → sign
JAN	1	00.00 → SCO
JAN	12	18.44 → SAG
MAY	14	03.40 → SCO
OCT	10	15.24 → SAG

JUPITER

mth	dy	time → sign
JAN	1	00.00 → VIR
JAN	18	02.12 → LEO
JUL	7	19.14 → VIR
DEC	13	02.20 → LIB

MOON

dy	jan	feb	mar	apr	may	jun	jul	aug	sep	oct	nov	dec	dy
1	17.31	LIB	SCO	SAG	CAP	PIS	ARI	11.15	23.14	08.24	22.24	12.59	1
2	VIR	13.34	SCO	04.37	01.27	PIS	22.26	GEM	LEO	VIR	SCO	SAG	2
3	21.44	SCO	08.09	CAP	AQU	07.04	TAU	13.32	23.20	10.01	SCO	22.36	3
4	LIB	SCO	SAG	17.24	13.15	ARI	TAU	CAN	VIR	LIB	04.56	CAP	4
5	LIB	00.13	20.32	AQU	PIS	13.22	02.26	13.27	VIR	13.19	SAG	CAP	5
6	06.00	SAG	CAP	AQU	22.05	TAU	GEM	LEO	00.04	SCO	14.24	10.15	6
7	SCO	13.08	CAP	04.37	ARI	16.09	03.20	12.50	LIB	19.46	CAP	AQU	7
8	17.32	CAP	09.19	PIS	ARI	GEM	CAN	VIR	03.26	SAG	CAP	22.57	8
9	SAG	CAP	AQU	12.46	03.24	16.42	02.42	13.50	SCO	SAG	02.19	PIS	9
10	SAG	01.52	20.11	ARI	TAU	CAN	LEO	LIB	10.46	05.48	AQU	PIS	10
11	06.34	AQU	PIS	18.03	06.00	16.45	02.34	18.20	SAG	CAP	14.51	10.37	11
12	CAP	12.52	PIS	TAU	GEM	LEO	VIR	SCO	21.46	18.09	PIS	ARI	12
13	19.19	PIS	04.26	21.29	07.21	18.03	04.54	SCO	CAP	AQU	PIS	19.15	13
14	AQU	21.48	ARI	GEM	CAN	VIR	LIB	03.00	CAP	AQU	01.36	TAU	14
15	AQU	ARI	10.32	GEM	08.52	21.58	10.56	SAG	10.28	06.25	ARI	TAU	15
16	06.47	ARI	TAU	00.15	LEO	LIB	SCO	14.47	AQU	PIS	09.12	00.06	16
17	PIS	04.48	15.11	CAN	11.40	LIB	20.38	CAP	22.34	16.35	TAU	GEM	17
18	16.17	TAU	GEM	03.00	VIR	05.03	SAG	CAP	PIS	ARI	13.45	01.52	18
19	ARI	09.50	18.47	LEO	16.25	SCO	SAG	03.38	PIS	ARI	GEM	CAN	19
20	23.11	GEM	CAN	06.17	LIB	14.55	08.40	AQU	08.47	00.07	16.17	02.11	20
21	TAU	12.50	21.31	VIR	23.26	SAG	CAP	15.47	ARI	TAU	CAN	LEO	21
22	TAU	CAN	LEO	10.36	SCO	SAG	21.28	PIS	17.01	05.28	18.10	02.56	22
23	03.05	14.10	23.53	LIB	SCO	02.43	AQU	PIS	TAU	GEM	LEO	VIR	23
24	GEM	LEO	VIR	16.44	08.46	CAP	AQU	02.29	23.25	09.23	20.32	05.39	24
25	04.20	15.05	VIR	SCO	SAG	15.26	09.50	ARI	GEM	CAN	VIR	LIB	25
26	CAN	VIR	03.00	SCO	20.11	AQU	PIS	11.23	GEM	12.27	VIR	11.09	26
27	04.06	17.20	LIB	01.25	CAP	AQU	20.54	TAU	04.00	LEO	00.11	SCO	27
28	LEO	LIB	08.18	SAG	CAP	03.54	ARI	17.59	CAN	15.09	LIB	19.20	28
29	04.17	22.45	SCO	12.44	08.52	PIS	ARI	GEM	06.49	VIR	05.34	SAG	29
30	VIR		16.56	CAP	AQU	14.43	05.40	21.51	LEO	18.10	SCO	SAG	30
31	06.56		SAG		21.09		TAU	CAN		LIB		05.37	31

SUN

mth	dy	time → sign
JAN	1	00.00 → CAP
JAN	20	07.39 → AQU
FEB	18	21.58 → PIS
MAR	20	21.16 → ARI
APR	20	08.41 → TAU
MAY	21	08.10 → GEM
JUN	21	16.20 → CAN
JUL	23	03.16 → LEO
AUG	23	10.07 → VIR
SEP	23	07.26 → LIB
OCT	23	16.24 → SCO
NOV	22	13.39 → SAG
DEC	22	02.49 → CAP

MERCURY

mth	dy	time → sign
JAN	1	00.00 → CAP
FEB	12	14.30 → AQU
MAR	4	11.34 → PIS
MAR	20	19.48 → ARI
APR	4	23.38 → TAU
JUN	12	13.40 → GEM
JUN	28	17.08 → CAN
JUL	12	19.41 → LEO
JUL	30	01.44 → VIR
OCT	6	11.09 → LIB
OCT	23	20.50 → SCO
NOV	11	18.00 → SAG
DEC	2	11.19 → CAP
DEC	28	17.30 → SAG

VENUS

mth	dy	time → sign
JAN	1	00.00 → SAG
JAN	12	20.23 → CAP
FEB	5	20.16 → AQU
MAR	1	20.39 → PIS
MAR	25	22.46 → ARI
APR	19	03.29 → TAU
MAY	13	11.08 → GEM
JUN	6	21.34 → CAN
JUL	1	10.42 → LEO
JUL	26	03.10 → VIR
AUG	20	00.44 → LIB
SEP	14	06.20 → SCO
OCT	10	01.16 → SAG
NOV	5	23.46 → CAP
DEC	6	15.26 → AQU

MARS

mth	dy	time → sign
JAN	1	00.00 → ARI
JAN	28	14.23 → TAU
MAR	17	21.32 → GEM
MAY	4	15.26 → CAN
JUN	21	12.11 → LEO
AUG	8	05.29 → VIR
SEP	24	04.31 → LIB
NOV	8	21.05 → SCO
DEC	23	01.25 → SAG

SATURN

mth	dy	time → sign
JAN	1	00.00 → SAG

JUPITER

mth	dy	time → sign
JAN	1	00.00 → LIB
FEB	19	15.23 → VIR
AUG	7	02.13 → LIB

MOON

dy	jan	feb	mar	apr	may	jun	jul	aug	sep	oct	nov	dec	dy
1	CAP	12.20	PIS	23.11	13.47	CAN	13.23	LIB	SAG	CAP	09.18	05.56	1
2	17.24	PIS	PIS	TAU	GEM	04.45	VIR	01.00	21.05	14.04	PIS	ARI	2
3	AQU	PIS	06.31	TAU	19.08	LEO	15.16	SCO	CAP	AQU	22.00	17.48	3
4	AQU	00.42	ARI	07.30	CAN	06.59	LIB	06.47	CAP	AQU	ARI	TAU	4
5	06.04	ARI	17.20	GEM	22.53	VIR	19.10	SAG	07.50	02.17	ARI	TAU	5
6	PIS	11.37	TAU	13.37	LEO	09.45	SCO	15.23	AQU	PIS	09.38	03.00	6
7	18.23	TAU	TAU	CAN	LEO	LIB	SCO	CAP	20.04	14.57	TAU	GEM	7
8	ARI	19.34	02.03	17.24	01.37	13.41	01.20	CAP	PIS	ARI	19.09	09.16	8
9	ARI	GEM	GEM	LEO	VIR	SCO	SAG	02.01	PIS	ARI	GEM	CAN	9
10	04.26	23.39	07.45	19.13	03.57	19.09	09.34	AQU	08.45	02.48	GEM	13.23	10
11	TAU	CAN	CAN	VIR	LIB	SAG	CAP	14.02	ARI	TAU	02.24	LEO	11
12	10.44	CAN	10.12	20.08	06.48	SAG	19.43	PIS	20.57	13.01	CAN	16.28	12
13	GEM	00.19>LEO	LEO	LIB	SCO	02.36	AQU	PIS	TAU	GEM	07.36	VIR	13
14	13.05	23.17	10.20	21.45	11.13	CAP	AQU	02.46	TAU	20.55	LEO	19.23	14
15	CAN	VIR	VIR	SCO	SAG	12.23	07.32	ARI	07.26	CAN	11.07	LIB	15
16	12.50	22.50	09.59	SCO	18.13	AQU	PIS	15.00	GEM	CAN	VIR	22.34	16
17	LEO	LIB	LIB	01.43	CAP	AQU	20.14	TAU	14.49	01.59	13.25	SCO	17
18	12.03	LIB	11.16	SAG	CAP	00.16	ARI	TAU	CAN	LEO	LIB	SCO	18
19	VIR	01.06	SCO	09.08	04.12	PIS	ARI	00.51	18.31	04.23	15.17	02.30	19
20	12.55	SCO	15.55	CAP	AQU	12.46	07.58	GEM	LEO	VIR	SCO	SAG	20
21	LIB	07.23	SAG	19.53	16.20	ARI	TAU	06.48	19.11	05.03	17.52	07.47	21
22	17.02	SAG	SAG	AQU	PIS	23.38	16.34	CAN	VIR	LIB	SAG	CAP	22
23	SCO	17.27	00.34	AQU	PIS	TAU	GEM	08.51	18.33	05.31	22.29	15.19	23
24	SCO	CAP	CAP	08.23	04.34	TAU	21.05	LEO	LIB	SCO	CAP	AQU	24
25	00.52	CAP	12.17	PIS	ARI	07.07	CAN	08.26	18.40	07.33	CAP	AQU	25
26	SAG	05.42	AQU	20.22	14.43	GEM	22.16	VIR	SCO	SAG	06.16	01.41	26
27	11.32	AQU	AQU	ARI	TAU	11.00	LEO	07.41	21.27	12.41	AQU	PIS	27
28	CAP	18.25	01.00	ARI	21.47	CAN	21.59	LIB	SAG	CAP	17.16	14.13	28
29	23.42		PIS	06.18	GEM	12.31	VIR	08.45	SAG	21.32	PIS	ARI	29
30	AQU		12.55	TAU	GEM	LEO	22.20	SCO	03.59	AQU	PIS	ARI	30
31	AQU		ARI		02.05		LIB	13.07		AQU		02.37	31

SUN

mth	dy	time → sign
JAN	1	00.00 → CAP
JAN	20	13.29 → AQU
FEB	19	03.48 → PIS
MAR	21	03.06 → ARI
APR	20	14.27 → TAU
MAY	21	13.51 → GEM
JUN	21	21.57 → CAN
JUL	23	08.50 → LEO
AUG	23	15.46 → VIR
SEP	23	13.09 → LIB
OCT	23	22.12 → SCO
NOV	22	19.29 → SAG
DEC	22	08.40 → CAP

MERCURY

mth	dy	time → sign
JAN	1	00.00 → SAG
JAN	14	10.03 → CAP
FEB	6	15.23 → AQU
FEB	24	21.44 → PIS
MAR	12	17.31 → ARI
APR	2	19.17 → TAU
APR	10	13.41 → ARI
MAY	17	01.53 → TAU
JUN	5	20.59 → GEM
JUN	20	02.20 → CAN
JUL	4	23.46 → LEO
JUL	26	10.08 → VIR
AUG	23	14.36 → LEO
SEP	11	01.08 → VIR
SEP	28	22.46 → LIB
OCT	16	08.52 → SCO
NOV	5	02.36 → SAG

VENUS

mth	dy	time → sign
JAN	1	00.00 → AQU
APR	6	16.00 → PIS
MAY	5	11.59 → ARI
JUN	1	04.07 → TAU
JUN	26	23.08 → GEM
JUL	22	05.26 → CAN
AUG	16	01.28 → LEO
SEP	9	12.36 → VIR
OCT	3	16.44 → LIB
OCT	27	16.26 → SCO
NOV	20	13.59 → SAG
DEC	14	10.55 → CAP

MARS

mth	dy	time → sign
JAN	1	00.00 → SAG
FEB	3	18.45 → CAP
MAR	17	07.17 → AQU
APR	27	02.32 → PIS
JUN	7	06.21 → ARI
JUL	21	07.11 → TAU
SEP	21	05.24 → GEM
OCT	29	00.01 → TAU

SATURN

mth	dy	time → sign
JAN	1	00.00 → SAG

JUPITER

mth	dy	time → sign
JAN	1	00.00 → LIB
JAN	13	12.42 → SCO
MAR	20	19.18 → LIB
SEP	7	08.48 → SCO

MOON

dy	jan	feb	mar	apr	may	jun	jul	aug	sep	oct	nov	dec	dy
1	TAU	04.40	CAN	06.01	LIB	02.53	CAP	12.11	ARI	TAU	08.09	LEO	1
2	12.23	CAN	18.27	VIR	16.14	SAG	19.44	PIS	19.24	14.50	CAN	LEO	2
3	GEM	07.37	LEO	05.54	SCO	05.23	AQU	23.14	TAU	GEM	17.02	05.18	3
4	18.22	LEO	19.15	LIB	16.43	CAP	AQU	ARI	TAU	GEM	LEO	VIR	4
5	CAN	08.11	VIR	05.16	SAG	10.35	03.57	ARI	08.07	02.00	22.45	09.31	5
6	21.23	VIR	18.35	SCO	19.23	AQU	PIS	12.04	GEM	CAN	VIR	LIB	6
7	LEO	08.23	LIB	06.07	CAP	19.24	15.18	TAU	18.22	09.50	VIR	11.28	7
8	22.59	LIB	18.35	SAG	CAP	PIS	ARI	TAU	CAN	LEO	01.16	SCO	8
9	VIR	10.03	SCO	10.00	01.29	PIS	ARI	00.16	CAN	13.49	LIB	12.02	9
10	VIR	SCO	20.56	CAP	AQU	07.20	04.09	GEM	00.41	VIR	01.30	SAG	10
11	00.52	14.11	SAG	17.41	11.27	ARI	TAU	09.25	LEO	14.44	SCO	12.46	11
12	LIB	SAG	SAG	AQU	PIS	20.12	15.46	CAN	03.19	LIB	01.03	CAP	12
13	04.02	20.55	02.36	AQU	23.58	TAU	GEM	14.43	VIR	14.11	SAG	15.38	13
14	SCO	CAP	CAP	04.38	ARI	TAU	GEM	LEO	03.44	SCO	01.54	AQU	14
15	08.49	CAP	11.28	PIS	ARI	07.31	00.15	17.07	LIB	14.09	CAP	22.12	15
16	SAG	05.51	AQU	17.23	12.50	GEM	CAN	VIR	03.49	SAG	05.53	PIS	16
17	15.13	AQU	22.41	ARI	TAU	16.04	05.31	18.17	SCO	16.23	AQU	PIS	17
18	CAP	16.39	PIS	ARI	TAU	CAN	LEO	LIB	05.16	CAP	13.56	08.45	18
19	23.22	PIS	PIS	06.16	00.14	22.04	08.41	19.50	SAG	22.04	PIS	ARI	19
20	AQU	PIS	11.17	TAU	GEM	LEO	VIR	SCO	09.13	AQU	PIS	21.38	20
21	AQU	05.02	ARI	18.03	09.23	LEO	11.11	22.48	CAP	AQU	01.28	TAU	21
22	09.41	ARI	ARI	GEM	CAN	02.22	LIB	SAG	16.03	07.19	ARI	TAU	22
23	PIS	18.05	00.16	GEM	16.14	VIR	13.57	SAG	AQU	PIS	14.30	10.09	23
24	22.03	TAU	TAU	03.46	LEO	05.41	SCO	03.38	AQU	19.10	TAU	GEM	24
25	ARI	TAU	12.20	CAN	21.00	LIB	17.25	CAP	01.33	ARI	TAU	20.33	25
26	ARI	05.52	GEM	10.44	VIR	08.30	SAG	10.28	PIS	ARI	03.00	CAN	26
27	10.56	GEM	21.53	LEO	23.55	SCO	21.53	AQU	13.07	08.07	GEM	CAN	27
28	TAU	14.17	CAN	14.40	LIB	11.11	CAP	19.25	ARI	TAU	13.51	04.33	28
29	21.47		CAN	VIR	LIB	SAG	CAP	PIS	ARI	CAN	22.41	LEO	29
30	GEM		03.45	16.06	01.33	14.32	03.52	PIS	01.58	GEM	22.41	10.41	30
31	GEM		LEO		SCO		AQU	06.35		GEM		VIR	31

SUN

mth	dy	time → sign
JAN	1	00.00 → CAP
JAN	20	19.19 → AQU
FEB	19	09.38 → PIS
MAR	21	08.55 → ARI
APR	20	20.17 → TAU
MAY	21	19.42 → GEM
JUN	22	03.50 → CAN
JUL	23	14.45 → LEO
AUG	23	21.43 → VIR
SEP	23	19.09 → LIB
OCT	24	04.11 → SCO
NOV	23	01.27 → SAG
DEC	22	14.35 → CAP

MERCURY

mth	dy	time → sign
JAN	1	00.00 → SAG
JAN	10	16.48 → CAP
JAN	30	15.42 → AQU
FEB	17	02.15 → PIS
MAR	5	11.53 → ARI
MAY	12	19.48 → TAU
MAY	28	17.35 → GEM
JUN	11	14.11 → CAN
JUN	28	16.31 → LEO
SEP	5	02.28 → VIR
OCT	21	01.20 → LIB
OCT	9	04.02 → SCO
OCT	31	01.16 → SAG
NOV	25	11.53 → SCO
DEC	13	15.42 → SAG

VENUS

mth	dy	time → sign
JAN	1	00.00 → CAP
JAN	7	08.17 → AQU
JAN	31	07.28 → PIS
FEB	24	10.53 → ARI
MAR	20	21.55 → TAU
APR	14	21.08 → GEM
MAY	10	15.45 → CAN
JUN	6	22.43 → LEO
JUL	8	12.08 → VIR
SEP	20	03.04 → LEO
SEP	25	08.06 → VIR
NOV	9	18.10 → LIB
DEC	7	16.42 → SCO

MARS

mth	dy	time → sign
JAN	1	00.00 → TAU
FEB	10	13.57 → GEM
APR	10	09.37 → CAN
JUN	1	02.24 → LEO
JUL	20	11.13 → VIR
SEP	5	22.42 → LIB
OCT	21	09.45 → SCO
DEC	3	18.09 → SAG

SATURN

mth	dy	time → sign
JAN	1	00.00 → SAG
JAN	5	13.24 → CAP

JUPITER

mth	dy	time → sign
JAN	1	00.00 → SCO
FEB	10	13.35 → SAG
APR	24	14.17 → SCO
OCT	5	14.45 → SAG

MOON

dy	jan	feb	mar	apr	may	jun	jul	aug	sep	oct	nov	dec	dy
1	15.21	SCO	08.33	22.42	11.58	ARI	TAU	07.23	LEO	22.08	SCO	20.11	1
2	LIB	03.11	SAG	AQU	PIS	16.37	12.05	CAN	08.31	LIB	10.02	CAP	2
3	18.42	SAG	12.05	AQU	22.19	TAU	GEM	17.09	VIR	23.54	SAG	20.35	3
4	SCO	06.29	CAP	06.23	ARI	TAU	GEM	LEO	12.56	SCO	10.05	AQU	4
5	20.55	CAP	17.16	PIS	ARI	05.35	00.03	LEO	LIB	SCO	CAP	AQU	5
6	SAG	10.40	AQU	16.33	10.39	GEM	CAN	00.29	15.53	00.54	12.14	00.16	6
7	22.50	AQU	AQU	ARI	TAU	17.44	10.08	VIR	SCO	SAG	AQU	PIS	7
8	CAP	16.50	00.25	ARI	23.34	CAN	LEO	05.56	18.20	02.38	17.35	07.59	8
9	CAP	PIS	PIS	04.32	GEM	CAN	18.15	LIB	SAG	CAP	PIS	ARI	9
10	01.52	PIS	09.54	TAU	GEM	04.19	VIR	09.59	21.04	06.12	PIS	18.56	10
11	AQU	01.55	ARI	17.25	11.57	LEO	VIR	SCO	CAP	AQU	02.10	TAU	11
12	07.39	ARI	21.37	GEM	CAN	12.50	00.26	12.58	CAP	12.06	ARI	TAU	12
13	PIS	13.47	TAU	GEM	22.40	VIR	LIB	SAG	00.43	PIS	13.04	07.22	13
14	17.10	TAU	TAU	05.48	LEO	18.42	04.33	15.18	AQU	20.20	TAU	GEM	14
15	ARI	TAU	10.30	CAN	LEO	LIB	SCO	CAP	05.54	ARI	TAU	20.00	15
16	ARI	02.39	GEM	15.55	06.38	21.38	06.42	17.53	PIS	ARI	01.16	CAN	16
17	05.33	GEM	22.28	LEO	VIR	SCO	SAG	AQU	13.16	06.40	GEM	CAN	17
18	TAU	13.50	CAN	22.27	11.06	22.14	07.42	21.59	ARI	TAU	13.56	07.58	18
19	18.16	CAN	CAN	VIR	LIB	SAG	CAP	PIS	23.12	18.40	CAN	LEO	19
20	GEM	20.38	07.22	VIR	12.22	22.01	09.05	PIS	TAU	GEM	CAN	18.29	20
21	GEM	LEO	LEO	01.19	SCO	CAP	AQU	04.51	TAU	GEM	02.04	VIR	21
22	04.47	LEO	12.28	LIB	11.51	23.00	12.42	ARI	11.16	07.22	LEO	VIR	22
23	CAN	02.06	VIR	01.34	SAG	AQU	PIS	14.58	GEM	CAN	12.08	02.29	23
24	12.12	VIR	14.27	SCO	11.22	AQU	19.53	TAU	23.49	19.03	VIR	LIB	24
25	LEO	04.29	LIB	00.59	CAP	03.09	ARI	TAU	CAN	LEO	18.42	07.00	25
26	17.12	LIB	14.53	SAG	13.09	PIS	ARI	03.18	CAN	LEO	LIB	SCO	26
27	VIR	06.14	SCO	01.32	AQU	11.28	06.43	GEM	10.36	03.48	21.21	08.15	27
28	20.54	SCO	15.31	CAP	18.42	ARI	TAU	15.33	LEO	VIR	SCO	SAG	28
29	LIB		SAG	04.55	PIS	23.11	19.23	CAN	18.04	08.42	21.12	07.38	29
30	LIB		17.49	AQU	PIS	TAU	GEM	CAN	VIR	LIB	SAG	CAP	30
31	00.05		CAP		04.18		GEM	01.33		10.14		07.15	31

SUN

mth	dy	time → sign
JAN	1	00.00 → CAP
JAN	21	01.10 → AQU
FEB	19	15.26 → PIS
MAR	20	14.42 → ARI
APR	20	02.06 → TAU
MAY	21	01.33 → GEM
JUN	21	09.42 → CAN
JUL	22	20.37 → LEO
AUG	23	03.34 → VIR
SEP	23	00.59 → LIB
OCT	23	10.02 → SCO
NOV	22	07.19 → SAG
DEC	21	20.26 → CAP

MERCURY

mth	dy	time → sign
JAN	1	00.00 → SAG
JAN	4	08.24 → CAP
JAN	23	06.16 → AQU
FEB	9	10.12 → PIS
APR	16	02.22 → ARI
MAY	4	16.45 → TAU
MAY	19	03.27 → GEM
JUN	2	20.31 → CAN
JUL	1	01.12 → LEO
JUL	6	01.23 → CAN
AUG	10	17.49 → LEO
AUG	27	03.11 → VIR
SEP	12	06.29 → LIB
OCT	1	17.17 → SCO
DEC	7	17.30 → SAG
DEC	27	07.21 → CAP

VENUS

mth	dy	time → sign
JAN	1	00.00 → SCO
JAN	2	08.43 → SAG
JAN	27	04.46 → CAP
FEB	20	16.45 → AQU
MAR	16	01.53 → PIS
APR	9	10.32 → ARI
MAY	3	19.56 → TAU
MAY	28	06.11 → GEM
JUN	21	16.34 → CAN
JUL	16	02.11 → LEO
AUG	9	10.54 → VIR
SEP	2	19.29 → LIB
SEP	27	05.12 → SCO
OCT	21	17.12 → SAG
NOV	15	08.57 → CAP
DEC	10	08.35 → AQU

MARS

mth	dy	time → sign
JAN	1	00.00 → SAG
JAN	14	04.54 → CAP
FEB	23	04.12 → AQU
APR	2	06.24 → PIS
MAY	11	07.23 → ARI
JUN	20	09.05 → TAU
AUG	2	04.25 → GEM
SEP	21	04.11 → CAN

SATURN

mth	dy	time → sign
JAN	1	00.00 → CAP

JUPITER

mth	dy	time → sign
JAN	1	00.00 → SAG
MAR	1	13.01 → CAP
JUN	10	01.46 → SAG
OCT	26	03.11 → CAP

MOON

dy	jan	feb	mar	apr	may	jun	jul	aug	sep	oct	nov	dec	dy
1	AQU	00.39	18.18	GEM	CAN	16.38	08.46	SCO	CAP	22.12	ARI	TAU	1
2	09.19	ARI	TAU	GEM	21.59	VIR	LIB	02.04	12.35	PIS	15.27	07.01	2
3	PIS	09.16	TAU	01.46	LEO	VIR	15.08	SAG	AQU	PIS	TAU	GEM	3
4	15.21	TAU	05.08	CAN	LEO	01.31	SCO	03.25	13.51	01.46	23.46	17.52	4
5	ARI	20.58	GEM	14.01	08.59	LIB	17.42	CAP	PIS	ARI	GEM	CAN	5
6	ARI	GEM	17.37	LEO	VIR	06.20	SAG	03.21	16.26	07.09	GEM	CAN	6
7	01.22	GEM	CAN	LEO	16.30	SCO	17.34	AQU	ARI	TAU	10.26	06.21	7
8	TAU	09.37	CAN	00.02	LIB	07.31	CAP	03.42	21.46	15.16	CAN	LEO	8
9	13.45	CAN	05.25	VIR	20.07	SAG	16.43	PIS	TAU	GEM	22.59	19.12	9
10	GEM	21.08	LEO	06.35	SCO	06.48	AQU	06.21	TAU	GEM	LEO	VIR	10
11	GEM	LEO	14.45	LIB	20.55	CAP	17.19	ARI	06.31	02.18	LEO	VIR	11
12	02.23	LEO	VIR	10.01	SAG	06.23	PIS	12.36	GEM	CAN	11.24	06.10	12
13	CAN	06.35	21.19	SCO	20.50	AQU	21.07	TAU	18.10	14.55	VIR	LIB	13
14	13.59	VIR	LIB	11.37	CAP	08.17	ARI	22.29	CAN	LEO	21.07	13.12	14
15	LEO	13.55	LIB	SAG	21.51	PIS	ARI	GEM	CAN	LEO	LIB	SCO	15
16	LEO	LIB	01.37	13.01	AQU	13.42	04.48	GEM	06.46	02.40	LIB	16.07	16
17	00.03	19.24	SCO	CAP	AQU	ARI	TAU	10.43	LEO	VIR	02.53	SAG	17
18	VIR	SCO	04.37	15.32	01.23	22.33	15.40	CAN	18.07	11.32	SCO	16.16	18
19	08.12	23.12	SAG	AQU	PIS	TAU	GEM	23.17	VIR	LIB	05.17	CAP	19
20	LIB	SAG	07.12	19.55	07.55	TAU	GEM	LEO	VIR	17.06	SAG	15.49	20
21	13.59	SAG	CAP	PIS	ARI	09.46	04.09	LEO	02.58	SCO	06.02	AQU	21
22	SCO	01.39	10.10	PIS	17.00	GEM	CAN	10.41	LIB	20.16	CAP	16.45	22
23	17.02	CAP	AQU	02.23	TAU	22.10	16.46	VIR	09.18	SAG	07.04	PIS	23
24	SAG	03.42	14.02	ARI	TAU	CAN	LEO	20.09	SCO	22.28	AQU	20.34	24
25	17.59	AQU	PIS	10.50	03.55	CAN	LEO	LIB	13.42	CAP	09.49	ARI	25
26	CAP	06.04	19.29	TAU	GEM	10.51	04.31	LIB	SAG	CAP	PIS	ARI	26
27	18.19	PIS	ARI	21.16	16.06	LEO	VIR	03.23	16.54	00.57	14.51	03.30	27
28	AQU	10.38	ARI	GEM	CAN	22.53	14.33	SCO	CAP	AQU	ARI	TAU	28
29	19.56	ARI	03.12	09.22	CAN	VIR	LIB	08.19	19.32	04.26	22.00	13.01	29
30	PIS		TAU	CAN	04.50	VIR	21.55	SAG	AQU	PIS	TAU	GEM	30
31	PIS		13.32		LEO		SCO	11.09		09.11		GEM	31

SUN

mth	dy	time → sign
JAN	1	00.00 → CAP
JAN	20	07.01 → AQU
FEB	18	21.17 → PIS
MAR	20	20.32 → ARI
APR	20	07.55 → TAU
MAY	21	07.23 → GEM
JUN	21	15.30 → CAN
JUL	23	02.24 → LEO
AUG	23	09.19 → VIR
SEP	23	06.43 → LIB
OCT	23	15.46 → SCO
NOV	22	13.08 → SAG
DEC	22	02.19 → CAP

MERCURY

mth	dy	time → sign
JAN	1	00.00 → CAP
JAN	14	18.59 → AQU
FEB	1	21.39 → PIS
FEB	24	20.23 → AQU
MAR	18	10.16 → PIS
APR	10	09.23 → ARI
APR	26	14.34 → TAU
MAY	10	16.34 → GEM
MAY	28	17.23 → CAN
AUG	4	01.17 → LEO
AUG	18	20.52 → VIR
SEP	4	22.32 → LIB
SEP	27	12.16 → SCO
OCT	22	02.29 → LIB
NOV	10	23.53 → SCO
NOV	30	22.55 → SAG
DEC	20	01.04 → CAP

VENUS

mth	dy	time → sign
JAN	1	00.00 → AQU
JAN	5	03.31 → PIS
FEB	2	04.44 → ARI
JUN	5	19.25 → TAU
JUL	7	04.32 → GEM
AUG	3	15.28 → CAN
AUG	29	14.18 → LEO
SEP	23	15.43 → VIR
OCT	18	19.58 → LIB
NOV	11	05.33 → SCO
DEC	5	03.40 → SAG
DEC	29	00.07 → CAP

MARS

mth	dy	time → sign
JAN	1	00.00 → CAN
FEB	5	00.28 → GEM
FEB	7	05.18 → CAN
MAY	6	01.15 → LEO
JUN	28	23.51 → VIR
AUG	17	00.42 → LIB
OCT	1	20.12 → SCO
NOV	13	21.55 → SAG
DEC	24	17.50 → CAP

SATURN

mth	dy	time → sign
JAN	1	00.00 → CAP

JUPITER

mth	dy	time → sign
JAN	1	00.00 → CAP
MAR	15	08.11 → AQU
AUG	12	08.47 → CAP
NOV	4	02.43 → AQU

MOON

dy	jan	feb	mar	apr	may	jun	jul	aug	sep	oct	nov	dec	dy
1	00.23	LEO	14.13	LIB	SCO	CAP	AQU	ARI	05.52	CAN	LEO	VIR	1
2	CAN	07.48	VIR	16.36	05.25	17.45	02.52	16.19	GEM	CAN	06.17	LIB	2
3	12.54	VIR	VIR	SCO	SAG	AQU	PIS	TAU	15.00	09.43	VIR	LIB	3
4	LEO	19.27	01.21	22.34	08.40	19.50	04.13	23.04	CAN	LEO	18.42	13.30	4
5	LEO	LIB	LIB	SAG	CAP	PIS	ARI	GEM	CAN	22.45	LIB	SCO	5
6	01.48	LIB	10.24	SAG	11.24	23.23	10.01	GEM	03.01	LIB	LIB	20.24	6
7	VIR	04.51	SCO	02.52	AQU	ARI	TAU	08.56	LEO	VIR	04.40	SAG	7
8	13.31	SCO	17.04	CAP	14.23	ARI	17.27	CAN	16.05	11.04	SCO	SAG	8
9	LIB	11.01	SAG	06.03	PIS	04.38	GEM	20.59	VIR	LIB	11.51	00.31	9
10	22.09	SAG	21.19	AQU	17.56	TAU	GEM	LEO	VIR	21.19	SAG	CAP	10
11	SCO	13.50	CAP	08.31	ARI	11.40	03.13	LEO	04.33	SCO	16.59	03.11	11
12	SCO	CAP	23.29	PIS	22.25	GEM	10.00	LIB	SCO	SCO	CAP	AQU	12
13	02.40	14.13	AQU	10.55	TAU	20.50	14.56	VIR	05.21	SAG	20.59	05.41	13
14	SAG	AQU	AQU	ARI	TAU	CAN	LEO	22.45	SCO	SAG	AQU	PIS	14
15	03.41	13.53	00.26	14.16	04.34	CAN	LEO	LIB	23.54	11.24	AQU	08.45	15
16	CAP	PIS	PIS	TAU	GEM	08.16	03.55	LIB	SAG	CAP	00.18	ARI	16
17	02.55	14.41	01.32	19.55	13.17	LEO	VIR	09.45	SAG	15.37	PIS	12.39	17
18	AQU	ARI	ARI	GEM	CAN	21.13	16.39	SCO	05.42	AQU	03.10	TAU	18
19	02.32	18.21	04.25	GEM	CAN	VIR	LIB	17.45	CAP	18.10	ARI	17.46	19
20	PIS	TAU	TAU	04.50	00.45	VIR	LIB	SAG	08.43	PIS	06.03	GEM	20
21	04.26	TAU	10.32	CAN	LEO	09.32	03.04	22.07	AQU	19.35	TAU	GEM	21
22	ARI	01.51	GEM	16.43	13.38	LIB	SCO	CAP	09.36	ARI	09.59	00.50	22
23	09.51	GEM	20.23	LEO	VIR	18.51	09.42	23.25	PIS	21.07	GEM	CAN	23
24	TAU	12.49	CAN	LEO	VIR	SCO	SAG	AQU	09.40	TAU	16.20	10.26	24
25	18.50	CAN	CAN	05.31	01.18	SCO	12.28	23.02	ARI	TAU	CAN	LEO	25
26	GEM	CAN	08.48	VIR	LIB	00.05	CAP	PIS	10.42	00.24	CAN	22.29	26
27	GEM	01.34	LEO	16.34	09.34	SAG	12.41	22.49	TAU	GEM	02.01	VIR	27
28	06.23	LEO	21.30	LIB	SCO	02.00	AQU	ARI	14.32	07.03	LEO	VIR	28
29	CAN		VIR	LIB	14.11	CAP	12.13	ARI	GEM	CAN	14.25	11.26	29
30	19.05		VIR	00.27	SAG	02.18	PIS	00.37	22.19	17.30	VIR	LIB	30
31	LEO		08.21		16.20		12.56	TAU		LEO		22.42	31

SUN

mth	dy	time → sign
JAN	1	00.00 → CAP
JAN	20	12.58 → AQU
FEB	19	03.15 → PIS
MAR	21	02.29 → ARI
APR	20	13.51 → TAU
MAY	21	13.16 → GEM
JUN	21	21.24 → CAN
JUL	23	08.18 → LEO
AUG	23	15.11 → VIR
SEP	23	12.35 → LIB
OCT	23	21.40 → SCO
NOV	22	19.02 → SAG
DEC	22	08.16 → CAP

MERCURY

mth	dy	time → sign
JAN	1	00.00 → CAP
JAN	7	15.08 → AQU
MAR	15	11.43 → PIS
APR	3	02.33 → ARI
APR	18	04.10 → TAU
MAY	3	06.05 → GEM
JUL	11	07.36 → CAN
JUL	26	18.50 → LEO
AUG	10	19.29 → VIR
AUG	29	15.48 → LIB
NOV	5	02.20 → SCO
NOV	23	17.31 → SAG
DEC	12	20.51 → CAP

VENUS

mth	dy	time → sign
JAN	1	00.00 → CAP
JAN	21	20.31 → AQU
FEB	14	18.09 → PIS
MAR	10	18.28 → ARI
APR	3	23.05 → TAU
APR	28	09.22 → GEM
MAY	23	02.47 → CAN
JUN	17	05.31 → LEO
JUL	12	22.33 → VIR
AUG	8	17.14 → LIB
SEP	7	00.11 → SCO

MARS

mth	dy	time → sign
JAN	1	00.00 → CAP
FEB	1	23.17 → AQU
MAR	12	07.59 → PIS
APR	19	16.52 → ARI
MAY	28	23.44 → TAU
JUL	9	03.42 → GEM
AUG	22	11.32 → CAN
OCT	11	23.45 → LEO

SATURN

mth	dy	time → sign
JAN	1	00.00 → CAP
JAN	3	19.15 → AQU

JUPITER

mth	dy	time → sign
JAN	1	00.00 → AQU
MAR	25	22.15 → PIS

MOON

dy	jan	feb	mar	apr	may	jun	jul	aug	sep	oct	nov	dec	dy
1	SCO	21.09	06.38	20.42	06.12	17.40	06.19	LEO	03.02	SCO	SAG	14.26	1
2	SCO	CAP	CAP	PIS	ARI	GEM	CAN	07.57	LIB	SCO	01.17	AQU	2
3	06.22	22.57	09.53	20.41	06.49	21.56	13.55	VIR	15.47	09.40	CAP	19.53	3
4	SAG	AQU	AQU	ARI	TAU	CAN	LEO	20.17	SCO	SAG	09.02	PIS	4
5	10.24	22.53	10.16	20.25	08.16	CAN	LEO	LIB	SCO	19.35	AQU	23.17	5
6	CAP	PIS	PIS	TAU	GEM	05.22	00.22	LIB	03.26	CAP	13.53	ARI	6
7	12.00	22.50	09.33	22.00	12.28	LEO	VIR	08.56	SAG	CAP	PIS	ARI	7
8	AQU	ARI	ARI	GEM	CAN	16.12	12.48	SCO	12.20	02.20	15.45	00.59	8
9	12.53	ARI	09.40	GEM	20.35	VIR	LIB	19.48	CAP	AQU	ARI	TAU	9
10	PIS	00.35	TAU	03.12	LEO	VIR	LIB	SAG	17.26	05.29	15.45	02.07	10
11	14.34	TAU	12.35	CAN	LEO	04.51	01.05	SAG	AQU	PIS	TAU	GEM	11
12	ARI	05.18	GEM	12.36	08.11	LIB	SCO	03.17	19.02	05.40	15.43	04.20	12
13	18.02	GEM	19.25	LEO	VIR	16.45	11.00	CAP	PIS	ARI	GEM	CAN	13
14	TAU	13.20	CAN	LEO	21.01	SCO	SAG	07.07	18.33	04.43	17.49	09.20	14
15	23.42	CAN	CAN	00.57	LIB	SCO	17.33	AQU	ARI	TAU	CAN	LEO	15
16	GEM	CAN	05.56	VIR	LIB	02.01	CAP	08.17	18.02	04.50	23.40	17.59	16
17	GEM	00.03	LEO	13.53	08.43	SAG	21.07	PIS	TAU	GEM	LEO	VIR	17
18	07.39	LEO	18.33	LIB	SCO	08.30	AQU	08.25	19.29	08.05	LEO	VIR	18
19	CAN	12.26	VIR	LIB	18.02	CAP	23.00	ARI	GEM	CAN	09.33	05.41	19
20	17.50	VIR	VIR	01.37	SAG	12.49	PIS	09.20	GEM	15.30	VIR	LIB	20
21	LEO	VIR	07.28	SCO	SAG	AQU	PIS	TAU	00.26	LEO	21.58	18.18	21
22	LEO	01.20	LIB	11.27	01.08	15.59	00.34	12.28	CAN	LEO	LIB	SCO	22
23	05.53	LIB	19.28	SAG	CAP	PIS	ARI	GEM	09.07	02.31	LIB	SCO	23
24	VIR	13.36	SCO	19.20	06.31	18.43	02.57	18.34	LEO	VIR	10.33	05.33	24
25	18.53	SCO	SCO	CAP	AQU	ARI	TAU	CAN	20.31	15.11	SCO	SAG	25
26	LIB	23.47	05.48	CAP	10.29	21.34	06.57	CAN	VIR	LIB	21.43	14.19	26
27	LIB	SAG	SAG	01.08	PIS	TAU	GEM	03.30	VIR	LIB	SAG	CAP	27
28	06.53	SAG	13.47	AQU	13.15	TAU	13.00	LEO	09.08	03.48	SAG	20.42	28
29	SCO		CAP	04.40	ARI	01.09	CAN	14.36	LIB	SCO	07.00	AQU	29
30	15.59		18.43	PIS	15.17	GEM	21.20	VIR	21.49	15.19	CAP	AQU	30
31	SAG		AQU		TAU		LEO	VIR		SAG		01.20	31

SUN

mth	dy	time → sign
JAN	1	00.00 → CAP
JAN	20	18.54 → AQU
FEB	19	09.09 → PIS
MAR	21	08.20 → ARI
APR	20	19.36 → TAU
MAY	21	18.58 → GEM
JUN	22	03.04 → CAN
JUL	23	13.59 → LEO
AUG	23	20.58 → VIR
SEP	23	18.23 → LIB
OCT	24	03.29 → SCO
NOV	23	00.50 → SAG
DEC	22	14.02 → CAP

MERCURY

mth	dy	time → sign
JAN	1	00.00 → CAP
JAN	2	01.11 → AQU
JAN	20	04.59 → CAP
FEB	15	10.09 → AQU
MAR	9	05.26 → PIS
MAR	26	03.52 → ARI
APR	9	22.04 → TAU
MAY	3	04.17 → GEM
MAY	10	20.39 → TAU
JUN	14	23.20 → GEM
JUL	4	03.00 → CAN
JUL	18	06.19 → LEO
AUG	3	09.20 → VIR
AUG	26	20.33 → LIB
SEP	16	20.29 → VIR
OCT	10	16.44 → LIB
OCT	28	19.54 → SCO
NOV	16	11.07 → SAG
DEC	6	05.17 → CAP

VENUS

mth	dy	time → sign
JAN	1	00.00 → SCO
JAN	6	17.35 → SAG
FEB	5	20.35 → CAP
MAR	4	11.42 → AQU
MAR	30	01.00 → PIS
APR	24	03.39 → ARI
MAY	19	01.21 → TAU
JUN	12	19.57 → GEM
JUL	7	11.18 → CAN
JUL	31	22.39 → LEO
AUG	25	05.49 → VIR
SEP	18	09.43 → LIB
OCT	12	11.50 → SCO
NOV	5	13.25 → SAG
NOV	29	15.21 → CAP
DEC	23	18.53 → AQU

MARS

mth	dy	time → sign
JAN	1	00.00 → LEO
JUN	3	06.30 → VIR
JUL	27	04.15 → LIB
SEP	12	09.11 → SCO
OCT	25	17.32 → SAG
DEC	5	09.03 → CAP

SATURN

mth	dy	time → sign
JAN	1	00.00 → AQU

JUPITER

mth	dy	time → sign
JAN	1	00.00 → PIS
APR	4	03.19 → ARI

MOON

dy	jan	feb	mar	apr	may	jun	jul	aug	sep	oct	nov	dec	dy
1	PIS	TAU	21.39	CAN	LEO	00.09	SCO	SAG	AQU	PIS	00.42 TAU	GEM	1
2	04.48	16.03	GEM	14.45	06.13	LIB	SCO	03.12	AQU	13.48	23.48	10.45	2
3	ARI	GEM	GEM	LE0	VIR	12.38	08.11	CAP	01.37	ARI	GEM	CAN	3
4	07.33	20.40	02.08	LEO	17.42	SCO	SAG	11.25	PIS	13.50	GEM	12.20	4
5	TAU	CAN	CAN	00.20	LIB	SCO	19.03	AQU	03.52	TAU	00.08	LEO	5
6	10.14	CAN	09.15	VIR	LIB	01.01	CAP	16.46	ARI	13.58	CAN	17.26	6
7	GEM	03.06	LEO	11.49	06.16	SAG	CAP	PIS	05.02	GEM	03.24	VIR	7
8	13.41	LEO	18.34	LIB	SCO	12.07	03.36	20.07	TAU	16.01	LEO	VIR	8
9	CAN	11.36	VIR	LIB	18.42	CAP	AQU	ARI	06.46	CAN	10.14	02.21	9
10	19.01	VIR	VIR	00.14	SAG	21.22	09.53	22.37	GEM	20.54	VIR	LIB	10
11	LEO	22.18	05.35	SCO	SAG	AQU	PIS	TAU	10.08	LEO	20.07	14.04	11
12	LEO	LIB	LIB	12.48	06.13	AQU	14.16	TAU	CAN	LEO	LIB	SCO	12
13	03.07	LIB	17.51	SAG	CAP	04.20	ARI	01.16	15.30	04.34	LIB	SCO	13
14	VIR	10.38	SCO	SAG	15.51	PIS	17.15	GEM	LEO	VIR	07.57	02.53	14
15	14.05	SCO	SCO	00.27	AQU	08.46	TAU	04.39	22.47	14.24	SCO	SAG	15
16	LIB	22.57	06.27	CAP	22.32	ARI	19.27	CAN	VIR	LIB	20.40	15.21	16
17	LIB	SAG	SAG	09.34	PIS	10.54	GEM	09.17	VIR	LIB	SAG	CAP	17
18	02.35	SAG	17.35	AQU	PIS	TAU	21.45	LEO	08.00	01.52	SAG	CAP	18
19	SCO	09.00	CAP	14.53	01.47	11.44	CAN	15.40	LIB	SCO	09.23	02.29	19
20	14.20	CAP	CAP	PIS	ARI	GEM	CAN	VIR	19.10	14.32	CAP	AQU	20
21	SAG	15.23	01.21	16.30	02.21	12.46	01.15	VIR	SCO	SAG	20.51	11.28	21
22	23.23	AQU	AQU	ARI	TAU	CAN	LEO	00.25	SCO	SAG	AQU	PIS	22
23	CAP	18.17	05.04	15.51	01.53	15.44	07.06	LIB	07.50	03.21	AQU	17.41	23
24	CAP	PIS	PIS	TAU	GEM	LEO	VIR	11.39	SAG	CAP	05.32	ARI	24
25	05.14	19.05	05.37	15.06	02.29	21.56	16.02	SCO	20.15	14.20	PIS	20.57	25
26	AQU	ARI	ARI	GEM	CAN	VIR	LIB	SCO	CAP	AQU	10.25	TAU	26
27	08.35	19.38	04.57	16.27	05.58	VIR	LIB	00.15	CAP	21.36	ARI	21.58	27
28	PIS	TAU	TAU	CAN	LEO	07.41	03.38	SAG	06.03	PIS	11.49	GEM	28
29	10.44		05.13	21.25	13.22	LIB	SCO	11.57	AQU	PIS	TAU	22.07	29
30	ARI		GEM	LEO	VIR	19.48	16.08	CAP	11.46	00.40	11.14	CAN	30
31	12.55		08.14		VIR		SAG	20.37		ARI		23.09	31

SUN

mth	dy	time → sign
JAN	1	00.00 → CAP
JAN	21	00.41 → AQU
FEB	19	14.57 → PIS
MAR	20	14.10 → ARI
APR	20	01.27 → TAU
MAY	21	00.50 → GEM
JUN	21	08.57 → CAN
JUL	22	19.53 → LEO
AUG	23	02.51 → VIR
SEP	23	00.17 → LIB
OCT	23	09.21 → SCO
NOV	22	06.39 → SAG
DEC	21	19.50 → CAP

MERCURY

mth	dy	time → sign
JAN	1	00.00 → CAP
FEB	10	21.30 → AQU
FEB	29	22.50 → PIS
MAR	16	23.55 → ARI
APR	2	00.58 → TAU
JUN	9	15.45 → GEM
JUN	24	17.17 → CAN
JUL	9	00.39 → LEO
JUL	27	11.35 → VIR
OCT	3	00.12 → LIB
OCT	20	07.11 → SCO
NOV	8	11.02 → SAG
NOV	30	19.30 → CAP
DEC	16	14.31 → SAG

VENUS

mth	dy	time → sign
JAN	1	00.00 → AQU
JAN	17	02.53 → PIS
FEB	10	21.10 → ARI
MAR	7	12.38 → TAU
APR	4	03.03 → GEM
MAY	9	03.15 → CAN
JUN	17	18.17 → GEM
AUG	5	08.52 → CAN
SEP	8	04.53 → LEO
OCT	5	18.10 → VIR
OCT	31	08.54 → LIB
NOV	25	01.25 → SCO
DEC	19	07.02 → SAG

MARS

mth	dy	time → sign
JAN	1	00.00 → CAP
JAN	13	06.14 → AQU
FEB	20	07.33 → PIS
MAR	29	11.24 → ARI
MAY	7	14.41 → TAU
JUN	17	11.43 → GEM
JUL	30	18.23 → CAN
SEP	15	05.22 → LEO
NOV	6	03.20 → VIR

SATURN

mth	dy	time → sign
JAN	1	00.00 → AQU
MAR	24	04.17 → PIS
SEP	16	21.04 → AQU
DEC	16	05.39 → PIS

JUPITER

mth	dy	time → sign
JAN	1	00.00 → ARI
APR	12	06.53 → TAU

MOON

dy	jan	feb	mar	apr	may	jun	jul	aug	sep	oct	nov	dec	dy
1	LEO	19.25	LIB	09.41	05.42	AQU	PIS	TAU	00.13	LEO	00.24	SCO	1
2	LEO	LIB	13.54	SAG	CAP	11.01	00.52	15.28	CAN	12.42	LIB	SCO	2
3	02.48	LIB	SCO	22.36	18.06	PIS	ARI	GEM	02.36	VIR	08.25	01.24	3
4	VIR	05.12	SCO	CAP	AQU	18.03	05.42	17.13	LEO	17.44	SCO	SAG	4
5	10.10	SCO	01.47	CAP	AQU	ARI	TAU	CAN	05.12	LIB	18.43	13.53	5
6	LIB	17.35	SAG	10.24	03.43	21.20	07.43	18.11	VIR	LIB	SAG	CAP	6
7	21.04	SAG	14.35	AQU	PIS	TAU	GEM	LEO	09.19	00.57	SAG	CAP	7
8	SCO	SAG	CAP	18.47	09.15	21.50	07.57	19.50	LIB	SCO	07.06	02.57	8
9	SCO	06.11	CAP	PIS	ARI	GEM	CAN	VIR	16.20	11.02	CAP	AQU	9
10	09.49	CAP	01.35	23.08	11.09	21.16	08.01	23.51	SCO	SAG	20.08	15.00	10
11	SAG	16.39	AQU	ARI	TAU	CAN	LEO	LIB	SCO	23.32	AQU	PIS	11
12	22.14	AQU	09.05	ARI	11.01	21.35	09.44	LIB	02.47	CAP	AQU	PIS	12
13	CAP	AQU	PIS	00.37	GEM	LEO	VIR	07.31	SAG	CAP	07.28	00.12	13
14	CAP	00.09	13.15	TAU	10.53	LEO	14.41	SCO	15.30	12.15	PIS	ARI	14
15	08.48	PIS	ARI	01.06	CAN	00.27	LIB	18.44	CAP	AQU	15.10	05.32	15
16	AQU	05.10	15.30	GEM	12.31	VIR	23.32	SAG	CAP	ARI	TAU	TAU	16
17	17.04	ARI	TAU	02.23	LEO	06.54	SCO	SAG	03.47	PIS	18.57	07.21	17
18	PIS	08.45	17.26	CAN	17.02	LIB	SCO	07.38	AQU	PIS	TAU	GEM	18
19	23.10	TAU	GEM	05.40	VIR	16.49	11.28	CAP	13.22	05.05	19.58	07.02	19
20	ARI	11.48	20.11	LEO	VIR	SCO	SAG	19.39	PIS	ARI	GEM	CAN	20
21	ARI	GEM	CAN	11.17	00.41	SCO	SAG	AQU	19.44	08.24	20.04	06.31	21
22	03.23	14.49	CAN	VIR	LIB	05.03	00.27	AQU	ARI	TAU	CAN	LEO	22
23	TAU	CAN	00.15	19.08	10.58	SAG	CAP	05.13	23.46	10.03	20.59	07.41	23
24	06.05	18.11	LEO	LIB	SCO	18.02	12.30	PIS	TAU	GEM	LEO	VIR	24
25	GEM	LEO	05.42	LIB	23.03	CAP	AQU	12.15	TAU	11.37	LEO	12.04	25
26	07.51	22.30	VIR	05.01	SAG	CAP	22.36	ARI	02.46	CAN	00.02	LIB	26
27	CAN	VIR	12.48	SCO	SAG	06.22	PIS	17.24	GEM	14.14	VIR	20.11	27
28	09.45	VIR	LIB	16.46	12.00	AQU	PIS	TAU	05.39	LEO	05.54	SCO	28
29	LEO	04.46	22.03	SAG	CAP	16.56	06.25	21.16	CAN	18.25	LIB	SCO	29
30	13.09		SCO	SAG	CAP	PIS	ARI	GEM	08.52	VIR	14.31	07.20	30
31	VIR		SCO		00.32		12.00	GEM		VIR		SAG	31

SUN

mth	dy	time → sign
JAN	1	00.00 → CAP
JAN	20	06.29 → AQU
FEB	18	20.48 → PIS
MAR	20	20.05 → ARI
APR	20	07.26 → TAU
MAY	21	06.50 → GEM
JUN	21	14.56 → CAN
JUL	23	01.48 → LEO
AUG	23	08.43 → VIR
SEP	23	06.06 → LIB
OCT	23	15.10 → SCO
NOV	22	12.30 → SAG
DEC	22	01.40 → CAP

MERCURY

mth	dy	time → sign
JAN	1	00.00 → SAG
JAN	13	03.12 → CAP
FEB	3	09.02 → AQU
FEB	21	05.40 → PIS
MAR	9	02.19 → ARI
MAY	15	13.19 → TAU
JUN	2	03.47 → GEM
JUN	16	02.04 → CAN
JUL	1	15.55 → LEO
JUL	31	08.08 → VIR
AUG	3	04.57 → LEO
SEP	8	17.14 → VIR
SEP	25	05.49 → LIB
OCT	12	21.15 → SCO
NOV	2	06.04 → SAG

VENUS

mth	dy	time → sign
JAN	1	00.00 → SAG
JAN	12	08.01 → CAP
FEB	5	07.42 → AQU
MAR	1	07.55 → PIS
MAR	25	09.54 → ARI
APR	18	14.31 → TAU
MAY	12	22.08 → GEM
JUN	6	08.39 → CAN
JUN	30	21.59 → LEO
JUL	25	14.52 → VIR
AUG	19	13.06 → LIB
SEP	13	19.50 → SCO
OCT	9	16.46 → SAG
NOV	5	19.36 → CAP
DEC	7	04.37 → AQU

MARS

mth	dy	time → sign
JAN	1	00.00 → VIR
JUN	29	01.12 → LIB
AUG	20	12.16 → SCO
OCT	4	06.46 → SAG
NOV	14	07.19 → CAP
DEC	23	05.36 → AQU

SATURN

mth	dy	time → sign
JAN	1	00.00 → PIS

JUPITER

mth	dy	time → sign
JAN	1	00.00 → TAU
APR	22	14.33 → GEM
SEP	21	04.39 → CAN
NOV	17	03.08 → GEM

MOON

dy	jan	feb	mar	apr	may	jun	jul	aug	sep	oct	nov	dec	dy
1	20.06	AQU	AQU	02.19	TAU	07.05	LEO	03.54	SCO	18.29	AQU	PIS	1
2	CAP	AQU	09.38	ARI	20.26	CAN	17.11	LIB	00.00	CAP	AQU	23.22	2
3	CAP	02.56	PIS	08.29	GEM	07.47	VIR	08.20	SAG	CAP	03.23	ARI	3
4	09.04	PIS	18.45	TAU	22.39	LEO	19.43	SCO	10.51	06.48	PIS	ARI	4
5	AQU	12.43	ARI	12.55	CAN	09.33	LIB	16.49	CAP	AQU	14.21	08.11	5
6	21.06	ARI	ARI	GEM	CAN	VIR	LIB	SAG	23.34	19.14	ARI	TAU	6
7	PIS	20.24	01.49	16.24	00.50	13.29	01.38	SAG	AQU	PIS	22.29	13.27	7
8	PIS	TAU	TAU	CAN	LEO	LIB	SCO	04.22	AQU	PIS	TAU	GEM	8
9	07.08	TAU	07.14	19.23	03.47	20.04	10.53	CAP	11.56	05.54	TAU	15.57	9
10	ARI	01.36	GEM	LEO	VIR	SCO	SAG	17.09	PIS	ARI	03.54	CAN	10
11	14.10	GEM	11.03	22.14	08.04	SCO	22.29	AQU	22.50	14.16	GEM	17.08	11
12	TAU	04.14	CAN	VIR	LIB	05.10	CAP	AQU	ARI	TAU	07.29	LEO	12
13	17.48	CAN	13.23	VIR	14.10	SAG	CAP	05.37	ARI	20.40	CAN	18.35	13
14	GEM	04.54	LEO	01.38	SCO	16.20	11.08	PIS	07.56	GEM	10.13	VIR	14
15	18.35	LEO	14.55	LIB	22.32	CAP	AQU	16.57	TAU	GEM	LEO	21.33	15
16	CAN	05.05	VIR	06.42	SAG	CAP	23.45	ARI	15.06	01.27	12.54	LIB	16
17	17.57	VIR	17.04	SCO	SAG	04.51	PIS	ARI	GEM	CAN	VIR	LIB	17
18	LEO	06.45	LIB	14.31	09.20	AQU	PIS	02.27	20.01	04.51	16.10	02.40	18
19	17.55	LIB	21.32	SAG	CAP	17.29	11.13	TAU	CAN	LEO	LIB	SCO	19
20	VIR	11.45	SCO	SAG	21.50	PIS	ARI	09.20	22.35	07.13	20.37	10.01	20
21	20.28	SCO	SCO	01.24	AQU	PIS	20.14	GEM	LEO	VIR	SCO	SAG	21
22	LIB	20.57	05.37	CAP	AQU	04.29	TAU	13.04	23.30	09.21	SCO	19.27	22
23	LIB	SAG	SAG	14.04	10.14	ARI	TAU	CAN	VIR	LIB	02.56	CAP	23
24	03.01	SAG	17.07	AQU	PIS	12.16	01.48	14.01	VIR	12.31	SAG	CAP	24
25	SCO	09.17	CAP	AQU	20.19	TAU	GEM	LEO	00.15	SCO	11.45	06.44	25
26	13.32	CAP	CAP	02.02	ARI	16.18	03.53	13.36	LIB	18.09	CAP	AQU	26
27	SAG	22.14	05.59	PIS	ARI	GEM	CAN	VIR	02.47	SAG	23.03	19.17	27
28	SAG	AQU	AQU	11.12	02.48	17.20	03.37	13.52	SCO	SAG	AQU	PIS	28
29	02.21		17.32	ARI	TAU	CAN	LEO	LIB	08.42	03.05	AQU	PIS	29
30	CAP		PIS	17.03	05.58	16.59	02.55	SCO	SAG	CAP	11.40	07.40	30
31	15.17		PIS		GEM		VIR	SCO		14.49		ARI	31

SUN

mth	dy	time → sign
JAN	1	00.00 → CAP
JAN	20	12.24 → AQU
FEB	19	02.39 → PIS
MAR	21	01.54 → ARI
APR	20	13.12 → TAU
MAY	21	12.33 → GEM
JUN	21	20.33 → CAN
JUL	23	07.25 → LEO
AUG	23	14.18 → VIR
SEP	23	11.45 → LIB
OCT	23	20.57 → SCO
NOV	22	18.15 → SAG
DEC	22	07.28 → CAP

MERCURY

mth	dy	time → sign
JAN	1	00.00 → SAG
JAN	7	18.27 → CAP
JAN	27	04.10 → AQU
FEB	13	10.19 → PIS
MAR	3	02.58 → ARI
MAR	22	02.34 → PIS
APR	17	21.34 → ARI
MAY	9	14.49 → TAU
MAY	24	17.59 → GEM
JUN	7	19.11 → CAN
JUN	26	19.07 → LEO
SEP	1	10.35 → VIR
SEP	17	08.17 → LIB
OCT	5	22.06 → SCO
OCT	30	07.38 → SAG
NOV	13	03.26 → SCO
DEC	11	15.29 → SAG

VENUS

mth	dy	time → sign
JAN	1	00.00 → AQU
FEB	6	12.45 → CAP
FEB	25	10.55 → AQU
APR	6	15.55 → PIS
MAY	5	04.33 → ARI
MAY	31	18.02 → TAU
JUN	26	11.43 → GEM
JUL	21	17.11 → CAN
AUG	15	12.47 → LEO
SEP	8	23.43 → VIR
OCT	3	03.41 → LIB
OCT	27	03.24 → SCO
NOV	20	01.05 → SAG
DEC	13	22.09 → CAP

MARS

mth	dy	time → sign
JAN	1	00.00 → AQU
JAN	30	07.12 → PIS
MAR	9	12.46 → ARI
APR	17	20.35 → TAU
MAY	28	22.14 → GEM
JUL	11	03.11 → CAN
AUG	25	15.55 → LEO
OCT	12	18.39 → VIR
DEC	4	00.56 → LIB

SATURN

mth	dy	time → sign
JAN	1	00.00 → PIS

JUPITER

mth	dy	time → sign
JAN	1	00.00 → GEM
MAY	5	14.41 → CAN
SEP	27	13.34 → LEO

MOON

dy	jan	feb	mar	apr	may	jun	jul	aug	sep	oct	nov	dec	dy
1	17.46	GEM	22.48	LEO	19.31	SCO	23.51	AQU	22.27	16.47	GEM	CAN	1
2	TAU	13.41	CAN	10.31	LIB	09.38	CAP	AQU	ARI	TAU	17.43	05.02	2
3	TAU	CAN	CAN	VIR	21.23	SAG	CAP	03.36	ARI	TAU	CAN	LEO	3
4	00.06	14.14	00.57	10.40	SCO	16.10	09.14	PIS	10.59	03.43	23.36	08.48	4
5	GEM	LEO	LEO	LIB	SCO	CAP	AQU	16.15	TAU	GEM	LEO	VIR	5
6	02.40	13.11	00.36 VIR	11.30	00.52	CAP	20.39	ARI	21.52	12.12	LEO	11.43	6
7	CAN	VIR	23.48	SCO	SAG	01.21	PIS	ARI	GEM	CAN	03.10	LIB	7
8	02.50	12.50	LIB	14.54	07.12	AQU	PIS	04.38	GEM	17.25	VIR	14.18	8
9	LEO	LIB	LIB	SAG	CAP	12.57	09.16	TAU	05.26	LEO	04.54	SCO	9
10	02.34	15.15	00.47	22.02	16.52	PIS	ARI	14.38	CAN	19.27	LIB	17.13	10
11	VIR	SCO	SCO	CAP	AQU	PIS	21.03	GEM	09.01	VIR	05.53	SAG	11
12	03.53	21.33	05.18	CAP	AQU	01.26	TAU	20.41	LEO	19.29	SCO	21.30	12
13	LIB	SAG	SAG	08.42	04.55	ARI	TAU	CAN	09.25	LIB	07.37	CAP	13
14	08.08	SAG	13.55	AQU	PIS	12.29	05.51	22.50	VIR	19.21	SAG	CAP	14
15	SCO	07.26	CAP	21.13	17.15	TAU	GEM	LEO	08.33	SCO	11.37	04.19	15
16	15.39	CAP	CAP	PIS	ARI	20.26	10.44	22.35	LIB	20.59	CAP	AQU	16
17	SAG	19.25	01.35	PIS	ARI	GEM	CAN	VIR	08.34	SAG	19.03	14.17	17
18	SAG	AQU	AQU	09.27	03.49	GEM	12.27	22.05	SCO	SAG	AQU	PIS	18
19	01.45	AQU	14.18	ARI	TAU	01.05	LEO	LIB	11.21	01.55	AQU	PIS	19
20	CAP	08.05	PIS	20.00	11.40	CAN	12.47	23.24	SAG	CAP	05.53	02.39	20
21	13.26	PIS	PIS	TAU	GEM	03.29	VIR	SCO	17.53	10.41	PIS	ARI	21
22	AQU	20.30	02.33	TAU	17.00	LEO	13.38	SCO	CAP	AQU	18.31	15.07	22
23	AQU	ARI	ARI	04.27	CAN	05.08	LIB	03.51	CAP	22.20	ARI	TAU	23
24	01.58	ARI	13.32	GEM	20.37	VIR	16.32	SAG	03.48	PIS	ARI	TAU	24
25	PIS	07.53	TAU	10.48	LEO	07.23	SCO	11.37	AQU	PIS	06.37	01.13	25
26	14.33	TAU	22.41	CAN	23.22	LIB	22.04	CAP	15.48	11.03	TAU	GEM	26
27	ARI	17.03	GEM	15.09	VIR	11.04	SAG	21.56	PIS	ARI	16.31	07.58	27
28	ARI	GEM	GEM	LEO	VIR	SCO	SAG	AQU	PIS	23.05	GEM	CAN	28
29	01.43		05.23	17.50	02.00	16.31	06.04	AQU	04.29	TAU	23.50	11.57	29
30	TAU		CAN	VIR	LIB	SAG	CAP	09.48	ARI	TAU	CAN	LEO	30
31	09.43		09.12		05.11		16.02	PIS		09.28		14.33	31

SUN

mth	dy	time → sign
JAN	1	00.00 → CAP
JAN	20	18.10 → AQU
FEB	19	08.26 → PIS
MAR	21	07.36 → ARI
APR	20	18.54 → TAU
MAY	21	18.14 → GEM
JUN	22	02.25 → CAN
JUL	23	13.16 → LEO
AUG	23	20.11 → VIR
SEP	23	17.38 → LIB
OCT	24	02.47 → SCO
NOV	23	00.04 → SAG
DEC	22	13.19 → CAP

MERCURY

mth	dy	time → sign
JAN	1	00.56 → CAP
JAN	19	17.09 → AQU
FEB	6	00.37 → PIS
APR	14	14.35 → ARI
MAY	1	23.26 → TAU
MAY	16	03.23 → GEM
MAY	31	18.06 → CAN
AUG	8	22.05 → LEO
AUG	24	06.16 → VIR
SEP	9	16.54 → LIB
SEP	30	01.46 → SCO
DEC	5	13.44 → SAG
DEC	24	20.36 → CAP

VENUS

mth	dy	time → sign
JAN	1	00.00 → CAP
JAN	6	19.37 → AQU
JAN	30	18.54 → PIS
FEB	23	22.30 → ARI
MAR	20	09.58 → TAU
APR	14	09.57 → GEM
MAY	10	06.01 → CAN
JUN	6	16.48 → LEO
JUL	8	22.14 → VIR
SEP	9	11.57 → LEO
OCT	1	18.09 → VIR
NOV	9	16.35 → LIB
DEC	7	08.48 → SCO

MARS

mth	dy	time → sign
JAN	1	00.00 → LIB
FEB	12	12.13 → SCO
MAR	31	06.19 → LIB
JUL	19	22.47 → SCO
SEP	10	01.41 → SAG
OCT	23	02.26 → CAP
DEC	1	20.22 → AQU

SATURN

mth	dy	time → sign
JAN	1	00.00 → PIS
MAR	3	21.13 → ARI

JUPITER

mth	dy	time → sign
JAN	1	00.00 → LEO
JAN	16	03.32 → CAN
MAY	23	08.28 → LEO
OCT	19	10.57 → VIR

MOON

dy	jan	feb	mar	apr	may	jun	jul	aug	sep	oct	nov	dec	dy
1	VIR	01.44	SCO	00.11	AQU	20.07	16.43	GEM	14.08	03.38	15.26	02.10	1
2	17.04	SCO	11.53	CAP	AQU	ARI	TAU	22.32	LEO	VIR	SCO	SAG	2
3	LIB	05.55	SAG	07.49	ARI	ARI	TAU	CAN	17.07	04.34	14.51	02.25	3
4	20.16	SAG	17.35	AQU	PIS	09.04	04.39	CAN	VIR	LIB	SAG	CAP	4
5	SCO	12.10	CAP	18.29	13.10	TAU	GEM	04.26	18.03	04.14	15.44	04.57	5
6	SCO	CAP	CAP	PIS	ARI	20.52	13.47	LEO	LIB	SCO	CAP	AQU	6
7	00.28	20.17	02.03	PIS	ARI	GEM	CAN	07.36	18.44	04.32	19.45	11.19	7
8	SAG	AQU	AQU	06.57	02.09	GEM	19.58	VIR	SCO	SAG	AQU	PIS	8
9	05.53	AQU	12.41	ARI	TAU	06.18	LEO	09.34	20.40	07.04	AQU	21.43	9
10	CAP	06.19	PIS	19.56	14.08	CAN	LEO	LIB	SAG	CAP	03.42	ARI	10
11	13.05	PIS	PIS	TAU	GEM	13.19	00.07	11.44	SAG	12.45	PIS	ARI	11
12	AQU	18.17	00.53	08.15	GEM	LEO	VIR	SCO	00.43	AQU	14.58	10.32	12
13	22.45	ARI	ARI	GEM	00.11	18.24	03.20	14.52	CAP	21.38	ARI	TAU	13
14	PIS	ARI	13.54	GEM	CAN	VIR	LIB	SAG	07.08	PIS	ARI	23.18	14
15	PIS	07.19	TAU	18.37	07.49	21.58	06.17	19.18	AQU	PIS	03.52	GEM	15
16	10.48	TAU	TAU	CAN	LEO	LIB	SCO	CAP	15.53	08.58	TAU	GEM	16
17	ARI	19.16	02.19	CAN	12.52	LIB	09.22	CAP	PIS	ARI	16.40	10.23	17
18	23.39	GEM	GEM	01.54	VIR	00.25	SAG	01.17	PIS	21.41	GEM	CAN	18
19	TAU	GEM	12.10	LEO	15.31	SCO	12.59	AQU	02.46	TAU	GEM	19.21	19
20	TAU	03.48	CAN	05.42	LIB	02.20	CAP	09.18	ARI	TAU	04.13	LEO	20
21	10.38	CAN	18.04	VIR	16.30	SAG	17.59	PIS	15.20	10.38	CAN	LEO	21
22	GEM	08.04	LEO	06.41	SCO	04.46	AQU	19.47	TAU	GEM	13.47	02.21	22
23	17.51	LEO	20.08	LIB	17.06	CAP	AQU	ARI	TAU	22.27	LEO	VIR	23
24	CAN	09.04	VIR	06.19	SAG	09.11	01.28	ARI	CAN	CAN	20.46	07.27	24
25	21.20	VIR	19.50	SCO	18.58	AQU	PIS	08.21	GEM	CAN	VIR	LIB	25
26	LEO	08.44	LIB	06.27	CAP	16.49	12.00	TAU	15.45	07.40	VIR	10.36	26
27	22.36	LIB	19.10	SAG	23.44	PIS	ARI	21.08	CAN	LEO	00.48	SCO	27
28	VIR	09.09	SCO	08.54	AQU	PIS	ARI	GEM	23.41	13.19	LIB	12.09	28
29	23.33		20.08	CAP	AQU	03.52	00.40	GEM	LEO	VIR	02.13	SAG	29
30	LIB		SAG	14.57	08.18	ARI	TAU	07.34	LEO	15.31	SCO	13.11	30
31	LIB		SAG		PIS		13.00	CAN		LIB		CAP	31

SUN

mth	dy	time → sign
JAN	1	00.00 → CAP
JAN	20	23.52 → AQU
FEB	19	14.12 → PIS
MAR	20	13.22 → ARI
APR	20	00.45 → TAU
MAY	21	00.07 → GEM
JUN	21	08.13 → CAN
JUL	22	19.05 → LEO
AUG	23	02.03 → VIR
SEP	22	23.27 → LIB
OCT	23	08.32 → SCO
NOV	22	05.45 → SAG
DEC	21	19.02 → CAP

SATURN

mth	dy	time → sign
JAN	1	00.00 → ARI

MERCURY

mth	dy	time → sign
JAN	1	00.00 → CAP
JAN	12	07.17 → AQU
FEB	1	12.58 → PIS
FEB	11	18.54 → AQU
MAR	17	14.42 → PIS
APR	7	01.01 → ARI
APR	22	16.18 → TAU
MAY	6	22.52 → GEM
MAY	29	22.44 → CAN
JUN	13	22.37 → GEM
JUL	13	01.30 → CAN
JUL	31	06.13 → LEO
AUG	15	00.54 → VIR
SEP	1	16.59 → LIB
SEP	28	14.43 → SCO
OCT	7	22.45 → LIB
NOV	8	11.04 → SCO
NOV	27	12.47 → SAG
DEC	16	14.14 → CAP

VENUS

mth	dy	time → sign
JAN	1	22.37 → SAG
JAN	26	17.35 → CAP
FEB	20	04.57 → AQU
MAR	15	13.32 → PIS
APR	8	21.45 → ARI
MAY	3	06.55 → TAU
MAY	27	17.06 → GEM
JUN	21	03.21 → CAN
JUL	15	12.57 → LEO
AUG	8	21.47 → VIR
SEP	2	06.37 → LIB
SEP	26	16.46 → SCO
OCT	21	05.19 → SAG
NOV	14	21.48 → CAP
DEC	9	22.42 → AQU

MARS

mth	dy	time → sign
JAN	1	00.00 → AQU
JAN	9	09.43 → PIS
FEB	17	03.12 → ARI
MAR	27	23.35 → TAU
MAY	8	14.20 → GEM
JUN	21	05.23 → CAN
AUG	5	17.00 → LEO
SEP	21	18.42 → VIR
NOV	9	06.23 → LIB
DEC	29	22.19 → SCO

JUPITER

mth	dy	time → sign
JAN	1	00.00 → VIR
FEB	27	03.22 → LEO
JUN	15	14.34 → VIR
NOV	15	22.58 → LIB

MOON

dy	jan	feb	mar	apr	may	jun	jul	aug	sep	oct	nov	dec	dy
1	15.24	PIS	ARI	TAU	GEM	LEO	VIR	02.11	13.22	AQU	16.51	08.58	1
2	AQU	14.39	ARI	06.40	01.50	LEO	16.10	SCO	CAP	AQU	ARI	TAU	2
3	20.35	ARI	10.27	GEM	CAN	03.52	LIB	05.11	16.19	03.21	ARI	21.06	3
4	PIS	ARI	TAU	19.13	12.54	VIR	20.20	SAG	06.57	AQU	PIS	03.01	GEM	4
5	PIS	02.15	23.17	CAN	LEO	09.49	SCO	06.57	20.27	10.35	TAU	GEM	5
6	05.45	TAU	GEM	CAN	20.58	LIB	22.05	CAP	PIS	ARI	14.48	09.43	6
7	ARI	15.09	GEM	05.28	VIR	12.30	SAG	08.37	PIS	20.07	GEM	CAN	7
8	18.02	GEM	11.21	LEO	VIR	SCO	22.24	AQU	02.49	TAU	GEM	22.02	8
9	TAU	GEM	CAN	12.04	01.21	12.42	CAP	11.45	ARI	TAU	03.26	LEO	9
10	TAU	02.34	20.27	VIR	LIB	SAG	23.03	PIS	12.06	07.43	CAN	LEO	10
11	06.54	CAN	LEO	15.01	02.30	12.05	AQU	17.53	TAU	GEM	15.45	08.59	11
12	GEM	10.50	LEO	LIB	SCO	CAP	AQU	23.54	23.54	20.23	LEO	VIR	12
13	17.54	LEO	01.51	15.32	01.53	12.46	02.03	ARI	GEM	CAN	LEO	17.08	13
14	CAN	16.02	VIR	SCO	SAG	AQU	PIS	03.36	GEM	CAN	01.55	LIB	14
15	CAN	VIR	04.23	15.23	01.30	16.42	08.51	TAU	12.28	08.08	VIR	21.31	15
16	02.09	19.21	LIB	SAG	CAP	PIS	ARI	15.51	CAN	LEO	08.26	SCO	16
17	LEO	LIB	05.33	16.23	03.22	PIS	19.30	GEM	23.25	16.58	LIB	22.27	17
18	08.11	22.00	SCO	CAP	AQU	00.50	TAU	GEM	LEO	VIR	11.06	SAG	18
19	VIR	SCO	06.54	19.57	08.53	ARI	TAU	04.15	LEO	22.05	SCO	21.32	19
20	12.47	SCO	SAG	AQU	PIS	12.25	08.13	CAN	07.15	LIB	11.04	CAP	20
21	LIB	00.48	09.34	AQU	18.14	TAU	GEM	14.40	VIR	LIB	SAG	20.59	21
22	16.28	SAG	CAP	02.45	ARI	TAU	20.31	LEO	12.00	00.05	10.20	AQU	22
23	SCO	04.12	14.16	PIS	ARI	01.22	CAN	22.21	LIB	SCO	CAP	23.01	23
24	19.23	CAP	AQU	12.32	06.15	GEM	CAN	VIR	14.39	00.32	11.02	PIS	24
25	SAG	08.37	21.15	ARI	TAU	13.43	06.55	VIR	SCO	SAG	AQU	PIS	25
26	21.57	AQU	PIS	ARI	19.12	CAN	LEO	03.45	16.30	01.13	14.52	05.02	26
27	CAP	14.42	PIS	00.22	GEM	CAN	15.10	LIB	SAG	CAP	PIS	ARI	27
28	CAP	PIS	06.32	TAU	GEM	00.30	VIR	07.38	18.44	03.43	22.26	14.57	28
29	01.06	23.14	ARI	13.11	07.43	LEO	21.32	SCO	CAP	AQU	ARI	TAU	29
30	AQU		17.55	GEM	CAN	09.26	LIB	10.40	22.11	08.54	ARI	TAU	30
31	06.16		TAU		18.53		LIB	SAG		PIS		03.11	31

SUN

mth	dy	time → sign
JAN	1	00.00 → CAP
JAN	20	05.33 → AQU
FEB	18	19.53 → PIS
MAR	20	19.08 → ARI
APR	20	06.24 → TAU
MAY	21	05.56 → GEM
JUN	21	13.55 → CAN
JUL	23	00.44 → LEO
AUG	23	07.43 → VIR
SEP	23	05.09 → LIB
OCT	23	14.13 → SCO
NOV	22	11.31 → SAG
DEC	22	00.48 → CAP

MERCURY

mth	dy	time → sign
JAN	1	00.00 → CAP
JAN	4	12.21 → AQU
MAR	12	15.23 → PIS
MAR	30	09.56 → ARI
APR	14	05.55 → TAU
APR	30	15.15 → GEM
JUL	8	03.58 → CAN
JUL	22	19.14 → LEO
AUG	7	04.27 → VIR
AUG	27	06.50 → LIB
OCT	7	02.55 → VIR
OCT	9	16.55 → LIB
NOV	1	16.52 → SCO
NOV	20	06.00 → SAG
DEC	9	13.22 → CAP

VENUS

mth	dy	time → sign
JAN	1	00.00 → AQU
JAN	4	20.06 → PIS
FEB	2	04.44 → ARI
JUN	6	01.43 → TAU
JUL	6	22.02 → GEM
AUG	3	05.34 → CAN
AUG	29	02.49 → LEO
SEP	23	03.22 → VIR
OCT	17	14.13 → LIB
NOV	10	16.46 → SCO
DEC	4	14.41 → SAG
DEC	28	11.08 → CAP

MARS

mth	dy	time → sign
JAN	1	00.00 → SCO
FEB	25	06.10 → SAG
SEP	21	06.22 → CAP
NOV	4	18.43 → AQU
DEC	15	14.33 → PIS

SATURN

mth	dy	time → sign
JAN	1	00.00 → ARI
APR	29	22.35 → TAU

JUPITER

mth	dy	time → sign
JAN	1	00.00 → LIB
MAR	30	21.50 → VIR
JUL	15	13.39 → LIB
DEC	16	15.43 → SCO

MOON

dy	jan	feb	mar	apr	may	jun	jul	aug	sep	oct	nov	dec	dy
1	GEM	10.29	LEO	20.03	09.49	21.07	06.49	19.55	TAU	GEM	11.35	08.14	1
2	15.53	LEO	LEO	LIB	SCO	CAP	AQU	ARI	19.23	14.52	LEO	VIR	2
3	CAN	20.40	04.07	LIB	11.19	21.03	07.26	ARI	GEM	CAN	LEO	19.17	3
4	CAN	VIR	VIR	00.22	SAG	AQU	PIS	02.02	GEM	CAN	00.00	LIB	4
5	03.54	VIR	11.34	SCO	11.57	23.13	11.16	TAU	06.57	03.25	VIR	LIB	5
6	LEO	05.00	LIB	02.57	CAP	PIS	ARI	11.49	CAN	LEO	09.59	02.30	6
7	14.42	LIB	16.56	SAG	13.28	PIS	18.53	GEM	19.36	15.21	LIB	SCO	7
8	VIR	11.18	SCO	05.04	AQU	04.36	TAU	23.57	LEO	VIR	16.18	05.42	8
9	23.32	SCO	20.48	CAP	17.04	ARI	TAU	CAN	LEO	VIR	SCO	SAG	9
10	LIB	15.23	SAG	07.46	PIS	13.06	05.31	CAN	07.20	00.48	19.30	06.20	10
11	LIB	SAG	23.40	AQU	23.09	TAU	GEM	12.38	VIR	LIB	SAG	CAP	11
12	05.32	17.28	CAP	11.41	ARI	23.48	17.47	LEO	17.01	07.19	21.08	06.27	12
13	SCO	CAP	CAP	PIS	ARI	GEM	CAN	LEO	LIB	SCO	CAP	AQU	13
14	08.19	18.30	02.09	17.13	07.28	GEM	CAN	00.32	LIB	11.33	22.53	07.56	14
15	SAG	AQU	AQU	ARI	TAU	11.52	06.29	VIR	00.25	SAG	AQU	PIS	15
16	08.39	20.03	05.04	ARI	17.41	CAN	LEO	10.51	SCO	14.35	AQU	11.56	16
17	CAP	PIS	PIS	00.43	GEM	CAN	18.42	LIB	05.42	CAP	01.52	ARI	17
18	08.17	23.48	09.27	TAU	GEM	00.35	VIR	18.54	SAG	17.21	PIS	18.35	18
19	AQU	ARI	ARI	10.28	05.30	LEO	VIR	SCO	09.14	AQU	06.32	TAU	19
20	09.21	ARI	16.20	GEM	CAN	12.53	05.20	SCO	CAP	20.26	ARI	TAU	20
21	PIS	07.02	TAU	22.17	18.12	VIR	LIB	00.12	11.31	PIS	12.52	03.28	21
22	13.43	TAU	TAU	CAN	LEO	23.03	13.04	SAG	AQU	PIS	TAU	GEM	22
23	ARI	17.41	02.12	CAN	LEO	LIB	SCO	02.49	13.22	00.17	20.59	14.08	23
24	22.13	GEM	GEM	10.51	06.07	LIB	17.10	CAP	PIS	ARI	GEM	CAN	24
25	TAU	GEM	14.18	LEO	VIR	05.31	SAG	03.36	15.55	05.32	GEM	CAN	25
26	TAU	06.11	CAN	21.57	15.07	SCO	18.09	AQU	ARI	TAU	07.10	02.21	26
27	09.53	CAN	CAN	VIR	LIB	08.00	CAP	04.03	20.29	13.00	CAN	LEO	27
28	GEM	18.12	02.37	VIR	20.05	SAG	17.35	PIS	TAU	GEM	19.22	15.20	28
29	22.36		LEO	05.43	SCO	07.44	AQU	05.57	TAU	23.13	LEO	VIR	29
30	CAN		12.54	LIB	21.30	CAP	17.30	ARI	04.05	CAN	LEO	VIR	30
31	CAN		VIR		SAG		PIS	10.50		CAN		03.18	31

SUN

mth	dy	time → sign
JAN	1	00.00 → CAP
JAN	20	11.26 → AQU
FEB	19	01.42 → PIS
MAR	21	00.52 → ARI
APR	20	12.15 → TAU
MAY	21	11.32 → GEM
JUN	21	19.43 → CAN
JUL	23	06.33 → LEO
AUG	23	13.34 → VIR
SEP	23	10.53 → LIB
OCT	23	20.08 → SCO
NOV	22	17.23 → SAG
DEC	22	06.32 → CAP

MERCURY

mth	dy	time → sign
JAN	1	00.00 → CAP
JAN	4	04.23 → AQU
JAN	4	11.53 → CAP
FEB	13	13.06 → AQU
MAR	5	20.13 → PIS
MAR	22	07.59 → ARI
APR	6	07.44 → TAU
JUN	13	12.46 → GEM
JUN	30	06.21 → CAN
JUL	14	08.09 → LEO
JUL	31	05.23 → VIR
OCT	7	18.04 → LIB
OCT	25	06.11 → SCO
NOV	13	01.17 → SAG
DEC	3	10.15 → CAP

VENUS

mth	dy	time → sign
JAN	1	00.00 → CAP
JAN	21	07.22 → AQU
FEB	14	05.03 → PIS
MAR	10	05.23 → ARI
APR	3	10.07 → TAU
APR	27	20.34 → GEM
MAY	22	14.16 → CAN
JUN	16	17.49 → LEO
JUL	12	12.17 → VIR
AUG	8	10.00 → LIB
SEP	7	01.55 → SCO

MARS

mth	dy	time → sign
JAN	1	00.00 → PIS
JAN	24	21.22 → ARI
MAR	7	01.35 → TAU
APR	18	18.46 → GEM
JUN	2	06.51 → CAN
JUL	18	06.44 → LEO
SEP	3	04.50 → VIR
OCT	20	10.49 → LIB
DEC	6	16.27 → SCO

SATURN

mth	dy	time → sign
JAN	1	00.00 → TAU

JUPITER

mth	dy	time → sign
JAN	1	00.00 → SCO
APR	30	06.29 → LIB
AUG	15	17.45 → SCO

MOON

dy	jan	feb	mar	apr	may	jun	jul	aug	sep	oct	nov	dec	dy
1	LIB	01.50	SAG	AQU	PIS	TAU	GEM	10.44	VIR	LIB	02.24	CAP	1
2	12.03	SAG	12.54	AQU	09.32	TAU	17.21	LEO	18.25	11.35	SAG	18.45	2
3	SCO	04.21	CAP	00.01	ARI	02.10	CAN	23.34	LIB	SCO	08.32	AQU	3
4	16.33	CAP	14.34	PIS	13.05	GEM	CAN	VIR	LIB	20.31	CAP	21.55	4
5	SAG	04.19	AQU	01.32	TAU	10.25	04.26	VIR	05.54	SAG	13.11	PIS	5
6	17.30	AQU	14.49	ARI	18.17	CAN	LEO	12.32	SCO	SAG	AQU	PIS	6
7	CAP	03.37	PIS	04.02	GEM	21.17	17.11	LIB	14.58	03.10	16.33	01.03	7
8	16.47	PIS	15.16	TAU	GEM	LEO	VIR	23.57	SAG	CAP	PIS	ARI	8
9	AQU	04.17	ARI	09.02	02.17	LEO	VIR	SCO	20.51	07.26	18.52	04.24	9
10	16.37	ARI	17.43	GEM	CAN	10.02	06.02	SCO	CAP	AQU	ARI	TAU	10
11	PIS	07.59	TAU	17.33	13.22	VIR	LIB	08.07	23.34	09.30	20.50	08.33	11
12	18.48	TAU	23.37	CAN	LEO	22.28	16.41	SAG	AQU	PIS	TAU	GEM	12
13	ARI	15.29	GEM	CAN	02.10	LIB	SCO	12.25	23.57	10.12	23.48	14.32	13
14	ARI	GEM	GEM	05.15	VIR	LIB	23.26	CAP	PIS	ARI	GEM	CAN	14
15	00.20	GEM	09.18	LEO	VIR	08.01	SAG	13.31	23.35	11.00	GEM	23.21	15
16	TAU	02.17	CAN	18.07	14.02	SCO	SAG	AQU	ARI	TAU	05.23	LEO	16
17	09.07	CAN	21.39	VIR	LIB	13.39	02.19	13.01	ARI	13.43	CAN	LEO	17
18	GEM	14.53	LEO	VIR	22.49	SAG	CAP	PIS	00.21	GEM	14.36	11.04	18
19	20.13	LEO	LEO	05.35	SCO	16.04	02.44	12.50	TAU	19.59	LEO	VIR	19
20	CAN	LEO	10.30	LIB	SCO	CAP	AQU	ARI	04.02	CAN	LEO	VIR	20
21	CAN	03.42	VIR	14.15	04.11	17.00	02.36	14.46	GEM	CAN	02.50	00.01	21
22	08.40	VIR	21.56	SCO	SAG	AQU	PIS	TAU	11.41	06.12	VIR	LIB	22
23	LEO	15.30	LIB	20.15	07.13	18.11	03.42	20.03	CAN	15.39	LIB	11.27	23
24	21.33	LIB	LIB	SAG	CAP	PIS	ARI	GEM	22.54	18.57	LIB	SCO	24
25	VIR	LIB	07.10	SAG	09.26	20.52	07.18	GEM	LEO	VIR	LIB	19.27	25
26	VIR	01.23	SCO	00.26	AQU	ARI	TAU	04.58	LEO	VIR	02.25	SAG	26
27	09.42	SCO	14.07	CAP	11.59	ARI	13.53	CAN	11.53	07.37	SCO	SAG	27
28	LIB	08.38	SAG	03.43	PIS	01.35	GEM	16.38	VIR	LIB	10.02	00.01	28
29	19.34		SAG	19.00	15.27	TAU	23.14	LEO	VIR	18.15	SAG	CAP	29
30	SCO		CAP	06.37	ARI	08.24	CAN	LEO	00.33	SCO	15.05	02.24	30
31	SCO		22.08		20.03		CAN	05.36		SCO		AQU	31

SUN

mth	dy	time → sign
JAN	1	00.00 → CAP
JAN	20	17.11 → AQU
FEB	19	07.23 → PIS
MAR	21	06.38 → ARI
APR	20	17.50 → TAU
MAY	21	17.15 → GEM
JUN	22	01.14 → CAN
JUL	23	12.16 → LEO
AUG	23	19.15 → VIR
SEP	23	16.49 → LIB
OCT	24	01.58 → SCO
NOV	22	23.11 → SAG
DEC	22	12.27 → CAP

MERCURY

mth	dy	time → sign
JAN	1	00.00 → CAP
JAN	2	23.32 → SAG
JAN	14	02.17 → CAP
FEB	7	20.53 → AQU
FEB	26	07.52 → PIS
MAR	14	04.47 → ARI
APR	1	14.17 → TAU
APR	18	21.52 → ARI
MAY	17	03.33 → TAU
JUN	7	06.45 → GEM
JUN	21	16.28 → CAN
JUL	6	08.53 → LEO
JUL	26	17.03 → VIR
AUG	29	20.45 → LEO
SEP	11	06.42 → VIR
SEP	30	09.12 → LIB
OCT	17	17.49 → SCO
NOV	6	06.52 → SAG

VENUS

mth	dy	time → sign
JAN	1	00.00 → SCO
JAN	7	01.01 → SAG
FEB	5	14.54 → CAP
MAR	4	02.24 → AQU
MAR	29	14.04 → PIS
APR	23	15.47 → ARI
MAY	18	12.48 → TAU
JUN	12	06.56 → GEM
JUL	6	22.02 → CAN
JUL	31	09.12 → LEO
AUG	24	16.22 → VIR
SEP	17	20.26 → LIB
OCT	11	22.48 → SCO
NOV	5	00.33 → SAG
NOV	29	02.41 → CAP
DEC	23	06.34 → AQU

MARS

mth	dy	time → sign
JAN	1	00.00 → SCO
JAN	23	01.26 → SAG
MAR	12	10.23 → CAP
MAY	3	20.49 → AQU
NOV	6	12.33 → PIS
DEC	26	18.22 → ARI

SATURN

mth	dy	time → sign
JAN	1	00.00 → TAU
JUN	18	16.22 → GEM

JUPITER

mth	dy	time → sign
JAN	1	00.00 → SCO
JAN	14	08.56 → SAG
JUN	5	02.32 → SCO
SEP	11	15.39 → SAG

MOON

dy	jan	feb	mar	apr	may	jun	jul	aug	sep	oct	nov	dec	dy
1	04.08	15.49	TAU	16.51	09.34	VIR	LIB	08.49	CAP	19.36	ARI	16.25	1
2	PIS	TAU	TAU	CAN	LEO	17.26	13.46	SAG	07.04	PIS	05.55	GEM	2
3	06.26	20.34	03.01	CAN	21.03	LIB	SCO	16.32	AQU	19.40	TAU	17.51	3
4	ARI	GEM	GEM	02.05	VIR	LIB	23.59	CAP	08.51	ARI	05.27	CAN	4
5	10.00	GEM	09.47	LEO	VIR	05.36	SAG	20.47	PIS	18.42	GEM	22.17	5
6	TAU	04.07	CAN	14.16	09.59	SCO	SAG	AQU	08.43	TAU	07.15	LEO	6
7	15.08	CAN	19.55	VIR	LIB	15.28	07.03	22.34	ARI	18.53	CAN	LEO	7
8	GEM	14.06	LEO	VIR	22.03	SAG	CAP	PIS	08.37	GEM	12.56	06.40	8
9	22.09	LEO	LEO	03.17	SCO	22.45	11.26	23.27	TAU	22.10	LEO	VIR	9
10	CAN	LEO	08.10	LIB	SCO	CAP	AQU	ARI	10.25	CAN	22.44	18.19	10
11	CAN	01.58	VIR	15.28	08.08	CAP	14.14	ARI	GEM	CAN	VIR	LIB	11
12	07.24	VIR	21.06	SCO	SAG	04.03	PIS	00.55	15.21	05.30	VIR	LIB	12
13	LEO	14.50	LIB	SCO	16.09	AQU	16.32	TAU	CAN	LEO	11.05	07.01	13
14	18.57	LIB	LIB	02.03	CAP	08.01	ARI	04.10	23.38	16.16	LIB	SCO	14
15	VIR	LIB	09.31	SAG	22.19	PIS	19.10	GEM	LEO	VIR	23.49	18.37	15
16	VIR	03.22	SCO	10.38	AQU	11.06	TAU	09.50	LEO	VIR	SCO	SAG	16
17	07.53	SCO	20.23	CAP	AQU	ARI	22.47	CAN	04.47	SCO	SCO	SAG	17
18	LIB	13.45	SAG	16.46	02.39	13.39	GEM	17.57	VIR	LIB	11.30	04.07	18
19	20.04	SAG	SAG	AQU	PIS	TAU	GEM	LEO	17.31	SAG	CAP	CAP	19
20	SCO	20.37	04.37	20.07	05.11	16.24	03.56	LEO	SCO	21.36	11.32		20
21	SCO	CAP	CAP	PIS	ARI	GEM	CAN	04.19	LIB	SCO	CAP	AQU	21
22	05.15	23.43	09.28	21.08	06.31	20.30	11.16	VIR	05.31	CAP	17.10	22
23	SAG	AQU	AQU	ARI	TAU	CAN	LEO	16.22	SCO	SAG	05.52	PIS	23
24	10.32	AQU	11.07	21.06	08.01	CAN	21.09	LIB	23.43	16.05	AQU	21.09	24
25	CAP	00.05›PIS	PIS	TAU	GEM	03.12	VIR	LIB	SAG	CAP	11.48	ARI	25
26	12.36	23.30	10.45	21.58	11.26	LEO	VIR	05.09	SAG	CAP	PIS	23.45	26
27	AQU	ARI	ARI	GEM	CAN	13.06	09.12	SCO	09.53	00.11	15.03	TAU	27
28	13.02	23.54	10.16	GEM	18.16	VIR	LIB	16.56	CAP	AQU	ARI	TAU	28
29	PIS		TAU	01.43	LEO	VIR	21.50	SAG	16.39	04.56	16.08	01.38	29
30	13.36		11.43	CAN	LEO	01.22	SCO	SAG	AQU	PIS	TAU	GEM	30
31	ARI		GEM		04.48		SCO	01.54		06.26		04.01	31

SUN

mth	dy	time → sign
JAN	1	00.00 → CAP
JAN	20	23.04 → AQU
FEB	19	13.13 → PIS
MAR	20	12.27 → ARI
APR	19	23.38 → TAU
MAY	20	22.56 → GEM
JUN	21	07.07 → CAN
JUL	22	18.03 → LEO
AUG	23	01.08 → VIR
SEP	22	22.37 → LIB
OCT	23	07.42 → SCO
NOV	22	05.04 → SAG
DEC	21	18.17 → CAP

MERCURY

mth	dy	time → sign
JAN	1	00.00 → SAG
JAN	11	18.13 → CAP
JAN	31	23.47 → AQU
FEB	18	12.55 → PIS
MAR	5	16.56 → ARI
MAY	12	23.42 → TAU
MAY	29	06.46 → GEM
JUN	12	02.52 → CAN
JUN	28	16.52 → LEO
SEP	5	11.38 → VIR
SEP	21	12.15 → LIB
OCT	9	11.11 → SCO
OCT	30	19.23 → SAG
NOV	29	07.08 → SCO
DEC	12	23.18 → SAG

VENUS

mth	dy	time → sign
JAN	1	00.00 → AQU
JAN	16	15.10 → PIS
FEB	10	10.07 → ARI
MAR	7	03.24 → TAU
APR	3	22.48 → GEM
MAY	10	13.53 → CAN
JUN	11	20.08 → GEM
AUG	6	01.21 → CAN
SEP	7	23.27 → LEO
OCT	5	08.38 → VIR
OCT	30	21.43 → LIB
NOV	24	13.23 → SCO
DEC	18	18.37 → SAG

MARS

mth	dy	time → sign
JAN	1	00.00 → ARI
FEB	10	14.11 → TAU
MAR	27	04.37 → GEM
MAY	12	13.23 → CAN
JUN	28	16.14 → LEO
AUG	15	00.44 → VIR
SEP	30	23.33 → LIB
NOV	15	22.12 → SCO
DEC	30	16.24 → SAG

SATURN

mth	dy	time → sign
JAN	1	00.00 → GEM
JAN	10	03.28 → TAU
FEB	21	14.33 → GEM

JUPITER

mth	dy	time → sign
JAN	1	00.00 → SAG
FEB	6	19.23 → CAP
JUL	24	16.32 → SAG
SEP	25	18.28 → CAP

MOON

dy	jan	feb	mar	apr	may	jun	jul	aug	sep	oct	nov	dec	dy
1	CAN	00.56	19.00	SCO	SAG	12.15	01.18	14.57	GEM	12.25	VIR	LIB	1
2	08.22	VIR	LIB	SCO	20.29	AQU	PIS	TAU	02.11	LEO	10.27	03.42	2
3	LEO	11.06	LIB	02.27	CAP	19.52	06.22	17.33	CAN	19.31	LIB	SCO	3
4	15.50	LIB	07.00	SAG	CAP	PIS	ARI	GEM	06.54	VIR	21.46	16.22	4
5	VIR	23.18	SCO	14.20	06.35	PIS	09.25	20.18	LEO	VIR	SCO	SAG	5
6	VIR	SCO	19.36	CAP	AQU	00.27	TAU	CAN	13.15	04.35	SCO	SAG	6
7	02.33	SCO	SAG	23.37	13.28	ARI	11.05	23.56	VIR	LIB	10.16	05.06	7
8	LIB	11.38	SAG	AQU	PIS	02.14	GEM	LEO	21.36	15.27	SAG	CAP	8
9	15.03	SAG	06.49	AQU	16.35	TAU	12.29	LEO	LIB	23.11	SCO	16.53	9
10	SCO	21.50	CAP	04.58	ARI	02.24	CAN	05.23	LIB	SCO	CAP	AQU	10
11	SCO	CAP	14.42	PIS	16.47	GEM	15.05	VIR	08.15	03.52	CAP	AQU	11
12	02.57	CAP	AQU	06.32	TAU	02.45	LEO	13.27	SCO	11.02	02.32	12
13	SAG	04.36	18.39	ARI	15.57	CAN	20.16	LIB	20.42	16.44	AQU	PIS	13
14	12.26	AQU	PIS	05.54	GEM	05.10	VIR	LIB	SAG	CAP	19.56	08.59	14
15	CAP	08.11	19.37	TAU	16.16	LEO	VIR	00.19	SAG	CAP	PIS	ARI	15
16	19.04	PIS	ARI	05.16	CAN	11.03	04.49	SCO	09.07	03.51	PIS	11.59	16
17	AQU	09.51	19.27	GEM	19.38	VIR	LIB	12.49	CAP	AQU	00.44	TAU	17
18	23.28	ARI	TAU	06.46	LEO	20.39	16.15	SAG	19.04	11.12	ARI	12.24	18
19	PIS	11.11	20.12	CAN	LEO	LIB	SCO	SAG	AQU	PIS	01.53	GEM	19
20	PIS	TAU	GEM	11.47	02.56	LIB	SCO	00.38	AQU	14.22	TAU	11.57	20
21	02.35	13.35	23.26	LEO	VIR	08.43	04.46	CAP	01.09	ARI	01.05	CAN	21
22	ARI	GEM	CAN	20.24	13.36	SCO	SAG	09.43	PIS	14.37	GEM	12.34	22
23	05.17	17.52	CAN	VIR	LIB	21.14	16.10	AQU	03.44	TAU	00.31	LEO	23
24	TAU	CAN	05.46	VIR	LIB	SAG	CAP	15.28	ARI	14.02	CAN	16.03	24
25	08.14	CAN	LEO	07.34	02.01	SAG	CAP	PIS	04.27	GEM	02.12	VIR	25
26	GEM	00.15	14.47	LIB	SCO	08.36	01.07	18.40	TAU	14.44	LEO	23.21	26
27	12.01	LEO	VIR	19.56	14.33	CAP	AQU	ARI	05.14	CAN	07.24	LIB	27
28	CAN	08.39	VIR	SCO	SAG	18.02	07.29	20.43	GEM	18.14	VIR	LIB	28
29	17.21	VIR	01.42	SCO	SAG	AQU	PIS	TAU	07.39	LEO	16.15	10.10	29
30	LEO		LIB	08.31	02.13	AQU	11.50	22.56	CAN	LEO	LIB	SCO	30
31	LEO		13.48		CAP		ARI	GEM		00.59		22.51	31

SUN

mth	dy	time → sign
JAN	1	00.00 → CAP
JAN	20	04.54 → AQU
FEB	18	19.02 → PIS
MAR	20	18.16 → ARI
APR	20	05.30 → TAU
MAY	21	04.55 → GEM
JUN	21	13.03 → CAN
JUL	22	23.56 → LEO
AUG	23	06.58 → VIR
SEP	23	04.21 → LIB
OCT	23	13.34 → SCO
NOV	22	10.54 → SAG
DEC	22	00.04 → CAP

MERCURY

mth	dy	time → sign
JAN	1	00.00 → SAG
JAN	4	14.47 → CAP
JAN	23	15.23 → AQU
FEB	9	19.33 → PIS
APR	16	21.18 → ARI
MAY	6	02.59 → TAU
MAY	20	17.26 → GEM
JUN	4	04.42 → CAN
JUN	27	06.46 → LEO
JUL	16	08.01 → CAN
AUG	11	12.21 → LEO
AUG	28	15.22 → VIR
SEP	13	16.11 → LIB
OCT	2	20.12 → SCO
DEC	8	21.29 → SAG
DEC	28	15.15 → CAP

VENUS

mth	dy	time → sign
JAN	1	00.00 → SAG
JAN	11	19.12 → CAP
FEB	4	18.43 → AQU
FEB	28	18.42 → PIS
MAR	24	20.34 → ARI
APR	18	01.05 → TAU
MAY	12	08.44 → GEM
JUN	5	19.20 → CAN
JUN	30	08.54 → LEO
JUL	25	02.13 → VIR
AUG	19	01.17 → LIB
SEP	13	09.05 → SCO
OCT	9	08.03 → SAG
NOV	5	15.39 → CAP
DEC	7	21.33 → AQU

MARS

mth	dy	time → sign
JAN	1	00.00 → SAG
FEB	12	05.43 → CAP
MAR	26	20.46 → AQU
MAY	8	04.25 → PIS
JUN	20	20.54 → ARI
AUG	12	14.42 → TAU
OCT	29	22.42 → ARI
DEC	24	08.26 → TAU

SATURN

mth	dy	time → sign
JAN	1	00.00 → GEM
AUG	1	22.40 → CAN

JUPITER

mth	dy	time → sign
JAN	1	00.00 → CAP
FEB	23	09.38 → AQU

MOON

dy	jan	feb	mar	apr	may	jun	jul	aug	sep	oct	nov	dec	dy
1	SAG	CAP	14.22	PIS	ARI	GEM	21.55	VIR	05.17	SAG	CAP	AQU	1
2	SAG	05.55	AQU	12.48	01.01	11.21	LEO	13.12	SCO	SAG	08.58	04.32	2
3	11.30	AQU	22.31	ARI	TAU	CAN	23.31	15.24	12.02	AQU	PIS	PIS	3
4	CAP	14.22	PIS	14.58	01.16	11.49	VIR	20.35	SAG	CAP	20.26	13.50	4
5	22.47	PIS	PIS	TAU	GEM	LEO	VIR	SCO	SAG	CAP	PIS	ARI	5
6	AQU	20.29	03.37	16.12	01.35	14.51	04.23	SCO	04.01	00.48	PIS	19.08	6
7	AQU	ARI	ARI	GEM	CAN	VIR	LIB	07.37	CAP	AQU	04.19	TAU	7
8	08.03	ARI	06.51	18.04	03.36	21.16	13.05	SAG	16.30	11.23	ARI	20.58	8
9	PIS	00.53	TAU	CAN	LEO	LIB	SCO	20.30	AQU	PIS	08.25	GEM	9
10	14.57	TAU	09.31	21.31	08.13	LIB	SCO	CAP	AQU	18.29	TAU	20.52	10
11	ARI	04.10	GEM	LEO	VIR	06.52	00.48	CAP	02.40	ARI	09.59	CAN	11
12	19.24	GEM	12.29	LEO	15.31	SCO	SAG	08.52	PIS	22.36	GEM	20.44	12
13	TAU	06.44	CAN	02.46	LIB	18.43	13.45	AQU	09.56	TAU	10.46	LEO	13
14	21.41	CAN	16.07	VIR	LIB	SAG	CAP	19.14	ARI	TAU	CAN	22.20	14
15	GEM	09.12	LEO	09.50	01.09	SAG	CAP	PIS	14.59	01.09	12.20	VIR	15
16	22.39	LEO	20.42	LIB	SCO	07.37	02.15	PIS	TAU	GEM	LEO	VIR	16
17	CAN	12.31	VIR	18.51	12.41	CAP	AQU	03.15	18.48	03.28	15.41	02.53	17
18	23.40	VIR	VIR	SCO	SAG	20.19	13.07	ARI	GEM	CAN	VIR	LIB	18
19	LEO	17.58	02.48	SCO	SAG	AQU	PIS	09.14	22.01	06.25	21.15	10.44	19
20	LEO	LIB	LIB	06.02	01.30	AQU	21.43	TAU	CAN	LEO	LIB	SCO	20
21	02.23	LIB	11.15	SAG	CAP	07.29	ARI	13.26	CAN	10.19	LIB	21.20	21
22	VIR	02.35	SCO	18.49	14.17	PIS	ARI	GEM	00.56	VIR	05.06	SAG	22
23	08.16	SCO	22.26	CAP	AQU	15.48	03.41	16.08	LEO	15.28	SCO	SAG	23
24	LIB	14.14	SAG	CAP	AQU	ARI	TAU	CAN	03.58	LIB	15.11	09.41	24
25	17.52	SAG	SAG	07.21	01.05	20.37	06.58	17.49	VIR	22.28	SAG	CAP	25
26	SCO	SAG	11.16	AQU	PIS	TAU	GEM	LEO	08.00	SCO	SAG	22.43	26
27	SCO	03.04	CAP	17.09	08.14	22.18	08.10	19.33	LIB	SCO	03.13	AQU	27
28	06.10	CAP	23.12	PIS	ARI	GEM	CAN	VIR	14.18	07.57	CAP	AQU	28
29	SAG		AQU	22.53	11.28	22.08	08.29	22.52	SCO	SAG	16.17	11.10	29
30	18.54		AQU	ARI	TAU	CAN	LEO	LIB	23.47	19.57	AQU	PIS	30
31	CAP		07.55		11.53		09.34	LIB		CAP		21.34	31

SUN

mth	dy	time → sign
JAN	1	00.00 → CAP
JAN	20	10.42 → AQU
FEB	19	00.57 → PIS
MAR	21	00.04 → ARI
APR	20	11.19 → TAU
MAY	21	10.34 → GEM
JUN	21	18.36 → CAN
JUL	23	05.35 → LEO
AUG	23	12.23 → VIR
SEP	23	09.58 → LIB
OCT	23	19.12 → SCO
NOV	22	16.34 → SAG
DEC	22	05.56 → CAP

MERCURY

mth	dy	time → sign
JAN	1	00.00 → CAP
JAN	16	03.52 → AQU
FEB	2	22.42 → PIS
MAR	2	17.48 → AQU
MAR	17	20.11 → PIS
APR	11	15.20 → ARI
APR	28	03.16 → TAU
MAY	12	04.55 → GEM
MAY	29	08.06 → CAN
AUG	5	11.41 → LEO
AUG	20	09.01 → VIR
SEP	6	05.48 → LIB
SEP	28	00.21 → SCO
OCT	26	23.22 → LIB
NOV	11	16.05 → SCO
DEC	2	06.17 → SAG
DEC	21	09.17 → CAP

VENUS

mth	dy	time → sign
JAN	1	00.00 → AQU
JAN	29	19.48 → CAP
FEB	28	14.25 → AQU
APR	6	14.13 → PIS
MAY	4	20.23 → ARI
MAY	31	07.16 → TAU
JUN	25	23.41 → GEM
JUL	21	04.38 → CAN
AUG	14	23.47 → LEO
SEP	8	10.24 → VIR
OCT	2	14.27 → LIB
OCT	26	14.11 → SCO
NOV	19	11.57 → SAG
DEC	13	09.12 → CAP

MARS

mth	dy	time → sign
JAN	1	00.00 → TAU
FEB	27	10.25 → GEM
APR	20	08.23 → CAN
JUN	9	00.54 → LEO
JUL	27	14.21 → VIR
SEP	12	19.15 → LIB
OCT	28	07.25 → SCO
DEC	10	22.17 → SAG

SATURN

mth	dy	time → sign
JAN	1	00.00 → CAN
JAN	7	20.19 → GEM
APR	18	22.22 → CAN

JUPITER

mth	dy	time → sign
JAN	1	00.00 → AQU
MAR	8	11.14 → PIS

MOON

dy	jan	feb	mar	apr	may	jun	jul	aug	sep	oct	nov	dec	dy
1	ARI	16.53	GEM	11.40	VIR	11.10	01.20	CAP	01.29	ARI	18.23	06.22	1
2	ARI	GEM	GEM	LEO	23.39	SCO	SAG	06.46	PIS	ARI	GEM	CAN	2
3	04.38	19.05	02.59	13.56	LIB	19.21	12.19	AQU	12.58	04.39	23.01	08.31	3
4	TAU	CAN	CAN	VIR	LIB	SAG	CAP	19.26	ARI	TAU	CAN	LEO	4
5	08.00	19.11	04.49	16.22	04.43	SAG	CAP	PIS	22.50	12.00	CAN	10.40	5
6	GEM	LEO	LEO	LIB	SCO	05.48	00.41	PIS	TAU	GEM	02.30	VIR	6
7	08.28	18.52	05.33	20.25	12.05	CAP	AQU	07.15	TAU	17.30	LEO	13.42	7
8	CAN	VIR	VIR	SCO	SAG	18.02	13.25	ARI	06.36	CAN	05.18	LIB	8
9	07.42	20.10	06.52	SCO	22.15	AQU	PIS	17.13	GEM	21.03	VIR	18.13	9
10	LEO	LIB	LIB	03.27	CAP	AQU	PIS	TAU	11.39	LEO	07.58	SCO	10
11	07.41	LIB	10.40	SAG	CAP	06.43	01.10	TAU	CAN	22.56	LIB	SCO	11
12	VIR	00.58	SCO	13.56	10.34	PIS	ARI	00.15	13.54	VIR	11.23	00.34	12
13	10.21	SCO	18.20	CAP	AQU	17.52	10.21	GEM	LEO	VIR	SCO	SAG	13
14	LIB	10.01	SAG	CAP	23.33	ARI	TAU	03.49	14.12	00.11	16.39	09.04	14
15	16.54	SAG	SAG	02.34	PIS	ARI	15.54	CAN	VIR	LIB	SAG	CAP	15
16	SCO	22.16	05.41	AQU	PIS	01.46	GEM	04.26	14.17	02.23	SAG	19.48	16
17	SCO	CAP	CAP	14.44	09.19	TAU	17.56	LEO	LIB	SCO	00.42	AQU	17
18	03.12	CAP	18.38	PIS	ARI	05.59	CAN	03.42	16.14	CAP	07.14	AQU	18
19	SAG	11.21	AQU	PIS	16.10	GEM	17.43	VIR	SCO	SAG	11.39	08.12	19
20	15.47	AQU	AQU	00.20	TAU	07.21	LEO	03.45	21.46	15.44	AQU	PIS	20
21	CAP	23.15	06.33	ARI	19.54	CAN	17.10	LIB	SAG	CAP	AQU	20.35	21
22	CAP	PIS	PIS	06.53	GEM	07.30	VIR	06.37	SAG	CAP	00.11	ARI	22
23	04.50	PIS	16.02	TAU	21.46	LEO	18.19	SCO	07.22	PIS	ARI	ARI	23
24	AQU	09.12	ARI	11.11	CAN	08.11	LIB	13.34	CAP	AQU	11.59	06.44	24
25	17.00	ARI	23.09	GEM	23.12	VIR	22.45	SAG	19.38	ARI	15.57	TAU	25
26	PIS	17.11	TAU	14.17	LEO	10.57	SCO	SAG	AQU	PIS	21.05	13.15	26
27	PIS	TAU	TAU	CAN	LEO	LIB	SCO	00.15	AQU	PIS	TAU	GEM	27
28	03.32	23.10	04.33	17.03	01.25	16.40	07.00	CAP	08.14	03.13	TAU	16.15	28
29	ARI		GEM	LEO	VIR	SCO	SAG	12.52	PIS	ARI	02.58	CAN	29
30	11.41		08.40	20.00	05.16	SCO	18.11	AQU	19.25	12.00	GEM	17.05	30
31	TAU		CAN		LIB		CAP	AQU		TAU		LEO	31

SUN

mth	dy	time → sign
JAN	1	00.00 → CAP
JAN	20	16.32 → AQU
FEB	19	06.51 → PIS
MAR	21	05.54 → ARI
APR	20	17.07 → TAU
MAY	21	16.27 → GEM
JUN	22	00.26 → CAN
JUL	23	11.27 → LEO
AUG	23	18.24 → VIR
SEP	23	15.50 → LIB
OCT	24	01.06 → SCO
NOV	22	22.37 → SAG
DEC	22	11.42 → CAP

MERCURY

mth	dy	time → sign
JAN	1	00.00 → CAP
JAN	8	21.54 → AQU
MAR	16	11.50 → PIS
APR	4	12.22 → ARI
APR	19	17.20 → TAU
MAY	4	11.55 → GEM
JUL	12	08.52 → CAN
JUL	28	08.05 → LEO
AUG	12	06.14 → VIR
AUG	30	17.20 → LIB
NOV	6	08.54 → SCO
NOV	25	01.44 → SAG
DEC	14	04.11 → CAP

VENUS

mth	dy	time → sign
JAN	1	00.00 → CAP
JAN	6	06.41 → AQU
JAN	30	06.05 → PIS
FEB	23	09.51 → ARI
MAR	19	21.42 → TAU
APR	13	22.23 → GEM
MAY	9	20.12 → CAN
JUN	6	10.57 → LEO
JUL	9	11.06 → VIR
SEP	2	15.36 → LEO
OCT	4	05.19 → VIR
NOV	9	13.54 → LIB
DEC	7	00.26 → SCO

MARS

mth	dy	time → sign
JAN	1	00.00 → SAG
JAN	21	18.32 → CAP
MAR	3	05.44 → AQU
APR	11	19.25 → PIS
MAY	21	08.14 → ARI
JUL	1	03.45 → TAU
AUG	14	20.36 → GEM
OCT	17	08.32 → CAN
NOV	25	18.21 → GEM

SATURN

mth	dy	time → sign
JAN	1	00.00 → CAN
SEP	17	04.44 → LEO

JUPITER

mth	dy	time → sign
JAN	1	00.00 → PIS
MAR	18	16.22 → ARI

MOON

dy	jan	feb	mar	apr	may	jun	jul	aug	sep	oct	nov	dec	dy
1	17.32	LIB	14.33	SAG	CAP	01.32	ARI	TAU	CAN	LEO	LIB	SCO	1
2	VIR	05.53	SCO	11.08	05.34	PIS	ARI	04.02	23.08	10.03	20.07	07.33	2
3	19.21	SCO	19.05	CAP	AQU	14.01	09.54	GEM	LEO	VIR	SCO	SAG	3
4	LIB	12.10	SAG	21.45	17.34	ARI	TAU	10.17	23.29	09.39	21.10	10.58	4
5	23.39	SAG	SAG	AQU	PIS	ARI	18.58	CAN	VIR	LIB	SAG	CAP	5
6	SCO	21.42	03.39	AQU	PIS	01.19	GEM	12.44	22.38	09.09	SAG	17.12	6
7	SCO	CAP	CAP	10.17	06.03	TAU	GEM	LEO	LIB	SCO	00.45	AQU	7
8	06.39	CAP	15.09	PIS	ARI	09.49	00.23	12.53	22.46	10.35	CAP	AQU	8
9	SAG	09.16	AQU	22.44	17.03	GEM	CAN	VIR	SCO	SAG	07.59	02.52	9
10	15.58	AQU	AQU	ARI	TAU	15.21	02.50	12.51	SCO	15.29	AQU	PIS	10
11	CAP	21.45	03.49	ARI	TAU	CAN	LEO	LIB	01.41	CAP	18.42	15.06	11
12	CAP	PIS	PIS	09.53	01.44	18.45	03.55	14.30	SAG	CAP	PIS	ARI	12
13	03.03	PIS	16.18	TAU	GEM	LEO	VIR	SCO	08.11	00.10	PIS	ARI	13
14	AQU	10.22	ARI	19.14	08.08	21.11	05.21	18.59	CAP	AQU	07.17	03.39	14
15	15.23	ARI	ARI	GEM	CAN	VIR	LIB	SAG	17.51	11.40	ARI	TAU	15
16	PIS	22.09	03.52	GEM	12.38	23.41	08.23	SAG	AQU	PIS	19.38	14.12	16
17	PIS	TAU	TAU	02.27	LEO	LIB	SCO	02.25	AQU	PIS	TAU	GEM	17
18	04.03	TAU	13.43	CAN	15.45	LIB	13.32	CAP	05.32	00.20	TAU	21.49	18
19	ARI	07.35	GEM	07.14	VIR	02.59	SAG	12.09	PIS	ARI	06.14	CAN	19
20	15.21	GEM	20.48	LEO	18.05	SCO	20.46	AQU	18.07	12.43	GEM	CAN	20
21	TAU	13.18	CAN	09.42	LIB	07.34	CAP	23.32	ARI	TAU	14.36	02.54	21
22	23.23	CAN	CAN	VIR	20.25	SAG	CAP	PIS	ARI	23.51	CAN	LEO	22
23	GEM	15.13	00.31	10.41	SCO	13.56	05.56	PIS	06.43	GEM	20.48	06.28	23
24	GEM	LEO	LEO	LIB	23.51	CAP	AQU	12.02	TAU	GEM	LEO	VIR	24
25	03.20	14.37	01.21	11.39	SAG	22.33	16.58	ARI	18.13	08.57	LEO	09.27	25
26	CAN	VIR	VIR	SCO	SAG	AQU	PIS	ARI	GEM	CAN	01.04	LIB	26
27	04.00	13.38	00.51	14.20	05.31	AQU	PIS	00.45	GEM	15.20	VIR	12.28	27
28	LEO	LIB	LIB	SAG	CAP	09.33	05.27	TAU	03.07	LEO	03.48	SCO	28
29	03.14		01.08	20.08	14.09	PIS	ARI	11.53	CAN	18.47	LIB	15.53	29
30	VIR		SCO	CAP	AQU	22.02	17.53	GEM	08.20	VIR	05.36	SAG	30
31	03.13		04.09		AQU		TAU	19.35		19.55		20.16	31

SUN

mth	dy	time → sign
JAN	1	00.00 → CAP
JAN	20	22.22 → AQU
FEB	19	12.40 → PIS
MAR	20	11.51 → ARI
APR	19	23.03 → TAU
MAY	20	22.25 → GEM
JUN	21	06.28 → CAN
JUL	22	17.13 → LEO
AUG	23	00.18 → VIR
SEP	22	21.48 → LIB
OCT	23	06.53 → SCO
NOV	22	04.22 → SAG
DEC	21	17.32 → CAP

SATURN

mth	dy	time → sign
JAN	1	00.00 → LEO
JAN	14	13.30 → CAN
JUN	5	05.28 → LEO

MERCURY

mth	dy	time → sign
JAN	1	00.00 → CAP
JAN	2	20.21 → AQU
JAN	25	01.36 → CAP
FEB	15	19.03 → AQU
MAR	9	12.04 → PIS
MAR	26	15.36 → ARI
APR	10	09.34 → TAU
APR	29	23.11 → GEM
MAY	19	19.25 → TAU
JUN	13	19.20 → GEM
JUL	4	14.13 → CAN
JUL	18	19.35 → LEO
AUG	3	16.43 → VIR
AUG	25	20.52 → LIB
SEP	21	07.15 → VIR
OCT	10	14.48 → LIB
OCT	29	04.55 → SCO
NOV	16	19.02 → SAG
DEC	6	09.25 → CAP

VENUS

mth	dy	time → sign
JAN	1	12.14 → SAG
JAN	26	06.13 → CAP
FEB	19	16.52 → AQU
MAR	15	00.59 → PIS
APR	8	08.52 → ARI
MAY	2	17.49 → TAU
MAY	27	03.47 → GEM
JUN	20	13.56 → CAN
JUL	14	23.34 → LEO
AUG	8	08.36 → VIR
SEP	1	17.44 → LIB
SEP	26	04.17 → SCO
OCT	20	17.24 → SAG
NOV	14	10.40 → CAP
DEC	9	12.50 → AQU

MARS

mth	dy	time → sign
JAN	1	00.00 → GEM
MAR	18	13.20 → CAN
MAY	16	11.33 → LEO
JUL	6	23.22 → VIR
AUG	24	05.43 → LIB
OCT	8	20.10 → SCO
NOV	20	23.50 → SAG

JUPITER

mth	dy	time → sign
JAN	1	00.00 → ARI
MAR	26	10.33 → TAU
AUG	23	10.37 → GEM
OCT	16	20.34 → TAU

MOON

dy	jan	feb	mar	apr	may	jun	jul	aug	sep	oct	nov	dec	dy
1	CAP	19.47	PIS	09.34	04.05	CAN	15.46	LIB	SAG	CAP	PIS	ARI	1
2	CAP	PIS	14.22	TAU	GEM	04.37	VIR	03.55	16.29	03.49	PIS	23.41	2
3	02.33	PIS	ARI	22.15	14.53	LEO	19.34	SCO	CAP	AQU	04.46	TAU	3
4	AQU	07.17	ARI	GEM	CAN	10.21	LIB	07.03	22.20	12.10	ARI	TAU	4
5	11.35	ARI	03.18	GEM	23.09	VIR	22.33	SAG	AQU	PIS	17.23	12.38	5
6	PIS	20.13	TAU	09.06	LEO	14.00	SCO	10.54	AQU	22.50	TAU	GEM	6
7	23.21	TAU	15.56	CAN	LEO	LIB	SCO	CAP	06.11	ARI	TAU	GEM	7
8	ARI	TAU	GEM	16.36	04.21	15.58	01.05	15.57	PIS	ARI	06.21	00.21	8
9	ARI	08.16	GEM	LEO	VIR	SCO	SAG	AQU	16.18	11.11	GEM	CAN	9
10	12.10	GEM	01.59	20.16	06.39	17.06	03.49	23.00	ARI	18.28	GEM	10.12	10
11	TAU	16.59	CAN	VIR	LIB	SAG	CAP	PIS	ARI	TAU	CAN	LEO	11
12	23.19	CAN	07.55	20.54	07.03	18.45	07.53	PIS	04.30	00.14	CAN	17.55	12
13	GEM	21.32	LEO	LIB	SCO	CAP	AQU	08.49	TAU	GEM	04.36	VIR	13
14	GEM	LEO	09.59	20.14	07.04	22.31	14.36	ARI	17.32	12.24	LEO	23.13	14
15	07.00	22.59	VIR	SCO	SAG	AQU	PIS	21.05	GEM	CAN	11.46	LIB	15
16	CAN	VIR	09.44	20.15	08.31	AQU	PIS	TAU	GEM	21.49	VIR	LIB	16
17	11.15	23.14	LIB	SAG	CAP	05.43	00.40	TAU	05.07	LEO	15.34	02.01	17
18	LEO	LIB	09.18	22.43	13.02	PIS	ARI	09.54	CAN	LEO	LIB	SCO	18
19	13.25	LIB	SCO	CAP	AQU	16.32	13.11	GEM	13.10	03.25	16.31	02.54	19
20	VIR	00.14	10.34	CAP	21.27	ARI	TAU	20.34	LEO	VIR	SCO	SAG	20
21	15.10	SCO	SAG	04.47	PIS	ARI	TAU	CAN	17.16	05.26	16.03	03.12	21
22	LIB	03.18	14.48	AQU	PIS	05.21	01.40	CAN	VIR	LIB	SAG	CAP	22
23	17.48	SAG	CAP	14.28	09.07	TAU	GEM	03.30	18.28	05.17	CAP	04.48	23
24	SCO	08.54	22.19	PIS	ARI	17.37	11.39	LEO	LIB	SCO	CAP	AQU	24
25	21.51	CAP	AQU	PIS	22.07	GEM	CAN	07.03	18.34	04.49	18.30	09.36	25
26	SAG	16.48	AQU	02.37	TAU	GEM	18.19	VIR	SCO	SAG	PIS	PIS	26
27	SAG	AQU	08.34	ARI	TAU	03.29	LEO	08.42	19.21	05.55	AQU	18.32	27
28	03.24	AQU	PIS	15.37	10.22	CAN	22.23	LIB	SAG	CAP	00.47	ARI	28
29	CAP	02.42	20.37	TAU	GEM	10.39	VIR	10.05	22.13	10.05	PIS	ARI	29
30	10.34		ARI	TAU	20.39	LEO	VIR	SCO	CAP	AQU	11.01	06.43	30
31	AQU		ARI		CAN		01.13	12.28		17.53		TAU	31

SUN

mth	dy	time → sign
JAN	1	00.00 → CAP
JAN	20	04.11 → AQU
FEB	18	18.30 → PIS
MAR	20	17.41 → ARI
APR	20	04.57 → TAU
MAY	21	04.18 → GEM
JUN	21	12.17 → CAN
JUL	22	23.04 → LEO
AUG	23	06.03 → VIR
SEP	23	03.25 → LIB
OCT	23	12.44 → SCO
NOV	22	10.04 → SAG
DEC	21	23.27 → CAP

MERCURY

mth	dy	time → sign
JAN	1	00.00 → CAP
FEB	10	23.53 → AQU
MAR	2	08.12 → PIS
MAR	18	11.53 → ARI
APR	3	02.46 → TAU
JUN	10	21.06 → GEM
JUN	26	07.03 → CAN
JUL	10	12.00 → LEO
JUL	28	10.18 → VIR
OCT	4	09.19 → LIB
OCT	21	16.22 → SCO
NOV	9	17.20 → SAG
DEC	1	06.42 → CAP
DEC	21	07.18 → SAG

VENUS

mth	dy	time → sign
JAN	1	00.00 → AQU
JAN	4	13.08 → PIS
FEB	2	05.48 → ARI
JUN	6	06.12 → TAU
JUL	6	15.09 → GEM
AUG	2	19.16 → CAN
AUG	28	15.10 → LEO
SEP	22	15.07 → VIR
OCT	17	01.36 → LIB
NOV	10	03.55 → SCO
DEC	4	01.44 → SAG
DEC	27	22.12 → CAP

MARS

mth	dy	time → sign
JAN	1	00.41 → CAP
FEB	9	11.44 → AQU
MAR	20	02.09 → PIS
APR	27	15.35 → ARI
JUN	6	03.16 → TAU
JUL	17	15.13 → GEM
SEP	1	00.22 → CAN
OCT	26	18.47 → LEO

SATURN

mth	dy	time → sign
JAN	1	00.00 → LEO
NOV	17	02.28 → VIR

JUPITER

mth	dy	time → sign
JAN	1	00.00 → TAU
APR	3	15.24 → GEM
AUG	20	12.30 → CAN
DEC	30	23.32 → GEM

MOON

dy	jan	feb	mar	apr	may	jun	jul	aug	sep	oct	nov	dec	dy
1	19.43	CAN	CAN	01.25	LIB	02.54	CAP	01.23	ARI	20.33	CAN	LEO	1
2	GEM	CAN	09.25	VIR	16.23	SAG	12.56	PIS	00.52	GEM	CAN	23.05	2
3	GEM	00.11	LEO	04.39	SCO	02.07	AQU	06.54	TAU	GEM	05.03	VIR	3
4	07.12	LEO	15.19	LIB	15.59	CAP	15.31	ARI	12.27	09.09	LEO	VIR	4
5	CAN	06.17	VIR	05.40	SAG	02.44	PIS	16.18	GEM	CAN	15.16	07.17	5
6	16.20	VIR	18.34	SCO	15.54	AQU	22.03	TAU	GEM	20.58	VIR	LIB	6
7	LEO	10.36	LIB	06.09	CAP	06.35	ARI	TAU	01.03	LEO	21.51	11.33	7
8	23.23	LIB	20.37	SAG	18.00	PIS	ARI	04.29	CAN	LEO	LIB	SCO	8
9	VIR	14.04	SCO	07.40	AQU	14.34	08.33	GEM	12.14	05.58	LIB	12.22	9
10	VIR	SCO	22.42	CAP	23.29	ARI	TAU	17.04	LEO	VIR	00.42	SAG	10
11	04.48	17.11	SAG	11.24	PIS	ARI	21.15	CAN	20.34	11.29	SCO	11.26	11
12	LIB	SAG	SAG	AQU	PIS	01.56	GEM	CAN	VIR	LIB	01.03	CAP	12
13	08.44	20.14	01.40	17.49	08.29	TAU	GEM	03.57	VIR	14.11	SAG	10.59	13
14	SCO	CAP	CAP	PIS	ARI	14.50	09.50	LEO	02.07	SCO	00.50	AQU	14
15	11.18	23.45	06.00	PIS	20.04	GEM	12.26	LIB	15.27	CAP	13.09	15
16	SAG	AQU	AQU	02.52	TAU	GEM	20.51	VIR	05.45	SAG	02.00	PIS	16
17	13.02	AQU	12.06	ARI	TAU	03.28	LEO	18.49	SCO	16.51	AQU	19.11	17
18	CAP	04.45	PIS	14.02	08.50	CAN	LEO	LIB	08.28	CAP	05.58	ARI	18
19	15.12	PIS	20.23	TAU	GEM	14.53	05.58	23.35	SAG	19.36	PIS	ARI	19
20	AQU	12.22	ARI	TAU	21.35	LEO	VIR	SCO	11.04	AQU	13.13	04.54	20
21	19.30	ARI	ARI	02.37	CAN	LEO	13.09	SCO	CAP	AQU	ARI	TAU	21
22	PIS	23.06	07.05	GEM	CAN	00.29	LIB	03.03	14.12	00.26	23.09	16.51	22
23	PIS	TAU	TAU	15.25	09.13	VIR	18.13	SAG	AQU	PIS	TAU	GEM	23
24	03.19	TAU	19.39	CAN	LEO	07.35	SCO	05.30	18.30	07.34	TAU	GEM	24
25	ARI	11.50	GEM	CAN	18.31	LIB	21.04	CAP	PIS	ARI	10.48	05.30	25
26	14.41	GEM	GEM	02.43	VIR	11.42	SAG	07.41	PIS	16.53	GEM	CAN	26
27	TAU	GEM	08.16	LEO	VIR	SCO	22.15	AQU	00.40	TAU	23.20	17.52	27
28	TAU	00.02	CAN	10.52	00.28	13.02	CAP	10.46	ARI	TAU	CAN	LEO	28
29	03.37		18.40	VIR	LIB	SAG	23.04	PIS	09.21	04.08	CAN	LEO	29
30	GEM		LEO	15.13	02.56	12.48	AQU	16.11	TAU	GEM	11.53	05.13	30
31	15.20		LEO		SCO		AQU	ARI		16.40		VIR	31

SUN

mth	dy	time → sign
JAN	1	00.00 → CAP
JAN	20	10.08 → AQU
FEB	19	00.26 → PIS
MAR	20	23.36 → ARI
APR	20	10.53 → TAU
MAY	21	10.04 → GEM
JUN	21	18.05 → CAN
JUL	23	05.05 → LEO
AUG	23	11.53 → VIR
SEP	23	09.23 → LIB
OCT	23	18.37 → SCO
NOV	22	16.02 → SAG
DEC	22	05.22 → CAP

MERCURY

mth	dy	time → sign
JAN	1	00.00 → SAG
JAN	13	20.10 → CAP
FEB	4	15.55 → AQU
FEB	22	16.14 → PIS
MAR	10	12.10 → ARI
MAY	16	08.23 → TAU
JUN	3	15.26 → GEM
JUN	17	15.47 → CAN
JUL	2	22.28 → LEO
JUL	27	06.07 → VIR
AUG	13	07.04 → LEO
SEP	9	19.23 → VIR
SEP	26	16.44 → LIB
OCT	14	05.30 → SCO
NOV	3	07.48 → SAG

VENUS

mth	dy	time → sign
JAN	1	00.00 → CAP
JAN	20	18.33 → AQU
FEB	13	16.03 → PIS
MAR	9	16.26 → ARI
APR	2	21.10 → TAU
APR	27	07.54 → GEM
MAY	22	02.03 → CAN
JUN	16	06.16 → LEO
JUL	12	02.16 → VIR
AUG	8	03.08 → LIB
SEP	7	05.04 → SCO

MARS

mth	dy	time → sign
JAN	1	00.00 → LEO
JAN	26	02.17 → CAN
APR	10	18.40 → LEO
JUN	14	02.26 → VIR
AUG	4	09.13 → LIB
SEP	19	20.55 → SCO
NOV	2	01.23 → SAG
DEC	12	17.33 → CAP

SATURN

mth	dy	time → sign
JAN	1	00.00 → VIR
JAN	5	00.58 → LEO
JUL	26	11.46 → VIR

JUPITER

mth	dy	time → sign
JAN	1	00.00 → GEM
APR	12	00.27 → CAN
SEP	5	08.16 → LEO

MOON

dy	jan	feb	mar	apr	may	jun	jul	aug	sep	oct	nov	dec	dy
1	14.31	SCO	13.02	CAP	09.00	ARI	19.37	CAN	20.46	14.17	SCO	20.44	1
2	LIB	07.13	SAG	00.05	PIS	03.50	GEM	CAN	VIR	LIB	10.03	CAP	2
3	20.35	SAG	15.58	AQU	14.27	TAU	GEM	02.10	VIR	21.48	SAG	21.35	3
4	SCO	08.50	CAP	03.20	ARI	13.53	07.33	LEO	07.15	SCO	12.40	AQU	4
5	22.03	CAP	17.50	PIS	21.52	GEM	CAN	14.29	GEM	SCO	CAP	23.36	5
6	SAG	09.04	AQU	07.51	TAU	GEM	20.13	VIR	15.38	03.06	15.04	PIS	6
7	22.55	AQU	19.45	ARI	TAU	01.30	LEO	VIR	SCO	SAG	AQU	PIS	7
8	CAP	09.47	PIS	14.21	07.18	CAN	LEO	01.30	21.39	06.52	18.06	03.39	8
9	22.05	PIS	23.08	TAU	14.07	08.44	LIB	SAG	CAP	PIS	22.11	ARI	9
10	AQU	12.56	ARI	23.27	18.41	LEO	VIR	10.11	SAG	09.42	PIS	09.50	10
11	22.50	ARI	ARI	GEM	CAN	LEO	19.48	SCO	01.20	AQU	ARI	TAU	11
12	PIS	19.50	05.18	GEM	CAN	02.35	LIB	15.43	CAP	12.12	ARI	17.54	12
13	PIS	TAU	TAU	10.59	07.17	VIR	LIB	SAG	03.08	PIS	03.35	GEM	13
14	03.05	TAU	14.48	CAN	12.55	LEO	03.47	18.03	AQU	15.06	TAU	GEM	14
15	ARI	06.24	GEM	23.30	19.15	LIB	SCO	CAP	04.09	ARI	10.45	03.50	15
16	11.30	GEM	GEM	LEO	VIR	19.28	07.50	18.15	PIS	19.22	GEM	CAN	16
17	TAU	18.56	02.49	LEO	VIR	SCO	SAG	AQU	05.50	TAU	20.16	15.37	17
18	23.06	CAN	CAN	10.44	04.24	22.01	08.33	18.04	ARI	TAU	CAN	LEO	18
19	GEM	CAN	15.12	VIR	LIB	SAG	CAP	PIS	09.43	02.05	CAN	LEO	19
20	GEM	07.09	LEO	18.53	09.39	21.52	07.41	19.29	TAU	GEM	08.09	04.34	20
21	11.50	LEO	LEO	LIB	SCO	CAP	AQU	ARI	16.56	11.52	LEO	VIR	21
22	CAN	17.39	01.49	23.39	11.31	21.07	07.26	ARI	GEM	CAN	20.57	16.40	22
23	CAN	VIR	VIR	SCO	SAG	AQU	PIS	00.06	GEM	CAN	VIR	LIB	23
24	00.02	VIR	09.41	SCO	11.41	21.57	09.46	TAU	03.31	00.04	VIR	LIB	24
25	LEO	02.03	LIB	02.00	CAP	PIS	ARI	08.31	CAN	LEO	08.07	01.32	25
26	10.56	LIB	15.01	SAG	12.10	PIS	15.50	GEM	16.01	12.32	LIB	SCO	26
27	VIR	08.28	SCO	03.27	AQU	01.53	TAU	19.59	LEO	VIR	15.38	06.07	27
28	20.08	SCO	18.37	CAP	14.37	ARI	TAU	CAN	LEO	22.51	SCO	SAG	28
29	LIB		SAG	05.28	PIS	09.21	01.31	CAN	04.11	LIB	19.23	07.15	29
30	LIB		21.23	AQU	19.52	TAU	GEM	08.40	VIR	LIB	SAG	CAP	30
31	03.03		CAP		ARI		13.28	LEO		05.52		06.53	31

SUN

mth	dy	time → sign
JAN	1	00.00 → CAP
JAN	20	16.04 → AQU
FEB	19	06.12 → PIS
MAR	21	05.22 → ARI
APR	20	16.38 → TAU
MAY	21	15.54 → GEM
JUN	21	23.58 → CAN
JUL	23	10.48 → LEO
AUG	23	17.42 → VIR
SEP	23	15.17 → LIB
OCT	24	00.25 → SCO
NOV	22	21.53 → SAG
DEC	22	11.15 → CAP

MERCURY

mth	dy	time → sign
JAN	1	00.00 → SAG
JAN	8	22.36 → CAP
JAN	28	12.52 → AQU
FEB	14	20.38 → PIS
MAR	3	21.35 → ARI
MAR	28	10.40 → PIS
APR	17	12.47 → ARI
MAY	10	22.03 → TAU
MAY	26	07.48 → GEM
JUN	9	06.32 → CAN
JUN	27	09.54 → LEO
SEP	2	21.39 → VIR
SEP	18	18.54 → LIB
OCT	7	03.55 → SCO
OCT	30	07.02 → SAG
NOV	18	03.08 → SCO
DEC	12	13.34 → SAG

VENUS

mth	dy	time → sign
JAN	1	00.00 → SCO
JAN	7	06.33 → SAG
FEB	5	09.16 → CAP
MAR	3	17.15 → AQU
MAR	29	03.17 → PIS
APR	23	04.05 → ARI
MAY	18	00.29 → TAU
JUN	11	18.15 → GEM
JUL	6	09.07 → CAN
JUL	30	20.05 → LEO
AUG	24	03.14 → VIR
SEP	17	07.21 → LIB
OCT	11	09.44 → SCO
NOV	4	11.50 → SAG
NOV	28	14.22 → CAP
DEC	22	18.25 → AQU

MARS

mth	dy	time → sign
JAN	1	00.00 → CAP
JAN	20	17.12 → AQU
FEB	27	20.22 → PIS
APR	7	01.08 → ARI
MAY	16	04.31 → TAU
JUN	26	01.51 → GEM
AUG	8	13.25 → CAN
SEP	24	21.28 → LEO
NOV	19	21.33 → VIR

SATURN

mth	dy	time → sign
JAN	1	00.00 → VIR

JUPITER

mth	dy	time → sign
JAN	1	00.00 → LEO
FEB	28	23.22 → CAN
APR	20	08.30 → LEO
SEP	29	10.13 → VIR

MOON

dy	jan	feb	mar	apr	may	jun	jul	aug	sep	oct	nov	dec	dy
1	AQU	ARI	ARI	GEM	CAN	22.41	19.08	SCO	11.33	AQU	10.09	TAU	1
2	07.08	22.03	07.09	GEM	CAN	VIR	LIB	22.05	CAP	AQU	ARI	23.02	2
3	PIS	TAU	TAU	06.24	01.56	VIR	LIB	SAG	13.59	00.23	11.16	GEM	3
4	09.41	TAU	12.58	CAN	LEO	11.12	05.57	SAG	AQU	PIS	TAU	GEM	4
5	ARI	05.33	GEM	17.58	14.41	LIB	SCO	02.23	14.03	00.28	13.26	04.01	5
6	15.17	GEM	22.34	LEO	VIR	21.05	12.55	CAP	PIS	ARI	GEM	CAN	6
7	TAU	16.06	CAN	LEO	VIR	SCO	SAG	03.28	13.29	00.45	18.24	12.09	7
8	23.42	CAN	CAN	06.52	02.47	SCO	16.07	AQU	ARI	TAU	CAN	LEO	8
9	GEM	CAN	10.47	VIR	LIB	03.14	CAP	03.05	14.12	03.07	CAN	23.33	9
10	GEM	04.25	LEO	18.45	12.10	SAG	16.59	PIS	TAU	GEM	03.14	VIR	10
11	10.14	LEO	23.42	LIB	SCO	06.23	AQU	03.10	17.54	09.09	LEO	VIR	11
12	CAN	17.18	VIR	LIB	18.25	CAP	17.23	ARI	GEM	15.20	CAN	12.29	12
13	22.16	VIR	VIR	04.16	SAG	08.06	PIS	05.21	GEM	19.12	VIR	LIB	13
14	LEO	VIR	11.41	SCO	22.25	AQU	18.57	TAU	01.27	LEO	VIR	LIB	14
15	LEO	05.37	LIB	11.18	CAP	09.56	ARI	10.41	CAN	LEO	04.16	00.08	15
16	11.10	LIB	21.49	SAG	CAP	PIS	22.43	GEM	12.25	07.51	LIB	SCO	16
17	VIR	16.12	SCO	16.23	01.26	12.52	TAU	19.17	LEO	VIR	15.29	08.36	17
18	23.40	SCO	SCO	CAP	AQU	ARI	TAU	CAN	LEO	20.44	SCO	SAG	18
19	LIB	23.51	05.38	22.02	04.18	17.18	04.59	CAN	01.15	LIB	23.56	13.54	19
20	LIB	SAG	SAG	AQU	PIS	TAU	GEM	06.28	VIR	LIB	SAG	CAP	20
21	09.51	SAG	10.56	22.41	07.30	23.23	13.40	LEO	14.11	08.02	SAG	17.13	21
22	SCO	04.00	CAP	PIS	ARI	GEM	CAN	19.11	LIB	SCO	06.01	AQU	22
23	16.08	CAP	13.52	PIS	11.20	GEM	CAN	VIR	LIB	17.09	CAP	19.50	23
24	SAG	05.12	AQU	00.51	TAU	07.24	00.30	VIR	01.54	SAG	10.37	PIS	24
25	18.27	AQU	15.04	ARI	16.28	CAN	LEO	08.13	SCO	SAG	AQU	22.40	25
26	CAP	04.52	PIS	03.27	GEM	17.47	13.01	LIB	11.36	00.11	14.17	ARI	26
27	18.12	PIS	15.47	TAU	23.51	LEO	VIR	20.12	SAG	CAP	PIS	ARI	27
28	AQU	04.54	ARI	07.49	CAN	LEO	VIR	SCO	18.40	05.16	17.17	02.08	28
29	17.25		17.36	GEM	CAN	06.14	02.06	SCO	CAP	AQU	ARI	TAU	29
30	PIS		TAU	15.11	10.08	VIR	LIB	05.39	22.49	08.29	19.54	06.32	30
31	18.11		22.08		LEO		13.46	SAG		PIS		GEM	31

SUN

mth	dy	time → sign
JAN	1	00.00 → CAP
JAN	20	21.44 → AQU
FEB	19	12.06 → PIS
MAR	20	11.13 → ARI
APR	19	22.24 → TAU
MAY	20	21.42 → GEM
JUN	21	05.44 → CAN
JUL	22	16.42 → LEO
AUG	22	23.46 → VIR
SEP	22	21.09 → LIB
OCT	23	06.12 → SCO
NOV	22	03.42 → SAG
DEC	21	16.53 → CAP

MERCURY

mth	dy	time → sign
JAN	1	00.00 → SAG
JAN	2	08.01 → CAP
JAN	21	02.17 → AQU
FEB	7	08.07 → PIS
APR	14	15.55 → ARI
MAY	2	10.58 → TAU
MAY	16	17.07 → GEM
MAY	31	22.09 → CAN
AUG	9	03.30 → LEO
AUG	24	18.44 → VIR
SEP	10	02.02 → LIB
SEP	30	01.16 → SCO
DEC	5	19.42 → SAG
DEC	25	04.47 → CAP

VENUS

mth	dy	time → sign
JAN	1	00.00 → AQU
JAN	16	03.34 → PIS
FEB	9	23.40 → ARI
MAR	6	18.54 → TAU
APR	3	19.43 → GEM
MAY	12	20.52 → CAN
JUN	5	05.42 → GEM
AUG	6	14.22 → CAN
SEP	7	17.59 → LEO
OCT	4	23.05 → VIR
OCT	30	10.33 → LIB
NOV	24	01.38 → SCO
DEC	18	06.23 → SAG

MARS

mth	dy	time → sign
JAN	1	00.00 → VIR
MAR	11	20.34 → LEO
MAY	4	02.20 → VIR
JUL	10	17.48 → LIB
AUG	29	05.40 → SCO
OCT	12	06.22 → SAG
NOV	22	01.32 → CAP
DEC	30	22.46 → AQU

SATURN

mth	dy	time → sign
JAN	1	00.00 → VIR
SEP	21	10.37 → LIB

JUPITER

mth	dy	time → sign
JAN	1	00.00 → VIR
OCT	27	10.30 → LIB

MOON

dy	jan	feb	mar	apr	may	jun	jul	aug	sep	oct	nov	dec	dy
1	12.29	LEO	VIR	LIB	22.22	CAP	AQU	ARI	01.50	CAN	12.18	07.13	1
2	CAN	15.21	VIR	05.21	SAG	19.29	05.48	16.55	GEM	19.57	VIR	LIB	2
3	20.47	VIR	10.40	SCO	SAG	AQU	PIS	TAU	06.39	LEO	VIR	20.00	3
4	LEO	VIR	LIB	16.35	07.14	AQU	08.46	20.10	CAN	LEO	00.31	SCO	4
5	LEO	04.04	23.22	SAG	CAP	00.10	ARI	GEM	14.22	LIB	06.19	SCO	5
6	07.48	LIB	SCO	SAG	14.03	PIS	11.30	GEM	LEO	VIR	13.19	07.57	6
7	VIR	16.46	SCO	01.43	AQU	03.23	TAU	01.12	LEO	18.30	SCO	SAG	7
8	20.38	SCO	10.38	CAP	18.33	ARI	14.33	CAN	00.31	LIB	SCO	18.12	8
9	LIB	SCO	SAG	08.00	PIS	05.29	GEM	08.23	VIR	01.25	SAG	CAP	9
10	LIB	03.19	19.02	AQU	20.44	TAU	18.44	LEO	12.22	07.15	SAG	CAP	10
11	08.55	SAG	CAP	11.07	ARI	07.22	CAN	17.54	LIB	SCO	12.15	02.36	11
12	SCO	10.12	23.45	PIS	21.24	GEM	CAN	VIR	LIB	19.37	CAP	AQU	12
13	18.17	CAP	AQU	11.40	TAU	10.29	01.03	VIR	01.06	SAG	21.10	09.03	13
14	SAG	13.19	AQU	ARI	22.07	CAN	LEO	05.32	SCO	SAG	AQU	PIS	14
15	23.51	AQU	01.10	11.11	GEM	16.22	10.11	LIB	13.28	06.37	AQU	13.21	15
16	CAP	13.54	PIS	TAU	GEM	LEO	VIR	18.15	SAG	CAP	03.21	ARI	16
17	CAP	PIS	00.41	11.41	00.52	LEO	21.55	SCO	23.45	14.53	PIS	15.36	17
18	02.25	13.43	ARI	GEM	CAN	01.47	LIB	SCO	CAP	AQU	06.21	TAU	18
19	AQU	ARI	00.13	15.11	07.14	VIR	LIB	06.07	CAP	19.31	ARI	16.39	19
20	03.33	14.35	TAU	CAN	LEO	13.55	10.33	SAG	06.30	PIS	06.51	GEM	20
21	PIS	TAU	01.47	22.52	17.32	LIB	SCO	15.11	AQU	20.43	TAU	18.03	21
22	04.52	17.58	GEM	LEO	VIR	LIB	21.42	CAP	09.27	ARI	06.27	CAN	22
23	ARI	GEM	06.55	LEO	VIR	02.26	SAG	20.32	PIS	19.55	GEM	21.34	23
24	07.31	GEM	CAN	10.12	06.11	SCO	SAG	AQU	09.37	TAU	07.18	LEO	24
25	TAU	00.34	15.58	VIR	LIB	13.02	05.45	22.43	ARI	19.17	CAN	LEO	25
26	12.11	CAN	LEO	23.09	18.37	SAG	CAP	PIS	08.53	GEM	11.23	04.32	26
27	GEM	10.10	LEO	LIB	SCO	20.46	10.34	23.11	TAU	21.00	LEO	VIR	27
28	19.02	21.53	03.52	LIB	SCO	CAP	AQU	ARI	09.21	CAN	19.37	15.05	28
29	CAN		VIR	11.35	05.05	CAP	13.11	23.41	GEM	CAN	VIR	LIB	29
30	CAN		16.49	SCO	SAG	02.04	PIS	TAU	12.46	02.38	VIR	LIB	30
31	04.08		LIB		13.14		14.53	TAU		LEO		03.36	31

SUN

mth	dy	time → sign
JAN	1	00.00 → CAP
JAN	20	03.35 → AQU
FEB	18	17.52 → PIS
MAR	20	17.07 → ARI
APR	20	04.15 → TAU
MAY	21	03.39 → GEM
JUN	21	11.42 → CAN
JUL	22	22.40 → LEO
AUG	23	05.34 → VIR
SEP	23	03.05 → LIB
OCT	23	12.16 → SCO
NOV	22	09.33 → SAG
DEC	21	22.52 → CAP

MERCURY

mth	dy	time → sign
JAN	1	00.00 → CAP
JAN	12	15.46 → AQU
JAN	31	17.34 → PIS
FEB	16	08.03 → AQU
MAR	18	04.33 → PIS
APR	8	09.13 → ARI
APR	24	05.31 → TAU
MAY	8	09.47 → GEM
MAY	28	17.04 → CAN
JUN	22	22.53 → GEM
JUL	12	21.08 → CAN
AUG	1	18.35 → LEO
AUG	16	12.44 → VIR
SEP	2	22.40 → LIB
SEP	27	11.04 → SCO
OCT	14	02.12 → LIB
NOV	9	13.14 → SCO
NOV	28	20.52 → SAG
DEC	17	22.21 → CAP

VENUS

mth	dy	time → sign
JAN	1	00.00 → SAG
JAN	11	06.46 → CAP
FEB	4	06.09 → AQU
FEB	28	06.04 → PIS
MAR	24	07.45 → ARI
APR	17	12.06 → TAU
MAY	11	19.44 → GEM
JUN	5	06.27 → CAN
JUN	29	20.20 → LEO
JUL	24	14.05 → VIR
AUG	18	13.45 → LIB
SEP	12	22.54 → SCO
OCT	9	00.04 → SAG
NOV	5	12.41 → CAP
DEC	8	20.56 → AQU

MARS

mth	dy	time → sign
JAN	1	00.00 → AQU
FEB	6	22.44 → PIS
MAR	17	02.25 → ARI
APR	25	07.17 → TAU
JUN	5	05.25 → GEM
JUL	18	08.43 → CAN
SEP	2	01.50 → LEO
OCT	21	01.47 → VIR
DEC	16	00.22 → LIB

SATURN

mth	dy	time → sign
JAN	1	00.00 → LIB

JUPITER

mth	dy	time → sign
JAN	1	00.00 → LIB
NOV	27	02.33 → SCO

MOON

dy	jan	feb	mar	apr	may	jun	jul	aug	sep	oct	nov	dec	dy
1	SCO	10.37	CAP	18.41	06.57	16.48	02.57	18.54	LIB	SCO	12.46	07.09	1
2	15.42	CAP	CAP	PIS	ARI	GEM	CAN	21.10	16.59	CAP	AQU		2
3	SAG	17.55	03.51	20.25	06.59	16.38	04.47	VIR	SCO	SAG	CAP	17.16	3
4	SAG	AQU	AQU	ARI	TAU	CAN	LEO	02.24	SCO	SAG	00.51	PIS	4
5	01.41	22.21	08.12	20.04	06.01	18.43	09.26	LIB	09.24	05.49	AQU	23.49	5
6	CAP	PIS	PIS	TAU	GEM	LEO	VIR	12.58	SAG	CAP	09.52	ARI	6
7	09.12	PIS	09.48	19.47	06.18	LEO	17.42	SCO	21.48	17.01	PIS	ARI	7
8	AQU	01.01	ARI	GEM	CAN	00.25	LIB	SCO	CAP	AQU	14.38	02.31	8
9	14.42	ARI	10.22	21.34	09.40	VIR	LIB	01.22	CAP	AQU	ARI	TAU	9
10	PIS	03.11	TAU	CAN	LEO	09.55	05.02	SAG	07.58	00.32	15.44	02.30	10
11	18.43	TAU	11.42	CAN	16.55	LIB	SCO	AQU	PIS	TAU	GEM	11
12	ARI	05.51	GEM	02.36	VIR	21.54	17.35	CAP	14.34	04.01	14.59	01.40	12
13	21.45	GEM	15.06	LEO	VIR	SCO	SAG	22.56	PIS	ARI	GEM	CAN	13
14	TAU	09.43	CAN	10.56	03.24	SCO	SAG	AQU	17.55	04.43	14.37	02.08	14
15	TAU	CAN	21.02	VIR	LIB	10.31	05.19	AQU	ARI	TAU	CAN	LEO	15
16	00.17	15.10	LEO	21.38	15.37	SAG	CAP	05.34	19.30	04.41	16.33	05.38	16
17	GEM	LEO	LEO	LIB	SCO	22.21	15.02	PIS	TAU	GEM	LEO	VIR	17
18	03.08	22.34	05.20	LIB	SCO	CAP	AQU	09.49	20.59	05.52	21.53	12.58	18
19	CAN	VIR	VIR	09.39	04.14	CAP	22.26	ARI	GEM	CAN	VIR	LIB	19
20	07.21	VIR	15.31	SCO	SAG	08.36	PIS	12.43	23.39	09.34	VIR	23.39	20
21	LEO	08.12	LIB	22.50	16.20	AQU	PIS	TAU	CAN	LEO	06.33	SCO	21
22	14.02	LIB	LIB	SAG	CAP	16.44	03.43	15.18	CAN	16.05	LIB	SCO	22
23	VIR	19.54	03.14	SAG	CAP	PIS	ARI	GEM	04.08	VIR	17.36	12.11	23
24	23.45	SCO	SCO	10.31	03.00	22.18	07.18	18.17	LEO	VIR	SCO	SAG	24
25	LIB	SCO	15.51	CAP	AQU	ARI	TAU	CAN	10.29	00.56	SCO	SAG	25
26	LIB	08.29	SAG	20.57	11.05	ARI	09.42	22.10	VIR	LIB	06.00	00.59	26
27	11.49	SAG	SAG	AQU	PIS	01.16	GEM	LEO	18.40	11.38	SAG	CAP	27
28	SCO	19.46	03.52	AQU	15.44	TAU	11.41	LEO	LIB	SCO	18.53	12.53	28
29	SCO		CAP	03.56	ARI	02.21	CAN	03.31	LIB	23.48	CAP	AQU	29
30	00.11		13.15	PIS	17.10	GEM	14.20	VIR	04.53	SAG	CAP	23.01	30
31	SAG		AQU		TAU		LEO	11.02		SAG		PIS	31

114

SUN

mth	dy	time → sign
JAN	1	00.00 → CAP
JAN	20	09.33 → AQU
FEB	18	23.47 → PIS
MAR	20	22.53 → ARI
APR	20	10.08 → TAU
MAY	21	09.25 → GEM
JUN	21	17.23 → CAN
JUL	23	04.16 → LEO
AUG	23	11.15 → VIR
SEP	23	08.44 → LIB
OCT	23	17.58 → SCO
NOV	22	15.20 → SAG
DEC	22	04.36 → CAP

MERCURY

mth	dy	time → sign
JAN	1	00.00 → CAP
JAN	5	16.46 → AQU
MAR	13	19.14 → PIS
MAR	31	20.56 → ARI
APR	15	18.54 → TAU
MAY	1	13.25 → GEM
JUL	9	11.26 → CAN
JUL	24	08.47 → LEO
AUG	8	14.07 → VIR
AUG	28	03.26 → LIB
NOV	3	01.11 → SCO
NOV	21	14.24 → SAG
DEC	10	20.02 → CAP

VENUS

mth	dy	time → sign
JAN	1	00.00 → AQU
JAN	23	02.53 → CAP
MAR	2	11.25 → AQU
APR	6	12.23 → PIS
MAY	4	12.27 → ARI
MAY	30	21.06 → TAU
JUN	25	12.13 → GEM
JUL	20	16.25 → CAN
AUG	14	11.09 → LEO
SEP	7	21.35 → VIR
OCT	2	01.33 → LIB
OCT	26	01.14 → SCO
NOV	18	23.03 → SAG
DEC	12	20.25 → CAP

MARS

mth	dy	time → sign
JAN	1	00.00 → LIB
AUG	3	11.32 → SCO
SEP	20	01.29 → SAG
OCT	31	23.22 → CAP
DEC	10	06.02 → AQU

SATURN

mth	dy	time → sign
JAN	1	00.00 → LIB
NOV	29	10.13 → SCO

JUPITER

mth	dy	time → sign
JAN	1	00.00 → SCO
DEC	26	01.46 → SAG

MOON

dy	jan	feb	mar	apr	may	jun	jul	aug	sep	oct	nov	dec	dy
1	PIS	TAU	TAU	CAN	23.45	LIB	SCO	09.36	AQU	PIS	TAU	GEM	1
2	06.33	20.20	01.50	13.36	VIR	21.12	14.25	CAP	16.11	08.06	TAU	10.58	2
3	ARI	GEM	GEM	LEO	VIR	SCO	SAG	22.17	PIS	ARI	00.23	CAN	3
4	11.02	22.28	04.48	18.18	06.32	SCO	SAG	AQU	PIS	13.09	GEM	11.26	4
5	TAU	CAN	CAN	VIR	LIB	08.31	03.15	AQU	00.24	TAU	01.59	LEO	5
6	12.48	23.50	07.50	VIR	15.24	SAG	CAP	09.23	ARI	16.39	CAN	13.32	6
7	GEM	LEO	LEO	00.26	SCO	21.12	16.03	PIS	06.27	GEM	04.10	VIR	7
8	13.01	LEO	11.27	LIB	SCO	CAP	AQU	18.21	TAU	19.39	LEO	18.11	8
9	CAN	02.15	VIR	08.33	02.17	CAP	AQU	ARI	10.57	CAN	07.40	LIB	9
10	13.21	VIR	16.34	SCO	SAG	10.08	03.35	ARI	GEM	22.44	VIR	LIB	10
11	LEO	07.02	LIB	19.07	14.50	AQU	PIS	01.00	14.18	LEO	12.46	01.34	11
12	15.37	LIB	LIB	SAG	CAP	21.44	12.49	TAU	CAN	LEO	LIB	SCO	12
13	VIR	15.16	00.17	SAG	CAP	PIS	ARI	05.22	16.46	02.09	19.42	11.27	13
14	21.17	SCO	SCO	07.41	03.44	PIS	19.00	GEM	LEO	VIR	SCO	SAG	14
15	LIB	SCO	11.03	CAP	AQU	06.20	TAU	07.40	18.57	06.23	SCO	23.15	15
16	LIB	02.45	SAG	20.18	14.46	ARI	22.03	CAN	VIR	LIB	04.52	CAP	16
17	06.46	SAG	23.47	AQU	PIS	11.07	GEM	08.40	22.02	12.21	SAG	CAP	17
18	SCO	15.36	CAP	AQU	22.04	TAU	22.46	LEO	LIB	SCO	16.21	12.12	18
19	19.00	CAP	CAP	06.19	ARI	12.34	CAN	09.40	LIB	21.02	CAP	AQU	19
20	SAG	CAP	11.53	PIS	ARI	GEM	22.35	VIR	03.32	SAG	CAP	AQU	20
21	SAG	03.15	AQU	12.23	01.22	12.13	LEO	12.22	SCO	SAG	05.20	00.56	21
22	07.51	AQU	21.01	ARI	TAU	CAN	23.20	LIB	12.30	08.38	AQU	PIS	22
23	CAP	12.09	PIS	14.59	01.54	11.57	VIR	18.21	SAG	CAP	17.43	11.34	23
24	19.25	PIS	PIS	TAU	GEM	LEO	VIR	SCO	SAG	21.36	PIS	ARI	24
25	AQU	18.17	02.37	15.48	01.38	13.36	02.45	SCO	00.31	AQU	PIS	18.37	25
26	AQU	ARI	ARI	GEM	CAN	VIR	LIB	04.11	CAP	AQU	03.07	TAU	26
27	04.49	22.32	05.39	16.43	02.27	18.30	09.58	SAG	13.21	09.12	ARI	21.49	27
28	PIS	TAU	TAU	CAN	LEO	LIB	SCO	16.42	AQU	PIS	08.31	GEM	28
29	11.58		07.44	19.09	05.43	LIB	20.48	CAP	AQU	17.25	TAU	22.12	29
30	ARI		GEM	CAN	VIR	03.02	SAG	CAP	00.18	ARI	10.36	CAN	30
31	17.03		10.09		12.02		SAG	05.23		22.04		21.33	31

SUN

mth	dy	time → sign
JAN	1	00.00 → CAP
JAN	20	15.14 → AQU
FEB	19	05.31 → PIS
MAR	21	04.36 → ARI
APR	20	15.50 → TAU
MAY	21	15.06 → GEM
JUN	21	23.07 → CAN
JUL	23	10.08 → LEO
AUG	23	17.07 → VIR
SEP	23	14.42 → LIB
OCT	23	23.56 → SCO
NOV	22	21.18 → SAG
DEC	22	10.32 → CAP

MERCURY

mth	dy	time → sign
JAN	1	13.36 → AQU
JAN	12	06.55 → CAP
FEB	14	09.37 → AQU
MAR	7	04.28 → PIS
MAR	23	20.09 → ARI
APR	7	17.05 → TAU
JUN	14	08.06 → GEM
JUL	1	19.14 → CAN
JUL	15	20.57 → LEO
AUG	1	10.22 → VIR
AUG	29	06.06 → LIB
SEP	6	02.30 → VIR
OCT	8	23.42 → LIB
OCT	26	15.47 → SCO
NOV	14	08.56 → SAG
DEC	4	11.26 → CAP

VENUS

mth	dy	time → sign
JAN	1	00.00 → CAP
JAN	5	17.56 → AQU
JAN	29	17.31 → PIS
FEB	22	21.32 → ARI
MAR	19	09.52 → TAU
APR	13	11.22 → GEM
MAY	9	10.57 → CAN
JUN	6	06.07 → LEO
JUL	10	05.25 → VIR
AUG	27	11.45 → LEO
OCT	5	19.33 → VIR
NOV	9	10.55 → LIB
DEC	6	16.14 → SCO

MARS

mth	dy	time → sign
JAN	1	00.00 → AQU
JAN	17	13.24 → PIS
FEB	25	00.17 → ARI
APR	5	14.07 → TAU
MAY	16	21.40 → GEM
JUN	29	06.54 → CAN
AUG	13	16.51 → LEO
SEP	30	00.23 → VIR
NOV	18	10.21 → LIB

SATURN

mth	dy	time → sign
JAN	1	00.00 → SCO
MAY	6	19.24 → LIB
AUG	24	11.43 → SCO

JUPITER

mth	dy	time → sign
JAN	1	00.00 → SAG

MOON

dy	jan	feb	mar	apr	may	jun	jul	aug	sep	oct	nov	dec	dy
1	LEO	09.47	LIB	16.20	11.01	AQU	PIS	07.37	GEM	12.54	23.31	09.41	1
2	21.49	LIB	23.51	SAG	CAP	19.42	14.47	TAU	02.53	LEO	LIB	SCO	2
3	VIR	14.32	SCO	SAG	23.09	PIS	ARI	14.43	CAN	14.15	LIB	14.56	3
4	VIR	SCO	SCO	02.30	AQU	PIS	ARI	GEM	04.47	VIR	01.53	SAG	4
5	00.44	23.28	07.15	CAP	AQU	06.59	00.05	18.09	LEO	14.42	SCO	22.28	5
6	LIB	SAG	SAG	15.06	11.44	ARI	TAU	CAN	04.36	LIB	06.09	CAP	6
7	07.16	SAG	18.29	AQU	PIS	15.05	05.41	18.37	VIR	16.06	SAG	CAP	7
8	SCO	11.33	CAP	AQU	22.16	TAU	GEM	LEO	04.13	SCO	13.31	08.39	8
9	17.14	CAP	CAP	03.30	ARI	19.37	07.50	17.49	LIB	20.21	CAP	AQU	9
10	SAG	CAP	07.30	PIS	ARI	GEM	CAN	VIR	05.49	SAG	CAP	20.53	10
11	SAG	00.40	AQU	13.37	05.36	21.32	07.54	17.51	SCO	SAG	00.10	PIS	11
12	05.26	AQU	19.47	ARI	TAU	CAN	LEO	LIB	11.08	SCO	04.30	AQU	PIS	12
13	CAP	13.02	PIS	20.59	10.03	22.21	07.43	20.44	SAG	CAP	12.41	09.17	13
14	18.26	PIS	PIS	TAU	GEM	LEO	VIR	SCO	20.34	16.00	PIS	ARI	14
15	AQU	23.46	06.00	TAU	12.48	23.38	09.10	SCO	CAP	AQU	PIS	19.33	15
16	AQU	ARI	ARI	02.15	CAN	VIR	LIB	03.33	CAP	AQU	00.36	TAU	16
17	07.02	ARI	14.04	GEM	15.01	VIR	13.38	SAG	08.45	04.41	ARI	TAU	17
18	PIS	08.30	TAU	06.14	LEO	02.36	SCO	13.59	AQU	PIS	10.06	02.23	18
19	18.08	TAU	20.20	CAN	17.37	LIB	21.31	CAP	21.30	16.18	TAU	GEM	19
20	ARI	14.52	GEM	09.26	VIR	07.59	SAG	CAP	PIS	ARI	16.45	06.02	20
21	ARI	GEM	GEM	LEO	21.11	SCO	SAG	02.25	PIS	ARI	GEM	CAN	21
22	02.36	18.31	00.52	12.12	LIB	15.55	08.11	AQU	09.10	01.47	21.10	07.44	22
23	TAU	CAN	CAN	VIR	LIB	SAG	CAP	15.10	ARI	TAU	CAN	LEO	23
24	07.40	19.46	03.43	14.04	02.17	SAG	20.26	PIS	19.12	CAN	CAN	09.01	24
25	GEM	LEO	LEO	LIB	SCO	02.08	AQU	PIS	TAU	GEM	00.19	VIR	25
26	09.28	19.49	05.18	19.04	09.27	CAP	AQU	03.08	TAU	14.47	LEO	11.18	26
27	CAN	VIR	VIR	SCO	SAG	14.07	09.11	ARI	03.24	CAN	03.02	LIB	27
28	09.10	20.30	06.48	SCO	19.07	AQU	PIS	13.38	GEM	18.50	VIR	15.27	28
29	LEO		LIB	01.28	CAP	AQU	21.21	TAU	09.24	LEO	05.57	SCO	29
30	08.35		09.57	SAG	CAP	02.52	ARI	21.49	CAN	21.33	LIB	21.44	30
31	VIR		SCO		07.00		ARI	GEM		VIR		SAG	31

SUN

mth	dy	time → sign
JAN	1	00.00 → CAP
JAN	20	21.04 → AQU
FEB	19	11.16 → PIS
MAR	20	10.22 → ARI
APR	19	21.38 → TAU
MAY	20	20.55 → GEM
JUN	21	05.02 → CAN
JUL	22	15.56 → LEO
AUG	22	23.00 → VIR
SEP	22	20.35 → LIB
OCT	23	05.43 → SCO
NOV	22	03.16 → SAG
DEC	21	16.22 → CAP

MERCURY

mth	dy	time → sign
JAN	1	00.00 → CAP
FEB	9	01.54 → AQU
FEB	27	18.07 → PIS
MAR	14	16.27 → ARI
MAR	31	20.25 → TAU
APR	25	11.45 → ARI
MAY	15	12.33 → TAU
JUN	7	15.42 → GEM
JUN	22	06.40 → CAN
JUL	6	18.53 → LEO
JUL	26	06.49 → VIR
SEP	30	19.41 → LIB
OCT	18	03.00 → SCO
NOV	6	12.09 → SAG
DEC	1	16.32 → CAP
DEC	7	20.46 → SAG

VENUS

mth	dy	time → sign
JAN	1	02.00 → SAG
JAN	25	18.49 → CAP
FEB	19	04.44 → AQU
MAR	14	12.36 → PIS
APR	7	20.13 → ARI
MAY	2	04.56 → TAU
MAY	26	14.40 → GEM
JUN	20	00.47 → CAN
JUL	14	10.31 → LEO
AUG	7	19.44 → VIR
SEP	1	05.07 → LIB
SEP	25	16.01 → SCO
OCT	20	05.46 → SAG
NOV	13	23.57 → CAP
DEC	9	03.26 → AQU

MARS

mth	dy	time → sign
JAN	1	00.00 → LIB
JAN	11	03.00 → SCO
AUG	17	19.38 → SAG
OCT	5	06.22 → CAP
NOV	15	18.18 → AQU
DEC	25	06.27 → PIS

SATURN

mth	dy	time → sign
JAN	1	00.00 → SCO

JUPITER

mth	dy	time → sign
JAN	1	00.00 → SAG
JAN	19	15.22 → CAP

MOON

dy	jan	feb	mar	apr	may	jun	jul	aug	sep	oct	nov	dec	dy
1	SAG	AQU	17.29	ARI	TAU	05.53	LEO	04.03	16.30	05.28	AQU	PIS	1
2	06.07	AQU	PIS	23.55	16.02	CAN	19.28	LIB	SAG	CAP	07.50	03.42	2
3	CAP	11.22	PIS	TAU	GEM	10.19	VIR	06.04	22.55	14.03	PIS	ARI	3
4	16.31	PIS	06.07	TAU	23.26	LEO	21.27	SCO	CAP	AQU	20.20	16.20	4
5	AQU	PIS	ARI	10.04	CAN	13.27	LIB	10.30	CAP	AQU	ARI	TAU	5
6	AQU	00.04	18.09	GEM	CAN	VIR	LIB	SAG	08.11	01.19	ARI	TAU	6
7	04.34	ARI	TAU	17.59	04.43	16.03	00.28	17.24	AQU	PIS	08.53	03.24	7
8	PIS	12.05	TAU	CAN	LEO	LIB	SCO	CAP	19.26	13.51	TAU	GEM	8
9	17.15	TAU	04.30	23.01	08.02	18.48	05.03	CAP	PIS	ARI	20.10	11.56	9
10	ARI	21.39	GEM	LEO	VIR	SCO	SAG	02.25	PIS	ARI	GEM	CAN	10
11	ARI	GEM	11.48	LEO	09.54	22.26	11.23	AQU	07.47	02.28	GEM	18.08	11
12	04.36	GEM	CAN	01.11	LIB	SAG	CAP	13.13	ARI	TAU	05.31	LEO	12
13	TAU	03.20	15.21	VIR	11.22	SAG	19.41	PIS	20.33	14.14	CAN	22.35	13
14	12.40	CAN	LEO	01.29	SCO	03.48	AQU	PIS	TAU	GEM	12.34	VIR	14
15	GEM	05.09	15.47	LIB	13.50	CAP	AQU	01.28	TAU	GEM	LEO	VIR	15
16	16.47	LEO	VIR	01.41	SAG	11.41	06.10	ARI	08.26	00.00	17.08	01.52	16
17	CAN	04.32	14.51	SCO	18.43	AQU	PIS	14.13	GEM	CAN	VIR	LIB	17
18	17.49	VIR	LIB	03.44	CAP	22.18	18.26	TAU	17.36	06.41	19.29	04.27	18
19	LEO	03.39	14.49	SAG	CAP	PIS	ARI	TAU	CAN	LEO	LIB	SCO	19
20	17.35	LIB	SCO	09.10	02.55	PIS	ARI	01.31	22.49	09.56	20.30	06.58	20
21	VIR	04.44	17.41	CAP	AQU	10.40	06.52	GEM	LEO	VIR	SCO	SAG	21
22	18.07	SCO	SAG	18.27	14.09	ARI	TAU	09.20	LEO	10.31	21.34	10.21	22
23	LIB	09.22	SAG	AQU	PIS	22.38	17.10	CAN	00.19 VIR	LIB	SAG	CAP	23
24	21.04	SAG	00.36	AQU	PIS	TAU	GEM	13.00	23.41	10.08	SAG	15.47	24
25	SCO	17.49	CAP	06.26	02.39	TAU	23.44	LEO	LIB	SCO	00.17	AQU	25
26	SCO	CAP	11.09	PIS	ARI	08.04	CAN	13.32	23.04	10.43	CAP	AQU	26
27	03.12	CAP	AQU	19.02	14.13	GEM	CAN	VIR	SCO	SAG	06.06	00.18	27
28	SAG	05.02	23.37	ARI	TAU	14.09	02.41	12.57	SCO	14.05	AQU	PIS	28
29	12.12	AQU	PIS	ARI	23.23	CAN	LEO	LIB	00.32	CAP	15.33	11.49	29
30	CAP		PIS	06.30	GEM	17.30	03.29	13.23	SAG	21.13	PIS	ARI	30
31	23.11		12.14		GEM		VIR	SCO		AQU		ARI	31

SUN

mth	dy	time	→	sign
JAN	1	00.00	→	CAP
JAN	20	02.55	→	AQU
FEB	18	17.08	→	PIS
MAR	20	16.15	→	ARI
APR	20	03.26	→	TAU
MAY	21	02.47	→	GEM
JUN	21	10.44	→	CAN
JUL	22	21.37	→	LEO
AUG	23	04.36	→	VIR
SEP	23	02.02	→	LIB
OCT	23	11.22	→	SCO
NOV	22	08.54	→	SAG
DEC	21	22.08	→	CAP

MERCURY

mth	dy	time	→	sign
JAN	1	00.00	→	SAG
JAN	11	18.28	→	CAP
FEB	1	07.49	→	AQU
FEB	18	23.42	→	PIS
MAR	7	00.07	→	ARI
MAY	14	02.11	→	TAU
MAY	30	19.47	→	GEM
JUN	13	16.11	→	CAN
JUN	29	19.37	→	LEO
SEP	6	19.39	→	VIR
SEP	22	23.14	→	LIB
OCT	10	18.54	→	SCO
OCT	31	16.44	→	SAG
DEC	4	19.20	→	SCO
DEC	12	11.04	→	SAG

VENUS

mth	dy	time	→	sign
JAN	1	00.00	→	AQU
JAN	4	06.22	→	PIS
FEB	2	08.25	→	ARI
JUN	6	08.52	→	TAU
JUL	6	08.06	→	GEM
AUG	2	09.10	→	CAN
AUG	28	03.36	→	LEO
SEP	22	02.53	→	VIR
OCT	16	13.07	→	LIB
NOV	9	15.08	→	SCO
DEC	3	13.02	→	SAG
DEC	27	09.13	→	CAP

MARS

mth	dy	time	→	sign
JAN	1	00.00	→	PIS
FEB	2	17.13	→	ARI
MAR	15	05.00	→	TAU
APR	26	09.24	→	GEM
JUN	9	10.42	→	CAN
JUL	25	04.14	→	LEO
SEP	10	01.45	→	VIR
OCT	27	15.31	→	LIB
DEC	14	18.48	→	SCO

SATURN

mth	dy	time	→	sign
JAN	1	00.00	→	SCO
NOV	17	02.23	→	SAG

JUPITER

mth	dy	time	→	sign
JAN	1	00.00	→	CAP
FEB	6	15.46	→	AQU

MOON

dy	jan	feb	mar	apr	may	jun	jul	aug	sep	oct	nov	dec	dy
1	00.36	GEM	15.23	LEO	21.21	SCO	18.22	AQU	05.42	00.35	GEM	CAN	1
2	TAU	05.59	CAN	10.25	LIB	07.33	CAP	12.33	ARI	TAU	08.31	00.59	2
3	12.00	CAN	21.28	VIR	21.17	SAG	21.36	PIS	17.28	13.36	CAN	LEO	3
4	GEM	11.02	LEO	10.54	SCO	08.34	AQU	21.43	TAU	GEM	19.04	09.14	4
5	20.18	LEO	23.43	LIB	20.56	CAP	AQU	ARI	TAU	GEM	LEO	VIR	5
6	CAN	13.09	VIR	10.10	SAG	11.52	03.40	ARI	06.27	01.59	LEO	14.33	6
7	CAN	VIR	23.47	SCO	22.11	AQU	PIS	09.41	GEM	02.18	CAN	LIB	7
8	01.28	14.10	LIB	10.18	CAP	18.47	13.21	TAU	18.10	11.33	VIR	16.56	8
9	LEO	LIB	23.47	SAG	CAP	PIS	ARI	22.31	CAN	LEO	05.52	SCO	9
10	04.40	15.49	SCO	12.57	02.38	PIS	ARI	GEM	CAN	17.09	LIB	17.13	10
11	VIR	SCO	SCO	CAP	AQU	05.24	01.44	GEM	02.27	VIR	06.31	SAG	11
12	07.13	19.09	01.29	19.04	10.56	ARI	TAU	09.28	LEO	19.12	SCO	16.59	12
13	LIB	SAG	SAG	AQU	PIS	18.11	14.23	CAN	06.52	LIB	05.52	CAP	13
14	10.07	SAG	05.55	AQU	22.25	TAU	GEM	16.57	VIR	19.13	SAG	18.15	14
15	SCO	00.27	CAP	04.30	ARI	TAU	GEM	LEO	08.34	SCO	05.53	AQU	15
16	13.48	CAP	13.11	PIS	ARI	06.45	00.54	21.15	LIB	19.06	CAP	22.50	16
17	SAG	07.36	AQU	16.18	11.23	GEM	CAN	VIR	09.17	SAG	08.25	PIS	17
18	18.29	AQU	22.50	ARI	TAU	17.22	08.25	23.44	SCO	20.35	AQU	PIS	18
19	CAP	16.38	PIS	ARI	TAU	CAN	LEO	LIB	10.40	CAP	14.42	07.36	19
20	CAP	PIS	PIS	05.12	00.01	CAN	13.29	LIB	SAG	CAP	PIS	ARI	20
21	00.38	PIS	10.20	TAU	GEM	01.32	VIR	01.51	13.49	00.54	PIS	19.41	21
22	AQU	03.43	ARI	18.01	11.05	LEO	17.10	SCO	CAP	AQU	00.42	TAU	22
23	09.02	ARI	23.06	GEM	CAN	07.32	LIB	04.36	19.11	08.27	ARI	TAU	23
24	PIS	16.27	TAU	GEM	19.54	VIR	20.16	SAG	AQU	PIS	13.07	08.45	24
25	20.05	TAU	TAU	05.26	LEO	11.48	SCO	08.24	AQU	18.47	TAU	GEM	25
26	ARI	TAU	12.02	CAN	LEO	LIB	23.12	CAP	02.50	ARI	TAU	20.44	26
27	ARI	05.11	GEM	14.10	02.06	14.37	SAG	13.31	PIS	ARI	02.08	CAN	27
28	08.53	GEM	23.13	LEO	VIR	SCO	SAG	AQU	12.43	06.59	GEM	CAN	28
29	TAU		CAN	19.24	05.40	16.30	02.21	20.25	ARI	TAU	14.23	06.44	29
30	21.01		CAN	VIR	LIB	SAG	CAP	PIS	ARI	19.59	CAN	LEO	30
31	GEM		06.51		07.07		06.25	PIS		GEM		14.43	31

SUN

mth	dy	time → sign
JAN	1	00.00 → CAP
JAN	20	08.44 → AQU
FEB	18	22.58 → PIS
MAR	20	22.03 → ARI
APR	20	09.16 → TAU
MAY	21	08.28 → GEM
JUN	21	16.30 → CAN
JUL	23	03.25 → LEO
AUG	23	10.26 → VIR
SEP	23	07.57 → LIB
OCT	23	17.11 → SCO
NOV	22	14.45 → SAG
DEC	22	04.05 → CAP

MERCURY

mth	dy	time → sign
JAN	1	00.00 → SAG
JAN	5	20.43 → CAP
JAN	25	00.34 → AQU
FEB	11	05.25 → PIS
MAR	3	07.22 → ARI
MAR	11	17.32 → PIS
APR	17	12.33 → ARI
MAY	7	12.34 → TAU
MAY	22	07.22 → GEM
JUN	5	14.06 → CAN
JUN	26	14.15 → LEO
JUL	23	21.53 → CAN
AUG	11	21.09 → LEO
AUG	30	03.28 → VIR
SEP	15	02.26 → LIB
OCT	4	00.19 → SCO
DEC	10	00.34 → SAG
DEC	29	23.14 → CAP

VENUS

mth	dy	time → sign
JAN	1	00.00 → CAP
JAN	20	05.34 → AQU
FEB	13	03.11 → PIS
MAR	9	03.35 → ARI
APR	2	08.19 → TAU
APR	26	19.11 → GEM
MAY	21	13.46 → CAN
JUN	15	18.55 → LEO
JUL	11	16.23 → VIR
AUG	7	20.44 → LIB
SEP	7	10.11 → SCO

MARS

mth	dy	time → sign
JAN	1	00.00 → SCO
FEB	2	06.19 → SAG
MAR	28	03.29 → CAP
OCT	9	01.13 → AQU
NOV	26	02.44 → PIS

SATURN

mth	dy	time → sign
JAN	1	00.00 → SAG

JUPITER

mth	dy	time → sign
JAN	1	00.00 → AQU
FEB	20	16.28 → PIS

MOON

dy	jan	feb	mar	apr	may	jun	jul	aug	sep	oct	nov	dec	dy
1	VIR	06.19	SCO	CAP	AQU	04.43	TAU	GEM	01.08	VIR	14.19	02.08	1
2	20.45	SCO	14.51	CAP	14.30	ARI	TAU	06.04	LEO	VIR	SCO	SAG	2
3	LIB	09.31	SAG	03.11	PIS	15.45	10.32	CAN	10.06	01.03	15.19	01.28	3
4	LIB	SAG	17.56	AQU	23.01	TAU	GEM	17.26	VIR	LIB	SAG	CAP	4
5	00.44	12.02	CAP	09.03	ARI	TAU	23.19	LEO	16.33	04.35	15.49	01.23	5
6	SCO	CAP	21.42	PIS	ARI	04.26	CAN	LEO	LIB	SCO	CAP	AQU	6
7	02.47	14.35	AQU	17.12	09.59	GEM	CAN	02.44	21.12	06.48	17.29	03.48	7
8	SAG	AQU	AQU	ARI	TAU	17.16	10.56	VIR	SCO	SAG	AQU	PIS	8
9	03.42	18.32	02.48	ARI	22.26	CAN	LEO	10.05	SCO	08.52	21.30	09.49	9
10	CAP	PIS	PIS	03.36	GEM	CAN	20.50	LIB	00.40	CAP	PIS	ARI	10
11	05.01	PIS	10.03	TAU	GEM	05.11	VIR	15.36	SAG	11.45	PIS	19.10	11
12	AQU	01.21	ARI	15.51	11.18	LEO	VIR	SCO	03.28	AQU	04.14	TAU	12
13	08.39	ARI	20.04	GEM	CAN	15.18	04.40	19.17	CAP	16.03	ARI	TAU	13
14	PIS	11.38	TAU	GEM	23.15	VIR	LIB	SAG	06.07	PIS	13.24	06.41	14
15	16.03	TAU	TAU	04.42	LEO	22.38	09.58	21.22	AQU	22.13	TAU	GEM	15
16	ARI	TAU	08.23	CAN	LEO	LIB	SCO	CAP	09.27	ARI	TAU	19.09	16
17	ARI	00.17	GEM	16.10	08.45	LIB	12.34	22.44	PIS	ARI	00.26	CAN	17
18	03.14	GEM	21.04	LEO	VIR	02.36	SAG	AQU	14.33	06.35	GEM	CAN	18
19	TAU	12.39	CAN	LEO	14.41	SCO	13.10	AQU	ARI	TAU	12.46	07.44	19
20	16.12	CAN	CAN	00.24	LIB	03.36	CAP	00.52	22.25	17.15	CAN	LEO	20
21	GEM	22.25	07.38	VIR	17.02	SAG	13.17	PIS	TAU	GEM	CAN	19.30	21
22	GEM	LEO	LEO	04.50	SCO	03.00	AQU	05.27	TAU	GEM	01.25	VIR	22
23	04.14	LEO	14.39	LIB	16.57	CAP	14.59	ARI	09.13	05.37	LEO	VIR	23
24	CAN	04.58	VIR	06.15	SAG	02.50	PIS	13.36	GEM	CAN	12.46	05.05	24
25	13.47	VIR	18.22	SCO	16.15	AQU	20.02	TAU	21.44	18.02	VIR	LIB	25
26	LEO	09.07	LIB	06.16	CAP	05.12	ARI	TAU	CAN	LEO	20.59	11.06	26
27	20.51	LIB	20.05	SAG	17.00	PIS	ARI	01.00	CAN	LEO	LIB	SCO	27
28	VIR	12.06	SCO	06.41	AQU	11.35	05.11	GEM	09.39	04.20	LIB	13.20	28
29	VIR		21.20	CAP	20.54	ARI	TAU	13.40	LEO	VIR	01.13	SAG	29
30	02.10		SAG	09.06	PIS	21.54	17.19	CAN	18.57	11.04	SCO	12.54	30
31	LIB		23.25		PIS		GEM	CAN		LIB		CAP	31

119

SUN

mth	dy	time → sign
JAN	1	00.00 → CAP
JAN	20	14.44 → AQU
FEB	19	04.52 → PIS
MAR	21	03.52 → ARI
APR	20	14.57 → TAU
MAY	21	14.10 → GEM
JUN	21	22.14 → CAN
JUL	23	09.06 → LEO
AUG	23	16.15 → VIR
SEP	23	13.46 → LIB
OCT	23	23.03 → SCO
NOV	22	20.29 → SAG
DEC	22	09.43 → CAP

SATURN

mth	dy	time → sign
JAN	1	00.00 → SAG

MERCURY

mth	dy	time → sign
JAN	1	00.00 → CAP
JAN	17	13.11 → AQU
FEB	4	02.31 → PIS
MAR	11	21.54 → AQU
MAR	13	21.12 → PIS
APR	12	20.23 → ARI
APR	29	15.35 → TAU
MAY	13	17.50 → GEM
MAY	30	04.24 → CAN
AUG	6	21.20 → LEO
AUG	21	21.37 → VIR
SEP	7	13.52 → LIB
SEP	28	17.24 → SCO
NOV	1	01.57 → LIB
NOV	11	21.54 → SCO
DEC	3	13.33 → SAG
DEC	22	17.40 → CAP

VENUS

mth	dy	time → sign
JAN	1	00.00 → SCO
JAN	7	10.23 → SAG
FEB	5	03.07 → CAP
MAR	3	07.52 → AQU
MAR	28	16.20 → PIS
APR	22	16.03 → ARI
MAY	17	11.56 → TAU
JUN	11	05.14 → GEM
JUL	5	19.50 → CAN
JUL	30	06.52 → LEO
AUG	23	14.00 → VIR
SEP	16	18.15 → LIB
OCT	10	20.49 → SCO
NOV	3	23.07 → SAG
NOV	28	01.54 → CAP
DEC	22	06.31 → AQU

MARS

mth	dy	time → sign
JAN	1	00.00 → PIS
JAN	8	12.25 → ARI
FEB	20	14.42 → TAU
APR	5	16.37 → GEM
MAY	21	03.05 → CAN
JUL	6	16.43 → LEO
AUG	22	19.57 → VIR
OCT	8	19.19 → LIB
NOV	24	03.02 → SCO

JUPITER

mth	dy	time → sign
JAN	1	00.00 → PIS
MAR	2	18.21 → ARI

MOON

dy	jan	feb	mar	apr	may	jun	jul	aug	sep	oct	nov	dec	dy
1	11.54	PIS	12.37	TAU	GEM	03.25	VIR	LIB	SAG	CAP	PIS	ARI	1
2	AQU	02.09	ARI	12.16	07.39	LEO	VIR	01.09	17.04	01.51	13.40	01.06	2
3	12.36	ARI	18.11	GEM	CAN	15.56	09.55	06.47	CAP	AQU	ARI	TAU	3
4	PIS	08.53	TAU	23.33	20.06	VIR	LIB	06.47	18.22	03.39	18.02	08.13	4
5	16.51	TAU	TAU	CAN	LEO	VIR	18.03	SAG	AQU	PIS	TAU	GEM	5
6	ARI	19.23	03.26	CAN	LEO	02.24	SCO	08.51	18.37	05.35	TAU	17.20	6
7	ARI	GEM	GEM	12.04	08.07	LIB	22.05	CAP	PIS	ARI	00.16	CAN	7
8	01.13	GEM	15.24	LEO	VIR	09.06	SAG	08.37	19.34	08.57	GEM	CAN	8
9	TAU	07.55	CAN	23.28	17.29	SCO	22.43	AQU	ARI	TAU	09.10	04.40	9
10	12.39	CAN	CAN	VIR	LIB	11.53	CAP	08.01	22.57	15.04	CAN	LEO	10
11	GEM	20.21	03.54	VIR	23.09	SAG	21.49	PIS	TAU	GEM	20.45	17.30	11
12	GEM	LEO	LEO	08.06	SCO	12.05	AQU	09.09	TAU	GEM	LEO	VIR	12
13	01.18	LEO	14.55	LIB	SCO	CAP	21.36	ARI	05.54	00.31	LEO	VIR	13
14	CAN	07.26	VIR	13.41	01.41	11.45	PIS	13.38	GEM	CAN	09.29	05.40	14
15	13.45	VIR	23.34	SCO	SAG	AQU	PIS	TAU	16.22	12.34	VIR	LIB	15
16	LEO	16.44	LIB	17.01	02.37	12.54	00.00	21.59	CAN	LEO	20.48	14.41	16
17	LEO	LIB	LIB	SAG	CAP	PIS	ARI	GEM	CAN	LEO	LIB	SCO	17
18	01.15	LIB	05.57	19.21	03.42	16.56	06.04	GEM	04.50	01.06	LIB	19.33	18
19	VIR	00.04	SCO	CAP	AQU	ARI	TAU	09.19	LEO	VIR	04.47	SAG	19
20	11.09	SCO	10.32	21.45	06.24	ARI	15.33	CAN	17.13	11.50	SCO	21.08	20
21	LIB	05.09	SAG	AQU	PIS	00.09	GEM	21.58	VIR	LIB	09.16	CAP	21
22	18.30	SAG	13.48	AQU	11.23	TAU	GEM	LEO	VIR	19.41	SAG	21.20	22
23	SCO	07.57	CAP	01.02	ARI	09.54	03.13	LEO	03.58	SCO	11.32	AQU	23
24	22.35	CAP	16.18	PIS	18.39	GEM	CAN	10.23	LIB	SCO	CAP	22.10	24
25	SAG	09.08	AQU	05.41	TAU	21.22	15.50	VIR	12.30	00.57	13.13	PIS	25
26	23.42	AQU	18.46	ARI	TAU	CAN	LEO	21.35	SCO	SAG	AQU	PIS	26
27	CAP	10.07	PIS	12.06	03.55	CAN	LEO	LIB	18.49	04.33	15.41	01.05	27
28	23.17	PIS	22.12	TAU	GEM	09.52	04.26	LIB	SAG	CAP	PIS	ARI	28
29	AQU		ARI	20.43	14.59	LEO	VIR	06.49	23.08	07.27	19.36	06.37	29
30	23.24		ARI	GEM	CAN	22.34	15.59	SCO	CAP	AQU	ARI	TAU	30
31	PIS		03.46		CAN		LIB	13.24		10.19		14.29	31

SUN

mth	dy	time → sign
JAN	1	00.00 → CAP
JAN	20	20.23 → AQU
FEB	19	10.35 → PIS
MAR	20	09.36 → ARI
APR	19	20.45 → TAU
MAY	20	19.56 → GEM
JUN	21	03.57 → CAN
JUL	22	14.54 → LEO
AUG	22	21.54 → VIR
SEP	22	19.25 → LIB
OCT	23	04.44 → SCO
NOV	22	02.14 → SAG
DEC	21	15.27 → CAP

MERCURY

mth	dy	time → sign
JAN	1	00.00 → CAP
JAN	10	05.27 → AQU
MAR	16	10.13 → PIS
APR	4	22.04 → ARI
APR	20	06.44 → TAU
MAY	4	19.40 → GEM
JUL	12	06.40 → CAN
JUL	28	21.19 → LEO
AUG	12	17.26 → VIR
AUG	30	20.25 → LIB
NOV	6	14.52 → SCO
NOV	25	10.04 → SAG
DEC	14	11.51 → CAP

VENUS

mth	dy	time → sign
JAN	1	00.00 → AQU
JAN	15	16.00 → PIS
FEB	9	13.01 → ARI
MAR	6	10.21 → TAU
APR	3	17.07 → GEM
MAY	17	16.26 → CAN
MAY	27	07.33 → GEM
AUG	6	23.24 → CAN
SEP	7	11.35 → LEO
OCT	4	13.15 → VIR
OCT	29	23.23 → LIB
NOV	23	13.31 → SCO
DEC	17	17.54 → SAG

MARS

mth	dy	time → sign
JAN	1	00.00 → SCO
JAN	8	15.17 → SAG
FEB	22	10.28 → CAP
APR	6	21.36 → AQU
MAY	22	07.30 → PIS
JUL	13	20.13 → ARI
OCT	23	22.21 → PIS
NOV	1	12.46 → ARI

SATURN

mth	dy	time → sign
JAN	1	00.00 → SAG
FEB	13	23.37 → CAP
JUN	10	05.11 → SAG
NOV	12	09.32 → CAP

JUPITER

mth	dy	time → sign
JAN	1	00.00 → ARI
MAR	8	15.32 → TAU
JUL	21	23.45 → GEM
NOV	30	20.37 → TAU

MOON

dy	jan	feb	mar	apr	may	jun	jul	aug	sep	oct	nov	dec	dy
1	GEM	18.06	LEO	08.05	01.39	20.58	07.30	17.53	TAU	22.39	LEO	VIR	1
2	GEM	LEO	13.06	LIB	SCO	CAP	AQU	ARI	08.11	CAN	LEO	VIR	2
3	00.17	LEO	VIR	18.26	08.52	23.34	08.33	20.24	GEM	CAN	04.02	00.56	3
4	CAN	06.54	VIR	SCO	SAG	AQU	PIS	TAU	15.37	08.31	VIR	LIB	4
5	11.47	VIR	01.32	SCO	13.54	AQU	10.37	TAU	CAN	LEO	17.04	12.51	5
6	LEO	19.36	LIB	02.29	CAP	02.00	ARI	01.43	CAN	21.01	LIB	SCO	6
7	LEO	LIB	12.27	SAG	17.37	PIS	14.27	GEM	02.14	VIR	LIB	21.55	7
8	00.35	LIB	SCO	08.19	AQU	05.04	TAU	09.52	LEO	VIR	04.46	SAG	8
9	VIR	06.42	20.59	CAP	20.39	ARI	20.16	CAN	14.48	10.03	SCO	SAG	9
10	13.17	SCO	SAG	12.10	PIS	09.02	GEM	20.26	VIR	LIB	14.06	04.07	10
11	LIB	14.36	SAG	AQU	23.23	TAU	GEM	LEO	VIR	21.58	SAG	CAP	11
12	23.39	SAG	02.31	14.24	ARI	14.14	04.08	LEO	03.51	SCO	21.12	08.25	12
13	SCO	18.36	CAP	PIS	ARI	GEM	CAN	08.46	LIB	SCO	CAP	AQU	13
14	SCO	CAP	05.08	15.47	02.22	21.19	14.11	VIR	16.07	07.58	CAP	11.53	14
15	05.58	19.25	AQU	ARI	TAU	CAN	LEO	21.52	SCO	SAG	02.36	PIS	15
16	SAG	AQU	05.42	17.31	06.31	CAN	LEO	LIB	SCO	15.44	AQU	15.03	16
17	08.15	18.44	PIS	TAU	GEM	06.57	02.17	LIB	02.25	CAP	06.34	ARI	17
18	CAP	PIS	05.45	21.10	13.05	LEO	VIR	10.12	SAG	21.05	PIS	18.11	18
19	08.02	18.35	ARI	GEM	CAN	19.03	15.22	SCO	09.45	AQU	09.12	TAU	19
20	AQU	ARI	07.05	GEM	22.51	VIR	LIB	19.55	CAP	23.58	ARI	21.43	20
21	07.27	20.51	TAU	04.04	LEO	VIR	LIB	SAG	13.43	PIS	11.02	GEM	21
22	PIS	TAU	11.21	CAN	LEO	07.57	03.13	SAG	AQU	PIS	TAU	GEM	22
23	08.31	TAU	GEM	14.34	11.12	LIB	SCO	01.49	14.51	00.59	13.12	02.35	23
24	ARI	02.42	19.27	LEO	VIR	18.58	11.42	CAP	PIS	ARI	GEM	CAN	24
25	12.36	GEM	CAN	LEO	23.49	SCO	SAG	04.05	14.29	01.22	17.20	09.57	25
26	TAU	12.12	CAN	03.16	LIB	SCO	16.07	AQU	ARI	TAU	CAN	LEO	26
27	20.02	CAN	06.54	VIR	LIB	02.18	CAP	04.01	14.29	02.55	CAN	20.27	27
28	GEM	CAN	LEO	15.37	10.06	SAG	17.25	PIS	TAU	GEM	00.52	VIR	28
29	GEM	00.12	19.49	LIB	SCO	06.00	AQU	03.29	16.43	07.28	LEO	VIR	29
30	06.11		VIR	LIB	16.57	CAP	17.23	ARI	GEM	CAN	12.00	09.09	30
31	CAN		VIR		SAG		PIS	04.22		16.03		LIB	31

SUN

mth	dy	time → sign
JAN	1	00.00 → CAP
JAN	20	02.06 → AQU
FEB	18	16.24 → PIS
MAR	20	15.29 → ARI
APR	20	02.37 → TAU
MAY	21	01.56 → GEM
JUN	21	09.54 → CAN
JUL	22	20.45 → LEO
AUG	23	03.43 → VIR
SEP	23	01.23 → LIB
OCT	23	10.34 → SCO
NOV	22	08.05 → SAG
DEC	21	21.25 → CAP

MERCURY

mth	dy	time → sign
JAN	1	00.00 → CAP
JAN	2	19.41 → AQU
JAN	29	04.04 → CAP
FEB	14	18.11 → AQU
MAR	10	18.06 → PIS
MAR	28	03.16 → ARI
APR	11	21.37 → TAU
APR	29	19.52 → GEM
MAY	28	22.53 → TAU
JUN	12	08.52 → GEM
JUL	6	00.51 → CAN
JUL	20	09.05 → LEO
AUG	5	00.54 → VIR
AUG	26	06.14 → LIB
SEP	26	15.28 → VIR
OCT	11	06.12 → LIB
OCT	30	13.53 → SCO
NOV	18	03.10 → SAG
DEC	7	14.32 → CAP

VENUS

mth	dy	time → sign
JAN	1	00.00 → SAG
JAN	10	18.10 → CAP
FEB	3	17.11 → AQU
FEB	27	16.59 → PIS
MAR	23	18.37 → ARI
APR	16	23.56 → TAU
MAY	11	06.28 → GEM
JUN	4	17.16 → CAN
JUN	29	07.21 → LEO
JUL	24	01.35 → VIR
AUG	18	01.58 → LIB
SEP	12	12.22 → SCO
OCT	8	16.04 → SAG
NOV	5	10.17 → CAP
DEC	10	04.51 → AQU

MARS

mth	dy	time → sign
JAN	1	00.00 → ARI
JAN	19	08.02 → TAU
MAR	11	08.43 → GEM
APR	29	04.30 → CAN
JUN	16	14.26 → LEO
AUG	3	13.25 → VIR
SEP	19	14.23 → LIB
NOV	4	05.14 → SCO
DEC	18	04.55 → SAG

SATURN

mth	dy	time → sign
JAN	1	00.00 → CAP

JUPITER

mth	dy	time → sign
JAN	1	00.00 → TAU
MAR	11	03.39 → GEM
JUL	30	23.22 → CAN

MOON

dy	jan	feb	mar	apr	may	jun	jul	aug	sep	oct	nov	dec	dy
1	21.34	SAG	SAG	AQU	PIS	TAU	GEM	LEO	VIR	20.53	SAG	CAP	1
2	SCO	23.30	08.58	AQU	11.50	22.02	09.19	LEO	01.47	SCO	SAG	17.42	2
3	SCO	CAP	CAP	01.37	ARI	GEM	CAN	07.19	LIB	SCO	02.47	AQU	3
4	07.11	CAP	13.36	PIS	11.55	GEM	14.37	VIR	14.23	09.29	CAP	AQU	4
5	SAG	02.51	AQU	01.51	TAU	00.17	LEO	18.28	SCO	SAG	12.09	00.48	5
6	13.14	AQU	14.59	ARI	12.03	CAN	23.04	LIB	SCO	20.45	AQU	PIS	6
7	CAP	03.52	PIS	01.07	GEM	05.28	VIR	LIB	02.51	CAP	18.25	05.11	7
8	16.31	PIS	14.36	TAU	14.19	LEO	VIR	07.05	SAG	CAP	PIS	ARI	8
9	AQU	04.18	ARI	01.31	CAN	14.29	10.30	SCO	13.13	05.06	21.08	06.59	9
10	18.31	ARI	14.25	GEM	20.23	VIR	LIB	19.02	CAP	AQU	ARI	TAU	10
11	PIS	05.45	TAU	04.58	LEO	VIR	23.09	SAG	20.02	09.37	21.09	07.15	11
12	20.36	TAU	16.16	CAN	LEO	02.31	SCO	SAG	AQU	PIS	TAU	GEM	12
13	ARI	09.22	GEM	12.31	06.30	LIB	SCO	04.16	23.08	10.41	20.19	07.49	13
14	23.36	GEM	21.27	LEO	VIR	15.11	10.31	CAP	PIS	ARI	GEM	CAN	14
15	TAU	15.40	CAN	23.39	19.07	SCO	SAG	09.59	23.38	09.52	20.51	10.41	15
16	TAU	CAN	CAN	VIR	LIB	SCO	19.01	AQU	ARI	TAU	CAN	LEO	16
17	03.57	CAN	06.13	VIR	LIB	02.12	CAP	12.46	23.22	09.19	CAN	17.19	17
18	GEM	00.33	LEO	12.31	07.48	SAG	CAP	PIS	TAU	GEM	00.45	VIR	18
19	09.57	LEO	17.39	LIB	SCO	10.41	00.35	13.59	TAU	11.09	LEO	VIR	19
20	CAN	11.34	VIR	LIB	18.52	CAP	AQU	ARI	00.16	CAN	08.54	03.45	20
21	18.02	VIR	VIR	01.13	SAG	16.57	04.07	15.10	GEM	16.47	VIR	LIB	21
22	LEO	VIR	06.24	SCO	SAG	AQU	PIS	TAU	03.50	LEO	20.25	16.18	22
23	LEO	00.05	LIB	12.38	03.54	21.36	06.41	17.39	CAN	LEO	LIB	SCO	23
24	04.32	LIB	19.10	SAG	CAP	PIS	ARI	GEM	10.44	02.15	LIB	SCO	24
25	VIR	12.57	SCO	12.15	11.01	PIS	09.10	22.13	LEO	VIR	09.13	04.37	25
26	17.02	SCO	SCO	CAP	AQU	01.06	TAU	CAN	20.32	14.11	SCO	SAG	26
27	LIB	SCO	06.54	CAP	16.13	ARI	12.15	CAN	VIR	LIB	21.30	15.10	27
28	LIB	00.29	SAG	05.33	PIS	03.45	GEM	05.12	VIR	LIB	SAG	CAP	28
29	05.49		16.26	AQU	19.25	TAU	16.32	LEO	08.15	02.56	SAG	23.38	29
30	SCO		CAP	10.03	ARI	06.08	CAN	14.29	LIB	SCO	08.26	AQU	30
31	16.30		22.45		20.59		22.41	VIR		15.23		AQU	31

SUN

mth	dy	time → sign
JAN	1	00.00 → CAP
JAN	20	08.02 → AQU
FEB	18	22.14 → PIS
MAR	20	21.20 → ARI
APR	20	08.27 → TAU
MAY	21	07.38 → GEM
JUN	21	15.33 → CAN
JUL	23	02.22 → LEO
AUG	23	09.23 → VIR
SEP	23	06.56 → LIB
OCT	23	16.17 → SCO
NOV	22	13.47 → SAG
DEC	22	03.08 → CAP

MERCURY

mth	dy	time → sign
JAN	1	00.00 → CAP
FEB	12	01.14 → AQU
MAR	3	17.15 → PIS
MAR	20	00.06 → ARI
APR	4	07.37 → TAU
JUN	12	00.27 → GEM
JUN	27	20.44 → CAN
JUL	11	23.42 → LEO
JUL	29	11.11 → VIR
OCT	5	17.46 → LIB
OCT	23	01.48 → SCO
NOV	11	00.02 → SAG
DEC	2	00.12 → CAP
DEC	25	22.54 → SAG

VENUS

mth	dy	time → sign
JAN	1	00.00 → AQU
JAN	16	15.21 → CAP
MAR	3	17.51 → AQU
APR	6	09.15 → PIS
MAY	4	03.52 → ARI
MAY	30	10.14 → TAU
JUN	25	00.16 → GEM
JUL	20	03.41 → CAN
AUG	13	22.09 → LEO
SEP	7	08.21 → VIR
OCT	1	12.13 → LIB
OCT	25	12.04 → SCO
NOV	18	09.58 → SAG
DEC	12	07.19 → CAP

MARS

mth	dy	time → sign
JAN	1	00.00 → SAG
JAN	29	14.21 → CAP
MAR	11	15.45 → AQU
APR	20	22.19 → PIS
MAY	31	07.20 → ARI
JUL	12	14.34 → TAU
AUG	31	11.30 → GEM
DEC	14	07.49 → TAU

SATURN

mth	dy	time → sign
JAN	1	00.00 → CAP

JUPITER

mth	dy	time → sign
JAN	1	00.00 → CAN
AUG	18	07.51 → LEO

MOON

dy	jan	feb	mar	apr	may	jun	jul	aug	sep	oct	nov	dec	dy
1	06.12	19.27	01.43	12.50	00.08	23.31	18.01	SAG	20.51	13.42	ARI	16.23	1
2	PIS	TAU	TAU	CAN	LEO	LIB	SCO	SAG	AQU	PIS	05.31	GEM	2
3	10.58	22.12	03.37	17.50	07.18	LIB	SCO	02.09	AQU	17.42	TAU	15.27	3
4	ARI	GEM	GEM	LEO	VIR	11.21	06.35	CAP	04.06	ARI	05.06	CAN	4
5	14.04	GEM	07.04	LEO	17.28	SCO	SAG	12.21	PIS	19.06	GEM	16.00	5
6	TAU	01.27	CAN	01.42	LIB	23.59	18.39	AQU	08.23	TAU	05.07	LEO	6
7	16.02	CAN	12.24	VIR	LIB	SAG	CAP	19.54	ARI	19.47	CAN	19.39	7
8	GEM	05.51	LEO	11.44	05.23	SAG	CAP	PIS	10.55	GEM	07.24	VIR	8
9	17.52	LEO	19.47	LIB	SCO	12.12	05.07	PIS	TAU	21.29	LEO	VIR	9
10	CAN	12.13	VIR	23.18	17.56	CAP	AQU	01.13	13.05	CAN	12.48	03.00	10
11	21.02	VIR	VIR	SCO	SAG	23.09	13.29	ARI	GEM	CAN	VIR	LIB	11
12	LEO	21.09	05.09	SCO	SAG	AQU	PIS	04.55	15.53	01.16	21.08	13.26	12
13	LEO	LIB	LIB	11.48	06.21	AQU	19.36	TAU	CAN	LEO	LIB	SCO	13
14	02.57	LIB	16.25	SAG	CAP	08.00	ARI	07.41	19.52	07.21	LIB	SCO	14
15	VIR	08.34	SCO	SAG	17.30	PIS	23.29	GEM	LEO	VIR	07.39	01.44	15
16	12.18	SCO	SCO	00.15	AQU	13.55	TAU	10.12	LEO	15.26	SCO	SAG	16
17	LIB	21.07	04.58	CAP	AQU	ARI	TAU	CAN	01.15	LIB	19.37	14.35	17
18	LIB	SAG	SAG	10.53	01.54	16.43	01.32	13.11	VIR	LIB	SAG	CAP	18
19	00.16	SAG	17.01	ARI	PIS	TAU	GEM	LEO	08.34	01.24	SAG	CAP	19
20	SCO	08.30	CAP	17.57	06.31	17.14	02.44	17.33	LIB	SCO	08.32	02.55	20
21	12.44	CAP	CAP	PIS	ARI	GEM	CAN	VIR	18.08	13.09	CAP	AQU	21
22	SAG	16.52	02.32	20.58	07.44	17.10	04.32	VIR	SCO	SAG	21.07	13.42	22
23	23.27	AQU	AQU	ARI	TAU	CAN	LEO	00.17	SCO	SAG	AQU	PIS	23
24	CAP	21.49	08.08	21.03	07.00	18.25	08.17	LIB	05.52	02.03	AQU	21.45	24
25	CAP	PIS	PIS	TAU	GEM	LEO	VIR	09.56	SAG	CAP	07.32	ARI	25
26	07.25	PIS	10.15	20.12	06.34	22.42	15.19	SCO	18.36	14.14	PIS	ARI	26
27	AQU	00.16	ARI	GEM	CAN	VIR	LIB	21.57	CAP	AQU	14.06	02.08	27
28	12.51	ARI	10.28	20.40	08.29	VIR	LIB	SAG	CAP	23.22	ARI	TAU	28
29	PIS		TAU	CAN	LEO	06.47	01.43	SAG	05.57	PIS	16.37	03.26	29
30	16.34		10.42	CAN	14.08	LIB	SCO	10.23	AQU	PIS	TAU	GEM	30
31	ARI		GEM		VIR		14.00	CAP		04.14		03.02	31

SUN

mth	dy	time	→ sign
JAN	1	00.00	→ CAP
JAN	20	13.44	→ AQU
FEB	19	03.55	→ PIS
MAR	21	03.05	→ ARI
APR	20	14.07	→ TAU
MAY	21	13.20	→ GEM
JUN	21	21.17	→ CAN
JUL	23	08.11	→ LEO
AUG	23	15.11	→ VIR
SEP	23	12.48	→ LIB
OCT	23	22.03	→ SCO
NOV	22	19.36	→ SAG
DEC	22	08.52	→ CAP

MERCURY

mth	dy	time	→ sign
JAN	1	00.00	→ SAG
JAN	14	08.05	→ CAP
FEB	5	22.22	→ AQU
FEB	24	02.38	→ PIS
MAR	11	22.42	→ ARI
MAY	16	22.45	→ TAU
JUN	5	02.23	→ GEM
JUN	19	05.40	→ CAN
JUL	4	06.04	→ LEO
JUL	26	13.00	→ VIR
AUG	19	21.45	→ LEO
SEP	10	17.14	→ VIR
SEP	28	03.25	→ LIB
OCT	15	14.01	→ SCO
NOV	4	10.44	→ SAG

VENUS

mth	dy	time	→ sign
JAN	1	00.00	→ CAP
JAN	5	05.05	→ AQU
JAN	29	04.47	→ PIS
FEB	22	09.07	→ ARI
MAR	18	21.43	→ TAU
APR	13	00.13	→ GEM
MAY	9	01.27	→ CAN
JUN	6	01.16	→ LEO
JUL	11	05.06	→ VIR
AUG	21	15.09	→ LEO
OCT	6	21.12	→ VIR
NOV	9	06.34	→ LIB
DEC	6	07.24	→ SCO
DEC	31	15.18	→ SAG

MARS

mth	dy	time	→ sign
JAN	1	00.00	→ TAU
JAN	21	01.27	→ GEM
APR	3	00.34	→ CAN
MAY	26	12.29	→ LEO
JUL	15	12.25	→ VIR
SEP	1	06.34	→ LIB
OCT	16	19.16	→ SCO
NOV	29	02.11	→ SAG

SATURN

mth	dy	time	→ sign
JAN	1	00.00	→ CAP
FEB	6	18.40	→ AQU

JUPITER

mth	dy	time	→ sign
JAN	1	00.00	→ LEO
SEP	12	06.23	→ VIR

MOON

dy	jan	feb	mar	apr	may	jun	jul	aug	sep	oct	nov	dec	dy
1	CAN	VIR	VIR	SCO	SAG	23.42	17.51	ARI	03.02	CAN	VIR	LIB	1
2	02.54	20.02	06.03	SCO	SAG	AQU	PIS	16.32	GEM	14.58	VIR	16.33	2
3	LEO	LIB	LIB	07.59	03.55	AQU	PIS	TAU	06.19	LEO	04.13	SCO	3
4	04.57	LIB	13.08	SAG	CAP	11.36	03.33	20.54	CAN	17.45	LIB	SCO	4
5	VIR	04.01	SCO	20.20	16.51	PIS	ARI	GEM	08.13	VIR	10.09	01.32	5
6	10.33	SCO	23.35	CAP	AQU	20.25	09.52	22.47	LEO	21.00	SCO	SAG	6
7	LIB	15.23	SAG	CAP	AQU	ARI	TAU	CAN	09.35	LIB	18.21	12.41	7
8	19.59	SAG	SAG	09.00	04.04	ARI	12.42	23.09	VIR	LIB	SAG	CAP	8
9	SCO	SAG	12.14	AQU	PIS	01.13	GEM	LEO	11.52	02.00	SAG	CAP	9
10	SCO	04.16	CAP	19.18	11.34	TAU	13.03	23.35	LIB	SCO	05.16	01.27	10
11	08.06	CAP	CAP	PIS	ARI	02.36	CAN	VIR	16.42	09.58	CAP	AQU	11
12	SAG	16.16	00.31	PIS	15.07	GEM	12.35	VIR	SCO	SAG	18.06	14.19	12
13	21.00	AQU	AQU	01.49	TAU	02.17	LEO	01.52	SCO	21.10	AQU	PIS	13
14	CAP	AQU	10.11	ARI	16.02	CAN	13.12	LIB	01.14	CAP	AQU	PIS	14
15	CAP	01.59	PIS	05.06	GEM	02.10	VIR	07.34	SAG	CAP	06.33	01.06	15
16	09.04	PIS	16.37	TAU	16.14	LEO	16.34	SCO	13.04	10.04	PIS	ARI	16
17	AQU	09.11	ARI	06.41	CAN	04.03	LIB	17.11	CAP	AQU	16.08	08.10	17
18	19.23	ARI	20.40	GEM	17.30	VIR	23.41	SAG	CAP	21.53	ARI	TAU	18
19	PIS	14.24	TAU	08.17	LEO	09.01	SCO	SAG	01.58	PIS	21.49	11.21	19
20	PIS	TAU	23.37	CAN	21.00	LIB	SCO	05.34	AQU	PIS	TAU	GEM	20
21	03.28	18.10	GEM	11.06	VIR	17.18	10.16	CAP	13.20	06.33	TAU	11.55	21
22	ARI	GEM	GEM	LEO	VIR	SCO	SAG	18.27	PIS	ARI	00.22	CAN	22
23	09.01	20.56	02.27	15.29	03.08	SCO	22.55	AQU	21.56	11.55	GEM	11.38	23
24	TAU	CAN	CAN	VIR	LIB	04.16	CAP	AQU	ARI	TAU	01.25	LEO	24
25	12.06	23.13	05.43	21.36	11.41	SAG	CAP	05.51	ARI	15.09	CAN	12.24	25
26	GEM	LEO	LEO	LIB	SCO	16.49	11.49	PIS	03.59	GEM	02.37	VIR	26
27	13.23	LEO	09.41	LIB	22.21	CAP	AQU	15.01	TAU	17.37	LEO	15.37	27
28	CAN	01.50	VIR	05.34	SAG	CAP	23.35	ARI	08.25	CAN	05.12	LIB	28
29	14.03		14.49	SCO	SAG	05.47	PIS	22.00	GEM	20.20	VIR	22.03	29
30	LEO		LIB	15.42	10.40	AQU	PIS	TAU	11.58	LEO	09.47	SCO	30
31	15.44		22.01		CAP		09.20	TAU		23.47		SCO	31

SUN

mth	dy	time → sign
JAN	1	00.00 → CAP
JAN	20	19.36 → AQU
FEB	19	09.47 → PIS
MAR	20	08.47 → ARI
APR	19	19.53 → TAU
MAY	20	19.13 → GEM
JUN	21	03.15 → CAN
JUL	22	14.11 → LEO
AUG	22	21.12 → VIR
SEP	22	18.44 → LIB
OCT	23	03.57 → SCO
NOV	22	01.24 → SAG
DEC	21	14.41 → CAP

MERCURY

mth	dy	time → sign
JAN	1	00.00 → SAG
JAN	10	01.48 → CAP
JAN	29	21.13 → AQU
FEB	16	07.04 → PIS
MAR	3	21.43 → ARI
APR	3	23.53 → PIS
APR	14	17.38 → ARI
MAY	11	04.11 → TAU
MAY	26	21.15 → GEM
JUN	9	18.27 → CAN
JUN	27	05.14 → LEO
SEP	3	08.03 → VIR
SEP	19	05.44 → LIB
OCT	7	10.12 → SCO
OCT	29	17.03 → SAG
NOV	21	19.43 → SCO
DEC	12	08.02 → SAG

VENUS

mth	dy	time → sign
JAN	1	00.00 → SAG
JAN	25	07.17 → CAP
FEB	18	16.43 → AQU
MAR	13	23.57 → PIS
APR	7	07.13 → ARI
MAY	1	15.42 → TAU
MAY	26	01.15 → GEM
JUN	19	11.23 → CAN
JUL	13	21.09 → LEO
AUG	7	06.22 → VIR
AUG	31	16.09 → LIB
SEP	25	03.32 → SCO
OCT	19	17.45 → SAG
NOV	13	12.48 → CAP
DEC	8	17.52 → AQU

MARS

mth	dy	time → sign
JAN	1	00.00 → SAG
JAN	9	09.32 → CAP
FEB	18	04.30 → AQU
MAR	28	02.15 → PIS
MAY	5	21.28 → ARI
JUN	14	15.56 → TAU
JUL	26	18.55 → GEM
SEP	12	06.11 → CAN

SATURN

mth	dy	time → sign
JAN	1	00.00 → AQU

JUPITER

mth	dy	time → sign
JAN	1	00.00 → VIR
OCT	10	13.38 → LIB

MOON

dy	jan	feb	mar	apr	may	jun	jul	aug	sep	oct	nov	dec	dy
1	07.30	CAP	AQU	PIS	19.09	GEM	22.15	VIR	SCO	SAG	12.43	09.23	1
2	SAG	14.09	AQU	03.04	TAU	11.58	LEO	08.17	SCO	17.29	AQU	PIS	2
3	19.09	AQU	09.11	ARI	TAU	CAN	22.37	LIB	00.50	CAP	AQU	21.49	3
4	CAP	AQU	PIS	11.18	00.28	13.35	VIR	11.16	SAG	CAP	01.13	ARI	4
5	CAP	02.51	20.07	TAU	GEM	LEO	VIR	SCO	10.06	04.53	PIS	ARI	5
6	07.59	PIS	ARI	17.33	04.09	15.28	00.27	17.57	CAP	AQU	13.19	08.16	6
7	AQU	14.15	ARI	GEM	CAN	VIR	LIB	SAG	22.08	17.38	ARI	TAU	7
8	20.52	ARI	05.05	22.18	07.07	18.33	04.53	SAG	AQU	PIS	23.19	15.37	8
9	PIS	23.36	TAU	CAN	LEO	LIB	SCO	04.00	AQU	PIS	TAU	GEM	9
10	PIS	TAU	12.03	CAN	09.56	23.27	12.17	CAP	10.56	05.36	TAU	20.05	10
11	08.22	TAU	GEM	01.46	VIR	SCO	SAG	16.06	PIS	ARI	06.49	CAN	11
12	ARI	06.08	16.50	LEO	13.05	SCO	22.16	AQU	23.02	15.48	GEM	22.47	12
13	17.00	GEM	CAN	04.09	LIB	06.29	CAP	AQU	ARI	TAU	12.19	LEO	13
14	TAU	09.31	19.20	VIR	17.15	SAG	CAP	04.51	ARI	TAU	CAN	LEO	14
15	21.55	CAN	LEO	06.10	SCO	15.50	10.03	PIS	09.47	00.08	16.23	00.56	15
16	GEM	10.15	20.13	LIB	23.22	CAP	AQU	17.11	TAU	GEM	LEO	VIR	16
17	23.26	LEO	VIR	09.10	SAG	CAP	22.44	ARI	18.40	06.36	19.28	03.33	17
18	CAN	09.47	20.55	SCO	SAG	03.19	PIS	ARI	GEM	CAN	VIR	LIB	18
19	22.57	VIR	LIB	14.40	08.13	AQU	PIS	04.10	GEM	11.01	22.03	07.20	19
20	LEO	10.05	23.20	SAG	CAP	16.00	11.07	TAU	00.59	LEO	LIB	SCO	20
21	22.22	LIB	SCO	23.40	19.44	PIS	ARI	12.36	CAN	13.27	LIB	12.42	21
22	VIR	13.11	SCO	CAP	AQU	PIS	21.36	GEM	04.19	VIR	00.52	SAG	22
23	23.42	SCO	05.13	CAP	AQU	04.03	TAU	17.36	LEO	14.39	SCO	20.04	23
24	LIB	20.26	SAG	11.38	08.25	TAU	TAU	CAN	05.08	LIB	05.01	CAP	24
25	LIB	SAG	15.09	AQU	PIS	13.28	04.44	19.15	VIR	16.04	SAG	CAP	25
26	04.32	SAG	CAP	AQU	19.52	TAU	GEM	LEO	04.55	SCO	11.38	05.43	26
27	SCO	07.33	CAP	00.20	ARI	19.14	08.08	18.46	LIB	19.29	CAP	AQU	27
28	13.20	CAP	03.44	PIS	ARI	GEM	CAN	VIR	05.44	SAG	21.19	17.28	28
29	SAG	20.34	AQU	11.13	04.16	21.42	08.39	18.11	SCO	SAG	AQU	PIS	29
30	SAG		16.23	ARI	TAU	CAN	LEO	LIB	09.33	02.18	AQU	PIS	30
31	01.07		PIS		09.19		08.01	19.38		CAP		06.07	31

SUN

mth	dy	time → sign
JAN	1	00.00 → CAP
JAN	20	01.21 → AQU
FEB	18	15.35 → PIS
MAR	20	14.44 → ARI
APR	20	01.47 → TAU
MAY	21	01.03 → GEM
JUN	21	09.00 → CAN
JUL	22	19.54 → LEO
AUG	23	02.50 → VIR
SEP	23	00.26 → LIB
OCT	23	09.36 → SCO
NOV	22	07.07 → SAG
DEC	21	20.23 → CAP

MERCURY

mth	dy	time → sign
JAN	1	00.00 → SAG
JAN	2	14 47 → CAP
JAN	21	11.23 → AQU
FEB	7	16.21 → PIS
APR	15	15.18 → ARI
MAY	3	21.51 → TAU
MAY	18	06.53 → GEM
JUN	2	03.52 → CAN
AUG	10	05.50 → LEO
AUG	26	07.03 → VIR
SEP	11	11.18 → LIB
OCT	1	02.13 → SCO
DEC	7	01.04 → SAG
DEC	26	12.48 → CAP

VENUS

mth	dy	time → sign
JAN	1	00.00 → AQU
JAN	3	23.51 → PIS
FEB	2	12.37 → ARI
JUN	6	10.01 → TAU
JUL	6	00.21 → GEM
AUG	1	22.36 → CAN
AUG	27	15.48 → LEO
SEP	21	14.27 → VIR
OCT	16	00.13 → LIB
NOV	9	02.10 → SCO
DEC	2	23.55 → SAG
DEC	26	20.07 → CAP

MARS

mth	dy	time → sign
JAN	1	00.00 → CAN
APR	27	23.30 → LEO
JUN	23	07.29 → VIR
AUG	12	01.14 → LIB
SEP	27	02.19 → SCO
NOV	9	05.32 → SAG
DEC	20	00.39 → CAP

SATURN

mth	dy	time → sign
JAN	1	00.00 → AQU
MAY	21	04.44 → PIS
JUN	30	08.13 → AQU

JUPITER

mth	dy	time → sign
JAN	1	00.00 → LIB
NOV	10	08.27 → SCO

MOON

dy	jan	feb	mar	apr	may	jun	jul	aug	sep	oct	nov	dec	dy
1	ARI	11.15	GEM	14.21	00.00	10.22	SAG	16.36	PIS	ARI	10.13	02.17	1
2	17.30	GEM	GEM	LEO	VIR	SCO	SAG	AQU	21.21	16.13	GEM	CAN	2
3	TAU	16.56	02.16	16.10	01.20	13.01	01.48	AQU	ARI	TAU	20.25	09.33	3
4	TAU	CAN	CAN	VIR	LIB	SAG	CAP	02.44	ARI	TAU	CAN	LEO	4
5	01.42	18.51	05.40	15.54	01.57	17.26	09.14	PIS	10.09	04.27	CAN	14.43	5
6	GEM	LEO	LEO	LIB	SCO	CAP	AQU	14.39	TAU	GEM	04.06	VIR	6
7	06.10	18.29	05.52	15.32	03.34	CAP	19.10	ARI	22.16	14.42	LEO	18.03	7
8	CAN	VIR	VIR	SCO	SAG	00.39	PIS	ARI	GEM	CAN	08.47	LIB	8
9	07.49	17.58	04.46	17.10	07.51	AQU	PIS	03.22	GEM	21.34	VIR	20.04	9
10	LEO	LIB	LIB	SAG	CAP	10.57	07.11	TAU	07.37	LEO	10.42	SCO	10
11	08.20	19.24	04.40	22.24	15.44	PIS	ARI	14.47	CAN	LEO	LIB	21.39	11
12	VIR	SCO	SCO	CAP	AQU	23.14	19.37	GEM	12.51	00.36	11.00	SAG	12
13	09.30	SCO	07.33	CAP	AQU	ARI	TAU	22.46	LEO	VIR	SCO	SAG	13
14	LIB	00.08	SAG	07.36	02.51	ARI	TAU	CAN	14.20	00.47	11.20	00.06	14
15	12.42	SAG	14.28	AQU	PIS	11.19	06.07	CAN	VIR	LIB	SAG	CAP	15
16	SCO	08.20	CAP	19.33	15.24	TAU	GEM	02.43	13.44	00.01	13.34	04.51	16
17	18.30	CAP	CAP	PIS	ARI	21.12	13.08	LEO	LIB	SCO	CAP	AQU	17
18	SAG	19.05	00.52	PIS	ARI	GEM	CAN	03.41	13.15	00.23	19.08	12.59	18
19	SAG	AQU	AQU	08.14	03.16	GEM	16.47	VIR	SCO	SAG	AQU	PIS	19
20	02.46	AQU	13.11	ARI	TAU	04.05	LEO	03.35	14.53	03.42	AQU	PIS	20
21	CAP	07.12	PIS	20.08	13.07	CAN	18.24	LIB	SAG	CAP	04.27	00.19	21
22	13.00	PIS	PIS	TAU	GEM	08.26	VIR	04.27	19.54	10.49	PIS	ARI	22
23	AQU	19.50	01.51	TAU	20.38	LEO	19.39	SCO	CAP	AQU	16.30	13.05	23
24	AQU	ARI	ARI	06.27	CAN	11.18	LIB	07.45	CAP	21.17	ARI	TAU	24
25	00.47	ARI	13.59	GEM	CAN	VIR	22.00	SAG	04.19	PIS	ARI	TAU	25
26	PIS	08.11	TAU	14.45	02.03	13.46	SCO	13.58	AQU	PIS	05.14	00.46	26
27	13.28	TAU	TAU	CAN	LEO	LIB	SCO	CAP	15.13	09.39	TAU	GEM	27
28	ARI	18.52	00.48	20.39	05.46	16.37	02.13	22.42	PIS	AQU	16.48	09.46	28
29	ARI		GEM	LEO	VIR	SCO	SAG	AQU	PIS	22.20	GEM	CAN	29
30	01.37		09.14	LEO	08.18	20.28	08.27	AQU	03.29	TAU	GEM	15.59	30
31	TAU		CAN		LIB		CAP	09.19		TAU		LEO	31

SUN

mth	dy	time → sign
JAN	1	00.00 → CAP
JAN	20	07.09 → AQU
FEB	18	21.22 → PIS
MAR	20	20.26 → ARI
APR	20	07.36 → TAU
MAY	21	06.46 → GEM
JUN	21	14.48 → CAN
JUL	23	01.44 → LEO
AUG	23	08.44 → VIR
SEP	23	06.16 → LIB
OCT	23	15.36 → SCO
NOV	22	13.09 → SAG
DEC	22	02.21 → CAP

MERCURY

mth	dy	time → sign
JAN	1	00.00 → CAP
JAN	14	00.28 → AQU
FEB	1	10.28 → PIS
FEB	21	15.18 → AQU
MAR	18	12.04 → PIS
APR	9	16.32 → ARI
APR	25	18.27 → TAU
MAY	9	21.05 → GEM
MAY	28	14.52 → CAN
JUL	2	23.18 → GEM
JUL	10	12.42 → CAN
AUG	3	06.09 → LEO
AUG	18	00.47 → VIR
SEP	4	04.56 → LIB
SEP	27	08.54 → SCO
OCT	19	06.19 → LIB
NOV	10	12.45 → SCO
NOV	30	04.39 → SAG
DEC	19	06.26 → CAP

VENUS

mth	dy	time → sign
JAN	1	00.00 → CAP
JAN	19	16.26 → AQU
FEB	12	14.05 → PIS
MAR	8	14.27 → ARI
APR	1	19.21 → TAU
APR	26	06.23 → GEM
MAY	21	01.27 → CAN
JUN	15	07.20 → LEO
JUL	11	06.30 → VIR
AUG	7	14.39 → LIB
SEP	7	17.11 → SCO

MARS

mth	dy	time → sign
JAN	1	00.00 → CAP
JAN	28	04.18 → AQU
MAR	7	11.20 → PIS
APR	14	18.13 → ARI
MAY	23	22.37 → TAU
JUL	3	22.34 → GEM
AUG	16	19.25 → CAN
OCT	4	15.53 → LEO
DEC	12	11.35 → VIR

SATURN

mth	dy	time → sign
JAN	1	00.00 → AQU
JAN	28	23.29 → PIS

JUPITER

mth	dy	time → sign
JAN	1	00.00 → SCO
DEC	9	10.43 → SAG

MOON

dy	jan	feb	mar	apr	may	jun	jul	aug	sep	oct	nov	dec	dy
1	20.15	LIB	14.43	SAG	16.34	PIS	ARI	11.05	CAN	LEO	LIB	SCO	1
2	VIR	07.49	SCO	03.38	AQU	18.31	14.23	GEM	15.37	06.39	20.19	07.13	2
3	23.31	SCO	16.54	CAP	AQU	ARI	TAU	22.22	LEO	VIR	SCO	SAG	3
4	LIB	11.14	SAG	09.45	00.47	ARI	TAU	CAN	20.33	08.56	19.46	06.43	4
5	LIB	SAG	21.24	AQU	PIS	07.14	03.12	CAN	VIR	LIB	SAG	CAP	5
6	02.29	16.02	CAP	18.51	12.01	TAU	GEM	06.31	22.57	09.22	20.02	07.52	6
7	SCO	CAP	CAP	PIS	ARI	20.03	14.17	LEO	LIB	SCO	CAP	AQU	7
8	05.34	22.16	04.15	PIS	ARI	GEM	CAN	11.42	LIB	09.47	22.48	12.24	8
9	SAG	AQU	AQU	06.09	00.50	GEM	22.43	VIR	00.26	SAG	AQU	PIS	9
10	09.16	AQU	13.09	ARI	TAU	07.22	LEO	15.07	SCO	11.44	AQU	21.03	10
11	CAP	06.23	PIS	18.48	13.43	CAN	LEO	LIB	02.25	CAP	05.04	ARI	11
12	14.25	PIS	23.59	TAU	GEM	16.29	04.48	17.56	SAG	16.09	PIS	ARI	12
13	AQU	16.49	ARI	TAU	GEM	LEO	VIR	SCO	05.44	AQU	14.44	08.56	13
14	22.04	ARI	ARI	04.48	01.27	23.16	09.15	20.53	CAP	23.18	ARI	TAU	14
15	PIS	ARI	12.27	GEM	CAN	VIR	LIB	SAG	10.42	PIS	ARI	22.00	15
16	PIS	05.20	TAU	19.41	10.58	VIR	12.35	SAG	AQU	PIS	02.44	GEM	16
17	08.42	TAU	TAU	CAN	LEO	03.48	SCO	00.18	17.31	08.56	TAU	GEM	17
18	ARI	18.05	01.29	CAN	17.31	LIB	15.09	CAP	PIS	ARI	15.41	10.25	18
19	21.22	GEM	GEM	04.45	VIR	06.20	SAG	04.34	PIS	20.34	GEM	CAN	19
20	TAU	GEM	12.54	LEO	20.54	SCO	17.30	AQU	02.30	TAU	GEM	21.13	20
21	TAU	04.27	CAN	09.58	LIB	07.32	CAP	10.27	ARI	TAU	04.21	LEO	21
22	09.35	CAN	20.39	VIR	21.51	SAG	20.38	PIS	13.47	09.28	CAN	LEO	22
23	GEM	10.48	LEO	11.40	SCO	08.37	AQU	18.55	TAU	GEM	15.33	06.01	23
24	18.55	LEO	LEO	LIB	21.43	CAP	AQU	ARI	TAU	22.15	LEO	VIR	24
25	CAN	13.27	00.14	11.18	SAG	11.10	01.56	ARI	02.41	CAN	LEO	12.27	25
26	CAN	VIR	VIR	SCO	22.17	AQU	PIS	06.13	GEM	CAN	00.09	LIB	26
27	08.38	14.06	00.46	10.48	CAP	16.44	10.31	TAU	15.12	09.05	VIR	16.17	27
28	LEO	LIB	LIB	SAG	CAP	PIS	ARI	19.07	CAN	LEO	05.22	SCO	28
29	03.39		00.15	12.05	01.19	PIS	22.13	GEM	CAN	16.21	LIB	17.45	29
30	VIR		SCO	CAP	AQU	02.07	TAU	GEM	00.55	VIR	07.21	SAG	30
31	05.34		00.41		08.03		TAU	07.00		19.46		17.57	31

127

SUN

mth	dy	time → sign
JAN	1	00.00 → CAP
JAN	20	13.04 → AQU
FEB	19	03.13 → PIS
MAR	21	02.13 → ARI
APR	20	13.26 → TAU
MAY	21	12.36 → GEM
JUN	21	20.32 → CAN
JUL	23	07.32 → LEO
AUG	23	14.37 → VIR
SEP	23	12.13 → LIB
OCT	23	21.32 → SCO
NOV	22	19.03 → SAG
DEC	22	08.19 → CAP

MERCURY

mth	dy	time → sign
JAN	1	00.00 → CAP
JAN	6	22.14 → AQU
MAR	14	21.33 → PIS
APR	2	07.29 → ARI
APR	17	07.52 → TAU
MAY	2	15.18 → GEM
JUL	10	16.59 → CAN
JUL	25	22.19 → LEO
AUG	10	00.14 → VIR
AUG	29	02.07 → LIB
NOV	4	08.54 → SCO
NOV	22	22.47 → SAG
DEC	12	02.56 → CAP

VENUS

mth	dy	time → sign
JAN	1	00.00 → SCO
JAN	7	12.10 → SAG
FEB	4	20.11 → CAP
MAR	2	22.13 → AQU
MAR	28	05.13 → PIS
APR	22	04.10 → ARI
MAY	16	23.26 → TAU
JUN	10	16.17 → GEM
JUL	5	06.39 → CAN
JUL	29	17.32 → LEO
AUG	23	00.45 → VIR
SEP	16	05.03 → LIB
OCT	10	07.48 → SCO
NOV	3	10.17 → SAG
NOV	27	13.24 → CAP
DEC	21	18.21 → AQU

MARS

mth	dy	time → sign
JAN	1	00.00 → VIR
JAN	22	23.32 → LEO
MAY	25	16.23 → VIR
JUL	21	09.16 → LIB
SEP	7	07.03 → SCO
OCT	20	21.14 → SAG
NOV	30	13.48 → CAP

SATURN

mth	dy	time → sign
JAN	1	00.00 → PIS

JUPITER

mth	dy	time → sign
JAN	1	00.00 → SAG

MOON

dy	jan	feb	mar	apr	may	jun	jul	aug	sep	oct	nov	dec	dy
1	CAP	08.05	PIS	16.59	11.53	CAN	LEO	01.23	16.57	01.10	13.17	00.51	1
2	18.39	PIS	23.30	TAU	GEM	19.17	11.35	LIB	SAG	CAP	PIS	ARI	2
3	AQU	14.13	ARI	TAU	GEM	LEO	VIR	07.29	19.45	03.59	19.21	09.40	3
4	21.49	ARI	ARI	04.49	00.45	LEO	19.55	SCO	CAP	AQU	ARI	TAU	4
5	PIS	ARI	08.50	GEM	CAN	05.46	LIB	11.14	21.47	07.35	ARI	20.35	5
6	PIS	00.09	TAU	17.40	12.55	VIR	LIB	SAG	AQU	PIS	03.35	GEM	6
7	04.56	TAU	20.55	CAN	LEO	13.13	01.19	12.52	AQU	12.42	TAU	GEM	7
8	ARI	12.44	GEM	CAN	22.33	LIB	SCO	CAP	00.08	13.55	GEM	08.44	8
9	15.58	GEM	GEM	05.16	VIR	17.03	03.37	13.28	PIS	20.05	GEM	CAN	9
10	TAU	GEM	09.40	LEO	VIR	SCO	SAG	AQU	04.14	TAU	GEM	21.24	10
11	TAU	01.17	CAN	13.39	04.30	17.50	03.43	14.46	ARI	TAU	01.57	LEO	11
12	04.57	CAN	20.28	VIR	LIB	SAG	CAP	11.21	06.10	CAN	14.37	LEO	12
13	GEM	11.31	LEO	18.20	06.53	17.05	03.21	18.41	TAU	GEM	14.37	09.26	13
14	17.20	LEO	LEO	LIB	SCO	CAP	AQU	ARI	21.48	18.20	LEO	VIR	14
15	CAN	18.52	03.54	20.13	06.58	16.52	04.37	ARI	GEM	CAN	LEO	19.09	15
16	CAN	VIR	VIR	SCO	SAG	AQU	PIS	02.25	GEM	CAN	02.02	LIB	16
17	03.36	VIR	08.18	20.52	06.36	19.13	09.23	TAU	10.16	06.46	VIR	LIB	17
18	LEO	00.00	LIB	SAG	CAP	PIS	ARI	13.40	CAN	10.18	01.07	SCO	18
19	11.39	LIB	10.52	21.54	07.39	PIS	18.20	GEM	22.20	17.11	LIB	SCO	19
20	VIR	03.55	SCO	CAP	AQU	01.29	TAU	GEM	LEO	VIR	14.40	03.13	20
21	17.54	SCO	12.57	CAP	11.40	ARI	TAU	02.24	LEO	SCO	SAG	SAG	21
22	LIB	07.13	SAG	00.38	PIS	11.35	06.23	CAN	08.01	15.56	15.56	02.46	22
23	22.32	SAG	SAG	AQU	19.13	TAU	GEM	14.13	VIR	LIB	SAG	CAP	23
24	SCO	10.11	CAP	05.51	ARI	TAU	19.16	LEO	14.50	04.06	15.48	01.52	24
25	SCO	CAP	19.10	PIS	ARI	00.02	CAN	23.50	LIB	SCO	CAP	AQU	25
26	01.37	13.14	AQU	13.41	05.47	GEM	CAN	VIR	19.20	05.56	16.15	02.45	26
27	SAG	AQU	AQU	ARI	TAU	12.56	07.07	VIR	SCO	SAG	AQU	PIS	27
28	03.26	17.16	00.18	23.53	18.07	CAN	LEO	07.15	22.30	07.15	18.59	07.06	28
29	CAP		PIS	TAU	GEM	CAN	17.12	LIB	SAG	CAP	PIS	ARI	29
30	05.03		07.26	TAU	GEM	01.02	VIR	12.51	SAG	09.23	PIS	15.21	30
31	AQU		ARI		06.59		VIR	SCO		AQU		TAU	31

SUN

mth	dy	time → sign
JAN	1	00.00 → CAP
JAN	20	18.51 → AQU
FEB	19	09.04 → PIS
MAR	20	08.01 → ARI
APR	19	19.13 → TAU
MAY	20	18.23 → GEM
JUN	21	02.23 → CAN
JUL	22	13.19 → LEO
AUG	22	20.21 → VIR
SEP	22	18.00 → LIB
OCT	23	03.16 → SCO
NOV	22	00.49 → SAG
DEC	21	14.03 → CAP

SATURN

mth	dy	time → sign
JAN	1	00.00 → PIS
APR	7	08.35 → ARI

MERCURY

mth	dy	time → sign
JAN	1	00.00 → CAP
JAN	1	18.08 → AQU
JAN	17	09.37 → CAP
FEB	15	02.46 → AQU
MAR	7	11.53 → PIS
MAR	24	08.02 → ARI
APR	8	03.12 → TAU
JUN	13	21.45 → GEM
JUL	2	07.35 → CAN
JUL	16	09.54 → LEO
AUG	1	16.17 → VIR
AUG	26	05.14 → LIB
SEP	12	09.31 → VIR
OCT	9	03.13 → LIB
OCT	27	01.01 → SCO
NOV	14	16.33 → SAG
DEC	4	13.48 → CAP

VENUS

mth	dy	time → sign
JAN	1	00.00 → AQU
JAN	15	04.32 → PIS
FEB	9	02.33 → ARI
MAR	6	02.04 → TAU
APR	3	15.24 → GEM
AUG	7	06.17 → CAN
SEP	7	05.05 → LEO
OCT	4	03.23 → VIR
OCT	29	12.02 → LIB
NOV	23	01.35 → SCO
DEC	17	05.34 → SAG

MARS

mth	dy	time → sign
JAN	1	00.00 → CAP
JAN	8	11.14 → AQU
FEB	15	11.36 → PIS
MAR	24	15.23 → ARI
MAY	2	18.26 → TAU
JUN	12	14.55 → GEM
JUL	25	18.35 → CAN
SEP	9	20.13 → LEO
OCT	30	07.20 → VIR

JUPITER

mth	dy	time → sign
JAN	1	00.00 → SAG
JAN	3	07.01 → CAP

MOON

dy	jan	feb	mar	apr	may	jun	jul	aug	sep	oct	nov	dec	dy
1	TAU	CAN	16.47	VIR	LIB	01.43	CAP	PIS	12.19	04.01	CAN	LEO	1
2	02.29	CAN	LEO	21.26	12.43	SAG	12.05	23.05	TAU	GEM	09.16	06.11	2
3	GEM	09.46	LEO	LIB	SCO	02.29	AQU	ARI	19.08	13.14	LEO	VIR	3
4	14.56	LEO	04.13	LIB	16.05	CAP	12.07	ARI	GEM	CAN	21.57	18.23	4
5	CAN	21.22	VIR	03.57	SAG	02.44	PIS	03.33	GEM	CAN	VIR	LIB	5
6	CAN	VIR	13.40	SCO	17.54	AQU	14.42	TAU	05.29	01.12	VIR	LIB	6
7	03.30	VIR	LIB	08.21	CAP	04.19	ARI	11.49	CAN	LEO	09.29	03.39	7
8	LEO	07.30	21.05	SAG	19.39	PIS	20.43	GEM	17.54	13.49	LIB	SCO	8
9	15.29	LIB	SCO	11.30	AQU	08.23	TAU	22.57	LEO	VIR	18.02	08.59	9
10	VIR	15.35	SCO	CAP	22.29	ARI	TAU	CAN	LEO	VIR	SCO	SAG	10
11	VIR	SCO	02.32	14.09	PIS	15.11	05.52	CAN	06.28	01.00	23.27	11.15	11
12	01.55	20.58	SAG	AQU	PIS	TAU	GEM	11.29	VIR	LIB	SAG	CAP	12
13	LIB	SAG	06.08	17.00	03.00	TAU	17.08	LEO	17.51	09.46	SAG	12.14	13
14	09.30	23.30	CAP	PIS	ARI	00.16	CAN	LEO	LIB	SCO	02.44	AQU	14
15	SCO	CAP	08.15	20.43	09.25	GEM	CAN	00.07	LIB	16.07	CAP	13.44	15
16	13.25	CAP	AQU	ARI	TAU	11.08	05.31	VIR	03.20	SAG	05.14	PIS	16
17	SAG	00.01	09.50	ARI	17.48	CAN	LEO	11.55	SCO	20.37	AQU	16.55	17
18	14.07	AQU	PIS	02.05	GEM	23.22	18.16	LIB	10.31	CAP	08.00	ARI	18
19	CAP	00.09	12.15	TAU	GEM	LEO	VIR	21.50	SAG	23.51	PIS	22.10	19
20	13.15	PIS	ARI	09.54	04.16	LEO	VIR	SCO	15.12	AQU	11.34	TAU	20
21	AQU	01.58	16.59	GEM	CAN	12.07	06.14	SCO	CAP	AQU	ARI	TAU	21
22	13.02	ARI	TAU	20.25	16.28	VIR	LIB	04.38	17.39	02.22	16.12	05.17	22
23	PIS	07.08	TAU	CAN	LEO	23.37	15.43	SAG	AQU	PIS	TAU	GEM	23
24	15.37	TAU	00.59	CAN	LEO	LIB	SCO	08.22	18.43	04.50	22.20	14.14	24
25	ARI	16.14	GEM	08.44	04.58	LIB	21.24	CAP	PIS	ARI	GEM	CAN	25
26	22.16	GEM	12.06	LEO	VIR	07.54	SAG	09.10	19.46	08.11	GEM	CAN	26
27	TAU	GEM	CAN	20.49	15.33	SCO	23.17	AQU	ARI	TAU	06.37	01.09	27
28	TAU	04.10	CAN	VIR	LIB	12.01	CAP	08.49	22.24	13.34	CAN	LEO	28
29	08.43	CAN	00.37	VIR	22.30	SAG	22.47	PIS	TAU	GEM	17.30	13.45	29
30	GEM		LEO	06.27	SCO	12.47	AQU	09.15	TAU	21.56	LEO	VIR	30
31	21.11		12.15		SCO		22.00	ARI		CAN		VIR	31

SUN

mth	dy	time	→ sign
JAN	1	00.00	→ CAP
JAN	20	00.41	→ AQU
FEB	18	14.55	→ PIS
MAR	20	13.53	→ ARI
APR	20	01.03	→ TAU
MAY	21	00.14	→ GEM
JUN	21	08.20	→ CAN
JUL	22	19.12	→ LEO
AUG	23	02.19	→ VIR
SEP	22	23.54	→ LIB
OCT	23	09.15	→ SCO
NOV	22	06.46	→ SAG
DEC	21	20.05	→ CAP

MERCURY

mth	dy	time	→ sign
JAN	1	00.00	→ CAP
FEB	9	05.50	→ AQU
FEB	28	03.51	→ PIS
MAR	16	04.14	→ ARI
APR	1	13.45	→ TAU
MAY	5	01.44	→ ARI
MAY	12	10.26	→ TAU
JUN	8	23.22	→ GEM
JUN	23	20.41	→ CAN
JUL	8	05.27	→ LEO
JUL	27	00.46	→ VIR
OCT	2	05.38	→ LIB
OCT	19	12.06	→ SCO
NOV	7	17.43	→ SAG
NOV	30	19.11	→ CAP
DEC	13	18.03	→ SAG

VENUS

mth	dy	time	→ sign
JAN	1	00.00	→ SAG
JAN	10	05.35	→ CAP
FEB	3	04.28	→ AQU
FEB	27	04.03	→ PIS
MAR	23	05.26	→ ARI
APR	16	09.44	→ TAU
MAY	10	17.20	→ GEM
JUN	4	04.17	→ CAN
JUN	28	18.38	→ LEO
JUL	23	13.12	→ VIR
AUG	17	14.32	→ LIB
SEP	12	02.18	→ SCO
OCT	8	08.25	→ SAG
NOV	5	08.53	→ CAP
DEC	12	04.39	→ AQU

MARS

mth	dy	time	→ sign
JAN	1	00.00	→ VIR
JAN	3	08.23	→ LIB
MAR	8	19.32	→ VIR
JUN	19	08.21	→ LIB
AUG	14	08.22	→ SCO
SEP	28	22.15	→ SAG
NOV	9	05.26	→ CAP
DEC	18	06.30	→ AQU

SATURN

mth	dy	time	→ sign
JAN	1	00.00	→ ARI

JUPITER

mth	dy	time	→ sign
JAN	1	00.00	→ CAP
JAN	21	15.25	→ AQU

MOON

dy	jan	feb	mar	apr	may	jun	jul	aug	sep	oct	nov	dec	dy
1	02.32	SCO	12.01	CAP	12.50	ARI	11.35	CAN	04.27	LIB	SCO	18.38	1
2	LIB	04.51	SAG	03.59	PIS	00.39	GEM	10.27	VIR	LIB	SCO	CAP	2
3	13.02	SAG	17.39	AQU	14.59	TAU	18.33	LEO	17.30	11.57	SAG	23.58	3
4	SCO	08.45	CAP	05.42	ARI	04.55	CAN	22.15	LIB	SCO	12.31	AQU	4
5	19.27	CAP	19.55	PIS	17.04	GEM	CAN	VIR	LIB	22.43	CAP	AQU	5
6	SAG	09.21	AQU	06.19	TAU	11.02	03.45	VIR	06.10	SAG	18.33	04.07	6
7	21.55	AQU	19.57	ARI	20.21	CAN	LEO	11.17	SCO	SAG	AQU	PIS	7
8	CAP	08.34	PIS	07.20	GEM	19.58	15.22	LIB	16.54	SAG	22.35	07.24	8
9	22.00	PIS	19.33	TAU	GEM	LEO	VIR	23.50	SAG	CAP	PIS	ARI	9
10	AQU	08.29	ARI	10.28	02.13	LEO	VIR	SCO	SAG	12.29	PIS	10.00	10
11	21.51	ARI	20.37	GEM	CAN	07.43	04.21	SCO	00.23	AQU	00.44	TAU	11
12	PIS	10.56	TAU	17.03	11.33	VIR	LIB	09.45	CAP	14.59	ARI	12.35	12
13	23.22	TAU	00.48	CAN	20.35	LIB	16.20	SAG	04.10	PIS	01.45	GEM	13
14	ARI	16.53	GEM	CAN	23.43	LIB	SCO	15.42	AQU	15.25	TAU	16.25	14
15	ARI	GEM	GEM	03.22	VIR	LIB	SCO	CAP	04.59	ARI	03.05	CAN	15
16	03.40	GEM	08.51	LEO	VIR	07.51	01.02	17.58	PIS	15.16	GEM	22.58	16
17	TAU	02.13	CAN	16.00	12.27	SCO	SAG	AQU	04.25	TAU	06.32	LEO	17
18	10.53	CAN	20.08	VIR	LIB	15.39	05.45	18.01	ARI	16.26	CAN	LEO	18
19	GEM	13.52	LEO	VIR	23.12	SAG	CAP	PIS	04.21	GEM	13.38	09.00	19
20	20.29	LEO	LEO	04.36	SCO	20.02	07.29	17.45	TAU	20.45	LEO	VIR	20
21	CAN	LEO	08.59	LIB	SCO	CAP	AQU	ARI	06.38	CAN	LEO	21.35	21
22	CAN	02.38	VIR	15.19	06.51	22.20	08.00	18.57	GEM	CAN	00.33	LIB	22
23	07.50	VIR	21.35	SCO	SAG	AQU	PIS	TAU	12.33	05.10	VIR	LIB	23
24	LEO	15.23	LIB	23.32	11.51	AQU	09.03	22.56	CAN	LEO	13.29	10.07	24
25	20.26	LIB	LIB	SAG	CAP	00.09	ARI	GEM	16.59	VIR	LIB	SCO	25
26	VIR	LIB	08.42	SAG	15.20	PIS	11.53	GEM	LEO	VIR	LIB	20.07	26
27	VIR	02.57	SCO	05.32	AQU	02.38	TAU	06.11	LEO	VIR	01.43	SAG	27
28	09.21	SCO	17.40	CAP	18.18	ARI	17.04	CAN	10.27	06.05	SCO	SAG	28
29	LIB		SAG	09.50	PIS	06.23	GEM	16.19	VIR	11.28	02.48	CAP	29
30	20.48		SAG	AQU	21.18	TAU	GEM	LEO	23.32	18.15	CAP		30
31	SCO		00.07		ARI		00.38	LEO		SCO		06.58	31

SUN

mth	dy	time → sign
JAN	1	00.00 → CAP
JAN	20	06.44 → AQU
FEB	18	20.55 → PIS
MAR	20	19.54 → ARI
APR	20	06.57 → TAU
MAY	21	06.02 → GEM
JUN	21	14.03 → CAN
JUL	23	00.52 → LEO
AUG	23	07.57 → VIR
SEP	23	05.34 → LIB
OCT	23	14.56 → SCO
NOV	22	12.31 → SAG
DEC	22	01.55 → CAP

MERCURY

mth	dy	time → sign
JAN	1	00.00 → SAG
JAN	12	16.23 → CAP
FEB	2	15.16 → AQU
FEB	20	10.22 → PIS
MAR	8	08.25 → ARI
MAY	15	02.10 → TAU
JUN	1	08.06 → GEM
JUN	15	05.33 → CAN
JUN	30	23.52 → LEO
SEP	8	01.56 → VIR
SEP	24	10.14 → LIB
OCT	12	02.45 → SCO
NOV	1	16.03 → SAG

VENUS

mth	dy	time → sign
JAN	1	00.00 → AQU
JAN	9	21.06 → CAP
MAR	4	16.14 → AQU
APR	6	05.36 → PIS
MAY	3	19.17 → ARI
MAY	29	23.32 → TAU
JUN	24	12.24 → GEM
JUL	19	15.14 → CAN
AUG	13	09.20 → LEO
SEP	6	19.26 → VIR
SEP	30	23.16 → LIB
OCT	24	23.03 → SCO
NOV	17	21.04 → SAG
DEC	11	18.33 → CAP

MARS

mth	dy	time → sign
JAN	1	00.00 → AQU
JAN	25	09.12 → PIS
MAR	4	16.10 → ARI
APR	13	01.21 → TAU
MAY	24	03.32 → GEM
JUL	6	09.09 → CAN
AUG	20	19.08 → LEO
OCT	7	12.17 → VIR
NOV	27	10.00 → LIB

SATURN

mth	dy	time → sign
JAN	1	00.00 → ARI
JUN	9	06.24 → TAU
OCT	25	18.55 → ARI

JUPITER

mth	dy	time → sign
JAN	1	00.00 → AQU
FEB	4	10.37 → PIS

MOON

dy	jan	feb	mar	apr	may	jun	jul	aug	sep	oct	nov	dec	dy
1	AQU	ARI	ARI	GEM	CAN	03.21	LIB	SCO	02.23	AQU	11.27	TAU	1
2	09.56	21.25	05.00	19.10	09.49	VIR	LIB	07.48	CAP	23.23	ARI	21.30	2
3	PIS	TAU	TAU	CAN	LEO	15.17	11.45	SAG	09.21	PIS	11.12	GEM	3
4	12.43	TAU	07.15	CAN	19.47	LIB	SCO	17.18	AQU	PIS	TAU	21.28	4
5	ARI	01.09	GEM	02.36	VIR	LIB	23.24	CAP	12.48	00.32>ARI	10.11	CAN	5
6	15.52	GEM	12.27	LEO	VIR	04.06	SAG	23.31	PIS	23.57	GEM	23.55	6
7	TAU	06.57	CAN	13.25	08.19	SCO	SAG	SAG	13.52	TAU	10.39	LEO	7
8	19.42	CAN	20.46	VIR	LIB	15.34	08.27	AQU	23.44	CAN	14.33	LEO	8
9	GEM	14.57	LEO	VIR	21.10	SAG	CAP	03.04	14.16	GEM	14.33	06.21	9
10	GEM	LEO	LEO	02.04	SCO	SAG	14.52	PIS	TAU	GEM	LEO	VIR	10
11	00.43	LEO	07.35	LIB	SCO	00.50	AQU	05.10	15.40	01.48	22.37	16.43	11
12	CAN	01.09	VIR	14.56	08.48	CAP	19.22	ARI	GEM	CAN	VIR	LIB	12
13	07.45	VIR	19.58	SCO	SAG	08.03	PIS	07.04	19.20	07.25	VIR	LIB	13
14	LEO	13.17	LIB	SCO	18.39	AQU	22.45	TAU	CAN	LEO	09.58	05.16	14
15	17.31	LIB	LIB	02.52	CAP	13.31	ARI	09.46	CAN	16.32	LIB	SCO	15
16	VIR	LIB	08.51	SAG	CAP	PIS	ARI	GEM	01.48	VIR	22.41	17.47	16
17	VIR	02.13	SCO	13.05	02.30	17.23	01.33	13.55	LEO	VIR	SCO	SAG	17
18	05.44	SCO	20.56	CAP	AQU	ARI	TAU	CAN	10.52	04.02	SCO	SAG	18
19	LIB	13.56	SAG	20.41	08.03	19.47	04.18	20.01	VIR	LIB	11.13	04.55	19
20	18.34	SAG	SAG	AQU	PIS	TAU	GEM	LEO	21.57	16.36	SAG	CAP	20
21	SCO	22.30	06.43	AQU	11.06	21.26	07.43	LEO	LIB	SCO	22.45	14.17	21
22	SCO	CAP	CAP	01.06	ARI	GEM	CAN	04.21	LIB	SCO	CAP	AQU	22
23	05.25	CAP	13.02	PIS	12.06	23.39	12.48	VIR	10.22	05.16	CAP	21.45	23
24	SAG	03.10	AQU	02.31	TAU	CAN	LEO	15.02	SCO	SAG	08.43	PIS	24
25	12.39	AQU	15.43	ARI	12.25	CAN	20.34	LIB	23.05	17.05	AQU	PIS	25
26	CAP	04.42	PIS	02.09	GEM	04.04	VIR	LIB	SAG	CAP	16.14	03.04	26
27	16.27	PIS	15.49	TAU	13.58	LEO	VIR	03.25	SAG	CAP	PIS	ARI	27
28	AQU	04.42	ARI	01.55	CAN	11.54	07.14	SCO	10.30	02.44	20.34	06.05	28
29	18.08		15.06	GEM	18.38	VIR	LIB	15.55	CAP	AQU	ARI	TAU	29
30	PIS		TAU	03.57	LEO	23.05	19.44	SAG	18.53	08.58	21.53	07.22	30
31	19.21		15.37		LEO		SCO	SAG		PIS		GEM	31

SUN

mth	dy	time → sign
JAN	1	00.00 → CAP
JAN	20	12.34 → AQU
FEB	19	02.44 → PIS
MAR	21	01.43 → ARI
APR	20	12.43 → TAU
MAY	21	11.50 → GEM
JUN	21	19.49 → CAN
JUL	23	06.42 → LEO
AUG	23	13.51 → VIR
SEP	23	11.33 → LIB
OCT	23	20.52 → SCO
NOV	22	18.27 → SAG
DEC	22	07.44 → CAP

MERCURY

mth	dy	time → sign
JAN	1	00.00 → SAG
JAN	7	02.01 → CAP
JAN	26	09.32 → AQU
FEB	12	15.29 → PIS
MAR	2	22.54 → ARI
MAR	18	09.23 → PIS
APR	17	22.07 → ARI
MAY	8	21.22 → TAU
MAY	23	21.23 → GEM
JUN	7	00.16 → CAN
JUN	26	15.39 → LEO
JUL	31	18.43 → CAN
AUG	11	04.25 → LEO
AUG	31	15.12 → VIR
SEP	16	12.53 → LIB
OCT	5	05.11 → SCO
OCT	30	20.08 → SAG
NOV	9	20.10 → SCO
DEC	11	02.09 → SAG
DEC	31	06.50 → CAP

VENUS

mth	dy	time → sign
JAN	1	00.00 → CAP
JAN	4	16.23 → AQU
JAN	28	16.17 → PIS
FEB	21	20.46 → ARI
MAR	18	09.57 → TAU
APR	12	13.17 → GEM
MAY	8	16.26 → CAN
JUN	5	21.25 → LEO
JUL	12	15.16 → VIR
AUG	15	14.12 → LEO
OCT	7	16.54 → VIR
NOV	9	02.18 → LIB
DEC	5	22.42 → SCO
DEC	31	04.52 → SAG

MARS

mth	dy	time → sign
JAN	1	00.00 → LIB
JAN	26	11.37 → SCO
MAY	5	21.27 → LIB
JUL	5	03.50 → SCO
SEP	2	19.18 → SAG
OCT	17	01.30 → CAP
NOV	26	06.43 → AQU

SATURN

mth	dy	time → sign
JAN	1	00.00 → ARI
MAR	1	01.38 → TAU

JUPITER

mth	dy	time → sign
JAN	1	00.00 → PIS
FEB	13	01.35 → ARI
JUN	28	09.41 → TAU
OCT	23	05.58 → ARI

MOON

dy	jan	feb	mar	apr	may	jun	jul	aug	sep	oct	nov	dec	dy
1	08.15	LEO	10.05	LIB	SCO	02.06	AQU	16.47	TAU	13.31	LEO	17.29	1
2	CAN	01.37	VIR	12.49	07.36	CAP	AQU	ARI	05.25	CAN	04.07	LIB	2
3	10.31	VIR	18.34	SCO	SAG	13.37	04.34	21.09	GEM	17.13	VIR	LIB	3
4	LEO	09.56	LIB	SCO	20.12	AQU	PIS	TAU	08.10	LEO	11.57	03.35	4
5	15.49	LIB	LIB	01.07	CAP	23.01	11.21	23.57	CAN	22.40	LIB	SCO	5
6	VIR	21.06	05.22	SAG	CAP	PIS	ARI	GEM	11.29	VIR	21.46	15.27	6
7	VIR	SCO	SCO	13.39	07.40	PIS	15.22	GEM	LEO	VIR	SCO	SAG	7
8	00.53	SCO	17.46	CAP	AQU	05.08	TAU	01.53	15.57	05.52	SCO	SAG	8
9	LIB	09.38	SAG	CAP	16.16	ARI	17.00	CAN	VIR	LIB	09.15	04.14	9
10	12.49	SAG	SAG	00.24	PIS	07.44	GEM	03.55	22.16	15.01	SAG	CAP	10
11	SCO	21.10	05.54	AQU	20.53	TAU	17.27	LEO	LIB	SCO	22.00	16.59	11
12	SCO	CAP	CAP	07.35	ARI	07.48	CAN	07.22	LIB	SCO	CAP	AQU	12
13	01.23	CAP	15.32	PIS	21.56	GEM	18.26	VIR	07.08	02.18	CAP	AQU	13
14	SAG	05.57	AQU	10.46	TAU	07.14	LEO	13.24	SCO	SAG	10.46	04.18	14
15	12.29	AQU	21.30	ARI	21.07	CAN	21.39	LIB	18.35	15.04	AQU	PIS	15
16	CAP	11.40	PIS	11.07	GEM	08.07	VIR	22.40	SAG	CAP	21.21	12.30	16
17	21.11	PIS	PIS	TAU	20.39	LEO	VIR	SCO	SAG	CAP	PIS	ARI	17
18	AQU	15.06	00.13	10.39	CAN	12.12	04.19	SCO	07.13	03.17	PIS	16.45	18
19	AQU	ARI	ARI	GEM	22.37	VIR	LIB	10.32	CAP	AQU	03.57	TAU	19
20	03.40	17.29	01.09	11.27	LEO	20.10	14.30	18.38	12.33	ARI	ARI	17.39	20
21	PIS	TAU	TAU	CAN	LEO	LIB	SCO	22.59	AQU	PIS	06.26	GEM	21
22	08.25	19.54	02.05	15.06	04.15	LIB	SCO	CAP	17.42	TAU	16.52	CAN	22
23	ARI	GEM	GEM	LEO	VIR	07.18	02.48	CAP	02.51	ARI	06.14	16.32	23
24	11.52	23.09	04.33	22.04	13.29	SCO	SAG	09.49	PIS	19.25	GEM	LEO	24
25	TAU	CAN	CAN	VIR	LIB	19.51	15.08	AQU	07.34	TAU	05.29	LEO	25
26	14.29	CAN	09.22	VIR	LIB	SAG	CAP	17.50	ARI	19.33	CAN	18.34	26
27	GEM	03.44	LEO	07.46	01.05	SAG	CAP	PIS	09.51	GEM	06.19	VIR	27
28	16.57	LEO	16.34	LIB	SCO	08.12	01.54	23.09	TAU	LEO	VIR	VIR	28
29	CAN		VIR	19.13	13.37	CAP	AQU	ARI	11.21	CAN	00.14		29
30	20.16		VIR	SCO	SAG	19.19	10.27	GEM	22.47	VIR	LIB		30
31	LEO		01.49		SAG		PIS	02.41		LEO		09.36	31

SUN

mth	dy	time → sign
JAN	1	00.00 → CAP
JAN	20	18.25 → AQU
FEB	19	08.31 → PIS
MAR	20	07.37 → ARI
APR	19	18.42 → TAU
MAY	20	17.49 → GEM
JUN	21	01.45 → CAN
JUL	22	12.43 → LEO
AUG	22	19.47 → VIR
SEP	22	17.25 → LIB
OCT	23	02.46 → SCO
NOV	22	00.16 → SAG
DEC	21	13.34 → CAP

MERCURY

mth	dy	time → sign
JAN	1	00.00 → CAP
JAN	18	22.22 → AQU
FEB	5	08.09 → PIS
APR	13	00.14 → ARI
APR	30	03.53 → TAU
MAY	14	07.13 → GEM
MAY	30	04.27 → CAN
AUG	7	05.45 → LEO
AUG	22	10.11 → VIR
SEP	7	22.24 → LIB
SEP	28	13.28 → SCO
NOV	7	07.25 → LIB
NOV	8	21.45 → SCO
DEC	3	20.26 → SAG
DEC	23	02.06 → CAP

VENUS

mth	dy	time → sign
JAN	1	00.00 → SAG
JAN	24	19.56 → CAP
FEB	18	04.45 → AQU
MAR	13	11.36 → PIS
APR	6	18.36 → ARI
MAY	1	02.47 → TAU
MAY	25	12.15 → GEM
JUN	18	22.18 → CAN
JUL	13	08.03 → LEO
AUG	6	17.33 → VIR
AUG	31	03.36 → LIB
SEP	24	15.28 → SCO
OCT	19	06.16 → SAG
NOV	13	02.11 → CAP
DEC	8	08.46 → AQU

MARS

mth	dy	time → sign
JAN	1	00.00 → AQU
JAN	4	03.13 → PIS
FEB	12	01.18 → ARI
MAR	23	01.33 → TAU
MAY	3	19.26 → GEM
JUN	16	12.45 → CAN
AUG	1	01.30 → LEO
SEP	17	00.25 → VIR
NOV	4	02.19 → LIB
DEC	23	14.42 → SCO

SATURN

mth	dy	time → sign
JAN	1	00.00 → TAU
AUG	10	02.36 → GEM
OCT	16	00.55 → TAU

JUPITER

mth	dy	time → sign
JAN	1	00.00 → ARI
FEB	14	21.31 → TAU
JUN	30	07.22 → GEM

MOON

dy	jan	feb	mar	apr	may	jun	jul	aug	sep	oct	nov	dec	dy
1	SCO	17.10	CAP	08.12	00.55	16.34	03.09	13.27	LIB	22.50	CAP	AQU	1
2	21.32	CAP	13.14	PIS	ARI	GEM	CAN	VIR	05.55	SAG	CAP	AQU	2
3	SAG	CAP	AQU	15.22	04.54	16.30	02.38	15.31	SCO	SAG	06.41	03.23	3
4	SAG	05.31	23.30	ARI	TAU	CAN	LEO	LIB	14.08	09.42	AQU	PIS	4
5	10.24	AQU	PIS	19.29	06.23	16.45	03.19	21.04	SAG	CAP	19.13	14.17	5
6	CAP	16.02	PIS	TAU	GEM	LEO	VIR	SCO	SAG	22.33	PIS	ARI	6
7	22.53	PIS	06.54	21.58	07.14	18.57	06.47	SCO	01.47	AQU	PIS	21.27	7
8	AQU	PIS	ARI	GEM	CAN	VIR	LIB	06.30	CAP	AQU	05.02	TAU	8
9	AQU	00.17	12.01	GEM	09.01	23.59	13.48	SAG	14.45	10.36	ARI	TAU	9
10	09.59	ARI	TAU	00.16	LEO	LIB	SCO	18.44	AQU	PIS	11.12	00.50	10
11	PIS	06.21	15.46	CAN	12.41	LIB	SCO	CAP	AQU	19.51	TAU	GEM	11
12	18.48	TAU	GEM	03.16	VIR	07.55	00.06	CAP	02.34	ARI	14.27	01.49	12
13	ARI	10.23	18.51	LEO	18.27	SCO	SAG	07.43	PIS	ARI	GEM	02.09	13
14	ARI	GEM	CAN	07.19	LIB	18.18	12.28	AQU	12.00	02.06	CAN	LEO	14
15	00.38	12.45	21.43	VIR	LIB	SAG	CAP	19.41	ARI	TAU	CAN	LEO	15
16	TAU	CAN	LEO	12.36	02.16	SAG	CAP	PIS	19.05	06.19	18.19	03.30	16
17	03.25	14.11	LEO	LIB	SCO	06.27	01.27	PIS	TAU	GEM	LEO	VIR	17
18	GEM	LEO	00.48	19.35	12.09	CAP	AQU	05.44	TAU	09.37	21.15	07.01	18
19	04.01	15.53	VIR	SCO	SAG	19.26	13.44	ARI	00.22	CAN	VIR	LIB	19
20	CAN	VIR	04.57	SCO	SAG	AQU	PIS	13.31	GEM	12.42	VIR	13.12	20
21	03.58	19.21	LIB	04.58	00.01	AQU	PIS	TAU	04.16	LEO	01.35	SCO	21
22	LEO	LIB	11.17	SAG	CAP	07.52	00.09	18.55	CAN	15.52	LIB	21.57	22
23	05.07	LIB	SCO	16.47	13.00	PIS	ARI	GEM	07.00	VIR	07.33	SAG	23
24	VIR	01.58	20.43	CAP	AQU	17.56	07.44	22.00	LEO	19.30	SCO	SAG	24
25	09.09	SCO	SAG	CAP	AQU	ARI	TAU	CAN	09.02	LIB	15.33	08.54	25
26	LIB	12.10	SAG	05.42	01.07	ARI	12.02	23.17	VIR	LIB	SAG	CAP	26
27	17.01	SAG	08.51	AQU	PIS	00.19	GEM	LEO	11.22	00.23	SAG	21.25	27
28	SCO	SAG	CAP	17.06	10.08	TAU	13.30	23.55	LIB	SCO	01.57	AQU	28
29	SCO	00.45	21.34	PIS	ARI	02.59	CAN	VIR	15.30	07.40	CAP	AQU	29
30	04.18		AQU	PIS	15.02	GEM	13.24	VIR	SCO	SAG	14.26	10.27	30
31	SAG		AQU		TAU		LEO	01.33		18.02		PIS	31

133

SUN

mth	dy	time → sign
JAN	1	00.00 → CAP
JAN	20	00.18 → AQU
FEB	18	14.29 → PIS
MAR	20	13.32 → ARI
APR	20	00.37 → TAU
MAY	20	23.45 → GEM
JUN	21	07.39 → CAN
JUL	22	18.28 → LEO
AUG	23	01.29 → VIR
SEP	22	23.06 → LIB
OCT	23	08.27 → SCO
NOV	22	06.02 → SAG
DEC	21	19.23 → CAP

MERCURY

mth	dy	time → sign
JAN	1	00.00 → CAP
JAN	10	13.27 → AQU
FEB	1	07.13 → PIS
FEB	6	19.59 → AQU
MAR	17	06.06 → PIS
APR	6	07.15 → ARI
APR	21	20.09 → TAU
MAY	6	04.54 → GEM
JUL	12	22.48 → CAN
JUL	30	10.19 → LEO
AUG	14	05.05 → VIR
SEP	1	00.38 → LIB
NOV	7	19.54 → SCO
NOV	26	18.25 → SAG
DEC	15	19.56 → CAP

VENUS

mth	dy	time → sign
JAN	1	00.00 → AQU
JAN	3	18.15 → PIS
FEB	2	19.15 → ARI
JUN	6	10.26 → TAU
JUL	5	16.45 → GEM
AUG	1	12.19 → CAN
AUG	27	04.14 → LEO
SEP	21	02.11 → VIR
OCT	15	11.44 → LIB
NOV	8	13.29 → SCO
DEC	2	11.13 → SAG
DEC	26	07.26 → CAP

MARS

mth	dy	time → sign
JAN	1	00.00 → SCO
FEB	14	20.07 → SAG
SEP	8	17.52 → CAP
OCT	27	17.21 → AQU
DEC	8	21.54 → PIS

SATURN

mth	dy	time → sign
JAN	1	00.00 → TAU
APR	20	22.06 → GEM

JUPITER

mth	dy	time → sign
JAN	1	00.00 → GEM
JUL	13	00.04 → CAN

MOON

dy	jan	feb	mar	apr	may	jun	jul	aug	sep	oct	nov	dec	dy
1	22.15	TAU	TAU	CAN	LEO	LIB	SCO	CAP	AQU	19.09	TAU	GEM	1
2	ARI	20.57	03.37	17.55	02.17	14.57	03.14	CAP	00.33	ARI	21.14	10.31	2
3	ARI	GEM	GEM	LEO	VIR	SCO	SAG	05.54	PIS	ARI	GEM	CAN	3
4	06.58	GEM	08.25	19.48	04.51	20.59	12.23	AQU	12.59	GEM	06.02	14.17	4
5	TAU	00.01	CAN	VIR	LIB	SAG	CAP	18.31	ARI	TAU	03.45	LEO	5
6	11.45	CAN	10.31	20.58	08.02	SAG	23.34	PIS	ARI	15.13	CAN	17.12	6
7	GEM	00.22	LEO	LIB	SCO	05.24	AQU	PIS	00.19	GEM	08.35	VIR	7
8	13.10	23.36	10.45	23.02	13.06	CAP	AQU	07.06	TAU	22.20	LEO	19.58	8
9	CAN	VIR	VIR	SCO	SAG	16.21	12.06	ARI	09.42	CAN	11.50	LIB	9
10	12.45	23.47	10.48	SCO	21.11	AQU	PIS	18.24	GEM	CAN	VIR	23.10	10
11	LEO	LIB	LIB	03.48	CAP	AQU	PIS	TAU	16.10	02.55	13.54	SCO	11
12	12.27	LIB	12.44	SAG	CAP	04.55	00.37	TAU	CAN	LEO	LIB	SCO	12
13	VIR	02.52	SCO	12.22	08.21	PIS	ARI	03.00	19.17	04.59	15.46	03.31	13
14	14.06	SCO	18.18	CAP	AQU	17.04	11.14	GEM	LEO	VIR	SCO	SAG	14
15	LIB	10.03	SAG	CAP	21.02	ARI	TAU	07.56	19.40	05.27	18.52	09.49	15
16	19.03	SAG	SAG	00.12	PIS	ARI	18.27	CAN	VIR	LIB	SAG	CAP	16
17	SCO	21.00	04.03	AQU	PIS	02.40	GEM	09.26	19.01	06.04	SAG	18.44	17
18	SCO	CAP	CAP	13.01	08.42	TAU	21.57	LEO	LIB	SCO	00.41	AQU	18
19	03.37	CAP	16.37	PIS	ARI	08.43	CAN	08.54	19.28	08.48	CAP	AQU	19
20	SAG	09.54	AQU	PIS	17.31	GEM	22.44	VIR	SCO	SAG	09.56	06.10	20
21	14.58	AQU	AQU	00.19	TAU	11.42	LEO	08.20	23.03	15.12	AQU	PIS	21
22	CAP	22.46	05.29	ARI	23.13	CAN	22.30	LIB	SAG	CAP	21.53	18.46	22
23	CAP	PIS	PIS	08.57	GEM	12.56	VIR	09.51	SAG	CAP	PIS	ARI	23
24	03.44	PIS	16.45	TAU	GEM	LEO	23.09	SCO	06.49	01.27	PIS	ARI	24
25	AQU	10.21	ARI	15.12	02.44	13.59	LIB	15.00	CAP	AQU	10.22	06.14	25
26	16.40	ARI	ARI	GEM	CAN	VIR	LIB	SAG	18.06	13.57	ARI	TAU	26
27	PIS	20.07	01.52	19.50	05.13	16.12	02.18	SAG	AQU	PIS	21.07	14.40	27
28	PIS	TAU	TAU	CAN	LEO	LIB	SCO	00.03	AQU	PIS	TAU	GEM	28
29	04.36		09.02	23.26	07.39	20.30	08.45	CAP	06.51	02.16	TAU	19.41	29
30	ARI		GEM	LEO	VIR	SCO	SAG	11.49	PIS	ARI	05.05	CAN	30
31	14.22		14.24		10.42		18.17	AQU		12.49		22.10	31

SUN

mth	dy	time → sign
JAN	1	00.00 → CAP
JAN	20	06.04 → AQU
FEB	18	20.15 → PIS
MAR	20	19.17 → ARI
APR	20	06.22 → TAU
MAY	21	05.30 → GEM
JUN	21	13.26 → CAN
JUL	23	00.16 → LEO
AUG	23	07.18 → VIR
SEP	23	04.57 → LIB
OCT	23	14.19 → SCO
NOV	22	11.55 → SAG
DEC	22	01.16 → CAP

SATURN

mth	dy	time → sign
JAN	1	00.00 → GEM

MERCURY

mth	dy	time → sign
JAN	1	00.00 → CAP
JAN	3	21.39 → AQU
FEB	4	04.19 → CAP
FEB	13	17.22 → AQU
MAR	11	23.35 → PIS
MAR	29	14.46 → ARI
APR	13	10.12 → TAU
APR	30	07.16 → GEM
JUL	7	10.37 → CAN
JUL	21	22.43 → LEO
AUG	6	09.52 → VIR
AUG	26	21.11 → LIB
OCT	2	09.26 → VIR
OCT	11	05.59 → LIB
OCT	31	22.44 → SCO
NOV	19	11.31 → SAG
DEC	8	20.22 → CAP

VENUS

mth	dy	time → sign
JAN	1	00.00 → CAP
JAN	19	03.44 → AQU
FEB	12	01.19 → PIS
MAR	8	01.43 → ARI
APR	1	06.41 → TAU
APR	25	17.58 → GEM
MAY	20	13.28 → CAN
JUN	14	20.18 → LEO
JUL	10	21.10 → VIR
AUG	7	09.10 → LIB
SEP	8	03.06 → SCO

MARS

mth	dy	time → sign
JAN	1	00.00 → PIS
JAN	18	22.55 → ARI
MAR	1	15.06 → TAU
APR	13	17.37 → GEM
MAY	28	11.44 → CAN
JUL	13	15.24 → LEO
AUG	29	14.39 → VIR
OCT	15	17.39 → LIB
DEC	1	14.28 → SCO

JUPITER

mth	dy	time → sign
JAN	1	00.00 → CAN
AUG	1	17.22 → LEO

MOON

dy	jan	feb	mar	apr	may	jun	jul	aug	sep	oct	nov	dec	dy
1	LEO	08.45	LIB	06.49	CAP	23.38	19.50	TAU	21.15	11.59	VIR	.11.16	1
2	23.35	LIB	18.52	SAG	CAP	PIS	ARI	TAU	CAN	LEO	01.29	SCO	2
3	VIR	10.36	SCO	11.59	04.45	PIS	ARI	03.48	CAN	14.53	LIB	11.59	3
4	VIR	SCO	21.56	CAP	AQU	11.53	08.17	GEM	02.38	VIR	01.11	SAG	4
5	01.25	15.22	SAG	21.08	15.47	ARI	TAU	12.03	LEO	14.52	SCO	13.40	5
6	LIB	SAG	SAG	AQU	PIS	ARI	19.02	CAN	04.17	LIB	01.02	CAP	6
7	04.42	23.10	04.49	AQU	PIS	00.08	GEM	16.28	VIR	13.58	SAG	17.55	7
8	SCO	CAP	CAP	08.59	04.23	TAU	GEM	LEO	03.58	SCO	03.00	AQU	8
9	09.59	CAP	14.57	PIS	ARI	10.30	02.38	18.04	LIB	14.22	CAP	AQU	9
10	SAG	09.16	AQU	21.42	16.33	GEM	CAN	VIR	03.49	SAG	08.28	01.47	10
11	17.19	AQU	AQU	ARI	TAU	18.16	07.09	18.39	SCO	17.46	AQU	PIS	11
12	CAP	20.54	02.57	ARI	TAU	CAN	LEO	LIB	05.45	CAP	17.43	12.59	12
13	CAP	PIS	PIS	09.56	03.05	23.41	09.42	20.02	SAG	CAP	PIS	ARI	13
14	02.42	PIS	15.35	TAU	GEM	LEO	VIR	SCO	10.49	00.52	PIS	ARI	14
15	AQU	09.27	ARI	20.57	11.34	LEO	11.40	23.26	CAP	AQU	05.39	01.44	15
16	14.01	ARI	ARI	GEM	CAN	03.25	LIB	SAG	18.55	11.08	ARI	TAU	16
17	PIS	21.59	04.02	GEM	17.53	VIR	14.14	SAG	AQU	PIS	18.25	13.44	17
18	PIS	TAU	TAU	06.02	LEO	06.12	SCO	05.16	AQU	23.15	TAU	GEM	18
19	02.36	TAU	15.21	CAN	22.02	LIB	18.03	CAP	05.19	ARI	TAU	23.31	19
20	ARI	08.51	GEM	12.22	VIR	08.43	SAG	13.18	PIS	ARI	06.26	CAN	20
21	14.48	GEM	GEM	LEO	VIR	SCO	23.27	AQU	17.12	11.58	GEM	CAN	21
22	TAU	16.17	00.07	15.36	00.20	11.43	CAP	23.12	ARI	TAU	16.49	06.50	22
23	TAU	CAN	CAN	VIR	LIB	SAG	CAP	PIS	ARI	TAU	CAN	LEO	23
24	00.29	19.37	05.14	16.23	01.39	16.02	06.41	PIS	05.56	00.18	CAN	12.06	24
25	GEM	LEO	LEO	LIB	SCO	CAP	AQU	10.49	TAU	GEM	01.01	VIR	25
26	06.18	19.48	06.45	16.16	03.21	22.37	16.06	ARI	18.28	11.11	LEO	15.54	26
27	CAN	VIR	VIR	SCO	SAG	AQU	PIS	23.33	GEM	CAN	06.43	LIB	27
28	08.32	18.48	06.05	17.14	06.55	AQU	PIS	TAU	GEM	19.21	VIR	18.42	28
29	LEO		LIB	SAG	CAP	08.02	03.40	TAU	05.03	LEO	09.55	SCO	29
30	08.41		05.22	21.04	13.36	PIS	ARI	11.46	CAN	LEO	LIB	21.02	30
31	VIR		SCO		AQU		16.18	GEM		00.00		SAG	31

SUN

mth	dy	time → sign
JAN	1	00.00 → CAP
JAN	20	11.54 → AQU
FEB	19	02.02 → PIS
MAR	21	01.01 → ARI
APR	20	12.04 → TAU
MAY	21	11.14 → GEM
JUN	21	19.12 → CAN
JUL	23	06.05 → LEO
AUG	23	13.09 → VIR
SEP	23	10.48 → LIB
OCT	23	20.10 → SCO
NOV	22	17.45 → SAG
DEC	22	07.05 → CAP

MERCURY

mth	dy	time → sign
JAN	1	00.00 → CAP
FEB	13	01.02 → AQU
MAR	5	02.06 → PIS
MAR	21	12.17 → ARI
APR	5	14.38 → TAU
JUN	13	01.35 → GEM
JUN	29	10.18 → CAN
JUL	13	12.11 → LEO
JUL	30	14.07 → VIR
OCT	7	01.30 → LIB
OCT	24	11.21 → SCO
NOV	12	07.21 → SAG
DEC	2	21.35 → CAP
DEC	30	19.53 → SAG

VENUS

mth	dy	time → sign
JAN	1	00.00 → SCO
JAN	7	13.09 → SAG
FEB	4	13.28 → CAP
MAR	2	12.41 → AQU
MAR	27	18.15 → PIS
APR	21	16.19 → ARI
MAY	16	11.00 → TAU
JUN	10	03.33 → GEM
JUL	4	17.40 → CAN
JUL	29	04.27 → LEO
AUG	22	11.37 → VIR
SEP	15	15.59 → LIB
OCT	9	18.57 → SCO
NOV	2	21.44 → SAG
NOV	27	01.09 → CAP
DEC	21	06.34 → AQU

MARS

mth	dy	time → sign
JAN	1	00.00 → SCO
JAN	17	04.24 → SAG
MAR	4	21.19 → CAP
APR	21	23.50 → AQU
JUN	17	02.27 → PIS
DEC	16	13.24 → ARI

SATURN

mth	dy	time → sign
JAN	1	00.00 → GEM
JUN	4	01.33 → CAN

JUPITER

mth	dy	time → sign
JAN	1	00.00 → LEO
AUG	27	09.28 → VIR

MOON

dy	jan	feb	mar	apr	may	jun	jul	aug	sep	oct	nov	dec	dy
1	23.44	AQU	AQU	ARI	TAU	21.29	13.14	VIR	SCO	SAG	AQU	PIS	1
2	CAP	19.56	03.27	ARI	TAU	CAN	LEO	06.49	18.33	03.22	19.53	10.57	2
3	CAP	PIS	PIS	08.21	03.28	CAN	20.17	LIB	SAG	CAP	PIS	ARI	3
4	03.58	PIS	13.31	TAU	GEM	07.26	VIR	10.14	21.52	07.46	PIS	22.31	4
5	AQU	05.45	ARI	21.25	15.43	LEO	VIR	SCO	CAP	AQU	05.04	TAU	5
6	10.58	ARI	ARI	GEM	CAN	14.52	01.21	13.12	CAP	14.21	ARI	TAU	6
7	PIS	18.00	01.37	GEM	CAN	VIR	LIB	SAG	02.16	PIS	16.30	11.27	7
8	21.16	TAU	TAU	09.37	01.48	19.31	04.45	16.03	AQU	23.09	TAU	GEM	8
9	ARI	TAU	14.39	CAN	LEO	LIB	SCO	CAP	08.08	ARI	TAU	GEM	9
10	ARI	06.46	GEM	18.55	08.32	21.40	06.49	19.25	PIS	ARI	05.16	00.12	10
11	09.49	GEM	GEM	LEO	VIR	SCO	SAG	AQU	16.10	10.06	GEM	CAN	11
12	TAU	17.20	02.13	LEO	11.43	22.13	08.22	AQU	ARI	TAU	18.11	11.42	12
13	22.09	CAN	CAN	00.08	LIB	SAG	CAP	00.20	ARI	22.46	CAN	LEO	13
14	GEM	CAN	10.07	VIR	12.15	22.39	10.39	PIS	02.51	GEM	CAN	21.08	14
15	GEM	00.06	LEO	01.43	SCO	CAP	AQU	08.01	TAU	GEM	05.49	VIR	15
16	07.57	LEO	13.54	LIB	11.44	CAP	15.15	ARI	15.33	11.42	LEO	VIR	16
17	CAN	03.24	VIR	01.17	SAG	00.42	PIS	18.54	GEM	CAN	14.38	03.48	17
18	14.30	VIR	14.44	SCO	12.04	AQU	23.21	TAU	GEM	22.42	VIR	LIB	18
19	LEO	04.49	LIB	00.53	CAP	05.58	ARI	TAU	04.08	LEO	19.43	07.21	19
20	18.33	LIB	14.39	SAG	15.02	PIS	ARI	07.42	CAN	LEO	LIB	SCO	20
21	VIR	06.10	SCO	02.21	AQU	15.07	10.49	GEM	14.04	06.02	21.25	08.17	21
22	21.24	SCO	15.34	CAP	21.42	ARI	TAU	19.46	LEO	VIR	SCO	SAG	22
23	LIB	08.47	SAG	06.59	PIS	ARI	23.43	CAN	20.06	09.28	21.04	07.56	23
24	LIB	SAG	18.49	AQU	PIS	03.16	GEM	CAN	VIR	LIB	SAG	CAP	24
25	00.10	13.12	CAP	15.03	08.00	TAU	GEM	04.50	22.50	10.10	20.33	08.14	25
26	SCO	CAP	CAP	PIS	ARI	16.14	11.24	LEO	LIB	SCO	CAP	AQU	26
27	03.27	19.26	00.52	PIS	20.34	GEM	CAN	10.28	23.53	09.56	21.49	11.11	27
28	SAG	AQU	AQU	01.56	TAU	GEM	20.18	VIR	SCO	SAG	AQU	PIS	28
29	07.31		09.27	ARI	TAU	03.53	LEO	13.42	SCO	10.38	AQU	18.10	29
30	CAP		PIS	14.28	09.33	CAN	LEO	LIB	00.58	CAP	02.26	ARI	30
31	12.45		20.06		GEM		02.28	16.01		13.42		ARI	31

SUN

mth	dy	time → sign
JAN	1	00.00 → CAP
JAN	20	17.44 → AQU
FEB	19	07.51 → PIS
MAR	20	06.50 → ARI
APR	19	17.52 → TAU
MAY	20	17.00 → GEM
JUN	21	00.58 → CAN
JUL	22	11.51 → LEO
AUG	22	18.55 → VIR
SEP	22	16.31 → LIB
OCT	23	01.50 → SCO
NOV	21	23.23 → SAG
DEC	21	12.43 → CAP

MERCURY

mth	dy	time → sign
JAN	1	00.00 → SAG
JAN	14	11.04 → CAP
FEB	7	04.21 → AQU
FEB	25	13.00 → PIS
MAR	12	09.46 → ARI
APR	1	02.28 → TAU
APR	13	01.25 → ARI
MAY	16	06.56 → TAU
JUN	5	12.49 → GEM
JUN	19	19.51 → CAN
JUL	4	14.53 → LEO
JUL	25	13.59 → VIR
AUG	25	01.34 → LEO
SEP	10	07.40 → VIR
SEP	28	14.14 → LIB
OCT	15	22.58 → SCO
NOV	4	14.41 → SAG

VENUS

mth	dy	time → sign
JAN	1	00.00 → AQU
JAN	14	17.17 → PIS
FEB	8	16.22 → ARI
MAR	5	18.14 → TAU
APR	3	14.58 → GEM
AUG	7	11.03 → CAN
SEP	6	22.17 → LEO
OCT	3	17.21 → VIR
OCT	29	00.41 → LIB
NOV	22	13.33 → SCO
DEC	16	17.11 → SAG

MARS

mth	dy	time → sign
JAN	1	00.00 → ARI
FEB	3	10.05 → TAU
MAR	21	07.41 → GEM
MAY	7	08.47 → CAN
JUN	23	20.52 → LEO
AUG	10	10.16 → VIR
SEP	26	09.17 → LIB
NOV	11	05.12 → SCO
DEC	25	16.06 → SAG

SATURN

mth	dy	time → sign
JAN	1	00.00 → CAN

JUPITER

mth	dy	time → sign
JAN	1	00.00 → VIR
SEP	25	03.26 → LIB

MOON

dy	jan	feb	mar	apr	may	jun	jul	aug	sep	oct	nov	dec	dy
1	05.03	GEM	CAN	LEO	18.04	SCO	18.02	AQU	ARI	TAU	14.54	10.51	1
2	TAU	14.04	CAN	02.46	LIB	07.53	CAP	04.36	ARI	18.56	CAN	LEO	2
3	17.59	CAN	09.19	VIR	20.40	SAG	17.23	PIS	00.17	GEM	CAN	23.01	3
4	GEM	CAN	LEO	07.53	SCO	07.13	AQU	08.01	TAU	GEM	03.33	VIR	4
5	GEM	00.51	17.19	LIB	21.09	CAP	18.27	ARI	10.26	LEO	06.55	VIR	5
6	06.40	LEO	VIR	10.25	SAG	07.11	PIS	15.27	GEM	CAN	15.01	08.47	6
7	CAN	09.04	22.32	SCO	21.18	AQU	23.04	TAU	22.51	VIR	19.24	LIB	7
8	17.39	VIR	LIB	11.51	CAP	09.39	ARI	TAU	CAN	LEO	23.24	14.45	8
9	LEO	15.14	LIB	SAG	22.47	PIS	ARI	02.34	CAN	LEO	LIB	SCO	9
10	LEO	LIB	02.04	13.34	AQU	15.50	07.52	GEM	11.07	06.01	LIB	16.55	10
11	02.39	19.59	SCO	CAP	AQU	ARI	TAU	15.21	LEO	VIR	04.06	SAG	11
12	VIR	SCO	04.58	16.34	02.53	ARI	19.46	CAN	21.18	13.33	SCO	16.43	12
13	09.39	23.36	SAG	AQU	PIS	01.38	GEM	CAN	VIR	LIB	05.58	CAP	13
14	LIB	SAG	07.53	21.25	10.03	TAU	GEM	03.31	VIR	18.11	SAG	16.11	14
15	14.34	SAG	CAP	PIS	ARI	13.45	08.42	LEO	04.55	SCO	06.34	AQU	15
16	SCO	02.15	11.11	PIS	19.58	GEM	CAN	13.50	LIB	20.59	CAP	17.25	16
17	17.19	CAP	AQU	04.25	TAU	GEM	20.57	VIR	10.26	SAG	07.40	PIS	17
18	SAG	04.28	15.27	ARI	TAU	02.38	LEO	22.10	SCO	23.08	AQU	21.53	18
19	18.25	AQU	PIS	13.44	07.48	CAN	LEO	LIB	14.31	CAP	10.39	ARI	19
20	CAP	07.28	21.30	TAU	GEM	15.06	07.45	LIB	SAG	CAP	PIS	ARI	20
21	19.12	PIS	ARI	TAU	20.36	LEO	VIR	04.38	17.36	01.39	16.12	05.53	21
22	AQU	12.46	ARI	01.11	CAN	LEO	16.40	SCO	CAP	AQU	ARI	TAU	22
23	21.30	ARI	06.11	GEM	CAN	02.11	LIB	09.10	20.11	05.14	ARI	16.33	23
24	PIS	21.31	TAU	13.57	09.08	VIR	23.09	SAG	AQU	PIS	00.17	GEM	24
25	PIS	TAU	17.36	CAN	LEO	10.51	SCO	11.48	22.56	10.25	TAU	GEM	25
26	03.07	TAU	GEM	CAN	19.53	LIB	SCO	CAP	PIS	ARI	10.26	04.39	26
27	ARI	09.23	GEM	02.15	VIR	16.14	02.49	13.09	PIS	17.39	GEM	CAN	27
28	12.47	GEM	06.24	LEO	VIR	SCO	SAG	AQU	02.58	TAU	22.12	17.15	28
29	TAU	22.13	CAN	12.01	03.24	18.17	03.59	14.34	ARI	TAU	CAN	LEO	29
30	TAU		18.08	VIR	LIB	SAG	CAP	PIS	09.25	03.12	CAN	LEO	30
31	01.19		LEO		07.09		03.55	17.47		GEM		05.34	31

SUN

mth	dy	time → sign
JAN	1	00.00 → CAP
JAN	19	23.23 → AQU
FEB	18	13.33 → PIS
MAR	20	12.35 → ARI
APR	19	23.38 → TAU
MAY	20	22.49 → GEM
JUN	21	06.47 → CAN
JUL	22	17.42 → LEO
AUG	23	00.47 → VIR
SEP	22	22.25 → LIB
OCT	23	07.44 → SCO
NOV	22	05.17 → SAG
DEC	21	18.36 → CAP

MERCURY

mth	dy	time → sign
JAN	1	00.00 → SAG
JAN	10	04.10 → CAP
JAN	30	05.38 → AQU
FEB	16	17.47 → PIS
MAR	5	01.35 → ARI
MAY	12	09.15 → TAU
MAY	28	10.45 → GEM
JUN	11	07.04 → CAN
JUN	28	04.02 → LEO
SEP	4	17.54 → VIR
SEP	20	16.41 → LIB
OCT	8	17.16 → SCO
OCT	30	09.03 → SAG
NOV	26	11.54 → SCO
DEC	12	21.21 → SAG

VENUS

mth	dy	time → sign
JAN	1	00.00 → SAG
JAN	9	16.57 → CAP
FEB	2	15.44 → AQU
FEB	26	15.09 → PIS
MAR	22	16.26 → ARI
APR	15	20.38 → TAU
MAY	10	04.16 → GEM
JUN	3	15.19 → CAN
JUN	28	05.55 → LEO
JUL	23	01.02 → VIR
AUG	17	03.06 → LIB
SEP	11	16.16 → SCO
OCT	8	01.02 → SAG
NOV	5	08.12 → CAP
DEC	15	15.58 → AQU

MARS

mth	dy	time → sign
JAN	1	00.00 → SAG
FEB	6	18.33 → CAP
MAR	20	18.03 → AQU
MAY	1	02.59 → PIS
JUN	12	02.31 → ARI
JUL	28	05.13 → TAU

SATURN

mth	dy	time → sign
JAN	1	00.00 → CAN
JUL	16	12.36 → LEO

JUPITER

mth	dy	time → sign
JAN	1	00.00 → LIB
OCT	26	02.54 → SCO

MOON

dy	jan	feb	mar	apr	may	jun	jul	aug	sep	oct	nov	dec	dy
1	VIR	06.52	SCO	03.49	AQU	00.09	TAU	12.53	LEO	VIR	07.30	SAG	1
2	16.21	SCO	18.31	CAP	14.44	ARI	20.27	CAN	19.57	14.25	SCO	SAG	2
3	LIB	12.22	SAG	06.32	PIS	06.21	GEM	CAN	VIR	LIB	13.56	01.43	3
4	LIB	SAG	22.13	AQU	18.37	TAU	GEM	01.11	VIR	LIB	SAG	CAP	4
5	00.01	14.33	CAP	08.46	ARI	14.37	07.08	LEO	07.53	00.04	18.18	03.37	5
6	SCO	CAP	23.50	PIS	ARI	GEM	CAN	13.55	LIB	SCO	CAP	AQU	6
7	03.45	14.27	AQU	11.29	00.02	GEM	19.12	VIR	18.11	07.29	21.32	05.45	7
8	SAG	AQU	AQU	ARI	TAU	00.47	LEO	VIR	SCO	SAG	AQU	PIS	8
9	04.12	14.00	00.34	15.51	07.30	CAN	LEO	02.10	SCO	12.45	AQU	09.03	9
10	CAP	PIS	PIS	TAU	GEM	12.41	07.58	LIB	02.04	CAP	00.24	ARI	10
11	03.08	15.22	02.04	22.56	17.21	LEO	VIR	12.36	SAG	16.06	PIS	13.47	11
12	AQU	ARI	ARI	GEM	CAN	LEO	20.10	SCO	06.58	AQU	03.23	TAU	12
13	02.51	20.19	06.06	GEM	CAN	01.23	LIB	19.48	CAP	18.06	ARI	20.01	13
14	PIS	TAU	TAU	09.04	05.18	VIR	LIB	SAG	09.03	PIS	07.03	GEM	14
15	05.28	TAU	13.45	CAN	LEO	13.00	05.52	23.14	AQU	19.40	TAU	GEM	15
16	ARI	05.19	GEM	21.18	17.47	LIB	SCO	CAP	09.25	ARI	12.11	04.02	16
17	12.07	GEM	GEM	LEO	VIR	21.25	11.36	23.40	PIS	22.05	GEM	CAN	17
18	TAU	17.14	00.45	LEO	VIR	SCO	SAG	AQU	09.44	TAU	19.43	14.19	18
19	22.25	CAN	CAN	09.28	04.31	SCO	13.27	22.53	ARI	TAU	CAN	LEO	19
20	GEM	CAN	13.18	VIR	LIB	01.46	CAP	PIS	11.49	02.45	CAN	LEO	20
21	GEM	05.56	LEO	19.28	11.50	SAG	12.56	TAU	23.02	GEM	06.11	02.40	21
22	10.43	LEO	LEO	LIB	SCO	02.53	AQU	ARI	17.08	10.42	LEO	VIR	22
23	CAN	17.45	01.11	LIB	15.39	CAP	12.13	ARI	GEM	CAN	18.43	15.27	23
24	23.22	VIR	VIR	02.26	SAG	02.37	PIS	01.59	GEM	21.50	VIR	LIB	24
25	LEO	VIR	11.01	SCO	17.12	AQU	13.24	TAU	02.12	LEO	VIR	LIB	25
26	LEO	04.00	LIB	06.47	CAP	03.04	ARI	08.44	CAN	LEO	06.59	02.05	26
27	11.25	LIB	18.30	SAG	18.11	PIS	17.55	GEM	14.04	06.59	LIB	SCO	27
28	VIR	12.22	SCO	09.34	AQU	05.52	TAU	18.58	LEO	16.34	08.45	28
29	22.14		23.58	CAP	20.10	ARI	TAU	CAN	LEO	22.16	SCO	SAG	29
30	LIB		SAG	11.55	PIS	11.46	02.03	CAN	02.45	LIB	22.33	11.36	30
31	LIB		SAG		PIS		GEM	07.15		LIB		CAP	31

SUN

mth	dy	time → sign
JAN	1	00.00 → CAP
JAN	20	05.17 → AQU
FEB	18	19.27 → PIS
MAR	20	18.27 → ARI
APR	20	05.27 → TAU
MAY	21	04.33 → GEM
JUN	21	12.27 → CAN
JUL	22	23.19 → LEO
AUG	23	06.24 → VIR
SEP	23	04.05 → LIB
OCT	23	13.28 → SCO
NOV	22	11.03 → SAG
DEC	22	00.24 → CAP

MERCURY

mth	dy	time → sign
JAN	1	00.00 → SAG
JAN	3	21.28 → CAP
JAN	22	20.43 → AQU
FEB	9	01.23 → PIS
APR	16	12.21 → ARI
MAY	5	08.29 → TAU
MAY	19	20.53 → GEM
JUN	3	11.22 → CAN
JUN	28	19.58 → LEO
JUL	10	20.20 → CAN
AUG	11	04.11 → LEO
AUG	27	19.32 → VIR
SEP	12	21.09 → LIB
OCT	2	04.40 → SCO
DEC	8	05.53 → SAG
DEC	27	20.56 → CAP

VENUS

mth	dy	time → sign
JAN	1	00.00 → AQU
JAN	1	20.21 → CAP
MAR	5	08.40 → AQU
APR	6	01.22 → PIS
MAY	3	10.26 → ARI
MAY	29	12.43 → TAU
JUN	24	00.33 → GEM
JUL	19	02.43 → CAN
AUG	12	20.22 → LEO
SEP	6	06.16 → VIR
SEP	30	10.03 → LIB
OCT	24	09.59 → SCO
NOV	17	08.04 → SAG
DEC	11	05.35 → CAP

MARS

mth	dy	time → sign
JAN	1	00.00 → TAU
FEB	17	22.45 → GEM
APR	14	01.00 → CAN
JUN	3	18.44 → LEO
JUL	22	18.54 → VIR
SEP	8	04.20 → LIB
OCT	23	16.39 → SCO
DEC	6	05.00 → SAG

SATURN

mth	dy	time → sign
JAN	1	00.00 → LEO

JUPITER

mth	dy	time → sign
JAN	1	00.00 → SCO
NOV	24	04.45 → SAG

MOON

dy	jan	feb	mar	apr	may	jun	jul	aug	sep	oct	nov	dec	dy
1	12.16	22.47	09.20	23.50	15.18	LEO	VIR	13.09	SAG	CAP	PIS	ARI	1
2	AQU	ARI	ARI	GEM	CAN	20.18	17.07	SCO	14.36	03.25	15.47	01.27	2
3	12.45	ARI	10.23	GEM	CAN	VIR	LIB	23.14	CAP	AQU	ARI	TAU	3
4	PIS	01.32	TAU	06.16	00.19	VIR	LIB	SAG	18.16	05.34	16.06	03.06	4
5	14.45	TAU	14.39	CAN	LEO	09.10	05.14	SAG	AQU	PIS	TAU	GEM	5
6	ARI	07.33	GEM	16.26	12.21	LIB	SCO	05.21	18.58	05.33	16.47	06.02	6
7	19.10	GEM	22.39	LEO	VIR	20.42	14.15	CAP	PIS	ARI	GEM	CAN	7
8	TAU	16.35	CAN	LEO	VIR	SCO	SAG	07.49	18.24	05.05	19.47	11.53	8
9	TAU	CAN	CAN	05.00	01.11	SCO	19.26	AQU	ARI	TAU	CAN	LEO	9
10	02.00	CAN	09.43	VIR	LIB	05.06	CAP	08.11	18.31	06.07	CAN	21.32	10
11	GEM	03.45	LEO	17.48	12.26	SAG	21.47	PIS	TAU	GEM	02.35	VIR	11
12	10.51	LEO	22.25	LIB	SCO	10.20	23.01	AQU	21.00	10.22	LEO	VIR	12
13	CAN	16.15	VIR	LIB	20.57	CAP	23.01	ARI	GEM	CAN	13.20	10.02	13
14	21.32	VIR	VIR	05.10	SAG	13.33	PIS	10.01	GEM	18.39	VIR	LIB	14
15	LEO	VIR	11.14	SCO	SAG	AQU	PIS	TAU	02.55	LEO	VIR	22.44	15
16	LEO	05.10	LIB	14.21	03.00	16.06	00.40	14.08	CAN	LEO	02.15	SCO	16
17	09.50	LIB	23.00	SAG	CAP	PIS	ARI	GEM	12.16	06.17	LIB	SCO	17
18	VIR	17.12	SCO	21.14	07.20	18.55	03.45	21.04	LEO	VIR	14.48	09.11	18
19	22.50	SCO	SCO	CAP	AQU	ARI	TAU	CAN	LEO	19.21	SCO	SAG	19
20	LIB	SCO	08.44	CAP	10.40	22.24	08.39	CAN	00.08	LIB	SCO	16.40	20
21	LIB	02.39	SAG	01.57	PIS	TAU	GEM	06.34	VIR	LIB	01.16	CAP	21
22	10.30	SAG	15.37	AQU	13.25	TAU	15.29	LEO	13.07	07.55	SAG	21.50	22
23	SCO	08.17	CAP	04.44	ARI	02.50	CAN	18.09	LIB	SCO	09.26	AQU	23
24	18.39	CAP	19.22	PIS	16.02	GEM	CAN	VIR	LIB	18.54	CAP	AQU	24
25	SAG	10.16	AQU	06.13	TAU	08.49	00.26	VIR	01.55	SAG	15.42	01.44	25
26	22.32	AQU	20.34	ARI	19.20	CAN	LEO	07.02	SCO	SAG	AQU	PIS	26
27	CAP	09.57	PIS	07.28	GEM	17.10	11.37	LIB	13.17	03.48	20.22	05.05	27
28	23.10	PIS	20.32	TAU	GEM	LEO	VIR	19.57	SAG	CAP	PIS	ARI	28
29	AQU		ARI	09.59	00.35	LEO	VIR	SCO	22.02	10.18	23.31	08.09	29
30	22.33		21.02	GEM	CAN	04.16	00.28	SCO	CAP	AQU	ARI	TAU	30
31	PIS		TAU		08.53		LIB	07.01		14.12		11.17	31

SUN

mth	dy	time → sign
JAN	1	00.00 → CAP
JAN	20	11.02 → AQU
FEB	19	01.10 → PIS
MAR	21	00.09 → ARI
APR	20	11.08 → TAU
MAY	21	10.13 → GEM
JUN	21	18.08 → CAN
JUL	23	05.01 → LEO
AUG	23	12.09 → VIR
SEP	23	09.53 → LIB
OCT	23	19.17 → SCO
NOV	22	16.51 → SAG
DEC	22	06.09 → CAP

MERCURY

mth	dy	time → sign
JAN	1	00.00 → CAP
JAN	15	09.26 → AQU
FEB	2	09.21 → PIS
FEB	27	03.01 → AQU
MAR	18	09.36 → PIS
APR	10	23.08 → ARI
APR	27	07.17 → TAU
MAY	11	09.18 → GEM
MAY	29	00.57 → CAN
AUG	4	17.16 → LEO
AUG	19	13.02 → VIR
SEP	5	12.04 → LIB
SEP	27	17.19 → SCO
OCT	24	03.37 → LIB
NOV	11	08.42 → SCO
DEC	1	12.22 → SAG
DEC	20	14.44 → CAP

VENUS

mth	dy	time → sign
JAN	1	00.00 → CAP
JAN	4	03.33 → AQU
JAN	28	03.34 → PIS
FEB	21	08.23 → ARI
MAR	17	22.02 → TAU
APR	12	02.16 → GEM
MAY	8	07.29 → CAN
JUN	5	18.00 → LEO
JUL	14	18.24 → VIR
AUG	9	01.13 → LEO
OCT	8	06.54 → VIR
NOV	8	21.07 → LIB
DEC	5	13.30 → SCO
DEC	30	18.03 → SAG

MARS

mth	dy	time → sign
JAN	1	00.00 → SAG
JAN	16	20.55 → CAP
FEB	26	01.34 → AQU
APR	6	08.50 → PIS
MAY	15	14.07 → ARI
JUN	24	21.28 → TAU
AUG	7	06.02 → GEM
SEP	28	23.56 → CAN
DEC	31	16.02 → GEM

SATURN

mth	dy	time → sign
JAN	1	00.00 → LEO
SEP	2	13.53 → VIR

JUPITER

mth	dy	time → sign
JAN	1	00.00 → SAG
DEC	18	20.13 → CAP

MOON

dy	jan	feb	mar	apr	may	jun	jul	aug	sep	oct	nov	dec	dy
1	GEM	05.16	LEO	15.44	10.42	SAG	CAP	PIS	05.37	GEM	04.49	VIR	1
2	15.15	LEO	21.33	LIB	SCO	15.10	05.25	20.44	TAU	16.58	LEO	VIR	2
3	CAN	14.35	VIR	LIB	22.49	CAP	AQU	ARI	07.31	CAN	12.46	06.02	3
4	21.15	VIR	VIR	04.37	SAG	23.16	10.53	23.17	GEM	22.28	VIR	LIB	4
5	LEO	VIR	09.26	SCO	SAG	AQU	PIS	TAU	11.09	LEO	23.48	18.32	5
6	LEO	02.16	LIB	16.58	09.22	AQU	14.58	TAU	CAN	LEO	LIB	SCO	6
7	06.19	LIB	22.18	SAG	CAP	05.25	ARI	02.02	17.00	07.04	LIB	SCO	7
8	VIR	15.11	SCO	SAG	17.49	PIS	17.55	GEM	LEO	VIR	12.19	07.12	8
9	18.16	SCO	SCO	03.37	AQU	09.27	TAU	05.37	LEO	17.59	SCO	SAG	9
10	LIB	SCO	10.38	CAP	23.33	ARI	20.11	CAN	01.11	LIB	SCO	18.52	10
11	LIB	03.02	SAG	11.24	PIS	11.30	GEM	10.43	VIR	LIB	01.00	CAP	11
12	07.09	SAG	20.36	AQU	PIS	TAU	22.40	LEO	11.32	06.15	SAG	CAP	12
13	SCO	11.43	CAP	15.40	02.20	12.25	CAN	18.04	LIB	SCO	13.02	05.02	13
14	18.12	CAP	CAP	PIS	ARI	GEM	CAN	VIR	23.38	18.59	CAP	AQU	14
15	SAG	16.36	02.53	16.48	02.50	13.46	02.45	VIR	SCO	SAG	23.31	13.16	15
16	SAG	AQU	AQU	ARI	TAU	CAN	LEO	04.05	SCO	SAG	AQU	PIS	16
17	01.50	18.31	05.31	16.12	02.35	17.26	09.40	LIB	12.22	07.04	AQU	18.54	17
18	CAP	PIS	PIS	TAU	GEM	LEO	VIR	16.14	SAG	07.16	PIS	ARI	18
19	06.17	19.07	05.43	15.52	03.39	LEO	19.55	SCO	23.53	16.53	PIS	21.39	19
20	AQU	ARI	ARI	GEM	CAN	00.47	LIB	SCO	CAP	AQU	11.25	TAU	20
21	08.49	20.04	05.16	17.51	07.58	VIR	LIB	04.45	CAP	23.04	ARI	22.15	21
22	PIS	TAU	TAU	CAN	LEO	11.45	08.19	SAG	08.19	PIS	12.20	GEM	22
23	10.53	22.43	06.08	23.39	16.27	LIB	SCO	15.21	AQU	PIS	TAU	22.19	23
24	ARI	GEM	GEM	LEO	VIR	LIB	20.31	CAP	12.56	01.25	11.30	CAN	24
25	13.30	GEM	09.50	LEO	VIR	00.28	SAG	22.36	PIS	ARI	GEM	23.53	25
26	TAU	03.49	CAN	09.25	04.17	SCO	SAG	AQU	14.24	01.08	11.08	LEO	26
27	17.11	CAN	17.05	VIR	LIB	12.25	06.23	AQU	ARI	TAU	CAN	LEO	27
28	GEM	11.31	LEO	21.46	17.12	SAG	CAP	02.35	14.18	00.12	13.24	04.45	28
29	22.17		LEO	LIB	SCO	22.06	13.15	PIS	TAU	GEM	LEO	VIR	29
30	CAN		03.28	LIB	SCO	CAP	AQU	04.26	14.35	00.51	19.45	13.38	30
31	CAN		VIR		05.08		17.42	ARI		CAN		LIB	31

SUN

mth	dy	time → sign
JAN	1	00.00 → CAP
JAN	20	16.45 → AQU
FEB	19	06.51 → PIS
MAR	20	05.50 → ARI
APR	19	16.52 → TAU
MAY	20	16.02 → GEM
JUN	21	00.01 → CAN
JUL	22	10.56 → LEO
AUG	22	18.04 → VIR
SEP	22	15.46 → LIB
OCT	23	01.10 → SCO
NOV	21	22.46 → SAG
DEC	21	12.05 → CAP

MERCURY

mth	dy	time → sign
JAN	1	00.00 → CAP
JAN	8	04.47 → AQU
MAR	14	22.47 → PIS
APR	2	17.46 → ARI
APR	17	21.08 → TAU
MAY	2	20.01 → GEM
JUL	10	20.18 → CAN
JUL	26	11.50 → LEO
AUG	10	10.52 → VIR
AUG	29	02.51 → LIB
NOV	4	16.01 → SCO
NOV	23	07.10 → SAG
DEC	12	10.14 → CAP

VENUS

mth	dy	time → sign
JAN	1	00.00 → SAG
JAN	24	08.07 → CAP
FEB	17	16.24 → AQU
MAR	12	22.53 → PIS
APR	6	05.37 → ARI
APR	30	13.36 → TAU
MAY	24	22.54 → GEM
JUN	18	08.50 → CAN
JUL	12	18.40 → LEO
AUG	6	04.21 → VIR
AUG	30	14.43 → LIB
SEP	24	03.01 → SCO
OCT	18	18.32 → SAG
NOV	12	15.26 → CAP
DEC	7	23.38 → AQU

MARS

mth	dy	time → sign
JAN	1	00.00 → GEM
MAR	4	10.02 → CAN
MAY	9	20.21 → LEO
JUL	1	16.23 → VIR
AUG	19	10.05 → LIB
OCT	4	04.35 → SCO
NOV	16	08.28 → SAG
DEC	27	07.32 → CAP

SATURN

mth	dy	time → sign
JAN	1	00.00 → VIR

JUPITER

mth	dy	time → sign
JAN	1	00.00 → CAP

MOON

dy	jan	feb	mar	apr	may	jun	jul	aug	sep	oct	nov	dec	dy
1	LIB	SAG	18.34	AQU	PIS	TAU	GEM	LEO	11.46	04.27	SAG	CAP	1
2	01.33	SAG	CAP	20.56	10.52	22.07	07.54	21.00	LIB	SCO	11.14	06.46	2
3	SCO	09.53	CAP	PIS	ARI	GEM	CAN	VIR	20.03	15.15	CAP	AQU	3
4	14.15	CAP	04.26	PIS	11.59	21.17	08.16	VIR	SCO	SAG	CAP	18.24	4
5	SAG	19.11	AQU	00.28	TAU	CAN	LEO	02.29	SCO	SAG	00.03	PIS	5
6	SAG	AQU	10.54	ARI	11.18	22.01	11.05	LIB	07.12	03.50	AQU	PIS	6
7	01.44	AQU	PIS	01.21	GEM	LEO	VIR	11.27	SAG	CAP	10.44	02.45	7
8	CAP	01.47	14.24	TAU	11.03	LEO	17.32	SCO	19.46	16.04	PIS	ARI	8
9	11.14	PIS	ARI	01.28	CAN	02.02	LIB	23.11	CAP	AQU	17.27	06.53	9
10	AQU	06.18	16.15	GEM	13.11	VIR	LIB	SAG	CAP	AQU	ARI	TAU	10
11	18.45	ARI	TAU	02.44	LEO	09.56	03.36	SAG	07.21	01.32	20.07	07.35	11
12	PIS	09.35	17.55	CAN	18.49	LIB	SCO	11.43	AQU	PIS	TAU	GEM	12
13	PIS	TAU	20.39	06.30	VIR	20.54	15.51	CAP	16.06	07.08	GEM	06.41	13
14	00.24	12.21	CAN	LEO	VIR	SCO	SAG	22.57	PIS	ARI	GEM	CAN	14
15	ARI	GEM	CAN	13.08	03.47	SCO	SAG	AQU	21.40	09.32	19.53	06.24	15
16	04.14	15.13	CAN	VIR	LIB	09.21	04.21	AQU	ARI	TAU	CAN	LEO	16
17	TAU	CAN	01.05	22.11	15.00	SAG	CAP	07.47	ARI	10.27	21.09	08.37	17
18	06.31	18.53	LEO	LIB	SCO	21.53	15.41	PIS	00.58	GEM	LEO	VIR	18
19	GEM	LEO	07.26	LIB	SCO	CAP	AQU	14.11	TAU	11.41	LEO	14.24	19
20	08.06	LEO	VIR	09.01	03.20	CAP	AQU	ARI	03.18	CAN	01.14	LIB	20
21	CAN	00.07	15.46	SCO	SAG	09.35	01.09	18.39	GEM	14.36	VIR	23.38	21
22	10.21	VIR	LIB	21.08	15.57	AQU	PIS	TAU	05.50	LEO	08.21	SCO	22
23	LEO	07.46	LIB	SAG	CAP	19.33	08.23	21.49	CAN	19.41	LIB	SCO	23
24	14.49	LIB	02.07	SAG	CAP	PIS	ARI	GEM	09.15	VIR	17.55	11.14	24
25	VIR	18.07	SCO	09.48	03.53	PIS	13.15	GEM	LEO	VIR	SCO	SAG	25
26	22.36	SCO	14.12	CAP	AQU	02.50	TAU	00.20	13.53	02.49	SCO	23.57	26
27	LIB	SCO	SAG	21.28	13.39	ARI	15.56	CAN	VIR	LIB	05.15	CAP	27
28	LIB	06.23	SAG	AQU	PIS	06.51	GEM	02.52	20.07	11.48	SAG	CAP	28
29	09.36	SAG	02.44	AQU	19.54	TAU	17.13	LEO	LIB	SCO	17.49	12.44	29
30	SCO		CAP	06.12	ARI	08.04	CAN	LIB	LIB	22.42	CAP	AQU	30
31	22.09		13.35		22.20		18.23	VIR		SAG		AQU	31

SUN

mth	dy	time → sign
JAN	1	00.00 → CAP
JAN	19	22.42 → AQU
FEB	18	12.48 → PIS
MAR	20	11.45 → ARI
APR	19	22.46 → TAU
MAY	20	21.52 → GEM
JUN	21	05.47 → CAN
JUL	22	16.37 → LEO
AUG	22	23.40 → VIR
SEP	22	21.20 → LIB
OCT	23	06.45 → SCO
NOV	22	04.24 → SAG
DEC	21	17.48 → CAP

SATURN

mth	dy	time → sign
JAN	1	00.00 → VIR
OCT	29	17.13 → LIB

MERCURY

mth	dy	time → sign
JAN	1	00.00 → CAP
JAN	1	09.53 → AQU
JAN	21	05.37 → CAP
FEB	14	15.41 → AQU
MAR	8	18.57 → PIS
MAR	25	19.57 → ARI
APR	9	14.23 → TAU
APR	30	22.30 → GEM
MAY	13	23.55 → TAU
JUN	14	02.49 → GEM
JUL	3	19.21 → CAN
JUL	17	23.09 → LEO
AUG	2	23.08 → VIR
AUG	25	20.19 → LIB
SEP	18	03.27 → VIR
OCT	10	03.47 → LIB
OCT	28	10.10 → SCO
NOV	16	00.30 → SAG
DEC	5	17.26 → CAP

VENUS

mth	dy	time → sign
JAN	1	00.00 → AQU
JAN	3	12.37 → PIS
FEB	3	03.42 → ARI
APR	11	12.50 → PIS
APR	24	07.19 → ARI
JUN	6	09.08 → TAU
JUL	5	08.24 → GEM
AUG	1	01.29 → CAN
AUG	26	16.13 → LEO
SEP	20	13.34 → VIR
OCT	14	22.48 → LIB
NOV	8	00.25 → SCO
DEC	1	22.05 → SAG
DEC	25	18.19 → CAP

MARS

mth	dy	time → sign
JAN	1	00.00 → CAP
FEB	4	15.57 → AQU
MAR	15	03.21 → PIS
APR	22	13.46 → ARI
MAY	31	21.20 → TAU
JUL	12	02.57 → GEM
AUG	25	17.17 → CAN
OCT	16	15.34 → LEO

JUPITER

mth	dy	time → sign
JAN	1	00.00 → CAP
JAN	5	15.43 → AQU

MOON

dy	jan	feb	mar	apr	may	jun	jul	aug	sep	oct	nov	dec	dy
1	00.28	22.10	03.34	16.31	00.57	15.18	04.20	SAG	03.44	PIS	ARI	14.25	1
2	PIS	TAU	TAU	CAN	LEO	LIB	SCO	08.09	AQU	PIS	00.46	GEM	2
3	09.51	TAU	08.00	19.34	04.38	22.45	14.12	CAP	15.59	09.22	TAU	16.02	3
4	ARI	02.16	GEM	LEO	VIR	SCO	SAG	21.09	PIS	ARI	04.54	CAN	4
5	15.47	GEM	11.08	23.03	09.52	SCO	SAG	AQU	PIS	16.34	GEM	17.08	5
6	TAU	04.07	CAN	VIR	LIB	08.25	02.09	AQU	02.15	TAU	07.44	LEO	6
7	18.13	CAN	13.25	VIR	16.49	SAG	CAP	09.36	ARI	21.48	CAN	19.07	7
8	GEM	04.44	LEO	03.23	SCO	20.01	15.05	PIS	10.19	GEM	10.24	VIR	8
9	18.15	LEO	15.35	LIB	SCO	CAP	AQU	20.24	TAU	GEM	LEO	22.48	9
10	CAN	05.39	VIR	09.24	01.50	CAP	AQU	ARI	16.18	01.49	13.31	LIB	10
11	17.42	VIR	18.47	SCO	SAG	08.54	03.45	ARI	GEM	CAN	VIR	LIB	11
12	LEO	08.34	LIB	18.02	13.10	AQU	PIS	04.51	20.21	05.04	17.23	04.33	12
13	18.34	LIB	LIB	SAG	CAP	21.33	14.41	TAU	CAN	LEO	LIB	SCO	13
14	VIR	14.52	00.24	SAG	CAP	PIS	ARI	10.27	22.40	07.46	22.25	12.26	14
15	22.31	SCO	SCO	05.28	02.02	PIS	22.31	GEM	LEO	VIR	SCO	SAG	15
16	LIB	SCO	09.23	CAP	AQU	07.53	TAU	13.14	23.57	10.31	SCO	22.33	16
17	LIB	00.54	SAG	18.20	14.18	ARI	TAU	CAN	VIR	LIB	05.23	CAP	17
18	06.21	SAG	21.20	AQU	PIS	14.22	02.42	13.58	VIR	14.24	SAG	CAP	18
19	SCO	13.26	CAP	AQU	23.31	TAU	GEM	LEO	01.27	SCO	15.02	10.40	19
20	17.31	CAP	CAP	05.56	ARI	17.01	03.52	14.01	LIB	20.50	CAP	AQU	20
21	SAG	CAP	10.08	PIS	ARI	GEM	CAN	VIR	04.53	SAG	CAP	23.43	21
22	SAG	02.07	AQU	14.10	04.41	17.13	03.29	15.13	SCO	SAG	03.12	PIS	22
23	06.19	AQU	21.09	ARI	TAU	CAN	LEO	LIB	06.40	AQU	PIS	PIS	23
24	CAP	13.01	PIS	18.47	06.35	16.51	03.24	19.17	SAG	CAP	16.09	11.41	24
25	18.58	PIS	PIS	TAU	GEM	LEO	VIR	SCO	22.20	19.09	PIS	ARI	25
26	AQU	21.25	05.04	21.03	06.59	17.48	05.27	SCO	CAP	AQU	PIS	20.27	26
27	AQU	ARI	ARI	GEM	CAN	VIR	LIB	03.17	CAP	AQU	03.12	TAU	27
28	06.13	ARI	10.10	22.39	07.46	21.26	10.57	SAG	11.08	07.46	ARI	TAU	28
29	PIS		TAU	CAN	LEO	LIB	SCO	14.45	AQU	PIS	10.35	01.14	29
30	15.26		13.37	CAN	10.19	LIB	20.11	CAP	23.27	17.57	TAU	GEM	30
31	ARI		GEM		VIR		SAG	CAP		ARI		02.46	31

SUN

mth	dy	time → sign
JAN	1	00.00 → CAP
JAN	20	04.29 → AQU
FEB	18	18.37 → PIS
MAR	20	17.34 → ARI
APR	20	04.31 → TAU
MAY	21	03.35 → GEM
JUN	21	11.30 → CAN
JUL	22	22.23 → LEO
AUG	23	05.28 → VIR
SEP	23	03.10 → LIB
OCT	23	12.37 → SCO
NOV	22	10.16 → SAG
DEC	21	23.40 → CAP

MERCURY

mth	dy	time → sign
JAN	1	00.00 → CAP
FEB	10	09.07 → AQU
MAR	1	13.29 → PIS
MAR	17	16.13 → ARI
APR	2	13.07 → TAU
JUN	10	05.42 → GEM
JUN	25	10.33 → CAN
JUL	9	16.30 → LEO
JUL	27	21.44 → VIR
OCT	3	15.05 → LIB
OCT	20	21.20 → SCO
NOV	8	23.45 → SAG
DEC	1	00.12 → CAP
DEC	18	14.55 → SAG

VENUS

mth	dy	time → sign
JAN	1	00.00 → CAP
JAN	18	14.36 → AQU
FEB	11	12.11 → PIS
MAR	7	12.35 → ARI
MAR	31	17.36 → TAU
APR	25	05.07 → GEM
MAY	20	01.06 → CAN
JUN	14	08.51 → LEO
JUL	10	11.33 → VIR
AUG	7	03.49 → LIB
SEP	8	15.46 → SCO
NOV	8	03.10 → LIB
NOV	30	00.34 → SCO

MARS

mth	dy	time → sign
JAN	1	00.00 → LEO
JUN	7	06.12 → VIR
JUL	29	23.48 → LIB
SEP	14	22.39 → SCO
OCT	28	06.49 → SAG
DEC	7	23.50 → CAP

SATURN

mth	dy	time → sign
JAN	1	00.00 → LIB
APR	7	18.45 → VIR
JUL	21	15.18 → LIB

JUPITER

mth	dy	time → sign
JAN	1	00.00 → AQU
JAN	18	02.12 → PIS
JUN	6	06.29 → ARI
SEP	9	04.50 → PIS

MOON

dy	jan	feb	mar	apr	may	jun	jul	aug	sep	oct	nov	dec	dy
1	CAN	VIR	VIR	SCO	SAG	05.09	01.11	ARI	00.20	CAN	03.52	LIB	1
2	02.42	13.43	00.32	16.54	10.01	AQU	PIS	08.14	GEM	18.22	VIR	14.45	2
3	LEO	LIB	LIB	SAG	CAP	17.35	13.45	TAU	06.52	LEO	05.20	SCO	3
4	02.54	16.57	02.12	SAG	20.53	PIS	ARI	16.55	CAN	20.01	LIB	18.00	4
5	VIR	SCO	SCO	01.08	AQU	PIS	ARI	GEM	09.46	VIR	06.17	SAG	5
6	04.59	SCO	07.37	CAP	AQU	05.51	00.30	21.51	LEO	19.53	SCO	23.17	6
7	LIB	00.05	SAG	12.52	09.35	ARI	TAU	CAN	09.54	LIB	08.29	CAP	7
8	10.01	SAG	17.14	AQU	PIS	15.42	07.52	23.24	VIR	19.53	SAG	CAP	8
9	SCO	10.45	CAP	AQU	21.30	TAU	GEM	LEO	09.02	SCO	13.38	07.31	9
10	18.11	CAP	CAP	01.49	ARI	22.12	11.39	23.02	LIB	22.10	CAP	AQU	10
11	SAG	23.25	05.43	PIS	ARI	GEM	CAN	VIR	09.22	SAG	22.33	18.42	11
12	SAG	AQU	AQU	13.32	06.49	GEM	12.55	22.44	SCO	SAG	AQU	PIS	12
13	04.55	AQU	18.45	ARI	TAU	01.51	LEO	LIB	12.53	04.18	AQU	PIS	13
14	CAP	12.24	PIS	22.56	13.19	CAN	13.16	LIB	SAG	10.25	07.16	14
15	17.18	PIS	PIS	TAU	GEM	03.55	VIR	00.27	20.31	14.25	PIS	ARI	15
16	AQU	PIS	06.33	TAU	17.47	LEO	14.25	SCO	CAP	AQU	23.00	18.50	16
17	AQU	00.31	ARI	06.09	CAN	05.42	LIB	05.35	CAP	AQU	ARI	TAU	17
18	06.18	ARI	16.30	GEM	21.07	VIR	17.43	SAG	07.36	02.53	ARI	TAU	18
19	PIS	10.56	TAU	11.40	LEO	08.14	SCO	14.18	AQU	PIS	10.05	03.38	19
20	18.37	TAU	TAU	CAN	23.59	LIB	23.50	CAP	20.16	15.24	TAU	GEM	20
21	ARI	18.48	00.29	15.43	VIR	12.15	SAG	CAP	PIS	ARI	18.47	09.23	21
22	ARI	GEM	GEM	LEO	VIR	SCO	SAG	01.39	PIS	ARI	GEM	CAN	22
23	04.41	23.30	06.17	18.25	02.51	18.11	08.40	AQU	08.48	02.31	GEM	12.52	23
24	TAU	CAN	CAN	VIR	LIB	SAG	CAP	14.12	ARI	TAU	01.15	LEO	24
25	11.12	CAN	09.40	20.18	06.18	SAG	19.39	PIS	20.18	11.49	CAN	15.15	25
26	GEM	01.09	LEO	LIB	SCO	02.22	AQU	PIS	TAU	GEM	06.02	VIR	26
27	14.03	LEO	10.58	22.30	11.17	CAP	AQU	02.50	TAU	19.15	LEO	17.39	27
28	CAN	00.53	VIR	SCO	SAG	12.53	08.01	ARI	06.12	CAN	09.35	LIB	28
29	14.11		11.22	SCO	18.45	AQU	PIS	14.36	GEM	CAN	VIR	20.51	29
30	LEO		LIB	02.37	CAP	AQU	20.43	TAU	13.47	00.40	12.16	SCO	30
31	13.24		12.42		CAP		ARI	TAU		LEO		SCO	31

143

SUN

mth	dy	time → sign
JAN	1	00.00 → CAP
JAN	20	10.20 → AQU
FEB	19	00.27 → PIS
MAR	20	23.22 → ARI
APR	20	10.19 → TAU
MAY	21	09.22 → GEM
JUN	21	17.18 → CAN
JUL	23	04.13 → LEO
AUG	23	11.22 → VIR
SEP	23	09.06 → LIB
OCT	23	18.32 → SCO
NOV	22	16.09 → SAG
DEC	22	05.32 → CAP

MERCURY

mth	dy	time → sign
JAN	1	00.00 → SAG
JAN	13	11.27 → CAP
FEB	3	22.20 → AQU
FEB	21	20.55 → PIS
MAR	9	17.48 → ARI
MAY	15	23.20 → TAU
JUN	2	20.04 → GEM
JUN	16	19.10 → CAN
JUL	2	05.39 → LEO
JUL	28	17.59 → VIR
AUG	8	09.49 → LEO
SEP	9	06.00 → VIR
SEP	25	21.10 → LIB
OCT	13	10.53 → SCO
NOV	2	16.56 → SAG

VENUS

mth	dy	time → sign
JAN	1	00.00 → SCO
JAN	7	12.32 → SAG
FEB	4	06.00 → CAP
MAR	2	02.40 → AQU
MAR	27	06.54 → PIS
APR	21	04.08 → ARI
MAY	15	22.14 → TAU
JUN	9	14.25 → GEM
JUL	4	04.19 → CAN
JUL	28	15.00 → LEO
AUG	21	22.12 → VIR
SEP	15	02.41 → LIB
OCT	9	05.51 → SCO
NOV	2	08.53 → SAG
NOV	26	12.38 → CAP
DEC	20	18.28 → AQU

MARS

mth	dy	time → sign
JAN	1	00.00 → CAP
JAN	15	22.43 → AQU
FEB	23	01.07 → PIS
APR	2	04.52 → ARI
MAY	11	07.05 → TAU
JUN	21	02.51 → GEM
AUG	3	09.23 → CAN
SEP	19	01.53 → LEO
NOV	11	04.17 → VIR

SATURN

mth	dy	time → sign
JAN	1	00.00 → LIB

JUPITER

mth	dy	time → sign
JAN	1	00.00 → PIS
JAN	22	17.14 → ARI
JUN	4	13.58 → TAU

MOON

dy	jan	feb	mar	apr	may	jun	jul	aug	sep	oct	nov	dec	dy
1	01.22	23.22	05.15	PIS	ARI	GEM	CAN	08.43	18.49	04.43	22.09	14.46	1
2	SAG	AQU	AQU	11.17	06.00	GEM	21.44	VIR	SCO	SAG	AQU	PIS	2
3	07.40	AQU	16.48	ARI	TAU	08.38	LEO	10.05	21.05	08.17	AQU	PIS	3
4	CAP	10.25	PIS	23.47	17.10	CAN	LEO	LIB	SAG	CAP	07.19	01.52	4
5	16.09	PIS	PIS	TAU	GEM	15.04	01.16	11.58	SAG	15.19	PIS	ARI	5
6	AQU	22.47	05.15	TAU	GEM	LEO	VIR	SCO	02.05	AQU	19.03	14.36	6
7	AQU	ARI	ARI	11.23	02.33	19.34	03.55	15.22	CAP	AQU	ARI	TAU	7
8	02.58	ARI	17.53	GEM	CAN	VIR	LIB	SAG	09.43	01.14	ARI	TAU	8
9	PIS	11.24	TAU	21.03	09.37	22.32	06.32	20.39	AQU	PIS	07.46	02.53	9
10	15.25	TAU	TAU	CAN	LEO	LIB	SCO	CAP	19.28	12.58	TAU	GEM	10
11	ARI	22.22	05.32	CAN	14.00	LIB	09.48	CAP	PIS	ARI	20.11	13.27	11
12	ARI	GEM	GEM	03.38	VIR	00.34	SAG	03.49	PIS	ARI	GEM	CAN	12
13	03.38	GEM	14.31	LEO	15.58	SCO	14.15	AQU	06.50	01.36	GEM	21.49	13
14	TAU	05.50	CAN	06.42	LIB	02.39	CAP	12.55	ARI	TAU	07.20	LEO	14
15	13.24	CAN	19.34	VIR	16.33	SAG	20.31	PIS	19.26	14.16	CAN	LEO	15
16	GEM	09.15	LEO	07.00	SCO	06.00	AQU	PIS	TAU	GEM	16.18	04.00	16
17	19.30	LEO	20.54	LIB	17.24	CAP	AQU	00.03	TAU	GEM	LEO	VIR	17
18	CAN	09.40	VIR	06.20	SAG	11.48	05.14	ARI	08.07	01.39	22.20	08.07	18
19	22.17	VIR	20.04	SCO	20.17	AQU	PIS	12.37	GEM	CAN	VIR	LIB	19
20	LEO	09.02	LIB	06.51	CAP	20.46	16.26	TAU	18.55	10.07	VIR	10.34	20
21	23.11	LIB	19.18	SAG	CAP	PIS	ARI	TAU	CAN	LEO	01.17	SCO	21
22	VIR	09.30	SCO	10.25	02.33	PIS	ARI	00.54	CAN	14.42	LIB	12.04	22
23	23.59	SCO	20.46	CAP	AQU	08.25	04.59	GEM	01.56	VIR	01.59	SAG	23
24	LIB	12.47	SAG	18.00	12.25	ARI	TAU	10.32	LEO	15.50	SCO	13.48	24
25	LIB	SAG	SAG	AQU	PIS	20.54	16.35	CAN	04.50	LIB	01.58	CAP	25
26	02.17	19.33	01.58	AQU	PIS	TAU	GEM	16.10	VIR	15.10	SAG	17.15	26
27	SCO	CAP	CAP	04.59	00.37	TAU	GEM	LEO	04.52	SCO	03.06	AQU	27
28	06.56	CAP	11.01	PIS	ARI	07.57	01.13	18.14	LIB	14.46	CAP	23.46	28
29	SAG		AQU	17.34	13.03	GEM	CAN	VIR	04.06	SAG	07.03	PIS	29
30	14.05		22.39	ARI	TAU	16.14	06.17	18.26	SCO	16.40	AQU	PIS	30
31	CAP		PIS		23.57		LEO	LIB		CAP		09.49	31

144

2012

SUN

mth	dy	time → sign
JAN	1	00.00 → CAP
JAN	20	16.11 → AQU
FEB	19	06.19 → PIS
MAR	20	05.16 → ARI
APR	19	16.13 → TAU
MAY	20	15.17 → GEM
JUN	20	23.10 → CAN
JUL	22	10.02 → LEO
AUG	22	17.08 → VIR
SEP	22	14.50 → LIB
OCT	23	00.15 → SCO
NOV	21	21.52 → SAG
DEC	21	11.13 → CAP

MERCURY

mth	dy	time → sign
JAN	1	00.00 → SAG
JAN	8	06.35 → CAP
JAN	27	18.13 → AQU
FEB	14	01.39 → PIS
MAR	2	11.42 → ARI
MAR	23	13.24 → PIS
APR	16	22.44 → ARI
MAY	9	05.16 → TAU
MAY	24	11.13 → GEM
JUN	7	11.17 → CAN
JUN	26	02.25 → LEO
SEP	1	02.34 → VIR
SEP	16	23.23 → LIB
OCT	5	10.37 → SCO
OCT	29	06.19 → SAG
NOV	14	07.44 → SCO
DEC	11	01.41 → SAG
DEC	31	14.04 → CAP

VENUS

mth	dy	time → sign
JAN	1	00.00 → AQU
JAN	14	05.49 → PIS
FEB	8	06.03 → ARI
MAR	5	10.26 → TAU
APR	3	15.19 → GEM
AUG	7	13.44 → CAN
SEP	6	14.49 → LEO
OCT	3	07.00 → VIR
OCT	28	13.06 → LIB
NOV	22	01.21 → SCO
DEC	16	04.40 → SAG

MARS

mth	dy	time → sign
JAN	1	00.00 → VIR
JUL	3	12.33 → LIB
AUG	23	15.26 → SCO
OCT	7	03.22 → SAG
NOV	17	02.38 → CAP
DEC	26	00.50 → AQU

SATURN

mth	dy	time → sign
JAN	1	00.00 → LIB
OCT	5	20.39 → SCO

JUPITER

mth	dy	time → sign
JAN	1	00.00 → TAU
JUN	11	17.24 → GEM

MOON

dy	jan	feb	mar	apr	may	jun	jul	aug	sep	oct	nov	dec	dy
1	ARI	19.16	GEM	08.37	VIR	12.32	SAG	09.57	PIS	23.27	GEM	CAN	1
2	22.17	GEM	15.09	LEO	VIR	SCO	22.52	AQU	05.38	TAU	GEM	CAN	2
3	TAU	GEM	CAN	13.54	02.05	12.34	CAP	13.59	ARI	TAU	07.44	01.58	3
4	TAU	06.05	23.19	VIR	LIB	SAG	CAP	PIS	15.42	11.48	CAN	LEO	4
5	10.45	CAN	LEO	15.33	02.21	12.32	00.27	21.00	TAU	GEM	19.40	11.53	5
6	GEM	13.25	LEO	LIB	SCO	CAP	AQU	ARI	TAU	GEM	LEO	VIR	6
7	21.06	LEO	03.28	15.19	01.40	14.18	04.30	ARI	04.11	00.46	LEO	18.36	7
8	CAN	17.34	VIR	SCO	SAG	AQU	PIS	07.29	GEM	CAN	04.36	LIB	8
9	CAN	VIR	04.51	15.13	02.01	19.23	12.15	TAU	16.50	11.56	VIR	21.52	9
10	04.36	19.55	LIB	SAG	CAP	PIS	ARI	20.12	CAN	LEO	09.36	SCO	10
11	LEO	LIB	05.25	17.03	05.04	PIS	23.32	GEM	CAN	19.25	LIB	22.23	11
12	09.45	22.02	SCO	CAP	AQU	04.22	TAU	GEM	03.02	VIR	11.11	SAG	12
13	VIR	SCO	06.55	21.49	11.43	ARI	TAU	08.29	LEO	23.03	SCO	21.44	13
14	13.29	SCO	SAG	AQU	PIS	16.23	12.28	CAN	09.32	LIB	10.53	CAP	14
15	LIB	00.57	10.25	AQU	21.47	TAU	GEM	18.06	VIR	LIB	SAG	21.54	15
16	16.35	SAG	CAP	05.39	ARI	TAU	GEM	12.56	00.07	10.37	AQU	AQU	16
17	SCO	05.04	16.13	PIS	ARI	05.25	00.32	LEO	LIB	SCO	CAP	AQU	17
18	19.30	CAP	AQU	16.00	10.05	GEM	CAN	00.34	14.47	SCO	00.27	00.49	18
19	SAG	10.29	AQU	ARI	TAU	17.35	10.14	VIR	SCO	SAG	AQU	PIS	19
20	22.41	AQU	00.06	ARI	23.07	CAN	LEO	04.47	16.35	01.42	16.56	07.44	20
21	CAP	17.32	PIS	04.06	GEM	CAN	17.25	LIB	SAG	CAP	PIS	ARI	21
22	CAP	PIS	09.58	TAU	GEM	03.48	VIR	07.55	19.22	05.03	PIS	18.26	22
23	02.54	PIS	ARI	17.06	11.32	LEO	22.39	SCO	CAP	AQU	01.13	TAU	23
24	AQU	02.49	21.44	GEM	CAN	11.44	LIB	10.51	23.34	11.01	ARI	TAU	24
25	09.12	ARI	TAU	GEM	22.13	VIR	LIB	SAG	AQU	PIS	12.19	07.15	25
26	PIS	14.31	TAU	05.43	LEO	17.16	02.30	14.00	AQU	19.32	TAU	GEM	26
27	18.29	TAU	10.44	CAN	LEO	LIB	SCO	CAP	05.25	ARI	TAU	20.08	27
28	ARI	TAU	GEM	16.12	06.07	20.34	05.19	17.40	PIS	ARI	00.59	CAN	28
29	ARI	03.28	23.08	LEO	VIR	SCO	SAG	AQU	13.15	06.16	GEM	CAN	29
30	06.30		CAN	23.03	10.47	22.05	07.31	22.32	ARI	TAU	13.56	07.46	30
31	TAU		CAN		LIB		CAP	PIS		18.41		LEO	31

OUTER PLANET SIGN TABLES

URANUS				
year	mth	dy	time	→ sign
1900	JAN	1	00.00	→ SAG
1904	DEC	20	13.01	→ CAP
1912	JAN	30	22.50	→ AQU
1912	SEP	4	16.28	→ CAP
1912	NOV	12	08.32	→ AQU
1919	APR	1	01.20	→ PIS
1919	AUG	16	21.51	→ AQU
1920	JAN	22	07.45	→ PIS
1927	MAR	31	17.14	→ ARI
1927	NOV	4	10.41	→ PIS
1928	JAN	13	08.10	→ ARI
1934	JUN	6	15.41	→ TAU
1934	OCT	10	00.07	→ ARI
1935	MAR	28	02.37	→ TAU
1941	AUG	7	15.30	→ GEM
1941	OCT	5	02.00	→ TAU
1942	MAY	15	04.13	→ GEM
1948	AUG	30	15.40	→ CAN
1948	NOV	12	13.20	→ GEM
1949	JUN	10	04.04	→ CAN
1955	AUG	24	17.57	→ LEO
1956	JAN	28	01.50	→ CAN
1956	JUN	10	01.42	→ LEO
1961	NOV	1	16.00	→ VIR
1962	JAN	10	05.54	→ LEO
1962	AUG	10	01.13	→ VIR
1968	SEP	28	16.01	→ LIB
1969	MAY	20	21.21	→ VIR
1969	JUN	24	10.26	→ LIB
1974	NOV	21	09.30	→ SCO
1975	MAY	1	17.41	→ LIB
1975	SEP	8	05.05	→ SCO
1981	FEB	17	08.42	→ SAG
1981	MAR	20	23.23	→ SCO
1981	NOV	16	12.07	→ SAG
1988	FEB	15	00.07	→ CAP
1988	MAY	27	01.20	→ SAG
1988	DEC	2	15.33	→ CAP
1995	APR	1	12.07	→ AQU
1995	JUN	9	01.42	→ CAP
1996	JAN	12	07.13	→ AQU
2003	MAR	10	20.54	→ PIS
2003	SEP	15	03.48	→ AQU
2003	DEC	30	09.15	→ PIS
2010	MAY	28	01.50	→ ARI
2010	AUG	14	03.32	→ PIS
2011	MAR	12	00.53	→ ARI

NEPTUNE				
year	mth	dy	time	→ sign
1900	JAN	1	00.00	→ GEM
1901	JUL	19	23.45	→ CAN
1901	DEC	25	13.20	→ GEM
1902	MAY	21	13.33	→ CAN
1914	SEP	23	20.20	→ LEO
1914	DEC	14	20.13	→ CAN
1915	JUL	19	13.30	→ LEO
1916	MAR	19	15.22	→ CAN
1916	MAY	2	10.38	→ LEO
1928	SEP	21	12.00	→ VIR
1929	FEB	19	11.21	→ LEO
1929	JUL	24	15.07	→ VIR
1942	OCT	3	17.10	→ LIB
1943	APR	17	10.55	→ VIR
1943	AUG	2	19.10	→ LIB
1955	DEC	24	15.23	→ SCO
1956	MAR	12	01.55	→ LIB
1956	OCT	19	09.21	→ SCO
1957	JUN	15	20.06	→ LIB
1957	AUG	6	08.23	→ SCO
1970	JAN	4	19.55	→ SAG
1970	MAY	3	01.30	→ SCO
1970	NOV	6	16.26	→ SAG
1984	JAN	19	02.31	→ CAP
1984	JUN	23	01.20	→ SAG
1984	NOV	21	13.20	→ CAP
1998	JAN	29	02.33	→ AQU
1998	AUG	23	00.26	→ CAP
1998	NOV	28	01.08	→ AQU
2011	APR	04	13.37	→ PIS
2011	AUG	05	03.12	→ AQU
2012	FEB	03	18.53	→ PIS

PLUTO				
year	mth	dy	time	→ sign
1900	JAN	1	00.00	→ GEM
1912	SEP	10	16.00	→ CAN
1912	OCT	20	08.30	→ GEM
1913	JUL	9	22.11	→ CAN
1913	DEC	28	04.23	→ GEM
1914	MAY	26	20.42	→ CAN
1937	OCT	7	12.26	→ LEO
1937	NOV	25	09.13	→ CAN
1938	AUG	3	18.20	→ LEO
1939	FEB	7	12.59	→ CAN
1939	JUN	14	04.50	→ LEO
1956	OCT	20	06.57	→ VIR
1957	JAN	15	02.19	→ LEO
1957	AUG	19	04.35	→ VIR
1958	APR	11	14.24	→ LEO
1958	JUN	10	19.26	→ VIR
1971	OCT	5	05.55	→ LIB
1972	APR	17	08.02	→ VIR
1972	JUL	30	11.13	→ LIB
1983	NOV	5	21.11	→ SCO
1984	MAY	18	14.47	→ LIB
1984	AUG	28	04.59	→ SCO
1995	JAN	17	10.10	→ SAG
1995	APR	21	01.38	→ SCO
1995	NOV	10	19.40	→ SAG
2008	JAN	26	03.45	→ CAP
2008	JUN	14	03.47	→ SAG
2008	NOV	27	02.06	→ CAP

THE PLANET-SIGN PROFILES

THE SUN, THE MOON AND THE PLANETS
THROUGH THE SIGNS OF THE ZODIAC

IMPORTANT TIPS

● The page layout of the Profiles should be self-explanatory. Appreciate that the sections with headings connected by arrows simply indicate that the meanings of the right-hand section follow on from the meanings of the left-hand one.

● There is a WHEN ALONE section at the bottom of each Planet-Sign Profile. I believe that being alone is a highly important state, which is criminally overlooked in many, if not most, texts concerning relationships. Please be aware that, apart from meaning literally on your own, I have also used the term ALONE to describe a state of being *alone but within a relationship*. Also, remember that OTHER also applies to people you have not yet met, who are 'out there'.

● Bear in mind when reading all the Profiles that what you read you may find yourself ascribing to Other rather than yourself. This is the phenomenon of *psychological projection* which this book refers to frequently, meaning that what we cannot recognize or accept in ourselves we find in someone else – for good or ill.

● Be sure to read the individual IMPORTANT TIPS at the start of each set of Profiles for that Planet. This will enable you to get the most out of the Profiles.

INDEX FOR SUN, MOON AND PLANETS THROUGH THE SIGNS

PLANETS ⇨	SUN	MOON	MERCURY	VENUS	MARS	JUPITER	SATURN	URANUS NEPTUNE PLUTO	ASCENDANT
Page number of desired Profile is given at the intersection of Sign row and Planet column.									
ZODIAC SIGNS ⇩ **TIPS** ⇨	149	163	177	185	199	213	227		263
ARIES	150	164	178	186	200	214	228	Not included – see page 241	264
TAURUS	151	165	178	187	201	215	229		265
GEMINI	152	166	179	188	202	216	230		266
CANCER	153	167	179	189	203	217	231		267
LEO	154	168	180	190	204	218	232		268
VIRGO	155	169	180	191	205	219	233		269
LIBRA	156	170	181	192	206	220	234		270
SCORPIO	157	171	181	193	207	221	235		271
SAGITTARIUS	158	172	182	194	208	222	236		272
CAPRICORN	159	173	182	195	209	223	237		273
AQUARIUS	160	174	183	196	210	224	238		274
PISCES	161	175	183	197	211	225	239		275

THE SUN

IMPORTANT TIPS

● With all Sun Signs it is important to bear in mind that they have to do with what you are *making* of a relationship in the sense of what your creative input is. For example, the helpfulness and precision of a Virgo Sun can make a relationship work because of a detailed attention to Other's needs that in turn aids the relationship itself. On the other hand, a negative input, such as a carping, know-it-all attitude in this case, would diminish Other and dry up the relationship.

● Unlike the other Planet-Sign Profiles, with the Sun I focus more upon the negatives and what you can do about them. This is because the Sun is symbolic of the ego and as such is responsible for many relationship differences.

● In the section of each Profile headed SO CAN FEEL WEAK (Admitting this brings Enlightenment), I use the word 'Enlightenment' in the sense of gaining a true sense and awareness of whatever the issue may be. You could also use the word SOLACE instead of Enlightenment, if you felt it to be more appropriate.

● Seeing that the Sun has so much to do with Father, occasionally it may be relevant, and extraordinarily enlightening, to read 'Other(s)' as meaning Father – your own, that is. If you are inclined to believe that your Soul chooses your parents, the results of doing this can be even more revealing.

SUN IN ARIES
The Brave Heart • The Impatient Heart

ROLES and GOALS

The will to *show a way forward* – boldly and assertively without being *arrogant or pushy*.
A life led in a spirit of *championing the underdog* – as opposed to always *wanting to win*.
Father is seen or expressed as one who is *honest and direct*, and/or *blunt and hard*.

YOU GENERATE	BUT CAN OVERWHELM
(How you Gain Respect)	*(How you Alienate Other)*

… a bright spontaneity that encourages Other to be more aware of simply being and to live in and for the moment.

… an independence and straightforwardness that is refreshing and makes Other want to go where you are going.

… an air of heroism as you protect the weak and fight for the oppressed.

… with a childish naïveté that is tiresome and short-sighted.

… with a simplistic attitude that overlooks the subtleties and sensitivities of Other, causing them to avoid what is boring, annoying or upsetting about you.

… by being arrogant and boastful, and coming on tough.

YOU OVEREMPHASIZE	SO CAN FEEL WEAK
(How you Lose Respect)	*(Admitting this brings Enlightenment)*

… your air of independence in order to be seen as you'd like to actually feel.

… how soon you will be able to achieve an objective, and so you fall short and appear ridiculous.

… a desire to win at all costs, rather than simply doing your best.

… when it is made only too clear what or who you depend upon, for whatever reason.

… when it seems that you are not getting anywhere.

… because you feel you have lost, when you could simply be learning a lesson.

WHEN ALONE …

… is probably for one of two reasons, but they both come under the heading of 'enforced independence'. The first one is that you have never allowed Other to see the 'Little Lamb' inside of you, and have only shown the forceful, independent Ram. People tire of such a seemingly two-dimensional nature and ultimately let you be as alone as you like to be thought independent. If you think you have 'chosen' to be on your own because of Other's failings, then you will have only your ego for company for some time.

The second reason is the converse of the first one – too much Lamb and not enough Ram. Failing to assert yourself and act independently, without approval from Other, becomes very unstimulating and burdensome for Other. They will be forced to look elsewhere for this, while still possibly maintaining a guilt-motivated link with you.

SUN IN TAURUS
The Steady Heart • The Stubborn Heart

ROLES and GOALS

The will to use generously your *sense of value* – without it descending into *possessiveness*.
A life led in a spirit of *radiating earthy stability* – as opposed to *lethargy* and *resisting change*.
Father is seen or expressed as one who is a *reliable provider*, and/or a *hedonistic materialist*.

YOU GENERATE

(How you Gain Respect)

… a feeling of natural stability that gives Other a sense of something permanent that they can build and rely upon.

… a sense of there being plenty of time to enjoy and accomplish things.

… a productiveness that is very reassuring and gives substance to the notion that life is good.

BUT CAN OVERWHELM

(How you Alienate Other)

… with an inability to grasp or accept abstract concepts that you perceive as having no 'real' value.

… with a sluggishness that is boring and a turn-off.

… by having many possessions but not appreciating the value of the intangibles of life.

YOU OVEREMPHASIZE

(How you Lose Respect)

… your sense of caution, which sometimes is really a fear of the unpredictable.

… your desire for physical gratification at the expense of the enduring bond you seek.

… the spiritual or philosophical side of life when really you are merely playing lip service to these aspects of existence.

SO CAN FEEL WEAK

(Admitting this brings Enlightenment)

… in the face of what appears to be Other threatening your sense of security.

… when feeling in danger of losing Other on a physical level – simply because that is nearly all you've focused upon.

… when made uncomfortably aware by Other of being a wolf in sheep's clothing.

WHEN ALONE …

… it is most probably because you have to find pastures new – even though it might feel that you have been put out to grass! But behind this the reason is only too down-to-earth: life with Other has become boring to the point of being impossible. You may have to accept that in some way you contributed to that boredom – possibly because you thought Other was a safe bet in the first place. Or they thought you were. Whatever the case, the salutary lesson is that a relationship without some pattern of growth and development in it is doomed to deadlock. And we are talking growth and development on a psychological or emotional level here, not just a physical/material one. The dynamics of relationship force us to confront our fears and shortcomings, which is something Taureans are averse to doing. And so finding yourself out of a relationship – or never having entered one at all – is owing to your stubborn resistance to change.

SUN IN GEMINI

The Friendly Heart • The Flippant Heart

ROLES and GOALS

The will to use generously your *levity and sense of humour* – without it devolving into *flippancy*.
A life led in a spirit of *interest and communication* – as opposed to *trivia and distraction*.
Father is seen or expressed as one who is *light and amusing*, and/or *fly or insubstantial*.

YOU GENERATE	BUT CAN OVERWHELM
(How you Gain Respect)	*(How you Alienate Other)*

… a sparkling display of wit and anecdotes that refreshes Other and relieves them of their heavier thoughts and feelings.

… a sense that things are easy to accomplish and that worrying is for fools.

… an air of deftness as you turn your hand to all manner of things with style and agility.

… with a superficiality that is paradoxically quite profound in that Other cannot penetrate it – only leave it, ultimately.

… with a cleverness that masks a deep inner doubt with regard to yourself and life in general, which Other inevitably spots.

… by knowing everything, but understanding little – least of all how Other feels.

YOU OVEREMPHASIZE	SO CAN FEEL WEAK
(How you Lose Respect)	*(Admitting this brings Enlightenment)*

… who and what you know – or, curiously, your lack of knowledge and contacts.

… your fear of commitment to the point of Other not wanting, or not being able, to commit to you.

… your reluctance to get right down to the real underlying truth of some issue, because it means you'll then have to stop flitting.

… in the face of not knowing what to say or how to behave.

… at the prospect of someone getting to know you well enough to discover that you do not love or know yourself that much.

… when you cannot rationalize or wander, which you do for fear of not being accepted for both sides of yourself.

WHEN ALONE …

… you have your other half for company. This can be your 'light twin' or your 'dark twin', but it is more usually the latter. Your dark twin is all the doubts and irrationalities that you find hard to accept and strive even harder to avoid. For this reason, Geminians try never to be out of relationship for too long. It is also why they have, or are tempted to have, more than one partner – or at least, keep their options open. But sooner or later, your dark twin, like your own shadow, will overtake you. The song 'Yesterday' by Gemini Paul McCartney says it all – '… I'm not half the man I used to be, there's a shadow hanging over me'. It is at such a time of being alone (all-one), that you must get to know and befriend what you have come to regard as unlovable in yourself. You will eventually realize that your dark twin was simply *in* the dark.

SUN IN CANCER

The Caring Heart • The Clinging Heart

ROLES and GOALS

The will to use generously your *sympathetic sense* – without being *doting* or *self-pitying*.
A life led in a spirit of *bestowing care and devotion* – as opposed to being a *mother hen*.
Father is seen or expressed as one who is *tender and kind*, and/or *weak and over-sentimental*.

YOU GENERATE	BUT CAN OVERWHELM
(How you Gain Respect)	*(How you Alienate Other)*

… an aura of gentleness and receptivity that makes Other feel safe, cared for, and as if they belong somewhere and to someone.

… a feeling of familiarity that implies an awareness of how Other feels.

… a sense of ambition and tenacity that ensures future security for Other and family.

… with a protectiveness that is suffocating, and an emotionality that is childish in the extreme.

… with a need to mother or be mothered, or blaming Other, the World, the weather.

… by desperately clinging to Other in the hope that they will supply what *you* have been promising.

YOU OVEREMPHASIZE	SO CAN FEEL WEAK
(How you Lose Respect)	*(Admitting this brings Enlightenment)*

… your discomfort with hard cold reality by consistently avoiding your responsibilities.

… your concern for Other when really it is your fear of losing Other; using Other's fears to keep them where you want them.

… your softly-softly approach in order to avoid confrontation with Other or some uncomfortable matter.

… in the face of what you have been conditioned to believe you cannot cope with – but with Other's help you can.

… when afraid of being neglected or abandoned as you possibly were in the past.

… when you fail to remember or realize that there is always someone or something, if not Other, who cares about you.

WHEN ALONE …

… it is probably because you have retreated so far into your shell that Other has given up and gone. Put another way, your refusal to look at certain emotional issues, stemming from your childhood, has meant that Other has no choice but to leave you to your own devices and get on with their own life. When a child sulks, sooner or later its parents just leave it in its room. Your dilemma is a Catch 22 one, for you have to come out your shell to find a healthier and more enjoyable form of protection. Tell yourself that being vulnerable and naked for a bit is infinitely better than having only your fears for company. A Hermit Crab tends to become a caricature of itself – all that is seen is its shell and not the sensitive soul within.

If, however, you are perfectly comfortable as a Hermit Crab, then who am I to winkle you out?

SUN IN LEO

The Noble Heart • The Tyrannical Heart

ROLES and GOALS

The will to use generously your *sense of privilege* – without it descending into *pomposity*.
A life led in a spirit of *radiating light and warmth* – as opposed to merely holding *centre-stage*.
Father is seen or expressed as one who is *powerful and noble*, and/or *downright cruel*.

YOU GENERATE	BUT CAN OVERWHELM
(How you Gain Respect)	*(How you Alienate Other)*
… an aura of certainty that enables Other to become more confident in themselves and their own abilities.	… with a patronizing attitude that causes Other to rebel against you in a way that gets to your most vulnerable area: your pride.
… a positive and cheerful glow that gives the impression that you have life under control.	… by having those around you conform to what you see as your idea of correct living.
… an air of dignity as you bear life's difficulties without complaint.	… by hardening yourself to Other's sensitive spots as well as your own.

YOU OVEREMPHASIZE	SO CAN FEEL WEAK
(How you Lose Respect)	*(Admitting this brings Enlightenment)*
… your need for admiration in order to gain a sense of importance and specialness.	… in the face of what appears to be Other's lack of attention or affection.
… what you see as your strengths because you can equate weakness with being unlovable.	… especially when you are afraid that your all too human weakness has been spotted.
… your convictions and 'rules', fearing that you'll lose your grip if you are magnanimous enough to loosen it.	… when you are unceremoniously 'cut' or 'banished', as a result of Other having to give you the truth but, because of your pride, not tell you it.

WHEN ALONE …

… it is unmistakably because it is the only way that you can feel in command of your own life.
The trouble with being a King or Queen is that to have a consort means being without any special privileges or perks such as you have come to regard as your divine right. The bedchamber may be royal, but what goes on in it can be decidedly common. In other words, emotions make equals of us all – and this can prove too much for your sense of pride and exclusiveness to abide. And so either you have ironically bowed out for want of being able to step down from your throne and relate in a human-to-human way, or your consort has had no other choice but to leave you with only that throne for company.
Either way it is time to reflect and accept.

SUN IN VIRGO
The Helpful Heart • The Critical Heart

ROLES and GOALS

The will to use generously your *sense of precision* – without it devolving into *pedantry*.
A life led in a spirit of *service and modesty* – as opposed to one of *drudge or self-doubt*.
Father is seen or expressed as one who is *thoughtful and attentive*, and/or *too exacting or lax*.

YOU GENERATE
(How you Gain Respect)

… an aura of authenticity that acts as an example to Other that it is possible to improve their life and be true to themselves.

… a sense of industriousness that encourages Other to become more efficient at their life's tasks, as well as your showing them better techniques for doing so.

… an air of self-control or inner restraint.

BUT CAN OVERWHELM
(How you Alienate Other)

… with a pat or know-it-all attitude that invites Other to leave you with only your apparent self-righteousness for company.

… with a workaholic life-style that misses the point that true efficiency leaves time for rest and recreation.

… with an inhibited nature that smacks of being afraid of life beyond your idea of it.

YOU OVEREMPHASIZE
(How you Lose Respect)

… your need to be seen and heard to be right – which could be wrong in itself!

… the importance of the practical at the expense of the natural or to the detriment of emotional priorities.

… your insistence on purity and correctness in Other, while overlooking that rough edges and imperfections are a fact of life.

SO CAN FEEL WEAK
(Admitting this brings Enlightenment)

… when you have no answer, reason or solution for something – and when you have to allow Other to help themselves.

… when your efforts appear not to be producing an obvious 'result'.

… when Other reflects personally on you as not being the 'perfect person' that you like to think you are but obviously are not.

WHEN ALONE …

… it is hardly surprising because Virgo is, after all, the Sign of the Hermit. The reason behind such withdrawal will be a feeling that you or Other is not good enough. When deliberate, such a retreat would be for reasons of 'getting your act together' or to become more sure of yourself as an individual before letting anyone else too close. In the case of involuntary isolation, it could be for the same reasons – but you just don't know it. But it is just as likely to be because you have still not removed the fly from your own ointment. This means that you continue to have, or rather believe you have, a dimension to your being that is too delicate and private to share. If so, you will be alone until you accept that this is a judgment you have made upon yourself (or Other), in order to avoid making any real changes in yourself.

SUN IN LIBRA

The Graceful Heart • The Superficial Heart

ROLES and GOALS

The will to use generously your *sense of justice* – without it devolving into *indecision*.
A life led in a spirit of *radiating harmony and beauty* – as opposed to merely being *'nice'*.
Father is seen or expressed as one who is *fair and diplomatic*, and/or *sitting on the fence*.

YOU GENERATE	BUT CAN OVERWHELM
(How you Gain Respect)	*(How you Alienate Other)*
… an aura of pleasantness that gives Other the feeling of being worth something.	… with a gloss of niceness that is purely for effect, and is in great need of sincerity.
… an impression of social ease, and of knowing the right faces and places as well possibly.	… with your dependence on others (rather than Other) to maintain your own feeling of being of any social worth and desirability.
… an air of aesthetic awareness or social harmony, or display artistic ability.	… by treating everything and everyone but Other with grace and consideration.

YOU OVEREMPHASIZE	SO CAN FEEL WEAK
(How you Lose Respect)	*(Admitting this brings Enlightenment)*
… your looks and/or style rather than emotional commitment – which amounts to using superficial means for superficial ends.	… with respect to the value or attractiveness of your inner being; know that exposing it will strengthen it.
… your tactfulness and willingness to compromise to the point of becoming a nonentity.	… when having to risk being disliked or disapproved of by Other; be true to yourself then so eventually will Other.
… the 'nice' or glamorous side of life at the expense of being real or substantial.	… when your 'muck' is raked up (*see* Venous Blood Syndrome on page 7).

WHEN ALONE …

… it is most likely for one of two reasons. The first reason for being alone is that you are having to discover yourself as an independent individual rather than an 'Other to or for Other' – which is like being a two-dimensional being, a human mirror and nothing else. In order to do this you will have to bring to the surface what appears to be some quite anti-social feelings and ideas. But this is okay as long as you stick with it and fashion such crude ore into fine steel. The second reason could be that you hold the belief that you are too odd or unacceptable to be in a relationship. This is as maybe, but being locked into such an incestuous and subjective relationship with yourself would prevent you from noticing that everyone, including a potential Other, is 'weird' too and has something to hide that they want discovered or uncovered by and with love.

SUN IN SCORPIO
The Deep Heart • The Cruel Heart

ROLES and GOALS

The will to use wisely your *penetrating insight* – so not let it descend into *selfish manipulation*.
A life led in a spirit of *emotional authenticity* – as opposed to merely being *obsessive*.
Father is seen or expressed as one who is *powerful and uncompromising*, and/or *destructive*.

YOU GENERATE
(How you Gain Respect)

… an unmistakably sexual vibration that reaches Other on a level beyond their inhibitions or conscious resistance.

… a laser-like perception of life and Other that is irresistible and deeply healing.

… an aura of intimacy that enables Other to be more in touch with their real feelings.

BUT CAN OVERWHELM
(How you Alienate Other)

… through sapping Other of their psychic and/or physical energy in order to subjugate them for your own darkly selfish reasons.

… by hitting Other where it hurts in order to vainly appease your own resentfulness.

… with a compulsion to have Other feel as deeply painful as you feel.

YOU OVEREMPHASIZE
(How you Lose Respect)

…: a conviction that you are absolutely right concerning an issue about which you are obviously biased.

… your desire to have someone exactly where you want them, be it very close, at a distance, or out of your life completely.

… Other's weaknesses – as a smoke screen to hide your own. Secretiveness.

SO CAN FEEL WEAK
(Admitting this brings Enlightenment)

… when you are not 100 per cent sure of yourself over any issue, especially an emotional one – but this is a weakness in itself.

… because you cannot bear to be unsure of where someone stands with you, and so you often enforce this with a finality that you later come to regret.

… about chinks in your own armour.

WHEN ALONE …

… it is because you have broken a taboo that most people observe to keep at bay anything they cannot manage psychologically. Like the pariah, you are cast out beyond the city walls of so-called polite society. The Other who does this could be one person in particular, a community, or your own family. As you stew in your own juice, it is down to your own formidable depth of insight to determine whether you were right or wrong in committing whatever deed it was that had you cast out – or what that deed was and whether you actually committed it at all. Scorpio has the arguable advantage of doing things out of a sense of inner conviction rather than out of a need for external approval. More often than not, the answer is that you have broken a taboo that was a cover-up for some species of emotional insincerity. What you have to face up to in the extremes of your isolation is that the underground river of truth will emerge when it will.

SUN IN SAGITTARIUS

The Enthusiastic Heart • The Arrogant Heart

ROLES and GOALS

The will to use generously your *sense of vision* – without it degenerating into *high and mightiness*.
A life led in a spirit of *infinite opportunity* – as opposed to *promising the impossible*.
Father is seen or expressed as one who is *expansive,* but may also be *unavailable*.

YOU GENERATE	**BUT CAN OVERWHELM**
(How you Gain Respect)	*(How you Alienate Other)*
… a creed of positive thinking which can open up possibilities for Other that they hitherto had not noticed or entertained.	… with plans and theories that if embarked upon create great confusion and possibly great loss.
… a cosmopolitan air of sophistication that grasps concepts and styles with ease.	… with a conceit that is trendiness posing as original or informed thinking.
… a philosophical and learned atmosphere that exhorts Other to greater things.	… with a lofty-mindedness that has little personal meaning or emotional significance.

YOU OVEREMPHASIZE	**SO CAN FEEL WEAK**
(How you Lose Respect)	*(Admitting this brings Enlightenment)*
… any facet of your personality which you mistakenly believe is a good advertisement for yourself.	… when you cannot or do not live up to your own prospectus. Know that greatness is made up of many small things.
… a careless, outspoken and laid-back attitude which is really just a denial of your own doubts and sensitivity.	… when Other spots the 'small you', which is the part that paradoxically makes the 'big you' more convincing.
… your conviction that you know the truth, have the technology, designed the T-shirt.	… when you haven't a clue where to go or who to turn to; so ask – or advertise!

WHEN ALONE …

… you are probably travelling light, and so being on your own suits you fine. If not, you are heavily weighed down with a lack of someone to carry your own sense of inferiority or throw it back at you. In fact, being alone for you is expressly in aid of making it clear to you that you are not as self-contained and self-sustaining as you like to think you are. A case of 'How the mighty are fallen'. This image is, in your case, like that of a lame horse – it needs the human touch to sort it out. It is this all too human aspect of your being that you can be inclined to forget or overlook as you fix your attention on some far-flung concept or objective. We all have that helpless little boy or girl somewhere inside of us, whom we lose sight of at our peril. The smallest of stones can make that horse lame – so watch your step in future.

SUN IN CAPRICORN

The Dutiful Heart • The Calculating Heart

ROLES and GOALS

The will to use constructively your *sense of order* – without it *crystallizing into rigidity*.
A life led in a spirit of *obedience to responsibility* – as opposed to merely being a *workhorse*.
Father is seen or expressed as one who is *thorough and objective*, and/or *cold and absent*.

YOU GENERATE

(How you Gain Respect)

… an aura of worldliness that offers Other a means of becoming more aware and stronger with regard to material status.

… a sense of matters being under control, born of your practical attitude and tried and true values.

… an air of seriousness that bespeaks dependability and single-mindedness.

BUT CAN OVERWHELM

(How you Alienate Other)

… with the stress you place upon form and position, especially when you try to pretend otherwise.

… with your reluctance to entertain a concept or innovation (that threatens your present reality) long enough for it to become a new reality.

… with a heaviness born of a need to control.

YOU OVEREMPHASIZE

(How you Lose Respect)

… the importance of having a quantifiable result and a logical reason for everything.

… strictness and economy for fear of anything emerging that is wild, original, or at least, not of your own making.

… your need to be top dog, or underdog by way of compensation, because being so keeps Other where you want them.

SO CAN FEEL WEAK

(Admitting this brings Enlightenment)

… when you have not got a plan, schedule or explanation for everything, while Other has probably survived quite well without.

… because you feel mechanical and dull as a result of not dipping into the Unknown.

… having a partner who is apparently beneath you or above you, or not having a partner at all (there being no takers).

WHEN ALONE …

… it is often so even when there is an Other in your life. Capricorn likes to have the *trappings* of normality and success, and so will invariably have a partner and/or family, etc, but how you actually feel on the inside can be a very different matter. You have a relatively sombre interior (hence the sense of aloneness, whoever you are with), and this needs the light and warmth of a spirited and childlike personality to keep the melancholia at bay. Your dilemma is that this is precisely the kind of personality that you tend not to trust and try to control. In your book, such free spirits are loose cannons, even though they are fun at first or at a distance. And so you are inclined to banish the very 'prison visitor' you like to see the most. If you do not realize this pattern sooner rather than later, your shaft of sunlight will either go behind a cloud for good, or they'll find someone more appreciative. If you are actually alone, it will be for this very reason.

SUN IN AQUARIUS

The Open Heart • The Indifferent Heart

ROLES and GOALS

The will to use generously your *sense of impartiality* – without your becoming *impersonal*.
A life led in a spirit of *liberation and reform* – as opposed to being *aloof or anti-social*.
Father is seen or expressed as one who is *cool and friendly*, and/or *icy and remote*.

YOU GENERATE	BUT CAN OVERWHELM
(How you Gain Respect)	*(How you Alienate Other)*
… a regard for Other's uniqueness and quirks of personality, thereby making them feel special.	… with your oddness, or by way of compensation, with your being a nonentity.
… an electric and unusual atmosphere that is a constant source of surprise.	… with an unpredictability that is born of your refusal to accept the limitations that make possible a measure of stability.
… an air of gentle detachment that does not judge Other, giving them space to be free.	… by a failure to tune into where Other is at emotionally.

YOU OVEREMPHASIZE	SO CAN FEEL WEAK
(How you Lose Respect)	*(Admitting this brings Enlightenment)*
… your idea that Other and the world in general should fit some kind of social or scientific theory.	… when having to live in the real world of material/emotional things, or even within your own physical body.
… an insistence that you be treated in some special way, and that you be unconditionally accepted for all your foibles.	… when you realize that this imperfect world will not offer you very much until you offer up your own imperfections.
… a set of values that often finds Other wanting, but always exonerates yourself.	… when nobody accepts or is impressed by your version of how things ought to be.

WHEN ALONE …

… it is because you have allowed detachment and eccentricity to run rife and develop like a virus until Other can no longer be bothered with trying to relate to the absurdly non-negotiable front you present. More than any other Sign, you are capable of making being alone into an art form. The trouble is that this might not amount to quite what you originally had in mind. Beneath all of your rationalizations of you-versus-the-world lies a deep fear of being seen to be just another human being, complete with emotionally tacky bits. But the paradox here is they are partly what make anyone special! And the more we look at and allow others to see our emotional interiors, the more we grow and develop as people, rather than remaining frozen at some icy altitude of emotional immunity. A failure to evolve and mature in this way can mean that Other changes but you do not – leaving you apparently outcast. You must track back to when in your life you cut out emotionally in the first place – and why, for it holds the key to how you got to be this way.

SUN IN PISCES

The Compassionate Heart • The Confused Heart

ROLES and GOALS

The will to use wisely your *great sensitivity* – without it collapsing into *over-susceptibility*.
A life led in a spirit of *inspiration and compassion* – as opposed to being or falling for *a victim*.
Father is seen or expressed as one who is *gentle and unassuming*, and/or *weak and unreal*.

YOU GENERATE		**BUT CAN OVERWHELM**
(How you Gain Respect)		*(How you Alienate Other)*

… an aura of emotional understanding that transcends Other's defences and reaches their heart.

… an emanation of peace and wistful charm that enchants, soothes and heals Other.

… an air of mystery and imagination that relieves Other from the mundanities of life.

… with a vulnerability or seductability that becomes virtually impossible to relate to or deal with; doormats get trodden on.

… with good intentions whose intensity conveys the bad feelings concealed within.

… with vague and deluded thinking that is created by your fear of facing the music.

YOU OVEREMPHASIZE		**SO CAN FEEL WEAK**
(How you Lose Respect)		*(Admitting this brings Enlightenment)*

… your openness to the feelings within and around you because you do not know what else to do with them.

… a desire to seek oblivion in drugs, alcohol, etc, rather than seeking honestly/spiritually.

… your passionate conviction that your impressions are the right ones – even when you find them unhelpful or contradictory.

… in the face of what appears to be Other's lack of comprehension of how you feel; so, at all costs, express those feelings better.

… when tempted by an easy way out, rather than confronting and identifying your inner fears – and then surrendering them.

… when having to admit that you are lost and do not know the way or the answer.

WHEN ALONE …

… it is very likely the only way that you can seal yourself off from the pain and misunderstanding that you feel when having to be in the world of people and things, or Other. Rather than simply being alone in the 'lonely' sense of the word, you could retreat into your own space where you can be alone and at one with the inner voice, your muse, guardian angel, or whatever comprises your inner reality – something which you can only tune into if you allow it to surface by accepting and letting go of the weaker or darker elements of your interior. Failing this or a similar course of action (or rather non-action), you could find yourself in a netherworld where you are neither in contact with Other or your inner being – aloneness indeed.
But all roads lead to Rome, meaning that aloneness, be it through retreat or escape, ultimately transports you to a place of peace or redemption – or at least, to a glimpse of some higher reason or meaning for the human condition, particularly your own.

161

THE MOON

IMPORTANT TIPS

- Moon Signs, when it comes right down to it, determine more than anything else the success or failure of our ability to relate positively and effectively. This is because the Moon represents the baggage of unmet emotional needs and childhood hurts that can so easily sabotage a relationship – without even knowing that that is what is happening until it is too late. So through studying your Moon Sign you may learn to respond positively and control those negative reactions that can escalate into terminal fallings-out. You can also learn what Other's emotional agenda is and, through understanding it and treating it with tenderness, create in them a far more secure sense of themselves and of being with you.

- Seeing that the Moon has so much to do with Mother, occasionally it may be relevant, and extraordinarily enlightening, to read 'Other(s)' as meaning Mother – your own, that is. If you are inclined to believe that your Soul chooses your parents, the results of doing this can be even more revealing.

MOON IN ARIES
The Brave Soul • The Impatient Soul

NATURE and NURTURE

The need to be *emotionally independent* – without being *emotionally insensitive*.
The instinct to *confront Other and break new ground* – but to avoid prolonged *strife*.
Mother is seen or expressed as one who is *strong and independent*, and/or *insular and inflexible*.

YOU NATURALLY RESPOND
(How you Create Comfort)

… towards Other with directness and childlike simplicity, thereby precipitating and clarifying emotional situations.

… spontaneously to complex or pressuresome predicaments in order to resolve them.

… to danger by pushing on through it.

BUT YOUR INNER CHILD REACTS
(How you Antagonize Other)

… with brief but frightening displays of temper when frustrated by what seem to be Other's blocking or evading tactics.

… impulsively to situations that really require some waiting and consideration of Other.

… to conflicts in a manner that actually exacerbates them.

YOU GRAVITATE TOWARDS
(How you are Unconsciously Drawn)

… Others who need to be led out of their apathy or victimhood.

… Others who try to tame, control or 'civilize' you, forcing you to assert and defend your own emotional space.

… wild, argumentative Others who reflect your own, possibly unconscious, need to fight for your right to be your own person.

BUT CAN GET CAUGHT UP IN
(How you Grow Emotionally)

… relationships with Others who, having been shown their teeth, bite you first.

… relationships where you are compromised and torn by the need to be emotionally recognized (having not been as a child).

… battles between 'worthy opponents' where the winners are those who define and defend their own and Others' 'soul-fields'.

WHEN ALONE …

… it is rather as if you are stuck or cast out into the wilderness, rather like an emotional scout behind the 'enemy's lines' (still in Other's emotional range but without the security of them being on your side). This means that your instinctual search for your own 'soul-field' – that is, where you have inner independence – has taken you to a place where by necessity you must have only yourself for company. How else could you win such a prize? Looked at from Other's standpoint – something which you may also have to learn in the process of determining and establishing your own – your apparent self-centredness has probably antagonized them to the point of leaving or neglecting you. Or their subsequent possessiveness has made you leave or distance yourself from them. If you have been alone like this for quite some time – or have even always been so – then that search for inner independence must have reached critical status.
Being a loner tends to go with the territory, ie your own and nobody else's territory,
for that is what you are after.

MOON IN TAURUS

The Steady Soul • The Stubborn Soul

NATURE and NURTURE

The need to be *physically satisfied*, but this may give rise to your being *psychologically unaware*.
The instinct to find *material security* – which could necessitate enduring *emotional limitations*.
Mother is seen or expressed as one who is a *provider*, but could also be a *(beast of) burden*.

YOU NATURALLY RESPOND

(How you Create Comfort)

… towards Other with a sense of emotional permanence and stability.

… in a physical, material or sensuous manner, providing Other with the necessary creature comforts.

… in a very real, substantial way, giving value for value.

BUT YOUR INNER CHILD REACTS

(How you Antagonize Other)

… with a great resistance to any change that might threaten, even when such changes are in aid of (re-)establishing security.

… by withholding or overlooking emotional and intangible favours.

… by wanting to possess Other as if they were personal property.

YOU GRAVITATE TOWARDS

(How you are Unconsciously Drawn)

… relationships that are based upon material stability and physical gratification, rather than, say, spiritual growth.

… the pleasures of the flesh, or Others who spice up your life, by way of compensation.

… Others who are in great need of material support or physical affection or attention.

BUT CAN GET CAUGHT UP IN

(How you Grow Emotionally)

… relationships where Other is more dependent upon what you have than what you are.

… relationships where stagnation and meaninglessness begin to reign, forcing you to review your motivations, or to stray.

… being heavily depended upon.

WHEN ALONE …

… or simply being made to feel alone, it will be down to one factor – worth. Taurus Moon emphasizes the importance of material stability and of relationships having a permanence to them. This is all very well, but 'man does not live by bread alone', meaning that what is also needed to keep a relationship alive are more intangible qualities like mutual creative involvement (as opposed to child-rearing), personal growth and change, or romance (whatever that might mean to you). And so there can come a time when the absence of one or more such qualities in your relationship starts to make the relationship 'bottom-heavy' in that it has all the 'things and trappings' but no zing or meaning to it. It just rumbles along, very slowly, and eventually comes to a halt. If you have not found a suitable Other at all, it will be because such overly basic values have prevented this from happening. Alternatively, you may lack a sense of self-worth and therefore not attract an Other. But it would still come down to assessing yourself merely by material values.

MOON IN GEMINI

The Friendly Soul • The Flippant Soul

NATURE and NURTURE

The need to be *in communication* with Other – but without resorting to *rationalizing emotions*.
The instinct to *acquire knowledge* – but to avoid *overlooking feelings*.
Mother is seen or expressed as one who is *quick and light-hearted*, and/or *shallow and cynical*.

YOU NATURALLY RESPOND	**BUT YOUR INNER CHILD REACTS**
(How you Create Comfort)	*(How you Antagonize Other)*
… with a carefree lightness that gives Other the impression of your being fun, interesting, and easy to be with.	… by skipping over or trivializing deep or difficult feelings that you or Other might be experiencing or presenting.
… to Other's problems and questions with a ready wit and an informed mind.	… with clever quips or fast and easy remedies that are ultimately ineffectual.
… with bright ideas and alternatives that refresh and stimulate Other.	… in a contrary way that disputes or twists much of what Other thinks or says.

YOU GRAVITATE TOWARDS	**BUT CAN GET CAUGHT UP IN**
(How you are Unconsciously Drawn)	*(How you Grow Emotionally)*
… Others who are emotionally uncomplicated and feel no need to plumb the depths of the soul.	…relationships which lack the 'X factor' or the opportunity to reach the part you find, through dissatisfaction, you want reached.
… Others who (also) appear to be flighty, naughty and hard to pin down.	… 'curiosity killed the cat' situations where you get in over your head and so have to become more emotionally earnest.
… Others who are mentally stimulating and 'in the know'.	… all head and no heart situations.

WHEN ALONE …

… it is more than likely because you find it hard to commit to a relationship deeply enough for it to be sustained, and you have flitted on to another flower, or are in the process of doing so. Having said this though, it is quite unusual for Moon in Gemini to be on its own because you are so adept at making new contacts, friends and lovers – as well as keeping things interesting. However, if you are alone, or caught between two Others, as it were, or if you are feeling alone within a relationship, it will be because of that reluctance to commit. Consequently, Other could give up on you for sitting on the fence too long, or no Other would be forthcoming at all because you are putting out this 'non-committal vibe'. Behind your fears of commitment is a predisposition to avoid confronting what is called the 'dark twin' – that is, the side to your personality that you don't want anyone to know about because you believe it to be unacceptable. But this is possibly down to your mother not recognizing this facet of your personality. So it is not really 'bad', but just made to feel that way through not being acknowledged when you were little.

MOON IN CANCER

The Caring Soul • The Clinging Soul

NATURE and NURTURE

The need to be *safe and secure* with Other – but this could become *dependent and suffocating*.
The instinct to make *home and family* – but there can be a *restrictive resistance to the unknown*.
Mother is seen or expressed as being *very maternal*, but could be *emotionally manipulative*.

YOU NATURALLY RESPOND

(How you Create Comfort)

… towards Other with a strong urge to make them feel they belong and are cared about.

… to Other's emotional situations with great sympathy and support.

… in a hospitable and congenial manner that puts Other at their ease.

BUT YOUR INNER CHILD REACTS

(How you Antagonize Other)

… with hurt and sulks if Other should not appreciate your subjective idea of what an emotional relationship should be like.

… by swamping Other with the attention that *you* need rather than the space *they* need.

… in a cloying and overly sentimental fashion in an attempt not to feel threatened.

YOU GRAVITATE TOWARDS

(How you are Unconsciously Drawn)

… Others who need mothering or supporting in an emotional way and/or who tie you to the home.

… Others who act as a mother figure to you in that they look after you instinctively.

… romantically minded Others who seem to be one or more of your dreams come true.

BUT CAN GET CAUGHT UP IN

(How you Grow Emotionally)

… relationships which lean on you with little thanks, recognition or return, thus forcing you to be more self-motivated or selfless.

… being overly dependent on Other who eventually wants their own space, and so then rebels.

… situations where you have mistakenly put all your eggs in one basket, so that you have to learn to cut your losses.

WHEN ALONE …

… it is usually a highly unpleasant experience for you, and so therefore something which you try to avoid at all costs. This is because for you life means always having someone close to you, be it a whole family or one Other in particular. You simply do not like being alone, and can often limit or undersell yourself because of such a need to belong. Being alone is rather like being a little bird who has been tossed out its nest by a cuckoo. But should this highly unwelcome situation come upon you, it will be because your self-diminishing neediness has reached a critical point where those needs must be looked at for what they are, and why they have come to rule your life so much. In 99.99 per cent of cases it will be something to do with your mother. She either gave you too much or not nearly enough – and so you would have to find a way of breaking those ties and being more, but not too, emotionally self-sufficient.

MOON IN LEO
The Noble Soul • The Vain Soul

NATURE and NURTURE

The need to *live in style* with Other – but this could mean being *greedy for ease and luxury*.
The instinct to *win admiration* – but without meriting this you'd be *always seeking attention*.
Mother is seen or expressed as one who is *unconditionally generous*, and/or *spoils the child*.

YOU NATURALLY RESPOND	**BUT YOUR INNER CHILD REACTS**
(How you Create Comfort)	*(How you Antagonize Other)*
… towards Other by making them feel very special, the 'only one'.	… with sulks and tantrums when Other does not find you beyond criticism.
… to children and party situations with playfulness and enthusiasm.	… with indignation and melodrama when things are not going your way.
… to Other or others generally in a warm, dignified and loyal fashion.	… by taking it very personally when Other is indifferent for reasons that possibly have nothing to do with you.

YOU GRAVITATE TOWARDS	**BUT CAN GET CAUGHT UP IN**
(How you are Unconsciously Drawn)	*(How you Grow Emotionally)*
… Others who appear to have a style or wherewithal that is above average.	… relationships which demand more of you as a person on all levels – emotional, physical, mental and spiritual.
… exciting, dramatic Others – especially when you are the focus of their attention.	… childish, jealousy-inducing scenarios that you must rise above or be sunk very low.
… Others who want to go up in the world and so are impressed by your classy style, and you cannot resist such admiration.	… relationships that bring you down to a more real, unglamorous, emotional level.

WHEN ALONE …

… you are like a banished king or queen. What could be wrong? Is no one good enough? How wronged you feel! At some point, given long enough, you may get round to asking yourself where *you* are going wrong. If so, this would be a highly important point in your emotional development. This would especially apply if you had been alone for quite some time, or have never been properly involved at all. If this is the case, it is most probably because you sense, possibly unconsciously, that you would have to get a lot more realistic on an emotional level than the romantic idea you have of love and relationship at present. If, however, you have recently separated, it is very likely that there were warning signs of trouble some time ago, but your ego refused to see or acknowledge them. In any event, you probably feel cheated and forsaken. But if you wish to avoid a similar scenario, then you must review your part in all this. This will have something to do with your being very generous to Other in some way, hence the forsaken feeling. But ask yourself what you were after in return, and was it realistic. If it was nothing, then why the bitterness?

MOON IN VIRGO
The Helpful Soul • The Critical Soul

NATURE and NURTURE

The need to be *clear* with and about Other – but this could make the relationship rather *sterile*.
The instinct for *establishing emotional order* – but this could amount to *denied feelings*.
Mother is seen or expressed as one who is *clean and efficient,* and/or *sour and restrictive*.

YOU NATURALLY RESPOND
(How you Create Comfort)

… towards Other with helpfulness and consideration, with a view to healing their ills and solving their problems.

… in a conscientious and attentive fashion, being of great practical value to Other.

… in a manner that is mindful of pure and correct behaviour.

BUT YOUR INNER CHILD REACTS
(How you Antagonize Other)

… in a sniffy and carping manner when Other finds your 'help' is more about your own neurotic ends than their welfare.

… by threatening to withdraw the input with which you have made yourself indispensable.

… with aversion or priggishness to anything Other does that is unfamiliar to you.

YOU GRAVITATE TOWARDS
(How you are Unconsciously Drawn)

… Others who are in some sort of fix and who could obviously benefit from your ministrations.

… messy or unhygienic scenes, or conversely, meticulously ordered ones.

… relationships where you can operate in a modest fashion or background capacity.

BUT CAN GET CAUGHT UP IN
(How you Grow Emotionally)

… relationships which become increasingly chaotic, forcing you to be more tolerant or to know where and how to draw the line.

… situations where you need to do all the tidying – or learn to be less tidy.

… relationships where Other takes you for granted, hopefully forcing you to express your deepest darkest feelings.

WHEN ALONE …

… it is because Other has ultimately been unable to meet your exacting requirements of them, or you have found yourself not good enough for Other, using the same exacting criteria. Either way, it could be time to change your criteria! But as is always the case with the Moon, there are deeply ingrained habits and maternal conditioning behind such requirements. So you are alone expressly in order to have a good look at yourself, sort your wheat from your chaff, but not be so discriminating as to put yourself permanently out of the running – or for that matter, to give up on yourself and go downhill with self-neglect by way of over-compensation. However, it has to be said that, as Virgo is the Sign of the Hermit, you are rather good at being all on your own – it sort of suits you. But be careful because, unlike the anchorites of old who would be avoiding the darkness of the Dark Ages they lived in, you would probably just be making a good job of avoiding your own inner darkness. Bring this into the light of consciousness, and stop judging.

MOON IN LIBRA

The Graceful Soul • The Superficial Soul

NATURE and NURTURE

The need to *have a partner* – but this could incline you sometimes to *not being yourself*.
The instinct to *be aesthetic and agreeable* – but could come across as *affected or insincere*.
Mother is seen or expressed as one who is *pleasant and peaceable*, and/or *capricious or unstable*.

YOU NATURALLY RESPOND	**BUT YOUR INNER CHILD REACTS**
(How you Create Comfort)	*(How you Antagonize Other)*
… towards Other with politeness and pleasantries, creating immediate harmony as you do so.	… to more honest but blunt displays from Other with hurt or outraged feelings.
… to conflict by trying to appease both sides, finding areas of common interest.	… by sitting on the fence when discomforted by being caught between two differing people, opinions or values.
… agreeably to artistic or aesthetically pleasing situations and Others.	… with disgust and ineffectuality in the face of ugliness or discord (because it reminds you unconsciously of your own).

YOU GRAVITATE TOWARDS	**BUT CAN GET CAUGHT UP IN**
(How you are Unconsciously Drawn)	*(How you Grow Emotionally)*
… Others who are equally observant of social rules, and are not too disposed to airing dirty laundry.	… relationships which go from bad to worse for want of one or both of you having a hard look at what is wrong in the first place.
… Others who respond to your flirtatious charms with a suggestion of excitement and even danger.	… relationships where you are out of your depth and (in danger of) getting your fingers burnt.
… anyone who appears to have (more) style and charisma (than Other).	… having, or not being able, to say no or make a decisive break with Other.

WHEN ALONE …

… it is probably not for long, if it ever happens at all. More than any other Moon Sign you need to have a partner, and so you make sure you do. So when you are alone for any duration it can feel lonely indeed. However, we often have to come to terms with our weaknesses – and a fear of being alone for long is one of yours. If you look back on your life so far, there has probably been very little time, compared with others, when you have been without a partner of some sort – and no gaps at all between some of them. Being alone for you equals not being attractive enough to get or have Other, which, in your emotional book, amounts to acute insecurity and worthlessness. So when and if you are alone for an extended period, it is because you really are having to learn some or all of the lessons outlined above.
Generally, this amounts to learning to be loved for what you are
as opposed to what you like to think you are.

MOON IN SCORPIO

The Deep Soul • The Paranoid Soul

NATURE and NURTURE

The need to be *intimately involved* with Other – inextricably linked to a *fear of abandonment*.
The instinct to *seek out the hidden* in Other – but equally a *dread of being exposed*.
Mother is seen or expressed as one who is *close and powerful*, and/or *denying and manipulative*.

YOU NATURALLY RESPOND

(How you Create Comfort)

… in a positive manner towards Other when you intuitively know them to be emotionally genuine.

… with passion and single-mindeness towards an Other who is attractive to you.

… quite irresistibly to an Other with a powerful personality.

BUT YOUR INNER CHILD REACTS

(How you Antagonize Other)

… by closing down completely at the first sign of emotional weakness in Other, which is a sign of emotional weakness in itself.

… with a fear of betrayal almost as soon as you are initially attracted to Other.

… when it suspects that the power it sees in Other could control you – and so the control games begin.

YOU GRAVITATE TOWARDS

(How you are Unconsciously Drawn)

… an Other who is in need of being emotionally transformed or taken in hand.

… situations where you have to prove your emotional tenacity and resilience.

… triangles of jealousy and other negative emotions.

BUT CAN GET CAUGHT UP IN

(How you Grow Emotionally)

… relationships with Others who turn out to be every bit as emotionally intense as you thought you were emotionally in command.

… complex or deeply distressing experiences that stand to purge and deepen your emotional make-up.

… having to establish once and for all where you stand emotionally.

WHEN ALONE …

… it is because it is simply the most effective state to be in for confronting you with your deepest and most central fear – abandonment and betrayal. Being alone is more often than not a testament to the self-fulfilling prophecy that you created. This is because you have a belief conditioned into you that sooner or later whoever you are with will leave you in the lurch or do the dirty on you in some way.
The ghastly truth, however, is that either you did not commit deeply and completely enough and so Other gives up out of sheer exhaustion, or you obsessively possessed Other under the guise of 'love', leaving them having to escape in order to breathe. If you are alone and you disagree with the above reasons, or they simply do not make sense to you, then it has to mean that you are in denial of your own emotional nature and make what is difficult to relate to even more so. Either that, or you have decided to sit this one out.

MOON IN SAGITTARIUS
The Gypsy Soul • The Naïve Soul

NATURE and NURTURE

The need to be *having fun* with Other – but this could find you being *emotionally indiscreet*.
The instinct to find a *positive direction* – but sometimes this could amount to *restlessness*.
Mother is seen or expressed as being *free and philosophical*, and/or *indulgent or sanctimonious*.

YOU NATURALLY RESPOND	BUT YOUR INNER CHILD REACTS
(How you Create Comfort)	*(How you Antagonize Other)*

… towards Other with great enthusiasm, giving Other a boost in the process.	… with offhandedness or dismissiveness when Other does not want to play your game.
… to Other in a manner that expects freedom of movement as well as allowing it.	… irresponsibly and outrageously when in any way restricted or obligated.
… in an innocent and trusting manner that brings out the best in Other.	… gullibly or opportunistically to any offer that appears to be better than what you currently have.

YOU GRAVITATE TOWARDS	BUT CAN GET CAUGHT UP IN
(How you are Unconsciously Drawn)	*(How you Grow Emotionally)*

… expansive, cosmopolitan Others where travel, abundance and sophistication are the style.	… relationships which promise far more than they deliver, showing you that indulgence or a want of ease makes for being a poor judge.
… Others who are outgoing and exciting, often with strong opinions and beliefs.	… situations that have no meaning and drive you to despair until you discover what you believe in for yourself.
… Others who are easy-going and fun to be with.	… a relationship with an unstable Other.

WHEN ALONE …

… it is most likely because you or Other have found your relationship too confining, or conversely too open-ended to feel secure in – and so something has to give. But because of this inclination of yours to want both security and freedom within a relationship, it is just as likely that you find yourself stuck with Other for reason of needing the one (security) but not enjoying it at all for reason of not getting the other (freedom) – that is, you are alone but with someone. The reason behind all this – if you have not already spotted it – is that you have been seeking a set of requirements in a partner that are contradictory at best or hypocritical at worst. In other words, don't expect or promise security when there is still some roaming to do on either of your parts. If you really are, or have been left, alone, then it is because you have to look for and find a more philosophical approach to relationship and/or a more spiritual reason for being. Until you do, you will be naïvely expecting Other to be more understanding than is presently possible for them.

MOON IN CAPRICORN

The Reliable Soul • The Deprived Soul

NATURE and NURTURE

The need to be *needed* by Other – but this could necessitate ongoing feelings of *rejection*.
The instinct to be *practically useful* – but this can be to compensate for a sense of *inadequacy*.
Mother is seen or expressed as being *serious and hard-working*, and/or *joyless and suppressive*.

YOU NATURALLY RESPOND	BUT YOUR INNER CHILD REACTS
(How you Create Comfort)	*(How you Antagonize Other)*
… towards Other with great caution but are very committed once decided.	… to opportunities for emotional experience with severe distrust (for fear of hurt).
… to Other's difficulties in an objective fashion and get down to sorting them.	… to Other in a reserved businesslike manner when sentiment and sympathy are needed.
…to Other with surprising passion when trust is won and familiarity established.	… by going very cold or merely dutiful at any sign of Other's interest waning.

YOU GRAVITATE TOWARDS	BUT CAN GET CAUGHT UP IN
(How you are Unconsciously Drawn)	*(How you Grow Emotionally)*
… Others who are professional or worldly, and rather conservative in at least one way.	… relationships with Others who withhold something, mirroring a childhood pattern of yours.
… Others who lend some warmth to your often rather chilly inner state.	… feeling dull and lacking in spirit and spontaneity in comparison to Other, while overlooking your priceless reliability.
… relationships where you can maintain some emotional control thereby establishing a stability and order which assist Other.	… boring or dead-end relationships because you never allow in a new or random element that could spice things up.

WHEN ALONE …

… it is either because it is the best or only way that you have found to control your emotional life, or you have become isolated within a relationship – which certainly makes you feel alone. But it is that need to control and not let emotions take their course which is behind both of these possibilities. And behind this is the likelihood that as a child you were never recognized as a feeling being – as a child in fact. Being left to become an adult too soon made you feel alone, but you accepted it at the time. Now, when you are alone again, it is to tell yourself not to be emotionally short-changed any more. Now you must dispel that cloud that hangs around inside of you, come out of the shadow it casts, and be a second-class emotional citizen no more. You'll probably always be one of life's survivors and supporters, but that does not mean to say that you have practically to prove that you are worth something in order to be loved and accepted.
Such is a lie and a sin against human feelings and the child within, and must be resisted at all costs as you claim your soul's due. Yes, you have a soul that must be recognized and appreciated for what it is.

MOON IN AQUARIUS

The Humanitarian Soul • The Detached Soul

NATURE and NURTURE

The need to be *your own person* with Other – which at times finds you *feeling on your own*.
The instinct to *emotionally experiment* – but Other could find you *emotionally disrespectful*.
Mother is seen or expressed as one who is *open and friendly*, and/or *remote and unmaternal*.

YOU NATURALLY RESPOND
(How you Create Comfort)

… towards Other by initially relating on a friendly, mental level while maintaining your emotional distance.

… to Other by using your natural psychological awareness to give them plenty of space to express themselves as they like.

… to Other with great tolerance and intuitive understanding.

BUT YOUR INNER CHILD REACTS
(How you Antagonize Other)

… by being unavailable should it detect the slightest sign of being needed by Other more than your inner child ever felt needed or loved.

… by not really responding at all – just hedging your bets as your mind plays with unreal ideas and infinite possibilities.

… by relating with your head rather than your heart or gut, thereby giving Other a false impression of yourself and your intentions.

YOU GRAVITATE TOWARDS
(How you are Unconsciously Drawn)

… relationships that first appear to put a minimum of pressure upon you to deliver emotionally.

… an unusual relationship set-up that appeals because its uniqueness constantly stimulates you and Other.

… any Other who excites you emotionally for reasons you cannot figure.

BUT CAN GET CAUGHT UP IN
(How you Grow Emotionally)

… relationship with an Other who fails to recognize your true emotional nature or needs – forcing you to recognize them yourself.

… relationships that are unpredictable and therefore feel insecure, or are boring because they're safe.

… situations that shock you into cutting out emotionally at critical times. Why?

WHEN ALONE …

… it is because you have made yourself unavailable – or more to the point, too unavailable. This probably harks back to some emotional break or trauma in childhood, and so you are quite inclined to continue to keep your emotional distance. But until you hop back into how you are really feeling – rather than how you think you are supposed to be feeling – you can perennially find yourself cut off from anyone who might really know you or get to know you. You are disposed to keeping yourself as an emotional cipher in order to prevent getting intimate enough to jog your memory back to that time in your early life when you got emotionally detached. But your unconscious keeps playing the same old records until you hear what they're saying, whether you are with someone or all alone.
Either way, you have to wake up to how you truly feel.

MOON IN PISCES
The Sensitive Soul • The Evasive Soul

NATURE and NURTURE

The need to be *selflessly involved* with Other – but this could necessitate acute *suffering*.
The instinct to *go with the flow* – but if there is too much pain you may crave *escape*.
Mother is seen or expressed as one who is willing to make *sacrifices*, but could play the *martyr*.

YOU NATURALLY RESPOND	BUT YOUR INNER CHILD REACTS
(How you Create Comfort)	*(How you Antagonize Other)*

(How you Create Comfort) | *(How you Antagonize Other)*

… towards Other with great sensitivity and empathy, thus finding a place in Other's heart and what goes on in Other's mind.

… to difficult and painful experiences in the spirit of redemption, for you know that suffering ultimately heals.

… to Other's longings, for they resonate with your own.

… with intense sulks, despair or evasion when it is discovered that your feelings are not understood at all. Therefore you must seek to understand/express them better yourself.

… with a refusal to face the hard facts of the situation.

… when it finds that Other's fantasy turned out to be your nightmare.

YOU GRAVITATE TOWARDS **BUT CAN GET CAUGHT UP IN**

(How you are Unconsciously Drawn) | *(How you Grow Emotionally)*

… Others who are weak or wounded, sensitive or poetic, and therefore seem in need of your selfless assistance.

… Others who initially promise to be your saviour and the answer to your dreams.

… Others who are sensitive and subtle, but possibly misfits or escapists – or mad.

… relationships which suck you dry, teaching you to be more discerning and self-preserving in future.

… trying desperately to maintain the illusion of how you initially thought Other and the relationship *ought* to be.

… sorting out reality from fantasy.

WHEN ALONE …

… it is most probably because you simply cannot take the risk of being hurt any more. However, if you are still hooked on Other and cannot seem to get free of them, your time alone would be best used building up a stronger sense of who you are as a separate individual, knowing where you begin and Other ends. This is a prime necessity for you, because without this strong sense of self, that 'melting into one' type of relationship that you crave can merely turn into an identity crisis (again). This is what that hurt actually stems from – getting addicted to Other as a substitute for something that should be your very own. And so some form of creative pursuit or spiritual quest is necessary to achieve this important objective of making one thing of yourself – for you certainly won't make one of yourself and Other until you have done so.

MERCURY

IMPORTANT TIPS

●   Note that each Mercury Profile only takes up half a page. This does not mean to say that they are only half as significant as the rest – how we *perceive and communicate* is well-known to be enormously important in relating. But Mercury is in many ways less complex than the other Planets because it does not have an emotional dimension to it. All the same, taking on board how you do and do not communicate can make the world of a difference – not because you have to change how you act or are or feel, but simply by looking at it the right way. You are then able to communicate what you are, think and feel, and consequently be better understood, as well as understanding what Other may be trying to get at.

MERCURY IN ARIES
The Forceful Mind • The Pushy Mind

PERCEPTION and COMMUNICATION

YOU SEE LIFE IN TERMS OF

(How you Communicate)

… thoughts and feelings as things to be acted upon. So you are not inclined to let issues with Other fester, and will broach them in a forthright and courageous way.

… there being a ready answer to problems as long as you grasp the nettle.

… confrontation being stimulating and emotionally relieving and revealing.

BUT TEND NOT TO SEE

(How you Fail to Communicate)

… that some issues concerning Other will only work out through time, and that trying to force a resolution only aggravates Other and makes matters worse.

… that you're interested only in getting what you want, and so the 'war' persists.

… the importance of what Other has to say or is trying to say.

MERCURY IN TAURUS
The Steady Mind • The Stubborn Mind

PERCEPTION and COMMUNICATION

YOU SEE LIFE IN TERMS OF

(How you Communicate)

… having to be practical and make sense, and so you approach matters concerning Other equipped with the ability to create and maintain material or physical stability.

… patiently and consistently considering what you see as all the relevant factors until a realistic and enduring solution is reached.

… nothing worth getting too upset by.

BUT TEND NOT TO SEE

(How you Fail to Communicate)

… deep emotional issues that require a more psychologically or spiritually informed awareness, giving rise to Other feeling blocked or misunderstood.

… that some issues need dealing with spontaneously or swiftly, otherwise matters are in danger of deteriorating.

… what is bothering Other.

Mercury is to a Relationship like what the Nervous System is to your Body

MERCURY IN GEMINI
The Clever Mind • The Crafty Mind

PERCEPTION and COMMUNICATION

YOU SEE LIFE IN TERMS OF	BUT TEND NOT TO SEE
(How you Communicate)	*(How you Fail to Communicate)*

… contrasts such as interesting or boring, bright or dull, relevant or inapplicable – and you do so quickly. And so you get to the point, or dismiss it, easily and swiftly.

… being only as good as what is mentally assimilated, then imparted to or shared with Other – you communicate with ease and enthusiasm, in fact.

… subtle or grey areas, issues that you have rationalized as insignificant, but really it is because they are the ones that you cannot deal with emotionally, and which inevitably give rise to difficulties with Other that your quick mind cannot simply cast aside.

… Other's point because it does not form part of the reality that interests you.

MERCURY IN CANCER
The Sympathetic Mind • The Moody Mind

PERCEPTION and COMMUNICATION

YOU SEE LIFE IN TERMS OF	BUT TEND NOT TO SEE
(How you Communicate)	*(How you Fail to Communicate)*

… comfortable and uncomfortable situations and ideas, and so you discuss matters with a view to creating a feeling of safety and avoiding confrontation. Other feels reassured by this, and so consequently is receptive to your point of view.

… being receptive to Other and thereby developing mutual understanding.

… what you do not want to see because certain issues remind you of feelings of insecurity that have more to do with the past (childhood) than the present. As Other tries to push their point home, disagreement and argument ensue, which is ironic, seeing that unpleasantness was what you were trying to avoid in the first place.

Mercury is to a Relationship like what the Nervous System is to your Body

MERCURY IN LEO
The Creative Mind • The Vain Mind

PERCEPTION and COMMUNICATION

 **YOU SEE LIFE IN TERMS OF**

(How you Communicate)

… having a strong, informed opinion that enables you to plan ahead and in a big way. And so Other is impressed and reassured by what you have to say.

… being respected for what you think, say and do, and giving due respect to Other for the same – so mutual respect is important for listening and being listened to.

BUT TEND NOT TO SEE

(How you Fail to Communicate)

… the finer but important details that are Other's concern, which when taken for granted could be used against you.

… the point that Other is making unless it flatters your ego. This can include the objective facts of a critical situation which you could choose to ignore at your peril.

MERCURY IN VIRGO
The Analytical Mind • The Worrisome Mind

PERCEPTION and COMMUNICATION

 YOU SEE LIFE IN TERMS OF

(How you Communicate)

… being right or wrong, and so you take great pains to ensure that you are in possession of the facts and can be trusted as a straight talker with an intelligent mind.

… being accurate and precise, so you look into the details of your own and Other's issues, separate the salient from the irrelevant and deliver clearly your findings.

BUT TEND NOT TO SEE

(How you Fail to Communicate)

… the wood for the trees and so have to spend a lonely night in the forest. This means that, correct though you may be, Other is only going to hear you when they feel valued by you for more than just being able to appreciate your fine sense of logic.

… that Other sometimes just wants to hang loose, or be silly or downright emotional.

Mercury is to a Relationship like what the Nervous System is to your Body

MERCURY IN LIBRA
The Fair Mind • The Superficial Mind

PERCEPTION and COMMUNICATION

YOU SEE LIFE IN TERMS OF **BUT TEND NOT TO SEE**

(How you Communicate)

… creating harmony and avoiding conflict, and so you are very skilful and diplomatic with Other, and aware of their position. Such awareness and flexibility can solve or even pre-empt relationship problems quite easily and efficiently.

… social and moral justice, which enables you to treat Other fairly.

(How you Fail to Communicate)

… that harmony is often created through conflict and confrontation. Consequently, you talk around the point which can infuriate Other – and then you start all over again!

… that maps are not the same as the places themselves – meaning that you relate from a theoretical base, not an emotionally real one.

MERCURY IN SCORPIO
The Penetrating Mind • The Paranoid Mind

PERCEPTION and COMMUNICATION

YOU SEE LIFE IN TERMS OF **BUT TEND NOT TO SEE**

(How you Communicate)

… underlying emotional truths and realities rather than merely how things appear on the surface. And so you are able to penetrate to Other's real or hidden motivations and consequently clarify them and resolve problems issuing from them.

… confidentiality, which inspires Other with trust and respect for your insights.

(How you Fail to Communicate)

… that Other is more straightforward and not so convoluted in their thinking and talking. Consequently, you make problems with Other which only exist in your suspicious, anguished and obsessed mind.

… that making secrets of things creates the very difficulties they were supposed to avoid; make a clean breast of things.

Mercury is to a Relationship like what the Nervous System is to your Body

MERCURY IN SAGITTARIUS
The Forthright Mind • The Gushy Mind

PERCEPTION and COMMUNICATION

YOU SEE LIFE IN TERMS OF	BUT TEND NOT TO SEE
(How you Communicate)	*(How you Fail to Communicate)*

… what has to be said because it creates problems when left unsaid. This clears the air and promotes broader awareness and understanding, even though it may shock or embarrass initially.

… everything being for the best ultimately, which is uplifting and guiding for Other.

… religious significance or ethical values.

… that saying something simply because it is preoccupying you can make a mountain out of a molehill, or get back from Other more than you bargained for.

… hard facts (that Other can see and tell).

… that your strong opinions and values blind you to those of Other, who then has no choice but to distance themself from you.

MERCURY IN CAPRICORN
The Methodical Mind • The Rigid Mind

PERCEPTION and COMMUNICATION

YOU SEE LIFE IN TERMS OF	BUT TEND NOT TO SEE
(How you Communicate)	*(How you Fail to Communicate)*

… tried and true procedures, thereby enabling you to grasp the essential facts of an issue and discuss things in a step-by-step, logical fashion that creates order.

… efficient or inefficient, useful or useless – and so you put across to Other what you set out to put across, as well as achieving an objective that you always have in mind.

… issues and factors concerning Other that fall outside of your rigidly set view of things; Other will ultimately take advantage of this if you fail to listen and learn from them.

… that Other may have plans that will only include you if you alter your agenda and criteria. So take time out to see someone who can help you achieve this.

Mercury is to a Relationship like what the Nervous System is to your Body

MERCURY IN AQUARIUS
The Original Mind • The Scatty Mind

PERCEPTION and COMMUNICATION

YOU SEE LIFE IN TERMS OF	BUT TEND NOT TO SEE
(How you Communicate)	*(How you Fail to Communicate)*

… truth and knowledge and so are able to make Other aware of issues and factors that are powerfully influential but not obvious.

… an unusual, free-thinking and non-judgmental way that allows Other to express themselves openly, thereby creating understanding almost magically.

… progressive *and* sentimental thinking.

… what Other is actually feeling because you are too busy with some theory of how things ought to be, or even how Other *ought* to be feeling.

… that Other is not so far-seeing as you are, or when you are being hare-brained.

… that Other cannot easily appreciate your apparently contradictory thought processes.

MERCURY IN PISCES
The Sensitive Mind • The Deluded Mind

PERCEPTION and COMMUNICATION

YOU SEE LIFE IN TERMS OF	BUT TEND NOT TO SEE
(How you Communicate)	*(How you Fail to Communicate)*

… myriad impressions from which you are able to gain uncannily accurate insights into Other's emotional and mental states, thereby making them feel that you are very much in tune with them.

… intuitive images rather than logical interpretations, so you express yourself best visually, poetically or suggestively.

… what the reality of a situation is when you become over-sensitized by your own desires and fears regarding Other, and so you consequently get the wrong end of the stick.

… how you bend the truth in order to avoid confronting what Other is thinking, feeling, saying or being, because mistakenly you fear your own weaknesses being brought to light.

Mercury is to a Relationship like what the Nervous System is to your Body

VENUS

IMPORTANT TIPS

● With all Venus Signs, LOVE can generally be attracted and expressed by consciously creating harmony through consideration and feeling for Other, and through artistic pursuits. The more individual or specific means are given according to each Sign.

● If you are MALE then your Venus Sign traits may be projected on to or sought after in FEMALES, which is fine if they are positive, but if they are negative it means that you'll need to study your Profile with a mind to admitting, claiming or expressing those traits for yourself. A poorly expressed or unexpressed Venus is rather like a personal quality that you have disregarded or suppressed because it is has been branded 'unmasculine' by your culture, only to find that someone else claims it and then appears to have you at a disadvantage. This is probably because you want back what you feel to be yours.

● The practice of some form of ART gives expression to Venus in a way that rewards you and others in its own right, rather than relying upon Other for such, thus avoiding disappointment or disharmony.

VENUS IN ARIES
The Bold Lover • The Impatient Lover

LOVE or FANCY?

Love for you is something that has to happen quickly, like at first sight, almost as if you are taken by storm. There also has to be a childlike, spontaneous quality to it that never settles down into an 'adult' rut of habit and predictability; love has to make something happen. The dark side to your particularly bright love nature is that you can be self-centred, impetuous and emotionally immature, causing you to give in to mere **Fancy**

YOU ATTRACT WITH°
(Use to Win Over)

… a forward but quite innocent seductiveness that is instantly beguiling.

… a wild and primal sexuality that suggests a romping, playful and uncomplicated sort of pleasure and love-making.

… a youthful appeal, whatever your actual age, that forces progress in some way.

YOU REPEL WITH°
(Avoid or Use to Drive Away)

… a selfish, demanding and minx-like nature that can drop Other quite unceremoniously.

… a reluctance, or possibly an inability, to give any more of yourself than is needed to keep Other where you want them.

… a Peter Pan complex that prevents you from accepting your social responsibilities.

YOU ARE ATTRACTED TO*
(How you are Won Over)

… forceful and demonstrative displays of interest and affection.

… Others who are independent with, to a degree, interests other than you.

… Others who have energetic or hectic social lives that are full of exciting and individualistic people.

YOU ARE REPELLED BY*
(What you are Turned Off by)

… limp, unsure or, worst of all, creepy types who lack passion or conviction for it reflects badly on your own vibrancy.

… fawning or clinging characters who want mothering or constant reassurance.

… fuddy-duddy social scenes and people that lack spontaneity and a bit of wildness.

WHEN ALONE …

… it could be because you have pushed one or more of the above negative traits to a point where noone is willing or able to commit to *you*. One of two choices here is to recognize that Other can keep your interest if you give them long enough to discover how to – but not too long, of course. The second choice is to settle for the fact that you are just too young at heart, or old in body, to find anyone who will last more than a week or so – if at all. The irony here is that sooner or later you will have to settle for something – the very thing you may believe you are so averse to. Alternatively, you could be alone because love has ended as suddenly as you like it to begin – kind of living by the sword and dying by it.

° *Especially if you are female.*

* *Especially if you are male.*

VENUS IN TAURUS

The Loyal Lover • The Possessive Lover

LOVE or FANCY?

Love for you is something that has to be physical, sensual and involve some material comforts and wherewithal too. You also want it to be solid and lasting, with possibly traditional or close-to-Nature undertones. However, without taking a look at the more spiritual aspects of relating you could be consigning yourself to being in a dull, gross and possessive relationship. Such blind indulgence would amount to mere **Fancy**

YOU ATTRACT WITH°	YOU REPEL WITH°
(Use to Win Over)	*(Avoid or Use to Drive Away)*
… a rich earthy appeal that promises pleasure and ultimate satisfaction.	… a possessiveness that prevents you from seeing who Other is as a person in their own right.
… a feeling that you are solid and reliable and not given to flightiness or unpredictability.	… a need for security that eclipses any sense of mystery or excitement.
… a natural beauty or handsomeness that is erotic but not threatening.	… jealousy born of lacking a sense of your inner worth.

YOU ARE ATTRACTED TO*	YOU ARE REPELLED BY*
(How you are Won Over)	*(What you are Turned Off by)*
… very tactile types who display a traditional sense of the romantic.	… a lack of physical affection or a poor sense of touch.
… Others who have artistic talent/awareness, especially good singing or speaking voices.	… philistines with no sense of beauty or love of Nature.
… natural qualities, good living, creature comforts, material stability.	… synthetic, ultra-modern or newfangled life-styles, and Others who have such.

WHEN ALONE ...

… it is quite likely that you are still actually with someone but are alone in the sense that Other is no longer the company they were, or even the company you wish to be in. The reason for this is that in concentrating, consciously or unconsciously, on having material stability or outer appeal in a relationship and partner, you have overlooked the importance of the inner person or quality. Your aloneness, whether you are still with someone or not, is in aid of forcing this spiritual or psychological consideration upon you. A variation upon this theme, which applies mainly if you are entirely alone, is that you hold Other to be some *object* of love that you wish to own or admire from afar. Such an attitude is bound to maintain that very distance interminably, so you need to get down to a more honest, physical level of loving and relating.

° *Especially if you are female.*

* *Especially if you are male.*

VENUS IN GEMINI
The Light-hearted Lover • The Fickle Lover

LOVE or FANCY?

Love for you is something that you do not want to become too dark or heavy; it should have just enough shade to keep you interested without feeling you have to probe and plumb the depths. However, carrying this lightness too far may well attract some kind of emotional crisis and confrontation, because an equal blending of the light and the dark is what makes the difference between real love and mere **Fancy**

YOU ATTRACT WITH°	YOU REPEL WITH°
(Use to Win Over)	*(Avoid or Use to Drive Away)*
… a cool wit and elusive charm.	… an icy breeze that probably originates from some deep inner doubt about your worth and attractiveness.
… a wide range of contacts which you seem to cultivate and maintain with enviable ease.	… a butterfly-like quality that commits you to noone in particular.
… a flirtatiousness that is balanced so well between sheer playfulness and really meaning it that it borders on being an art form.	… a capriciousness that is addicted to teasing and avoiding any real emotional contact.

YOU ARE ATTRACTED TO*	YOU ARE REPELLED BY*
(How you are Won Over)	*(What you are Turned Off by)*
… a clever mind and a way with words.	… a lack of mental and verbal sparkle.
… someone who will keep the flame of love alive and interesting with the occasional unexpected breeze, even though this might mean the occasional tornado.	… anything that smacks of settling down into some well-worn groove as the 'comfortable' couple.
… plenty of variety, especially where sex is concerned.	… sex or romance that has no curiosity for what has not yet been tried.

WHEN ALONE …

… it is because noone can pin you down. The fact of the matter is that this probably suits you … at least some of the time. Another reason could be that you have not been developing or exercising your natural wit and cheeky charm enough to attract a likely suitor. As ever with Gemini, there are two sides or ways of looking at the situation. In other words, you are either being too light or not light enough. Your style is, after all, of the 'keep 'em guessing' variety, so playing it too straight would be counter-productive. If you feel alone, as distinct from actually being alone, it is very likely because you are not allowing into discussion a certain issue you are uncomfortable with – and no other points of contact can be made until this one is addressed.

° Especially if you are female.

* Especially if you are male.

VENUS IN CANCER

The Sentimental Lover • The Insecure Lover

LOVE or FANCY?

Love for you is something that is very dependent upon home, family and security, no matter how wild
or adventurous you may like to think you are. A case of 'love me, love my family' – and loving
Other's family would be just as important. You are also romantic in a dreamy sort of way.
But such a mix of the cosy and the ideal could be pretty hard to find or maintain,
for they may reflect childhood longings that amount to mere **Fancy**

YOU ATTRACT WITH°	YOU REPEL WITH°
(Use to Win Over)	*(Avoid or Use to Drive Away)*
… tenderness and a familiar charm that makes Other feel both excited and comfortable.	… a misuse of your ability to get inside Other in the form of emotional blackmail.
… an extremely caring and compassionate nature that protects and nurtures Other.	… a suffocating and clingy neediness that makes Other want to get as far from you as you try to be close to them.
… domestic skills such as cooking, décor and warm hospitality.	… being a stay-at-home or blindly depending on Other to keep the home-fires burning.

YOU ARE ATTRACTED TO*	YOU ARE REPELLED BY*
(How you are Won Over)	*(What you are Turned Off by)*
… Others who appreciate the importance of home and family life.	… brashness or a rejection of anything or anyone that you feel for; being made to feel unwelcome or taken for granted.
… soulful Others who possibly have some affliction for you to sympathize with.	… a lack of sensitivity, especially towards children, animals and Nature – and yourself.
… cuddly romance rather than thrusting passion – at least once you have exhausted this cultural myth.	… impersonal sex.

WHEN ALONE …

… it could be that you have done the very thing to Other that you cannot bear being done to you: taken
them for granted in some way. Most likely you have been enjoying the emotional or material security of a
relationship long enough for you not to notice that it's there. Consequently, you have looked for something
more exciting elsewhere, or Other has found someone more appreciative elsewhere. Conversely, you have
clung too closely and fussed and fawned over Other to the point when they just had to get away –
or this is how Other has been with you and you have had to run. A third reason is simply that you have
been after the dream lover which an ordinary mortal can never be;
you must track back to your childhood for why.

° *Especially if you are female.*

* *Especially if you are male.*

VENUS IN LEO

The Generous Lover • The Selfish Lover

LOVE or FANCY?

Love for you is something that must be playful, passionate and courtly. Nothing or noone should be as important as the lover and the beloved. A king and his queen in a garden of blissful romance. However, such an absolute and all-consuming sense of love may well be impossible to maintain when not tempered with a measure of reality. Failing to do this would set you up for a fall when such 'love' is shown to be mere **Fancy**

YOU ATTRACT WITH°	YOU REPEL WITH°
(Use to Win Over)	*(Avoid or Use to Drive Away)*

… ardent expressions of romantic interest which Other finds irresistible.

… radiantly bestowing upon Other all manner of gifts and favours.

… a style, beauty or sense of fun that makes Other feel very privileged and proud to be with you, especially in company.

… the feeling you give Other when they are made to realize that they cannot live up to the unattainable romantic ideal you have projected on to them.

… vain, selfish interest and overbearing possessiveness posing as loyalty.

… game-playing or flaunting yourself.

YOU ARE ATTRACTED TO*	YOU ARE REPELLED BY*
(How you are Won Over)	*(What you are Turned Off by)*

… an Other you can feel proud of.

… an Other who sees past your impressive outer display and appreciates the vulnerability they find inside of you.

… classic, romantic courtship; playing imaginative love and sex games.

… being made to feel embarrassed.

… an Other who does not notice or respect your deeper feelings, merely because you do not make them public or obvious.

… crude, impersonal, second-rate expressions of interest; insulting behaviour.

WHEN ALONE …

… it is because you have become so preoccupied with 'love's shine' rather than its inner glow that Other sooner or later appears lack-lustre and wanting – and so you dismiss them. Then, for the same reason, you simply no longer attract an Other or the right kind of Other. Metaphorically, the gilt that you put on the gingerbread has worn off and you do not have enough faith in real and ordinary love to show the real and ordinary you that lies beneath that gilt. So it is vitally important that you look at the reasons for your doubting the worth of that real, ordinary – and probably wounded – you. The lion's pride tends to prevent it from being seen when it is wounded, but this is a mistake for the wound can fester when not tended – which can make you unapproachable, if not unattractive. Show this true you and the true Other will appear.

° *Especially if you are female.*

* *Especially if you are male.*

VENUS IN VIRGO

The Reliable Lover • The Exacting Lover

LOVE or FANCY?

Love for you is something that has an excruciatingly fine line between being true and false, acceptable and unacceptable. You have a very delicate and discerning sensibility, but you do not want it crushed or abused by indiscriminate treatment. This very critical inner state can attract just what you want, or find noone at all who measures up, or by way of compensating for such fastidiousness, cause you to succumb to some mere **Fancy**

YOU ATTRACT WITH°	**YOU REPEL WITH°**
(Use to Win Over)	*(Avoid or Use to Drive Away)*
… an air of reserve or unattainability that gives the lie to your private sensuality.	… a standoffishness which peculiarly can sometimes become quite amoral.
… a fine sense of aesthetic detail, be it artistic, cosmetic or sartorial.	… a fussiness or priggishness that can turn out to be a blind to your own self-doubt.
… a sense of health and helpfulness which you offer Other in a quiet, modest and practical fashion.	… a clinical approach and opportunistic motivation with regard to how and why you show an interest in Other.

YOU ARE ATTRACTED TO*	**YOU ARE REPELLED BY***
(How you are Won Over)	*(What you are Turned Off by)*
… Others with above average intelligence and a discerning eye.	… a lack of a fine mental understanding, concerning you or some other subject.
… an Other who shares with you some specific interest or occupation, possibly employing special methods.	… lazy slobs or at least an absence of common ground with regard to work and ways of doing things.
… cleanliness and health-consciousness.	… sordidness, or strangely, punctiliousness.

WHEN ALONE …

… it is because noone can live up to your rather exacting standards. And by the very nature of such fastidiousness you can be alone more often than most – even to the point of being left on the shelf. Such bachelor/spinsterhood may, like classic example Cliff Richard, be very much to your liking, suiting your sense of purity and keeping yourself to yourself. However, if you do not think you are ready for such abstinence, then you are going to have to adjust those standards. This does not mean you have to become wanton – although occasionally you can be by way of relief from your own restraints. It is a case of being more exacting as to what those standards are rather than them just being exacting in themselves. This means that you must ask yourself what you feel is unhealthy or unreasonable about your own sexual attitude and emotional requirements and rectify that before you can expect a suitable Other to appear or remain.

° Especially if you are female.

* Especially if you are male.

VENUS IN LIBRA

The Charming Lover • The Superficial Lover

LOVE or FANCY?

Love for you is something that has to be evidently civil, beautiful and harmonious – a classical love that graces your life and the society you live in like a piece of music or a work of art. You draw this sense of love from deep levels of your soul, but paradoxically it can distance you from actually feeling love on a personal level, making it hard for you to utterly commit, and causing you to seduce with and be seduced by mere **Fancy**

YOU ATTRACT WITH°	YOU REPEL WITH°
(Use to Win Over)	*(Avoid or Use to Drive Away)*

… a gentle, sophisticated and aesthetic charm that can make Other feel treated how they've always wanted to be treated.

… a social style and contacts; the improved life-style these promise or bring.

… being true to some definite standard of relating and social behaviour.

… an inability to resist the temptation of using and enjoying your natural appeal through flirting, thus appearing insincere to Other.

… a blind adherence to social etiquette and norms so as to mask emotional ineptitude.

… an intolerance of honest displays of emotion, such being seen as bad manners.

YOU ARE ATTRACTED TO*	YOU ARE REPELLED BY*
(How you are Won Over)	*(What you are Turned Off by)*

… beauty, be it of looks or personality.

… an Other who is your equal, in terms of complementing you, rather than of social standing.

… harmony and tastefulness, be it in the living room, the kitchen or the bedroom.

… Others who do not appeal to your refined sense of values and appearance.

… an Other who lacks the social graces or at least refuses to learn any (from you?).

… any kind of aesthetic, moral or cultural wasteland; coarseness.

WHEN ALONE …

… or dissatisfied, it is because noone measures up to your impossible standards. More to the point, however pleasing and graceful these standards may be, they do not fulfil Other's emotional needs – or your own for that matter. It is equally possible that you have applied these high social and aesthetic standards to your own personality and found it wanting and unfit for relationship. The barrier you have to get through is a superficial idea of love and relating. This does not mean that you are shallow and incapable of loving, but that you use surface values like looks and behaviour as your criteria because you are not sure of your own inner worth and lovability. Libra, the Scales, can 'tip' things the other way and find you rejecting social and aesthetic values to some degree, but this would be you simply rebelling against them in an attempt to find your own emotional truth. But carried too far, this could find you more alone than ever. Truth is beauty.

° *Especially if you are female.*

* *Especially if you are male.*

VENUS IN SCORPIO

The Intense Lover • The Desperate Lover

LOVE or FANCY?

Love for you is something that has a fated quality about it, created or matched by a deep passion that involves you as if under the influence of some sort of potion. Often despite your better judgment you are drawn down and into a dark well of emotional fascination, towards some outcome you apparently have no control over unless you resist it from the first. Therefore be very careful that such attraction is not mere **Fancy**

YOU ATTRACT WITH°	YOU REPEL WITH°
(Use to Win Over)	*(Avoid or Use to Drive Away)*
… a subtle and compelling charm that draws Other to you powerfully and inexplicably.	… a sinister underlying intention that, when detected, leads to a fight for survival.
… an aura of sexual confidence that, one way or the other, lives up to itself.	… your perverted way of satisfying your degenerate needs and appetites.
… a totally focused and uncompromising attention to Other, rather like a snake fixing its prey.	… a sexual or emotional overkill that if not resisted at the outset can destroy love or any finer feelings that Other might have.

YOU ARE ATTRACTED TO*	YOU ARE REPELLED BY*
(How you are Won Over)	*(What you are Turned Off by)*
… powerful types of Other, who are often in need of emotional deepening or transformation, along with yourself probably.	… blandness and a fear of plunging into one's emotional depths.
… relationships that involve secrecy and/or the breaking of sexual or social taboos.	… Others who play it too safe and are unwilling to explore the unexplored.
… relationships that claim body and soul.	… relationships which bind you but do not emotionally fulfil you.

WHEN ALONE …

… one reason could be that you are unprepared to commit to a relationship of any depth of meaning for you know that it will demand painful confrontations with your most intimate fears and obsessions. It could even be that you are involved in a relationship for material or practical reasons but which is lacking any soul connection or emotional satisfaction – and so you are alone in a psychological sense. Often, money may have become a substitute for love in that you are manipulated by it in some way. Conversely, your aloneness could take the form of feeling deeply for someone who cannot or will not match such depth. The reason behind this is that you are pledged at some profound level to remind Other of the ultimate supremacy that considerations of the soul must take. In all of these cases, the long and lonely night of soul that you endure will firstly be reminding *you* of this spiritual truth. 'Who feels it, knows it.'

° Especially if you are female.   ** Especially if you are male.*

VENUS IN SAGITTARIUS

The Adventurous Lover • The Wanton Lover

LOVE or FANCY?

Love for you is something that should be exciting and rapturous, yet at the same time have meaning and even some deeply moral or religious quality about it. Basically you want to satisfy equally both your body and your soul or mind, and you will pursue such an objective enthusiastically and uninhibitedly. Troubles arise when the lusts or needs of your body leave the idealism of your mind behind, or vice versa, either being mere **Fancy**

YOU ATTRACT WITH°
(Use to Win Over)

… a demonstrative, honest and open manner.

… a light-hearted, party mood that immediately gives Other a sense of fun being in the offing.

… a sense that you have definite and intelligent ethical standards.

YOU REPEL WITH°
(Avoid or Use to Drive Away)

… an immodesty and seductiveness that eventually becomes counter-productive.

… loose morals – and impersonal affection to match.

… hypocritical efforts to get Other to behave in the upright manner that you feel you yourself ought to, but fail to.

YOU ARE ATTRACTED TO*
(How you are Won Over)

… Others who are emotionally sophisticated and/or mentally informed.

… Others who have an enterprising and expansive approach to life, or have exotic connections or are of foreign origin.

… Others who have a playful streak but have principles as well.

YOU ARE REPELLED BY*
(What you are Turned Off by)

… small-minded, dull or dishonest Others who lack experience or a sense of adventure.

… provincialism or parochialism.

… Others who are too reserved, inhibited or sanctimonious.

WHEN ALONE …

… it is for one of two reasons, or possibly both. The first is that you give or promise a lot but overlook the details, and so eventually you are disappointed or Other is. This implies that you get carried away with your own enthusiastic idea of love and Other and so fail to see – possibly because you do not want to – the small or unsensational side to Other's character and life. This in turn suggests that you do not acknowledge the same in yourself because you somehow believe it to be unlovable. The second reason why you could find yourself alone in an unwelcome way, is that your and Other's beliefs or moral values do not agree. You have an interesting mixture of both wild and ethical behaviour which is quite hard to understand or accept – unless you yourself do. Until then you are unlikely to attract an Other whose values harmonize with yours.

° *Especially if you are female.*

* *Especially if you are male.*

VENUS IN CAPRICORN

The Dutiful Lover • The Inhibited Lover

LOVE or FANCY?

Love for you is something that has to be tried to be true, and so you favour the conventional values of fidelity and duty, and the passing of time through commitment and probably the enduring institution of marriage in order to establish a relationship or Other as reliable and worthwhile. When carried too far, however, such hide-bound relating can cause you to want some sort of release, but be careful this is not merely some **Fancy**

YOU ATTRACT WITH°

(Use to Win Over)

… a serious and considered attitude which bespeaks dependability and substance.

… commitment and involvement with matters besides Other, such as a profession or worthwhile goal.

… a resourcefulness and possible affluence that promises ease in the material world.

YOU REPEL WITH°

(Avoid or Use to Drive Away)

… an inhibited and distrustful approach towards emotional matters.

… a cold self-containment that betrays the fact that Other is just another responsibility in a life of duties and commitments.

… putting money and status above feelings, especially those of and for Other.

YOU ARE ATTRACTED TO*

(How you are Won Over)

… a mature, responsible and utterly trustworthy Other.

… an Other who has an elusive or mysterious quality that you cannot put your finger on – or control, for that matter.

… an Other who is a firm, recognizable member of your social or cultural group.

YOU ARE REPELLED BY*

(What you are Turned Off by)

… sloppy, irresolute types who are looking for someone to use as a step up life's ladder.

… those too eager to fit in with your plans and opinions, for in truth you only trust and respect an Other who is their own person.

… situations where you feel ill at ease because there are too many 'unknowns'.

WHEN ALONE …

… it is because you have not trusted anyone to come close enough to discover the real you. This is not to do with you making yourself known as a personality with all your various strengths and weaknesses too, but more a case of revealing your very soul to Other, and trusting them with it in a real way. You can be very adept at presenting yourself in an apparently candid fashion, but this can be a bit like paying lip-service to emotional honesty. In other words, for all your apparently straight dealing, you always hold back the very part of yourself that is chaotic and lost, or at least is what you regard as such. This is the part that love and love only can heal, but it is love that you ultimately do not trust. You too often mistake the formalities and conditions placed upon love as love itself – so it is no wonder you do not trust it and find yourself alone.

° *Especially if you are female.*

* *Especially if you are male.*

VENUS IN AQUARIUS

The Liberated Lover • The Indifferent Lover

LOVE or FANCY?

Love for you is something that should never tie you down. Other has to be a friend to you just as much as anything else, be that lover, spouse, etc. What all this amounts to is that you see love in terms of ideals and principles rather than needs or passions, although at times it can be quite confusing as to what is really motivating you. Freedom and honesty are your bywords, but they could become an excuse to say and do what you **Fancy**

YOU ATTRACT WITH°	YOU REPEL WITH°
(Use to Win Over)	*(Avoid or Use to Drive Away)*
… a package of the unusual, unique and friendly which makes a light go on inside Other that they didn't even know was there.	… an aloofness and lack of personal feeling towards Other that in time will attract the same from Other – in earnest.
… an easy-going and non-possessive attitude which is like a breath of fresh air.	… a complete disregard for loyalty towards Other, when it suits you.
… a socially progressive attitude that is open to new ideas and values.	… an odd and/or theoretical, as opposed to realistic, version of how one should relate.

YOU ARE ATTRACTED TO*	YOU ARE REPELLED BY*
(How you are Won Over)	*(What you are Turned Off by)*
… Others who are people in their own right and maybe stand out from the crowd.	… being put into a set category or expected to behave according to the norm.
… freedom-loving Others who have their own specially devised rules for living.	… Others who toe the party line and cannot think for themselves.
… unusual, experimental or open relationship set-ups.	… an inability to share thoughts, feelings and even bodies.

WHEN ALONE …

… it is because your insistence on the freedom to do as you or Other chooses eventually causes relationships to become dysfunctional or non-starters. Relationships run on a fuel called human emotion, whatever else you may think they ought to run on. In the name of doing what you think is your own thing you have probably overlooked what really is. So, sooner or later, you are made to feel what it is like to be without anyone to feel for you, or you are alone with someone who is no longer able to feel that much for you. In the second case, Other probably hangs in there for their own unique reasons, while you hang in there because a feeling is keeping you there despite what you think. Apart from this, your free and experimental style of relating is bound to experience periodic gaps, rather like being short of guinea pigs!

° *Especially if you are female.*

* *Especially if you are male.*

VENUS IN PISCES

The Compassionate Lover • The Deluded Lover

LOVE or FANCY?

Love for you is something that is all-encompassing and unconditional, extending to all forms of life, not just the human. You are thereby able to tune into the very soul of Other, inspiring and releasing talents and relieving pain and longing. However, you can be taken down to levels of acute suffering by such self-sacrificing devotion or addiction for it may indicate little love for yourself and as such is delusory to the point of sheer **Fancy**

YOU ATTRACT WITH°
(Use to Win Over)

… a pervasive charm that evokes in Other romantic feelings and soulful longings.

… creative or healing talents that enchant Other, making them fan, follower or slave.

… a compassionate and seemingly selfless sensitivity that tunes into exactly what Other wants or needs at the time.

YOU REPEL WITH°
(Avoid or Use to Drive Away)

… a seductiveness that works overtime to meet unrealistic and fanciful expectations.

… a switching back and forth between total submission and wanton evasiveness.

… an almost insane idealizing of Other, or preoccupation with them, that eventually makes them (want to) run away from you.

YOU ARE ATTRACTED TO*
(How you are Won Over)

… glamorous, wayward, otherworldly Others who weave a spell.

… an Other who is unavailable because you are into dreaming rather than having.

… losers and sad cases because they appeal to your compassionate soul.

YOU ARE REPELLED BY*
(What you are Turned Off by)

… harsh, brassy, over-confident Others who are only into material things.

… a dream that is in danger of coming true, because you'll then have to live up to it.

… Others who take advantage of you – or at least you should be!

WHEN ALONE …

… it is because it's Nature's way of giving you an emotional cold turkey. You are so prone to becoming addicted to Other, or rather your idea of them, that isolating you and denying you a 'fix' is the only realistic way of getting you to face the music and own up to the facts. Until you realize and appreciate that you are being victim to some notion or feeling that has more to do with your own soul or past hurts than it does with Other, then you will be forcibly and unavoidably 'on the wagon'. An alternative to this, or possibly a stage or so further on from it, is that you are learning to 'suffer nobly', which means that you are having to turn the other cheek for the overall good, whatever that might mean to you. For instance, your suffering may be the only way that Other can learn a lesson that they have long been avoiding.

° *Especially if you are female.*

* *Especially if you are male.*

MARS

IMPORTANT TIPS

● ANGER is the word I use as a general description for the negative expressions of Mars, and can be read to include firstly physical, emotional or verbal violence to self or Other, abuse and unacceptable lust, and secondly over- or under-activity, suppression of desire and self-assertion, and the physical complaints that are symptomatic of these conditions (inflammation, tension, irritability, wounds, and those that relate to the heart, head, muscles and adrenal glands). Anger, simply as an expression of losing one's temper, is, to be realistic, unavoidable at times – indeed it can be quite necessary, effective and therapeutic, rather like a safety valve – but one should endeavour eventually to 'clear' oneself of even this anger. Here is a brief breakdown of key anger-making issues for each Mars (and Sun) Sign:

ARI	Being thwarted	LEO	Dishonour	SAG	Attack on one's beliefs
TAU	Jealousy, loss	VIR	Unreasonableness	CAP	Laziness, feebleness
GEM	Poor communication	LIB	Injustice	AQU	Abuse of rights
CAN	Insecurity, fear	SCO	Emotional insincerity	PIS	Insensitivity

● With all Mars Signs, ENERGY can generally be created and maintained, and ANGER worked off or avoided, through healthy exercise, dancing, yoga, tai chi, (dangerous) sports and sexual activity. More individual or specific means are given according to each Sign.

● If you are FEMALE then your Mars Sign traits may be projected on to or sought after in MALES, which is fine if they are positive, but if they are negative it means that you'll need to study your Profile with a mind to admitting, claiming or expressing those traits for yourself. An unexpressed Mars is rather like a personal weapon that you have discarded for fear of using it, only to find that someone else picks it up and uses it against you.

MARS IN ARIES
The Bold Suitor • The Impetuous Suitor

ENERGY or ANGER?

Energy is created and maintained through honest and direct means that breed quick results, rather than through complex strategies and convoluted agendas. Decisions are best made impulsively, and if proved wrong, swiftly proceed with whatever's next, without looking back. Although lack of forethought can create problems, it is best to use these manners of assertion, or energy can remain as, or devolve into, **Anger**

YOU ATTRACT WITH*
(Use to Win Over)

... a self-assured and energetic manner that comes right to the point, gets things started.

... a direct sexual approach that excites because it leaves no room for mistaking your desires.

... a fearless, independent streak that puts you way out in front of competition.

YOU REPEL WITH*
(Avoid or Use to Drive Away)

... an arrogance and pushiness that completely overlooks finer points and feelings.

... a coarse and unsubtle, even violent, way which sets out to make sexual conquests.

... an inability to share and co-operate.

YOU ARE ATTRACTED TO°
(How you are Won Over)

... heroic types, or situations where the competition is stiff and you therefore stand to make the most heroic impression.

... sexual objectives that can be swiftly achieved, or those who can swiftly achieve sexual objectives.

... athletic, adventurous, leader types.

YOU ARE REPELLED BY°
(What you are Turned Off by)

... faintheartedness and low-key situations where there is no competition or prize worth fighting for.

... being treated as a sexual object – or *not* being treated as one, depending on your mood or gender.

... limp types with no get-up-and-go.

WHEN ALONE ...

... it can be for reasons which are as complex as you usually like to keep or have things straightforward. In other words, your direct, even pushy, sexual nature can be a problem in that it turns people off, or if you do not accept or recognize this go-for-it side of your personality, then you can be consistently put off by it in others to the point of there being no comers, or at least, none that you find attractive. This second point is far more likely to be the case if you are female. And so the remedy here is to be a bit more softly-softly if you are the former, and to swallow your finer feelings and be more to the point and honest with yourself if you are the latter. Your problem could of course be a combination of the two, in which case be more circumspect, but not so much that the object of your desires is not clear about your feelings or intentions.

---

* Especially if you are male.   *° Especially if you are female.*

MARS IN TAURUS

The Sensuous Suitor • The Jealous Suitor

ENERGY or ANGER?

Energy is created and maintained over a drawn-out period as long as you have a material goal.
Laid-back initially, it takes a lot to turn you on, but once aroused it takes even more to turn you off.
The same applies to your temper: if you are frustrated in pursuit or possession of what you desire,
it is like a red rag to a Bull; what was previously steady and productive devolves into
a destructive and hard-to-subdue **Anger**

YOU ATTRACT WITH*	YOU REPEL WITH*
(Use to Win Over)	*(Avoid or Use to Drive Away)*
… an earthy, sensuous and a throbbing sexuality; great stamina.	… a jealous and possessive nature that is blind to reason; won't let up.
… an advantageous material position, or at least, a sound ability and commitment regarding such things.	… an opportunistic obsession with the physical/material aspects of life that bar any appreciation of the spiritual or intangible.
… a solid dependability that stands its ground, defends you and yours.	… a stubborn, intractable and unrelenting attitude that is its own worst enemy.

YOU ARE ATTRACTED TO°	YOU ARE REPELLED BY°
(How you are Won Over)	*(What you are Turned Off by)*
… Others who promise stability of some kind or other, who have substance and produce solid results.	… material insufficiency and promises that are not met.
… traditionally sexual types and situations, perhaps even where chauvinism has a place, to some degree.	… woolly, newfangled ideas and values concerning sexual roles (or that do not have a discernibly practical purpose).
… physical permanence and unhurriedness.	… Others or relationships that are prone to change and upset.

WHEN ALONE …

… it is, for one reason, because you are having to take stock of yourself physically and materially, and learn
to be your own master where such matters are concerned. Conversely (or possibly as an eventuality of the
first reason), the almost excessive importance that you place upon money and physical gratification could
have isolated you from fruitful relationship, and maybe made you rather sluggish or complacent too.
Ultimately then, in either respect, you may have to take some fall in the form of losing what or who you
hold most dear. This would force you to focus upon issues of physical and/or material satisfaction in order to
appreciate their true value or limitations. If you have always, or for some time, been alone, then this states
that such a revaluation is a priority concerning what you want and how you go about getting it.

* Especially if you are male.
° Especially if you are female.

MARS IN GEMINI

The Eloquent Suitor • *The Tricky Suitor*

ENERGY or ANGER?

Energy is created and maintained through the use of your intellect and words, and also your hands. Tactical pursuits like debate and chess also keep sharp your most valued weapons – your mind and tongue. Your rapier-like wit and lively nervous system need diverse and speedy input and stimulation, or they can devolve into biting sarcasm and defensive cynicism, such being the usual forms taken by any **Anger**

YOU ATTRACT WITH*	YOU REPEL WITH*
(Use to Win Over)	*(Avoid or Use to Drive Away)*

… the gift of the gab; being in the know and on the go.

… a lively, adolescent-like wit and charm that dazzles and flatters with ease and a kind of 'you can't pin me down' vibe.

… manual skills and an agile body, displaying versatility in more than one field.

… a fly, roguish nature that palls as fast as it initially impresses.

… a cold, unfeeling streak that cannot stay the emotional course; all head and all talk – at least, apparently.

… a fidgety or distracted temperament that never gets to, or steers around, the point.

YOU ARE ATTRACTED TO°	YOU ARE REPELLED BY°
(How you are Won Over)	*(What you are Turned Off by)*

… lively situations where there is plenty of opportunity to interact in a quick, light and verbal fashion.

… Others who have ready wit and a flashy sense of humour.

… where you are challenged to show your mental muscle or to keep them guessing.

… dull, homey, predictable situations where nothing is happening at that very moment.

… Others who cannot get their mind into gear and who are too slow to appreciate the pace of life as you like it.

… a lack of stimulation; safe scenarios where everything and everyone is a known quantity.

WHEN ALONE …

… it is because you have found the pace of your love or sex life too nerve-wracking to continue with. The reason behind this is that you have been driven simultaneously by a desire to satisfy your feelings on the one hand, and a fear of actually encountering them on the other. So when you do get what you desire you then have to control it with your wits in a bid to avoid feeling what you are afraid of feeling. You set up reasons and schedules that pre-empt that dreaded encounter with your own emotional truth. This psychological split may well express itself as a love triangle. So being alone is telling you that it is time to stop living life on these two diverging lines of thinking and feeling, and to take stock of your inner fears and feelings with a view to understanding them. Then and only then will you be ready to emerge again into the fray.

* Especially if you are male.   *° Especially if you are female.*

MARS IN CANCER

The Emotional Suitor • The Moody Suitor

ENERGY or ANGER?

Energy is created and maintained when used to create security and by keeping attuned to your moods and giving vent to them in the form of emotionally charged activities like music and dance. You prefer indirect ways of asserting yourself and your wishes, but if this means it becomes unclear as to what you want or where you stand you may then blame or resent Other, giving rise to sulks and then inexplicable **Anger**

YOU ATTRACT WITH*	YOU REPEL WITH*
(Use to Win Over)	*(Avoid or Use to Drive Away)*

YOU ATTRACT WITH*

(Use to Win Over)

… a passionate aura that is all the more so for being held back or indirectly expressed.

… an instinct for how to approach Other's most susceptible emotional and sexual areas.

… a feeling of strength and protectiveness about you that Other responds to powerfully yet quite unconsciously.

YOU REPEL WITH*

(Avoid or Use to Drive Away)

… hidden, brooding moods which only emerge when you have got past first base.

… an inclination to emotionally blackmail or manipulate Other by playing upon their vulnerable spots.

… a clingy and possessive nature that betrays an initially apparent independence.

YOU ARE ATTRACTED TO°

(How you are Won Over)

… Others who have the emotional or material wherewithal to make you feel secure enough to do your own thing.

… Others with a strong home or family feel or who seem able to be part of your own.

… Other sexually when you feel safe or when it plays a part in furthering security.

YOU ARE REPELLED BY°

(What you are Turned Off by)

… insecure or rootless scenarios; Others who undermine you with personal insults.

… Others who do not warm to your family or domestic scene.

… Other sexually when they remind you of your own insecurities; sexual hunger.

WHEN ALONE …

… it is probably because your security needs and sexual desires have been working at cross purposes. Instinctively, you are inclined to go for an Other whom you feel secures and protects you in some way. The trouble is that if you are a male, you probably thought that it was just a sexual thing, only to find that your sexual needs are denied at the first sign of insecurity. If you are female, you have probably used sex as a means of getting security, but later find that Other was not as safe and secure as you thought. The upshot of either case is a breakdown of emotional and/or sexual rapport – something which can eventually find you out on your own. Be more clear and honest about your intentions and you will then get a relationship to match in that it and Other will give you both satisfaction and security.

* Especially if you are male.

° Especially if you are female.

MARS IN LEO
The Royal Suitor • The Conceited Suitor

ENERGY or ANGER?

Energy is created and maintained through striving towards something that makes you feel pride and respect for yourself and/or Other. Finding the noble thing to do can be extremely important when you are having to fight your way through or out of a compromising or pressurized situation.
Merely pretending that you are getting what you want with boasts and flourishes
in spite of fair criticism are signs of incipient **Anger**

YOU ATTRACT WITH*	YOU REPEL WITH*
(Use to Win Over)	*(Avoid or Use to Drive Away)*
… a very confident and stylish way of asserting and displaying yourself.	… a pompous, vain self-righteousness that is blind to constructive and important advice.
… a dignified and highly honourable manner of conducting yourself, especially when under emotional pressure.	… steamrollering anyone or anything that gets in your way; pure egotism posing as superiority.
… an impressive and chivalrous sexuality that comes across as relaxed and in command.	… an imperious sexuality that demands its self-styled and self-elected rights.

YOU ARE ATTRACTED TO°	YOU ARE REPELLED BY°
(How you are Won Over)	*(What you are Turned Off by)*
… Others who admire your social style and/or creative talents; the spotlight.	… cynical or overly critical Others who fail to appreciate the drama of life.
… the Other who can be your 'king' or 'queen' in the sense that they are respectful, honourable and someone to be proud of.	… low-key or lacklustre Others or situations that put you in a bad light, or that drag you down to their level.
… sexual or confrontational situations where your prowess and dignity win the day.	… mean-spirited, back-stabbing means of getting what is wanted.

WHEN ALONE …

… it is because you have been banished by either pricing yourself out of the market, or you have been upstaged as a result of not admitting to your failings or doing anything about them – at least not until it was too late. And bear in mind that being 'alone' can also mean that you are still with an Other but are not getting what you want. How long you spend in exile therefore has everything to do with facing up to your ego's delusions of grandeur, because they are at the root of your aloneness. Of all the Mars Signs, yours can find it the hardest to eat humble-pie – but when you do recognize what's best all round, you will be amazed at how swiftly things gets turned around. A case of having to stoop to conquer.

---

* Especially if you are male.   *° Especially if you are female.*

MARS IN VIRGO

The Accurate Suitor • The Fastidious Suitor

ENERGY or ANGER?

Energy is created or maintained through working very hard at improving your knowledge and technique and also at what gets in the way of your achieving satisfaction or effectiveness. In the process, avoid being too hard on yourself or Other for this would lead to endless disappointment. For you, such dissatisfaction and frustration are expressions of your anger at feeling so constrained or hard-put, or of what drives you to that **Anger**

YOU ATTRACT WITH*	YOU REPEL WITH*
(Use to Win Over)	*(Avoid or Use to Drive Away)*
… a finely attuned attentiveness that makes Other feel picked out for some special quality and reason.	… a fussy and critical eye that leaves no room for mistakes and therefore none for naturalness and spontaneity either.
… an ability to hit the right spot sexually, along with a certain delicacy of touch.	… sexually inhibiting behaviour; being very exacting and/or repressed regarding sex.
… a thorough and methodical way of running things.	… workaholism; obsession with doing things at the 'right' time and in the 'right' place.

YOU ARE ATTRACTED TO°	YOU ARE REPELLED BY°
(How you are Won Over)	*(What you are Turned Off by)*
… an Other who is reliable, practical, clean, hardworking and intellectually astute.	… bores who are always right.
… a certain unreachability in Other, for to you – whether you know it or not – such is the essence of desirability.	… Others who make it too easy for you to get what you want from them because it must mean it is not worth much.
… precision in manner of dress, movement, and verbal or facial expression.	… fumbling inappropriate behaviour or anything else that fails to hit your own small and critical spot.

WHEN ALONE …

… it is because noone has yet been born who can fill all of your requirements long enough for you to realize that it is your list of requirements that's at fault. Curiously, you may have become quite indiscriminate in your choice of Others to relieve your sense of aloneness, but this would simply be a case of going from one extreme to the other – the commonest human trait of the lot. A more profound reason for your being alone, particularly if it has been for quite some time, is that your 'sexual dust' is having to settle.
This means that your attitude to sex has certain impurities or misconceptions about it that puts a bar upon your attracting it – that is, until you clean up your act or get something straight. If this is the case, be careful not to be so self-critical that such denial shows like a skin disease for that would ironically prolong the process.

* Especially if you are male.   *° Especially if you are female.*

MARS IN LIBRA

The Agreeable Suitor • The Indecisive Suitor

ENERGY or ANGER?

Energy is created and maintained through establishing and keeping a just balance between what you want and have a right to and what Other wants and has a right to – and fighting for what determines that balance. The great danger is that such fair and conciliatory behaviour can make you indecisive and err in favour of granting Other more than is their due, then resenting it, with the subsequent disharmony driving you to **Anger**

YOU ATTRACT WITH*	YOU REPEL WITH*
(Use to Win Over)	*(Avoid or Use to Drive Away)*
… a well-mannered and considerate approach (initially at least) that evokes a pleasant response from Other.	… a half-heartedness that has at its root a fear of moving from a notion of love to the real thing.
… charming, skilful and discreet courtship rather than a seductive kill.	… a limpness that is owing to a fear of entering into a state of challenge or conflict.
… elegant and fashionably aware sexual advances.	… emotionally absent blandishments that fail to cut the sexual mustard.

YOU ARE ATTRACTED TO°	YOU ARE REPELLED BY°
(How you are Won Over)	*(What you are Turned Off by)*
… civilized, harmonious Others and social scenarios that have well-defined or subtle boundaries of acceptable behaviour.	… awkward scenes where you are not sure what is expected of you and/or given no opportunity to take the lead yourself.
… hot-headed, wilful Others who challenge you to be more forceful and decisive.	… protracted conflicts as a major ingredient of a relationship.
… a relationship that fits in with your social life and mutual friends.	… an Other who is incapable of adapting to whatever social environment they're in.

WHEN ALONE …

… it is because you have been too busy trying to find or live up to an idea that you have of love and sex as opposed to what they actually are in reality. Part and parcel of such an idea – or ideal, more like – is your fear of having seen, or having to show, a more raw and self-interested side to your self – and to your masculinity if you are male. The myth that one has to be well-behaved in the form of some kind of paragon of sexual and romantic virtue can make you so nice and considerate that it hurts – and eventually leaves you with noone to prove it to. The fact is that what is seriously lacking here is the honest and straightforward emotions that attract and keep the interest of mere mortals. In the end, and especially while you are alone, you have to discover that you simply cannot please Other *all* the time if you are to satisfy your own desires.

* Especially if you are male.   *° Especially if you are female.*

MARS IN SCORPIO

The Passionate Suitor • The Cruel Suitor

ENERGY or ANGER?

Energy is created and maintained through the uncompromising and undeviating pursuit of whatever it is that you truly desire. Such should include powerful or front-line occupations, the military, getting closer to any place of power (internal or external), creating deep change, especially with regard to how you make known and satisfy your desires – or it can remain as or devolve into a highly destructive **Anger**

YOU ATTRACT WITH*
(Use to Win Over)

… an intense sexual effectiveness that does not necessarily have anything to do with how you look.

… a forcefulness that brooks no opposition.

… an intrepidity that shrinks from no challenge; a spiritual stamina that makes it through the night.

YOU REPEL WITH*
(Avoid or Use to Drive Away)

… a poisonous and destructive resentfulness.

… a negative opinion of anyone whose weaknesses remind you of your own.

… a disinclination to honestly confront the enemy within, and so forgive those who (appear to) have been hostile towards you; ruthless vengefulness.

YOU ARE ATTRACTED TO°
(How you are Won Over)

… powerful people and relationships that inevitably get very close to you, and transform you – despite your reservations.

… charismatic types and/or dangerous situations that demand your complete and utter involvement.

… breaking (sexual) taboos, thus forcing confrontations.

YOU ARE REPELLED BY°
(What you are Turned Off by)

… wimpishness and superficiality.

… fainthearted attempts to win you body and soul, something which alone can merit a relationship worthy of your involvement.

… your own self-disgust born of a reluctance to bite the bullet and take the plunge – into a relationship or your own Shadow.

WHEN ALONE …

… it is because you have been denying or suppressing those strong desires, especially for some kind of personal transformation, to which the above refers. Indeed, you could be 'alone' even though you are in a relationship. This is because you feel you must experience some kind of emotional pressure or pain to maintain an ongoing sense of being intensely involved – but you have rigged it, probably unconsciously, so that no crisis or confrontation occurs. But inevitably it will, whether you are alone or not. So you must own up to this dark and powerful streak, and note how it has affected Other in the past, and thereby attract a relationship and partner that does it justice – or renew the one you are or were in as a result of taking stock of your provocativeness and overhauling your manner of expressing it.

* Especially if you are male.

° Especially if you are female.

MARS IN SAGITTARIUS

The Ardent Suitor • The Unruly Suitor

ENERGY or ANGER?

Energy is created and maintained through enthusiastically pursuing whatever or whoever has meaning for you. It is absolutely essential that you have the space, time and freedom to explore your interests and desires, but wisely rather than wildly. To a degree, physical exertion will siphon off your prodigious energy. Being or feeling cooped-up or held back by anything or anyone will drive you to mighty and self-justifying **Anger**

YOU ATTRACT WITH*	YOU REPEL WITH*
(Use to Win Over)	*(Avoid or Use to Drive Away)*
… a spirited and very confident way of going about things.	… an overwhelming boisterousness that proves to be more energy than sense.
… a crusading or progressive energy that encourages and exhorts Other to enjoy and further themselves.	… a self-righteous, might-is-right attitude that arrogantly assumes that Other always wants what you want, should believe what you believe.
… a lusty and vigorous sexuality embracing both human virtues and animal passions.	… immoral and bigoted (sexual) behaviour.

YOU ARE ATTRACTED TO°	YOU ARE REPELLED BY°
(How you are Won Over)	*(What you are Turned Off by)*
… energetic Others who seem to be going somewhere in life.	… limp-wristed types and affairs that are going nowhere.
… adventures, outdoor pursuits, fun and games, and generally horsing around.	… pedestrian, provincial Others who like to play it safe, possibly forcing you to break away yourself from such confinement.
… the pageant of life, exploring and hotly debating far-reaching subjects like history, mythology, religion and law	… life becoming too mundane with no sense of it having any greater or higher meaning.

WHEN ALONE …

… it is most probably because you have run out of road, meaning that either you got to a point where the road of life split and you both went your own ways, or that the road you were on was not going anywhere so Other left it or you did. Having said all of this though, you are one of the least likely Mars Signs to find themselves alone for long. Like a horse that has lost track of its herd, you gallop off and away until you have found a new one. You are not one to hang around on your own pondering the why and the wherefore – Others, like life, are opportunities not to be missed. However, there is another possible reason for being alone, and that is that you got on your high horse one day and then Other called your bluff, and you couldn't back down. But until you do, you will stay alone – be positively avoided in fact.

* Especially if you are male.   *° Especially if you are female.*

MARS IN CAPRICORN
The Persistent Suitor • The Hard Suitor

ENERGY or ANGER?

Energy is created and maintained through deciding upon an objective, planning a route to attain it, and not suffering any nonsense or weaknesses along the way. Because you are so controlled, and can easily settle into sexual abstinence if you have to, you are not one to fly off the handle very often or at least not without having some purpose in doing so. But should Other step across a certain line, yours is a cold, unforgiving **Anger**

YOU ATTRACT WITH*	YOU REPEL WITH*
(Use to Win Over)	*(Avoid or Use to Drive Away)*
… an earthy and persistent single-mindedness that makes for being reliable and capable of functioning well in the material world.	… an inclination to cut off from the more personal and sentimental side of life should it suit your purposes.
… sexual stamina and effectiveness; general staying power.	… being the sex machine who thinks mainly in terms of performance; being sexually straight, boring or repressed.
… an aura of discipline and self-control; being independent and not in the least squeamish.	… a hard, pull-your-socks-up, attitude.

YOU ARE ATTRACTED TO°	YOU ARE REPELLED BY°
(How you are Won Over)	*(What you are Turned Off by)*
… soft, sentimental, playful Others who are capable of thawing you out and getting you to let your hair down.	… soppy, fawning types who come to depend too much upon your worldliness.
… a long-term relationship where solid foundations can be laid down through time.	… flash-in-the-pan relationships that have no real substance or potential for building it into something greater like a family or social cornerstone.
… an Other who is efficient in their own right, a professional type.	… immature time-wasters.

WHEN ALONE …

… it is because you either run too tight a ship, or you are overly conservative in your desires and expectations. And so you are inclined to narrow down your field of possibilities for reasons of being a bit too Spartan on the one hand, or too straight, duty-bound or unexciting on the other. You can be self-sufficient to the point of making a virtue out of it and so become cold, dry and self-contained. You need to let Other into your more fragile and emotional interior and let them feel that they have a strength that you need and have not got. This means trusting enough to let down your guard and not be so in control of yourself and Other. You may well need a professional therapist to help you let go in this important respect.

---

* Especially if you are male.

° Especially if you are female.

MARS IN AQUARIUS
The Inventive Suitor • The Odd Suitor

ENERGY or ANGER?

Energy is created and maintained through making sure that you can pursue your possibly quite unusual, quirky, abstract aims in equally unusual, quirky, abstract ways. You like to make your mind up as you go along, not keeping to a set schedule or route if you can help it. This appears erratic to Other, but it's actually your free-wheeling way of doing things. If denied, your usually cool temperament can turn into sudden, laser-like **Anger**

YOU ATTRACT WITH*
(Use to Win Over)

… an unusual, unclassifiable approach that is exciting because there is an 'anything-can-happen' feel to it.

… the feeling about you that you are your own person.

… an interest and urge to involve yourself in progressive, innovative or New Age projects.

YOU REPEL WITH*
(Avoid or Use to Drive Away)

… a lack of sexual substance or any real willingness to commit yourself.

… a perverse, odd or peculiar quality about you that is symptomatic of similar notions and feelings, or that hides indecisiveness.

… a lot of far-flung ideas and intentions, but little else.

YOU ARE ATTRACTED TO°
(How you are Won Over)

… friendly sexual (mind)games that do not necessarily lead to anything more serious.

… any Other who appeals to your taste for the unusual, unconventional, complex or even off-the-wall.

… group or team activities rather than solely one-to-one.

YOU ARE REPELLED BY°
(What you are Turned Off by)

… having your sexuality presumed upon simply because it is open or unusual.

… meat-and-potato types who bore you and fail to appreciate your uniqueness and the intricacies of your personality.

… being forced to interact more intimately than is comfortable to you.

WHEN ALONE …

… it is because your desires, and your way of expressing them, are possibly too rarefied for a suitable Other to be available at the present time. Maybe you do not realize how unusual your tastes are, and have been trying to find an Other who is straight or ordinary, giving rise to disappointments. Or you have failed to relate to Other properly for the same reason, and consequently things won't have worked out. The more you accept the erratic and out-of-the-ordinary nature of what turns you on, the more, paradoxically, you will have to turn you on. Deny it, and it will be denied you. So go out on a limb, maybe use computer dating in a spirit of experimentation. If you are fully aware of your quirkiness, and are alone within or without a relationship, the time has come to 'out' yourself and surprise yourself into a (re)new(ed) relationship.

* Especially if you are male.   *° Especially if you are female.*

MARS IN PISCES
The Sensitive Suitor • The Vulnerable Suitor

ENERGY or ANGER?

Energy is created or maintained through following your dreams and understanding the laws that govern them. This means to say that your desires spring from your psyche or imagination more than from your body, and so you tend to find satisfaction through images and suggestion, like in photography and dance, for example. Without recognizing this subtlety of your desire, frustration, abuse and distress become your **Anger**

YOU ATTRACT WITH*	YOU REPEL WITH*
(Use to Win Over)	*(Avoid or Use to Drive Away)*
… a subtle mixture of gentleness and drive, sexuality and mystery – what could be called charisma, in fact.	… a volatile and tentative approach which smacks of having something to hide and of not being willing or able to follow through.
… an ability to get under Other's skin with some indefinable quality of your being.	… a seductiveness or seductability that is treacherous because it is misguided.
… artistic or healing talent.	… confusion over how to express yourself (sexually).

YOU ARE ATTRACTED TO°	YOU ARE REPELLED BY°
(How you are Won Over)	*(What you are Turned Off by)*
… exotic and/or mysterious situations and Others.	… brash or crude Others.
… the dance of life – and those that tend to lead you a dance, because, despite common sense, that is what turns you on.	… anything that is too simplistic in that it follows a path so logical and straight as to be a total turn-off.
… environments that are quiet, quaint, peaceful, inspiring or subtly healing.	… harsh, violent, noisy places where there is no sense of the fragility and subtlety of your/human sensitivity.

WHEN ALONE …

… it is because you have never been definite enough about being with someone – in particular or in general. Alternatively, or additionally, it can be quite difficult for Other to determine quite where it is you are coming from, and what it is you really want, especially in the sexual sense. Because of all this, you never quite manage to focus yourself and your energies, and this in turn leads to Other not being able to focus upon you – which means that you wind up alone. So it is not because you are undesirable – far from it – but because maybe you think you are too strange for anyone to accept all of you. And so you make sure they don't see all of you, one way or the other, which eventually means Other won't see you at all. Allow yourself to be led by something spiritual, rather than foolishly trying to lead yourself, and Other will follow.

---

* Especially if you are male.

° Especially if you are female.

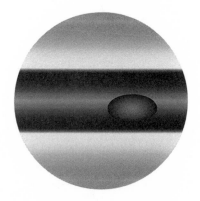

JUPITER

IMPORTANT TIPS

●   That great Jupiterian, the mystic poet William Blake, wrote that 'the Road of Excess leads to the Palace of Wisdom'. This simply means that by following our natural appetites and visions to the utmost we will eventually, through the highs and lows of real experience, discover the true meaning of things, and what we are really after. The Chinese philosopher, Lao-Tzu, presaged Blake with a line of similar meaning: 'If you first wish to contract something, you must first let it fully expand'. So when reading the Profiles, bear all this in mind – particularly with respect to the section headed BUT MAY BE EXCESSIVELY. Here you will find that what was originally an excess of yours can become a virtue. For example, someone with Jupiter in Taurus may have been excessively greedy and wasteful, gone to the limit, and then become a great advocate of natural economy and law.

●   By being true to your Jupiter Sign process, you will grow and prosper, and expand beyond your present limitations – quite magically, in some cases. In terms of relationship especially, whatever beliefs or opinions you might feel you disagree with in Other, by looking at them more carefully, hopefully you will see that they may have a vital point that you have been missing – to your cost. I always prefix these points with ☟☟☟ in the section headed BUT DISAGREE WITH.

JUPITER IN ARIES

The Spontaneous Giver • The Imprudent Giver

VIRTUES and PLEDGES

The goodness to *put your cards on the table* – yet to avoid being *foolish or naïve*.
The morality to be *respectful of Other's beliefs* and resist being *intolerant*.
The reverence to *allow Other to assert themself freely* – yet without then *taking advantage*.

YOU CAN BE TRUSTED TO	BUT MAY BE EXCESSIVELY
… promote or encourage Other's efforts and intentions to make something of themselves in their own right.	… enthusiastic about something simply because it is individualistic without it necessarily having much real worth.
… champion Others who are not afraid to stand up for what they believe in.	… impatient and even scathing of Other when they are not too sure of their standpoint.
… stand alone with your principles or take up a leading or central position when the occasion demands it.	… arrogant and wasteful when the complexity of a situation calls for caution.

YOU BELIEVE	BUT DISAGREE WITH
(What Promotes Growth and Enthusiasm)	*(What you are Put Off/Held Back by)*
… that luck and faith are things that you attain through your own efforts, and that the courage of your convictions and fighting for them is what makes them grow stronger.	… Other believing that everything comes to he or she who waits, or that the meek shall inherit the Earth, or similar philosophies of passivity.
… that life looks after those that live it.	♣♣♣ Point to watch: Sometimes one has to wait and take a back seat for a while; maybe Other can show you how to spot the right moment.
… in taking advantage of opportunities on impulse.	

WHEN ALONE …

… it is most probably because you have taken your independence to its logical conclusion – or extreme, more like. And if you are in some sort of leadership position, such a place is, as they say, often a lonely one to be in. In either case, you have to weigh the advantages against the disadvantages. It could be said that Jupiter in Aries eventually forces one to come to some sort of philosophy of acceptance regarding independence or leadership, and the aloneness that can go with it. If, however, you find this unacceptable, the spell of aloneness can be broken if you are prepared to share the nature of that aloneness with an Other who is preferably also a leader or a loner for then they'll properly understand your predicament. What all this amounts to is that when you do this you have to surrender the authority you have as a leader, or the inaccessibility of a loner, and exchange it for a personal respect for one another, a respect that is rather like that of comrades-in-arms. Even though you may be fighting different battles, your wounds are the same.

JUPITER IN TAURUS

The Substantial Giver • The Conceited Giver

VIRTUES and PLEDGES

The goodness to be *jovial and good-humoured* – without becoming too *physically indulgent*.
The morality to be *charitable and generous* – without being *smug or wasteful*.
The reverence for *Mother Nature's laws and abundance* – without being a *'green bore'*.

YOU CAN BE TRUSTED TO	BUT MAY BE EXCESSIVELY
… enjoy sensually what you have on a physical or material level, be it great or small.	… parsimonious or blind to the joys of living simply but enjoyably.
… give what you can in terms of food, drink, shelter, financial support – or even of your own body, if it comforts or pleasures Other.	… hedonistic, sexually irresponsible and greedy; squandering resources that could have been better used.
… steadily, if in some cases slowly, accumulate sufficient material wherewithal.	… keen on money, or conversely, short of money because of a lack of awareness regarding in-flow and out-flow.

YOU BELIEVE	BUT DISAGREE WITH
(What Promotes Growth and Enthusiasm)	*(What you are Put Off/Held Back by)*
… that life is based upon what is actually happening on the physical or material level of existence. This does not necessarily mean that you cannot believe in things you cannot touch and see – but it might. It would be more enlightening to say that you believed in Nature, the body, and Providence.	… Other leading a life that is not based upon solid or time-tested beliefs and values, or that follows a purely theoretical, and therefore fanciful and useless, philosophy.
	❗❗❗ Point to watch: A material philosophy needs an abstract one, and vice versa, for a more complete understanding.

WHEN ALONE …

… it is because, to one degree or another, you do not understand the nature of the invisible lines of force that connect you with the rest of life, and maybe one Other in particular. You are not naturally disposed to recognizing the psychic effect that one human being has upon another. You probably think that you are, but as I have said, it is significantly a matter of the degree to which you are aware of the nature of these psychic links. Put it this way, whatever feelings you are putting out, Other (known or to be) will be picking up on them – consciously, but mostly unconsciously. Now if you do not fully appreciate the exact nature of those invisible, unconscious feelings, then Other will mirror them back to you. So, for example, if you do not feel lovable or understood at some level, there will be no Other to love you or understand you at that level either.

Discover such buried feelings, and reconcile yourself with them, and Other will do so too. Similarly, praying (an invisible thing) will connect you with those invisible lines, and draw (an)Other in.

JUPITER IN GEMINI
The Information Giver • The Doubt Giver

VIRTUES and PLEDGES

The goodness to *judge everyone on their own merit* – yet to avoid *superficial appraisal.*
The morality to be *intellectually honest* in your relationships, and so avoid being *contrary.*
The reverence for *the written and spoken word* – but placing little value on *gossip and rumour.*

YOU CAN BE TRUSTED TO	BUT MAY BE EXCESSIVELY
… know at least a little about everything and everyone, and have an opinion concerning all of them.	… concerned with, and dabbling in, the affairs of others, trying to manage their lives and tell them how to behave.
… have a healthy sense of scepticism regarding any matter so that that you do not go overboard about anything or anyone, checking out the facts first.	… questioning so that nothing ever gets given the benefit of the doubt, so all you have is an array of contradictions, no solid feelings, and little or no faith.
… not be gullible intellectually.	… gullible emotionally.

YOU BELIEVE	BUT DISAGREE WITH
(What Promotes Growth and Enthusiasm)	*(What you are Put Off/Held Back by)*
… in the right, ability and opportunity to go where one pleases, talk to whom one wants, and generally to be a 'citizen of the world'.	… Other stuffing themselves away in some corner or being similarly self-absorbed.
… in the principle of 'thinking globally and acting locally' and the 'global village', and in the Internet.	… only entertaining a narrow band of contacts and therefore possibilities.
… in the power of reason.	‼️ Point to watch: Only by looking within, into the realm of feelings, will you know who you truly are on the outside.

WHEN ALONE …

… it is a very unusual event because you are, by your very nature, a contact-maker. So when you are alone – or at least, or rather especially, when you admit to being alone but still with an Other – it has to be for quite a serious reason. Most probably, such aloneness is forcing you to look more deeply into yourself in order to find out why you are like you are – alone, that is. By the nature of the beast, little else would have forced you to do so – after all, with all those people and things to explore on the outside, why should you have to go looking within? This does not mean to say that you haven't done any inner searching – of course you have – but it is the degree of depth that is the crucial issue now. Without going deeper than before into your make-up, you are not going to find out why you now feel so disconnected from (any) Other. You can be sure that the reasons will be found within, and hopefully this very book is helping you in this. Understanding how the inner state creates the outer one is now an important issue for your Jupiter Sign.

JUPITER IN CANCER
The Natural Giver • The Self-indulgent Giver

VIRTUES and PLEDGES

The goodness to *treat everyone as deserving of care* – yet to avoid *indiscriminate doting.*
The morality to *uphold family values and integrity* – without becoming *restricted and resentful.*
The reverence for *the generosity and receptivity of the Feminine* – but without being *too subjective.*

YOU CAN BE TRUSTED TO	BUT MAY BE EXCESSIVELY
… create a familiar, comfortable and hospitable environment which enables Other to grow and prosper.	… mollycoddling and indulging, to the point of preventing development in Other.
… protect the weak from the oppressiveness of the world at large, thereby giving them a chance to find their feet.	… protective and 'understanding' of Other, possibly in a bid to have your own shortcomings overlooked.
… instinctively tune in to the most basic, but sometimes subtle, needs of Other.	… aware of Other's weakness rather than their strengths, and, albeit unconsciously, playing upon them, drawing comfort from them.

YOU BELIEVE	BUT DISAGREE WITH
(What Promotes Growth and Enthusiasm)	*(What you are Put Off/Held Back by)*
… that safety and comfort and sustenance should be the birthright of everyone. This should be mainly provided by mother and the family unit, but not exclusively. 'Family' can also be taken to mean your nation, peer group, club, etc, and ultimately Humanity itself.	… Other putting politics and business, or any external non-emotional issues, before personal feelings and sentiments.
… in Mother Nature.	… the State not taking care of people if they cannot feed or home themselves.
	‼‼ Point to watch: Overall welfare at times has to be tough on the individual.

WHEN ALONE …

… it is because you had to get left with only yourself for comfort. In this way you have to become aware of how it is far more difficult to care about yourself that it is to care about Other. If this is incomprehensible to you, then I am afraid that you still have some way to go – so endeavour to understand because, more than any other Jupiter Sign, you can be flummoxed as to why you are alone and lonely when you are such a kind and considerate person. The main reason is that you have tended to bestow all manner of help and support upon Other when really you were wanting to do it for yourself. Other may have lapped this all up, which was like appreciation of you – or they abused or rejected it, which would confirm feelings of your not being worth caring about. Also, you could forgive Other because that would give you permission to forgive yourself indiscriminately – 'nothing wrong with me' sort of thing. But there is – you do not care about yourself enough! So imagine you are Other, take stock of them, and nurse them/yourself back to health.

JUPITER IN LEO

The Generous Giver • The Pretentious Giver

VIRTUES and PLEDGES

The goodness to *share your good feelings or fortune* – yet without being *patronizing*.
The morality to be *honourable and dignified* in your relationships – without being *pompous*.
The reverence for anything or anyone *bright and creative* – yet without being *élitist*.

YOU CAN BE TRUSTED TO	BUT MAY BE EXCESSIVELY
… encourage and further the creative efforts of Other, using whatever resources you can afford in order to do so.	… expectant that Other will deliver whatever will make you look more important, powerful and sexy.
… think big and live life with a sense of there being something great and magnificent about it, or at least you will admonish those who are mean-spirited and have little minds.	… patronizing or defamatory whenever Other does not live up to the high standard that you set for yourself – which you probably have not lived up to either.
… keep your 'important' promises.	… dismissive of annoying commitments.

YOU BELIEVE	BUT DISAGREE WITH
(What Promotes Growth and Enthusiasm)	*(What you are Put Off/Held Back by)*
… that there is something bright, honourable, creative and divine in human beings – or at least, some of them. For at the same time you believe in a hierarchy, in that certain people are more gifted and evolved than others, and so are obliged to set a good example.	… any excuse for behaving in a manner that is beneath one's dignity.
… in the Sun as God.	… in radical socialism, communism or anything that disregards and overrules the sovereignty of the individual.
	‼‼ Point to watch: The double standard of wanting privilege for self and equality for all.

WHEN ALONE …

… it is, for one reason, because it is the only way that you can truly rule your own roost. Furthermore, this would be because your rules for living are probably idiosyncratic to the point of it being impossible for Other to live up to or with. Alternatively, you are alone so that you may have the space and time to devise that set of rules, those individual principles, and then like the first case, realize that you have them and what they imply. Other – whether from the past or whether you are still involved with them for some reason (possibly concerning the law or children) – was or is still battling with your rules. If they have a set of their own rules too (with Jupiter in Leo too possibly), then you will have a protracted battle that could ensure that one or both of you stay alone. But THE rule of Jupiter in Leo in called *noblesse oblige*, which means that rank imposes obligations. In other words, if you want to be free (of this battle) to find someone else, or simply for peace of mind, see the conflict as beneath your dignity, accept your losses, and gracefully withdraw.

JUPITER IN VIRGO
The Helpful Giver • The Critical Giver

VIRTUES and PLEDGES

The goodness to *make the most out of the least* – yet to avoid *embittered complaining*.
The morality to be *upright and pure* in your relationships – without being *puritanical*.
The reverence for *personal space and solitude* – yet without being *anti-social*.

YOU CAN BE TRUSTED TO	BUT MAY BE EXCESSIVELY

… help Other to develop their potential through study and attention to detail.

… live a reasonably healthy and moderate life, with possibly only occasional, compensatory binges.

… live up to your responsibilities – for the sake of your love of order, not necessarily for the love of Other.

… demanding that Others do things/work exactly your way, with the consequence that you are inclined to attract either narrow-minded sycophants or wanton rebels.

… orderly, so that by way of balance, Other is correspondingly chaotic.

… envious of others that appear (not surprisingly) to have an easier lifestyle.

YOU BELIEVE	BUT DISAGREE WITH
(What Promotes Growth and Enthusiasm)	*(What you are Put Off/Held Back by)*

… that life is based upon reason, so you hold that good thoughts and deeds will eventually attract good fortune, and bad thoughts and deeds will ultimately result in bad fortune. Through appealing to this philosophy, your sense of reason, Other can get you to accept, enthuse over or forgive most things.

… Other leading a life that does not appear to have a pure and well-defined set of goals and principles.

❦❦❦ Point to watch: How you 'define' is limited by what you know – or rather what you don't. Other could be aware of things which your closely constructed beliefs overlook.

WHEN ALONE …

… it is most likely because you really need or actually want to be. Virgo is the Sign of the Hermit so, with the Planet of Growth here, it is during times of being on your own that you can get to do what you want or have to do. Everyday or incidental patches of being alone with yourself for relatively short periods of time should be cherished and made good use of. Actually being alone, in the sense of being without a mate or companion, could mean that you are being forced to get down to that project or task you have been putting off. Or possibly to consider in solitude the meaning for your existence, especially in terms of the work you do or are supposed to be doing, and what kind of relationship you would wish to be in. Fate is utterly intelligent; it does not leave you all on your own just for the hell of it. A darker reason for your being alone, which we have to consider, is that you are simply a misanthrope, that you dislike people generally. If so, you are alone to see the error of your ways – for you too are a person, one of the people.

JUPITER IN LIBRA

The Gracious Giver • The Insincere Giver

VIRTUES and PLEDGES

The goodness to *bring peace where there is strife* – yet to avoid *glossing over.*
The morality to be *true to Other* in your heart, not just *for appearances only.*
The reverence for *Other's beliefs and values* – yet without *loss of individual identity.*

YOU CAN BE TRUSTED TO	BUT MAY BE EXCESSIVELY
… be true to the whole idea of partnership, in the sense of it being the main thing to make sense of life – the good companion.	… reluctant to have a deeper look at the underlying energies that are involved between two people because it would mean looking at your own dirty laundry.
… honour Other, be they in the present or past, for you are aware that any negative feelings will cast a shadow.	… attached to anyone you have ever had relationship with, thereby confusing and compromising the current ones.
… adhere to certain principles of justice, and of social and aesthetic standards.	… misguided by conventional morality.

YOU BELIEVE	BUT DISAGREE WITH
(What Promotes Growth and Enthusiasm)	*(What you are Put Off/Held Back by)*
… that life is or should be based upon principles of justice and fair play. This especially applies in relationship for you are aware that a lack of moral sense is at the root of all relationship problems.	… Other doing whatever they please without any consideration for you – and vice versa.
… that as long as balance and harmony are created, within and without, all will be well.	… a lack of social propriety and beauty in everyday life.
	❢❢❢ Point to watch: If you truly believe in harmony then Other will make you aware that you have to go through conflict in order to get there.

WHEN ALONE …

… it is most likely because you are in a contradictory, self-cancelling state of being. On the one hand, you are in great need, consciously or unconsciously, of some deeply moving and intensely intimate relationship. On the other hand, however, you are resisting – again consciously or unconsciously – anything that plunges you into those same emotional depths because you know that they will force you to look more closely at yourself. What you fail to recognize is that you have it within you to balance these two extremes. This means that you allow yourself to go deeper enough into your emotional stuff, but you gracefully pull out if it rocks the boat too much – just enough to restore equilibrium, but no more. Conversely, if you should start to feel heavy or depressed it is because you have been being playing it too light (again), glossing over heavy issues and so remaining deadlocked. If this is the case, 'loosen your safety straps' by taking more risks emotionally – like following your heart or loins, and/or having some form of deep and ruthless therapy.

JUPITER IN SCORPIO

The Total Giver • The Manipulative Giver

VIRTUES and PLEDGES

The goodness to *understand and transform evil* – yet to avoid getting on a *power trip*.
The morality to be *true to the ultimate good* – and to eliminate *questionable motives*.
The reverence for the *powers of the unconscious* – without becoming *spooked or obsessive*.

YOU CAN BE TRUSTED TO	BUT MAY BE EXCESSIVELY
… leave no stone unturned in your pursuit of whatever or whoever you are passionately involved with.	… manipulative in order to get Other where you think you want them.
… be in touch with deep qualities and hidden causes in life and eventually be able to employ them to some beneficial end.	… concerned with the underlying meaning of things so that Other feels trapped in your web of intrigue, psychology or esoterica.
… pledge yourself absolutely once every snag has been experienced and eliminated.	… looking for the ultimate origin of things, and so miss the obvious, find it too difficult, go for the money, get disillusioned, start over …

YOU BELIEVE	BUT DISAGREE WITH
(What Promotes Growth and Enthusiasm)	*(What you are Put Off/Held Back by)*
… that all of life originates and issues from some hidden, unconscious or soul realm of existence, and so you relate to Other in an equally deep and serious fashion, seeing them as an important part in the process of the workings of your unconscious mind.	… the idea that relationships are random and are simply about the pursuit of pleasure and security and family-raising.
… in fated, deeply committed relationships.	❗❗❗ Point to watch: As this is an idea that is believed (at least, unconsciously) by most people, you may not know that you actually disagree with it.

WHEN ALONE …

… it is most likely because you do not believe you can survive the pain and intensity of a close relationship – ever or again. To deal with this state, you then see it going in one of two extreme directions – as is the wont of planets in Scorpio. The first avenue is deciding to follow a life of sexual abstinence where you focus all your (sexual) energies into some spiritual discipline. The other option, which is really all you're left with if you do not find the first acceptable, is to muddle through as you resist plunging into either dark pool. It takes very little reflection to see that this is actually a pretty dire course to take, because it hurts more than anything. So short of taking the road of abstention where you believe in something that will help manage your feelings for you, you have to believe that something will look after you, carry you and guide you through the treacherous reefs of intimate relating. What all this is saying is believe that you are positively transformed through emotional pain, and that your real enemy is thinking that there is a soft option.

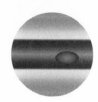

JUPITER IN SAGITTARIUS

The Expansive Giver • The Hollow Giver

VIRTUES and PLEDGES

The goodness to *create good vibrations* – yet without becoming *smug or complacent.*
The morality to *practise and promote ethical behaviour* – without being *sanctimonious.*
The reverence for *some Higher Power guiding us all* – and avoiding *going astray.*

YOU CAN BE TRUSTED TO	BUT MAY BE EXCESSIVELY
… take the highest moral ground that you are aware of, or at least …	… pompous and assume a kind of spiritual superiority, as if you know something that most Others do not.
… find the easiest way out of or through a tricky situation, and to be optimistic most of the time, or failing that…	… irresponsible in dealing with your more mundane circumstances, trusting things to work when really it is Others who make sure that they do.
… seek out some good reason for, or higher meaning to, life that will promote faith and optimism.	… God-trusting or God-denying.

YOU BELIEVE	BUT DISAGREE WITH
(What Promotes Growth and Enthusiasm)	*(What you are Put Off/Held Back by)*
… that life is a continuous process of growth and expansion on all levels of existence, leading to ultimate bliss. However, if you fail to see your part in this for some reason, it can make you feel resentful and forsaken, like 'If there is a God and he's not doing much for me, I must be damned'.	… Other disagreeing with you over matters of morality, religion, God, etc.
	… taking a negative viewpoint for that is inclined to remind you of your own doubts.
	❗❗❗ Point to watch: All rivers meet up in the ocean, all beliefs (or non-beliefs even) eventually amount to the same basic truths.

WHEN ALONE …

… you are probably out in the wilderness somewhere in an effort, consciously or unconsciously, to find out what you believe, or if there is something or someone to believe in (any more). If you are looking for someone to believe in then you are setting yourself up for a fall (again). It is vital for you to understand that a belief in some Higher Power or overall guiding intelligence is natural to you. But, owing to the nature of God, religion, etc, you may have become heavily disenchanted at some stage. But still that inner memory or notion that there is a God persists, but because you have denied it on the inside you look for it on the outside in some Other. But, being a mere mortal, Other cannot deliver what you are after, falls from grace in your eyes, and confirms your doubts. The whole thing could be the reverse way around, with you being the 'believer' who attracts an Other who worships you only to inevitably see or make you fall from grace. Your aloneness, arrived at either way, is God's way of getting you to see what God's truth is.

JUPITER IN CAPRICORN

The Constructive Giver • The Conditional Giver

VIRTUES and PLEDGES

The goodness to *live up to material responsibilities* – without it becoming a *slog*.
The morality to *uphold traditional values* – without them being *restrictive*.
The reverence for *time-worn customs and rituals* – yet without incurring a *loss of meaning*.

YOU CAN BE TRUSTED TO

… keep to certain tried and true methods and patterns in one or more areas of your life, even though they may not be that obvious.

… deliver what you promise, mainly because you don't promise what you cannot deliver.

… endure and make the most of times of difficulty or scarcity.

BUT MAY BE EXCESSIVELY

… dependent upon the rules and regulations laid down by someone else, be that Other or the State, or whoever appears to have the authority.

…reactionary towards this.

… cautious in what you give out, and then expect something back in return.

… caught up in the seeking of status, and overlooking your true worth in the process.

YOU BELIEVE

(What Promotes Growth and Enthusiasm)

… that life is basically a proving ground, a working situation, and that any kind of luxury must be well-deserved.

… that any spiritual belief should be based upon and around practical needs and natural laws and cycles.

… that 'by their works shall ye know them'.

BUT DISAGREE WITH

(What you are Put Off/Held Back by)

… fanciful or newfangled beliefs and ideas that have no proper roots in older systems.

… giving time or space to anyone who is all talk and no walk.

♉♉♉ Point to watch: Today's radicals are tomorrow's conservatives; constructive criticism is better than outright dismissal.

WHEN ALONE …

… it is as if you yourself have barred yourself from rewarding and sustainable relationships by imposing certain limiting conditions, or by allowing yourself to be subjected to them. This has something to do with the idea that you are what you believe you are – an idea that Jupiter in Capricorn will possibly sniff at. If you believe you are not capable of having a successful relationship then that is what the case will be. From your point of view there are probably some very practical and logical reasons for being on your own. But it is the other way around – you are choosing these restrictive circumstances, when the real reasons are to do with more emotional and internal qualities of your being. In short, you attract apparently limited or limiting relationships that reflect how you are limiting yourself – because you do not want to explore an area where you have no control. I recommend you look for the real reasons for being alone under your other Planet-Sign positions, especially the Moon and Venus if you are male, or the Sun and Mars if you are female.

JUPITER IN AQUARIUS
The Freedom Giver • The Erratic Giver

VIRTUES and PLEDGES

The goodness to be *open-minded* – and avoid being *too abstract*.
The morality to be *non-judgmental and impartial* – yet to avoid being *distant and aloof*.
The reverence for *equal rights* – yet without becoming bound by *political correctness*.

YOU CAN BE TRUSTED TO	BUT MAY BE EXCESSIVELY

… aspire to the ideal of everyone having the right to be who they are, and, more significantly, to be free to grow into that person, through whatever process of success and failure that it takes.

… resist dogmatism and anything or anyone that restricts the development of human potential, individually or collectively.

… liberal, to the point that Other finds it very difficult to get an honest, human emotional reaction from you. This can drive them to great extremes to shock you into one.

… open-ended morally – and unpredictable, anything from tight to loose. Other can find this so hard to relate to that they rebel.

YOU BELIEVE	BUT DISAGREE WITH
(What Promotes Growth and Enthusiasm)	*(What you are Put Off/Held Back by)*

… that life is what you think it to be, and so the freer and less biased your mind is then the more easily and healthily you will grow and progress. This implies that you are free to imagine God to be whatever you want 'it' to be, including the belief in the non-existence of God.

… the Universal Mind.

… fundamentalists who think they're right and everyone else is wrong.

… anything that denies the essential quality of human nature: free will.

‼️ Point to watch: Being averse to giving a definite form to your beliefs could amount to a lack of conviction generally.

WHEN ALONE …

… it is most likely because you have put or got yourself into a state of mind that that has 'immunized' itself against relationships. This you have done because intuition or experience tells you that being emotionally involved with another human being is painful and upsetting for it tests your theories of life to a point where they do not hold water any more. It is far easier to keep your philosophy intact when there is no Other to challenge it by putting you through emotional hoops where your intellectual theories provide no answers and bring no comfort. And so the deeper reason for your being alone is that you are having to stretch your mentality and morality to accommodate your emotional needs and desires. Double standards must be identified and reconciled, concepts of personal rights expanded to include the rights of Other to disagree with whose concepts. What is contradictory best be read as being paradoxical (believing in nothing is a belief in itself), or being a challenge (Other's chauvinism versus your liberalism, or vice versa).

JUPITER IN PISCES
The Unconditional Giver • The Whimsical Giver

VIRTUES and PLEDGES

The goodness to *give up the lesser for the sake of the greater* – and to avoid *self-pity.*
The morality to *follow your heart* in your relationships – without being *self-deluding.*
The reverence for *the best in human nature* – yet without being *gullible.*

YOU CAN BE TRUSTED TO	BUT MAY BE EXCESSIVELY

… appreciate the sensitive and soulful in Other and to respond to them in a creative and imaginative way.

… be kind and compassionate towards any suffering.

… put your own needs and fears on hold when Other's state or circumstances genuinely require help and reassurance.

… fantasy-prone – entertaining very unreal possibilities concerning Other.

… emotional and allow yourself precariously to be carried along by the tide of events.

… indiscriminate and impractical when it comes to understanding the wider implications of succumbing to what Other needs or promises.

YOU BELIEVE	BUT DISAGREE WITH
(What Promotes Growth and Enthusiasm)	*(What you are Put Off/Held Back by)*

… in rapture as the main indicator of anything or anyone being of true and lasting value. Such feelings would include blissful extremes of sorrow and pain and poignancy.

… that compassion, when all is said and done, is the ultimate response to the human condition.

… anything or anyone that does not inspire you or include a sense of the sublime.

… a clinical approach to the human condition.

♆♆♆ Point to watch: Fervour, especially of the religious variety, although so convincing at the time, can often lead to disaster.

WHEN ALONE …

… it is because you have over-emphasized or under-emphasized the expression of the above traits. If you have over-emphasized, you have misguidedly been wearing your heart on your sleeve at the same time as not being aware of the weaknesses and shortcomings of human nature. Consequently, you have been let down and hurt, leaving you to retreat into your own grotto of self-protection. But the best protection for the heart is that it be strong in the faith that all is for the best, and to eliminate self-importance. If you have under-emphasized the above-described qualities (quite possibly as a result of over-emphasizing them), you have therefore limited your possibilities to the point of being emotionally unavailable. This would be a case of your not being prepared to take the highs with the lows and settling for the safe and mediocre – which amounts to being alone or stuck with an oppressive or boring Other. Jupiter in Pisces is very much a case of 'Take away my demons and you take away my angels' as Dante so exquisitely put it.

SATURN

IMPORTANT TIPS

- The section on each page headed YOU COMMIT TO is focal because the Saturnian principles of Responsibility and Stability are absolutely dependent upon Commitment. So it is important to understand that COMMIT means a *conscious and constructive* act as opposed to merely falling in love or finding a security niche.

- There is an irony to your Saturn Profile in that the very Others or relationships that you ARE/SHOULD BE WARY OF are often what YOU CAN GET STUCK WITH ⟶ AS YOU ARE LEARNING whatever lessons they pose or set you.

- Read your Saturn Profile very carefully and you will see that your Saturn Sign is the great key to a fulfilling and lasting relationship because it is based upon something far more substantial than romantic love or unconscious or emotional neediness.

- TIME is an extremely important aspect of anything to do with Saturn. With respect to relationships, this means giving them time to develop as you work through the TASKS and OBLIGATIONS that are the concerns of your Saturn Profile.

SATURN IN ARIES
The Independent Rock • The Independence Block

TASKS and OBLIGATIONS

The discipline to *do things on your own account* – but not be *anti-social*.
Time taken/allowed to *develop powers of self-assertion* – thus assuaging *feelings of inadequacy*.
Building relationships that are *respectful of individuality* – yet do not become *separative*.

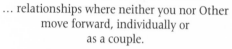

YOU CAN GET STUCK WITH	AS YOU ARE LEARNING TO
… relationships where neither you nor Other move forward, individually or as a couple.	… do what you want to do without Other or Other's approval.
… an Other who appears to keep you as and where they want you; strife-torn situations.	… become your own person, often through making your own mistakes.
… projects and relationships that come to nothing.	… be *patient* and allow things to develop step by step rather than having one or two energetic but ineffectual stabs.

YOU COMMIT TO	BUT ARE/SHOULD BE WARY OF
(How you are Won Over)	*(What you are Put Off/Oppressed by)*
… an Other who respects you as an individual and allows you to exercise your own will and discover your own strengths and weaknesses.	… Others who take you over, even though it may seem like they are taking some weight off your shoulders.
… an Other with a strong character who can act independently of you, even though you may at first find this threatening.	… overly forceful Others who selfishly do their own thing and expect you to sit tight or tag along.
… challenging situations and relationships.	… relationship prospects that are beyond your capabilities.

WHEN ALONE …

… it is because you have chosen the ultimately most appropriate and straightforward way of living up to the task that Saturn in Aries has set you: independence. Without anyone – or anything – to lean on or blame, you finally are forced to confront your own weaknesses as just that – your own. Alternatively, you could be alone because you are aware, through experience or instinct, that independence is far harder to maintain when you are with someone else. In fact, to be really honest, independence when there is no Other in your life is a bit like being a fire-fighter when there are no fires around. If you are alone but in a relationship, in the sense that you lead separate lives more or less, this is okay if it suits you – but I would venture to say that it doesn't really. This scenario is one of 'mock independence' where you are still dependent upon one another to ascribe your difficulties, inhibitions or hang-ups to. For example, wishing you could go off and do your own thing but you cannot because Other wouldn't like it. Saturn in Aries calls for brutal honesty.

SATURN IN TAURUS

The Steady Rock • The Money Block

TASKS and OBLIGATIONS

The discipline to *consolidate self-worth and finances* – and so not be *materially dependent*.
Time taken/allowed to *establish material security* – thus assuaging *fears of being without*.
Building relationships that are *physically loyal* – yet not *boringly predictable*.

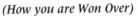

YOU CAN GET STUCK WITH	AS YOU ARE LEARNING TO
… relationships where you are very dependent upon Other for your material welfare and position.	… either become more materially self-sufficient, or to be happy with what you have got.
… an Other who has little or no material wherewithal and is dependent upon you.	… be generous but prudent with regard to Other.
… situations where money becomes a major issue and a block to emotional accord.	… look at what is emotionally lacking in your relationship, which the material state reflects.

YOU COMMIT TO	BUT ARE/SHOULD BE WARY OF
(How you are Won Over)	*(What you are Put Off/Oppressed by)*
… an Other who is materially stable, or is at least practical and has the potential to be so.	… feckless types who always seem to be one step (or less) away from ruin.
… an Other who is not at all well off materially, thereby calling upon you to organize or alleviate such matters.	… Others who are merely interested in you for your money or position, or conversely, who think they can buy you.
… an Other who is aware of your true worth and loves you solely for that, and will pass any tests that set out to prove this point.	… situations where money and what it can buy seem to be the only criteria of worth.

WHEN ALONE …

… it is mainly for one of two reasons. Firstly, being alone is in aid of forcing you to take serious stock of your material position, earning power, and whatever talents you have. Behind this is a case of your never really realizing or making the most of what you've got. Perhaps there was always an Other there to support you or bail you out. Secondly, it would be a case of having everything that money can buy – and nothing else. And so aloneness would eventually confront you with the realization that it is only the non-material or spiritual qualities of life that have any true and lasting worth. And like the first case, it may now be time for you to develop your own potential. If you are alone but still in a relationship, then it would be a kind of mixture of the above two cases. That is to say that you are staying together for material reasons only and consequently not discovering or appreciating the true worth of yourself or Other.

SATURN IN GEMINI

The Friendly Rock • The Communication Block

TASKS and OBLIGATIONS

The discipline to *say what you have to say and say it well* – not just *talking for the sake of it.*
Time taken/allowed to *establish lines of communication* – thus assuaging *misunderstandings.*
Building relationships that are *mentally stimulating* – yet not *lacking emotional rapport.*

YOU CAN GET STUCK WITH	**AS YOU ARE LEARNING TO**
… an Other who insists on there being a logical explanation for everything, or who won't listen to your logical explanations.	… create an understanding that is based upon empathy and/or touch.
… situations where no amount of thinking or talking seems to resolve issues.	… think through a problem until you really know what the issue is – then you probably won't have to say much or anything.
… an Other who refuses, or is unable, to talk or listen.	… be sure of your own mind and act upon what it tells you.

YOU COMMIT TO	**BUT ARE/SHOULD BE WARY OF**
(How you are Won Over)	*(What you are Put Off/Oppressed by)*
… an Other who is able to see and make contact with both the light and the dark, the bright and the unsure sides of your personality, and accept both of them.	… Others who are too enthusiastic about or impressed by just one facet of your being.
… an Other with whom you can talk about anything, and then not need to talk at all.	… interactions that are rife with misunderstandings or which stumble from querying the meaning and significance of one word to the next.
… an Other to whom you feel no need to explain or excuse yourself.	… uncomfortable silences.

WHEN ALONE …

… you probably have noone but your own 'dark twin' to interact with, which is why you prefer to be in anyone or anything's company rather than just your own. Your dark twin is the side of your personality which you prefer not to look at with more than a cursory glance. This is why knowing plenty of facts and figures, as well as always having someone to talk to (at, more like) are important to you for they fill your brain with seemingly useful and absorbing items. Your dark twin is 'jammed'. But it is your dark twin that holds the key to your success, as long as you communicate with it rather than seeking anything or anyone to distract you from it. It is just that over the years, especially the early ones, you were led to believe that this part of you was dumb, untalented, unattractive, etc, when really it was sensitive, original and attractive in a way that whoever labelled you thus found threatening.
So being alone can be your great breakthrough.

SATURN IN CANCER

The Caring Rock • The Caring Block

TASKS and OBLIGATIONS

The discipline to *fulfil family and emotional responsibilities* – yet not be *hardhearted*.
Time taken/allowed to *establish roots of shared feelings* – thus assuaging *depressive moods*.
Building relationships that are *mutually nurturing* – yet do not foster *co-dependency*.

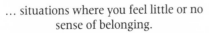

YOU CAN GET STUCK WITH	AS YOU ARE LEARNING TO
… situations where you feel little or no sense of belonging.	… build a solid or inner core of emotional security and/or a material stability that is not overly dependent upon Other.
… relationships where you or Other are very needy, clinging or pathetic in some way.	… develop 'feminine' qualities such as empathy or emotional understanding.
… uncomfortable set-ups owing to there being too much emotional 'cross-fire' or preoccupation; dysfunctional families.	… limit your concern for Other by considering your emotional rights too.

YOU COMMIT TO	BUT ARE/SHOULD BE WARY OF
(How you are Won Over)	*(What you are Put Off/Oppressed by)*
… an Other who, seeing past your emotional defences, recognizes and takes seriously your innermost feelings and sentiments, and can express genuine emotions themselves.	… gushing or mawkish displays of emotion.
… an Other who can control their feelings without suppressing yours or their own.	… oversentimentality or any expression of seemingly 'false' emotion that echoes childhood experiences; being mothered or restricted by family ties.
… being nurtured without being made to feel emotionally blackmailed/compromised.	… any situation or relationship that threatens to be a repeat performance of your own family's nature or difficulties.

WHEN ALONE ...

… it is most probably owing to your not being willing or able to express, involve or commit yourself emotionally – for one or more of the above reasons. Emotional isolation is a very necessary part of your life pattern, because it is through this that you get in touch with your often buried feelings. Try to avoid getting into either a downward spiral of self-pity on the one hand, or on the other, denying the feelings that you have, for this would prevent the possibility of new or renewed relationship. What we fear comes upon us – so sooner or later you had or have to get in touch with those needs and sensibilities that have been confused by certain fears of feeling or difficulty in feeling. Then you will attract *who* and *what* you need. You have an inclination to keep a stiff upper lip where your feelings are concerned, but without even realizing that you are doing so. Your emotions are rather like a cushion that has been sat upon for so long it has become compressed and forgotten how springy it was.
So go easy on yourself and try to plump yourself up a bit.

SATURN IN LEO
The Noble Rock • The Vanity Block

TASKS and OBLIGATIONS

The discipline to *conduct yourself in a dignified fashion* – but without *putting on an act*.
Time taken/allowed to *develop your creative potentials* – thus assuaging *feelings of insignificance*.
Building relationships based upon *mutual respect* – yet avoiding *rejection of criticism*.

YOU CAN GET STUCK WITH	AS YOU ARE LEARNING TO
… relationships where you feel subjugated or somehow inferior, possibly with little say in how things are done.	… recognize your own sense of authority and that you will be ultimately more admired for this than merely being impressive.
… Others who leave all the donkey-work to you, or expect you to put on a show all the time, no matter what.	… be content within yourself rather than being so dependent upon Other's esteem.
… an autocratic or even tyrannical Other.	… realize there is a 'boss' inside you that needs honestly to come out into the open.

YOU COMMIT TO	BUT ARE/SHOULD BE WARY OF
(How you are Won Over)	*(What you are Put Off/Oppressed by)*
… an Other who respects your power and authority and helps you express them, but does not let you lord it over them.	… an Other who worships you – because they are expecting something of you that you've yet to make real in yourself.
… a relationship in which you feel you have a definite role and a decent life-style.	… Others who admire you solely for superficial things like looks or style.
… an Other who has a healthy sense of personal pride, is creative in some way, and who is good with children.	… any Other who lacks integrity or is not prepared to take on the responsibilities of being a partner or parent.

WHEN ALONE …

… it is because you are being forced to take stock of who you really are as distinct from the impression that you give. Pride is the great issue with Saturn in Leo, especially because you probably feel that you are not someone who is that subject to it (unless you have Sun or Moon in Leo too). No, the subtlety with Saturn in Leo pride is that it is *defensive* pride, which means to say that your pride is in a part of yourself that you have been unsure of for quite some time. This is not as cryptic as it sounds. There is a sensitive and creative part of your personality which probably got sat upon early on in life and you have been protecting it ever since with a fear of criticism and a confident front. The trouble then becomes that you give Other the impression you are as strong as you feel you ought to have been, and Other then suppresses you or is in awe of you. In effect then, one or both of you thinks that the other is dictatorially ruling the roost – followed by strife and/or separation. Know that you have a natural authority, then exercise it moderately.

SATURN IN VIRGO

The Helpful Rock • The Critical Block

TASKS and OBLIGATIONS

The discipline to be *discriminating* – but without becoming *neurotically perfectionistic*.
Time taken/allowed to *implement necessary improvements* – thus avoiding *depression/ill-health*.
Building relationships that are *mutually helpful* – yet do not degenerate into *constant carping*.

YOU CAN GET STUCK WITH	AS YOU ARE LEARNING TO
… relationships where you find yourself in a subordinate position, or at least one where you have less control than you'd like.	… be of service to Other, purely because there is something that needs to be done and which only you can do so well.
… relationships that become so oppressive that you have to hide yourself away somewhere, possibly into (over)work.	… make a time and a place for yourself that does not simply become a retreat from looking at your emotional shortcomings.
… Others who deny you what you want.	… enjoy yourself (physically) without guilt.

YOU COMMIT TO	BUT ARE/SHOULD BE WARY OF
(How you are Won Over)	*(What you are Put Off/Oppressed by)*
… an Other who has a definite sense of purity but is also quite sensual, touching the border between 'right' and 'wrong'.	… Others who are morally offensive to you, be they too tight or too loose – but then again you may be there to teach them.
… an Other who respects your work and your physical space.	… Others who attempt to take over your life.
… a relationship where you know exactly what is and what is not expected of you, and Other of them.	… vague, messy or hoping-against-hope types of relationship – that is, unless you are prepared to make it work at any cost.

WHEN ALONE …

… it is because you are more or less allergic to being in close proximity to anyone for that long. But what lies behind this seemingly impossible dilemma is the fact that there is something about you that just has to be left untouched. The trouble is that you are not usually aware of this until an Other starts to invade that space in some way. You then experience this as *total* invasion and you are driven to *totally* retreat – or, by way of projection, Other becomes unavailable, that is, Other retreats because you don't. Then when such retreat becomes unbearable, you indiscriminately throw yourself back into the emotional fray, only to eventually retreat again, *ad nauseam*. So now that you are alone again, ascertain exactly that part of you that you wish to keep to yourself and why, rather than finding out the usual, hard way.
You will find that this 'virgin territory' of yours is a part that is in need of healing, so see to it.
Metaphorically, this is like a boil that gets periodically bashed and more and more sore
while you're dancing with someone. So lance it.

SATURN IN LIBRA

The Just Rock • The Decision Block

TASKS and OBLIGATIONS

The discipline to *fulfil your loving duty to Other* – but not just be *bound by convention*.
Time taken/allowed to *establish right relations* – thus avoiding *untenable relationships*.
Building relationships that are *true to themselves* – and are not just relationships *in name only*.

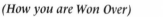

YOU CAN GET STUCK WITH

… a relationship that starts out well but becomes increasingly dull, meaningless and confining.

… doing a balancing act between the Other whom you have to be with and the Other whom you want to be with.

… an Other for fear of being alone.

AS YOU ARE LEARNING TO

… enter into relationship for reasons of conscious choice rather than just because it is 'what one does'.

… face the fact that you only find yourself reflected in Other; if you are split within yourself there will be more than one Other.

… be true to yourself.

YOU COMMIT TO

(How you are Won Over)

… an Other who is as willing to commit themselves as you are; how much is that?

… an Other whom you know and feel will make an honest person out of you, and who wants you to make an honest person out of them (honest=honest with oneself).

… an Other of serious intent and gracious demeanour, and with some doubts.

BUT ARE/SHOULD BE WARY OF

(What you are Put Off/Oppressed by)

… thinking that simply having a certificate of marriage will make it work.

… an Other who has all the right qualities and credentials; the less cracks there seem to be then the more there will be.

… any Other who is utterly convinced that you are made for one another, or conversely, who is constantly undecided.

WHEN ALONE …

… it is basically because you are having to review and consider what relationships are all about, for you as an individual in terms of your experience, and also more generally with regard and in contrast to your social milieu. It is more than likely that your initial attitude to relationship was very much moulded by your class, racial and cultural background. This is the social 'programme' which has you unconsciously believe that a certain Other, at a certain age, and from a certain social category, is certainly the one for you. If my records are anything to go by, one person in 20 with Saturn in Libra remains happily and faithfully married to their original marriage partner. So the chances are that at some point you will be looking at just yourself in the mirror – and hopefully realizing that any partner is entirely to do with what you see there.
What is honest and real will attract just that, in the same way that what is denied and bound up in fantasy will conjure up frustration, deceit and disillusionment.

SATURN IN SCORPIO
The Potent Rock • The Sexual Block

TASKS and OBLIGATIONS

The discipline to *control powerful urges* – without becoming *repressed*.
Time taken/allowed to *detect the inner truth* – thus assuaging *feelings of jealousy*.
Building relationships that are *deeply trusting* – in order to avoid *treachery*.

YOU CAN GET STUCK WITH	AS YOU ARE LEARNING TO
… a relationship which is tied together only by joint finances and possessions, and/or children; power games.	… establish what truly matters to you; having ruthlessly to cut your losses would be the testament to your sincerity in this.
… relationships which are doomed from the start – there being a third party, internal problem or some other obstacle to union.	… stop using excuses for not taking the plunge into an intimate relationship.
… an Other for fear of making the break.	… be on your own, so at last you can break the taboo of getting to know who you are.

YOU COMMIT TO	BUT ARE/SHOULD BE WARY OF
(How you are Won Over)	*(What you are Put Off/Oppressed by)*
… an Other whom you feel at a very deep level you are willing to spend your life with, for whom you would literally die or suffer death.	… any signs that if push comes to shove Other will not be at your side.
… a relationship that has a genuinely fulfilling sexual dimension.	… sexual incompatibility, or sexual problems and inhibitions – but these may very well be the actual reason for a relationship, that is, to become aware of them and sort them out.
… an Other with whom you mutually share all of your secrets.	… a lack of confidentiality and/or an Other who is censorious/indiscreet about you.

WHEN ALONE …

… it is because there is a hidden, and probably sexual, side to your nature that effectively repels Other, although paradoxically that same side can initially attract Other. But this is not as paradoxical as it sounds because sexual energy by its very nature both attracts and repels, without one's looks, mind or bank balance having any bearing upon it. Sexual energy is somewhat like an emanation that issues from one like a scent. That scent can be strong or weak, pleasant or unpleasant. Often Other can be drawn to it if it is strong only to find later that it is not pleasant, in the sense that there is an undertone that says 'stay away, I am not really sexually available' (for whatever reason). But it is the word 'sexually' that needs defining, for it has a specific meaning here. It is saying that you are not ready or able to get close enough to Other on a psychological level – that is, there is something deep in your soul that needs healing, possibly purging. Sexual relationships may well actually do this, but if your scent precludes this, then seek psychological help.

SATURN IN SAGITTARIUS

The Faithful Rock • The 'God' Block

TASKS and OBLIGATIONS

The discipline to *adhere to an evolving moral code* – but without becoming *dogmatic*.
Time taken/allowed to *explore life's meaning* – thus assuaging *inner doubts*.
Building relationships that are *adventurous* – yet do not encourage *amorality*.

YOU CAN GET STUCK WITH	AS YOU ARE LEARNING TO
… relationships which are held together mostly by guilt posing as obligation.	… develop a more balanced, broad and generous sense of what life expects of you.
… relationships that are strife-torn, especially owing to conflicts of belief.	… turn the other cheek in the faith that whatever is right will eventually win through; avoid self-righteousness.
… holding the baby or feeling that you have got the raw end of a deal, that you have been unjustly treated.	… discover that you are able to manage impeccably all that is set you.

YOU COMMIT TO	BUT ARE/SHOULD BE WARY OF
(How you are Won Over)	*(What you are Put Off/Oppressed by)*
… an Other who has beliefs and ethical values similar to your own, and who is forever seeking with an open mind.	… Others who are too set in their ways religiously and are closed to the exploration of any other systems of belief.
… an Other with whom you can travel, both inwardly and outwardly.	… an Other who is stuck in some quasi-religious or sectarian backwater.
… an Other who has a strong faith in the ultimate good, and whose principles are well-defined but tolerant.	… an Other who preaches and is lacking in tolerance, or who has traits of character that you yourself find hard to tolerate.

WHEN ALONE …

… it is because you are having to learn to be more flexible and easy-going. You may believe that you are so, but upon reflection you would realize that you do have some quite tight expectations of what you or Other should be. You or someone else has set down some rather too well-defined parameters of acceptable attitudes and behaviour. The trouble is that this took place very early on in life – or you were actually born with them – and so consequently it is never very long before Other does something which grates upon those predefined beliefs and standards. Effectively, you class yourself out of the relationship stakes, or you get stuck with someone who is simply a reflection of how stuck you are with those very standards. As these self-justifying convictions of yours are relatively unconscious, you would notice them better if you wrote down what you do not allow Other to be or do. Pushing back these limitations, which were originally put there to protect you from the unknown, would greatly increase your chances of successful relationship.

SATURN IN CAPRICORN

The Veritable Rock • The Status Block

TASKS and OBLIGATIONS

The discipline to *take on material and professional responsibilities* – but not become *hard-bitten*.
Time taken/allowed to *establish the purpose of a relationship* – but avoiding merely *hollow status*.
Building relationships where you have *well-defined roles* – yet don't become *coldly businesslike*.

YOU CAN GET STUCK WITH	AS YOU ARE LEARNING TO
… dull and meaningless relationships which are maintained merely for the sake of status or avoiding being seen to fail.	… grasp the fact that the only mistakes in life are the ones that you do not learn from; come clean and make a fresh start.
… an Other who is seriously incapable of managing life in the material world.	… prove that you can be the one in charge; be the one who provides stability.
… Others who want to control you and keep tabs on you.	… be more in control of yourself; make your own boundaries clear and firm.

YOU COMMIT TO	BUT ARE/SHOULD BE WARY OF
(How you are Won Over)	*(What you are Put Off/Oppressed by)*
… an Other who has their own firmly established sense of duty, discipline, responsibility or professional position.	… Others who have yet to find out the meaning of duty and responsibility – especially if they are kidding themselves (and you) in this respect.
… an Other who is old enough to be mature and know their place in the world.	… Others who have more growing up to do than their actual age merits.
… an Other who is objective and self-contained enough to keep emotional considerations in perspective.	… Others who are easily swayed and too dependent upon your approval.

WHEN ALONE …

… it is, for one reason, owing to the fact that you are having to get a clearer idea of yourself as a separate identity. This would especially be the case if you have an emphasis on Water Signs (Cancer, Scorpio and Pisces) because you would be learning to contain yourself rather than be contained – or kept down and in, more like – by an Other. Another reason for being alone would be quite the opposite in that you had made yourself too self-contained to the point where no Other could get near enough to you to be actually with you in the emotional sense. Yet another reason, which could spring from the first two, is that you have become cynical about Others in general, and cannot see any possibility of a relationship ever working. Of course, keeping yourself to yourself would ensure this, which is like trying to make an omelette without cracking the eggs. So, alone, you are establishing a strong enough shell to contend with Other; then/or, you must allow your shell to be broken into, or at least cracked a little.

SATURN IN AQUARIUS

The Principled Rock • The Originality Block

TASKS and OBLIGATIONS

The discipline to *ascertain and stick to your principles* – but not be *judgmental*.
Time taken/allowed to *creatively develop idiosyncrasies* – and so avoid *suppressing originality*.
Building relationships that *revere each other's uniqueness* – and so do not foster *alienation*.

YOU CAN GET STUCK WITH	AS YOU ARE LEARNING TO
… relationships that do not allow you to be yourself with all your peculiarities upfront; Others who insist that you behave in a formal fashion that is acceptable to whoever they regard as being the 'right people'.	… be your true self through having it forced to the surface by being trapped in the midst of false and shallow values/people.
… highly unusual or unconventional relationships that are highly inconvenient.	… go through a zigzag process whereby you are shunted this way and that until you eventually arrive with the right Other in the right place at the right time.

YOU COMMIT TO	BUT ARE/SHOULD BE WARY OF
(How you are Won Over)	*(What you are Put Off/Oppressed by)*
… an Other who allows you to go through many twists and turns as you endeavour to discover who you really are as a unique individual.	… Others who get embarrassed by your peculiarities and, worse still, become censorious about them.
… an Other who is way outside of your background's idea of acceptability, but knows the real you.	… going overboard for an Other simply because they are the type your mother or father warned you against.
… an Other who is positively unusual.	… pretentiousness in any shape or form, particularly a pretence at liberality.

WHEN ALONE …

… it is quite likely owing to your being what could be called a 'social rarity', in that you do not fit easily into one of the usual niches that society provides. Put plainly, the odds of your finding a suitable Other are not so much against you, but dependent upon your having arrived at a thorough awareness and acceptance of your own distinctly unique personality. This will take time for you to arrive at, but when you do, that 1,000 – 1 chance will seem immaterial as that one Other in a thousand pops into your life. However, the real quirk here is that you can be inclined to look and go for someone who is as conventional as you like to think you are, or who is as odd as you hope you are not. Consequently, you can persist in making the odds longer than they actually are. Yet another permutation is where you find the right Other but they seem too unusual for you, that is, they are reflecting back at you your own unusualness which you are denying. Given time, and an honest awareness of your idiosyncrasies, you should find the lid to fit your kettle.

SATURN IN PISCES
The Subtle Rock • The Sensitivity Block

TASKS and OBLIGATIONS

The discipline to *admit to weaknesses and blind-spots* – but not be *self-effacing*.
Time taken/allowed to *appreciate the subtle and elusive* – thus preventing *misunderstandings*.
Building relationships that are based upon *mutual acceptance* – yet do not foster *evasiveness*.

YOU CAN GET STUCK WITH	AS YOU ARE LEARNING TO
… Others who are slippery, vague, hopeless cases who are hard to pin down.	… be of selfless help to Other, which may include having to be very tough on them.
… Others who are ruled by logic and deny the existence of anything mystical or scientifically unexplainable.	… look into and develop the more mystical and illogical side of life and yourself, yet making sure that you are not being fanciful.
… Others who are safe but boring, and/or who seek oblivion in drink or drugs.	… take a good look at how you are possibly avoiding your own issues.

YOU COMMIT TO	BUT ARE/SHOULD BE WARY OF
(How you are Won Over)	*(What you are Put Off/Oppressed by)*
… an Other with whom you feel subtle but undeniable ties that probably involve the making of some kind of sacrifice.	… Others who have a hard luck story that appeals to your sense of guilt or worthlessness which may be posing as your wanting to 'save' Other.
… an Other who accepts you unconditionally, has no ulterior motives and does not play on your feelings.	… confidence tricksters, recognizable by their appeal to your sympathy or idealism.
… an Other who is creative, sensitive and spiritual, and/or quiet and gentle.	… loud, brash, flashy types who make all manner of unrealistic claims and promises.

WHEN ALONE …

… it is very likely because you have yet to come to the realization that there is a subtle, spiritual dimension to relationships – or that there ought to be. Because you are inclined to deny the invisible and scientifically unverifiable in life and yourself, you also try to keep your relationships simpler and more straightforward than it is possible for them to be. You may very well attempt to keep them simple to the point of them being purely physical or 'nothing serious', or with someone who agrees with or embodies your acceptable version of existence, but who is unacceptably dull, coarse or insensitive. So aloneness for you is really a testament to your denial of your own sensitivity and what you see as the emotional chaos that such sensitivity implies.

But it is only through admitting and accepting your soul and its sensitivity that you will attract a kindred spirit. And that kindred spirit will be able to soothe those chaotic emotions and help you to accept yourself, while you find yourself bringing a subtle but powerful meaning to their life too.

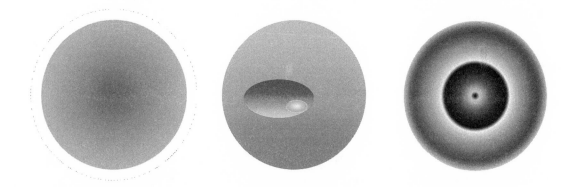

URANUS, NEPTUNE
AND PLUTO

● Because these Outer Planets spend so long (approximately 7,14 and 20 years respectively) in each Sign, the actual Sign qualities are spread out over a whole generation and have, in themselves, little meaning as far as personal relating is concerned. However, you will need to know their Sign positions for determining:

The significance of Ruling Planets (*see* page 276)

Sign-to-Sign and Planet-to-Planet Interaction in Chapter Three

Relationship Themes and Dynamics in Chapter Four

● If you wish to know about the generational effects of the Outer Planets, I refer you to my previous book *Do It Yourself Astrology* (Element Books). If you wish to know how they affect you individually you would need to find out their House positions and the Aspects they make to the other Planets in your Birthchart. This can be done by applying to one of the organizations given on the last page, or to myself.

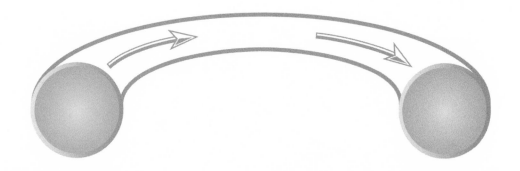

RISING SIGN – SETTING SIGN

RISING SIGN – SETTING SIGN

The Rising Sign or ASCendant is simply the Zodiacal Sign that is rising in the East at the time of birth, and the Setting Sign, or DEScendant, is the one that is setting in the West at that time. The ASCendant and DEScendant are therefore always in opposite Signs. For example, anyone who has Virgo Rising (ASCendant in Virgo) would always have Pisces Setting (DEScendant in Pisces) because Virgo and Pisces are opposite Signs. This can be seen graphically on the CHARTWHEEL. Also, be aware that the Rising Sign is seen to be on the left, and the Setting Sign on the right.

What the RISING SIGN represents and describes is SELF-EXPRESSION, that is, what it is about an individual that is presented to the world as their IDENTITY, CHARACTER or IMAGE. The event this stems from is BIRTH, when what you APPEAR to be EMERGES into the world.

What the SETTING SIGN represents and describes is the equal and opposite reaction to this expression of Self. It is OTHER – which could be anything or anyone other than Self, be it a motorcar that bumps into you at a road junction, a pet, or the general public – but more usually it is that 'significant other': one's PARTNER, SPOUSE or, as they are so often appropriately called, one's OTHER or BETTER HALF. And as a birthchart is a map of potential, the Setting Sign can tell us what to look for if we do not have a better half – for they are out there somewhere waiting for us! Furthermore, it can also show us what it is about our Self that we prefer to see in Other – because it is unconsciously felt to be too good or too bad to exist in our Self. This is the timeworn situation of falling in love with somebody when we see in them what we really like and identify with, and then falling out of love when we see in them what we do not like and do not want to identify with.

In psychology this is called PROJECTION. This is a very apt term. Imagine life and yourself as a motion picture show. There is the *film,* which is your life story being played out; the *screen* upon which it appears to happen in the form of external events and relationships; and then there is the *lens* through which you focus your attention. Everything that appears to be happening in your life (screen) has actually been created by you (film and lens) consciously or unconsciously. This is a very profound and powerful idea, because it means that it is within our *own* control as to how we see our partners and others generally, and ultimately what we determine as their actual nature. The reason why this hasn't caught on as permanent cultural and social custom is because in order for it to work you have to *own* not only what you see as pleasant and positive in Other as being a reflection of or complement to yourself, but also what is nasty and negative. (*See also* The Venous Blood Syndrome on page 7.)

A diagrammatic view of this profound model of the relationship between Self and Other, along with their astrological correspondences of Rising and Setting Sign, is given below.

PROJECTOR = SELF = RISING SIGN   SCREEN = OTHER = SETTING SIGN

The whole issue of psychological projection is a theme running throughout this book, and I particularly refer you to THE MIRROR on page 485, where you can immediately experience this as the basic internal principle of relating. The Mirror is seen astrologically in terms of the Sun as the Life of an individual being reflected by the Mirror of the Moon which is symbolic of all responses and reactions to Life or Solar expression. Here though, with respect to the Rising Sign and the Setting Sign, we can see how this basic principle operates externally for the individual, how we get back what we put out as that equal and opposite reaction. The Sun and Moon are incorporated into this model in terms of the Sun being the *light* in the projector that makes the whole show possible (that is, your life itself), and the Moon as being the screen which reflects that light.

The meanings for all Rising and Setting Signs are given in THE RISING AND SETTING SIGN PROFILES which begin on page 263 after you have been shown how to work them out. Each Profile is set out with the Rising Sign on the left and the Setting Sign on the right at the top of the page. There then follows a twofold positive/negative, title for the SELF or Rising Sign – that is, your expressed image of yourself – and also for the OTHER or Setting Sign – that is, what you are inclined to attract back as a complement or reaction to that Self, your PROJECTED SELF in fact. This could also be regarded as your alter ego. I then go on to describe and explain how this Interaction between Self and Other pans out according to how you are seeing it – or projecting it.

You will find that the more you claim what the DEScendant or Setting Sign describes as belonging to your Self rather than to Other, then the more Other will automatically integrate, agree and harmonize with you. This is simply because you have chosen to integrate, agree and harmonize with a part of yourself that you have hitherto disowned and projected. This is particularly true with regard to the SHADOW aspect of the Rising/Setting Sign Interaction which is also included on each page profile. A good example of someone taking back their Shadow projection, or introjecting as it is called, was Diana, Princess of Wales. She had Sagittarius Rising/Gemini Setting and, through owning her 'inferiority' rather than projecting it on to Prince Charles, she gained the common touch for which she was and still is famous. Note, however, how much initially she needed to suffer her own sense of inferiority in order to convert it. Also, it would seem that Other for Diana was the World rather than one person. When she found that One Other, it was time to leave and make her final and lasting impression on our World – like the Setting Sun. She was born just before Sunset.

In my practice as an astrological consultant, I have lost count of the number of times I have described a client's partner to them – to which they nod in affirmation – only then to remind them that I am seeing that description in *their* birthchart! Having said this, I must point out that such a description is not entirely gleaned from the Setting Sign alone, although it is so often the same as the Sun or Moon Sign of the partner. As you will have hopefully seen so far, and will see more of later, the Planet-Sign positions also depict the kind of partners and relationships we attract.

WORKING OUT YOUR RISING SIGN/SETTING SIGN

Turn to the next page for instructions on how to read the Tables that follow. The actual descriptions of what each Rising Sign/Setting Sign means follow the Tables in the RISING AND SETTING SIGN PRO-FILES. The Tables just give you the Rising Sign, as the Profiles are set out from Aries Rising through to Pisces Rising, with the appropriate Setting Signs included.

RISING SIGN TABLES AND HOW TO USE THEM

SIGN-NAME ABBREVIATIONS

Aries	ARI	**Leo**	LEO	**Sagittarius**	SAG
Taurus	TAU	**Virgo**	VIR	**Capricorn**	CAP
Gemini	GEM	**Libra**	LIB	**Aquarius**	AQU
Cancer	CAN	**Scorpio**	SCO	**Pisces**	PIS

The Tables show Rising Signs for each hour of the day, on the hour. For our purposes here it is only necessary to list them for every three days, and I must stress that this method is greatly simplified. To calculate an absolutely accurate Ascendant, things like Longitude and Latitude and Sidereal Time have to be taken into consideration by a trained astrologer or using a computer program. If you do not already know your Ascendant I recommend that you obtain it through contacting one of the astrological bodies (including myself) given at the back of the book. If you obtain your 'Cross Aspects' described later on in the book in Part Two, you will also be supplied with your precise Ascendant, along with other accurate astrological data such as House positions.

For the time being though, using our *example BIRTH TIME and DATE of 5 AUGUST 1955 at 4.30pm British Summer Time (BST) in OXFORD, ENGLAND*, we carry on as follows:

1 If you were born during Summer Time (or during some out-of-the-ordinary time standard such as when the United Kingdom went over to Central European Time between 1968 and 1972), it is best to convert this back to the usual Standard Time – that is, the time as it was before being changed. Such is the case with our example, so we take off one hour as BST is one hour ahead of GMT. This gives us 3.30pm.

UNKNOWN BIRTH TIME

If you do not know your birth time, try reading all of the Rising Sign Profiles and select which you think is most likely. If you have a vague birth time, look up all Rising Signs occurring during that period and study all of those Profiles and make your choice. I must emphasize though, that this method is not always that easy or that reliable (there can be Planets in Signs creating a similar effect), but it gives you a clue.

2 Go to the Tables and look for the date nearest to the one in question. *For our example this will actually be AUG 5.* You will see that there are two strips of entries for all dates. The upper or shaded strip has AM birth times in the top half of it, and the corresponding Rising Sign and its degree in the bottom half. The lower or non-shaded strip has PM birth times in the top half of it, and again, Rising Sign and degree in the bottom half. *In our example we look along the lower strip, as the birth time is PM, for the Hour nearest 3.30pm. This could be 3 or 4, and the Rising Sign given below each is SAG 10 and SAG 23 respectively. Using the Sign-Name Abbreviation given above, we know that in either case our example was born with SAGittarius Rising.*

3 Now for the degree. There are 30 degrees of arc to each Sign of the Zodiac. This is because there are 360 degrees in a circle, and 12 Signs in the Zodiac (360 divided by 12 = 30). The first degree, or 01, is just past the thirtieth degree of the previous Sign.

4 Because this method of Rising Sign calculation has been greatly simplified, and is therefore approximate, if the Rising Sign you come up with is near the beginning (01–05 degrees) or near the end (26–30) of a Sign, then consider that, in the former case, the preceding Sign may be your Rising Sign, and in the latter, the following may be your Rising Sign. Read the Profiles for both and see which one is the most suitable. For the order of the Signs, look at the top of this page where they are listed in three columns reading downwards. If our example were born at 4am on the same day (after having deducted the hour for Summer Time) we would look on the upper or AM strip for AUG 5, and find that the Rising Sign and Degree is CAN 29 or 29 degrees of Cancer Rising. Being near the end of that Sign there is also the possibility of the Ascendant being the Sign after, which is LEO. Or if born at 7am that day, we would have VIR 05, meaning that it might be Leo Rising, the Sign before VIRgo.

5 INTERPOLATION – If you know what this means then use it to determine a more accurate Rising Sign and degree – that is, adjust the intervals between the birth times and between the birth dates, and between the times, dates and degrees given in the Tables. *In our example, we saw that 3.30pm gives us SAG 10 for 3pm, and SAG 23 for 4pm. A simple interpolation here would give us SAG 16 as this is the approximate midpoint between SAG 10 and SAG 23, as 3.30pm is the midpoint between 3 and 4pm.*

6 Having worked out your Rising Sign or ASCendant, you can now enter it on the CHARTWHEEL as you did with the Sun, Moon and Planets earlier on. As you do so, be sure also to insert your DEScendant exactly in the OPPOSITE Sign to your Rising Sign. Use the abbreviations ASC for your Rising Sign and DES for your Setting Sign as in the CHARTWHEEL Example 1 on page 29. *NOW* read your Rising/Setting Sign Profile in the pages following the tables, but be sure first to read the IMPORTANT TIPS on page 263.

RISING SIGN TABLES

JAN 1 – AM	1	2	3	4	5	6	7	8	9	10	11	12noon
Sign/Degree	LIB 20	SCO 02	SCO 14	SCO 26	SAG 08	SAG 21	CAP 04	CAP 19	AQU 07	AQU 28	PIS 23	ARI 18

JAN 1 – PM	1	2	3	4	5	6	7	8	9	10	11	12midnight
Sign/Degree	TAU 12	GEM 01	GEM 18	CAN 02	CAN 15	CAN 28	LEO 09	LEO 21	VIR 03	VIR 15	VIR 27	LIB 09

JAN 4 – AM	1	2	3	4	5	6	7	8	9	10	11	12noon
Sign/Degree	LIB 23	SCO 04	SCO 16	SCO 28	SAG 10	SAG 23	CAP 07	CAP 22	AQU 11	PIS 03	PIS 28	ARI 23

JAN 4 – PM	1	2	3	4	5	6	7	8	9	10	11	12midnight
Sign/Degree	TAU 16	GEM 05	GEM 21	CAN 05	CAN 17	LEO 01	LEO 12	LEO 23	VIR 05	VIR 17	VIR 29	LIB 11

JAN 7 – AM	1	2	3	4	5	6	7	8	9	10	11	12noon
Sign/Degree	LIB 25	SCO 07	SCO 18	SAG 01	SAG 13	SAG 26	CAP 10	CAP 26	AQU 15	PIS 07	ARI 03	ARI 28

JAN 7 – PM	1	2	3	4	5	6	7	8	9	10	11	12midnight
Sign/Degree	TAU 20	GEM 08	GEM 23	CAN 07	CAN 20	LEO 02	LEO 14	LEO 26	VIR 08	VIR 20	LIB 02	LIB 14

JAN 10 – AM	1	2	3	4	5	6	7	8	9	10	11	12noon
Sign/Degree	LIB 27	SCO 09	SCO 21	SAG 03	SAG 15	SAG 28	CAP 13	CAP 29	AQU 19	PIS 12	ARI 08	TAU 02

JAN 10 – PM	1	2	3	4	5	6	7	8	9	10	11	12midnight
Sign/Degree	TAU 23	GEM 11	GEM 26	CAN 10	CAN 22	LEO 04	LEO 16	LEO 28	VIR 10	VIR 22	LIB 04	LIB 16

JAN 13 – AM	1	2	3	4	5	6	7	8	9	10	11	12noon
Sign/Degree	LIB 29	SCO 11	SCO 23	SAG 05	SAG 18	CAP 01	CAP 16	AQU 03	AQU 23	PIS 17	ARI 14	TAU 07

JAN 13 – PM	1	2	3	4	5	6	7	8	9	10	11	12midnight
Sign/Degree	TAU 27	GEM 14	GEM 29	CAN 12	CAN 25	LEO 07	LEO 19	VIR 01	VIR 12	VIR 24	LIB 06	LIB 18

JAN 16 – AM	1	2	3	4	5	6	7	8	9	10	11	12noon
Sign/Degree	SCO 02	SCO 14	SCO 26	SAG 08	SAG 20	CAP 04	CAP 19	AQU 07	AQU 28	PIS 22	ARI 18	TAU 11

JAN 16 – PM	1	2	3	4	5	6	7	8	9	10	11	12midnight
Sign/Degree	GEM 01	GEM 17	CAN 02	CAN 15	CAN 27	LEO 09	LEO 21	VIR 03	VIR 15	VIR 27	LIB 09	LIB 21

JAN 19 – AM	1	2	3	4	5	6	7	8	9	10	11	12noon
Sign/Degree	SCO 04	SCO 16	SCO 28	SAG 10	SAG 23	CAP 07	CAP 22	AQU 10	PIS 02	PIS 27	ARI 22	TAU 15

JAN 19 – PM	1	2	3	4	5	6	7	8	9	10	11	12midnight
Sign/Degree	GEM 04	GEM 20	CAN 04	CAN 17	LEO 01	LEO 11	LEO 23	VIR 05	VIR 17	VIR 29	LIB 11	LIB 23

JAN 22 – AM	1	2	3	4	5	6	7	8	9	10	11	12noon
Sign/Degree	SCO 06	SCO 18	SAG 01	SAG 12	SAG 25	CAP 09	CAP 25	AQU 14	PIS 07	ARI 02	ARI 27	TAU 19

JAN 22 – PM	1	2	3	4	5	6	7	8	9	10	11	12midnight
Sign/Degree	GEM 08	GEM 23	CAN 07	CAN 20	LEO 02	LEO 14	LEO 26	VIR 08	VIR 19	LIB 01	LIB 13	LIB 25

JAN 25 – AM	1	2	3	4	5	6	7	8	9	10	11	12noon
Sign/Degree	SCO 09	SCO 21	SAG 03	SAG 15	SAG 28	CAP 12	CAP 29	AQU 18	PIS 12	ARI 07	TAU 02	TAU 23

JAN 25 – PM	1	2	3	4	5	6	7	8	9	10	11	12midnight
Sign/Degree	GEM 11	GEM 26	CAN 10	CAN 22	LEO 04	LEO 16	LEO 28	VIR 10	VIR 22	LIB 04	LIB 16	LIB 28

JAN 28 – AM	1	2	3	4	5	6	7	8	9	10	11	12noon
Sign/Degree	SCO 11	SCO 23	SAG 05	SAG 17	CAP 01	CAP 15	AQU 02	AQU 23	PIS 17	ARI 12	TAU 06	TAU 27

JAN 28 – PM	1	2	3	4	5	6	7	8	9	10	11	12midnight
Sign/Degree	GEM 14	GEM 29	CAN 12	CAN 25	LEO 07	LEO 18	VIR 01	VIR 12	VIR 24	LIB 06	LIB 18	SCO 01

JAN 31 – AM	1	2	3	4	5	6	7	8	9	10	11	12noon
Sign/Degree	SCO 13	SCO 25	SAG 07	SAG 20	CAP 03	CAP 18	AQU 06	AQU 27	PIS 22	ARI 17	TAU 11	GEM 01

JAN 31 – PM	1	2	3	4	5	6	7	8	9	10	11	12midnight
Sign/Degree	GEM 17	CAN 02	CAN 15	CAN 27	LEO 09	LEO 21	VIR 03	VIR 14	VIR 26	LIB 09	LIB 21	SCO 02

FEBRUARY

FEB 3 – AM	1	2	3	4	5	6	7	8	9	10	11	12noon
Sign/Degree	SCO 16	SCO 28	SAG 10	SAG 22	CAP 06	CAP 22	AQU 10	PIS 02	PIS 27	ARI 22	TAU 15	GEM 04

FEB 3 – PM	1	2	3	4	5	6	7	8	9	10	11	12midnight
Sign/Degree	GEM 20	CAN 04	CAN 17	CAN 29	LEO 11	LEO 23	VIR 05	VIR 17	VIR 29	LIB 11	LIB 23	SCO 05

FEB 6 – AM	1	2	3	4	5	6	7	8	9	10	11	12noon
Sign/Degree	SCO 18	SAG 02	SAG 12	SAG 25	CAP 09	CAP 25	AQU 14	PIS 06	ARI 02	ARI 27	TAU 19	GEM 07

FEB 6 – PM	1	2	3	4	5	6	7	8	9	10	11	12midnight
Sign/Degree	GEM 23	CAN 07	CAN 20	LEO 02	LEO 14	LEO 25	VIR 07	VIR 19	LIB 01	LIB 13	LIB 25	SCO 07

FEB 9 – AM	1	2	3	4	5	6	7	8	9	10	11	12noon
Sign/Degree	SCO 20	SAG 02	SAG 15	SAG 28	CAP 12	CAP 29	AQU 18	PIS 11	ARI 07	TAU 02	TAU 23	GEM 11

FEB 9 – PM	1	2	3	4	5	6	7	8	9	10	11	12midnight
Sign/Degree	GEM 26	CAN 09	CAN 22	LEO 04	LEO 16	LEO 28	VIR 10	VIR 22	LIB 04	LIB 16	LIB 28	SCO 09

FEB 12 – AM	1	2	3	4	5	6	7	8	9	10	11	12noon
Sign/Degree	SCO 23	SAG 05	SAG 17	CAP 01	CAP 15	AQU 02	AQU 22	PIS 16	ARI 12	TAU 06	TAU 26	GEM 14

FEB 12 – PM	1	2	3	4	5	6	7	8	9	10	11	12midnight
Sign/Degree	GEM 29	CAN 12	CAN 24	LEO 06	LEO 18	VIR 01	VIR 12	VIR 24	LIB 06	LIB 18	SCO 01	SCO 12

FEB 15 – AM	1	2	3	4	5	6	7	8	9	10	11	12noon
Sign/Degree	SCO 25	SAG 07	SAG 20	CAP 03	CAP 18	AQU 06	AQU 27	PIS 21	ARI 17	TAU 10	GEM 01	GEM 17

FEB 15 – PM	1	2	3	4	5	6	7	8	9	10	11	12midnight
Sign/Degree	CAN 02	CAN 14	CAN 27	LEO 09	LEO 21	VIR 02	VIR 14	VIR 26	LIB 08	LIB 20	SCO 02	SCO 14

FEB 18 – AM	1	2	3	4	5	6	7	8	9	10	11	12noon
Sign/Degree	SCO 27	SAG 10	SAG 22	CAP 06	CAP 21	AQU 10	PIS 01	PIS 26	ARI 22	TAU 14	GEM 04	GEM 20

FEB 18 – PM	1	2	3	4	5	6	7	8	9	10	11	12midnight
Sign/Degree	CAN 04	CAN 17	LEO 01	LEO 11	LEO 23	VIR 05	VIR 17	VIR 29	LIB 11	LIB 23	SCO 05	SCO 16

FEB 21 – AM	1	2	3	4	5	6	7	8	9	10	11	12noon
Sign/Degree	SAG 01	SAG 12	SAG 25	CAP 09	CAP 25	AQU 14	PIS 06	ARI 01	ARI 26	TAU 19	GEM 07	GEM 23

FEB 21 – PM	1	2	3	4	5	6	7	8	9	10	11	12midnight
Sign/Degree	CAN 07	CAN 19	LEO 02	LEO 13	LEO 25	VIR 07	VIR 19	LIB 01	LIB 13	LIB 25	SCO 07	SCO 19

FEB 24 – AM	1	2	3	4	5	6	7	8	9	10	11	12noon
Sign/Degree	SAG 02	SAG 14	SAG 27	CAP 12	CAP 28	AQU 18	PIS 11	ARI 06	TAU 01	TAU 22	GEM 10	GEM 26

FEB 24 – PM	1	2	3	4	5	6	7	8	9	10	11	12midnight
Sign/Degree	CAN 09	CAN 22	LEO 04	LEO 16	LEO 27	VIR 09	VIR 21	LIB 03	LIB 15	LIB 27	SCO 09	SCO 21

FEB 27 – AM	1	2	3	4	5	6	7	8	9	10	11	12noon
Sign/Degree	SAG 05	SAG 17	CAP 01	CAP 15	AQU 02	AQU 22	PIS 16	ARI 11	TAU 06	TAU 26	GEM 14	GEM 28

FEB 27 – PM	1	2	3	4	5	6	7	8	9	10	11	12midnight
Sign/Degree	CAN 12	CAN 24	LEO 06	LEO 18	VIR 01	VIR 12	VIR 24	LIB 06	LIB 18	SCO 01	SCO 11	SCO 23

MAR 2 – AM	1	2	3	4	5	6	7	8	9	10	11	12noon
Sign/Degree	SAG 07	SAG 20	CAP 03	CAP 18	AQU 05	AQU 26	PIS 21	ARI 16	TAU 10	GEM 01	GEM 17	CAN 01
MAR 2 – PM	1	2	3	4	5	6	7	8	9	10	11	12midnight
Sign/Degree	CAN 14	CAN 27	LEO 08	LEO 20	VIR 02	VIR 14	VIR 26	LIB 08	LIB 20	SCO 02	SCO 14	SCO 26
MAR 5 – AM	1	2	3	4	5	6	7	8	9	10	11	12noon
Sign/Degree	SAG 09	SAG 22	CAP 06	CAP 21	AQU 09	PIS 01	PIS 26	ARI 21	TAU 14	GEM 03	GEM 20	CAN 04
MAR 5 – PM	1	2	3	4	5	6	7	8	9	10	11	12midnight
Sign/Degree	CAN 17	CAN 29	LEO 11	LEO 23	VIR 04	VIR 16	VIR 28	LIB 10	LIB 22	SCO 04	SCO 16	SCO 28
MAR 8 – AM	1	2	3	4	5	6	7	8	9	10	11	12noon
Sign/Degree	SAG 12	SAG 25	CAP 09	CAP 24	AQU 13	PIS 06	ARI 01	ARI 26	TAU 18	GEM 07	GEM 22	CAN 06
MAR 8 – PM	1	2	3	4	5	6	7	8	9	10	11	12midnight
Sign/Degree	CAN 19	LEO 01	LEO 13	LEO 25	VIR 07	VIR 19	LIB 01	LIB 13	LIB 25	SCO 07	SCO 18	SAG 01
MAR 11 – AM	1	2	3	4	5	6	7	8	9	10	11	12noon
Sign/Degree	SAG 14	SAG 27	CAP 12	CAP 28	AQU 17	PIS 10	ARI 06	TAU 01	TAU 22	GEM 10	GEM 25	CAN 09
MAR 11 – PM	1	2	3	4	5	6	7	8	9	10	11	12midnight
Sign/Degree	CAN 22	LEO 04	LEO 15	LEO 27	VIR 09	VIR 21	LIB 03	LIB 15	LIB 27	SCO 09	SCO 21	SAG 03
MAR 14 – AM	1	2	3	4	5	6	7	8	9	10	11	12noon
Sign/Degree	SAG 17	CAP 01	CAP 15	AQU 02	AQU 22	PIS 15	ARI 11	TAU 05	TAU 26	GEM 13	GEM 28	CAN 11
MAR 14 – PM	1	2	3	4	5	6	7	8	9	10	11	12midnight
Sign/Degree	CAN 24	LEO 06	LEO 18	VIR 01	VIR 12	VIR 24	LIB 06	LIB 18	SCO 01	SCO 11	SCO 23	SAG 05
MAR 17 – AM	1	2	3	4	5	6	7	8	9	10	11	12noon
Sign/Degree	SAG 19	CAP 03	CAP 18	AQU 05	AQU 26	PIS 20	ARI 16	TAU 10	GEM 01	GEM 16	CAN 01	CAN 14
MAR 17 – PM	1	2	3	4	5	6	7	8	9	10	11	12midnight
Sign/Degree	CAN 26	LEO 08	LEO 20	VIR 02	VIR 14	VIR 26	LIB 08	LIB 20	SCO 02	SCO 14	SCO 25	SAG 08
MAR 20 – AM	1	2	3	4	5	6	7	8	9	10	11	12noon
Sign/Degree	SAG 22	CAP 05	CAP 21	AQU 09	PIS 01	PIS 26	ARI 21	TAU 14	GEM 03	GEM 19	CAN 03	CAN 16
MAR 20 – PM	1	2	3	4	5	6	7	8	9	10	11	12midnight
Sign/Degree	CAN 29	LEO 11	LEO 22	VIR 04	VIR 16	VIR 28	LIB 10	LIB 22	SCO 04	SCO 16	SCO 28	SAG 10
MAR 23 – AM	1	2	3	4	5	6	7	8	9	10	11	12noon
Sign/Degree	SAG 24	CAP 08	CAP 24	AQU 13	PIS 05	ARI 01	ARI 26	TAU 18	GEM 06	GEM 22	CAN 06	CAN 19
MAR 23 – PM	1	2	3	4	5	6	7	8	9	10	11	12midnight
Sign/Degree	LEO 01	LEO 13	LEO 25	VIR 07	VIR 19	LIB 01	LIB 13	LIB 25	SCO 06	SCO 18	SAG 01	SAG 12
MAR 26 – AM	1	2	3	4	5	6	7	8	9	10	11	12noon
Sign/Degree	SAG 27	CAP 11	CAP 28	AQU 17	PIS 10	ARI 06	TAU 01	TAU 22	GEM 10	GEM 25	CAN 09	CAN 21
MAR 26 – PM	1	2	3	4	5	6	7	8	9	10	11	12midnight
Sign/Degree	LEO 03	LEO 15	LEO 27	VIR 09	VIR 21	LIB 03	LIB 15	LIB 27	SCO 09	SCO 21	SAG 03	SAG 15
MAR 29 – AM	1	2	3	4	5	6	7	8	9	10	11	12noon
Sign/Degree	CAP 01	CAP 14	AQU 01	AQU 21	PIS 15	ARI 11	TAU 05	TAU 26	GEM 13	GEM 28	CAN 11	CAN 24
MAR 29 – PM	1	2	3	4	5	6	7	8	9	10	11	12midnight
Sign/Degree	LEO 06	LEO 18	VIR 01	VIR 11	VIR 23	LIB 05	LIB 17	LIB 29	SCO 11	SCO 23	SAG 05	SAG 17

APRIL

APR 1 – AM	1	2	3	4	5	6	7	8	9	10	11	12noon
Sign/Degree	CAP 03	CAP 17	AQU 05	AQU 26	PIS 20	ARI 16	TAU 09	TAU 29	GEM 16	CAN 01	CAN 14	CAN 26

APR 1 – PM	1	2	3	4	5	6	7	8	9	10	11	12midnight
Sign/Degree	LEO 08	LEO 20	VIR 02	VIR 14	VIR 26	LIB 08	LIB 20	SCO 02	SCO 13	SCO 25	SAG 07	SAG 20

APR 4 – AM	1	2	3	4	5	6	7	8	9	10	11	12noon
Sign/Degree	CAP 05	CAP 21	AQU 09	PIS 01	PIS 25	ARI 20	TAU 13	GEM 03	GEM 19	CAN 03	CAN 16	CAN 28

APR 4 – PM	1	2	3	4	5	6	7	8	9	10	11	12midnight
Sign/Degree	LEO 10	LEO 22	VIR 04	VIR 16	VIR 28	LIB 10	LIB 22	SCO 04	SCO 16	SCO 28	SAG 10	SAG 22

APR 7 – AM	1	2	3	4	5	6	7	8	9	10	11	12noon
Sign/Degree	CAP 08	CAP 24	AQU 13	PIS 05	ARI 01	ARI 25	TAU 17	GEM 06	GEM 22	CAN 06	CAN 19	LEO 01

APR 7 – PM	1	2	3	4	5	6	7	8	9	10	11	12midnight
Sign/Degree	LEO 13	LEO 25	VIR 06	VIR 18	LIB 01	LIB 12	LIB 24	SCO 06	SCO 18	SAG 01	SAG 12	SAG 25

APR 10 – AM	1	2	3	4	5	6	7	8	9	10	11	12noon
Sign/Degree	CAP 11	CAP 27	AQU 17	PIS 10	ARI 05	TAU 01	TAU 22	GEM 09	GEM 25	CAN 08	CAN 21	LEO 03

APR 10 – PM	1	2	3	4	5	6	7	8	9	10	11	12midnight
Sign/Degree	LEO 15	LEO 27	VIR 09	VIR 21	LIB 03	LIB 15	LIB 27	SCO 09	SCO 20	SAG 02	SAG 15	SAG 28

APR 13 – AM	1	2	3	4	5	6	7	8	9	10	11	12noon
Sign/Degree	CAP 14	AQU 01	AQU 21	PIS 15	ARI 10	TAU 04	TAU 25	GEM 13	GEM 28	CAN 11	CAN 24	LEO 06

APR 13 – PM	1	2	3	4	5	6	7	8	9	10	11	12midnight
Sign/Degree	LEO 17	LEO 29	VIR 11	VIR 23	LIB 05	LIB 17	LIB 29	SCO 11	SCO 23	SAG 05	SAG 17	CAP 01

APR 16 – AM	1	2	3	4	5	6	7	8	9	10	11	12noon
Sign/Degree	CAP 17	AQU 04	AQU 25	PIS 19	ARI 15	TAU 09	TAU 29	GEM 16	CAN 01	CAN 14	CAN 26	LEO 08

APR 16 – PM	1	2	3	4	5	6	7	8	9	10	11	12midnight
Sign/Degree	LEO 20	VIR 02	VIR 13	VIR 25	LIB 07	LIB 19	SCO 01	SCO 13	SCO 25	SAG 07	SAG 20	CAP 03

APR 19 – AM	1	2	3	4	5	6	7	8	9	10	11	12noon
Sign/Degree	CAP 20	AQU 08	AQU 29	PIS 25	ARI 20	TAU 13	GEM 02	GEM 19	CAN 03	CAN 16	CAN 28	LEO 10

APR 19 – PM	1	2	3	4	5	6	7	8	9	10	11	12midnight
Sign/Degree	LEO 22	VIR 04	VIR 16	VIR 28	LIB 10	LIB 22	SCO 04	SCO 16	SCO 27	SAG 10	SAG 22	CAP 06

APR 22 – AM	1	2	3	4	5	6	7	8	9	10	11	12noon
Sign/Degree	CAP 24	AQU 12	PIS 04	ARI 01	ARI 25	TAU 17	GEM 06	GEM 22	CAN 06	CAN 18	LEO 01	LEO 13

APR 22 – PM	1	2	3	4	5	6	7	8	9	10	11	12midnight
Sign/Degree	LEO 24	VIR 06	VIR 18	LIB 01	LIB 12	LIB 24	SCO 06	SCO 18	SAG 01	SAG 12	SAG 25	CAP 09

APR 25 – AM	1	2	3	4	5	6	7	8	9	10	11	12noon
Sign/Degree	CAP 27	AQU 16	PIS 09	ARI 05	ARI 29	TAU 21	GEM 09	GEM 25	CAN 08	CAN 21	LEO 03	LEO 15

APR 25 – PM	1	2	3	4	5	6	7	8	9	10	11	12midnight
Sign/Degree	LEO 27	VIR 09	VIR 21	LIB 03	LIB 15	LIB 27	SCO 08	SCO 20	SAG 02	SAG 14	SAG 27	CAP 12

APR 28 – AM	1	2	3	4	5	6	7	8	9	10	11	12noon
Sign/Degree	AQU 01	AQU 21	PIS 14	ARI 10	TAU 04	TAU 25	GEM 12	GEM 27	CAN 11	CAN 23	LEO 05	LEO 17

APR 28 – PM	1	2	3	4	5	6	7	8	9	10	11	12midnight
Sign/Degree	LEO 29	VIR 11	VIR 23	LIB 05	LIB 17	LIB 29	SCO 11	SCO 23	SAG 05	SAG 17	CAP 01	CAP 15

MAY 1 – AM	1	2	3	4	5	6	7	8	9	10	11	12noon
Sign/Degree	AQU 04	AQU 25	PIS 19	ARI 15	TAU 09	TAU 29	GEM 15	CAN 01	CAN 13	CAN 26	LEO 08	LEO 20

MAY 1 – PM	1	2	3	4	5	6	7	8	9	10	11	12midnight
Sign/Degree	VIR 01	VIR 13	VIR 25	LIB 07	LIB 19	SCO 01	SCO 13	SCO 25	SAG 07	SAG 19	CAP 03	CAP 18

MAY 4 – AM	1	2	3	4	5	6	7	8	9	10	11	12noon
Sign/Degree	AQU 08	AQU 29	PIS 24	ARI 20	TAU 13	GEM 02	GEM 19	CAN 03	CAN 16	CAN 28	LEO 10	LEO 22

MAY 4 – PM	1	2	3	4	5	6	7	8	9	10	11	12midnight
Sign/Degree	VIR 04	VIR 16	VIR 28	LIB 10	LIB 22	SCO 04	SCO 15	SCO 27	SAG 09	SAG 22	CAP 06	CAP 21

MAY 7 – AM	1	2	3	4	5	6	7	8	9	10	11	12noon
Sign/Degree	AQU 12	PIS 04	PIS 29	ARI 24	TAU 17	GEM 06	GEM 21	CAN 05	CAN 18	LEO 01	LEO 12	LEO 24

MAY 7 – PM	1	2	3	4	5	6	7	8	9	10	11	12midnight
Sign/Degree	VIR 06	VIR 18	LIB 01	LIB 12	LIB 24	SCO 06	SCO 18	SAG 01	SAG 12	SAG 25	CAP 09	CAP 24

MAY 10 – AM	1	2	3	4	5	6	7	8	9	10	11	12noon
Sign/Degree	AQU 16	PIS 09	ARI 04	ARI 29	TAU 21	GEM 09	GEM 24	CAN 08	CAN 21	LEO 03	LEO 15	LEO 26

MAY 10 – PM	1	2	3	4	5	6	7	8	9	10	11	12midnight
Sign/Degree	VIR 08	VIR 20	LIB 02	LIB 14	LIB 26	SCO 08	SCO 20	SAG 02	SAG 14	SAG 27	CAP 11	CAP 28

MAY 13 – AM	1	2	3	4	5	6	7	8	9	10	11	12noon
Sign/Degree	AQU 20	PIS 14	ARI 09	TAU 04	TAU 25	GEM 12	GEM 27	CAN 11	CAN 23	LEO 05	LEO 17	LEO 29

MAY 13 – PM	1	2	3	4	5	6	7	8	9	10	11	12midnight
Sign/Degree	VIR 11	VIR 23	LIB 05	LIB 17	LIB 29	SCO 10	SCO 22	SAG 04	SAG 17	CAP 01	CAP 14	AQU 01

MAY 16 – AM	1	2	3	4	5	6	7	8	9	10	11	12noon
Sign/Degree	AQU 24	PIS 19	ARI 14	TAU 08	TAU 28	GEM 15	CAN 01	CAN 13	CAN 25	LEO 07	LEO 19	VIR 01

MAY 16 – PM	1	2	3	4	5	6	7	8	9	10	11	12midnight
Sign/Degree	VIR 13	VIR 25	LIB 07	LIB 19	SCO 01	SCO 13	SCO 25	SAG 07	SAG 19	CAP 03	CAP 18	AQU 05

MAY 19 – AM	1	2	3	4	5	6	7	8	9	10	11	12noon
Sign/Degree	AQU 29	PIS 24	ARI 19	TAU 12	GEM 02	GEM 18	CAN 03	CAN 16	CAN 28	LEO 10	LEO 22	VIR 03

MAY 19 – PM	1	2	3	4	5	6	7	8	9	10	11	12midnight
Sign/Degree	VIR 15	VIR 27	LIB 09	LIB 21	SCO 03	SCO 15	SCO 27	SAG 09	SAG 22	CAP 05	CAP 21	AQU 09

MAY 22 – AM	1	2	3	4	5	6	7	8	9	10	11	12noon
Sign/Degree	PIS 04	PIS 29	ARI 24	TAU 16	GEM 05	GEM 21	CAN 05	CAN 18	LEO 01	LEO 12	LEO 24	VIR 06

MAY 22 – PM	1	2	3	4	5	6	7	8	9	10	11	12midnight
Sign/Degree	VIR 18	LIB 01	LIB 12	LIB 24	SCO 06	SCO 17	SCO 29	SAG 12	SAG 24	CAP 08	CAP 24	AQU 13

MAY 25 – AM	1	2	3	4	5	6	7	8	9	10	11	12noon
Sign/Degree	PIS 08	ARI 04	ARI 29	TAU 20	GEM 09	GEM 24	CAN 08	CAN 20	LEO 03	LEO 14	LEO 26	VIR 08

MAY 25 – PM	1	2	3	4	5	6	7	8	9	10	11	12midnight
Sign/Degree	VIR 20	LIB 02	LIB 14	LIB 26	SCO 08	SCO 20	SAG 02	SAG 14	SAG 27	CAP 11	CAP 28	AQU 17

MAY 28 – AM	1	2	3	4	5	6	7	8	9	10	11	12noon
Sign/Degree	PIS 13	ARI 09	TAU 03	TAU 24	GEM 12	GEM 27	CAN 10	CAN 23	LEO 05	LEO 17	LEO 29	VIR 11

MAY 28 – PM	1	2	3	4	5	6	7	8	9	10	11	12midnight
Sign/Degree	VIR 23	LIB 05	LIB 17	LIB 28	SCO 10	SCO 22	SAG 04	SAG 16	CAP 01	CAP 14	AQU 01	AQU 21

MAY 31 – AM	1	2	3	4	5	6	7	8	9	10	11	12noon
Sign/Degree	PIS 18	ARI 14	TAU 08	TAU 28	GEM 15	CAN 01	CAN 13	CAN 25	LEO 07	LEO 19	VIR 01	VIR 13

MAY 31 – PM	1	2	3	4	5	6	7	8	9	10	11	12midnight
Sign/Degree	VIR 25	LIB 07	LIB 19	SCO 01	SCO 13	SCO 24	SAG 06	SAG 19	CAP 02	CAP 17	AQU 05	AQU 26

JUNE

	1	2	3	4	5	6	7	8	9	10	11	12noon
JUN 3 – AM Sign/Degree	PIS 23	ARI 19	TAU 12	GEM 02	GEM 18	CAN 02	CAN 15	CAN 28	LEO 10	LEO 21	VIR 03	VIR 15

	1	2	3	4	5	6	7	8	9	10	11	12midnight
JUN 3 – PM Sign/Degree	VIR 27	LIB 09	LIB 21	SCO 03	SCO 15	SCO 27	SAG 09	SAG 21	CAP 05	CAP 21	AQU 09	PIS 01

	1	2	3	4	5	6	7	8	9	10	11	12noon
JUN 6 – AM Sign/Degree	PIS 28	ARI 24	TAU 16	GEM 05	GEM 21	CAN 05	CAN 18	LEO 01	LEO 12	LEO 24	VIR 06	VIR 18

	1	2	3	4	5	6	7	8	9	10	11	12midnight
JUN 6 – PM Sign/Degree	LIB 01	LIB 12	LIB 24	SCO 05	SCO 17	SCO 29	SAG 11	SAG 24	CAP 08	CAP 24	AQU 12	PIS 05

	1	2	3	4	5	6	7	8	9	10	11	12noon
JUN 9 – AM Sign/Degree	ARI 03	ARI 28	TAU 20	GEM 08	GEM 24	CAN 08	CAN 20	LEO 02	LEO 14	LEO 26	VIR 08	VIR 20

	1	2	3	4	5	6	7	8	9	10	11	12midnight
JUN 9 – PM Sign/Degree	LIB 02	LIB 14	LIB 26	SCO 08	SCO 20	SAG 02	SAG 14	SAG 27	CAP 11	CAP 27	AQU 17	PIS 10

	1	2	3	4	5	6	7	8	9	10	11	12noon
JUN 12 – AM Sign/Degree	ARI 08	TAU 03	TAU 24	GEM 12	GEM 27	CAN 10	CAN 23	LEO 05	LEO 17	LEO 28	VIR 10	VIR 22

	1	2	3	4	5	6	7	8	9	10	11	12midnight
JUN 12 – PM Sign/Degree	LIB 04	LIB 16	LIB 28	SCO 10	SCO 22	SAG 04	SAG 16	SAG 29	CAP 14	AQU 01	AQU 21	PIS 14

	1	2	3	4	5	6	7	8	9	10	11	12noon
JUN 15 – AM Sign/Degree	ARI 13	TAU 07	TAU 28	GEM 15	GEM 29	CAN 13	CAN 25	LEO 07	LEO 19	VIR 01	VIR 13	VIR 25

	1	2	3	4	5	6	7	8	9	10	11	12midnight
JUN 15 – PM Sign/Degree	LIB 07	LIB 19	SCO 01	SCO 12	SCO 24	SAG 06	SAG 19	CAP 02	CAP 17	AQU 04	AQU 25	PIS 19

	1	2	3	4	5	6	7	8	9	10	11	12noon
JUN 18 – AM Sign/Degree	ARI 18	TAU 12	GEM 01	GEM 18	CAN 02	CAN 15	CAN 27	LEO 09	LEO 21	VIR 03	VIR 15	VIR 27

	1	2	3	4	5	6	7	8	9	10	11	12midnight
JUN 18 – PM Sign/Degree	LIB 09	LIB 21	SCO 03	SCO 15	SCO 27	SAG 09	SAG 21	CAP 05	CAP 20	AQU 08	PIS 01	PIS 24

	1	2	3	4	5	6	7	8	9	10	11	12noon
JUN 21 – AM Sign/Degree	ARI 23	TAU 16	GEM 05	GEM 21	CAN 05	CAN 18	LEO 01	LEO 12	LEO 24	VIR 05	VIR 17	LIB 01

	1	2	3	4	5	6	7	8	9	10	11	12midnight
JUN 21 – PM Sign/Degree	LIB 11	LIB 23	SCO 05	SCO 17	SCO 29	SAG 11	SAG 24	CAP 08	CAP 24	AQU 12	PIS 04	ARI 01

	1	2	3	4	5	6	7	8	9	10	11	12noon
JUN 24 – AM Sign/Degree	ARI 28	TAU 20	GEM 08	GEM 24	CAN 07	CAN 20	LEO 03	LEO 14	LEO 26	VIR O8	VIR 20	LIB 02

	1	2	3	4	5	6	7	8	9	10	11	12midnight
JUN 24 – PM Sign/Degree	LIB 14	LIB 26	SCO 08	SCO 19	SAG 01	SAG 14	SAG 26	CAP 11	CAP 27	AQU 16	PIS 09	ARI 05

	1	2	3	4	5	6	7	8	9	10	11	12noon
JUN 27 – AM Sign/Degree	TAU 02	TAU 24	GEM 11	GEM 26	CAN 10	CAN 22	LEO 05	LEO 16	LEO 28	VIR 10	VIR 22	LIB 04

	1	2	3	4	5	6	7	8	9	10	11	12midnight
JUN 27 – PM Sign/Degree	LIB 16	LIB 28	SCO 10	SCO 22	SAG 04	SAG 16	SAG 29	CAP 14	AQU 01	AQU 21	PIS 14	ARI 10

	1	2	3	4	5	6	7	8	9	10	11	12noon
JUN 30 – AM Sign/Degree	TAU 07	TAU 27	GEM 14	GEM 29	CAN 12	CAN 25	LEO 07	LEO 19	VIR 01	VIR 12	VIR 24	LIB 06

	1	2	3	4	5	6	7	8	9	10	11	12midnight
JUN 30 – PM Sign/Degree	LIB 18	SCO 01	SCO 12	SCO 24	SAG 06	SAG 19	CAP 02	CAP 17	AQU 04	AQU 25	PIS 19	ARI 15

JULY

	1	2	3	4	5	6	7	8	9	10	11	12noon
JUL 3 – AM Sign/Degree	TAU 11	GEM 01	GEM 17	CAN 02	CAN 15	CAN 27	LEO 09	LEO 21	VIR 03	VIR 15	VIR 27	LIB 09

	1	2	3	4	5	6	7	8	9	10	11	12midnight
JUL 3 – PM Sign/Degree	LIB 21	SCO 03	SCO 15	SCO 26	SAG 08	SAG 21	CAP 05	CAP 20	AQU 08	AQU 29	PIS 24	ARI 19
JUL 6 – AM Sign/Degree	TAU 15	GEM 04	GEM 20	CAN 05	CAN 17	LEO 01	LEO 12	LEO 23	VIR 05	VIR 17	VIR 29	LIB 11
JUL 6 – PM Sign/Degree	LIB 23	SCO 05	SCO 17	SCO 29	SAG 11	SAG 24	CAP 08	CAP 23	AQU 12	PIS 04	PIS 29	ARI 24
JUL 9 – AM Sign/Degree	TAU 19	GEM 08	GEM 23	CAN 07	CAN 20	LEO 02	LEO 14	LEO 26	VIR 08	VIR 20	LIB 02	LIB 14
JUL 9 – PM Sign/Degree	LIB 25	SCO 07	SCO 19	SAG 01	SAG 13	SAG 26	CAP 10	CAP 27	AQU 16	PIS 09	ARI 04	ARI 29
JUL 12 – AM Sign/Degree	TAU 23	GEM 11	GEM 26	CAN 10	CAN 22	LEO 04	LEO 16	LEO 28	VIR 10	VIR 22	LIB 04	LIB 16
JUL 12 – PM Sign/Degree	LIB 28	SCO 10	SCO 21	SAG 03	SAG 16	SAG 29	CAP 13	AQU 01	AQU 20	PIS 14	ARI 09	TAU 04
JUL 15 – AM Sign/Degree	TAU 27	GEM 14	GEM 29	CAN 12	CAN 25	LEO 07	LEO 18	VIR 01	VIR 12	VIR 24	LIB 06	LIB 18
JUL 15 – PM Sign/Degree	SCO 01	SCO 12	SCO 24	SAG 06	SAG 18	CAP 02	CAP 16	AQU 04	AQU 24	PIS 19	ARI 14	TAU 08
JUL 18 – AM Sign/Degree	GEM 01	GEM 17	CAN 02	CAN 15	CAN 27	LEO 09	LEO 21	VIR 03	VIR 15	VIR 27	LIB 09	LIB 21
JUL 18 – PM Sign/Degree	SCO 03	SCO 14	SCO 26	SAG 08	SAG 21	CAP 04	CAP 20	AQU 08	AQU 29	PIS 24	ARI 19	TAU 12
JUL 21 – AM Sign/Degree	GEM 04	GEM 20	CAN 04	CAN 17	CAN 29	LEO 11	LEO 23	VIR 05	VIR 17	VIR 29	LIB 11	LIB 23
JUL 21 – PM Sign/Degree	SCO 05	SCO 17	SCO 29	SAG 11	SAG 23	CAP 07	CAP 23	AQU 11	PIS 04	PIS 29	ARI 24	TAU 16
JUL 24 – AM Sign/Degree	GEM 07	GEM 23	CAN 07	CAN 20	LEO 02	LEO 14	LEO 25	VIR 07	VIR 19	LIB 01	LIB 13	LIB 25
JUL 24 – PM Sign/Degree	SCO 07	SCO 19	SAG 01	SAG 13	SAG 26	CAP 10	CAP 26	AQU 16	PIS 08	ARI 04	ARI 29	TAU 20
JUL 27 – AM Sign/Degree	GEM 11	GEM 26	CAN 09	CAN 22	LEO 04	LEO 16	LEO 28	VIR 10	VIR 22	LIB 04	LIB 16	LIB 28
JUL 27 – PM Sign/Degree	SCO 09	SCO 21	SAG 03	SAG 16	SAG 29	CAP 13	AQU 01	AQU 20	PIS 13	ARI 09	TAU 03	TAU 24
JUL 30 – AM Sign/Degree	GEM 14	GEM 29	CAN 12	CAN 24	LEO 06	LEO 18	VIR 01	VIR 12	VIR 24	LIB 06	LIB 18	SCO 01
JUL 30 – PM Sign/Degree	SCO 12	SCO 24	SAG 06	SAG 18	CAP 01	CAP 16	AQU 03	AQU 24	PIS 18	ARI 14	TAU 08	TAU 28

AUGUST

AUG 2 – AM	1	2	3	4	5	6	7	8	9	10	11	12noon
Sign/Degree	GEM 17	CAN 01	CAN 14	CAN 27	LEO 09	LEO 21	VIR 03	VIR 14	VIR 26	LIB 08	LIB 20	SCO 02

AUG 2 – PM	1	2	3	4	5	6	7	8	9	10	11	12midnight
Sign/Degree	SCO 14	SCO 26	SAG 08	SAG 21	CAP 04	CAP 19	AQU 07	AQU 29	PIS 23	ARI 19	TAU 12	GEM 01

AUG 5 – AM	1	2	3	4	5	6	7	8	9	10	11	12noon
Sign/Degree	GEM 20	CAN 04	CAN 17	CAN 29	LEO 11	LEO 23	VIR 05	VIR 17	VIR 29	LIB 11	LIB 23	SCO 05

AUG 5 – PM	1	2	3	4	5	6	7	8	9	10	11	12midnight
Sign/Degree	SCO 16	SCO 28	SAG 10	SAG 23	CAP 07	CAP 23	AQU 11	PIS 03	PIS 28	ARI 25	TAU 16	GEM 05

AUG 8 – AM	1	2	3	4	5	6	7	8	9	10	11	12noon
Sign/Degree	GEM 23	CAN 07	CAN 19	LEO 02	LEO 13	LEO 25	VIR 07	VIR 19	LIB 01	LIB 13	LIB 25	SCO 07

AUG 8 – PM	1	2	3	4	5	6	7	8	9	10	11	12midnight
Sign/Degree	SCO 19	SAG 01	SAG 13	SAG 26	CAP 10	CAP 26	AQU 15	PIS 08	ARI 03	ARI 28	TAU 20	GEM 08

AUG 11 – AM	1	2	3	4	5	6	7	8	9	10	11	12noon
Sign/Degree	GEM 26	CAN 09	CAN 22	LEO 04	LEO 16	LEO 28	VIR 10	VIR 21	LIB 03	LIB 15	LIB 27	SCO 09

AUG 11 – PM	1	2	3	4	5	6	7	8	9	10	11	12midnight
Sign/Degree	SCO 21	SAG 03	SAG 15	SAG 28	CAP 13	AQU 01	AQU 19	PIS 13	ARI 08	TAU 03	TAU 24	GEM 12

AUG 14 – AM	1	2	3	4	5	6	7	8	9	10	11	12noon
Sign/Degree	GEM 28	CAN 12	CAN 24	LEO 06	LEO 18	VIR 01	VIR 12	VIR 24	LIB 06	LIB 18	SCO 01	SCO 12

AUG 14 – PM	1	2	3	4	5	6	7	8	9	10	11	12midnight
Sign/Degree	SCO 23	SAG 05	SAG 18	CAP 01	CAP 16	AQU 03	AQU 24	PIS 18	ARI 13	TAU 07	TAU 28	GEM 15

AUG 17 – AM	1	2	3	4	5	6	7	8	9	10	11	12noon
Sign/Degree	CAN 01	CAN 14	CAN 27	LEO 09	LEO 20	VIR 02	VIR 14	VIR 26	LIB 08	LIB 20	SCO 02	SCO 14

AUG 17 – PM	1	2	3	4	5	6	7	8	9	10	11	12midnight
Sign/Degree	SCO 26	SAG 08	SAG 20	CAP 04	CAP 19	AQU 07	AQU 28	PIS 23	ARI 18	TAU 11	GEM 01	GEM 18

AUG 20 – AM	1	2	3	4	5	6	7	8	9	10	11	12noon
Sign/Degree	CAN 04	CAN 17	CAN 29	LEO 11	LEO 23	VIR 05	VIR 17	VIR 29	LIB 11	LIB 23	SCO 04	SCO 16

AUG 20 – PM	1	2	3	4	5	6	7	8	9	10	11	12midnight
Sign/Degree	SCO 28	SAG 10	SAG 23	CAP 07	CAP 22	AQU 11	PIS 03	PIS 28	ARI 23	TAU 16	GEM 05	GEM 21

AUG 23 – AM	1	2	3	4	5	6	7	8	9	10	11	12noon
Sign/Degree	CAN 06	CAN 19	LEO 01	LEO 13	LEO 25	VIR 07	VIR 19	LIB 01	LIB 13	LIB 25	SCO 07	SCO 19

AUG 23 – PM	1	2	3	4	5	6	7	8	9	10	11	12midnight
Sign/Degree	SAG 01	SAG 13	SAG 26	CAP 10	CAP 26	AQU 15	PIS 07	ARI 03	ARI 28	TAU 20	GEM 08	GEM 24

AUG 26 – AM	1	2	3	4	5	6	7	8	9	10	11	12noon
Sign/Degree	CAN 09	CAN 22	LEO 04	LEO 16	LEO 28	VIR 09	VIR 21	LIB 03	LIB 15	LIB 27	SCO 09	SCO 21

AUG 26 – PM	1	2	3	4	5	6	7	8	9	10	11	12midnight
Sign/Degree	SAG 03	SAG 15	SAG 28	CAP 13	CAP 29	AQU 19	PIS 12	ARI 08	TAU 02	TAU 24	GEM 11	GEM 26

AUG 29 – AM	1	2	3	4	5	6	7	8	9	10	11	12noon
Sign/Degree	CAN 12	CAN 24	LEO 06	LEO 18	VIR 01	VIR 12	VIR 24	LIB 06	LIB 18	SCO 01	SCO 11	SCO 23

AUG 29 – PM	1	2	3	4	5	6	7	8	9	10	11	12midnight
Sign/Degree	SAG 05	SAG 18	CAP 01	CAP 16	AQU 03	AQU 23	PIS 17	ARI 13	TAU 07	TAU 27	GEM 14	GEM 29

SEP 1 – AM	1	2	3	4	5	6	7	8	9	10	11	12noon
Sign/Degree	CAN 14	CAN 27	LEO 08	LEO 20	VIR 02	VIR 14	VIR 26	LIB 08	LIB 20	SCO 02	SCO 14	SCO 26

SEP 1 – PM	1	2	3	4	5	6	7	8	9	10	11	12midnight
Sign/Degree	SAG 08	SAG 20	CAP 04	CAP 19	AQU 07	AQU 28	PIS 22	ARI 18	TAU 11	GEM 01	GEM 17	CAN 02

SEP 4 – AM	1	2	3	4	5	6	7	8	9	10	11	12noon
Sign/Degree	CAN 17	CAN 28	LEO 11	LEO 23	VIR 04	VIR 16	VIR 28	LIB 10	LIB 22	SCO 04	SCO 16	SCO 28

SEP 4 – PM	1	2	3	4	5	6	7	8	9	10	11	12midnight
Sign/Degree	SAG 10	SAG 23	CAP 07	CAP 22	AQU 10	PIS 02	PIS 27	ARI 23	TAU 15	GEM 04	GEM 20	CAN 04

SEP 7 – AM	1	2	3	4	5	6	7	8	9	10	11	12noon
Sign/Degree	CAN 19	LEO 01	LEO 13	LEO 25	VIR 07	VIR 19	LIB 01	LIB 13	LIB 25	SCO 07	SCO 18	SAG 01

SEP 7 – PM	1	2	3	4	5	6	7	8	9	10	11	12midnight
Sign/Degree	SAG 12	SAG 25	CAP 09	CAP 25	AQU 14	PIS 07	ARI 02	ARI 27	TAU 19	GEM 08	GEM 23	CAN 07

SEP 10 – AM	1	2	3	4	5	6	7	8	9	10	11	12noon
Sign/Degree	CAN 21	LEO 04	LEO 15	LEO 27	VIR 09	VIR 21	LIB 03	LIB 16	LIB 27	SCO 09	SCO 21	SAG 03

SEP 10 – PM	1	2	3	4	5	6	7	8	9	10	11	12midnight
Sign/Degree	SAG 15	SAG 28	CAP 12	CAP 29	AQU 19	PIS 12	ARI 07	TAU 02	TAU 23	GEM 11	GEM 26	CAN 10

SEP 13 – AM	1	2	3	4	5	6	7	8	9	10	11	12noon
Sign/Degree	CAN 24	LEO 06	LEO 18	VIR 01	VIR 11	VIR 23	LIB 05	LIB 17	LIB 29	SCO 11	SCO 23	SAG 05

SEP 13 – PM	1	2	3	4	5	6	7	8	9	10	11	12midnight
Sign/Degree	SAG 17	CAP 01	CAP 15	AQU 03	AQU 23	PIS 17	ARI 12	TAU 06	TAU 27	GEM 14	GEM 29	CAN 12

SEP 16 – AM	1	2	3	4	5	6	7	8	9	10	11	12noon
Sign/Degree	CAN 26	LEO 08	LEO 20	VIR 02	VIR 14	VIR 26	LIB 08	LIB 20	SCO 02	SCO 14	SCO 25	SAG 07

SEP 16 – PM	1	2	3	4	5	6	7	8	9	10	11	12midnight
Sign/Degree	SAG 20	CAP 03	CAP 19	AQU 06	AQU 27	PIS 22	ARI 17	TAU 11	GEM 01	GEM 17	CAN 02	CAN 15

SEP 19 – AM	1	2	3	4	5	6	7	8	9	10	11	12noon
Sign/Degree	CAN 29	LEO 11	LEO 22	VIR 04	VIR 16	VIR 28	LIB 10	LIB 22	SCO 04	SCO 16	SCO 28	SAG 10

SEP 19 – PM	1	2	3	4	5	6	7	8	9	10	11	12midnight
Sign/Degree	SAG 23	CAP 06	CAP 22	AQU 10	PIS 02	PIS 27	ARI 22	TAU 15	GEM 04	GEM 20	CAN 04	CAN 17

SEP 22 – AM	1	2	3	4	5	6	7	8	9	10	11	12noon
Sign/Degree	LEO 01	LEO 13	LEO 25	VIR 07	VIR 19	LIB 01	LIB 13	LIB 24	SCO 06	SCO 18	SAG 01	SAG 12

SEP 22 – PM	1	2	3	4	5	6	7	8	9	10	11	12midnight
Sign/Degree	SAG 25	CAP 09	CAP 25	AQU 14	PIS 07	ARI 02	ARI 27	TAU 19	GEM 07	GEM 23	CAN 07	CAN 20

SEP 25 – AM	1	2	3	4	5	6	7	8	9	10	11	12noon
Sign/Degree	LEO 03	LEO 15	LEO 27	VIR 09	VIR 21	LIB 03	LIB 15	LIB 27	SCO 09	SCO 20	SAG 02	SAG 15

SEP 25 – PM	1	2	3	4	5	6	7	8	9	10	11	12midnight
Sign/Degree	SAG 28	CAP 12	CAP 29	AQU 18	PIS 11	ARI 07	TAU 02	TAU 23	GEM 11	GEM 26	CAN 09	CAN 22

SEP 28 – AM	1	2	3	4	5	6	7	8	9	10	11	12noon
Sign/Degree	LEO 06	LEO 18	LEO 29	VIR 11	VIR 23	LIB 05	LIB 17	LIB 29	SCO 11	SCO 23	SAG 05	SAG 17

SEP 28 – PM	1	2	3	4	5	6	7	8	9	10	11	12midnight
Sign/Degree	CAP 01	CAP 15	AQU 02	AQU 23	PIS 16	ARI 12	TAU 06	TAU 27	GEM 14	GEM 29	CAN 12	CAN 24

OCTOBER

	1	2	3	4	5	6	7	8	9	10	11	12noon
OCT 1 – AM Sign/Degree	LEO 08	LEO 20	VIR 02	VIR 14	VIR 26	LIB 08	LIB 20	SCO 02	SCO 13	SCO 25	SAG 07	SAG 20

	1	2	3	4	5	6	7	8	9	10	11	12midnight
OCT 1 – PM Sign/Degree	CAP 03	CAP 18	AQU 06	AQU 27	PIS 21	ARI 16	TAU 10	GEM 01	GEM 17	CAN 02	CAN 14	CAN 27
OCT 4 – AM Sign/Degree	LEO 10	LEO 22	VIR 04	VIR 16	VIR 28	LIB 10	LIB 22	SCO 04	SCO 16	SCO 28	SAG 10	SAG 22
OCT 4 – PM Sign/Degree	CAP 06	CAP 22	AQU 10	PIS 02	PIS 26	ARI 22	TAU 15	GEM 04	GEM 20	CAN 04	CAN 17	CAN 29
OCT 7 – AM Sign/Degree	LEO 13	LEO 24	VIR 06	VIR 18	LIB 01	LIB 12	LIB 24	SCO 06	SCO 18	SAG 01	SAG 12	SAG 25
OCT 7 – PM Sign/Degree	CAP 09	CAP 25	AQU 14	PIS 06	ARI 01	ARI 27	TAU 19	GEM 07	GEM 23	CAN 07	CAN 19	LEO 02
OCT 10 – AM Sign/Degree	LEO 15	LEO 27	VIR 09	VIR 21	LIB 03	LIB 15	LIB 27	SCO 08	SCO 20	SAG 02	SAG 15	SAG 28
OCT 10 – PM Sign/Degree	CAP 12	CAP 28	AQU 18	PIS 11	ARI 07	TAU 01	TAU 23	GEM 10	GEM 26	CAN 09	CAN 22	LEO 04
OCT 13 – AM Sign/Degree	LEO 17	LEO 29	VIR 11	VIR 23	LIB 05	LIB 17	LIB 29	SCO 11	SCO 23	SAG 05	SAG 17	CAP 01
OCT 13 – PM Sign/Degree	CAP 15	AQU 02	AQU 22	PIS 16	ARI 12	TAU 06	TAU 26	GEM 14	GEM 28	CAN 12	CAN 24	LEO 06
OCT 16 – AM Sign/Degree	LEO 20	VIR 01	VIR 13	VIR 25	LIB 08	LIB 19	SCO 01	SCO 13	SCO 25	SAG 07	SAG 20	CAP 03
OCT 16 – PM Sign/Degree	CAP 18	AQU 06	AQU 27	PIS 21	ARI 17	TAU 10	GEM 01	GEM 17	CAN 01	CAN 14	CAN 27	LEO 09
OCT 19 – AM Sign/Degree	LEO 22	VIR 04	VIR 16	VIR 28	LIB 10	LIB 22	SCO 04	SCO 15	SCO 27	SAG 09	SAG 22	CAP 06
OCT 19 – PM Sign/Degree	CAP 21	AQU 09	PIS 01	PIS 26	ARI 21	TAU 14	GEM 03	GEM 20	CAN 04	CAN 17	CAN 29	LEO 11
OCT 22 – AM Sign/Degree	LEO 24	VIR 06	VIR 18	LIB 01	LIB 12	LIB 24	SCO 06	SCO 18	SAG 01	SAG 12	SAG 25	CAP 09
OCT 22 – PM Sign/Degree	CAP 25	AQU 13	PIS 06	ARI 01	ARI 26	TAU 18	GEM 07	GEM 23	CAN 06	CAN 19	LEO 01	LEO 13
OCT 25 – AM Sign/Degree	LEO 27	VIR 08	VIR 20	LIB 02	LIB 14	LIB 26	SCO 08	SCO 20	SAG 02	SAG 14	SAG 27	CAP 12
OCT 25 – PM Sign/Degree	CAP 28	AQU 18	PIS 11	ARI 06	TAU 17	TAU 22	GEM 10	GEM 25	CAN 09	CAN 22	LEO 04	LEO 16
OCT 28 – AM Sign/Degree	LEO 29	VIR 11	VIR 23	LIB 05	LIB 17	LIB 29	SCO 11	SCO 22	SAG 04	SAG 17	CAP 01	CAP 15
OCT 28 – PM Sign/Degree	AQU 02	AQU 22	PIS 16	ARI 11	TAU 05	TAU 26	GEM 13	GEM 28	CAN 12	CAN 24	LEO 06	LEO 18
OCT 31 – AM Sign/Degree	VIR 01	VIR 13	VIR 25	LIB 07	LIB 19	SCO 01	SCO 13	SCO 25	SAG 07	SAG 19	CAP 03	CAP 18
OCT 31 – PM Sign/Degree	AQU 05	AQU 26	PIS 21	ARI 16	TAU 10	GEM 01	GEM 16	CAN 01	CAN 14	CAN 26	LEO 08	LEO 20

NOV 3 – AM	1	2	3	4	5	6	7	8	9	10	11	**12noon**
Sign/Degree	VIR 04	VIR 16	VIR 28	LIB 10	LIB 22	SCO 03	SCO 15	SCO 27	SAG 09	SAG 22	CAP 06	CAP 21

NOV 3 – PM	1	2	3	4	5	6	7	8	9	10	11	**12midnight**
Sign/Degree	AQU 09	PIS 01	PIS 26	ARI 21	TAU 14	GEM 03	GEM 19	CAN 04	CAN 17	CAN 29	LEO 11	LEO 23

NOV 6 – AM	1	2	3	4	5	6	7	8	9	10	11	**12noon**
Sign/Degree	VIR 06	VIR 18	LIB 01	LIB 12	LIB 24	SCO 06	SCO 18	SCO 29	SAG 12	SAG 24	CAP 08	CAP 24

NOV 6 – PM	1	2	3	4	5	6	7	8	9	10	11	**12midnight**
Sign/Degree	AQU 13	PIS 05	ARI 01	ARI 26	TAU 18	GEM 07	GEM 23	CAN 06	CAN 19	LEO 01	LEO 13	LEO 25

NOV 9 – AM	1	2	3	4	5	6	7	8	9	10	11	**12noon**
Sign/Degree	VIR 08	VIR 20	LIB 02	LIB 14	LIB 26	SCO 08	SCO 20	SAG 02	SAG 14	SAG 27	CAP 11	CAP 28

NOV 9 – PM	1	2	3	4	5	6	7	8	9	10	11	**12midnight**
Sign/Degree	AQU 17	PIS 10	ARI 06	TAU 01	TAU 22	GEM 10	GEM 25	CAN 09	CAN 21	LEO 03	LEO 15	LEO 27

NOV 12 – AM	1	2	3	4	5	6	7	8	9	10	11	**12noon**
Sign/Degree	VIR 11	VIR 23	LIB 05	LIB 17	LIB 29	SCO 10	SCO 22	SAG 04	SAG 17	CAP 01	CAP 14	AQU 01

NOV 12 – PM	1	2	3	4	5	6	7	8	9	10	11	**12midnight**
Sign/Degree	AQU 21	PIS 15	ARI 11	TAU 05	TAU 26	GEM 13	GEM 28	CAN 11	CAN 24	LEO 06	LEO 18	LEO 29

NOV 15 – AM	1	2	3	4	5	6	7	8	9	10	11	**12noon**
Sign/Degree	VIR 13	VIR 25	LIB 07	LIB 19	SCO 01	SCO 13	SCO 24	SAG 07	SAG 19	CAP 02	CAP 17	AQU 05

NOV 15 – PM	1	2	3	4	5	6	7	8	9	10	11	**12midnight**
Sign/Degree	AQU 26	PIS 20	ARI 16	TAU 09	TAU 29	GEM 16	CAN 01	CAN 14	CAN 26	LEO 08	LEO 20	VIR 02

NOV 18 – AM	1	2	3	4	5	6	7	8	9	10	11	**12noon**
Sign/Degree	VIR 15	VIR 27	LIB 09	LIB 21	SCO 03	SCO 15	SCO 27	SAG 09	SAG 22	CAP 05	CAP 21	AQU 09

NOV 18 – PM	1	2	3	4	5	6	7	8	9	10	11	**12midnight**
Sign/Degree	PIS 01	PIS 25	ARI 21	TAU 14	GEM 03	GEM 19	CAN 03	CAN 16	CAN 29	LEO 10	LEO 22	VIR 04

NOV 21 – AM	1	2	3	4	5	6	7	8	9	10	11	**12noon**
Sign/Degree	VIR 18	LIB 01	LIB 12	LIB 24	SCO 06	SCO 17	SCO 29	SAG 11	SAG 24	CAP 08	CAP 24	AQU 13

NOV 21 – PM	1	2	3	4	5	6	7	8	9	10	11	**12midnight**
Sign/Degree	PIS 05	ARI 01	ARI 25	TAU 18	GEM 06	GEM 22	CAN 06	CAN 19	LEO 01	LEO 13	LEO 25	VIR 07

NOV 24 – AM	1	2	3	4	5	6	7	8	9	10	11	**12noon**
Sign/Degree	VIR 20	LIB 02	LIB 14	LIB 26	SCO 08	SCO 20	SAG 02	SAG 14	SAG 27	CAP 11	CAP 27	AQU 17

NOV 24 – PM	1	2	3	4	5	6	7	8	9	10	11	**12midnight**
Sign/Degree	PIS 10	ARI 05	TAU 01	TAU 22	GEM 10	GEM 25	CAN 09	CAN 21	LEO 03	LEO 15	LEO 27	VIR 09

NOV 27 – AM	1	2	3	4	5	6	7	8	9	10	11	**12noon**
Sign/Degree	VIR 22	LIB 04	LIB 16	LIB 28	SCO 10	SCO 22	SAG 04	SAG 16	CAP 01	CAP 14	AQU 01	AQU 21

NOV 27 – PM	1	2	3	4	5	6	7	8	9	10	11	**12midnight**
Sign/Degree	PIS 15	ARI 10	TAU 05	TAU 25	GEM 13	GEM 28	CAN 11	CAN 24	LEO 06	LEO 17	LEO 29	VIR 11

NOV 30 – AM	1	2	3	4	5	6	7	8	9	10	11	**12noon**
Sign/Degree	VIR 25	LIB 07	LIB 19	SCO 01	SCO 12	SCO 24	SAG 06	SAG 19	CAP 02	CAP 17	AQU 05	AQU 25

NOV 30 – PM	1	2	3	4	5	6	7	8	9	10	11	**12midnight**
Sign/Degree	PIS 20	ARI 15	TAU 09	GEM 01	GEM 16	CAN 01	CAN 14	CAN 26	LEO 08	LEO 20	VIR 02	VIR 14

DECEMBER

DEC 3 – AM	1	2	3	4	5	6	7	8	9	10	11	12noon
Sign/Degree	VIR 27	LIB 09	LIB 21	SCO 03	SCO 15	SCO 27	SAG 09	SAG 21	CAP 05	CAP 20	AQU 08	PIS 01

DEC 3 – PM	1	2	3	4	5	6	7	8	9	10	11	12midnight
Sign/Degree	PIS 25	ARI 20	TAU 13	GEM 03	GEM 19	CAN 03	CAN 16	CAN 28	LEO 10	LEO 22	VIR 04	VIR 16

DEC 6 – AM	1	2	3	4	5	6	7	8	9	10	11	12noon
Sign/Degree	LIB 01	LIB 12	LIB 23	SCO 05	SCO 17	SCO 29	SAG 11	SAG 24	CAP 08	CAP 24	AQU 12	PIS 04

DEC 6 – PM	1	2	3	4	5	6	7	8	9	10	11	12midnight
Sign/Degree	ARI 01	ARI 25	TAU 17	GEM 06	GEM 22	CAN 06	CAN 19	LEO 01	LEO 13	LEO 24	VIR 06	VIR 18

DEC 9 – AM	1	2	3	4	5	6	7	8	9	10	11	12noon
Sign/Degree	LIB 02	LIB 14	LIB 26	SCO 08	SCO 19	SAG 01	SAG 14	SAG 27	CAP 11	CAP 27	AQU 16	PIS 09

DEC 9 – PM	1	2	3	4	5	6	7	8	9	10	11	12midnight
Sign/Degree	ARI 05	TAU 01	TAU 21	GEM 09	GEM 25	CAN 08	CAN 21	LEO 03	LEO 15	LEO 27	VIR 09	VIR 21

DEC 12 – AM	1	2	3	4	5	6	7	8	9	10	11	12noon
Sign/Degree	LIB 04	LIB 16	LIB 28	SCO 10	SCO 22	SAG 04	SAG 16	SAG 29	CAP 14	AQU 01	AQU 21	PIS 14

DEC 12 – PM	1	2	3	4	5	6	7	8	9	10	11	12midnight
Sign/Degree	ARI 10	TAU 04	TAU 25	GEM 12	GEM 27	CAN 11	CAN 23	LEO 05	LEO 17	LEO 29	VIR 11	VIR 23

DEC 15 – AM	1	2	3	4	5	6	7	8	9	10	11	12noon
Sign/Degree	LIB 07	LIB 19	SCO 01	SCO 12	SCO 24	SAG 06	SAG 19	CAP 02	CAP 17	AQU 04	AQU 25	PIS 19

DEC 15 – PM	1	2	3	4	5	6	7	8	9	10	11	12midnight
Sign/Degree	ARI 15	TAU 09	TAU 29	GEM 16	CAN 01	CAN 13	CAN 26	LEO 08	LEO 20	VIR 01	VIR 13	VIR 25

DEC 18 – AM	1	2	3	4	5	6	7	8	9	10	11	12noon
Sign/Degree	LIB 09	LIB 21	SCO 03	SCO 15	SCO 26	SAG 09	SAG 21	CAP 05	CAP 20	AQU 08	PIS 01	PIS 24

DEC 18 – PM	1	2	3	4	5	6	7	8	9	10	11	12midnight
Sign/Degree	ARI 20	TAU 13	GEM 02	GEM 19	CAN 03	CAN 16	CAN 28	LEO 10	LEO 22	VIR 04	VIR 16	VIR 28

DEC 21 – AM	1	2	3	4	5	6	7	8	9	10	11	12noon
Sign/Degree	LIB 11	LIB 23	SCO 05	SCO 17	SCO 29	SAG 11	SAG 24	CAP 08	CAP 23	AQU 12	PIS 04	ARI 01

DEC 21 – PM	1	2	3	4	5	6	7	8	9	10	11	12midnight
Sign/Degree	ARI 25	TAU 17	GEM 06	GEM 22	CAN 06	CAN 18	LEO 01	LEO 12	LEO 24	VIR 06	VIR 18	LIB 01

DEC 24 – AM	1	2	3	4	5	6	7	8	9	10	11	12noon
Sign/Degree	LIB 14	LIB 26	SCO 08	SCO 19	SAG 01	SAG 14	SAG 26	CAP 11	CAP 27	AQU 16	PIS 09	ARI 04

DEC 24 – PM	1	2	3	4	5	6	7	8	9	10	11	12midnight
Sign/Degree	ARI 29	TAU 21	GEM 09	GEM 25	CAN 08	CAN 21	LEO 03	LEO 15	LEO 27	VIR 08	VIR 20	LIB 02

DEC 27 – AM	1	2	3	4	5	6	7	8	9	10	11	12noon
Sign/Degree	LIB 16	LIB 28	SCO 10	SCO 22	SAG 04	SAG 16	SAG 29	CAP 14	AQU 01	AQU 20	PIS 14	ARI 09

DEC 27 – PM	1	2	3	4	5	6	7	8	9	10	11	12midnight
Sign/Degree	TAU 04	TAU 25	GEM 12	GEM 27	CAN 11	CAN 23	LEO 05	LEO 17	LEO 29	VIR 11	VIR 23	LIB 05

DEC 30 – AM	1	2	3	4	5	6	7	8	9	10	11	12noon
Sign/Degree	LIB 18	SCO 01	SCO 12	SCO 24	SAG 06	SAG 18	CAP 02	CAP 17	AQU 04	AQU 25	PIS 19	ARI 14

DEC 30 – PM	1	2	3	4	5	6	7	8	9	10	11	12midnight
Sign/Degree	TAU 08	TAU 28	GEM 15	CAN 01	CAN 13	CAN 25	LEO 08	LEO 19	VIR 01	VIR 13	VIR 25	LIB 07

RISING AND SETTING SIGN PROFILES

IMPORTANT TIPS for understanding the layout and terms used

●   Remember that your Rising Sign represents what you immediately show to the world, that is your persona, image or SELF, which is the word used to indicate this in the Profiles. The reaction you get back to this is symbolized by your Setting Sign which could be described as your partner, your other or better half, your alter ego, the kind of relationship you attract, other people (and things) generally, or simply as OTHER, the word used in the Profiles and throughout this book. Often you will find that the Other in your life has the Sun, Moon or some other emphasis in the same Sign as your Setting Sign.

●   THE INTERACTION shows how these two parts of your life/personality encounter and react to one another.

●   Your SHADOW is a description of that part of yourself which you deny, suppress or misapprehend – and then project – which, when acknowledged, owned and accepted can actually help you to resolve problems of relating and self-expression.

●   STYLE OF RELATIONSHIP describes the kind of partnership which, despite what you may believe, is best for your welfare and development.

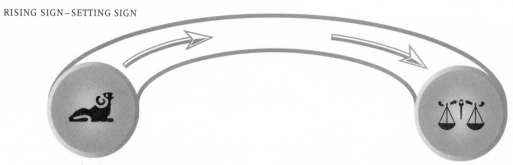

ARIES RISING • LIBRA SETTING

SELF Go-getter or Bulldozer   Diplomat or Yes-person **OTHER**

THE INTERACTION

You take on the role of leader, so invariably you act first, decide what's to be done, and get things moving. Other acts as a counterbalance to this, depending upon how agreeable they find it, and whether it fits in with the general consensus or not. Other will usually try to be diplomatic in the face of your unequivocal stance. If Other is particularly unsure of their own standpoint they will go along – happily or not – with whatever your decision or action happens to be. If or when they have a more definite opinion, and they are not entirely happy with your tack, they will deal with your forcefulness in the following way. First they'll try to get you to see their own or another's position; failing that they'll argue a bit, and failing that they'll use passive resistance. But any soppiness or superficiality on Other's part would be vigorously attacked by you.

SHADOW = INDECISION

You are uncomfortable with having to wait things out, or with letting things develop outside of your initiative. It is as if you see any passivity or too much consideration of other people's opinions as flabby indecisiveness, and as being a sure sign of asking to be beaten to the punch. But what you see as precarious indecision is really a weighing of the pros and cons of a situation, a look at any possible repercussions, and a generally more harmonious manner. Taking this on board would prevent the strife, dissatisfaction and even disaster which your pushiness or impetuosity can attract.

STYLE OF RELATIONSHIP

Balanced and fair, with yourself and Other having equal say in all matters – very much the partnership, in fact. Despite what you might think to the contrary – that being your way of thinking – other people tend or like to see you both as a couple, a social touchstone, even an example of how a relationship ought to work. What you need – despite your wilfulness, or rather because of it – is quite a conventional relationship, the social unit which your milieu comes to rely upon as 'always being there'. All this acts as a stabilizer to your dynamic persona, and as a safe haven to which you may return after one of your sorties.

WHEN ALONE ...

… it is because your selfish and inconsiderate behaviour has caught up with you and there are no takers. But your pushiness, although it can sometimes be downright rude or thoughtless, does not as a rule have any malice behind it. It is just that having to get your oar in first can lead to you being the only one on board. Seeing that the kind of Other you attract is usually a deferential, socially aware person, they will probably put up with you for quite some time, then unexpectedly turn the tables on you. It is important for you to soften your hard edge enough to let your softness show, rather than being seen by Other as a challenge or a threat.

MARS *is your Ruling Planet*   VENUS *is Other's Ruling Planet*

See page 276 for how they both interact in your chart

TAURUS RISING • SCORPIO SETTING

SELF Sensualist or Hedonist

Delver or Demon **OTHER**

THE INTERACTION

You are very much a creature of Nature and the physical senses, exuding an aura of permanence and constancy. You do not like to be hurried or pushed into anything unknown or too new, and are happiest when surrounded by whatever is familiar to you. No matter how you actually look, there is a tactile, even huggable, feel about you – an animal magnetism, in fact. But it is just this slow and physically strong presence that attracts an Other who is not content to leave things as they are. Other is more inclined to dig beneath your placid or stubborn surface in search of the soul and passion that they detect underneath. This ruffles you as much as it excites you – and there's the rub. It is as if you need that 'sting' to stop you from sliding into the mud of your resistance to change – and the sting that works best is sexual in nature. But should Other push you too far, or excite you too much even, you dig your hooves in deeper than ever.

SHADOW = INTENSITY

You are uncomfortable with feelings that are too arousing or provocative – a bit like a red rag to a bull, one could say. Your reaction to such intensity of feeling is to bear your weight down upon it, which means to flatten it with earthy logic, simply not to acknowledge it or even see it. But the more you deny your Shadow, the more you will attract what you'll interpret as disruption. Your pleasure-seeking and sensual persona is bound to evoke deep passions in Other, so it would be wise to understand the secret and psychological workings of human nature then they won't take your earthy straightforwardness unawares.

STYLE OF RELATIONSHIP

A deeply committed relationship is definitely the fodder for you, the type of partnership that can endure quite heavy conflicts or tests of fidelity. At times you may feel trapped and manipulated by such an arrangement, as if you have been bought body and soul. But yours is a rich and fertile pairing, the kind that produces and provides. Rather like a farm that is dependent upon its soil, you have to keep nurturing it, occasionally turning it over, ploughing the goodness back in to regenerate it, letting it lie fallow, etc. Indeed, the seasonal cycle of birth and rebirth, prospering and dying, epitomizes your style of relationship.

WHEN ALONE ...

... it is simply because you have not been prepared to accept the deep commitment and mutual possession that this Rising/Setting combination demands. Possibly you fear your depths being plumbed, or that Other would not like what they found beneath your attractive surface. Because of that surface you have no difficulty attracting a mate, but you make the mistake of doubting the profound value of what lies beneath it. After all, a garden is only as good as its soil.

 VENUS *is your Ruling Planet*   PLUTO *is Other's Ruling Planet*

See page 276 for how they both interact in your chart

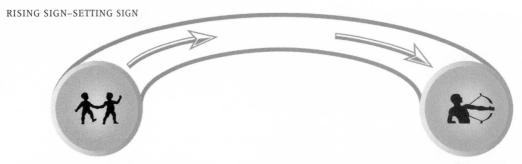

GEMINI RISING • SAGITTARIUS SETTING

SELF Enquirer or Dabbler Teacher or Preacher **OTHER**

THE INTERACTION

You approach life in the spirit of enquiry, like the eternal student. You love making connections between one thing and another, without necessarily having to feel any sense of where it is all heading or what it all means. You are also a keen maker of contacts, priding yourself on being acquainted with all types of individual and scene. Not surprisingly, you are equipped with quick wits and word-power. Quite what all this amounts to – that is, who is doing all this talking, thinking and enquiring – can be very elusive. And so you attract an Other intent on teaching you to become some kind of comprehensive whole. Because of this, Other can organize you into an entity of more meaning and emotional integrity – if you let them. However, this can make you feel preached at, and you may wriggle even more in order to remain the free agent you identify with being, even chopping and changing identities to facilitate this.

SHADOW = SUPERIORITY

Your friendliness and conversational ease give the lie to the fact that behind such affability there languishes a quite aloof and even supercilious being. It is as if there is a dimension to your personality that you feel is apart from the world, that noone can ever reach or understand. But because this is your Shadow and as such is denied, you wind up feeling there is a part of you that you must keep out of sight, and so you use your agile tongue and wit to throw Other off the scent. If you accepted your Shadow, you would find that it is not so much superiority but more a sense of your higher self – looking out for you, in spite of yourself.

STYLE OF RELATIONSHIP

You love a relationship that feels as if it is going somewhere. The trouble is, with your dilettante-like nature, you will interpret this quite literally as going on a trip or travelling abroad with someone. Really this means that your relationship has to amount to something in a philosophical or even religious sense, like a moral statement. It is as if the relationship is a hair-clasp that holds together all the disparate strands of your Mercurial temperament. Without understanding or accepting this style, you had better resign yourself to a series of inconsequential affairs posing as a love life – the sum being less than the total of the parts.

WHEN ALONE ...

... you will, apart from anything else, have your alter ego for company. And this is the clue as to why you are alone: you are disinclined to allow an Other to see the side to your nature which is the 'dark twin' – that is, the one whom you assume would not be accepted by Other. You may know in your heart what characterizes this dark twin, and it could be described somewhere in these pages under the influence of some Planet. But whatever it is like, let it out so that it might grow to be seen, known, loved and transformed.

MERCURY *is your Ruling Planet* JUPITER *is Other's Ruling Planet*

See page 276 for how they both interact in your chart

CANCER RISING • CAPRICORN SETTING

`SELF` Carer or Cowerer   Worldly One or Wet Blanket `OTHER`

THE INTERACTION

You are all 'feelers', picking up the emotional climate around you with instinctual ease. It can seem at times that you are purely response and reaction to whoever you are with or wherever you are. This can result in your not being at all sure whether it is your feeling or someone else's. In any event, you have to respond in some way, usually giving care or sympathy, or needing it – or you simply withdraw into your famous shell until it is 'safe' to come out again. With such moodiness being the hallmark of your identity, you are inclined to attract an Other who is more emotionally controlled, restrained or repressed even. They may also be somewhat older than you, biologically or psychologically, and therefore more adult or worldly. Other provides you with the equipment and technique that make it possible to function in the harsh material world at which your childlike persona can blanch. If Other's more mature stance appears cold or calculating to you though, you will give a commensurate display of fearfulness and/or withdrawal.

SHADOW = IMPERSONALITY

Your dreamy, sensitive and sentimental response to life makes you react negatively to anything that appears to be coldly realistic and unfeeling. But that is often all it is – a *reaction* that interprets a businesslike and objective approach to things as being alien and unfamiliar, and therefore uncaring. Such a subjective response has at its root a feeling of insecurity that has your mother, father and childhood as the reason behind it. Take a step back and see that this impersonal attitude is the very objectivity, seriousness and sober sense of purpose that you need to learn and acquire so as to feel more safe and secure in the world.

STYLE OF RELATIONSHIP

You require a traditional type of relationship where each of you has a clear sense of their role and position in it. This may feel restrictive and limiting at first, but eventually, and paradoxically, this feeling of having and knowing your boundaries and responsibilities is what makes you feel secure and protected enough to go out and explore your potential and make the most of yourself. An open, easy-come-easy-go kind of relationship would not give you this. As the Chinese proverb says, 'Limitation is the key to freedom'.

WHEN ALONE ...

... it is very likely because you have not accepted the limitations (or lessons) of a relationship in the way outlined above. Without doing this, a relationship, or Other, can wither on the vine. Seeking some kind of unrealistic 'freedom' can be the culprit behind this, and the reason behind that can be a very basic and unconscious distrust of finding any Other whom you can rely upon at all. Alternatively, not taking a tough enough 'impersonal' stance with Other can leave you feeling emotionally exhausted, if not on your own.

THE MOON *is your Ruling Planet*   SATURN *is Other's Ruling Planet*

See page 276 for how they both interact in your chart   267

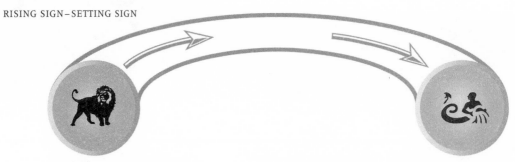

LEO RISING • AQUARIUS SETTING

SELF **Showman or Show-off**   **Observer or Outsider** **OTHER**

THE INTERACTION

Like a King or Queen you express yourself with apparent confidence and style, with a regal air that names the game and sets the rules. This attracts Other who, like a court jester, responds positively only when you are aware of what is popular and have at heart the interests of Other. Failing this, you are met with cool indifference, mockery or outright rebellion. Conversely, Other's views and theories about life and society, if only slightly tinged with political correctness, are shot down by you with a blast of passionate self-justification. When, on the other hand, Other's populist point is expressed in such a way as to make it clear that noting it would lead to elevating your individual position, then you graciously and happily accept it.

SHADOW = ORDINARINESS

You have a dread of being merely one amongst the grey mass of human society, so it rankles when Other shows signs of being a member of this large and unexclusive club and subscribes to fitting in but at the same time wants to be slightly different. Such naffness is what you yourself live in fear of being accused of. But being a bit so-called ordinary can paradoxically be quite quirky and, more to the point, render you less self-conscious and more at ease with the world. This is like the monarch who is far more popular with his subjects because he is seen to be like them than if he held himself apart from and above them.

STYLE OF RELATIONSHIP

Unusual and unprecedented types of interaction, with the accent on freedom, are what suit you, despite the hassle and unpredictability they engender. It is as if you are inventing a set of values that will suit you and Other exclusively. This quality of your relationship reflects what poet Kahlil Gibran advised any couple: 'Let the winds of the heavens dance between you.' In other words, don't ever fall into complacency by thinking you really know, let alone own, one another, or shock and upset will descend upon you. In any event, you are inclined to run hot and cold, go on/off, as needs for freedom and companionship alternate.

WHEN ALONE ...

… or without success in or recognition from the world at large, it is no doubt because you have been sticking stubbornly to an egocentric viewpoint or value system that failed to appeal to Other. So Other had to follow the only course open to them in the face of such overt self-righteousness. If in future you begin to show that behind your magnificent façade you are an ordinary, feeling human being, then Other – either in their current form or a new one – will be only too pleased to bask in your light or appreciate your creative expressions. Just so long as your bright persona is not just a defence system against a world you feel does not understand you. The truth is that it will not do so as long as you fail to show the mere human inside.

THE SUN *is your Ruling Planet*   URANUS *is Other's Ruling Planet*

          See page 276 for how they both interact in your chart

VIRGO RISING • PISCES SETTING

SELF Servant or Slave   Saviour or Victim **OTHER**

THE INTERACTION

You approach life with a view to improving the quality of it in some way, and so you have an eye for detail and, more's the point, a eye for what is flawed, unclean, untidy or unhealthy. Consequently, you are almost constantly on the go – there is always something or someone that needs seeing to from where you stand. This means that Other will very often fall into this category of what 'needs seeing to'. So Other may be vague, unkempt, absent-minded, weak, or in some way in need of practical attention – or at least, that is how they'll seem to you. And this is the point, because you can make a rod for your back with all manner of lame duck, hopeless case, addict or invalid becoming your Other – or workload rather – simply because you see Other as something in need of your attention. Other's response to this will be to be even more vague and unkempt, for you are only too willing to take the strain. But if you dropped your critical gaze for long enough you might see that Other is showing a way to be more accepting and laid back about life.

SHADOW = CONFUSION

Your need for things to be 'just so' masks a fear of collapse and confusion. Put more accurately, your Shadow is actually a profound doubt that life and Other will be all right without your constant attention, especially to those details. You find it hard to trust the fact that in life some things (just have to) work themselves out in their own way and time. As if to show you that you can no more control Other than a sailor can control the sea, the 'confusion' can leak in with your being particularly messy in one area of your life, and quite indiscriminate in some of your relationships. Pick what you ought to let go of – then do so.

STYLE OF RELATIONSHIP

A mixture of purity and 'anything goes' would be a shorthand if somewhat contradictory description of your ideal relationship. Unconditional with distinct no-go areas would be another. What all this amounts to is that you are attempting to find that perfect relationship, and the nearer you get to it, the more you appreciate that such a thing is a paradox. And the further you get from it, the more impossible it seems. The answer is to keep working at it until you have distilled that blend of discernment and acceptance.

WHEN ALONE ...

... it is simply because you have priced yourself out of the market. Virgo is the Sign of the Hermit so you are more likely than most to get left on the shelf – out of choice, you'd protest. You may well like it that way, but if you did you'd hardly be reading this book – unless you were sorting someone else out. More to the point though, you are inclined to find noone quite right because there is some deeply-seated flaw of your own which you have classified as untouchable or hopeless. Not so – just simply in need of practice!

 MERCURY *is your Ruling Planet*   NEPTUNE *is Other's Ruling Planet*

See page 276 for how they both interact in your chart

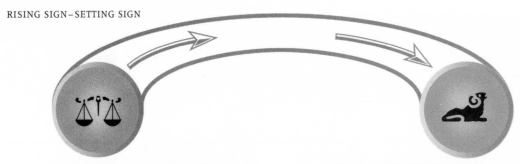

LIBRA RISING • ARIES SETTING

SELF Diplomat or Yes-person   Go-getter or Bulldozer **OTHER**

THE INTERACTION

You want to make yourself out to be an agreeable and sociable person. Having a partner in life is more important for you than any other Rising Sign for it is a testament to this aspiration. Furthermore, you are willing to bend over backwards, make all sorts of compromises, and endlessly groom yourself in order to achieve this end of being the Other to an Other. This is all very well and very pleasant too, but the irony is that you attract someone who forces you ultimately to stand up for yourself and to be your own person, and not just someone who harmonizes with someone else. Other to you can be quite disagreeable or lacking in the social graces, and could learn from your innate good manners and powers of diplomacy. But Other may be particularly acid should your style be merely a fashionable but superficial display of socially correct verbiage and mannerisms. However, there is also the possibility that Other will play along with you (such is our culture's programming to please and gain approval) and that eventually and shockingly the raw and crude reality of each of you will burst out, presenting your very real sense of harmony with a very real challenge.

SHADOW = AGGRESSION

If you often find yourself being unjustifiably attacked or mistreated by Other, you can be sure that you are being caught in your own Shadow. The image of charm and pleasantness that you project can fool you into thinking that there isn't an offensive bone in your body – or at least, apart from the ones that you choose to be aware of. But the fact is, being so nice is asking to be pushed around – which is a way of getting Other to act out the aggression that you have but only otherwise experience as anger, frustration or illness. Getting off the fence, stating your case, and being prepared to engage in conflict would resolve matters.

STYLE OF RELATIONSHIP

It is desirable that both you and Other regard yourselves and each other as individuals in your own right. So a healthy sense of competitiveness is to be encouraged for it helps to keep each of you mindful of your individual worth and effectiveness. Being physically active, together and individually, is also recommended. Without creating or maintaining this theme, outright and destructive conflict could surface.

WHEN ALONE ...

… it because the time has come for you to develop and come to terms with yourself as an individual being – that is, someone who has only themselves to contend with life. Although, or rather because, you need a partner more than most, it is inevitable that you will encounter such aloneness quite acutely at some point in your self-development. Naturally, such a state will not come upon you, or be embarked upon, easily – but it should be seen as a positive turning point, with a better relationship following upon it in due course.

VENUS *is your Ruling Planet*   MARS *is Other's Ruling Planet*

See page 276 for how they both interact in your chart

SCORPIO RISING • TAURUS SETTING

SELF Delver or Vampire

Sensualist or Hedonist **OTHER**

THE INTERACTION

Your persona is like a probe, seeking out whatever lies beneath surface appearances to satisfy your hunger for passions, secrets, intrigues and powerful emotions. At the same time you cloak your own feelings and intentions, becoming as impenetrable as you are penetrating. Other finds this intensely suggestive approach and personal style quite irresistible, succumbing like a hypnotist's subject or even a lamb (or Bull) to the slaughter. This is until it dawns on Other that they are not so sure about being under your spell, or who you are behind that cloak – and whether there's a dagger there too. At this point, when Other comes to suspect your secretiveness and the intentions behind it, they will dig their heels in and become impassive, immovable, intransigent – but still remain. In turn, this is the juncture when you must realize that you want Other to resist you because it is a sign that they are solid and loyal enough not to be perturbed by your sexual power plays and extremes of emotion. Great fulfilment can follow upon this 'deal' being made.

SHADOW = GULLIBILITY

Considering that shady areas are what you are drawn to, it is not surprising to find that your own Shadow is quite ironic. All your secretiveness, devious ploys and the tabs you keep on Other leave you curiously unaware of the obvious about yourself – that if you behave secretively then you must have an area of your personality that is particularly vulnerable. And you can be so busy protecting it that you can be caught unawares; what you feared most comes upon you. So when you identify and admit this vulnerable area, what was gullibility then becomes an intense candour which Other finds extremely binding and endearing.

STYLE OF RELATIONSHIP

A steady, traditional, almost 'down on the farm' kind of set-up suits you. What you may find wanting in the area of psychological acuteness or emotional intensity is made up for in a peaceful and natural relationship that is more concerned with creature comforts and natural appetites and values.

WHEN ALONE ...

... it is often the case that you are actually in a relationship but are alone within your heavily protective shell. You are caught between the need for an intimate relationship where Other knows your darkest secrets, and a fear of that vulnerability being disclosed. If you err in favour of the latter, you effectively shut Other out from your emotional interior. Inevitably Other will make the best of their own space which effectively and progressively has less and less to do with you. If you are entirely on your own the same equation applies: to be as close to (an)Other as you need to be necessitates being aware enough of your own emotional hang-ups to trust Other with them, rather than manipulating Other through a knowledge of *their* hang-ups.

PLUTO *is your Ruling Planet*   VENUS *is Other's Ruling Planet*

See page 276 for how they both interact in your chart

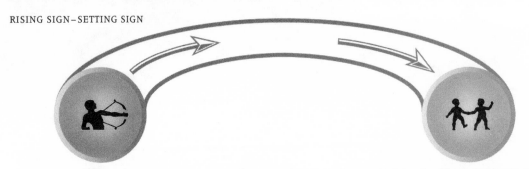

SAGITTARIUS RISING • GEMINI SETTING

SELF Teacher or Preacher

Enquirer or Dabbler **OTHER**

THE INTERACTION

Like the superior being that you are inclined to present yourself as, you express yourself with a larger than life sense of confidence and apparent self-assurance. This attracts Other who, as the eternal gatherer of pieces of information, is impressed by your seemingly broad and effortless grasp of all manner of things. Other sees your persona as a role model for how to give off a cosmopolitan air that makes them look as knowledgeable as they potentially or actually are. However, should Other become aware that behind any particular facet of your self-advertisement there is no product to live up to it, then a kind of intellectual scorn towards what is seen as smugness or pretentiousness on your part can colour their idea of you. Conversely, Other's array of endless but unrelated bytes of information, which is simply diversity, is helpful to you just as long as it doesn't annoy you.

SHADOW = INFERIORITY

What can really bug you about Other is a certain downmarket, irrelevant or inept quality, with a worrisome nature to match. But this is actually a reflection of your fear of being provincial or in *doubt*. Remind yourself that such 'inferiority' is an example to you of the common touch and concerns that would greatly complement, even complete, your talent for seeing the bigger picture. Being honest about your doubts will put Other at their ease and, consequently, they will feel more confident in themselves.

STYLE OF RELATIONSHIP

Variety and not getting too tied down are important to you. But so too is having the commitment to a lasting relationship. This contradiction is symbolized by having dualistic Gemini on your Descendant. The resolution to this dilemma is to accept the fact that you lead a two-tone lifestyle and hope that Other will love you for the adventurous and exciting being that you are. Having more than one partner would be stretching this a bit, but if such is the case, it would mean that you found it hard to be honest and share all of your light and shade with just one Other. Then again it could fall to your partner to act out any suppressed duplicity or lack of commitment on your part!

WHEN ALONE ...

... it is most likely because you have simply found it so hard to commit yourself to a relationship that you have either been given up as a hopeless case, or that you have never dared take any sort of plunge even into the shallows of a relationship. When it comes down to it, you hate being alone, for then you have to confront what is at the root of relationship problems: your own inconsistencies as opposed to those you see as belonging to Other. Sooner or later, this is the one plunge you will have to take – into your depths.

JUPITER *is your Ruling Planet*   MERCURY *is Other's Ruling Planet*

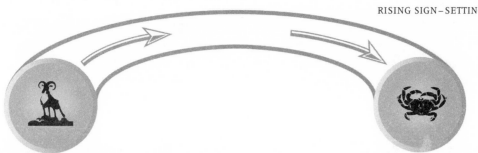

CAPRICORN RISING • CANCER SETTING

SELF **Worldly One or Wet Blanket**   **Carer or Cowerer** OTHER

You approach virtually everything and everyone in a tactical, businesslike manner; you certainly do not lead with your feelings. You generate an aura of material, political awareness and if anything needs organizing you'll be the first to offer – or rather start doing so without even being asked. Life to you is something to be managed and controlled, so when it comes to emotionally relating or social interplay you're not exactly one to let rip and let your hair down. Dependability and respectability are what you have on offer, not passion and drama. This is not to say that you have no sense of fun, but even that would have a certain limit placed upon it. Other cannot help but respond to all this serious, grown-up stuff in a commensurately emotional, childlike and needy fashion. Either that, or you are not about to get much response at all other than an equally restrained display. Hopefully then, Other will get you to melt and loosen up a bit, and appreciate that life can be a soulful adventure and not a matter-of-fact affair where you squash Other at one sign too many of playful romanticism or unscripted unworldliness. This would be a mistake because you need their caring, sympathetic and comparatively immature input to get past your tough hide of an exterior.

SHADOW = NAÏVETÉ

You live in dread of losing the control of keeping what's really on the inside becoming visible on the outside. You feel that to appear unworldly or naïve would amount to some kind of self-demolition. And because you are petrified of letting this child in you show, what you see as that guileless part of you becomes increasingly like a time-bomb of a baby that one day is going to bawl the house down. This means that if you do not confess to having that naïve and innocent part to you, the part which Other truly loves, a time will come when it causes you to make the very gaffe that destroys what you have so painstakingly built up.

STYLE OF RELATIONSHIP

A home-from-home, traditional type of relationship where you and Other each know your respective roles, duties and boundaries. Family values and sentimentality should be the life blood of your relationship. If such appears claustrophobic to you, or just doesn't seem to happen in this day and age, then you must be still on some wide arc of self-discovery that will lead back to this basic set-up – one day, soon or far off.

WHEN ALONE …

… it is because you have yet to realize that relationships are born and maintained in the unconscious mind, that very pool of emotions and longings which you work so hard to keep under control. You are like a dam that holds all the water in to generate power for material use but without any natural flow which would bring about fertility and growth. Open the sluices, release your emotions, relinquish control, surrender your fears!

SATURN *is your Ruling Planet*   THE MOON *is Other's Ruling Planet*

See page 276 for how they both interact in your chart   273

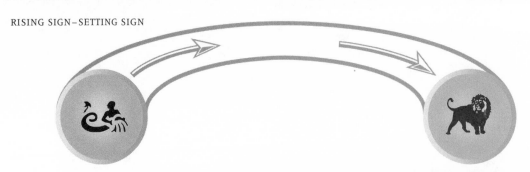

AQUARIUS RISING • LEO SETTING

SELF **Observer or Outsider** **Showman or Show-off** **OTHER**

THE INTERACTION

Your approach is cool but friendly. A person's intellect and social or political viewpoint is what appears to interest you most, for you engage on that level first and foremost. Emotional and sexual vibrations are kept beneath your surface, ranging in depth from merely needing scratching to reveal rich, intense feelings, to being virtually unavailable or even non-existent. This measure of how emotionally accessible you are is critical with regard to how Other responds or reacts to you. They may coast along with your apparently airy coolness for quite some time until either they explode with boredom or frustration – or you do. In either case, it is this distance that you create and keep between Other and your true inner feelings that is responsible for this kind of reaction. Consciously or unconsciously, Other is trying to show you that it's all right to have human emotions, to have highs and lows and not just hover in some safe and socially acceptable place in between. On the other hand, your impartial and intuitive assessment of Other's nature and worth, and life in general, is something which Other should take note of – so express it with some confidence and style!

SHADOW = ELITISM

Unless there are Leo planets in your chart, you are inclined to feel uncomfortable with sticking out in a crowd or having a high profile. You cringe if Other should be showy, exclusive or blow their own trumpet. This is a sign of a classic kind of Shadow because it misses or obscures your own sense of specialness. Possibly you choose to display your uniqueness by appearing unusual or unconventional, but in a fashion that is acceptable in itself – that is, you are 'conventionally unconventional' or put on an act in a professional capacity. In truth, what you might regard as elitism in Other is just your own specialness which is unexpressed or suppressed because you doubt it for some reason. Let it show and it will grow!

STYLE OF RELATIONSHIP

As if to confirm much of the above, you like your relationship with Other to be special or in a class all of its own. An 'ordinary' or lacklustre relationship is not for you, and even if you think it is, it's not what you'll get. In fact a fiery, dramatic relationship is quite likely because it serves to keep you in touch with your ego and emotions, things which you are inclined to disassociate from in order to appear 'civilized'.

WHEN ALONE ...

… it is a logical outcome of your being too detached – that is, you become completely detached. You may well like this state of being, but more than most Rising Signs, you are pulled back into relationship again quite quickly and easily – in the same way that cool air draws in heat. If it then gets too hot for you again, you detach and retract, and so and so on, in an on/off fashion. But generally you are quite constant in this.

 URANUS *is your Ruling Planet*   THE SUN *is Other's Ruling Planet*

See page 276 for how they both interact in your chart

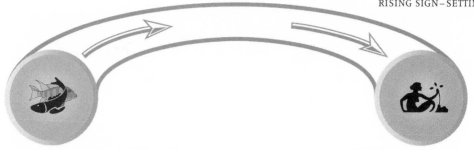

PISCES RISING • VIRGO SETTING

SELF Saviour or Victim   Servant or Slave **OTHER**

THE INTERACTION

You are very sensitive, as if the whole surface of your skin were picking up on Other and the environment in general. You channel or deal with this in a creative/mystical or evasive/dreamy fashion. You're not quite sure where you begin and Other ends, and will dart off into the shadows if things get too barbed emotionally. Yet at the same time there are some things about Other that you find very hard to resist – are addicted to, in fact. Other will probably view all this popping in and out as chaotic and in need of sorting out. This of course can make you even more evasive, but if you value Other's perspective, you will receive their practical assistance. In return, you are quite dedicated to Other, helping or healing them in a subtle, psychic way. Negatively, Other can become a slave to your elusive charm as they try to order your chaos. More than most Rising/Setting combinations, this one depends upon meeting one another half way.

SHADOW = SCEPTICISM

Other's critical attitude toward you is really the form your Shadow takes. This means that for all your vague and dreamy manner there lurks behind it a scientific and sceptical attitude that finds it hard to accept certain things, but not anything, that does not have a rational explanation. You still like to maintain an area where you can be totally illogical, so it can be pretty difficult to determine where you're coming from. Suffice to say that making clear what you accept and what you question would itself clarify relationships.

STYLE OF RELATIONSHIP

More than anything, you require a relationship that is crystal clear about its own nature and status. The trouble is that you can confuse having such a thing as an impingement on your freedom to meander where you will. This can be a big mistake for vague relationships for you are rather like what uncharted waters are to a rudderless boat. A clean, wholesome and definite arrangement is, despite your suspicions or apparent aversions, your best bet. A sailor without a home port can eventually get lost or washed up.

WHEN ALONE ...

... or adrift more like, it is down to one or more of the illusions described above. Be it your need to roam the Seven Seas of the yet to be experienced, your over-sensitivity that makes you allergic to being close to an Other, or one of your many brands of evasiveness – they all have behind them one thing. This is your fear of facing your own music – that is, your own hurts, egotism, lack of faith, or anything else that strands you between the devil and the deep blue sea. The flip in your own slippery tail is that in being alone you are ultimately forced to face this music of yours. And when you do, you'll know the score and thereby attract the Other who can and will help you in just the way that you need to be helped.

NEPTUNE *is your Ruling Planet*   MERCURY *is Other's Ruling Planet*

See page 276 for how they both interact in your chart   275

RULING PLANETS

At the foot of each page that describes a Rising/Setting Sign, you will have seen what is YOUR RULING PLANET (that which is said to rule your Rising Sign) and what is Other's Ruling Planet (the Planet which rules your Setting Sign – what I call the SETTING RULER). Your Ruling Planet is a further significator of the way in which your Self operates, and the Setting Ruler the manner in which Other appears to do so in response to Self. Remember here that 'Other' is the embodiment of your Projected Self, and not actually some 'other' in particular, even though they will appear that way. Perhaps this is best understood when we realize that one person can appear quite different to different people – because different people have different Projected Selves. There are a number of ways you can use this information.

1 Simply review or look at what is the Sign position for both the Ruling Planet and the Setting Ruler in the PLANET-SIGN PROFILES, or look at the general meaning of that Planet in PLANETS OF LOVE in the General Introduction. *In our example, Jack has JUPiter as his Ruling Planet which we see he has placed in Leo, and this, along with the general nature of Jupiter, would further describe his manner of Self-Expression. Conversely, he has Gemini Setting giving Other's Ruler as MERcury. The qualities of this planet and its Sign position (in his chart) then reveal more about his type of partner, relationships and way of relating.*

2 Having established the Signs in which your Ruling Planet and your Setting Ruler are placed, we can then look at the relationship between those two Signs to get some idea of how readily and in what way the Self will see Other as being a part of It, which will in turn colour how Self and Other – or simply how you and your partner – can integrate and relate. This is a case of the ATTITUDE that one has towards relationship going a long way to predetermining the success or failure of it. Look at the CHARTWHEEL where you have entered your Planet-Sign positions, locate the Sign of the Ruling Planet and the Sign of the Setting Ruler, and then count how many Signs they are apart. By 'Signs apart', I mean that you take the next Sign on from the one in question as being one Sign apart from it, two Signs on as being two Signs apart, etc. For instance, if your Ruling Planet was in Virgo and your Setting Ruler in Gemini, then *taking the shortest route*, they would be *three* Signs apart. On the next page, you see a chart to enable you to understand what the relationship between your Ruling Planet and Setting Ruler means in terms of YOUR BASIC UNDERLYING ATTITUDE TOWARDS RELATIONSHIP. *In our example, Jack's JUPiter (Ruling Planet) and MERcury (Setting Ruler) are in the SAME SIGN (NONE apart), so his Self would see Other as being very much a part of him, as being united for better or worse, but possibly not see where real differences exist.*

3 Ruling Planets can be used to find out how the interpretations of Planet-Sign positions – as given in the Planet-Sign Profiles – can be subtly altered by the Sign position of the Planet that rules any given Sign. In astrology this is called DISPOSITION. We will use our example and the Table, SIGNS AND THEIR RULERS on the next page, to demonstrate this. *Take Jill's VENus in GEMini. This sounds quite breezy and capable of emotional detachment – but in reality, Jill is obviously not quite like this; she has a light touch emotionally, but is not what you'd regard as being without empathy or sympathy. So, we look to the Table for what Planet rules Venus's Sign, Gemini, and we see that it is MERcury. We then check out the Sign placement of her Mercury, and find that it is in CANcer. Cancer is a particularly emotional and sympathetic Sign, which explains this subtle shift from what one would initially expect from Venus in Gemini, where Mercury is said to DISPOSIT Venus. We can then take this even further by looking at the Dispositor of Mercury, which is the Moon, which Jill has in Scorpio, which lays further claim to her Venus being more emotional than its Sign position suggests.* And so on and so on, sometimes coming back to the Planet you started with, or just one Planet called the Final Dispositor which is like the head of a chain of command.

YOUR UNDERLYING ATTITUDE TO RELATIONSHIP

SIGNS APART OF RULING AND SETTING PLANET	HOW YOUR SELF SEES AND THEREFORE BASICALLY RELATES TO OTHER
NONE (SAME SIGN)	As being very much a part of yourself, being united for better or worse, making for quite an intense and convincing bond. But this possibly egocentric view would fail to see where real differences lie, which could lead to confusion arising later as one or both of you feel unrecognized for the individuals that you are.
ONE	Initially as being close, but differences can later appear and by contrast be seen to be compromising. This can be avoided by adopting a respectful distance at the outset, that is not assuming you know who that person is or what they mean to you. There could be a distinct part of them you will not recognize or even like.
TWO	As being manageable as long as reason prevails. When however, things become more emotional and therefore less rational, there could be an inclination towards escapism, infidelity, and a rationalizing of feelings. Yours is a positive attitude as long as this pitfall is avoided, and emotions are worked through on their own terms and within the relationship.
THREE	As being in conflict and very different on some basic level. The challenge here is therefore one of seeing very clearly what Other represents as a part of yourself, and consciously acknowledging it and living it out, otherwise strife-torn, abortive or non-existent relationships will be your lot. Much depends here upon the degree of relating and social skills indicated by the Planet-Sign positions, especially in order to avoid alienation.
FOUR	As being basically compatible, and that harmony should exist. This can give rise to a rather romantic or idealistic overlay that refuses to see where there are real problems within a relationship which in turn could give rise to sizeable disillusionment. Basically though, a very healthy attitude to relationship, giving rise to steadfastness.
FIVE	As there always being something that will make the relationship feel incomplete or compromise it – and that is what appears to happen or be the case. To make things work, a compromise has to be made in the sense of accepting the fact that perfection is something to aspire towards rather than insist upon as being ready-made.
SIX (OPPOSITE SIGNS)	As being at odds, unavailable, unsuitable, unrecognizable, untenable, not even existing. Like THREE, for a relationship to be given a fair chance, or to happen at all, there is a great need to see what it is in Other that is reflecting a part of yourself that you do not want to see or own – and vice versa. In this case though, it should be a bit easier because the 'attraction between opposites' is more apparent. But there is still a see-saw, on-off, alienating effect created by such an attitude.

SIGNS AND THEIR RULERS

SIGN	RULER	SIGN	RULER
ARIes	MARs	LIBra	VENus
TAUrus	VENus	SCOrpio	MARs/PLUto*
GEMini	MERcury	SAGittarius	JUPiter
CANcer	MOOn	CAPricorn	SATurn
LEO	SUN	AQUarius	SATurn/URAnus*
VIRgo	MERcury	PISces	NEPtune/JUPiter*

* Choice of Ruler

PART TWO

The nature of the Chemistry between one person and another

•

The Themes and Dynamics of the Relationship itself

•

Simple *calculation* and some *application*

Chapter Three
THE INTERACTION

We were born to join and dance,
Head over heels, life and limb entwining,
To meet again, by a fleeting chance,
With the Bells of Time all chiming
In our hearts and minds –
Reason drowned by Rhyme.

from *VENUS – Planet of Attraction, Loving and Relating*

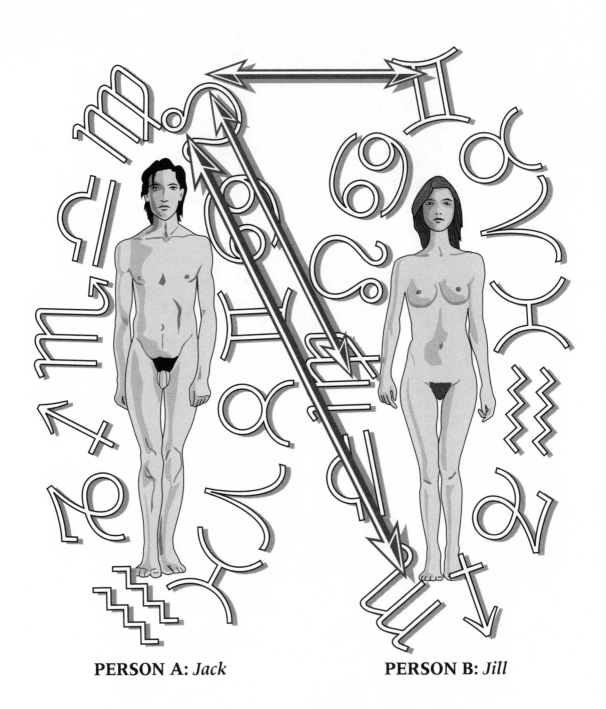

PERSON A: *Jack*   **PERSON B:** *Jill*

Picture 4: **Sign-to-Sign Interaction**

THE INTERACTION

This part of the book enables you to find out how one person interacts with another. I have chosen the word 'Interaction' because it aptly describes the way that astrology views and determines how the Planets and Signs of two Birthcharts respond to one another. In fact, the way in which people actually do respond to one another is often described as the 'chemistry' between them. As is invariably the case, astrological metaphor is paralleled by common metaphor – simply because they both reflect the truth of the matter! Again, you will see that the detail from Picture 1 (page 6) beautifully illustrates this Interaction. To fully appreciate and understand any Interaction between two people, it is strongly suggested that you look at both as Individuals first, using Chapter Two.

And so, to explore this chemistry – how the ingredients or make-up of the One interact with those of the Other – we will go about it here in two ways:

Sign-to-Sign Interaction
and
Planet-to-Planet Interaction

… and if you are of a seriously self-contemplating disposition, there is also a third way of looking at, or rather internally experiencing, Interaction. It is called …

The Mirror

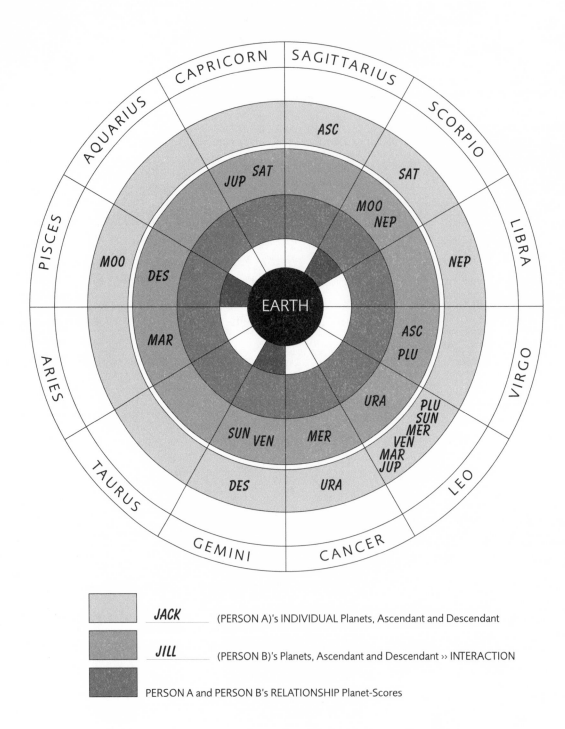

Chartwheel – Example 2

SIGN-TO-SIGN INTERACTION

As explained in Chapter Two, the Planets energize each Sign. So the more Planetary energy there is in any Sign in an individual's Birthchart, then the more influence that Sign will have on that individual's personality. In effect, however, there is usually more than one Sign that is emphasized over the others. So, one way in which we can see how two people interact is firstly by assessing which Sign or Signs are most emphasized in their respective Birthcharts, and then seeing how these individual sets of emphasized Signs interact with one another. *See* Picture 4 for a symbolic illustration of Sign-to-Sign Interaction.

WORKING IT OUT – SIX STEPS TO GREATER UNDERSTANDING

1 First, go to the CHARTWHEEL where you plotted in the various Sign positions of the Planets, ASCendant and DEScendant at the beginning of Chapter Two. These positions should be the ones written in the ring shaded like this   on the CHARTWHEEL, and they refer to Person A, who is possibly yourself. Now look up in the TABLES all the Sign positions of the Planets and ASCendant for Person B, who is the partner, or Other, to Person A. Again, as with Person A, we enter these positions on to the CHARTWHEEL, but this time in the next ring in from Person A's, which is shaded like this   and separated from it with a narrow white ring, for ease of reading. Also, we insert Person B's name to the right of the box shaded in the same way, just below the CHARTWHEEL itself. As with A, remember to enter B's DEScendant opposite their ASCendant. There should be 12 positions in all for each – check. *In our example, Person B is called Jill, born on 6 June 1960 at 1.10pm in England. Jill's Planet, ASCendant and DEScendant Sign positions are shown marked in on the CHARTWHEEL – EXAMPLE 2 opposite, along with Person A's or Jack's.*

2 Having completed this, now fill in the SIGN-TO-SIGN INTERACTION CHART on page 286 (there's also one at the back of the book for you to photocopy*) in the following manner. Looking at the CHARTWHEEL, first focus on the segment for the Sign of ARIes at the far left. If either A or B have any Planets, ASCendants or DEScendants there, enter them in the ARIes row on the CHART, and under the relevant name. Abbreviate the Planets, etc, to their first three letters, as before, as this greatly facilitates the process. Then, just to the right of the Planet's name, also enter the Point Score for that Planet, which you will find at the foot of the CHART along with the Point Scores for all the other Planets, etc. (Ignore the last column, THEME, which is used in Chapter Four.) *In our example, Jack has no Planets in ARIes, but Jill does, and it is MARs, which has a Point Score of 3. So the SIGN-TO-SIGN INTERACTION CHART for our example would so far look like this:*

PERSON A: *Jack*   PERSON B: *Jill*

S I G N	PERSON A's PLANETS (incl. ASC and DES)	+	PERSON B's PLANETS (incl. ASC and DES)	+	THEME Double the lower or equal point scores
ARIes			*MAR 3*		
TAUrus					

*It is best to photocopy this and all other CHARTS, as a separate sheet is easier to fill in and you will have spares for other pairs.

SIGN-TO-SIGN INTERACTION (AND RELATIONSHIP THEME) CHART

PERSON A: PERSON B:

S I G N	PERSON A's PLANETS (incl. ASC and DES)	+	PERSON B's PLANETS (incl. ASC and DES)	+	THEME Double the lower or equal point scores
ARIes					
TAUrus					
GEMini					
CANcer					
LEO					
VIRgo					
LIBra					
SCOrpio					
SAGittarius					
CAPricorn					
AQUarius					
PISces					

POINT SCORES: SUN, MOOn, ASCendant, DEScendant=4 each. MERcury, VENus, MARs=3 each. JUPiter, SATurn=2 each. URAnus, NEPtune, PLUto=1 each.

3 Now, going around the CHARTWHEEL in an anti-clockwise direction, we come to TAUrus. Check to see whether it has any Planets etc there belonging to either Person A or B. If so enter them on the CHART in the Taurus row, under the relevant name, along with their appropriate Point Scores. Then proceed to GEMini and record any Planets, ASCendants or DEScendants found in that Sign for each person. Continue through all the Signs up to PISces, recording all the Planets, etc (along with their Point Scores) that you find in each, for both people.

4 Add up the Point Scores for each Sign, for both people separately, and enter the total in the space provided in the column headed +. *For our example, the completed SIGN-TO-SIGN INTERACTION CHART is shown overleaf.*

5 You are now ready to assess which of UP TO THREE Signs are most emphasized for each person *individually*. Mark or ring the significant point scores for each Sign as you go.
• Look and see if there is any one Sign for Person A that has an obvious highest score – that is, by six or more points than the other Signs in their chart.
• Failing this, look and see if there are just two or three scores that are higher than the rest.
• If there is an even spread of scores over a number of Signs, choose the ones that have the SUN, MOOn, ASCendant or DEScendant placed in them.
• Generally speaking, total scores of three or less are not considered.
Repeat the process for Person B.

6 Now you should have a set of one to three emphasized Signs for Person A, and likewise for Person B. Go to THE SIGN-TO-SIGN PROFILES which begin on page 289, find the page that is headed with one of the Signs emphasized in A's Birthchart, and read below it how that Sign interacts with all the Signs that are emphasized in B's Birthchart. If you wanted to, you could read the whole thing from Person B's perspective.

    In our example, we see that Jack has an outright highest score of 16 points in LEO, whereas Jill has three highest scores of GEMini (seven points), VIRgo and SCOrpio (both five points). Note that Jill has four points in PISces where her DEScendant is, making a close fourth place. In such a case, it could be worthwhile including it as a highest score and incorporate it when reading up the Sign-to-Sign Profiles. For this example, we would find the page headed THE SIGN OF LEO INTERACTS WITH (page 294) and read the rows beginning GEMINI GOOD-NATUREDLY, VIRGO DELICATELY and SCORPIO DANGEROUSLY. If, for the sake of further example, Person A had a second highest score as well, say in Pisces, then you would go to the page headed THE SIGN OF PISCES INTERACTS WITH and read all the rows referring to B's emphasized Signs (Gemini, Virgo and Scorpio).

    If Jill wanted to look at it all from her perspective, she would have to read the pages about Gemini, Virgo and Scorpio and how they interacted with Leo. But in this case, it is simpler just to read the Leo page.

Please note that these are *not* Charts merely for finding out how Sun Signs or Moon Signs get on with one another. Although using them in this way could prove very informative, it could give an incomplete, even inaccurate, picture. They are designed to help in understanding the Interaction between Signs that are emphasized in one person's Birthchart with the Signs that are emphasized in another's, as described above. They are also to help in seeing a Planet-to-Planet Interaction in the context of the Signs in which each Planet is placed (*see* page 308), and for interpreting Relationship Dynamics when you get to Chapter Four – The Relationship.

SIGN-TO-SIGN INTERACTION (AND RELATIONSHIP THEME) CHART
EXAMPLE

PERSON A: *Jack*   PERSON B: *Jill*

SIGN	PERSON A's PLANETS (incl. ASC and DES)	+	PERSON B's PLANETS (incl. ASC and DES)	+	THEME Double the lower or equal point scores
ARIes			MAR 3	3	
TAUrus					
GEMini	DES 4	4	SUN 4 VEN 3	(7)	
CANcer	URA 1	1	MER 3	3	
LEO	SUN 4 MAR 3 MER 3 JUP 2 VEN 3 PLU 1	(16)	URA 1	1	
VIRgo			ASC 4 PLU 1	(5)	
LIBra	NEP 1	1			
SCOrpio	SAT 2	2	MOO 4 NEP 1	(5)	
SAGittarius	ASC 4	4			
CAPricorn			JUP 2 SAT 2	4	
AQUarius					
PISces	MOO 4	4	DES 4	4	

POINT SCORES: SUN, MOOn, ASCendant, DEScendant=4 each. MERcury, VENus, MARs=3 each. JUPiter, SATurn=2 each. URAnus, NEPtune, PLUto=1 each.

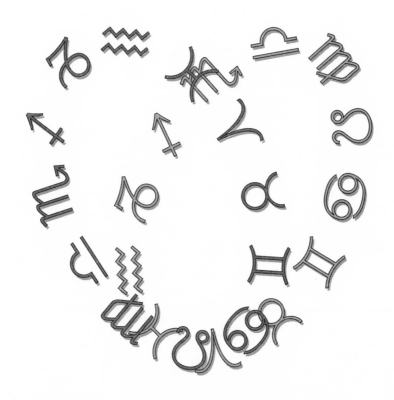

THE SIGN-TO-SIGN
PROFILES

THE SIGN OF **ARIES** INTERACTS WITH

ARIES – *Impulsively*

TWO LEADERS – Everything depends upon your sharing the same goals and principles. At the positive extreme, you will charge through life together in an uncomplicated way, getting where you want to get to as a couple, and as independent beings. If your directions are too dissimilar though, you are probably one of the record-holders for short-lived relationships!

TAURUS – *Compromisingly*

THE LEADER AND THE BANKER – Your criteria are so different. Aries sees life in terms of going ahead no matter what; Taurus in terms of weighing the cost and hanging on to what they've got. Meeting halfway could create a relationship that satisfies both basic needs and the urge to go forward. But a forceful ego and a stubborn one are, as a rule, never about to do so.

GEMINI – *Easily*

THE LEADER AND THE JESTER – This is a youthful pairing with the highs and lows that such speed, enthusiasm and self-interest engender. As far as it goes, this can be stimulating and uncomplicated. You are both agile and freedom-loving enough to avoid a heavily passionate or intense involvement. Outside attractions could change all this, however.

CANCER – *Uncomfortably*

THE LEADER AND THE MATRIARCH – Such classic extremes as Arian independence and Cancerian dependence can only find anything approaching harmony in a very traditional set-up where the Ram is male and wins the bread, and the Crab is female and keeps the home. Failing this, Arian selfishness and Cancerian neediness can only torment one another.

LEO – *Heroically*

THE LEADER AND THE MONARCH – Much can be achieved and with plenty of fun and excitement too. But this can become a problem if the interaction turns into a competition to see who can dominate or win the most. When both of you are directing your prodigious energies towards a common goal, guided by similar principles, all goes well.

VIRGO – *Determinedly*

THE LEADER AND THE ADVISOR – The problem for Virgo is that Aries will not listen and jumps in headfirst, and then, maybe, will listen when it's too late. So Aries should learn to listen, weigh Virgo's advice carefully, and then act – or not. Virgo is learning to be more forceful, be more sure of their own counsel, and ultimately to act upon it themselves.

LIBRA – *Confrontationally*

THE LEADER AND THE DIPLOMAT – You can work as a team as long as Aries is allowed to forge ahead in their straightforward way, while Libra irons out the bumps caused by this. Also, Libra's pleasantness and Aries' forcefulness can temper one another. But without recognizing how different you are, it can be felt as uncouthness and niceness grating horribly.

SCORPIO – *Explosively*

THE LEADER AND THE SPY – This is rather like fire and ice meeting up; a lot of passionate hissing and melting at first, but inevitably your elemental natures compromise one another, causing rage and resentment. Scorpio comes disdainfully to see Aries' straightforwardness as stupid, and Aries cannot abide Scorpio's covert behaviour. Gut-wrenching honesty is needed.

SAGITTARIUS – *Enterprisingly*

THE LEADER AND THE PRIEST – This marries together a strong sense of being after something in life with the justification for getting it. Consequently, you have the wherewithal to go far and achieve a great deal. If this sounds more like an enterprise than a relationship, then you have spotted that a sense of personal intimacy could be amiss – but does this matter?

CAPRICORN – *Conflictingly*

THE LEADER AND THE PRESIDENT – Together you have the makings of success, but it is more likely that one of you feels superior to the other – usually Capricorn over Aries. So ultimately, as neither of you is one to be bested, rebellion or resistance, or locked horns, is a strong likelihood. A common goal, or enemy, might help to unite you.

AQUARIUS – *Progressively*

THE LEADER AND THE REFORMIST – This is a relationship that can really go places, change things, set new standards, etc. You are both independent and freedom-loving, and so respect each other's space and wishes. There is a dark side to such undeniable brightness and lightness, however: the little needy child hiding in one or both of you can get overlooked.

PISCES – *Inappropriately*

THE LEADER AND THE MESSIAH – Aries wants to win, Pisces is prepared to turn the other cheek. Aries takes direct action, Pisces uses passive resistance. It might initially seem that one of you is saving the other – but later it gets confusing as to who is saviour and who is victim. A case of tragically mistaken identities – unless you explode your respective myths.

THE SIGN OF **TAURUS** INTERACTS WITH

ARIES – *Compromisingly*

THE BANKER AND THE LEADER – Your criteria are so different. Aries sees life in terms of going ahead no matter what; Taurus in terms of weighing the cost and hanging on to what they've got. Meeting halfway could create a relationship that satisfies both basic needs and the urge to go forward. But a forceful ego and a stubborn one are, as a rule, never about to do so.

TAURUS – *Solidly*

TWO BANKERS – Hopefully you started off together on the right foot, because if you didn't it is unlikely to get any better. Why? Because two Bulls are twice as unlikely to change as one! But Nature and Her rhythms being what they are, you are likely to attract or encounter someone or something that forces you to change. This way lies true prosperity.

GEMINI – *Awkwardly*

THE BANKER AND THE JESTER – The image here is of the Bull peacefully grazing his field when along comes a bee to buzz around his head. Taurus provides and abides, while Gemini stops things from getting too settled. You both need what the other supplies, but a failure to realize and accept this would attract greater threats to Taurus' stability and Gemini's freedom.

CANCER – *Comfortably*

THE BANKER AND THE MATRIARCH – This is a bit like the farmer and his wife; a natural, traditional and productive arrangement of things. There will also be other timeworn elements as well though – like possessiveness and jealousy, and classic gender roles with their pluses and minuses. But these are as Nature's price for this wholesome combination.

LEO – *Difficultly*

THE BANKER AND THE MONARCH – This is a solid and lasting combination, but it is unlikely to be without its storms. It is essential that you each appreciate what the other is providing. Taurus could be seen as providing the 'stage' or steadiness, and Leo the 'drama' or excitement. Without such an agreement no amount of pleasure or wealth will compensate.

VIRGO – *Agreeably*

THE BANKER AND THE ADVISOR – This is a very harmonious combination. Taurus provides and Virgo maintains – and should Taurus get too bogged down in material things, Virgo coaxes them towards the finer things of life in the delicate manner they appreciate. The Bull's part is kindly to keep Virgo mindful of the wood when the trees get in their way.

LIBRA – *Indulgently*

THE BANKER AND THE DIPLOMAT – Because you both like set procedures and ways of doing things, it would be a wonder if you ever gelled in a natural, emotional sense. Yours is more of an arrangement that has the pleasures of the flesh and society as a substitute for anything more profound. As far as this goes, you can enjoy this sedate and stable arrangement.

SCORPIO – *Powerfully*

THE BANKER AND THE SPY – The Bull wants to keep things stable and as they are; the Scorpion wants to get down to the hidden emotional roots of why they are. The Earth and the Underworld are embedded together, yet they jealously guard their own realms. For this passionate involvement to work each must respect how different yet interdependent they are.

SAGITTARIUS – *Disagreeably*

THE BANKER AND THE PRIEST – At first Sag looks like an exciting prospect to the Bull, but before too long they just don't deliver what Taurus thought they were promised. To Sag, Taurus initially seems to be the anchor they need, but they wind up feeling tethered by them. A healthy exchange could occur, if your different currencies or value systems would allow it.

CAPRICORN – *Prosperously*

THE BANKER AND THE PRESIDENT – You make a stable, industrious and eventually affluent couple, and enjoy together the pleasures of the flesh. Both of you have a style of living that is power-based, with Cap initiating projects and Taurus maintaining funds. As long as neither of you becomes greedy or philistine, you will last and last, happily and securely.

AQUARIUS – *Unsuitably*

THE BANKER AND THE REFORMIST – As Taurus effectively 'invests' in a relationship, they get extra-possessive when Aquarius shows signs of going out on a limb, as is their wont. Earth and Air co-exist rather than unite as seen in the differing priorities of Taurean physical needs and Aquarian mental abstractions. Both being stubborn, you persist – mostly in vain.

PISCES – *Symbiotically*

THE BANKER AND THE MESSIAH – This has all the joy and security of a fertile island set in a mysterious sea. You provide one another with what each needs: the Fish get something solid to contain and feed them; the Bull is kept alive to the wonders of life. Only your egotistic extremes of playing it too safe or of being too evasive could scotch this potentially fine match.

THE SIGN OF **GEMINI** INTERACTS WITH

ARIES – *Easily*

THE JESTER AND THE LEADER – This is a youthful pairing with the highs and lows that such speed, enthusiasm and self-interest engender. As far as it goes, this can be stimulating and uncomplicated. You are both agile and freedom-loving enough to avoid a heavily passionate or intense involvement. Outside attractions could change all this, however.

TAURUS – *Compromisingly*

THE JESTER AND THE BANKER – The image here is of the Bull peacefully grazing his field when along comes a bee to buzz around his head. Taurus provides and abides, while Gemini stops things from getting too settled. You both need what the other supplies, but a failure to realize and accept this would attract greater threats to Taurus' stability and Gemini's freedom.

GEMINI – *Nimbly*

TWO JESTERS – This can be a case of who's fooling who as you both weave in and out of contact. As long as neither of you crave anything more emotionally profound and do not look too deeply into things, life can be a breeze. But should such avoiding of each other's heartland cease to satisfy, then that breeze could stiffen into an icy gale. Two butterflies.

CANCER – *Tentatively*

THE JESTER AND THE MATRIARCH – Like blossom and fruit respectively, one must leave the tree and the other must stay on it until ripe. You are part of the same process but you do not gel at all easily. Gemini being out and about to bring home fresh ideas and people, while Cancer keeps the home, could work. But if the Crab clings, the Twins might not come home at all.

LEO – *Good-naturedly*

THE JESTER AND THE MONARCH – This is a playful interaction. It may appear to be on Leo's terms, but actually Gemini's clever sense of humour, love of variety, and the detachment that goes with it, has the Lion by the tail at times. Overall, quite a subtle interaction for it engenders a tacit understanding based on Leo's power and Gemini's wit.

VIRGO – *Annoyingly*

THE JESTER AND THE ADVISOR – Both of you have a lot to say, but because each of you has different agendas or priorities a lot does not get understood. Virgo thinks practically, Gemini thinks for its own sake. And with all this thinking and talking there can be little room for any real emotional interplay. Still, you can learn a lot from one another, and have fun too.

LIBRA – *Smartly*

THE JESTER AND THE DIPLOMAT – You both have your own, yet compatible, ways of deftly manipulating things into appearing easier than they really are. And so you support one another in this to the extent of actually making things easier than they ought to be! As long as you are both happy to live and love so cerebrally, without profound emotions, all will be fine.

SCORPIO – *Abrasively*

THE JESTER AND THE SPY – Gemini makes light of things, while Scorpio makes heavy of them. A deal could be struck here, but the Twins' lightness is seen by Scorpio as flippancy and emotional insincerity. Gemini regards Scorpio's depth as treacherous and hard work, so they wriggle even more. There can be a peculiar intrigue here, but not a bond to relax with.

SAGITTARIUS – *Curiously*

THE JESTER AND THE PRIEST – This is not such an unlikely combination as it appears. Gemini's streetwise wit can keep Sag from being pious and out-of-touch, while Sag can provide the Twins with an overall view or philosophy that can knit together their scattered thoughts. Failing this though, Sag could look down on Gemini, who then snaps at Sag's heels.

CAPRICORN – *Condescendingly*

THE JESTER AND THE PRESIDENT – On a material level, Cap is infinitely more astute and powerful than the Twins, whom they tolerate to keep them informed and amused. But Gemini may secretly regard Cap as a boring goat whom they'll milk for what they've got and then be off. A mutual recognition of the real people would help, IF you both gave it the time.

AQUARIUS – *Cerebrally*

THE JESTER AND THE REFORMIST – You are both very much on the same wavelength, seeing life as a thing of the mind, spinning endless word plays and abstract concepts into a fabric which you agree on as being reality. The pattern you weave together makes sense and is fun, yet it may not be that fulfilling emotionally. But that is probably all right by both of you.

PISCES – *Adaptively*

THE JESTER AND THE MESSIAH – At some rarefied level you are akin, attuned, as you both are, to the truth that we reach the sublime through a blending of humour and humility. But unless you are spiritually disciplined, such can find you all froth and no substance. Something needs to keep you both down-to-earth – possibly the friends you delight, or a child.

THE SIGN OF **CANCER** INTERACTS WITH

ARIES – *Uncomfortably*

THE MATRIARCH AND THE LEADER – Such classic extremes as Arian independence and Cancerian dependence can only find anything approaching harmony in a very traditional set-up where the Ram is male and wins the bread, and the Crab is female and keeps the home. Failing this, Arian selfishness and Cancerian neediness can only torment one another.

TAURUS – *Comfortably*

THE MATRIARCH AND THE BANKER – This is a bit like the farmer and his wife; a natural, traditional and productive arrangement of things. There will also be other timeworn elements as well though – like possessiveness and jealousy, and classic gender roles with their pluses and minuses. But these are as Nature's price for this wholesome combination.

GEMINI – *Tentatively*

THE MATRIARCH AND THE JESTER – Like fruit and blossom respectively, one must stay on the tree until ripe and the other must leave it. You are part of the same process but you do not gel at all easily. Gemini being out and about to bring home fresh ideas and people, while Cancer keeps the home, could work. But if the Crab clings, the Twins might not come home at all.

CANCER – *Caringly*

TWO MATRIARCHS – Your instinctual need and sense of security, along with a warm and personal manner, ensures that you are Nature's veritable nest-builders and family-raisers. But as ever with same-Sign combinations, you get the best and the worst of them. In your case, beware of coddling you and yours to the point where your individual beings are lost sight of.

LEO – *Dramatically*

THE MATRIARCH AND THE MONARCH – Leo gives a sparkle to Cancer's security-oriented and possibly limited lifestyle; Cancer provides a sense of family and belonging. Unless this exchange is appreciated, Leo will soon feel suffocated by such 'familiarity', and the Crab can come to resent and feel threatened by the Lion's love of excitement.

VIRGO – *Naturally*

THE MATRIARCH AND THE ADVISOR – You are 'Mother Nature's own' in that together you create a comfortable, efficient and caring environment, be that in the home or wherever. The downside to this is that you can live in each other's pockets to the point of suffocation. The occasional outing would offset the 'risk of too much safety' in this excellent combination.

LIBRA – *Warily*

THE MATRIARCH AND THE DIPLOMAT – Cancer needs security and Libra wants peace, which is a good foot to start out on. But whereas security is maintained by containing things, peace is sought by opening things up, being more gregarious – and this is where you can fail to understand one another. For harmony and comfort, respect your individual roles in this.

SCORPIO – *Emotionally*

THE MATRIARCH AND THE SPY – You can work very well together as long as you agree on emotional priorities, and avoid feeling that you should be everything to one another, an impression you initially give and receive. This should be sorted sooner rather than later, for being highly emotional, you could find yourselves with neither room nor mood to negotiate.

SAGITTARIUS – *Inconveniently*

THE MATRIARCH AND THE PRIEST – The home and the open road do not really ever meet, except perhaps in a caravan. Cancer clings to the safe and familiar, whereas Sag aspires to far-flung horizons. To Cancer, Sag is insecurity incarnate. To Sag, Cancer is like an open prison. Unless you can be more open or gypsy-like, your divergent values will separate you.

CAPRICORN – *Complementarily*

THE MATRIARCH AND THE PRESIDENT – Ideally you could make a quite 'complete' combination, with Cap looking after the worldly affairs and Cancer tending to the domestic ones, the ends being family and reputation. What clinches this is accepting that Cancer puts feelings first, and Cap practicalities – and occasionally to take a leaf from each other's book.

AQUARIUS – *Adversely*

THE MATRIARCH AND THE REFORMIST – As a rule, your values and goals are too different to make any kind of match. Cancer wants to maintain the status quo; Aquarius wants to change it. Cancer comes from the gut – Aquarius from the head. The fact that you are interacting at all indicates that you need to learn from one another – otherwise disaster!

PISCES – *Sensitively*

THE MATRIARCH AND THE MESSIAH – This combination is what the world needs more of! Your abilities to tune into and respect each other's feelings, dreams and fears is the mainstay here. What is more, you thrive on all this sympathy and compassion emanating out to family, friends and the world at large. Be sure though, to allow each other to follow their respective dream.

THE SIGN OF **LEO** INTERACTS WITH

ARIES – *Heroically*

THE MONARCH AND THE LEADER – Much can be achieved and with plenty of fun and excitement too. But this can become a problem if the interaction turns into a competition to see who can dominate or win the most. When both of you are directing your prodigious energies towards a common goal, guided by similar principles, all goes well.

TAURUS – *Difficultly*

THE MONARCH AND THE BANKER – This is a solid and lasting combination, but it is unlikely to be without its storms. It is essential that you each appreciate what the other is providing. Taurus could be seen as providing the 'stage' or steadiness, and Leo the 'drama' or excitement. Without such an agreement no amount of pleasure or wealth will compensate.

GEMINI – *Good-Naturedly*

THE MONARCH AND THE JESTER – This is a playful interaction. It may appear to be on Leo's terms, but actually Gemini's clever sense of humour, love of variety, and the detachment that goes with it, has the Lion by the tail at times. Overall, quite a subtle interaction for it engenders a tacit understanding based on Leo's power and Gemini's wit.

CANCER – *Dramatically*

THE MONARCH AND THE MATRIARCH – Leo gives a sparkle to Cancer's security-oriented and possibly limited lifestyle; Cancer provides a sense of family and belonging. Unless this exchange is appreciated, Leo will soon feel suffocated by such 'familiarity', and the Crab can come to resent and feel threatened by the Lion's love of excitement.

LEO – *Respectfully*

TWO MONARCHS – That you interact 'respectfully' is mandatory rather than natural. Without determining your respective areas of rulership, like who rules the home, finances, children, etc, then fierce competition for the spotlight will lead to tears and strife, or simply living in different 'kingdoms'. Get 'who rules what' right and bliss rules!

VIRGO – *Delicately*

THE MONARCH AND THE ADVISOR – This can work when Leo admits their need for one they can trust to keep them informed of what they should be aware of. In return, Leo gives Virgo much-needed confidence, making them the power behind the throne. But if Virgo presumes upon this they could incur royal displeasure – be banished even – but Leo may regret it.

LIBRA – *Graciously*

THE MONARCH AND THE DIPLOMAT – This should be quite a graceful interaction because Libra defers to Leo's will, and Leo values Libra's social skills, especially those that iron out the bumps created by any royal gaffes. Libra loves the sense of being a part of something grand and dignified. But Libra beware of a sense of impotency, and Leo, of frustration.

SCORPIO – *Dangerously*

THE MONARCH AND THE SPY – These powerful Signs can be jealously at odds. To lessen the conflict, what Leo frowns upon as Scorpio's underhandedness can best be seen as a psychological awareness in need of Leo's generosity of spirit, whereas what Scorpio scorns as Leo's highhandedness can best be seen merely as naïveté in need of Scorpionic insight.

SAGITTARIUS – *Magnanimously*

THE MONARCH AND THE PRIEST – You both have your own 'affairs of state' to occupy you, and so your lives together can resemble a pageant with all the fun and colour that this engenders. Both are 'big' Signs, so a grand lifestyle can be enjoyed, but in order to prevent estrangement, care should be taken to observe 'small' things like tact and hidden insecurities.

CAPRICORN – *Pragmatically*

THE MONARCH AND THE PRESIDENT – You both like sticking to certain forms and social conventions, for this is what maintains the rule and order that you love. However, trust and patience will be needed to relate to the sensitive soul in each of you that exists behind that power mask, and to wait for it to emerge. If not, relations can become decidedly frosty.

AQUARIUS – *Reactively*

THE MONARCH AND THE REFORMIST – This is the hardest of opposites to (re)unite, but also the most important. This is because it is the gulf between the privileged and the lowly that creates most of the world's ills. If the Heart of Leo can be noble and generous, and the Mind of Aquarius honest and truthful – then, and only then, will peace truly reign.

PISCES – *Considerately*

THE MONARCH AND THE MESSIAH – Fish turning the other cheek can seem like they are giving the Lion *carte blanche* to rule as they please. After a while though, the Fish are seen to have their own following which insidiously threatens Leo. Leo best see Pisces as an example of the power of humility, and Pisces regard Leo as a role model for how to face the music.

THE SIGN OF **VIRGO** INTERACTS WITH

ARIES – *Determinedly*

THE ADVISOR AND THE LEADER – The problem for Virgo is that Aries will not listen and jumps in headfirst, and then, maybe, will listen when it's too late. So Aries should learn to listen, weigh Virgo's advice carefully, and then act – or not. Virgo is learning to be more forceful, be more sure of their own counsel, and ultimately to act upon it themselves.

TAURUS – *Agreeably*

THE ADVISOR AND THE BANKER – This is a very harmonious combination. Taurus provides and Virgo maintains – and should Taurus get too bogged down in material things, Virgo coaxes them towards the finer things of life in the delicate manner they appreciate. The Bull's part is kindly to keep Virgo mindful of the wood when the trees get in their way.

GEMINI – *Annoyingly*

THE ADVISOR AND THE JESTER – Both of you have a lot to say, but because each of you has different agendas or priorities a lot does not get understood. Virgo thinks practically, Gemini thinks for its own sake. And with all this thinking and talking there can be little room for any real emotional interplay. Still, you can learn a lot from one another, and have fun too.

CANCER – *Naturally*

THE ADVISOR AND THE MATRIARCH – You are 'Mother Nature's own' in that together you create a comfortable, efficient and caring environment, be that in the home or wherever. The downside to this is that you can live in each other's pockets to the point of suffocation. The occasional outing would offset the 'risk of too much safety' in this excellent combination.

LEO – *Delicately*

THE ADVISOR AND THE MONARCH – This can work when Leo admits their need for one they can trust to keep them informed of what they should be aware of. In return, Leo gives Virgo much-needed confidence, making them the power behind the throne. But if Virgo presumes upon this they could incur royal displeasure – be banished even – but Leo may regret it.

VIRGO – *Critically*

TWO ADVISORS – For a Sign that loves sanity, this combination can be preciousness gone mad! Everything is checked and scrutinized, fixed when it doesn't need fixing, to the point that life is all preparation and no living. An eternal dress rehearsal. However, if you can put up with this, such joint efficiency and precision will benefit *someone else* very much indeed.

LIBRA – *Pedantically*

THE ADVISOR AND THE DIPLOMAT – As you both have a definite sense of how things should be done, you can get along very well – at first. Eventually though your lives can become so 'correct' that the more messy and untidy emotions that are the reality of a real relationship are banished to the closet. Regularly clearing *that* out together would help.

SCORPIO – *Exactingly*

THE ADVISOR AND THE SPY – Virgo's prudence can teach Scorpio the wisdom of leaving some stones unturned, whereas Scorpio's emotional insight can stop Virgo from being such a goody-two-shoes. But this interchange will work only if you both consciously agree to this kind of 'deal'. Yet even if you do, such mutual cleansing and purging can exhaust you both.

SAGITTARIUS – *Disappointingly*

THE ADVISOR AND THE PRIEST – What starts out as Virgo's admiration for Sagittarian optimism and largesse, can develop into rank annoyance as their promises come to nothing. To all this, Sag just heaves a sigh and/or teases some more. For it to work, it must be recognized that Virgo's sense of detail and Sag's feel for the whole can complement one another.

CAPRICORN – *Efficiently*

THE ADVISOR AND THE PRESIDENT – This is a classic match – where would one be without the other?! Success depends ultimately on each person knowing their ground – something you both excel in. But as you categorize and compartmentalize, make time and room for some earthy fun and nonsense too – then you'll be in clover in more ways than one.

AQUARIUS – *Idiosyncratically*

THE ADVISOR AND THE REFORMIST – Both of you are highly individualistic, which can be your bane or your boon. Bane – if you think you should be the same *type* of individuals, a contradiction in terms giving rise to constant aggravation. Boon – if you give each other the space and time to find and be yourselves, to be two unique human beings more than a couple.

PISCES – *Humbly*

THE ADVISOR AND THE MESSIAH – The two of you can really help one another to enjoy sensitivity combined with order. The pitfall to avoid is Virgo's concern for detail missing the feel of a thing, and Pisces over-reacting to just that. You share the same concept of how good life should be – just appreciate that you see and approach this from opposing viewpoints.

295

THE SIGN OF **LIBRA** INTERACTS WITH

ARIES – *Confrontationally*

THE DIPLOMAT AND THE LEADER – You can work as a team as long as Aries is allowed to forge ahead in their straightforward way, while Libra irons out the bumps caused by this. Also, Libra's pleasantness and Aries' forcefulness can temper one another. But without recognizing how different you are, it can be felt as uncouthness and niceness grating horribly.

TAURUS – *Indulgently*

THE DIPLOMAT AND THE BANKER – Because you both like set procedures and ways of doing things, it would be a wonder if you ever gelled in a natural, emotional sense. Yours is more of an arrangement that has the pleasures of the flesh and society as a substitute for anything more profound. As far as this goes, you can enjoy this sedate and stable arrangement.

GEMINI – *Smartly*

THE DIPLOMAT AND THE JESTER – You both have your own, but compatible, ways of deftly manipulating things into appearing easier than they really are. And so you support one another in this to the extent of actually making things easier than they ought to be! As long as you are both happy to live and love so cerebrally, without profound emotions, all will be fine.

CANCER – *Warily*

THE DIPLOMAT AND THE MATRIARCH – Cancer needs security and Libra wants peace, which is a good foot to start out on. But whereas security is maintained by containing things, peace is sought by opening things up, being more gregarious – and this is where you can fail to understand one another. For harmony and comfort, respect your individual roles in this.

LEO – *Graciously*

THE DIPLOMAT AND THE MONARCH – This should be quite a graceful interaction because Libra defers to Leo's will, and Leo values Libra's social skills, especially those that iron out the bumps created by any royal gaffes. Libra loves the sense of being a part of something grand and dignified. But Libra beware of a sense of impotency, and Leo, of frustration.

VIRGO – *Pedantically*

THE DIPLOMAT AND THE ADVISOR – As you both have a definite sense of how things should be done, you can get along very well – at first. Eventually though your lives can become so 'correct' that the more messy and untidy emotions that are the reality of a real relationship are banished to the closet. Regularly clearing *that* out together would help.

LIBRA – *Deferentially*

TWO DIPLOMATS – You are confronted with having to know how to respond, relate in awkward situations, and socially conduct yourselves in general. If you are good at this, you are either particularly gracious and naturally well-mannered, or you are being superficial at the expense of emotional sincerity. Or somewhere between the two. The decision is yours!

SCORPIO – *Demandingly*

THE DIPLOMAT AND THE SPY – You are more than likely working at cross-purposes, with Libra wanting a fair and respectable match, but Scorpio desiring something of a deeper and darker hue. Libra's pleasant overtures are seen as superficial and trashed by Scorpio, who is then treated with kid gloves, making them even more spiky. Be genuine – but just, too.

SAGITTARIUS – *Reasonably*

THE DIPLOMAT AND THE PRIEST – You are both adept at observing the ways of the society that you live in, and so you successfully conduct your relationship in accordance with its written and unwritten laws. Sometimes this means you are both coming from your heads rather than your hearts, which can diminish passion – but that's the price you pay for order.

CAPRICORN – *Formally*

THE DIPLOMAT AND THE PRESIDENT – This is a very 'correct' pairing that does not allow much room for the highly passionate or free-and-easy. Because of this conventional style you are able to build and fashion a respectable life together. But if there are any signs of dissatisfaction on either side, then it's time to be more emotionally aware and outspoken.

AQUARIUS – *Thoughtfully*

THE DIPLOMAT AND THE REFORMIST – If this could get off the ground then great things could be achieved and even some new social ground broken. You could be an example to others of how two people can harmonize as a pair yet still be individuals in their own right. But first you'd have to come out of your heads and into your bodies – from theory to reality.

PISCES – *Kindly*

THE DIPLOMAT AND THE MESSIAH – Libran indecisiveness and Piscean evasiveness can give the illusion of compatibility as you appear to fit in with each other, not wanting to face the dark or difficult bits. But if you do decide to really get down to the business of honest relating, you do so with fairness and sensitivity – otherwise it can interminably insubstantial.

THE SIGN OF **SCORPIO** INTERACTS WITH

ARIES – *Explosively*

THE SPY AND THE LEADER – This is rather like fire and ice meeting up; a lot of passionate hissing and melting at first, but inevitably your elemental natures compromise one another, causing rage and resentment. Scorpio comes disdainfully to see Aries' straightforwardness as stupid, and Aries cannot abide Scorpio's covert behaviour. Gut-wrenching honesty is needed.

TAURUS – *Powerfully*

THE SPY AND THE BANKER – The Bull wants to keep things stable and as they are; the Scorpion wants to get down to the hidden emotional depths of why they are. The Earth and the Underworld are embedded together, yet they jealously guard their own realms. For this passionate involvement to work each must respect how different yet interdependent they are.

GEMINI – *Abrasively*

THE SPY AND THE JESTER – Scorpio makes heavy of things, while Gemini makes light of them. A deal could be struck here, but the Twins' lightness is seen by Scorpio as flippancy and emotional insincerity. Gemini regards Scorpio's depth as treacherous and hard work, so they wriggle even more. There can be a peculiar intrigue here, but not a bond to relax with.

CANCER – *Emotionally*

THE SPY AND THE MATRIARCH – You can work very well together as long as you agree on emotional priorities, and avoid feeling that you should be everything to one another, an impression you initially give and receive. This should be sorted sooner rather than later, for being highly emotional, you could find yourselves with neither room nor mood to negotiate.

LEO – *Dangerously*

THE SPY AND THE MONARCH – These powerful Signs can be jealously at odds. To lessen the conflict, what Leo frowns upon as Scorpio's underhandedness can best be seen as a psychological awareness in need of Leo's generosity of spirit, whereas what Scorpio scorns as Leo's highhandedness can best be seen merely as naïveté in need of Scorpionic insight.

VIRGO – *Exactingly*

THE SPY AND THE ADVISOR – Virgo's prudence can teach Scorpio the wisdom of leaving some stones unturned, whereas Scorpio's emotional insight can stop Virgo from being such a goody-two-shoes. But this interchange will work only if you both consciously agree to this kind of 'deal'. Yet even if you do, such mutual cleansing and purging can exhaust you both.

LIBRA – *Demandingly*

THE SPY AND THE DIPLOMAT – You are more than likely working at cross-purposes, with Libra wanting a fair and respectable match, but Scorpio desiring something of a deeper and darker hue. Libra's pleasant overtures are seen as superficial and trashed by Scorpio, who is then treated with kid gloves, making them even more spiky. Be genuine – but just, too.

SCORPIO – *Intensely*

TWO SPIES – You understand each other because you both inhabit the same world of deep feelings and dark secrets. If you can steer your way around the spectre of betrayal that tries to threaten your essential trust, then you will have a lasting and unmistakable bond. It would be wise to check out/respect the chinks in each other's armour before they become liabilities.

SAGITTARIUS – *Suspiciously*

THE SPY AND THE PRIEST – You both love power, but whereas Sag expresses it openly, Scorpio uses it covertly. Your definitions of truth are very different. This makes it hard to read one another, so embarrassments and subterfuges are the awkward result. The reason you are together is for Sag to learn some tact, and Scorpio some candour. If not, 'paranoia'.

CAPRICORN – *Beneficially*

THE SPY AND THE PRESIDENT – You can be very useful to one another. This does not sound very romantic, but then it wouldn't, for you are a businesslike, no-nonsense pair. Yet it falls to Scorpio to remind Cap that they are an emotional being after all, while Cap teaches Scorp that they misuse their emotional wiles at their peril. A powerful pairing, for good or ill.

AQUARIUS – *Frustratingly*

THE SPY AND THE REFORMIST – Your agendas are so very different that you are liable to confound one another. Scorpio wants intrigue and emotional satisfaction; Aquarius is more intent upon exposing the 'truth' and things adding up mentally. Unless you can both recognize the validity of each other's requirements, you will both become exasperated.

PISCES – *Intuitively*

THE SPY AND THE MESSIAH – You have a strong bond but a strange one. There are deep and mysterious elements to your relationship that only reveal themselves in the fullness of time – and then maybe not at all. Being both intuitive and emotional, you are attuned to this submerged agenda and remain true to it and each other – barring the occasional reef, that is.

THE SIGN OF **SAGITTARIUS** INTERACTS WITH

ARIES – *Enterprisingly*

THE PRIEST AND THE LEADER – This marries together a strong sense of being after something in life with the justification for getting it. Consequently, you have the wherewithal to go far and achieve a great deal. If this sounds more like an enterprise than a relationship, then you have spotted that a sense of personal intimacy could be amiss – but does this matter?

TAURUS – *Disagreeably*

THE PRIEST AND THE BANKER – At first Sag looks like an exciting prospect to the Bull, but before too long they just don't deliver what Taurus thought they were promised. To Sag, Taurus initially seems to be the anchor they need, but they wind up feeling tethered by them. A healthy exchange could occur, if your different currencies or value systems would allow it.

GEMINI – *Curiously*

THE PRIEST AND THE JESTER – This is not such an unlikely combination as it appears. Gemini's streetwise wit can keep Sag from being pious and out-of-touch, while Sag can provide the Twins with a overall view or philosophy that can knit together their scattered thoughts. Failing this though, Sag could look down on Gemini, who then snaps at Sag's heels.

CANCER – *Inconveniently*

THE PRIEST AND THE MATRIARCH – The home and the open road do not really ever meet, except perhaps in a caravan. Cancer clings to the safe and familiar, whereas Sag aspires to far-flung horizons. To Cancer, Sag is insecurity incarnate. To Sag, Cancer is like an open prison. Unless you can be more open or gypsy-like, your divergent values will separate you.

LEO – *Magnanimously*

THE PRIEST AND THE MONARCH – You both have your own 'affairs of state' to occupy you, and so your lives together can resemble a pageant with all the fun and colour that this engenders. Both are 'big' Signs, so a grand lifestyle can be enjoyed, but in order to prevent estrangement, care should be taken to observe 'small' things like tact and hidden insecurities.

VIRGO – *Disappointingly*

THE PRIEST AND THE ADVISOR – What starts out as Virgo's admiration for Sagittarian optimism and largesse can develop into rank annoyance as their promises come to nothing. To all this, Sag just heaves a sigh and/or teases some more. For it to work, it must be recognized that Virgo's sense of detail and Sag's feel for the whole can complement one another.

LIBRA – *Reasonably*

THE PRIEST AND THE DIPLOMAT – You are both adept at observing the ways of the society that you live in, and so you successfully conduct your relationship in accordance with its written and unwritten laws. Sometimes this means you are both coming from your heads rather than your hearts, which can diminish passion – but that's the price you pay for order.

SCORPIO – *Suspiciously*

THE PRIEST AND THE SPY – You both love power, but whereas Sag expresses it openly, Scorpio uses it covertly. Your definitions of truth are very different. This makes it hard to read one another, so embarrassments and subterfuges are the awkward result. The reason you are together is for Sag to learn some tact, and Scorpio some candour. If not, 'paranoia'.

SAGITTARIUS – *Idealistically*

TWO PRIESTS – As long as you believe in something and each other, and respect each other's beliefs if they are different, then you can be a model relationship in that you are an example of two people progressing onwards and upwards together. This is like two hitched horses that keep looking ahead at their own paths, avoiding jealous or hypocritical sideward glances.

CAPRICORN – *Competitively*

THE PRIEST AND THE PRESIDENT – You think you grate upon one another because Cap sees Sag as over-optimistic and Sag regards Cap as a wet blanket. The real reason why you can fall out so easily though is because you both want to run the show. With Sag's vision and Cap's practicality you could team up and clean up. But nothing less than greed bars the way.

AQUARIUS – *Liberally*

THE PRIEST AND THE REFORMIST – As you both like the freedom to explore life and yourselves, this works well as you are likely to allow the same to each other – hopefully avoiding bigotry. In the process though, your freedom to do your own thing can cause you to float apart and have only a pretend relationship. Until then, you can certainly hit some high spots.

PISCES – *Deceptively*

THE PRIEST AND THE MESSIAH – You are both into vision and belief as the mainstays of existence, and because of this, your faith, far-flung ideas and easy-goingness can take you, quite ecstatically, some way together. But unless something forces a truly honest showdown, then a mixture of vagueness, indulgence and impracticality can find you undoing one another.

THE SIGN OF **CAPRICORN** INTERACTS WITH

ARIES – *Conflictingly*

THE PRESIDENT AND THE LEADER – Together you have the makings of success, but it is more likely that one of you feels superior to the other – usually Capricorn over Aries. So ultimately, as neither of you is one to be bested, rebellion or resistance, or locked horns, are a strong likelihood. A common goal, or enemy, might help to unite you.

TAURUS – *Prosperously*

THE PRESIDENT AND THE BANKER – You make a stable, industrious and eventually affluent couple, and enjoy together the pleasures of the flesh. Both of you have a style of living that is power-based, with Cap initiating projects and Taurus maintaining funds. As long as neither of you becomes greedy or philistine, you will last and last, happily and securely.

GEMINI – *Condescendingly*

THE PRESIDENT AND THE JESTER – On a material level, Cap is infinitely more astute and powerful than the Twins, whom they tolerate to keep them informed and amused. But Gemini may secretly regard Cap as a boring goat whom they'll milk for what they've got and then be off. A mutual recognition of the real people would help, IF you both gave it the time.

CANCER – *Complementarily*

THE PRESIDENT AND THE MATRIARCH – Ideally you could make a quite 'complete' combination, with Cap looking after the worldly affairs and Cancer tending to the domestic ones, the ends being family and reputation. What clinches this is accepting that Cancer puts feelings first, and Cap practicalities – and occasionally to take a leaf from each other's book.

LEO – *Pragmatically*

THE PRESIDENT AND THE MONARCH – You both like sticking to certain forms and social conventions, for this is what maintains the rule and order that you love. However, trust and patience will be needed to relate to the sensitive soul in each of you that exists behind that power mask, and to wait for it to emerge. If not, relations can become decidedly frosty.

VIRGO – *Efficiently*

THE PRESIDENT AND THE ADVISOR – This is a classic match – where would one be without the other? Success depends ultimately on each person knowing their ground – something you both excel in. But as you categorize and compartmentalize, make time and room for some earthy fun and nonsense too – then you'll be in clover in more ways than one.

LIBRA – *Formally*

THE PRESIDENT AND THE DIPLOMAT – This is a very 'correct' pairing that does not allow much room for the highly passionate or free-and-easy. Because of this conventional style you are able to build and fashion a respectable life together. But if there are any signs of dissatisfaction on either side, then it's time to be more emotionally aware and outspoken.

SCORPIO – *Beneficially*

THE PRESIDENT AND THE SPY – You can be very useful to one another. This does not sound very romantic, but then it wouldn't, for you are a businesslike, no-nonsense pair. Yet it falls to Scorpio to remind Cap that they are an emotional being after all, while Cap teaches Scorp that they misuse their emotional wiles at their peril. A powerful pairing, for good or ill.

SAGITTARIUS – *Competitively*

THE PRESIDENT AND THE PRIEST – You think you grate upon one another because Cap sees Sag as over-optimistic and Sag regards Cap as a wet blanket. The real reason why you can fall out so easily though is because you both want to run the show. With Sag's vision and Cap's practicality you could team up and clean up. But nothing less than greed bars the way.

CAPRICORN – *Undemonstratively*

TWO PRESIDENTS – Some would say that this is more of a corporate merger than a relationship, and it is true that your quality of life together may get measured by joint status, or merely by how often you can fit one another into each of your schedules. It may take some kind of crunch, but when you discover the heart and soul of one another – success!

AQUARIUS – *Politically*

THE PRESIDENT AND THE REFORMIST – On the face of it, this is not a good mix – Cap's plans and pitch can be queered by Aquarian liberality, which in turn feels cramped by the Goat's conservatism. But the very fact that you are interacting at all points to the likelihood of Cap needing to update and loosen up, and of Aquarius having to get real and organized.

PISCES – *Auspiciously*

THE PRESIDENT AND THE MESSIAH – When Cap appreciates how much they need and profit from Piscean imagination and emotional sensitivity, and Pisces accepts the value of Cap's worldly hard-headedness, then this can be like Heaven and Earth happily meeting one another. So brook neither Piscean vagueness and evasiveness, nor Capricornian purblindness.

THE SIGN OF **AQUARIUS** INTERACTS WITH

ARIES – *Progressively*

THE REFORMIST AND THE LEADER – This is a relationship that can really go places, change things, set new standards, etc. You are both independent and freedom-loving, and so respect each other's space and wishes. There is a dark side to such undeniable brightness and lightness, however: the little needy child hiding in one or both of you can get overlooked.

TAURUS – *Unsuitably*

THE REFORMIST AND THE BANKER – As Taurus effectively 'invests' in a relationship, they get extra-possessive when Aquarius shows signs of going out on a limb, as is their wont. Earth and Air co-exist rather than unite as seen in the differing priorities of Taurean physical needs and Aquarian mental abstractions. Both being stubborn, you persist – mostly in vain.

GEMINI – *Cerebrally*

THE REFORMIST AND THE JESTER – You are both very much on the same wavelength, seeing life as a thing of the mind, spinning endless word plays and abstract concepts into a fabric which you agree on as being reality. The pattern you weave together makes sense and is fun, yet it may not be that fulfilling emotionally. But that is probably all right by both of you.

CANCER – *Adversely*

THE REFORMIST AND THE MATRIARCH – As a rule, your values and goals are too different to make any kind of match. Cancer wants to maintain the status quo; Aquarius wants to change it. Cancer comes from the gut – Aquarius from the head. The fact that you are interacting at all indicates that you need to learn from one another – otherwise disaster!

LEO – *Reactively*

THE REFORMIST AND THE MONARCH – This is the hardest of opposites to (re)unite, but also the most important. This is because it is the gulf between the lowly and the privileged that creates most of the world's ills. If the Heart of Leo can be noble and generous, and the Mind of Aquarius honest and truthful – then, and only then, will peace truly reign.

VIRGO – *Idiosyncratically*

THE REFORMIST AND THE ADVISOR – Both of you are highly individualistic, which can be your bane or your boon. Bane – if you think you should be the same type of individual, a contradiction in terms, giving rise to constant aggravation. Boon – if you give each other the space and time to find and be yourselves, to be two unique human beings more than a couple.

LIBRA – *Thoughtfully*

THE REFORMIST AND THE DIPLOMAT – If this could get off the ground then great things could be achieved and even some new social ground broken. You could be an example to others of how two people can harmonize as a pair yet still be individuals in their own right. But first you'd have to come out of your heads and into your bodies – from theory to reality.

SCORPIO – *Frustratingly*

THE REFORMIST AND THE SPY – Your agendas are so very different that you are liable to confound one another. Scorpio wants intrigue and emotional satisfaction; Aquarius is more intent upon exposing the 'truth' and things adding up mentally. Unless you can both recognize the validity of each other's requirements, you will both become exasperated.

SAGITTARIUS – *Liberally*

THE REFORMIST AND THE PRIEST – As you both like the freedom to explore life and yourselves, this works well as you are likely to allow the same to each other – hopefully avoiding bigotry. In the process though, your freedom to do your own thing can cause you to float apart and have only a pretend relationship. Until then, you can certainly hit some high spots.

CAPRICORN – *Politically*

THE REFORMIST AND THE PRESIDENT – On the face of it, this is not a good mix – Cap's plans and pitch can be queered by Aquarian liberality, which in turn feels cramped by the Goat's conservatism. But the very fact that you are interacting at all points to the likelihood of Cap needing to update and loosen up, and of Aquarius having to get real and organized.

AQUARIUS – *Coolly*

TWO REFORMISTS – You can work so well together because you are both living in your minds where awkward things like bodies and feelings do not intrude too much. The stuff of life is discussed and reviewed, with only an occasional dip into the physical or emotional. But this doesn't 'hold water' when there simply is no longer anything there to keep you together.

PISCES – *Hopefully*

THE REFORMIST AND THE MESSIAH – You can start out with similar idealistic intentions, but the very vagueness and airiness of such notions catches up with you later and you are no longer sure who or what you are to one another. Maybe one or both of you thought the other would change. Maybe you did in your own way. But it's never too late … Maybe.

THE SIGN OF **PISCES** INTERACTS WITH

ARIES – *Inappropriately*

THE MESSIAH AND THE LEADER – Aries wants to win, Pisces is prepared to turn the other cheek. Aries takes direct action, Pisces uses passive resistance. It might initially seem that one of you is saving the other – but later it gets confusing as to who is saviour and who is victim. A case of tragically mistaken identities – unless you explode your respective myths.

TAURUS – *Symbiotically*

THE MESSIAH AND THE BANKER – This has all the joy and security of a fertile island set in a mysterious sea. You provide one other with what each needs: the Fish get something solid to contain and feed them; the Bull is kept alive to the wonders of life. Only your egotistic extremes of playing it too safe or of being too evasive could scotch this potentially fine match.

GEMINI – *Adaptively*

THE MESSIAH AND THE JESTER – At some rarefied level you are akin, attuned, as you both are, to the truth that we reach the sublime through a blending of humour and humility. But unless you are spiritually disciplined, such can find you all froth and no substance. Something needs to keep you both down-to-earth – possibly the friends you delight, or a child.

CANCER – *Sensitively*

THE MESSIAH AND THE MATRIARCH – This combination is what the world needs more of! Your abilities to tune into and respect each other's feelings, dreams and fears is the mainstay here. What is more, you thrive on all this sympathy and compassion emanating out to family, friends and the world at large. Be sure though, to allow each other to follow your respective dreams.

LEO – *Considerately*

THE MESSIAH AND THE MONARCH – Fish turning the other cheek can seem like they are giving the Lion *carte blanche* to rule as they please. After a while though, the Fish are seen to have their own following which insidiously threatens Leo. Leo best see Pisces as an example of the power of humility, and Pisces regard Leo as a role model for how to face the music.

VIRGO – *Humbly*

THE MESSIAH AND THE ADVISOR – The two of you can really help one another to enjoy sensitivity combined with order. The pitfall to avoid is Virgo's concern for detail missing the feel of a thing, and Pisces over-reacting to just that. You share the same concept of how good life should be – just appreciate that you see and approach this from opposing viewpoints.

LIBRA – *Kindly*

THE MESSIAH AND THE DIPLOMAT – Libran indecisiveness and Piscean evasiveness can give the illusion of compatibility as you appear to fit in with each other, not wanting to face the dark or difficult bits. But if you do decide to really get down to the business of honest relating, you do so with fairness and sensitivity – otherwise it can interminably insubstantial.

SCORPIO – *Intuitively*

THE MESSIAH AND THE SPY – You have a strong bond but a strange one. There are deep and mysterious elements to your relationship that only reveal themselves in the fullness of time – and then maybe not at all. Being both intuitive and emotional, you are attuned to this submerged agenda and remain true to it and each other – barring the occasional reef, that is.

SAGITTARIUS – *Deceptively*

THE MESSIAH AND THE PRIEST – You are both into vision and belief as the mainstays of existence, and because of this, your faith, far-flung ideas and easy-goingness can take you, quite ecstatically, some way together. But unless something forces a truly honest showdown, then a mixture of vagueness, indulgence and impracticality can find you undoing one another.

CAPRICORN – *Auspiciously*

THE MESSIAH AND THE PRESIDENT – When Cap appreciates how much they need and profit from Piscean imagination and emotional sensitivity, and Pisces accepts the value of Cap's worldly hard-headedness, then this can be like Heaven and Earth happily meeting one another. So brook neither Piscean vagueness and evasiveness, nor Capricornian purblindness.

AQUARIUS – *Hopefully*

THE MESSIAH AND THE REFORMIST – You can start out with similar idealistic intentions, but the very vagueness and airiness of such notions catches up with you later and you are no longer sure who or what you are to one another. Maybe one or both of you thought the other would change. Maybe you did in your own way. But it's never too late … Maybe.

PISCES – *Dreamily*

TWO MESSIAHS – This is more like two martyrs, unfortunately. And the 'cause' to which you sacrifice your lives can be alcohol, drugs, your 'dream', or to another who is even more of a victim than you both feel yourselves to be. Then again, you might just make it if you quit the self-pity or addictiveness, and truly got down to realizing that vision you first beheld.

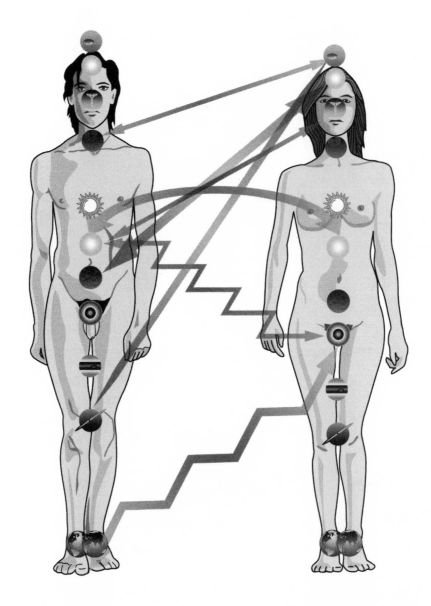

PERSON A: *Jack*   **PERSON B:** *Jill*

Picture 5: **Planet-to-Planet Interaction**

PLANET-TO-PLANET INTERACTION

We now take an important step closer to the heart of understanding the Interaction between two people. In a relationship of any kind, the Planets in one person's Birthchart are interacting with the Planets in the other person's Birthchart. In astrology, the study of this is called Synastry, and it could be said to describe the most potent chemistry between one person and another. The Planets, as symbols of various parts of the one individual, affect and are affected by those of the other individual. Picture 5 symbolically illustrates this Planet-to-Planet Interaction.

There are FOUR BASIC TYPES of Interaction that can occur between one Planet and another. The astrological term for these types of Interaction is ASPECT when between Planets in an individual's chart, or CROSS-ASPECT when used to describe the Interaction between a Planet in one person's chart and a Planet in another person's chart – but often the mere term 'Aspect' is used for both. Aspects are determined by one Planet being an approximate number of degrees apart from another Planet on the CHARTWHEEL, but you need not concern yourself with this technicality.

CROSS-ASPECT TYPE	MEANING IN A RELATIONSHIP	° apart
CONjoining	Intensifying • Uniting • Binding • Energizing	0°
CHAllenging	Conflicting • Strength-demanding or -producing	90°
SUPporting	Harmonizing • Co-operative • Prospering	120°
OPPosing	Contrasting • Awareness-producing or -demanding	180°

WORKING IT OUT – JUST ONE STEP TO EVEN GREATER UNDERSTANDING

This involves quite exact and complex calculations, so I have not included them in the scope of this book, because you would not be able to 'do it yourself' unless you were a trained astrologer. I recommend that you order your CROSS-ASPECTS from me, or some other agency. In either case, this will, or should, be of little cost.

There are at least three good reasons for obtaining your CROSS-ASPECTS:

1 Your Cross-Aspects delineate the PLANET-TO-PLANET INTERACTIONS which accurately describe the chemistry between any two people, and therefore provide you with very valuable, helpful and reliable information.

2 Your Cross-Aspects also determine which PLANET-TO-PLANET INTERACTIONS are the most powerful and significant. These most exact and precise Interactions are called CLOSE ONES, and they form the core of a relationship.

3 Your PLANET-TO-PLANET INTERACTIONS will enable you to work out your FINAL FOCUS in the next section. This explains what your relationship is essentially all about, for each person individually and as a couple.

In the meantime, whether or not you are going to obtain your Cross-Aspects, you can, if you wish, go straight to Chapter Four – The Relationship, not forgetting to look in The Mirror on page 485 on the way!

When you receive your CROSS-ASPECTS from me, you will then be able simply to read up what these Interactions mean by consulting the PLANET-TO-PLANET PROFILES which begin on page 306. Also, for each Interaction, I will tell you what page to go straight to in this book rather that having to look each one up. To order your CROSS-ASPECTS from me, simply fill in the Order Form on page 526 at the back of the book.

You may also obtain these Cross-Aspects between Person A's and Person B's Birthcharts through contacting one of the astrological organizations given at the back of this book. They will be able to put you in touch with a suitable astrologer or astrological service. You may, of course, know of one already.

However, the Cross-Aspects they give will not be laid out in exactly the same way as those which I provide, as mine are laid out with the context of this book in mind. To get an approximation of it though, simply ask for the Cross-Aspects between Person A and Person B (as per birth details, and from both A's and B's perspectives), and stating, if possible, those Cross-Aspects which are within an orb of three degrees. Those Cross-Aspects which are within three degrees will be the same as the CLOSE ONES (*see* opposite).

The actual terms used to describe the Aspects will differ from the terms used above. Where we have used the term CONjoining they could use the term 'Conjunct' or 'in Conjunction with'; CHAllenging they would use the term 'Square' or 'Squaring'; SUPporting they would use the term 'Trine' or 'Trining'; OPPosing they could use the term 'in Opposition to'.

In addition, the astrologer or astrological service might supply you with certain other Cross-Aspects, which are most likely to be the 'Sextile' which is like a milder form of the Trine, and the Quincunx which is somewhere between the Square and the Opposition, which you may adapt for interpretation. They may also include Aspects to each person's Midheaven or MC, which is an astrological point not covered in this book.

WHEN YOU OBTAIN YOUR CROSS-ASPECTS FROM ME

They will be set out as on the page opposite, *as per our example of Jack (Person A) and Jill (Person B)*. As soon as you receive your own CROSS-ASPECTS, you can read all of these Interactions in the PLANET-TO-PLANET PROFILES in the light of the knowledge that they are the most significant and accurate indications for the relationship between the two people in question. Also included in your CROSS-ASPECTS will be the Interactions from B's perspective (*like the example of Jill on page 480*), as well as the exact Planet-Sign and Ascendant positions for each person.

When you receive your CROSS-ASPECTS, go to the interpretations of what they actually mean in the PLANET-TO-PLANET PROFILES. First though, go to the PLANET-TO-PLANET PROFILES – HOW TO USE THEM on the following page. The PROFILES themselves begin on page 317 with SUN Interactions and run right through to ASCendant Interactions in the same order used previously.

If you have not yet got your Cross-Aspects, you may like to look through the Planet-to-Planet Profiles to get some idea of the kind of information you have or could have in store for you.

CROSS-ASPECTS

From the perspective of Jack (Person A) to Jill (Person B)

INTERACTION	QUALITY OF ASPECT*	PAGE
A's SUN SUPporting B's MARs	*EASY*	*327*
A's SUN CONjoining B's URAnus	*HARD AND EASY*	*332*
A's SUN CHAllenging B's NEPtune	*HARD – Teardrop*	*336*
A's MOOn SUPporting B's MOOn	*EASY – Heart*	*345*
A's MOOn SUPporting B's MERcury	*EASY*	*347*
A's MOOn CHAllenging B's VENus	*HARD*	*348*
A's MOOn SUPporting B's NEPtune	*EASY – Heart*	*359*
A's MOOn OPPosing B's PLUto	*HARD – Teardrop, Key*	*362*
A's MERcury SUPporting B's MARs	*EASY*	*371*
A's MERcury CONjoining B's URAnus	*HARD AND EASY*	*376*
A's MERcury CHAllenging B's NEPtune	*HARD*	*378*
A's VENus CHAllenging B's MOOn	*HARD*	*348*
A's VENus CHAllenging B's NEPtune	*HARD – Cupid, Teardrop*	*397*
A's MARs SUPporting B's MARs	*EASY*	*405*
A's MARs CONjoining B's URAnus	*HARD AND EASY – Cupid*	*412*
A's JUPiter CHAllenging B's MOOn	*HARD*	*352*
A's JUPiter CONjoining B's URAnus	*EASY*	*424*
A's JUPiter CHAllenging B's NEPtune	*HARD*	*426*
A's SATurn CHAllenging B's URAnus	*HARD*	*436*
A's SATurn CONjoining B's NEPtune	*HARD AND EASY*	*438*
A's URAnus CHAllenging B's MOOn	*HARD – Teardrop*	*356*
A's URAnus CHAllenging B's NEPtune	*HARD*	*448*
A's NEPtune CONjoining B's MOOn	*HARD AND EASY – Cupid, Heart, Teardrop, Key*	*358*
A's NEPtune OPPosing B's MARs	*HARD – Cupid*	*413*
A's PLUto SUPporting B's MARs	*EASY*	*415*
A's PLUto SUPporting B's JUPiter	*EASY*	*429*
A's PLUto CONjoining B's PLUto	*HARD AND EASY*	*464*
A's ASCendant CHAllenging B's PLUto	*HARD – Cupid*	*466*

*
EASY = usually SUPporting (*see* page 303 for meaning).
HARD = usually CHAllenging (*see* page 303 for meaning).
HARD AND EASY = usually CONjoining or OPPosing (*see* page 303 for meaning).
Cupid = precipitating, mutually attracting, falling in love/lust, necessary for relationship to happen.
Heart = positive and lasting, marriage/partnership material.
Teardrop = involving suffering, acutely/profoundly emotional.
Key (Contact) = highly significant interactions.

Of the above, the following are **CLOSE ONES:**

INTERACTION	QUALITY OF ASPECT*	PAGE
A's MOOn SUPporting B's MOOn	EASY – Heart	345
A's MOOn SUPporting B's MERcury	EASY	347
A's MOOn SUPporting B's NEPtune	EASY – Heart	359
A's MOOn OPPosing B's PLUto	HARD – Teardrop, Key	362
A's VENus CHAllenging B's MOOn	HARD	348
A's VENus CHAllenging B's NEPtune	HARD – Cupid, Teardrop	397
A's MARs CONjoining B's URAnus	HARD AND EASY – Cupid	410
A's ASCendant CHAllenging B's PLUto	HARD – Cupid	466

HOW TO USE
THE PLANET-TO-PLANET PROFILES

1 If you have obtained your CROSS-ASPECTS from me, you will now have a list of all the Cross-Aspects or Planet-to-Planet Interactions between Person A and Person B, along with the page numbers in this book where you will find the interpretation or PROFILE of each one. Take the first one on either list and simply go to the page indicated in the PLANET-TO-PLANET PROFILES.

If you have acquired your Cross-Aspects from someone other than me, then you will have to look up where an Interaction is by using the PLANET-TO-PLANET PROFILES INDEX which starts on page 309. If it is A's SUN then go to the section in the Index headed *A's SUN*. There then follow four separate lists for each of the four possible Interactions or Aspects that A's SUN could be making to B's Planets. Select the list that refers to the Aspect in question, find B's Planet, and immediately to the right (→) you will see the title of the Profile for that Interaction, followed by the relevant page number. *With our example, Person A's (Jack's) first Planet-to-Planet Interaction is his SUN SUPporting Person B's (Jill's) MARs. Looking this up in the way described above we see that it is on page 327 and that the Profile for this is called SUN SUPPORTING MARS.* NOTE: Sometimes you will find that the actual name of the Profile that the Index or my Cross-Aspects give is the reverse way around. *From our example, if you look up, say, Jack/A's Ascendant Challenging Jill/B's Pluto, you are directed to PLUTO CHALLENGING ASCENDANT.*

2 When you have found the Profile itself, enter the name of each person in the spaces provided beneath the relevant Planet. *In the case of our example, SUN SUPPORTING MARS, the beginning of this PROFILE would then look like this:*

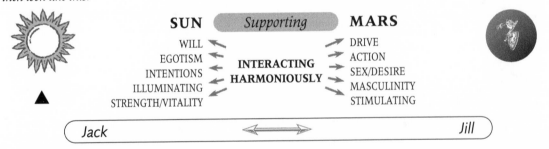

If the Profile is the reverse way around as *in the example of Jack/A's Ascendant Challenging Jill/B's Pluto being described as PLUTO CHALLENGING ASCENDANT, make sure you put Jill or B's name to the left under PLUTO, and Jack or A's name to the right under ASCENDANT, like this:*

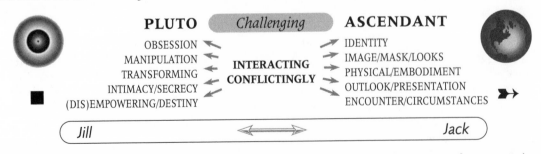

NOW when the text refers to a Planet, you'll know that it is referring to the Person whose name is on the same side of the Profile as that Planet.

3 NO ONE CROSS-ASPECT OR PLANET-TO-PLANET INTERACTION MAKES OR BREAKS A RELATIONSHIP. IT IS BEST TO REGARD THE HARD ONES AS 'DEMAND', AND THE EASY ONES AS 'SUPPLY' – AND DO YOUR BEST TO MAKE SURE THAT ONE MEETS THE OTHER.

4 To help you instantly recognize the basic significance of any particular Cross-Aspect or Interaction – as given to the left and/or right of the Title of that Interaction, or at the start of the text – **here is a**

KEY TO THE PLANET-TO-PLANET PROFILE SYMBOLS

▲ = EASY ASPECTS = usually SUPporting (*see* page 303 for meaning).

■ = HARD ASPECTS = usually CHAllenging (*see* page 303 for meaning).

▲■ = HARD AND EASY ASPECTS = usually CONjoining or OPPosing (*see* page 303 for meaning).

➤➤ = CUPID ASPECTS = precipitating, mutually attracting, falling in love/lust, necessary for a one-to-one relationship to actually happen.

♥ = HEART ASPECTS = positive and lasting, marriage/partnership material.

♦ = TEARDROP ASPECTS = involving suffering, acutely/profoundly emotional.

⚷ = KEY CONTACTS = highly significant Interactions.

⇔ = ASPECTS where Person A's Planet is interchangeable with Person B's Planet.

NOTE: To a very significant extent, ALL CROSS-ASPECTS ARE INTERCHANGEABLE.

DW = DOUBLE WHAMMY. Mark this in yourself when you find an Aspect going both ways. *In our example, Jack's Venus is Challenging Jill's Moon, and so too is Jill's Venus Challenging Jack's Moon.* You will automatically discover DWs because you will find yourself entering your names twice for the same Aspect. This kind of interaction has a marked influence upon a relationship.

5 MUTUALITY – It is important to be aware that all four Aspect types are *mutual* in that when, say, Person A has VENus CHAllenging B's NEPtune, then B's Neptune is also CHAllenging A's VENus, whether consciously or unconsciously. (*See* point 9 overleaf for an example of this.)

6 TYPES OF RELATIONSHIP – I have placed the main focus upon romantic/sexual relationships because, in my experience, these are what people are most concerned about. But at the same time I have indicated significant issues regarding other types of relationships, such as family, friendship and even business, when it has been appropriate to do so. Overall, however, I have worded the Profiles in a way which can, with a little bit of imagination and reading between the lines, be applied to any kind of relationship.

7 CLOSE ONES – Take special note of these Interactions for they form the core of a relationship, and are like a 'tight fit' in terms of either ease or difficulty, depending on the type of Cross-Aspect.

8 USING THE INTERACTION KEYWORDS – The Interaction Keywords are what you see beneath the two Planets in question, either side of a bundle of two-way arrows superimposed with the word describing what that Interaction is basically about. This is a graphic depiction of the two people's personal energies interacting. Using this is not absolutely necessary for understanding the Profiles – all you have to do is read the text and hopefully you will be enlightened about one aspect of the relationship. However, familiarizing yourself with how to use the Interaction Keywords in KEYWORD CORNER on page 483 will greatly expand upon what you get out of the Profiles.

In our Jack and Jill example, and using the Profile above, PLUTO CHALLENGING ASCENDANT, we can use the Keywords in many ways, but here are a few.

• For what is basically a Challenging Interaction, we can extract positive objectives or themes from the Keywords. Jill could EMPOWER Jack's IDENTITY – that is, make him more aware of his physical presence and PRESENTATION.

Or Jack's PHYSICAL nature and PRESENTATION could be seen to Interact with Jill in a way she found very INTIMATE and EMPOWERING. And note how this could escalate as each of them fed one another in this way.

• Jill may MANIPULATE Jack's IMAGE in such a way that TRANSFORMED his sense of IDENTITY to such an extent that was DISEMPOWERING for him. Behind all this could be Jill's OBSESSION with his LOOKS. *See how the plot can thicken – with just one Interaction.*

• Using the Keywords given for the Planets in KEYWORD CORNER on page 483 (and more extensively in PLANETS OF LOVE in Chapter One), you will be able to explore any given Interaction, and find very personal patterns of some complexity. *In our example, Jack and Jill's ENCOUNTER TRANSFORMED their CIRCUMSTANCES through a CRISIS that brought them to an EMPOWERING INTIMACY.*

9 ADVANCED USE OF INTERACTIONS – After you have studied the Profiles for an Interaction, you may gain further insights by looking at the Sign-to-Sign Interaction for any Interactions that have been determined as particularly important or interesting. Ascertain the Sign for each Planet in question, and refer to the SIGN-TO-SIGN PROFILES (beginning on page 289) in the same way as described in the SIGN-TO-SIGN INTERACTION section earlier in Chapter Three.

In our example, suppose you wanted to look at the Sign-to-Sign Interaction of Jack's MOOn SUPorting Jill's MERcury. We know that his MOOn is in PISces and that her MERcury is in CANcer. So we just go to the page in the Sign-to-Sign Profiles headed THE SIGN OF PISCES INTERACTS WITH – and then look at the row that begins CANCER INTUITIVELY, and read the text that describes the Interaction in terms of these two Signs rather than just the two Planets, thus augmenting your sense of it.

You can now read even more meaning into any Interaction by discovering what any Planet in one person's Birthchart is saying or doing to a Planet in another's. This you do by taking Keywords and/or the relevant Planet-Sign Profile from the former and applying them to the latter by using the Interaction name. This is best explained through our example again. *Take Jack's SATurn CHAllenging Jill's URAnus. But Jack wants to see what it means in terms of how Jill affects him, so let's look at it the other way around as Jill's URAnus CHAllenging Jack's SATurn. So take a couple of Keywords for URAnus, say, AWAKENING and PROVOCATION, and then apply them to the meaning of Jack's SATurn in terms of the general meaning of that Planet (in Planets of Love) and, most appropriately, in terms of its Sign position, which is SCOrpio. So looking at what it says for SATurn in SCOrpio (on page 235) we'll find just what it is in Jack's life and personality that is being AWAKENED and PROVOKED by Jill's URAnus CHALLENGING him in this way! You can then check out what Jill's URAnus means through the other Keywords, like her INTUITION and UNUSUALNESS, and in the general descriptions of this Planet on page 11 in PLANETS OF LOVE.*

THE PLANET-TO-PLANET PROFILES INDEX

PAGE NUMBERS IN ITALICS denote that that Interaction is entitled with the Planets the other way around, eg Moon Supporting Sun is called Sun Supporting Moon, and listed among the Sun Interactions.

A's SUN

CONjoining

B's SUN → SUN CONJOINING SUN	318
B's MOOn → SUN CONJOINING MOON	320
B's MERcury → SUN CONJOINING MERCURY	322
B's VENus → SUN CONJOINING VENUS	324
B's MARs → SUN CONJOINING MARS	326
B's JUPiter → SUN CONJOINING JUPITER	328
B's SATurn → SUN CONJOINING SATURN	330
B's URAnus → SUN CONJOINING URANUS	332
B's NEPtune → SUN CONJOINING NEPTUNE	335
B's PLUto → SUN CONJOINING PLUTO	337
B's ASCendant → SUN CONJOINING ASCENDANT	339

SUPporting

B's SUN → SUN SUPPORTING SUN	319
B's MOOn → SUN SUPPORTING MOON	321
B's MERcury → SUN SUPPORTING MERCURY	323
B's VENus → SUN SUPPORTING VENUS	325
B's MARs → SUN SUPPORTING MARS	327
B's JUPiter → SUN SUPPORTING JUPITER	329
B's SATurn → SUN SUPPORTING SATURN	331
B's URAnus → SUN SUPPORTING URANUS	334
B's NEPtune → SUN SUPPORTING NEPTUNE	336
B's PLUto → SUN SUPPORTING PLUTO	338
B's ASCendant → SUN SUPPORTING ASCENDANT	340

CHAllenging

B's SUN → SUN CHALLENGING SUN	318
B's MOOn → SUN CHALLENGING MOON	321
B's MERcury → SUN CHALLENGING MERCURY	323
B's VENus → SUN CHALLENGING VENUS	325
B's MARs → SUN CHALLENGING MARS	327
B's JUPiter → SUN CHALLENGING JUPITER	329
B's SATurn → SUN CHALLENGING SATURN	331
B's URAnus → SUN CHALLENGING URANUS	333
B's NEPtune → SUN CHALLENGING NEPTUNE	336
B's PLUto → SUN CHALLENGING PLUTO	338
B's ASCendant → SUN CHALLENGING ASCENDANT	340

OPPosing

B's SUN → SUN OPPOSING SUN	319
B's MOOn → SUN OPPOSING MOON	322
B's MERcury → SUN OPPOSING MERCURY	324
B's VENus → SUN OPPOSING VENUS	326
B's MARs → SUN OPPOSING MARS	328
B's JUPiter → SUN OPPOSING JUPITER	330
B's SATurn → SUN OPPOSING SATURN	332
B's URAnus → SUN OPPOSING URANUS	334
B's NEPtune → SUN OPPOSING NEPTUNE	337
B's PLUto → SUN OPPOSING PLUTO	339
B's ASCendant → SUN OPPOSING ASCENDANT	341

A's MOON

CONjoining

B's SUN → SUN CONJOINING MOON	*320*
B's MOOn → MOON CONJOINING MOON	344
B's MERcury → MOON CONJOINING MERCURY	346
B's VENus → MOON CONJOINING VENUS	348
B's MARs → MOON CONJOINING MARS	350
B's JUPiter → MOON CONJOINING JUPITER	352
B's SATurn → MOON CONJOINING SATURN	354
B's URAnus → MOON CONJOINING URANUS	356
B's NEPtune → MOON CONJOINING NEPTUNE	358
B's PLUto → MOON CONJOINING PLUTO	360
B's ASCendant → MOON CONJOINING ASCENDANT	362

SUPporting

B's SUN → SUN SUPPORTING MOON	*319*
B's MOOn → MOON SUPPORTING MOON	345
B's MERcury → MOON SUPPORTING MERCURY	347
B's VENus → MOON SUPPORTING VENUS	349
B's MARs → MOON SUPPORTING MARS	351
B's JUPiter → MOON SUPPORTING JUPITER	353
B's SATurn → MOON SUPPORTING SATURN	355
B's URAnus → MOON SUPPORTING URANUS	357
B's NEPtune → MOON SUPPORTING NEPTUNE	359
B's PLUto → MOON SUPPORTING PLUTO	361
B's ASCendant → MOON SUPPORTING ASCENDANT	363

CHAllenging

B's SUN → SUN CHALLENGING MOON	*321*
B's MOOn → MOON CHALLENGING MOON	344
B's MERcury → MOON CHALLENGING MERCURY	346
B's VENus → MOON CHALLENGING VENUS	348
B's MARs → MOON CHALLENGING MARS	350
B's JUPiter → MOON CHALLENGING JUPITER	352
B's SATurn → MOON CHALLENGING SATURN	354
B's URAnus → MOON CHALLENGING URANUS	356
B's NEPtune → MOON CHALLENGING NEPTUNE	358
B's PLUto → MOON CHALLENGING PLUTO	360
B's ASCendant → MOON CHALLENGING ASCENDANT	363

OPPosing

B's SUN → SUN OPPOSING MOON	*322*
B's MOOn → MOON OPPOSING MOON	345
B's MERcury → MOON OPPOSING MERCURY	347
B's VENus → MOON OPPOSING VENUS	349
B's MARs → MOON OPPOSING MARS	351
B's JUPiter → MOON OPPOSING JUPITER	353
B's SATurn → MOON OPPOSING SATURN	355
B's URAnus → MOON OPPOSING URANUS	357
B's NEPtune → MOON OPPOSING NEPTUNE	359
B's PLUto → MOON OPPOSING PLUTO	362
B's ASCendant → MOON OPPOSING ASCENDANT	364

A's MERCURY

CONjoining

B's SUN → SUN CONJOINING MERCURY — 322
B's MOOn → MOON CONJOINING MERCURY — 346
B's MERcury → MERCURY CONJOINING MERCURY — 366
B's VENus → MERCURY CONJOINING VENUS — 368
B's MARs → MERCURY CONJOINING MARS — 370
B's JUPiter → MERCURY CONJOINING JUPITER — 372
B's SATurn → MERCURY CONJOINING SATURN — 374
B's URAnus → MERCURY CONJOINING URANUS — 376
B's NEPtune → MERCURY CONJOINING NEPTUNE — 378
B's PLUto → MERCURY CONJOINING PLUTO — 380
B's ASCendant → MERCURY CONJOINING ASCENDANT — 382

CHAllenging

B's SUN → SUN CHALLENGING MERCURY — 323
B's MOOn → MOON CHALLENGING MERCURY — 346
B's MERcury → MERCURY CHALLENGING MERCURY — 366
B's VENus → MERCURY CHALLENGING VENUS — 368
B's MARs → MERCURY CHALLENGING MARS — 370
B's JUPiter → MERCURY CHALLENGING JUPITER — 372
B's SATurn → MERCURY CHALLENGING SATURN — 374
B's URAnus → MERCURY CHALLENGING URANUS — 376
B's NEPtune → MERCURY CHALLENGING NEPTUNE — 378
B's PLUto → MERCURY CHALLENGING PLUTO — 381
B's ASCendant → MERCURY CHALLENGING ASCENDANT — 383

SUPporting

B's SUN → SUN SUPPORTING MERCURY — 323
B's MOOn → MOON SUPPORTING MERCURY — 347
B's MERcury → MERCURY SUPPORTING MERCURY — 367
B's VENus → MERCURY SUPPORTING VENUS — 369
B's MARs → MERCURY SUPPORTING MARS — 371
B's JUPiter → MERCURY SUPPORTING JUPITER — 373
B's SATurn → MERCURY SUPPORTING SATURN — 375
B's URAnus → MERCURY SUPPORTING URANUS — 377
B's NEPtune → MERCURY SUPPORTING NEPTUNE — 379
B's PLUto → MERCURY SUPPORTING PLUTO — 381
B's ASCendant → MERCURY SUPPORTING ASCENDANT — 383

OPPosing

B's SUN → SUN OPPOSING MERCURY — 324
B's MOOn → MOON OPPOSING MERCURY — 347
B's MERcury → MERCURY OPPOSING MERCURY — 367
B's VENus → MERCURY OPPOSING VENUS — 369
B's MARs → MERCURY OPPOSING MARS — 371
B's JUPiter → MERCURY OPPOSING JUPITER — 373
B's SATurn → MERCURY OPPOSING SATURN — 375
B's URAnus → MERCURY OPPOSING URANUS — 377
B's NEPtune → MERCURY OPPOSING NEPTUNE — 380
B's PLUto → MERCURY OPPOSING PLUTO — 382
B's ASCendant → MERCURY OPPOSING ASCENDANT — 384

A's VENUS

CONjoining

B's SUN → SUN CONJOINING VENUS — 324
B's MOOn → MOON CONJOINING VENUS — 348
B's MERcury → MERCURY CONJOINING VENUS — 368
B's VENus → VENUS CONJOINING VENUS — 386
B's MARs → VENUS CONJOINING MARS — 388
B's JUPiter → VENUS CONJOINING JUPITER — 390
B's SATurn → VENUS CONJOINING SATURN — 392
B's URAnus → VENUS CONJOINING URANUS — 394
B's NEPtune → VENUS CONJOINING NEPTUNE — 397
B's PLUto → VENUS CONJOINING PLUTO — 399
B's ASCendant → VENUS CONJOINING ASCENDANT — 401

CHAllenging

B's SUN → SUN CHALLENGING VENUS — 325
B's MOOn → MOON CHALLENGING VENUS — 348
B's MERcury → MERCURY CHALLENGING VENUS — 368
B's VENus → VENUS CHALLENGING VENUS — 386
B's MARs → VENUS CHALLENGING MARS — 388
B's JUPiter → VENUS CHALLENGING JUPITER — 390
B's SATurn → VENUS CHALLENGING SATURN — 392
B's URAnus → VENUS CHALLENGING URANUS — 395
B's NEPtune → VENUS CHALLENGING NEPTUNE — 397
B's PLUto → VENUS CHALLENGING PLUTO — 399
B's ASCendant → VENUS CHALLENGING ASCENDANT — 401

SUPporting

B's SUN → SUN SUPPORTING VENUS — 325
B's MOOn → MOON SUPPORTING VENUS — 349
B's MERcury → MERCURY SUPPORTING VENUS — 369
B's VENus → VENUS SUPPORTING VENUS — 387
B's MARs → VENUS SUPPORTING MARS — 389
B's JUPiter → VENUS SUPPORTING JUPITER — 391
B's SATurn → VENUS SUPPORTING SATURN — 393
B's URAnus → VENUS SUPPORTING URANUS — 395
B's NEPtune → VENUS SUPPORTING NEPTUNE — 398
B's PLUto → VENUS SUPPORTING PLUTO — 400
B's ASCendant → VENUS SUPPORTING ASCENDANT — 402

OPPosing

B's SUN → SUN OPPOSING VENUS — 326
B's MOOn → MOON OPPOSING VENUS — 349
B's MERcury → MERCURY OPPOSING VENUS — 369
B's VENus → VENUS OPPOSING VENUS — 387
B's MARs → VENUS OPPOSING MARS — 389
B's JUPiter → VENUS OPPOSING JUPITER — 391
B's SATurn → VENUS OPPOSING SATURN — 393
B's URAnus → VENUS OPPOSING URANUS — 396
B's NEPtune → VENUS OPPOSING NEPTUNE — 398
B's PLUto → VENUS OPPOSING PLUTO — 400
B's ASCendant → VENUS OPPOSING ASCENDANT — 402

A's MARS

CONjoining

B's SUN → SUN CONJOINING MARS 326
B's MOOn → MOON CONJOINING MARS 350
B's MERcury → MERCURY CONJOINING MARS 370
B's VENus → VENUS CONJOINING MARS 388
B's MARs → MARS CONJOINING MARS 404
B's JUPiter → MARS CONJOINING JUPITER 406
B's SATurn → MARS CONJOINING SATURN 408
B's URAnus → MARS CONJOINING URANUS 410
B's NEPtune → MARS CONJOINING NEPTUNE 412
B's PLUto → MARS CONJOINING PLUTO 414
B's ASCendant → MARS CONJOINING ASCENDANT 416

CHAllenging

B's SUN → SUN CHALLENGING MARS 327
B's MOOn → MOON CHALLENGING MARS 350
B's MERcury → MERCURY CHALLENGING MARS 370
B's VENus → VENUS CHALLENGING MARS 388
B's MARs → MARS CHALLENGING MARS 404
B's JUPiter → MARS CHALLENGING JUPITER 406
B's SATurn → MARS CHALLENGING SATURN 408
B's URAnus → MARS CHALLENGING URANUS 410
B's NEPtune → MARS CHALLENGING NEPTUNE 412
B's PLUto → MARS CHALLENGING PLUTO 415
B's ASCendant → MARS CHALLENGING ASCENDANT 417

SUPporting

B's SUN → SUN SUPPORTING MARS 327
B's MOOn → MOON SUPPORTING MARS 351
B's MERcury → MERCURY SUPPORTING MARS 371
B's VENus → VENUS SUPPORTING MARS 389
B's MARs → MARS SUPPORTING MARS 405
B's JUPiter → MARS SUPPORTING JUPITER 407
B's SATurn → MARS SUPPORTING SATURN 409
B's URAnus → MARS SUPPORTING URANUS 411
B's NEPtune → MARS SUPPORTING NEPTUNE 413
B's PLUto → MARS SUPPORTING PLUTO 415
B's ASCendant → MARS SUPPORTING ASCENDANT 417

OPPosing

B's SUN → SUN OPPOSING MARS 328
B's MOOn → MOON OPPOSING MARS 351
B's MERcury → MERCURY OPPOSING MARS 371
B's VENus → VENUS OPPOSING MARS 389
B's MARs → MARS OPPOSING MARS 405
B's JUPiter → MARS OPPOSING JUPITER 407
B's SATurn → MARS OPPOSING SATURN 409
B's URAnus → MARS OPPOSING URANUS 411
B's NEPtune → MARS OPPOSING NEPTUNE 413
B's PLUto → MARS OPPOSING PLUTO 416
B's ASCendant → MARS OPPOSING ASCENDANT 418

A's JUPITER

CONjoining

B's SUN → SUN CONJOINING JUPITER 328
B's MOOn → MOON CONJOINING JUPITER 352
B's MERcury → MERCURY CONJOINING JUPITER 372
B's VENus → VENUS CONJOINING JUPITER 390
B's MARs → MARS CONJOINING JUPITER 406
B's JUPiter → JUPITER CONJOINING JUPITER 420
B's SATurn → JUPITER CONJOINING SATURN 422
B's URAnus → JUPITER CONJOINING URANUS 424
B's NEPtune → JUPITER CONJOINING NEPTUNE 426
B's PLUto → JUPITER CONJOINING PLUTO 428
B's ASCendant → JUPITER CONJOINING ASCENDANT 430

CHAllenging

B's SUN → SUN CHALLENGING JUPITER 329
B's MOOn → MOON CHALLENGING JUPITER 352
B's MERcury → MERCURY CHALLENGING JUPITER 372
B's VENus → VENUS CHALLENGING JUPITER 390
B's MARs → MARS CHALLENGING JUPITER 406
B's JUPiter → JUPITER CHALLENGING JUPITER 420
B's SATurn → JUPITER CHALLENGING SATURN 422
B's URAnus → JUPITER CHALLENGING URANUS 424
B's NEPtune → JUPITER CHALLENGING NEPTUNE 426
B's PLUto → JUPITER CHALLENGING PLUTO 428
B's ASCendant → JUPITER CHALLENGING ASCENDANT 430

SUPporting

B's SUN → SUN SUPPORTING JUPITER 329
B's MOOn → MOON SUPPORTING JUPITER 353
B's MERcury → MERCURY SUPPORTING JUPITER 373
B's VENus → VENUS SUPPORTING JUPITER 391
B's MARs → MARS SUPPORTING JUPITER 407
B's JUPiter → JUPITER SUPPORTING JUPITER 421
B's SATurn → JUPITER SUPPORTING SATURN 423
B's URAnus → JUPITER SUPPORTING URANUS 425
B's NEPtune → JUPITER SUPPORTING NEPTUNE 427
B's PLUto → JUPITER SUPPORTING PLUTO 429
B's ASCendant → JUPITER SUPPORTING ASCENDANT 431

OPPosing

B's SUN → SUN OPPOSING JUPITER 330
B's MOOn → MOON OPPOSING JUPITER 353
B's MERcury → MERCURY OPPOSING JUPITER 373
B's VENus → VENUS OPPOSING JUPITER 391
B's MARs → MARS OPPOSING JUPITER 407
B's JUPiter → JUPITER OPPOSING JUPITER 421
B's SATurn → JUPITER OPPOSING SATURN 423
B's URAnus → JUPITER OPPOSING URANUS 425
B's NEPtune → JUPITER OPPOSING NEPTUNE 427
B's PLUto → JUPITER OPPOSING PLUTO 429
B's ASCendant → JUPITER OPPOSING ASCENDANT 431

A's SATURN

CONjoining

B's SUN → SUN CONJOINING SATURN   330
B's MOOn → MOON CONJOINING SATURN   354
B's MERcury → MERCURY CONJOINING SATURN   374
B's VENus → VENUS CONJOINING SATURN   392
B's MARs → MARS CONJOINING SATURN   408
B's JUPiter → JUPITER CONJOINING SATURN   422
B's SATurn → SATURN CONJOINING SATURN   434
B's URAnus → SATURN CONJOINING URANUS   436
B's NEPtune → SATURN CONJOINING NEPTUNE   438
B's PLUto → SATURN CONJOINING PLUTO   440
B's ASCendant → SATURN CONJOINING ASCENDANT   442

SUPporting

B's SUN → SUN SUPPORTING SATURN   331
B's MOOn → MOON SUPPORTING SATURN   355
B's MERcury → MERCURY SUPPORTING SATURN   375
B's VENus → VENUS SUPPORTING SATURN   393
B's MARs → MARS SUPPORTING SATURN   409
B's JUPiter → JUPITER SUPPORTING SATURN   423
B's SATurn → SATURN SUPPORTING SATURN   435
B's URAnus → SATURN SUPPORTING URANUS   437
B's NEPtune → SATURN SUPPORTING NEPTUNE   439
B's PLUto → SATURN SUPPORTING PLUTO   441
B's ASCendant → SATURN SUPPORTING ASCENDANT   443

CHAllenging

B's SUN → SUN CHALLENGING SATURN   331
B's MOOn → MOON CHALLENGING SATURN   354
B's MERcury → MERCURY CHALLENGING SATURN   374
B's VENus → VENUS CHALLENGING SATURN   392
B's MARs → MARS CHALLENGING SATURN   408
B's JUPiter → JUPITER CHALLENGING SATURN   422
B's SATurn → SATURN CHALLENGING SATURN   434
B's URAnus → SATURN CHALLENGING URANUS   436
B's NEPtune → SATURN CHALLENGING NEPTUNE   438
B's PLUto → SATURN CHALLENGING PLUTO   440
B's ASCendant → SATURN CHALLENGING ASCENDANT   442

OPPosing

B's SUN → SUN OPPOSING SATURN   332
B's MOOn → MOON OPPOSING SATURN   355
B's MERcury → MERCURY OPPOSING SATURN   375
B's VENus → VENUS OPPOSING SATURN   393
B's MARs → MARS OPPOSING SATURN   409
B's JUPiter → JUPITER OPPOSING SATURN   423
B's SATurn → SATURN OPPOSING SATURN   435
B's URAnus → SATURN OPPOSING URANUS   437
B's NEPtune → SATURN OPPOSING NEPTUNE   439
B's PLUto → SATURN OPPOSING PLUTO   441
B's ASCendant → SATURN OPPOSING ASCENDANT   443

A's URANUS

CONjoining

B's SUN → SUN CONJOINING URANUS   332
B's MOOn → MOON CONJOINING URANUS   356
B's MERcury → MERCURY CONJOINING URANUS   376
B's VENus → VENUS CONJOINING URANUS   394
B's MARs → MARS CONJOINING URANUS   410
B's JUPiter → JUPITER CONJOINING URANUS   424
B's SATurn → SATURN CONJOINING URANUS   436
B's URAnus → URANUS CONJOINING URANUS   446
B's NEPtune → URANUS CONJOINING NEPTUNE   447
B's PLUto → URANUS CONJOINING PLUTO   449
B's ASCendant → URANUS CONJOINING ASCENDANT   451

SUPporting

B's SUN → SUN SUPPORTING URANUS   334
B's MOOn → MOON SUPPORTING URANUS   357
B's MERcury → MERCURY SUPPORTING URANUS   377
B's VENus → VENUS SUPPORTING URANUS   395
B's MARs → MARS SUPPORTING URANUS   411
B's JUPiter → JUPITER SUPPORTING URANUS   425
B's SATurn → SATURN SUPPORTING URANUS   437
B's URAnus → URANUS SUPPORTING URANUS   446
B's NEPtune → URANUS SUPPORTING NEPTUNE   448
B's PLUto → URANUS SUPPORTING PLUTO   450
B's ASCendant → URANUS SUPPORTING ASCENDANT   452

CHAllenging

B's SUN → SUN CHALLENGING URANUS   333
B's MOOn → MOON CHALLENGING URANUS   356
B's MERcury → MERCURY CHALLENGING URANUS   376
B's VENus → VENUS CHALLENGING URANUS   395
B's MARs → MARS CHALLENGING URANUS   410
B's JUPiter → JUPITER CHALLENGING URANUS   424
B's SATurn → SATURN CHALLENGING URANUS   436
B's URAnus → URANUS CHALLENGING URANUS   446
B's NEPtune → URANUS CHALLENGING NEPTUNE   448
B's PLUto → URANUS CHALLENGING PLUTO   450
B's ASCendant → URANUS CHALLENGING ASCENDANT   452

OPPosing

B's SUN → SUN OPPOSING URANUS   334
B's MOOn → MOON OPPOSING URANUS   357
B's MERcury → MERCURY OPPOSING URANUS   377
B's VENus → VENUS OPPOSING URANUS   396
B's MARs → MARS OPPOSING URANUS   411
B's JUPiter → JUPITER OPPOSING URANUS   425
B's SATurn → SATURN OPPOSING URANUS   437
B's URAnus → URANUS OPPOSING URANUS   447
B's NEPtune → URANUS OPPOSING NEPTUNE   449
B's PLUto → URANUS OPPOSING PLUTO   451
B's ASCendant → URANUS OPPOSING ASCENDANT   453

A's NEPTUNE

CONjoining

B's SUN → SUN CONJOINING NEPTUNE	335
B's MOOn → MOON CONJOINING NEPTUNE	358
B's MERcury → MERCURY CONJOINING NEPTUNE	378
B's VENus → VENUS CONJOINING NEPTUNE	397
B's MARs → MARS CONJOINING NEPTUNE	412
B's JUPiter → JUPITER CONJOINING NEPTUNE	426
B's SATurn → SATURN CONJOINING NEPTUNE	438
B's URAnus → URANUS CONJOINING NEPTUNE	447
B's NEPtune → NEPTUNE CONJOINING NEPTUNE	456
B's PLUto → NEPTUNE CONJOINING PLUTO	457
B's ASCendant → NEPTUNE CONJOINING ASCENDANT	459

SUPporting

B's SUN → SUN SUPPORTING NEPTUNE	336
B's MOOn → MOON SUPPORTING NEPTUNE	359
B's MERcury → MERCURY SUPPORTING NEPTUNE	379
B's VENus → VENUS SUPPORTING NEPTUNE	398
B's MARs → MARS SUPPORTING NEPTUNE	413
B's JUPiter → JUPITER SUPPORTING NEPTUNE	427
B's SATurn → SATURN SUPPORTING NEPTUNE	439
B's URAnus → URANUS SUPPORTING NEPTUNE	448
B's NEPtune → NEPTUNE SUPPORTING NEPTUNE	456
B's PLUto → NEPTUNE SUPPORTING PLUTO	458
B's ASCendant → NEPTUNE SUPPORTING ASCENDANT	460

CHAllenging

B's SUN → SUN CHALLENGING NEPTUNE	336
B's MOOn → MOON CHALLENGING NEPTUNE	358
B's MERcury → MERCURY CHALLENGING NEPTUNE	378
B's VENus → VENUS CHALLENGING NEPTUNE	397
B's MARs → MARS CHALLENGING NEPTUNE	412
B's JUPiter → JUPITER CHALLENGING NEPTUNE	426
B's SATurn → SATURN CHALLENGING NEPTUNE	438
B's URAnus → URANUS CHALLENGING NEPTUNE	448
B's NEPtune → NEPTUNE CHALLENGING NEPTUNE	456
B's PLUto → NEPTUNE CHALLENGING PLUTO	458
B's ASCendant → NEPTUNE CHALLENGING ASCENDANT	460

OPPosing

B's SUN → SUN OPPOSING NEPTUNE	337
B's MOOn → MOON OPPOSING NEPTUNE	359
B's MERcury → MERCURY OPPOSING NEPTUNE	380
B's VENus → VENUS OPPOSING NEPTUNE	398
B's MARs → MARS OPPOSING NEPTUNE	413
B's JUPiter → JUPITER OPPOSING NEPTUNE	427
B's SATurn → SATURN OPPOSING NEPTUNE	439
B's URAnus → URANUS OPPOSING NEPTUNE	449
B's NEPtune → NEPTUNE OPPOSING NEPTUNE	457
B's PLUto → NEPTUNE OPPOSING PLUTO	458
B's ASCendant → NEPTUNE OPPOSING ASCENDANT	461

A's PLUTO

CONjoining

B's SUN → SUN CONJOINING PLUTO	337
B's MOOn → MOON CONJOINING PLUTO	360
B's MERcury → MERCURY CONJOINING PLUTO	380
B's VENus → VENUS CONJOINING PLUTO	399
B's MARs → MARS CONJOINING PLUTO	414
B's JUPiter → JUPITER CONJOINING PLUTO	428
B's SATurn → SATURN CONJOINING PLUTO	440
B's URAnus → URANUS CONJOINING PLUTO	449
B's NEPtune → NEPTUNE CONJOINING PLUTO	457
B's PLUto → PLUTO CONJOINING PLUTO	464
B's ASCendant → PLUTO CONJOINING ASCENDANT	465

SUPporting

B's SUN → SUN SUPPORTING PLUTO	338
B's MOOn → MOON SUPPORTING PLUTO	361
B's MERcury → MERCURY SUPPORTING PLUTO	381
B's VENus → VENUS SUPPORTING PLUTO	400
B's MARs → MARS SUPPORTING PLUTO	415
B's JUPiter → JUPITER SUPPORTING PLUTO	429
B's SATurn → SATURN SUPPORTING PLUTO	441
B's URAnus → URANUS SUPPORTING PLUTO	450
B's NEPtune → NEPTUNE SUPPORTING PLUTO	458
B's PLUto → PLUTO SUPPORTING PLUTO	464
B's ASCendant → PLUTO SUPPORTING ASCENDANT	466

CHAllenging

B's SUN → SUN CHALLENGING PLUTO	338
B's MOOn → MOON CHALLENGING PLUTO	360
B's MERcury → MERCURY CHALLENGING PLUTO	381
B's VENus → VENUS CHALLENGING PLUTO	399
B's MARs → MARS CHALLENGING PLUTO	415
B's JUPiter → JUPITER CHALLENGING PLUTO	428
B's SATurn → SATURN CHALLENGING PLUTO	440
B's URAnus → URANUS CHALLENGING PLUTO	450
B's NEPtune → NEPTUNE CHALLENGING PLUTO	458
B's PLUto → PLUTO CHALLENGING PLUTO	464
B's ASCendant → PLUTO CHALLENGING ASCENDANT	466

OPPosing

B's SUN → SUN OPPOSING PLUTO	339
B's MOOn → MOON OPPOSING PLUTO	362
B's MERcury → MERCURY OPPOSING PLUTO	382
B's VENus → VENUS OPPOSING PLUTO	400
B's MARs → MARS OPPOSING PLUTO	416
B's JUPiter → JUPITER OPPOSING PLUTO	429
B's SATurn → SATURN OPPOSING PLUTO	441
B's URAnus → URANUS OPPOSING PLUTO	451
B's NEPtune → NEPTUNE OPPOSING PLUTO	458
B's PLUto → PLUTO OPPOSING PLUTO	464
B's ASCendant → PLUTO OPPOSING ASCENDANT	467

A's ASCENDANT

CONjoining

B's SUN → SUN CONJOINING ASCENDANT | *339*
B's MOOn → MOON CONJOINING ASCENDANT | *362*
B's MERcury → MERCURY CONJOINING ASCENDANT | *382*
B's VENus → VENUS CONJOINING ASCENDANT | *401*
B's MARs → MARS CONJOINING ASCENDANT | *416*
B's JUPiter → JUPITER CONJOINING ASCENDANT | *430*
B's SATurn → SATURN CONJOINING ASCENDANT | *442*
B's URAnus → URANUS CONJOINING ASCENDANT | *451*
B's NEPtune → NEPTUNE CONJOINING ASCENDANT | *459*
B's PLUto → PLUTO CONJOINING ASCENDANT | *465*
B's ASCendant → ASCENDANT CONJOINING ASCENDANT | 470

SUPporting

B's SUN → SUN SUPPORTING ASCENDANT | *340*
B's MOOn → MOON SUPPORTING ASCENDANT | *363*
B's MERcury → MERCURY SUPPORTING ASCENDANT | *383*
B's VENus → VENUS SUPPORTING ASCENDANT | *402*
B's MARs → MARS SUPPORTING ASCENDANT | *417*
B's JUPiter → JUPITER SUPPORTING ASCENDANT | *431*
B's SATurn → SATURN SUPPORTING ASCENDANT | *443*
B's URAnus → URANUS SUPPORTING ASCENDANT | *452*
B's NEPtune → NEPTUNE SUPPORTING ASCENDANT | *460*
B's PLUto → PLUTO SUPPORTING ASCENDANT | *466*
B's ASCendant → ASCENDANT SUPPORTING ASCENDANT | 471

CHAllenging

B's SUN → SUN CHALLENGING ASCENDANT | *340*
B's MOOn → MOON CHALLENGING ASCENDANT | *363*
B's MERcury → MERCURY CHALLENGING ASCENDANT | *383*
B's VENus → VENUS CHALLENGING ASCENDANT | *401*
B's MARs → MARS CHALLENGING ASCENDANT | *417*
B's JUPiter → JUPITER CHALLENGING ASCENDANT | *430*
B's SATurn → SATURN CHALLENGING ASCENDANT | *442*
B's URAnus → URANUS CHALLENGING ASCENDANT | *452*
B's NEPtune → NEPTUNE CHALLENGING ASCENDANT | *460*
B's PLUto → PLUTO CHALLENGING ASCENDANT | *466*
B's ASCendant → ASCENDANT CHALLENGING ASCENDANT | 470

OPPosing

B's SUN → SUN OPPOSING ASCENDANT | *341*
B's MOOn → MOON OPPOSING ASCENDANT | *364*
B's MERcury → MERCURY OPPOSING ASCENDANT | *384*
B's VENus → VENUS OPPOSING ASCENDANT | *402*
B's MARs → MARS OPPOSING ASCENDANT | *418*
B's JUPiter → JUPITER OPPOSING ASCENDANT | *431*
B's SATurn → SATURN OPPOSING ASCENDANT | *443*
B's URAnus → URANUS OPPOSING ASCENDANT | *453*
B's NEPtune → NEPTUNE OPPOSING ASCENDANT | *461*
B's PLUto → PLUTO OPPOSING ASCENDANT | *467*
B's ASCendant → ASCENDANT OPPOSING ASCENDANT | 471

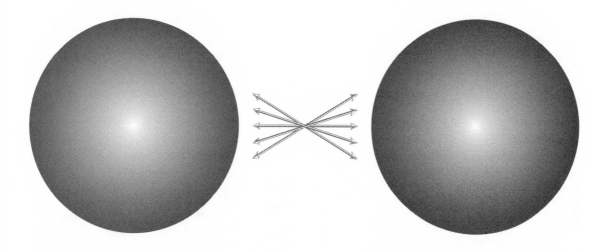

THE PLANET-TO-PLANET PROFILES

These are the Heart
of the Book…

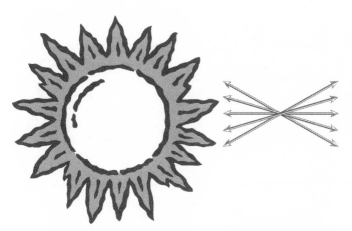

THE SUN

**INTERACTING
WITH**

THE SUN
THE MOON
MERCURY
VENUS
MARS
JUPITER

SATURN
URANUS
NEPTUNE
PLUTO
ASCENDANT

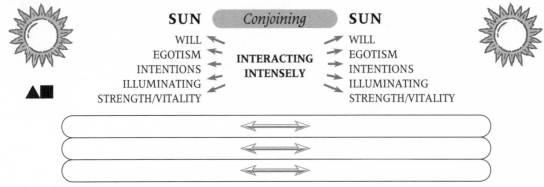

This means that your birthdays are within a week or so of one another, and that your Sun Signs could very well be the same. If they are the same, the strong similarity in your basic make-ups is of course noticeable. The best and the worst of your shared Sun Sign is expressed, experienced and intensified by your being together. The Air Signs, Gemini, Libra and Aquarius, profit from this intensification because they are naturally co-operative. The first two Fire Signs, Aries and Leo, would tend to bring out the competitive streak in one another – for good or ill. The third Fire Sign, Sagittarius, has an expansive, philosophical and impersonal quality, so they lope along rather well. The Earth Signs, Taurus, Virgo and Capricorn, are more territory conscious, which could give rise to problems – but apart from that, very stable, and a lot would get done. Virgo to Virgo could be a bit exacting though. Finally, the Water Signs, Cancer, Scorpio and Pisces: once two Crabs have locked claws there is probably no parting them, and Scorpios nest down, but if they do fall out, Hiroshima's got nothing on it! Pisceans tend to lose sight of one another. If you are not the same Sign, then you will be one Sign apart, which means that some kind of compromise will have to be made at some point. This is because your similarities can blind you to your dissimilarities and find you in an awkward place where the best way out is to meet each other half way. All in all, same Sign or not, this is a pretty positive Interaction, but a common goal or direction, with some rules for how to go about getting there, should be seen as the important thing.

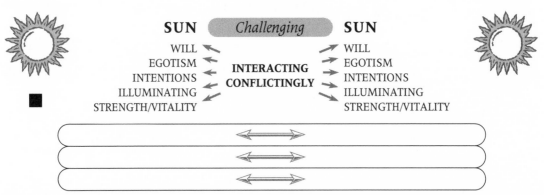

Your individual wills are at odds with each other and so your life tracks tend in different directions. This can lead to interminable battles as you both try to get your own way, sapping one another's strength in the process. From a positive standpoint, it means that you can each become stronger in your own right as you continually wrestle for supremacy, or better still, accept what one Sun Sign can learn or gain from another. However, unless you are the kind of people to whom harmony is not that important, or you actually need someone to keep you on your mettle, then do not expect to work together or live in each other's pockets. This Interaction can exist in longstanding relationships, but it would seem that, apart from the reasons just given, it would be between people that both have ego problems of some kind. For example, one would need to learn humility, whereas the other is learning to become more sure of themselves – the hard way.

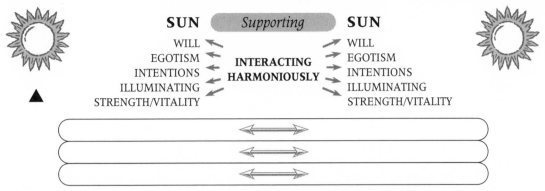

You are basically very compatible – but such a statement needs some further definition that focuses on the word 'basically'. This Interaction gives you a sound foundation upon which to build your relationship and anything that might issue from it, like children or a product/creation. Whatever else might happen along the way, as your relationship is built and progresses, there will always be this basic understanding to refer to and be reassured by. But Sun Supporting Sun does not indicate or determine the more individualistic qualities of your overall Interaction. This is done by other planetary pairings, which can amount to anything from a wonderful mansion to an abandoned shell!

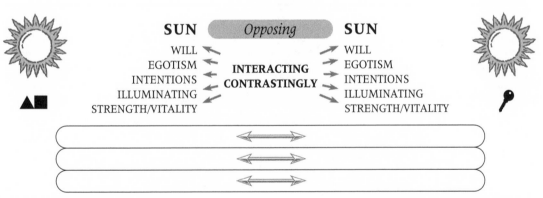

Here you have a classic case of opposites attracting one another. So although you are strongly drawn to one another at the outset, as time goes by you find that you each have quite distinct 'ego zones' and the one will object quite vehemently to theirs being invaded and managed by the other – or even seeming to be. This amounts to an exercise in respecting each other's space and way of living. Having avoided this pitfall, which could otherwise result in quite serious rifts being caused, you can create a very complementary relationship that presents a complete front and life-style to anyone, be it children, employees or others in general. A blending of the best of each of your Sun Sign's qualities is the goal to aim for. A great deal also depends upon emotional harmony and reasonable communication being provided by other Interactions.

Look at the Sign-to-Sign Profiles for the Signs involved in any Interaction   319

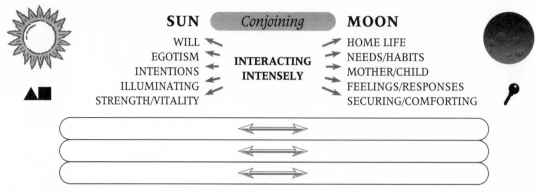

SUN *Conjoining* **MOON**

WILL
EGOTISM
INTENTIONS
ILLUMINATING
STRENGTH/VITALITY

**INTERACTING
INTENSELY**

HOME LIFE
NEEDS/HABITS
MOTHER/CHILD
FEELINGS/RESPONSES
SECURING/COMFORTING

Whatever your sexes, ages or positions in life, this Interaction gives you a definite feeling of being connected in some way, if not many ways. There is a feeling of familiarity, despite anything else that might or might not be happening between the two of you. It is as if the Sun person has the Moon person 'fixed in their beam', as if they are illuminating their inner or emotional being. Depending on other factors, particularly sexual or status ones, this can make the Moon person feel overwhelmed or greatly impressed by the Sun, or somehow inferior or even at their command. As the Moon reflects this back, the Sun feels this happening and, depending on what kind of ego they have, can feel empowered and then become anything from dominating to feeling strangely or uncomfortably superior. At another level – when there are plenty of other strong Interactions – you may feel like soul-mates. After a short while though, it can make a great difference as to what sex the Sun and the Moon are. When the Sun is male and the Moon female, the above descriptions lean towards the positive, for the male Solar 'radiating' and the female Lunar 'receiving' are in their natural and comfortable roles. In fact, if this is the case, it almost acts as a demonstration of this phenomenon, flying in the face of contemporary ideas of men and women being the same (as distinct from equal). When it is reversed, the female can uncomfortably feel that the man should be making the moves but he doesn't for he is waiting, possibly quite awkwardly, for her to do so. If the man should make the move, the woman then feels equally uncomfortable. Then again, it could be a case of your actually getting something out of such a role-reversal. But here too, yet this time not so obviously, the basic differences between male and female are experienced. If you are both the same sex, then you might say the Sun determines who is the 'male' and the Moon the 'female'. There is also a sense of the Sun as being the 'parent' and the Moon as being the 'child'. This may literally be the case, and this Interaction would then be highly suitable. However, an older 'child' and a younger 'parent' could be curiously enlightening or plain awkward. To sum up, basic connectedness is what this Interaction is all about, but other more personal and idiosyncratic Interactions would indicate whether such a basis has anything worth building upon it.

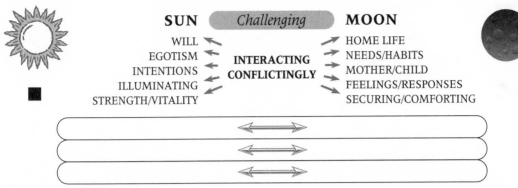

SUN *Challenging* **MOON**

WILL
EGOTISM   **INTERACTING**
INTENTIONS   **CONFLICTINGLY**
ILLUMINATING
STRENGTH/VITALITY

HOME LIFE
NEEDS/HABITS
MOTHER/CHILD
FEELINGS/RESPONSES
SECURING/COMFORTING

This makes for a basic incompatibility. You would need to have a great deal going for your relationship in terms of external and superficial worth, or conversely, inner and spiritual worth, in order to override this one. The Sun person cannot seem to appreciate where the Moon person is coming from emotionally. Consequently, they often offend, confuse or dominate the Moon person without even knowing it. The Moon person's background and personal habits do not fit in with the Sun's life-style. Another, and decidedly better, way of overcoming, or at least diminishing, the negative effects of this Interaction, is for the Moon to become very aware of how and why they react to the Sun's way of being. In the meantime, the Sun would have to learn to observe how the Moon is feeling and avoid stepping on their toes. Even so, this is not a desirable Interaction, especially between parents for they put out mixed messages and double standards to their children – unless these problems are dealt with in the manner suggested.

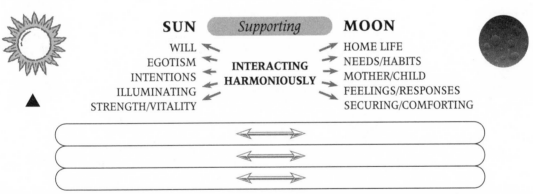

SUN *Supporting* **MOON**

WILL
EGOTISM   **INTERACTING**
INTENTIONS   **HARMONIOUSLY**
ILLUMINATING
STRENGTH/VITALITY

HOME LIFE
NEEDS/HABITS
MOTHER/CHILD
FEELINGS/RESPONSES
SECURING/COMFORTING

This is one of the most basically harmonious Interactions, and favours any kind of relationship, be it romantic, family, business or between friends. The Sun person is the 'leader' here, and Moon is quite happy to follow that lead. Because of traditional gender roles, it is more effective when a male is the Sun and a female the Moon. Nevertheless, if the reverse, it may well be that the male is in need of someone to show the way, and he knows it, and therefore accepts it. In return, the Moon's instinctively positive response to the Sun gives them a sense of being on the right course in life. However, because this Interaction has this 'basic' quality of harmony, it does not define or take into consideration the more idiosyncratic qualities of the relationship, be they positive or negative. It simply promises that, come what may, there will be an essential harmony between the two of you.

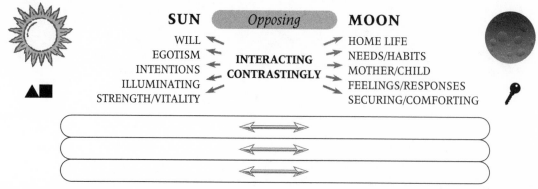

This Interaction is like the Full Moon – when the Sun is diametrically opposite the Moon and illuminating the whole of its face. The Moon person is therefore very much in the thrall of the Sun person, dependent upon their words and actions for feeling whatever they feel. The Sun person is bestowing upon the Moon the attention, warmth and sheer vitality that they need to feel alive and comfortable – or they could simply overwhelm them and have them dangling on a string. The Moon person can either accept this gladly or sadly, or retreat into some area of safety where the Sun's ego can't get at them. A great deal can be learned by the Sun as to how they affect others with their will and ego, for the Moon picks up every little nuance and reflects it back to the Sun. The Moon, on the other hand, is made to feel acutely aware of every little emotional feature – particularly childhood or childish patterns of behaviour. So much depends upon the spirit in which this illuminating and reflecting is performed. This Interaction is far more manageable when the male is the Sun partner because traditionally it is his role to 'do', and when the Moon is the female for traditionally it is her role to 'be' in response. When the reverse way around, you could both feel out of your traditional roles to the extent that the female Sun is having to be both mother and partner to the other, while the male Moon feels rather weak and powerless and in danger of crumbling. But if the female Sun can get the hang of having such power and use it benevolently, and the male Moon get the feel of how effective being passive can be, then all will be well. Even so, and common though this aspect is in marriages, it is rather demanding. But then it does promise a great reward: increased awareness of what and who you are, and of life itself.

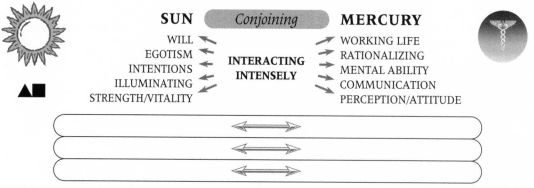

This poses the importance of communication, but does not indicate in itself whether or not it is good or bad communication. If as a pair you have a sound mental rapport indicated elsewhere, then this Interaction will give it more strength and energy. If you have a poor intellectual link, or ongoing emotional conflict, then this will make it all the more exasperating – simply because efficient communication is more sorely needed. The Sun person, one way or the other, will highlight the mental condition of the Mercury person. This can take the form of aiding and encouraging their mental muscle, and/or belittling any weakness that the Sun perceives them as having. Work issues can also be spotlighted in these ways. The Mercury person, if they have a strong intellect, will give as good as they get, be it positive or negative. Ideas can fly like sparks, just as readily as disputes. To create the former, some mutual respect and understanding is called for, especially where it comes to appreciating where either person has an educational or mental work background that is better or worse than average.

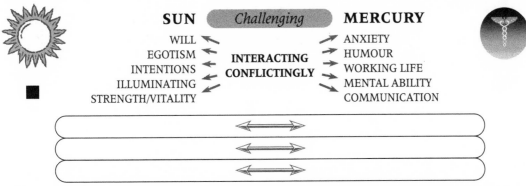

SUN *Challenging* **MERCURY**

WILL
EGOTISM
INTENTIONS
ILLUMINATING
STRENGTH/VITALITY

**INTERACTING
CONFLICTINGLY**

ANXIETY
HUMOUR
WORKING LIFE
MENTAL ABILITY
COMMUNICATION

The two of you often talk or think at cross-purposes, so arranging day-to-day activities can prove to be irritatingly difficult. Another reason for this may be that the Mercury person's daily schedule does not fit the Sun person's plans. All of these little annoyances can build up to being a sizeable problem. It is well known that good communication is one of the most important elements of a successful relationship – and, to varying degrees, this aspect denies you this. To complicate matters, the Sun may view Mercury as intellectually inferior and disorganized, whereas Mercury thinks the Sun pompous and overbearing. It could even be the other way around – the Sun feeling mentally inferior – and so their ego overcompensates. The truth is that the Sun individual is shedding light on the Mercury affairs of the other, and Mercury cleverly or caustically comments on the Sun's life generally. In this way, both of you reveal not only shortcomings but positive avenues that could be taken to improve your minds and lives generally and your working lives in particular. But the superior stance the Sun takes can make Mercury defensive and so not benefit from their light, such as it is, by not taking them seriously. This can even reach a point where Mercury sees the Sun merely as a figure of fun, which causes the Sun to look down on them even more. If the Sun could learn to be more noble and less conceited it would pre-empt this defensive reaction.

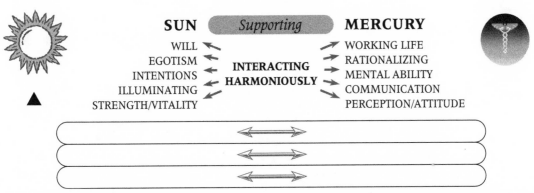

SUN *Supporting* **MERCURY**

WILL
EGOTISM
INTENTIONS
ILLUMINATING
STRENGTH/VITALITY

**INTERACTING
HARMONIOUSLY**

WORKING LIFE
RATIONALIZING
MENTAL ABILITY
COMMUNICATION
PERCEPTION/ATTITUDE

You have no trouble communicating, especially with regard to the more objective or non-emotional issues of life. This is a good aspect for intellectual companionship, and so also favours any working partnership. Whether or not such good mental rapport touches upon the more nitty-gritty aspects of your relationship would rest with the quality of any Interaction involving the Moon, Mars, Saturn and Pluto in each of your charts. But you can certainly assist one another in the development of your minds and careers, giving confidence to one another in these areas as you do so.

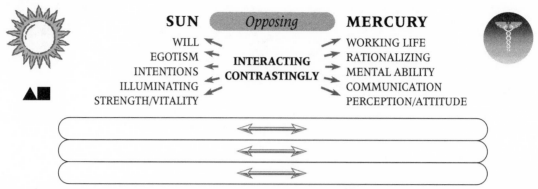

SUN *Opposing* **MERCURY**

WILL		WORKING LIFE
EGOTISM	**INTERACTING**	RATIONALIZING
INTENTIONS	**CONTRASTINGLY**	MENTAL ABILITY
ILLUMINATING		COMMUNICATION
STRENGTH/VITALITY		PERCEPTION/ATTITUDE

Essentially, the Sun person feels in a superior position to the Mercury person. This is because Mercury only has their point of view to offer the Sun or confront them with, whereas the Sun has their whole will and life-style with which to either overwhelm, ignore or approve of Mercury. Of course, if Mercury is very sure of themselves mentally and the Sun person's will is not that developed, it would be a different story – but it would not amount to a balanced or satisfying relationship. This Interaction is therefore about the Sun taking on board what Mercury has to say, and not just resisting or criticizing out of wounded or threatened pride. Mercury, on the other hand, should see themselves as some sort of advisor to a dignitary, and not presume upon their mental connection or prowess. Bearing all this in mind, you can learn a great deal from one another.

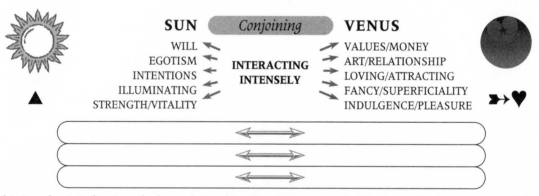

SUN *Conjoining* **VENUS**

WILL		VALUES/MONEY
EGOTISM	**INTERACTING**	ART/RELATIONSHIP
INTENTIONS	**INTENSELY**	LOVING/ATTRACTING
ILLUMINATING		FANCY/SUPERFICIALITY
STRENGTH/VITALITY		INDULGENCE/PLEASURE

This is a classic indication of a love relationship. The Venus person bathes in the Sun's expression of their personality, responding with an appreciation and affection that is immediately pleasing and attractive to the Sun person. Simultaneously, the Venus person feels warmed and filled with loving energy from the Sun person. As long as this mutual admiration and pleasure in each other's company does not devolve into a fanciful and superficially romantic relationship, where heavier emotions build up unattended to, then you can develop a loving, caring and creative relationship. Such an Interaction also greatly favours any artistic endeavours that you might be involved in for it is evident that you make pleasing 'music' together, literally or figuratively. Socializing and having fun together are also strong points, again as long as they do not become so indulgent or hedonistic that you lose sight of each other as individual emotional beings.

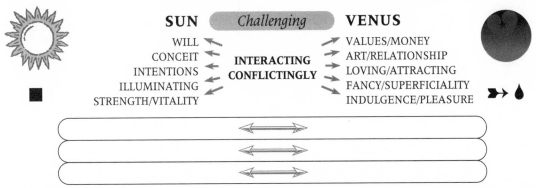

SUN *Challenging* **VENUS**

WILL
CONCEIT — **INTERACTING**
INTENTIONS **CONFLICTINGLY**
ILLUMINATING
STRENGTH/VITALITY

VALUES/MONEY
ART/RELATIONSHIP
LOVING/ATTRACTING
FANCY/SUPERFICIALITY
INDULGENCE/PLEASURE

This Interaction can amount to being one of Cupid's most capricious darts. You are drawn together for relatively superficial and indulgent reasons, but at the time it will have seemed quite, even intensely, romantic. But as time goes by the differences between you make it uncomfortably clear that your values and intentions are at odds with one another. The Venus person seems less and less able to please the Sun person, and the Sun feels that Venus is beneath them. It would seem that the Sun's point of view is obscured by their chagrin at not having things as they like them, while Venus expresses the very traits which rub this in. Love and vanity make poor companions, with the result that there is no real understanding or sympathy between you – or at least, it is not provided by this aspect on its own. If the Sun person could be less egotistical and the Venus person more sure of their worth then all would be well, but the very nature of this Interaction spells out that this is probably just not the case – yet ultimately these are the respective lessons you have to learn, with or without one another.

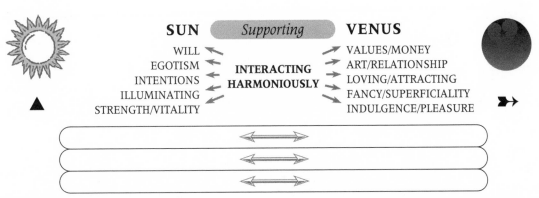

SUN *Supporting* **VENUS**

WILL
EGOTISM **INTERACTING**
INTENTIONS **HARMONIOUSLY**
ILLUMINATING
STRENGTH/VITALITY

VALUES/MONEY
ART/RELATIONSHIP
LOVING/ATTRACTING
FANCY/SUPERFICIALITY
INDULGENCE/PLEASURE

Being together brings out a heightened sense of fun and harmony. Not only that, but you find each other attractive in an easy sort of way. There is a great deal that you readily agree upon, and so others like to be around you – be they friends, children or business associates. There can even be a feeling of wealth about you that may very well attract that very thing if other Interactions support this. Hopefully there are dynamic and challenging aspects between you that drive you to achieve something, because this Interaction can incline you to being a bit lazy, even complacent. But apart from that, you have a delightful and enjoyable chemistry that graces any situation, but especially social gatherings such as parties.

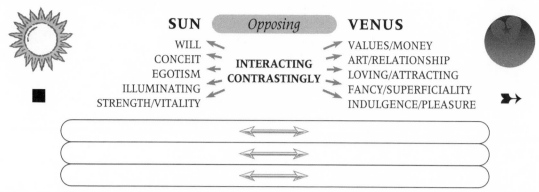

SUN *Opposing* **VENUS**

WILL
CONCEIT
EGOTISM
ILLUMINATING
STRENGTH/VITALITY

**INTERACTING
CONTRASTINGLY**

VALUES/MONEY
ART/RELATIONSHIP
LOVING/ATTRACTING
FANCY/SUPERFICIALITY
INDULGENCE/PLEASURE

This is an odd Interaction for it means that your attraction and affection for one another is blighted by a certain sense of distance and dissatisfaction. It is as if one, or both, of you is drawn to something in the other which you later find is not really to your liking, but you seem stuck with each other all the same. If it is just one of you that experiences this, then the relationship can also wind up being decidedly one-sided. The most likely reason for either case is that vanity and superficial appeal have become ensnared by one another. In other words, you are being confronted with the perils of superficial or romantic notions of love and the only way of putting matters right is either by deepening your love through recognizing what it really is that you feel genuinely for in each other, or to accept the fact that you have been the victims of your own fancies and call it a day. If there are other commitments, such as having children, then the former course would appear to be compulsory – or at least, something you must try very hard at.

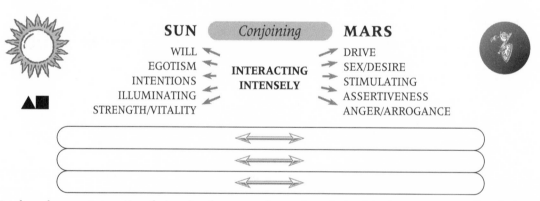

SUN *Conjoining* **MARS**

WILL
EGOTISM
INTENTIONS
ILLUMINATING
STRENGTH/VITALITY

**INTERACTING
INTENSELY**

DRIVE
SEX/DESIRE
STIMULATING
ASSERTIVENESS
ANGER/ARROGANCE

You have here an Interaction that makes for a sexual or active relationship, but not necessarily a loving or affectionate one. In itself then, this aspect gives you a greater energy together as a couple than you'd have individually, and so you can get a lot done, go many places together, and, if it is a sexual relationship, find each other very stimulating. Whatever the case, you arouse one another. You can also be quite competitive. But there comes a point where a lack of care and tenderness can cause you actually to wear one another out. This can also be the case if you do not allow one another the time and space to do your own thing as individuals. Mars is, after all, the God of War, so fighting can easily replace passion and the enjoyment of the physical aspects of life. If you find that the sexual or sporting/competitive area is 'hot' for you, make sure that there are also some harmonious and intellectual connections between you. Otherwise it will just become rather basic and dissatisfying, if not downright combative. Your combined energies can, as I say, achieve a great deal in whatever field you choose, but there is always a danger of pushing yourselves or others, or both, too hard.

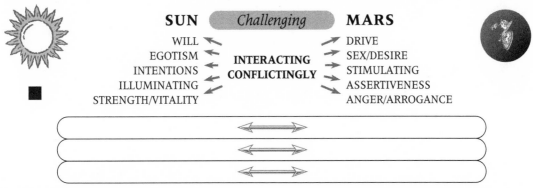

SUN *Challenging* **MARS**

WILL	DRIVE
EGOTISM	**INTERACTING**	SEX/DESIRE
INTENTIONS	**CONFLICTINGLY**	STIMULATING
ILLUMINATING	ASSERTIVENESS
STRENGTH/VITALITY	ANGER/ARROGANCE

This Interaction represents a battle zone in your relationship which unfortunately is likely to spread to other areas as well. And talking of battles, there is a 'soldierly' or masculine quality to the way you interact generally. So there can be an impulsive, 'let's go and do it' approach to things, but little receptivity, tenderness or passivity. This is especially noticeable if yours is a sexual relationship, meaning that it can be very exciting and immediate up until the point where it becomes too coarse or one-dimensional for one or both of you. But more basically, your egos are at war with one another, and only a good amount of harmonious Interaction could prevent this Interaction from making your lives a misery of conflict, which may even include physical combat. Going back to the 'soldier' analogy, the Sun person treats the Mars person as the squaddie who has to be constantly told what to do. This riles Mars to the point that they eventually mutiny in some way. Or they may simply snap at the heels of the Sun in a terrier-like fashion, thereby attracting more scorn and bossiness from the Sun. Through this Interaction you could each learn a lot about how effective you are, or need to be, in asserting or defending yourself. Ideally you should learn this after a battle or two, rather than living an ongoing war together.

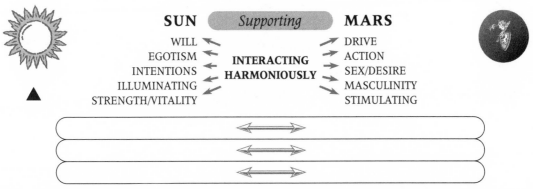

SUN *Supporting* **MARS**

WILL	DRIVE
EGOTISM	**INTERACTING**	ACTION
INTENTIONS	**HARMONIOUSLY**	SEX/DESIRE
ILLUMINATING	MASCULINITY
STRENGTH/VITALITY	STIMULATING

This is a very positive Interaction for it means that your intentions and actions are in sync with each other. And so activities and projects are executed swiftly, enthusiastically and efficiently. There is also a natural sexual harmony between you, at least on a purely physical level of expression. In fact, this Interaction is quite basic for it makes it clear who wants what, who's on top, etc. If this can be accepted as enough then this Interaction would act as a strong contribution to your relationship being lasting and satisfying. You are able to keeps things simple with a kind of 'go for it or forget it' attitude. This can ease and overcome many difficulties that might arise, but not those of a more complex psychological variety. The asset of this Interaction is that it makes you as a couple quite brisk, as long as it does not cause you to skip more subtle issues. Sporting activities are also something you may enjoy together or even excel in.

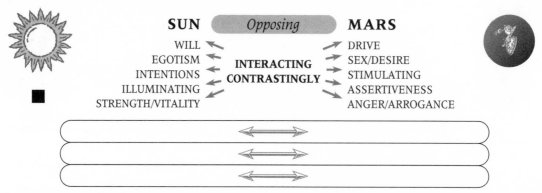

SUN | *Opposing* | MARS

WILL | | DRIVE
EGOTISM | **INTERACTING** | SEX/DESIRE
INTENTIONS | **CONTRASTINGLY** | STIMULATING
ILLUMINATING | | ASSERTIVENESS
STRENGTH/VITALITY | | ANGER/ARROGANCE

The Sun person makes the Mars person more aware of their independence (or lack of it) and sexuality. The Sun may not do this consciously. They may in fact do so inadvertently by treating Mars as a lesser being, somewhat like an officer would regard one of his men. And so Mars may have to strike out on their own, but this is precisely how they find themselves – and is the meaning of this Interaction, for Mars at least. However, it probably will not go as simply as this. The Sun will have their ego pricked by Mars's fighting back, and try to stop them going or get them back. But Mars is not what they want back, it is their self-esteem. And so the basic competition or incompatibility that is the core of this Interaction plays itself out in this way, with many a fight and a lonely space in between. This aspect is not one of love in the romantically or generally accepted sense of being close and together, for it is stressing the need for each of you to be an independent individual in your own right, sometimes in quite a crude and hard way. If yours is a sexual relationship, this hardness and lack of love can be quite noticeable – and add to the separativeness of this Interaction. This aspect can exist in long, ongoing relationships, but other things will be holding you together while the battle persists as some form of keeping you both on your toes, or more seriously, as a means of bringing home the importance of independence within a relationship, something which one of you is resisting and the other contesting.

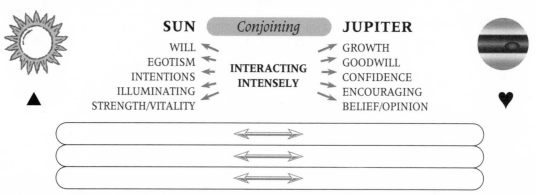

SUN | *Conjoining* | JUPITER

WILL | | GROWTH
EGOTISM | **INTERACTING** | GOODWILL
INTENTIONS | **INTENSELY** | CONFIDENCE
ILLUMINATING | | ENCOURAGING
STRENGTH/VITALITY | | BELIEF/OPINION

You have an affinity with each other that is very healthy and honest. Not only are you mutually supportive and encouraging, but as a couple you both go out of your way to be helpful and generous towards others. Owing to this, and a generally good feel about the pair of you, you are popular. Naturally enough, this Interaction favours being parents or anyone in authority, not least because there is always a benign quality about you and between you. This is one of the few Interactions that is entirely positive, and it goes a long way to overcoming friction and disagreement indicated elsewhere. This could be further aided by the fact that, together or individually, you might follow some definite moral code or spiritual discipline. It must be pointed out that this is not an emotional Interaction – it can even be quite impersonal – and so it does not in itself indicate romance, just that good feeling. This all promises that – mentally or spiritually, materially or emotionally – to some degree you will grow, as partners or as individuals, as a result of your time together.

The greatest act of love is to love the unlovable ...

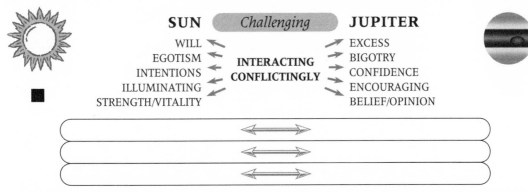

SUN *Challenging* **JUPITER**

WILL		EXCESS
EGOTISM	**INTERACTING**	BIGOTRY
INTENTIONS	**CONFLICTINGLY**	CONFIDENCE
ILLUMINATING		ENCOURAGING
STRENGTH/VITALITY		BELIEF/OPINION

The beliefs and philosophy of the Jupiter person either get in the way of the Sun person freely expressing themselves or make them want continually to get the better of them. At the same time, you both encourage each other's excesses, wasting quite a lot of energy and time as you do so. Your relationship can eventually take on a 'believers versus infidels' quality as you progressively mount one 'holy crusade' after another against each other. It has to be said that you can have quite a lot of fun and horseplay together, but will also regularly fall out with each other. Each of you just has to be right all the time, and so a true intimacy is not made possible, at least, not by this Interaction. Distance and travel can also be a part of this Interaction that brings adventure, but it exacerbates, or simply externalizes, differences in philosophy or cultural outlook. Your conflicting egos and beliefs drive formidable wedges between you. This aspect of your relationship is quite 'male', which tends, on its own account, to exclude the presence of sympathy and tolerance.

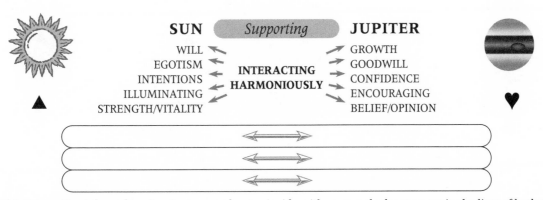

SUN *Supporting* **JUPITER**

WILL		GROWTH
EGOTISM	**INTERACTING**	GOODWILL
INTENTIONS	**HARMONIOUSLY**	CONFIDENCE
ILLUMINATING		ENCOURAGING
STRENGTH/VITALITY		BELIEF/OPINION

This Interaction is bound to give rise to, or at least coincide with, personal advancement in the lives of both of you. The hallmark of this excellent aspect is that you help one another to improve your personal lots in a way that is altruistic. There is no thought of doing what one of you does for the other as requiring or deserving any sort of 'payment' – although one paying the other for something to help them out is a good example of the generosity that this coupling engenders. This is all the more significant when considering that it is not just each other's individual ambitions that you each assist, but rather something for the both of you. Of course, it could be said that what helps the one in a partnership also helps the other, and indeed this is the essence of such a coupling – but in a more far-reaching way than either of you may yet appreciate. As planetary symbols, the Sun and Jupiter are all about prospering and growing – but in a wonderfully impersonal way. So this aspect of your relationship is a real gift, a boost to, or restoring of, a belief that life is something great, holy even. You also make good travelling companions for you believe that the road (of life) will take you where it will – together or apart, as you have a respect for each other's freedom.

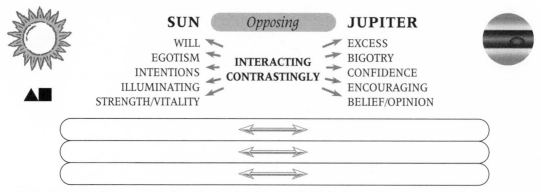

SUN	*Opposing*	JUPITER
WILL		EXCESS
EGOTISM	**INTERACTING**	BIGOTRY
INTENTIONS	**CONTRASTINGLY**	CONFIDENCE
ILLUMINATING		ENCOURAGING
STRENGTH/VITALITY		BELIEF/OPINION

As both of these planets are inclined to be bright and playful, there is a general atmosphere of good-naturedness between the two of you. But this is called upon again and again to overcome or diffuse the strong clashes that occur between the Sun person's ego and life-style, and the Jupiter person's philosophy and beliefs. The Sun is all too likely to regard Jupiter as a hypocritical know-it-all, preaching and moralizing. On the other hand Jupiter sees the Sun as too proud for their own good, and unable to view things from what they regard as their superior mental overview. The fact remains that you are poles apart in these important respects, and that it would be wise to take the differences on board and, by contrast, benefit from getting a clearer idea of your individual standpoints. Then you will each become more sure of that standpoint and not waste time and energy trying to defend or prove it to the opposing camp. Jupiter may need to remind themself that are three ways of teaching: by example, by example and by example. And the Sun will be subtly reminded of how enlightening Jupiter's view can be when it is no longer so readily offered – or available at all.

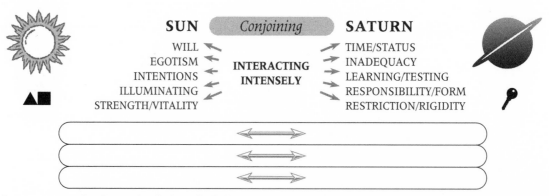

SUN	*Conjoining*	SATURN
WILL		TIME/STATUS
EGOTISM	**INTERACTING**	INADEQUACY
INTENTIONS	**INTENSELY**	LEARNING/TESTING
ILLUMINATING		RESPONSIBILITY/FORM
STRENGTH/VITALITY		RESTRICTION/RIGIDITY

The Sun person brightens the dark or doubtful areas of Saturn's personality or life, while Saturn gives the Sun a sense of purpose and position in life. Negatively, however, Saturn can darken, resent or suppress what is bright in the Sun, while the Sun can make Saturn feel (even more) dull or inadequate by comparison. There is also something rather timely about your coming together, which is why it is a Key Contact. There is a serious reason for your being involved. This is not a romantic connection in itself – it could very much be a business relationship – but it is highly significant. Both of you should become more worldly and responsible as a result of interacting; this may even mark a first step towards adulthood, parenthood or maturity. As long as you both appreciate that the Sun-half provides the light and confidence, and that Saturn provides the sense of order and limitation – and do not allow one to dazzle or blot out the other – then this can contribute to a very stable and long-lasting, or simply learning, relationship.

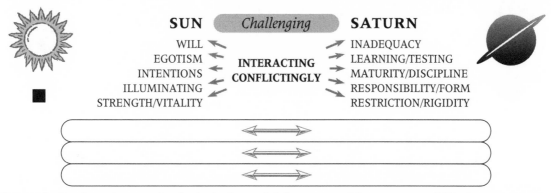

You are inclined to trigger each other's doubts and defences – so this can prove a difficult aspect to your relationship. It is rather as if one of you is the 'monarch' (Sun) and the other is 'president/prime minister' (Saturn). You both have or want a sense of power and position, and feel that the other threatens it in some way. The Sun person is brighter and more outgoing in the use and expression of themselves and their way of life. The Saturn person is more conservative, traditional, and toes some sort of party line. Possibly the common ground that you do have is one or each of you wishing to maintain your individual integrity. And so it would be fruitful to earn each other's respect through showing that you both stick to your principles – even though they are very different – and defer to the other if they have honourably proved their point. All this will take time, which poses the necessity of there being a commitment to a duty that goes beyond your ego conflict – like being parents, for example. Basically, a balance needs to be struck between the Sun's expansive and generous nature, and Saturn's restraining and cautious one. You both have an important contribution to make to whatever is the substance of your relationship, but the Sun is being forced to learn that restrictions can have great value, and Saturn to trust that matters will unfold creatively and should not be controlled too much. Failing to understand these apparently opposing laws of good 'government' can cause one or both of you, or the relationship itself, to fall from grace.

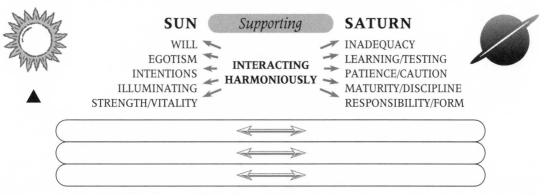

This Interaction lends itself well to any kind of organization. As a couple you can function in a businesslike way, with each determining and knowing what roles to play or responsibilities to fulfil. This is by no means a romantic connection for it emphasizes the importance of the mundane and material side of life. Because of this, as a couple you can create stability and durability as far as any other emotional contacts will allow or demand. In terms of what you do for each other, the Sun person can bring some light and play into the overly serious or even downcast areas of the Saturn person's life, while the Sun is given a sense of order and tradition by Saturn. If the Saturn person is the older of the two of you then this coupling will accentuate these positive attributes, which means that the sense of order provided by that individual is more likely to be quite real and substantial. In any event, the stability and order, which is the hallmark of this Interaction, can be attained if the two of you establish some rules and limitations that you are both happy to keep to. Notwithstanding other Interactions, this aspect does confer mutual trust and reliability.

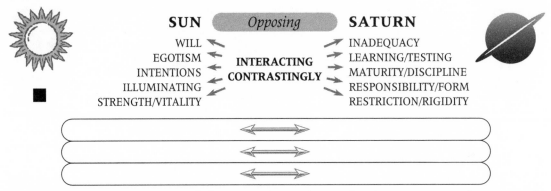

SUN *Opposing* **SATURN**

WILL	INADEQUACY
EGOTISM	LEARNING/TESTING
INTENTIONS	MATURITY/DISCIPLINE
ILLUMINATING	RESPONSIBILITY/FORM
STRENGTH/VITALITY	RESTRICTION/RIGIDITY

INTERACTING CONTRASTINGLY

With what they think they are sure of, the Sun person confronts what the Saturn person is not sure of in themselves. Alternatively, or as a response to this confrontation by the Sun, Saturn will suppress and dampen the Sun's self-expression – they may even sense what is coming from the Sun unconsciously, and withdraw or suppress them from the outset. This very inharmonious and unromantic Interaction probably occurs at a time in their life when the Sun person needs to learn to be sure enough of themselves so as not to over-compensate by over-asserting their strong points at the expense of another person's weak ones. Conversely, Saturn needs to take a good hard look at the weaker side of their personality, rather then leaving it to rot in the shadows. This is a 'Light versus Shade' Interaction; Saturn can resent the brightness and apparently strident confidence of the Sun person, while the Sun finds the Saturn person fearful, too cautious or boringly conservative. Saturn re-presents the Sun's shadow or weak side, whereas Saturn's shadow is re-presented by the bright Sun. Both planets have to do with authority, but of different types (*see* Sun Challenging Saturn above). As such, it makes for a poor boss/employer, teacher/student or parent/child relationship – simply because it will not be clear who is actually in charge. As previously stated, so much depends on how sure of their pitch each person is. If one is truly confident then they will feel no need to get into a conflict of wills with the other. But the very nature of this Interaction seems to attract individuals and couples who have yet to attain this kind of true self-assuredness.

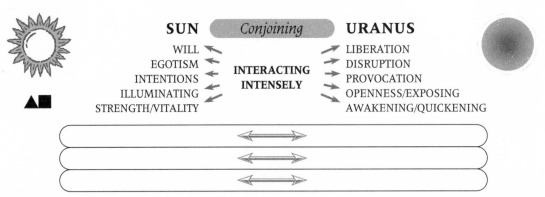

SUN *Conjoining* **URANUS**

WILL	LIBERATION
EGOTISM	DISRUPTION
INTENTIONS	PROVOCATION
ILLUMINATING	OPENNESS/EXPOSING
STRENGTH/VITALITY	AWAKENING/QUICKENING

INTERACTING INTENSELY

This is a bit like sunshine and lightning coming into exciting and flashy contact. You can both feel very plugged into one another, but it is rather like trying to hold a 10,000 volt charge steady. This is an odd Interaction because it seems to promise or threaten so much but, like lightning or sunshine, it can be gone in an instant. However, for as long as you can stay steady enough or even manage to be in each other's presence, you can both experience some strange and extraordinary sensations – some thrilling, some uncomfortable. There is also an underlying sense of 'where is this supposed to be going?' and 'what happens next?'. This of course adds to the crackle and sizzle between the two of you, but it also points to the innate instability of this contact – at least, for any kind of ongoing emotional relationship. It has to be said that this is very

If a relationship is tired, bored or lost, pretend you have just met ...

unlikely, a word that could also be used to describe you as a couple should you become one. But still this sort of electromagnetic connection persists. It may be that this unusual Interaction is only really for doing unusual things, like some kind of magical or esoteric activity, or just for having fun. Or perhaps it would put one or both of you in touch with an alternative side to life. One of you may be an outsider while the other is quite conventional, and you both have something to show one another in this respect. In the end, this Interaction is rather like a firework display, lots of ooh-ing and aah-ing, but rather anticlimactic. Keeping or living up to what it so erratically promises would necessitate having a decidedly odd life-style, one that precludes the normal routines that make things manageable but at times comparatively dull. Whether or not it occurs to either of you, there is the notion that your encounter should have happened, or will happen, at another time, another place. More to the point though, it is some kind of 'wake-up call' to both of you, right here and now.

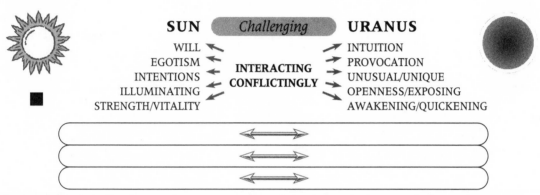

SUN *Challenging* **URANUS**

WILL	INTUITION
EGOTISM	PROVOCATION
INTENTIONS	UNUSUAL/UNIQUE
ILLUMINATING	OPENNESS/EXPOSING
STRENGTH/VITALITY	AWAKENING/QUICKENING

INTERACTING CONFLICTINGLY

The Sun person is inclined to see the Uranus person as being interestingly eccentric, but at the same time as being a bit of a loose cannon. Uranus, for their part, has mixed feelings of admiration and rebelliousness towards the Sun. This Interaction could be called 'Royalists versus Republicans'. Uranus is especially outraged by any signs of autocracy from the Sun, and will do all they can to rattle their cage. In return, the Sun will patronizingly humour Uranus or, depending upon the Sun's personal influence or social position, cause them to feel an outcast and an outsider whose ideas are totally off the wall. But Uranus will respond to this with renewed revolutionary zeal. This can amount to anything from actually sabotaging the Sun's position to more subtle psychological tactics, such as detaching themselves in a way that piques the Sun's pride. In the end, the Sun needs to be more honourable, and Uranus absolutely truthful. The Sun is, or appears to be, in the 'ruling position', and as such, should grant Uranus credit where it is due for their laser-like perception of how things actually are. And if Uranus is reacting and uptight, then they themselves should wake up to the fact that this is because they are unable to detach themselves, and so are therefore part of the problem that they are so ready to accuse the Sun of creating.

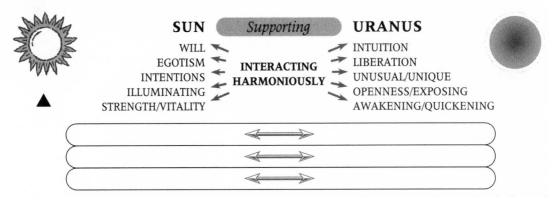

SUN *Supporting* **URANUS**

SUN		URANUS
WILL		INTUITION
EGOTISM	**INTERACTING**	LIBERATION
INTENTIONS	**HARMONIOUSLY**	UNUSUAL/UNIQUE
ILLUMINATING		OPENNESS/EXPOSING
STRENGTH/VITALITY		AWAKENING/QUICKENING

You have a very positive Interaction because it has something that all too many relationships lack: a true sense of friendship. This means that you allow each other room to be yourselves, are open with one another, and that there is little or no possessiveness about each other. The Uranus person has a liberating and awakening effect upon the Sun person, giving them new ideas and directions. Alternative or metaphysical subjects are very likely to be the means through which this effect happens, and you may well have met in a situation that was related to such matters. Groups involved in esoteric or unusual pursuits can be a significant part of your time together. In return, the Sun individual validates or furthers the Uranus individual's more original expressions and qualities, rather like a monarch would patronize an artist. All of this positive Interaction makes for a mutual attraction, mentally and/or physically, yet it does not necessarily confer the emotional stability that ensures a lasting tie. Paradoxically though, because you are always surprising one another with hitherto unknown facets of your characters, this relationship has a self-refreshing quality about it. Whatever the case though, that outstanding friendship should remain.

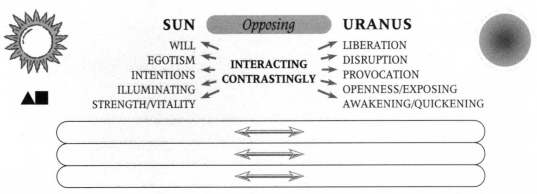

SUN *Opposing* **URANUS**

SUN		URANUS
WILL		LIBERATION
EGOTISM	**INTERACTING**	DISRUPTION
INTENTIONS	**CONTRASTINGLY**	PROVOCATION
ILLUMINATING		OPENNESS/EXPOSING
STRENGTH/VITALITY		AWAKENING/QUICKENING

You have an exciting but unstable Interaction which demands a great deal of space and freedom for both of you. At least as far as this aspect is concerned, your relationship could never be described as cosy! The Uranus person takes exception to the Sun's overbearing nature and intuitively discovers ways of putting a spoke in their wheel. But the more they rattle the Sun person's cage, the more dictatorial the Sun becomes by way of reaction, and so on and so on. If both of you have a bit of humility and willingness to learn from one another, you can become aware of the ways in which you might queer your own pitches, rather than others'. Such a positive way of dealing with this Interaction would also need to find the Sun person somehow eliciting respect from the Uranus person. And Uranus would have to put the Sun really on the spot to make them understand that they hadn't got all their bases covered. From out of all this a mutually enlightening friendship could emerge, but a lasting intimate relationship would be a rarity.

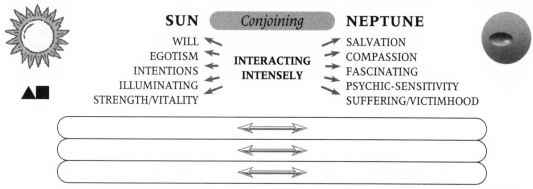

SUN *Conjoining* **NEPTUNE**

WILL	**INTERACTING**	SALVATION
EGOTISM	**INTENSELY**	COMPASSION
INTENTIONS		FASCINATING
ILLUMINATING		PSYCHIC-SENSITIVITY
STRENGTH/VITALITY		SUFFERING/VICTIMHOOD

⟺ The range of feelings and experiences that this Interaction can create in and for you both is vast. Perhaps the spectrum could be described as stretching between the spiritual and creative at one end, to the addictive and confusing at the other. This spectrum of feeling and experience could itself be called one of mutual fascination or inspiration. But then again it could be or become quite one-sided where one of you is, or is seen to be, in a weak position (probably Neptune, but not always) and the other in a strong one (probably the Sun, but not always). So one scenario could be that one of you is fascinated by the other for some reason – bewitching eyes, a psychic sense of having met in a previous life, artistic talent, or some such thing – but the other is not that interested. Or you could both be under each other's spell and lose all sight of the real world and its responsibilities. Or you embark together on some kind of inner journey. Or one of you is by a peculiar twist of circumstances having to help the other with some affliction or addiction. The list is endless, but it will always be somewhere on that spectrum. And underlying whatever the scenario might be, consciously or unconsciously, there is some mysterious or karmic tie, or a debt to be repaid, or something to be lived out for reasons that are hard to fathom. Because of all this, deception and/or illusion are quite likely to be somewhere on the menu. A more precise reason for this could be that one of you is trying to keep to something, while the other is trying to avoid it. This Interaction can take you to Heaven and then to Hell and then back to Earth. A spiritual or creative reason for your being together is the healthiest and sanest way of handling this Interaction. This means to say that seeking enlightenment or relief, for yourselves or others, gives your relationship the path that it is designed for. Imagination and sensitivity create the chemistry between you, and it is highly important that you use them both wisely and constructively, guided by something inner or divine, rather than let either of them get the better of you.

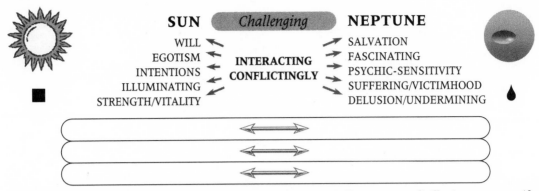

SUN   *Challenging*   **NEPTUNE**

WILL		SALVATION
EGOTISM	**INTERACTING**	FASCINATING
INTENTIONS	**CONFLICTINGLY**	PSYCHIC-SENSITIVITY
ILLUMINATING		SUFFERING/VICTIMHOOD
STRENGTH/VITALITY		DELUSION/UNDERMINING

⟺ Your relationship can start off as a fatal fascination but eventually encounter disillusionment – or, if not dealt with, even end in it. This is because one or both of you, on first meeting the other, will present their most attractive and glamorous side of themselves, blended with whatever the other expects this to be. This is a bit like sunshine sparkling on and off the surface of water. But come nightfall there can be just a dull grey limpid mass – that is, sooner or later the mirage evaporates and the real and vulnerable person remains. Unless one of you is some kind of spiritual master (in which case they wouldn't have been taken in first of all) they will then find that what they thought was a knight in shining armour or a damsel in distress is by comparison rather pathetic. But, continuing with the Sun-reflected-on-the-water metaphor, they are really seeing what is pathetic about themselves. But again, both of you will most likely try to bluff your way out of this uncomfortable realization, which is when the real trouble begins. One of you (probably, but not always, the Sun person) takes on the role of the one in charge and can make the other's life a misery by treating them like a slave, fool or fall guy. If not doing so already, then one or both of you may seek solace in some form of escape from the oppression – like alcohol, drugs or work, or eventually from out of the relationship altogether. However, this could prove difficult, because both of you are addicted to your own illusions of strength (Sun/ego) and weakness (Neptune/victim), which this Interaction so uncomfortably represents. Consequently, all manner of deception (self, unconscious or otherwise) can creep into the cracks that this Interaction opens up. So unless some rigorous creative, spiritual or therapeutic discipline is, or already has been, embarked upon by both of you, your relationship will become a leaky vessel that has only one fate.

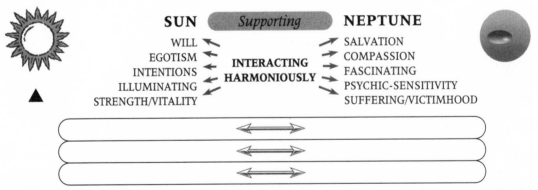

SUN   *Supporting*   **NEPTUNE**

WILL		SALVATION
EGOTISM	**INTERACTING**	COMPASSION
INTENTIONS	**HARMONIOUSLY**	FASCINATING
ILLUMINATING		PSYCHIC-SENSITIVITY
STRENGTH/VITALITY		SUFFERING/VICTIMHOOD

You have quite a spiritual or dreamy connection, and so flow together or apart as the current of life allows. Notwithstanding any other more passionate or possessive Interactions, you accept this gentle ebbing and flowing. Imagination, dance, music and the otherworldly can be elements that make up your relationship in a positive and creative way. One to one, the Sun person affirms and sheds light upon the Neptune person's sensitive areas, thereby helping them to express and deal with them better. Reciprocally, Neptune treats the Sun with the respect and sensitivity that causes them to feel more sure of themselves. There is a mutual blessing going on here, something which may not be that obvious to others, simply because the process is patently subtle. However, because there is a psychic link between you, others who are psychically attuned will pick up on it. This is not a robust connection by any means, but it knows how to go around obstacles – if you let it.

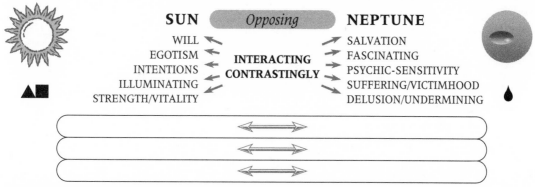

SUN *Opposing* **NEPTUNE**

WILL	**INTERACTING**	SALVATION
EGOTISM	**CONTRASTINGLY**	FASCINATING
INTENTIONS		PSYCHIC-SENSITIVITY
ILLUMINATING		SUFFERING/VICTIMHOOD
STRENGTH/VITALITY		DELUSION/UNDERMINING

⟺ The Sun is bright and outgoing and set upon creating an impression, proving a point, and being seen to be important. Neptune, on the other hand, is mysterious and diffuse, passive and evasive. Positively, you can both tune into the ethereal and theatrical, the musical and romantic, feeding each other's dreams and fantasies. Negatively, the Neptune person is inclined to dodge and deceive in the face of what they feel to be the Sun's glaring and invasive ego as it attempts to pin Neptune to the wall, spotlighting their weaknesses. Neptune then responds with more evasiveness and fabrication as they reel against their delicate feelings being thus assaulted. If there are other Interactions which bestow some respect and decent communication, the two of you may eventually tune into the fact that you are both not only as sensitive as one another, but that you also have similar difficulties expressing or protecting that sensitivity. This is, after all, a psychic Interaction, and if paranoia can be avoided on one or both of your parts, then a subtle and curiously strong bond can develop. Having said this though, there is always the chance of some hidden hurt slipping in or of a mutual blind-spot being encouraged, thereby sabotaging that bond. This Interaction very much depends on respecting each other's emotional wounds and the sensitivity that attracted them or the distressed circumstances that inflicted them.

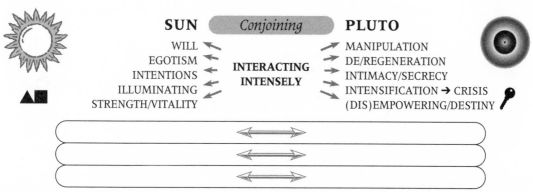

SUN *Conjoining* **PLUTO**

WILL	**INTERACTING**	MANIPULATION
EGOTISM	**INTENSELY**	DE/REGENERATION
INTENTIONS		INTIMACY/SECRECY
ILLUMINATING		INTENSIFICATION ➔ CRISIS
STRENGTH/VITALITY		(DIS)EMPOWERING/DESTINY

This is a journey into the Underworld – with or without a torch! The Pluto person takes the Sun down to levels of experience they would not have agreed to visiting had they first seen a brochure. Pluto sees the Sun as the light they want in their lives, but that too often means that they try to convert and remake the Sun person in the image of what they feel their hero/heroine ought to be. Psychologically speaking, the hero/heroine may be what they feel their father is or ought to have been like. Depending on what their father was/is actually like, they can also resent and even despise the Sun – especially if the Sun is forced to brandish their torch in order to maintain their individuality. If, however, such psychological complexes do not loom or are suitably dealt with, then this Interaction can take on the form of a mutually empowering and regenerative relationship. But it has to be said that some sort of purging has to take place first as your respective ego defence systems are given the once over – the reason being that they get in the way of the vibrant intimacy that is the true and deep intention of this Interaction. Whether this happens or not, you are each bound to become somewhat closer to your real selves, if not each other. In the fullness of time, you will realize how deeply affected you have been by the experience of being involved – or even nearly involved – with one another.

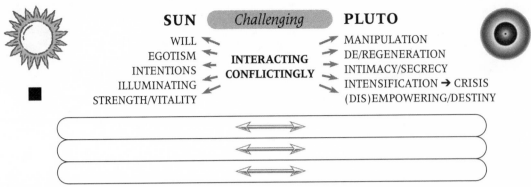

SUN *Challenging* **PLUTO**

SUN		PLUTO
WILL		MANIPULATION
EGOTISM	**INTERACTING**	DE/REGENERATION
INTENTIONS	**CONFLICTINGLY**	INTIMACY/SECRECY
ILLUMINATING		INTENSIFICATION → CRISIS
STRENGTH/VITALITY		(DIS)EMPOWERING/DESTINY

There is probably a great intimacy between the two of you, but this in itself becomes a problem, especially if this is a sexual relationship. In fact the sexual dimension is the main area of conflict and power struggle, and consequently where your relationship could come to grief. At first the feeling of being invaded and taken over is sexually attractive, particularly if the Pluto person is male. But eventually one or both of you, but most likely the Sun person, feels laid bare and robbed of their own will. Pluto, on the other hand, is rather like a moth drawn to a flame, but the intensity of such a pull can be interpreted by the Sun as being deliberately forceful – and it may be. In any event, this Interaction demands that both of you attain a more conscious awareness of the powerful effect that you can have on others generally, and on each other in particular. It may come as a surprise that every human being has this power potential in them, but it takes this kind of Interaction to spell out what kind of influence this can exert. So this intense and powerful contact is all too often destructive in some way, either partially or of the whole relationship. Basically, it is manifesting the dangers of any negative course either of you have set out upon – probably quite unconsciously, and possibly before your relationship even started. Underhand or morally questionable motives on the part of either of you are inevitably brought to a point of crisis. Whether or not you survive such a crisis as a couple, there is still a deep and lasting effect and lesson built into this relationship.

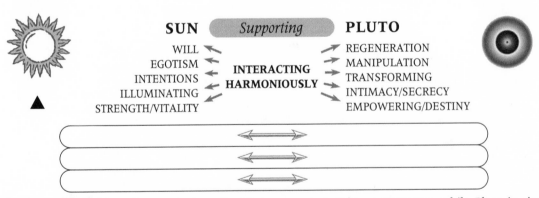

SUN *Supporting* **PLUTO**

SUN		PLUTO
WILL		REGENERATION
EGOTISM	**INTERACTING**	MANIPULATION
INTENTIONS	**HARMONIOUSLY**	TRANSFORMING
ILLUMINATING		INTIMACY/SECRECY
STRENGTH/VITALITY		EMPOWERING/DESTINY

The Sun individual benefits greatly from the Pluto person's insights or resources, while Pluto is given much needed confidence by the Sun's convincing appreciation or admiration of those very things. Together you can be the new broom that sweeps clean, clearing away obstacles to your progress and well-being, either individually or as a couple – or even for the area of society in which you operate. This is a mutually regenerative relationship and, other Interactions considered, can make for a longstanding and self-renewing partnership. With the support of similar Interactions, great wealth and/or power can be attained. In any event, you will both be the better for knowing one another.

... expecting it to last forever can be the death of a relationship ...

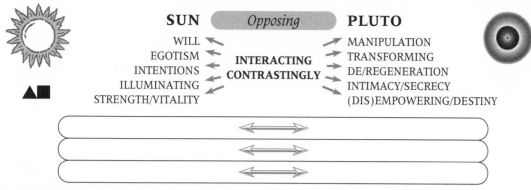

The Pluto individual inevitably tries to mould or transform the Sun person. What motives and values they have for doing this are the crucial issue, for they make the difference between it being a Svengali type of approach which can rob the Sun person of their own will and individuality, or through connecting very deeply with the core of the Sun's being, empowering them and giving them a far stronger sense of their own will. More often than not though, the nature of this Interaction will lie somewhere in between. This can mean that the Sun person, through resisting Pluto's negative or selfish attempts to change them, actually strengthens them and gets them more in touch with their own individuality. Before this occurs, however, the Sun might be taken quite low, especially with regard to moral or sexual behaviour. Alternatively, the Sun should endeavour to recognize and validate Pluto's positive moves to change and empower them, for the reason behind any of their negative efforts is a lurking doubt in their own personal influence. Whatever the case, Pluto can or should become more aware of their own power-plays and motivations to transform the Sun person. Ironically, the more that the Sun's will is empowered by Pluto, then the more they can resist and even boss around the Pluto individual. This can be the case from the outset if it is the Pluto person that is the less confident of the two of you. As long as this balance of power is understood and maintained, this Interaction can make for a mutually empowering relationship – but a battle of wills is an integral, and potentially healthy, part of this process.

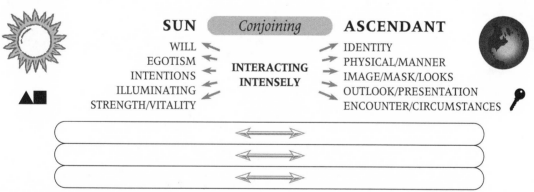

Your meeting should mark a new beginning for one or both of you. The Sun person is rather like a beam of light which shows the Ascendant person the path towards what they are supposed to become. If the Ascendant is looking for some way forward (or out), either consciously or unconsciously, encountering the Sun is a bit like a light being switched on for them. Not only are they made to see their way ahead more clearly, they also get a clearer idea of what their current circumstances are about. In fact this may come before seeing their way ahead, but only a little. Naturally enough, such a ready and positive response to their ego causes the Sun to behave in a confident and magnanimous fashion. Consequently, the two of you get off to a good, even dynamic, start which can, as I say, lead to a new path for one or both of you, either together or individually. A possible downside to all this bright Interaction could be that your respective egos and images become so intensified as to make you act rashly, and you both take on more than you originally thought you were taking on. So eventually competitiveness and being too much in each other's faces may be a problem. However, if there are other fast and furious Interactions between you, then the immediacy of this one will be irresistible. Sometimes life is running along rails, and all you can do is apply the brakes a bit, but if Fate wants you to switch tracks – you will. Seeing that this Interaction leads to a far stronger sense of yourselves and your abilities, you may as well toot your whistle and move on down the line – but watch out for amber or red signals!

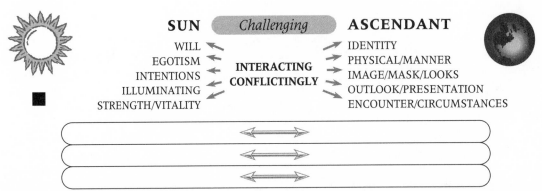

They may not show it, but the Ascendant person feels a little in the shadow of the Sun person. To them the Sun seems to have more going for them, rather like a child would feel when comparing themself to an adult. Probably unbeknown to the Ascendant though, the Sun feels the same about them. And so you have a mild contest of wills here, which, if owned up to, can lead to a rather clear idea of who you each are in your own right. Failing this, this Interaction will give rise to a petty competitiveness with each of you egocentrically trying to score points off one another.

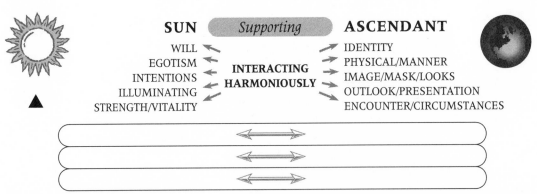

⇔ The Sun person makes the Ascendant feel more confident about their personal expression and appearance by helping them improve it, or simply appreciating it. Because of this positive effect, the Sun person feels that they have something going for them too. This healthy interchange can also work the other way around. Either way, this Interaction contributes a good feeling to any romantic or marital relationship. You are both confirming each other's existence and therefore get along consistently well.

The nature of all Interactions depends upon ...

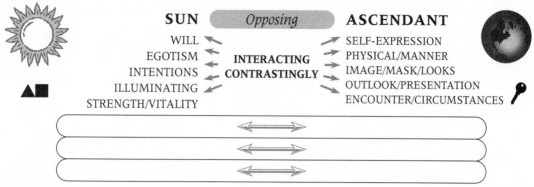

SUN *Opposing* **ASCENDANT**

WILL		SELF-EXPRESSION
EGOTISM	**INTERACTING**	PHYSICAL/MANNER
INTENTIONS	**CONTRASTINGLY**	IMAGE/MASK/LOOKS
ILLUMINATING		OUTLOOK/PRESENTATION
STRENGTH/VITALITY		ENCOUNTER/CIRCUMSTANCES

This is one of the two most significant Interactions of all (the other being Sun Conjoining Ascendant). This is because the will or ego of the Sun person finds its Mirror or Shadow in the manner and presentation of the Ascendant person – and vice versa. (If you wish to refresh your idea of these concepts of Mirror and Shadow, generally and personally, read or re-read about Rising and Setting Signs on page xxx, and your Rising and Setting Sign Profiles which begin on page xxx). Essentially, the Sun person is the Ascendant person's 'other half' – or at least, seems to be. Depending on the Ascendant person's level of self-awareness, they may or may not like some of this because it reflects back a part of themselves they have yet to come to terms with: their Shadow. The same is the case for the Sun person, with the Ascendant person embodying *their* other half. What the Sun person puts out unconsciously (that is, what is different or the opposite to what they are intending) is played back to them as the Ascendant person's manner of self-expression; and similarly, they may or may not like some of this. But just because you are embodying or reflecting each other's other half, there is a strong attraction between you – at least initially. As time goes by, seeing each of your alter egos externalized in the other in this way can provide a feeling of being made complete by each other. But as I have just pointed out, it can at times be objectionable to one or both of you. The great secret for success here, is to 'take back your projection', that is, to recognize and accept that it is your 'other half', warts and all, that makes you a more complete, and a stronger and better, person. In turn, this would possibly give you a relationship to match. As ever, a great deal depends upon the other Interactions between the two of you. But even if this does not turn out to be a marriage or meeting of soul-mates, this Interaction can so sharpen your sense of who you are or appear to be that, as a result of it, you are more able to recognize and attract someone who really is your other half – because of having learned what this really is in you.

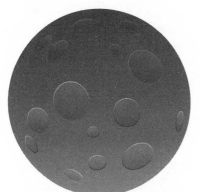

THE MOON

INTERACTING WITH

MOON   SATURN
MERCURY   URANUS
VENUS   NEPTUNE
MARS   PLUTO
JUPITER   ASCENDANT

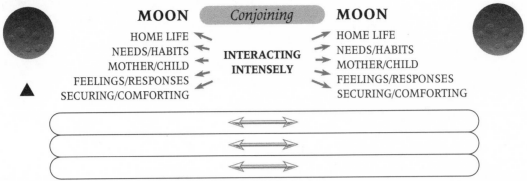

Your emotional rhythms and dispositions are very alike, which means that you not only mirror each other's highs but also your lows. You crest together and you trough together! Yet because you are so emotionally in step, you kind of surf side-by-side through these troughs and peaks. It also has to be said that a great deal depends upon the actual Moon Sign(s) in question, which will usually be the same. Check out the positive qualities and help one another to make them more so. Check out the negative qualities and make a pledge to each other to keep a wary eye out for getting simultaneously caught in any downward spiral. The trick here is not to go over the top when you're both on a high, otherwise the inevitable low could wipe you both out for a while or more. By and large though, you are excellently and instinctively well matched – peas in a pod, type of thing. Whatever or whoever is under your care should count themselves lucky – troughs notwithstanding!

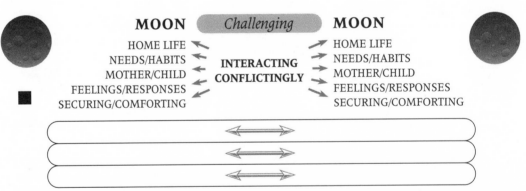

Your backgrounds and habits are different, possibly at odds with each other – or alternatively, there may actually be some sort of friction from the past. It is therefore difficult for you to get in step regarding such things as home and family life, and day-to-day co-existence. It is hard for you to find a 'flow' that allows you to relax into a life together. There may well be sympathy for one another, but it can be awkwardly expressed – possibly because of the general inconvenience that this Interaction brings. Consequently, this Interaction can cause a stale feeling to creep into the relationship – because there is not the fundamental 'soil' for it to grow in. It is very likely that your relationship has another agenda other than the Lunar, settling down, home-from-home type of thing. Sexual interest or family conflict could be the agenda. Indeed, the emotional difference between you can actually be sexually stimulating, but obviously the shelf-life of the relationship itself can be limited – unless of course you are both, rightly or wrongly, prepared to live with such basic emotional discord, and perhaps learn from it.

No one Interaction makes or breaks a relationship

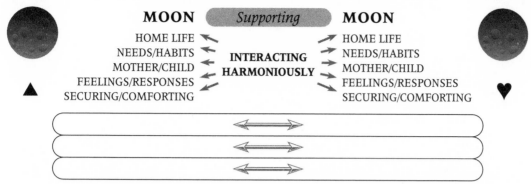

MOON *Supporting* **MOON**

HOME LIFE
NEEDS/HABITS
MOTHER/CHILD
FEELINGS/RESPONSES
SECURING/COMFORTING

**INTERACTING
HARMONIOUSLY**

HOME LIFE
NEEDS/HABITS
MOTHER/CHILD
FEELINGS/RESPONSES
SECURING/COMFORTING

This is one of the most basically favourable Interactions for it bestows upon the relationship personal and emotional harmony. Both of you feel relaxed and at ease in each other's company. So this strongly contributes to the underlying stability that is needed for a domestic, familial, intimate or business relationship – or, for that matter, any kind of relationship. As individuals you see eye-to-eye on such basic issues as what are deemed to be the really important values and qualities of a wholesome and healthy life. This is especially positive for bringing up children because as parents your united front on basic values gives your offspring a balanced and confident feeling about themselves and life. In fact, between the two of you there is a mutual emotional nurturing going on that can do much to heal your individual past wounds. Others find it comfortable to be around you, too. The child in the one of you brings out the child in the other – and thereby you find it easy to play with one another.

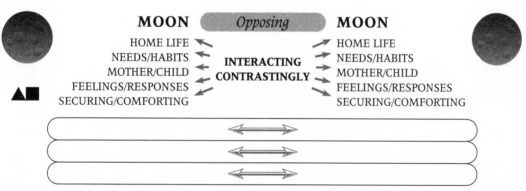

MOON *Opposing* **MOON**

HOME LIFE
NEEDS/HABITS
MOTHER/CHILD
FEELINGS/RESPONSES
SECURING/COMFORTING

**INTERACTING
CONTRASTINGLY**

HOME LIFE
NEEDS/HABITS
MOTHER/CHILD
FEELINGS/RESPONSES
SECURING/COMFORTING

You are involved in an Interaction of emotional extremes. You each bring out the other's feelings, good and bad, simply because they are so different. This serves to make you more aware of what kind of emotional animals you each are, but it can be a bit like a game of emotional poker as each of you keeps raising the bet. Eventually, it can become only too obvious that emotionally you are on different sides of the tracks. If you have harmony and good communication elsewhere, or a strong sense of yourselves as individuals, then your contrasting personalities can actually complement one another. You can then be a pair who 'cover the board' in whatever area it might be – social, creative or family. Two halves making a whole, in fact. And yet, the trouble with 'two halves' is that they meet but do not necessarily interpenetrate; you complement one another but do not integrate with each other. A great deal depends upon the Signs your respective Moons are in, and what you actually need from a relationship. If you both want to be a 'social unit' then this combination can, as I say, meet and cater for extremes externally. If, however, you need to feel more closely intertwined as an intimate couple in your own right, then Moon Opposing Moon will feel like the chalk and cheese that it is.

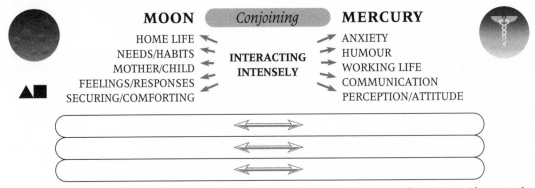

MOON *Conjoining* MERCURY

HOME LIFE		ANXIETY
NEEDS/HABITS	INTERACTING	HUMOUR
MOTHER/CHILD	INTENSELY	WORKING LIFE
FEELINGS/RESPONSES		COMMUNICATION
SECURING/COMFORTING		PERCEPTION/ATTITUDE

⟺ There is great immediacy and spontaneity in how you connect with one another. It is as if a part of one of you is plugged into a part of the other. If this sounds sexual it is not supposed to be, for this Interaction in itself has no specific indication of your being that way involved or attracted. However, such is your mutual ability to tune into each other and communicate what you find there, either verbally or kinaesthetically, that a sexual relationship – if you have one – would certainly not find you lost for words. Then again, just talking for the sake of it can be a bit of a waste of this excellent rapport that you possess – rather like watching television with the colour and contrast turned right down. In other words, the link between you is a sophisticated one, and is supposed to be used for conveying something of value and meaning. Because of this smart 'wire' that you have between you, you would also make a good team in any work situation. Again though, a constant 'brother/sister/schoolkid' kind of banter could drive colleagues nuts. If you have avoided or got out of this possible 'loop' of gossip, giggles or meaninglessness, then you can do wonders for helping each other – as well as friends, family and associates – by putting straight any emotional or intellectual problems you or they might have. In the process, however, Mercury should avoid being too dry and lacking in empathy as they rationalize the Moon's feelings in an attempt to clarify them, and the Moon should make some effort to keep their feelings in check and not be too subjective or become stuck in a rut. All the same, this Interaction is a testament to the saying 'A trouble shared is a trouble halved', or for that matter, 'Two heads are better than one'.

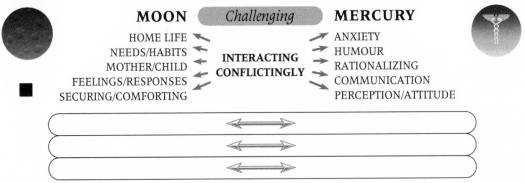

MOON *Challenging* MERCURY

HOME LIFE		ANXIETY
NEEDS/HABITS	INTERACTING	HUMOUR
MOTHER/CHILD	CONFLICTINGLY	RATIONALIZING
FEELINGS/RESPONSES		COMMUNICATION
SECURING/COMFORTING		PERCEPTION/ATTITUDE

⟺ This Interaction is particularly interchangeable, but I give here the usual roles that the Moon and Mercury play. This Interaction seriously affects the day-to-day affairs of both of you because the Moon person lives life in a more instinctive, emotionally-led fashion, while the Mercury person bases their activities on logic and work routines. There can therefore be disagreements over mundane issues like what food to eat, how to run domestic matters, personal cleanliness, use of time, etc. Habits such as the proverbial 'leaving the cap off the toothpaste' can aggravate the Mercury individual, while this kind of order seems irrelevant to the Moon person. The Moon may be seen as lazy and dominated by emotional issues such as past involvements and family problems, while Mercury is regarded as clinical and insensitive. If some kind of domestic or mundane, and therefore emotional, harmony is to exist, then Mercury has either to get accustomed to doing all those little tasks which the Moon leaves undone, or become a little bit more laid-back with respect to these issues. On the other hand, the Moon could learn to organize their lives partly along rational lines rather than solely on instinctual ones, and recognize the advantages of the everyday maintenance of things. This Interaction is very much a case of meeting each other half way, which is the basic remedy for all conflicts. With such a sense of grace, each of you can benefit from learning from the other: Mercury to become more emotionally aware in the sense of being perceptive of feelings rather than merely being technically 'right'; and the Moon to appreciate that having some kind of method or intellectual overview would actually assuage the emotional aggravation that Mercury gets blamed for inflicting with their demand for mental order.

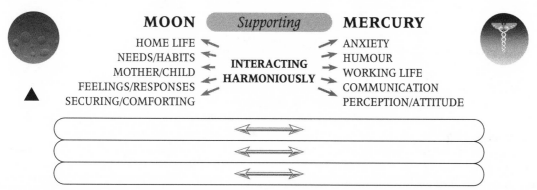

You have no trouble in communicating how you feel or the point either of you wish to make to the other. The difficult Interactions that you have with one another are to a large degree sorted out because you are able to be rational about matters but without becoming divorced from the emotional issues involved. As a rule, the Mercury individual is the one who contributes a clear mental viewpoint, while the Moon person provides a sense of emotional awareness and security, which aids the rational thinking of Mercury. Similarly, Mercury helps clarify the Moon's feelings, while the Moon helps out when Mercury gets stuck in their head. This Interaction also favours the work environment and makes for a common touch with regard to sensing what appeals to others in general, and what they feel comfortable with. Obviously, this can greatly benefit both the jobs and the emotional security of you as a couple, and for the same reasons you could work together well. Running through all this there is an ongoing banter and sense of childlike fun.

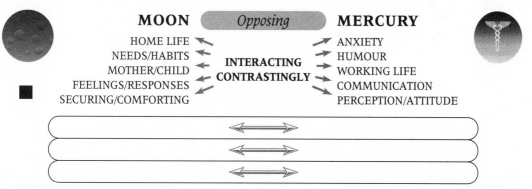

⟺ Because you approach one another from very different perspectives, there is the strong likelihood of mutual misunderstanding. It is a bit like trying to connect with each other's fingertips in the dark. In effect, the Mercury person uses a rational, intellectual approach where the Moon person is needing or expecting an emotional or sympathetic one, and vice versa, with Mercury not being able to identify what the Moon's pitch is. Consequently, Mercury perceives the Moon as vague or moody, while the Moon can experience Mercury as unfeeling or critical. As usual, this Interaction will not be operating all the time, especially if there are more positive Interactions between you, but it can tend to kick in at those times when your opposing expectations give rise to getting the wrong end of the stick at the crucial moment. Eventually, such perennial 'mis-connections' can render untenable an ongoing, everyday relationship. In small or occasional doses though, this Interaction can be quite stimulating or amusing.

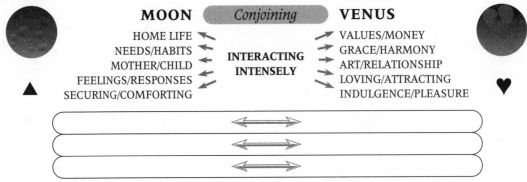

MOON *Conjoining* **VENUS**

HOME LIFE	VALUES/MONEY
NEEDS/HABITS	GRACE/HARMONY
MOTHER/CHILD	ART/RELATIONSHIP
FEELINGS/RESPONSES	LOVING/ATTRACTING
SECURING/COMFORTING	INDULGENCE/PLEASURE

INTERACTING INTENSELY

You have a feeling for each other that is both sympathetic and affectionate, caring and loving. If this sounds good, you're right, it is! This Interaction favours love, marriage, friendship and family relationships like no other. The natural occurrence of what could loosely be termed 'native' pursuits is something that you draw great pleasure from, as well as providing it for others. Such things are singing, dancing, crafts, artistic expression, etc – but all done on a personal or domestic level, and not necessarily a professional one. This is a very gentle and 'female' Interaction because you both tune into what is lovable and likeable, rather than desirable and admirable. The former qualities are accommodating and flexible, whereas the latter can be brittle and distance-inducing. For this reason, this Interaction very much favours female-to-female relationships. If there is a 'but' to this lovely Interaction, it is the possible excess of this 'femaleness', for it can incline you to be too passive as a couple. So unless there are some more dynamic Interactions between you, this means that you can get led down whatever path presents itself rather than be consciously self-directing or discriminating, with the result that pleasure and comfort-seeking become your sole directive, and aimlessness your only product. Apart from that possible hitch, together and with each other, you are 'Sweet and lovely, sweeter than the roses in May ...'.

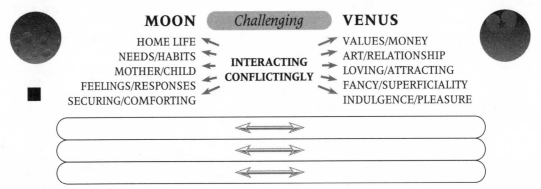

MOON *Challenging* **VENUS**

HOME LIFE	VALUES/MONEY
NEEDS/HABITS	ART/RELATIONSHIP
MOTHER/CHILD	LOVING/ATTRACTING
FEELINGS/RESPONSES	FANCY/SUPERFICIALITY
SECURING/COMFORTING	INDULGENCE/PLEASURE

INTERACTING CONFLICTINGLY

Needs for pleasure (Venus) and security (Moon), and the clash between them, strongly colour this aspect of your relationship. Such motivations, valid as far as they go, do not make for a deeper bond, or most importantly, a respect and recognition for each other as individuals in your own right. At one level, and also beneath the surface, you are each in the relationship for different reasons. At a superficial level you may both appear to be getting what you want or need, but sooner or later such will not be enough – for one or both of you. Of course, other Interactions may supply this, but because this one represents such a pull towards comfort and pleasure you may not even notice what else you have, or have not, got going for you – until one of you suddenly stops supplying the cushions or candy, or some crisis strikes. This means that one of you (probably Venus) goes cold or even looks elsewhere – while the Moon withdraws or sulks. Another possible hitch can be your relationship being complicated by the mother or family of one or both of you, or the domestic set-up, compromising your social/love life. Behind any or all such difficulties is the fact that, in one important area at least, you are not emotionally or socially in tune. Paradoxically though, because this Interaction is very 'female', it makes for a basic and instinctual empathy, whatever your sex, that can tolerate and accommodate a great deal of strife, within or outside your relationship. This also means that you are hospitable to others. But it is this very 'accommodation' that can gloss over the gritty issues that one day will have to surface.

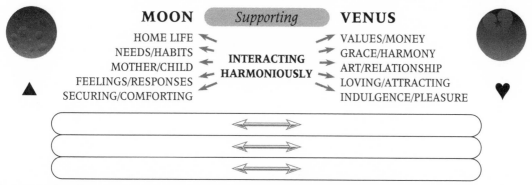

MOON *Supporting* **VENUS**

HOME LIFE VALUES/MONEY
NEEDS/HABITS GRACE/HARMONY
MOTHER/CHILD **INTERACTING** ART/RELATIONSHIP
FEELINGS/RESPONSES **HARMONIOUSLY** LOVING/ATTRACTING
SECURING/COMFORTING INDULGENCE/PLEASURE

There is a soft and gracious feeling between the two of you, which others around you appreciate as well. This lends itself particularly well to romantic, family or friendly relationships or any dealings with the public, but because this Interaction is quite 'female' in quality, it places the accent upon affection rather than sex. The man, if there is one, in your relationship, is able to get in touch with his female side through this partnership. So both of you are receptive and tender towards one another, showing respect for each other's sensitivity. Again, because this is very 'yin' in feel, such empathy could be entirely passive and not necessarily acted upon. If there are more dynamic or passionate Interactions indicated elsewhere, then this one provides a soft base for those harder desires. The home and family of the Moon person can be beautified or graced by the Venus person, and the Moon person provides a vehicle or receptacle for Venus's loving feelings. The word 'pleasant' sums up this Interaction.

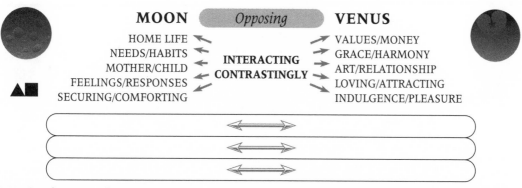

MOON *Opposing* **VENUS**

HOME LIFE VALUES/MONEY
NEEDS/HABITS GRACE/HARMONY
MOTHER/CHILD **INTERACTING** ART/RELATIONSHIP
FEELINGS/RESPONSES **CONTRASTINGLY** LOVING/ATTRACTING
SECURING/COMFORTING INDULGENCE/PLEASURE

⟺ Having these two Planets opposing one another creates a soft and tender attraction for each other, but it has an inclination to find you not quite knowing who's supposed to make a move towards anything more dynamic than simply liking and feeling affectionate towards one another. If, because of a more intense feeling between you, things become more intimate, this Interaction can cause one of you to want to back out. If you are both fairly emotionally aware, then you will probably both realize you were mistaken in your intentions. If not, however, in the same way that making that move initially towards one another was awkward, it can be equally awkward trying to pull apart, which in turn can wind up with one of you feeling upset and unwanted. Underlying all of this is the probability that the Moon person is motivated by security needs, but the Venus person by pleasure or social ones. Another expression of this combination of such conflicting needs is that you both become rather indulgent and hedonistic, maybe by way of compensation. When all is said and done, this Interaction has really only the makings of 'just good friends', and very sociable and lively ones at that!

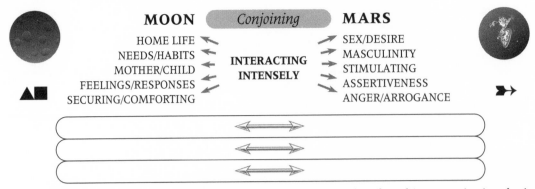

There is a strong and basic reaction to one another – very possibly sexual. In fact, this Interaction is so basic as to be almost primitive for it embodies the meeting of the two most fundamental drives – desire and need. If the Mars person is male and the Moon person female, then this mutual attraction is usually more intense. It would also be more straightforward than the other way around, in which case the male Moon would be having to respond passively to an unusually assertive Mars female. In any event, such a strong tug towards one another seems to defy any more social or sensitive considerations about your becoming intimately involved. It is plain that there is no problem with mutual attraction here, but when the initial burst of animal enthusiasm is over, and the relationship tries or has to settle down to something more humdrum and domestic, then trouble can begin. One expression of this could be that the two of you keep trying to maintain that original intensity which then leads to a sense of urgency and/or disappointment. Another could be that the mundanities of life take over and these hot feelings have no choice but to burst out as anger or aggression in one of you (probably Mars) which elicits a hurt or threatened feeling from the other (probably Moon). Positive aspects will balance and maintain this rather fruity bond, whereas negative ones will lead to ongoing conflict, frustration and hurt – and eventually, and maybe gratefully, separation.

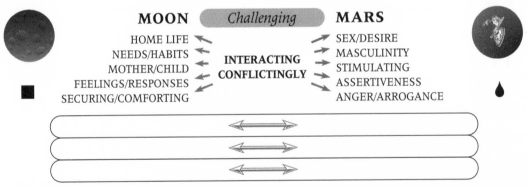

If in close proximity for any length of time, you will bring out the worst in each other: the Moon's over-sensitivity born of childhood and past experiences, and Mars's residual anger and desire to get and act in spite of circumstances. If you are contemplating getting together for a protracted period, be warned and give yourselves a trial period with 'get-out clauses' – or just back off altogether. Barbed remarks and acutely hurt feelings having already arisen would be a danger sign here. If you are already in such a situation it is because your respective unconscious minds deemed it necessary. This means that you both had to become more aware of your emotional fears and impulses, and these very things drew you together. So it is a case of the fat being in the fire. Ideally, and put simply, the Moon person needs to toughen up a bit and not be so phased by the slings and arrows of emotional life – or alternatively not be so comfy or complacent. Equally, the Mars person had best get in touch with their anger and the reasons for it in some way other than using the Moon as a punch-bag. Both of you, if you value your relationship or yourselves at all, may well need to seek professional help in dealing with your respective emotional difficulties. Two hurt children are only too able to hurt one another – and other children, perhaps your own.

Sometimes you'll find that one person's Planet is interchangeable with the other's

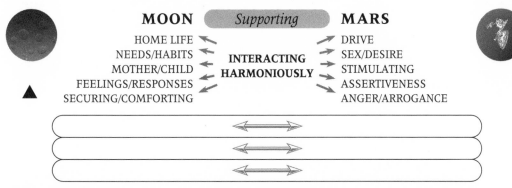

MOON *Supporting* MARS

HOME LIFE → ← DRIVE
NEEDS/HABITS → **INTERACTING** ← SEX/DESIRE
MOTHER/CHILD → **HARMONIOUSLY** ← STIMULATING
FEELINGS/RESPONSES → ← ASSERTIVENESS
SECURING/COMFORTING → ← ANGER/ARROGANCE

You have a vibrant Interaction here that enables you, individually or as a couple, to get a lot done for you tend to energize one another. Mars acts as a ramrod to the Moon who otherwise may have stayed at home and not achieved or experienced much. On the other hand, the Moon can show fiery Mars how fun can be had in a more private and cosy way. Naturally, this aspect is more favourable when Mars is male and the Moon is female, for they are then in their traditional roles. But this description can give a limited idea of the great scope that the 'energetic accord' of this Interaction affords you both. Sexually, for example, you can be equally physical and emotional, and instinctively lose yourselves in the heat of passion. But just because the Moon and Mars are such instinctual drives (security and sex, need and desire), there is a danger you could consume yourselves, so some moderation would keep the fires burning nicely.

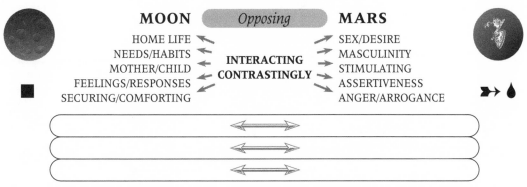

MOON *Opposing* MARS

HOME LIFE → ← SEX/DESIRE
NEEDS/HABITS → **INTERACTING** ← MASCULINITY
MOTHER/CHILD → **CONTRASTINGLY** ← STIMULATING
FEELINGS/RESPONSES → ← ASSERTIVENESS
SECURING/COMFORTING → ← ANGER/ARROGANCE

⟺ In a non-domestic relationship, or one where you are not with one another day-in-day-out, this Interaction adds a frisson of emotional tension, which gives the relationship a charge of emotional reality – a bit like a live chat show. However, if yours is a live-in, family or working relationship, then you're in for a rough ride. The Mars person is always hitting, deliberately or inadvertently, the Moon's tender spots. Mars sees the Moon as too soft and emotionally motivated. Mars wants action, the Moon needs comfort. But psychological projection is particularly rife here, for Mars is hitting out at the Moon as they see in them their own dependency and vulnerability. And the Moon would love to be as spontaneous and forceful as Mars, but they dare not be, and so justify this by seeing Mars as insensitive. Unconscious motivations are the main theme here. Because of this, there is liable to be a strong sexual attraction, but this can too often be the interpretation or expression you both give this Interaction at the outset. In other words, you are drawn to one another for reasons of unconscious programmes in each of you that set one another off. But owing to the Moon's inclination to avoid such confrontations, and to Mars's putting it on someone else, such a 'hot' Interaction has to be given a site that is acceptable to you both – sex. So it should not be so surprising when you find that your passion is a mixed blessing, as it cooks up both delicious and ghastly dishes. As they say, if you can't stand the heat, then stay out of the kitchen. But once in, you probably won't be able to get out – at least until you know what's cooking!

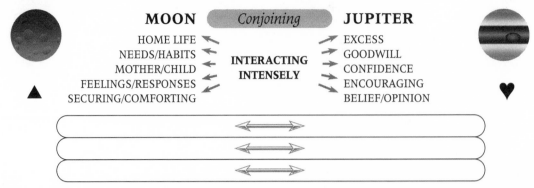

There is a great and natural feeling of understanding for one another. Whatever might be occurring in your lives, together or individually, it is always within both of you to explore it if it is positive, or to accommodate it if it is not. There exists an innate faith and trust in one another, to whatever degree it needs to be there. For these reasons, this Interaction has more the nature of furthering and maintaining a relationship rather than initiating or creating one. And so, if your relationship is ongoing, then you can be sure that together you will progressively overcome any difficulties, and prosper in the process. It also favours child-rearing and caring for the spiritual or physical health of anyone or anything – as long as you avoid doting on each other and pious do-gooding or proselytising. But do not expect this aspect alone to fire you up. Indeed, the ultimate expression or energy of this Interaction may go beyond emotional and physical gratification, as it leans more and more towards altruism and philanthropy. Kindness towards one another, and to those around you, is the great key to emotional well-being bestowed upon you by the benign effect of this Interaction.

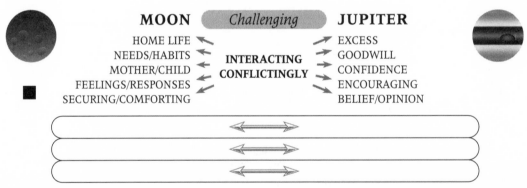

⇔ Although there is a measure of kindness and consideration between the two of you, it is inclined to become a case of emotionally indulging or doting on one another, or conversely a vague discord caused by the phoniness of such misplaced 'care'. In truth, one of you is after security and home-life (Moon) while the other is after freedom and adventure (Jupiter) – but these can be interchangeable. And so a false sense of security or togetherness can grow out of this. It is as if this Interaction happens to make it known to one or both of you that what you have been brought up to need or believe in is not actually appropriate for you as individuals. This is not a particularly hard 'hard' aspect – but it can cause emotional confusion. Exploring what you both really need or believe could reveal that you are more in tune than you thought – or a lot less, which is possibly why you'd be disinclined to undertake such exploration.

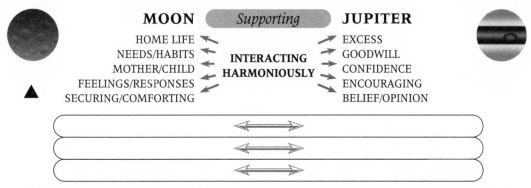

There exists a 'good feeling' between the two of you. This has its roots in the fact that you mean each other no harm at a deeply instinctual and moral level. Put more positively, you are generous and considerate towards one another, and genuinely care what becomes of each other. Together you are in touch with some of the best of human nature. You nurture or encourage each other's development, be it emotionally or materially, mentally or spiritually. Obviously, this Interaction goes a long way towards sorting out or preventing any strife or misunderstanding caused by other Interactions. In fact, owing to the passivity of this Interaction, it may well need some kind of challenge – from within or without your relationship – to call it into being. Such kindness that you create and have between you will also be of inestimable value in looking after or teaching others.

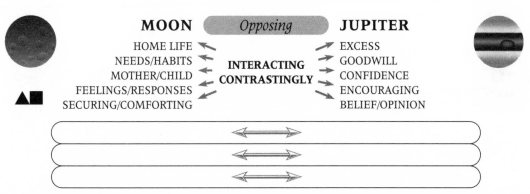

⟷ To a certain degree, this is the opposite of a blessing in disguise. In other words, you both have a genuine desire to help one another, but are misguided as to the form such support takes. For example, the Moon person senses the apparent confidence or faith of the Jupiter person, wants to be part of it, so then goes about indulging them in the unconscious attempt to achieve that. The Jupiter person interprets this as the Moon being an acolyte worthy of indulging in return – possibly by confidently encouraging some questionable habits and metaphorically patting them on the head. Such a peculiar Interaction has a simple truth behind it: Jupiter's beliefs are detrimental to the security of the Moon, and the Moon's responses give Jupiter a false idea of those beliefs' value. This Interaction ultimately forces the Moon person to be more aware of their own needs and more in command of satisfying them, and the Jupiter person to be more sure of their ethics and beliefs before imposing them on someone who too readily accepts them in their need for security or their need to care.

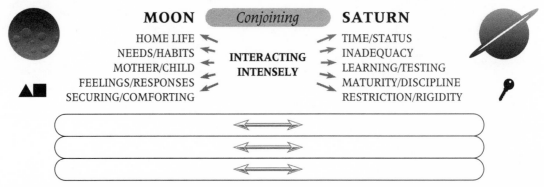

This is an important Interaction, but unfortunately not for the most cheerful of reasons. Whereas the Moon person expresses their feelings only too naturally with respect to their Moon Sign, the Saturn person has a commensurately difficult time positively expressing their Saturn Sign qualities (*see* page 227 for Saturn Profiles). The writing on the wall with this contact is saying that both of you have an important lesson to learn from each other. The Moon person needs to discipline their emotions and be more mature, less childish, in this area. Saturn, on the other hand, could take some lessons from the Moon in how to live up to their Saturn Sign potentials. The trouble here is that the Moon feels suppressed or chilled by what is really only Saturn's inadequacy in this respect, for Saturn, in the face of the Moon's emotional ease, feels awkward and in need of controlling the Moon's behaviour. And so a downward spiral is only too likely if the two of you are not emotionally very objective. For this to happen, there will certainly also have to be a good supply of mutually loving and caring Interactions present, because this Interaction certainly doesn't fit that bill. This has been called a 'fated contact' because it is quite timely in the sense of both people having to become more conscious of free-flowing feelings on the Moon's part, and inhibitions on Saturn's. Family responsibilities and domestic arrangements can be a very likely area for these lessons and difficulties to surface, as too can Saturn's professional duties getting in the way of the Moon's needs, and vice versa. Having said all of this, if the writing on the wall is read and obeyed, a very stable and mutually responsible, though possibly somewhat sober, relationship can be established.

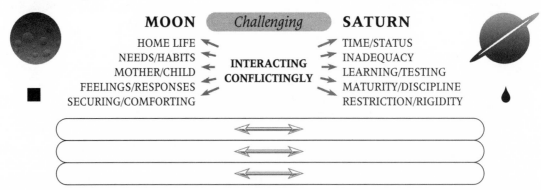

This is a highly unsympathetic Interaction, even though the Moon may at first feel some of Saturn's pain. But as time goes by it becomes apparent that there is a no-go area between the two of you – rather like a patch of black ice. If, for some reason or other, you are initially reluctant to engage, it is probably because of an instinct that senses this 'black ice' and so you avoid coming any closer. If this is not the case, however, the 'black ice' can create quite a cold and uncaring feeling between you that can eat away like a cancer at the rest of the relationship. The reasons for this are most likely ingrained fears and inhibitions on Saturn's part, and previously unmet or indulged childhood needs on the Moon's. In other words, negative parental conditioning is dragged to the surface and reiterated under this aspect. The Moon can play out the fearful side of their mother, while Saturn expresses their father's doubts. This mixture, unless you are prepared to go to great effort and depth, is unfortunately separative. Nonetheless, it does teach you this important lesson because that was what was there to be learned. It also goes some way to teaching you both the value of caution.

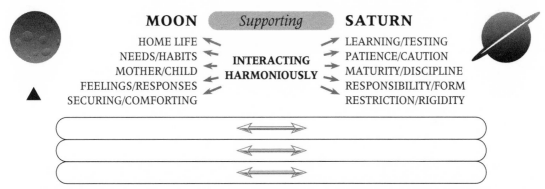

MOON *Supporting* **SATURN**

HOME LIFE	LEARNING/TESTING
NEEDS/HABITS	PATIENCE/CAUTION
MOTHER/CHILD	MATURITY/DISCIPLINE
FEELINGS/RESPONSES	RESPONSIBILITY/FORM
SECURING/COMFORTING	RESTRICTION/RIGIDITY

INTERACTING HARMONIOUSLY

At a very basic level you can rely upon one another: the Moon person for being there emotionally, domestically and, if necessary, maternally; the Saturn person for being materially and professionally committed. Either of you could actually fill both bills. This could be called a 'meat and potatoes' aspect for it provides those essentials of responsibility, duty and durability for home, family or business. Good, solid, lasting stuff. However, unless your coming together was 'arranged' there would have to be more interesting or romantic Interactions for you to have come together at all. Then again, this down-home sort of feeling between the two of you may remain just a notion if there are serious conflicts or illusions about and between the two of you. But whenever the boat rocks on choppy seas, this aspect serves as excellent ballast – but it isn't the kind to get you launched in the first place. Perhaps this Interaction favours a traditional type of partnership with, for instance, the man being Saturn and the breadwinner, and with the woman being the mother and homemaker.

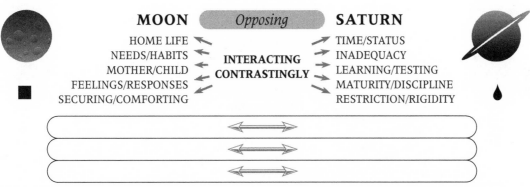

MOON *Opposing* **SATURN**

HOME LIFE	TIME/STATUS
NEEDS/HABITS	INADEQUACY
MOTHER/CHILD	LEARNING/TESTING
FEELINGS/RESPONSES	MATURITY/DISCIPLINE
SECURING/COMFORTING	RESTRICTION/RIGIDITY

INTERACTING CONTRASTINGLY

The sense of order and social correctness of the Saturn person is totally at odds with the natural behaviour and free-flowing responses of the Moon person. The result is that the Moon feels controlled and thwarted by Saturn, experiencing them as being judgmental and unsympathetic. Saturn sees the Moon as childish and irresponsible. It would seem that, as is so often the case with hard Interactions with Saturn, a difficult lesson is here in the learning. And because it is a difficult lesson, this Interaction can go on for a considerable period of time – until the lesson has been learned or the inherent difficulties make the relationship untenable. The lesson itself is that each of you should learn to accept that what is different to oneself is not wrong. Yet at the same time, Saturn probably does have a point in that the Moon person needs to grow up and get the hang of the way of the world. Conversely, Saturn needs to let the child in them out more, have more fun, and remember their dreams – as per the Moon person's example. The actual reasons for becoming involved at all are most likely down to insecurity on the Moon's part, and loneliness on Saturn's – a sad, but not very promising, recipe. If there was enough objectivity, a deal could be made here. But alas, objectivity is the very thing the Moon is learning, and Saturn would have to shoulder most of the worldly responsibilities.

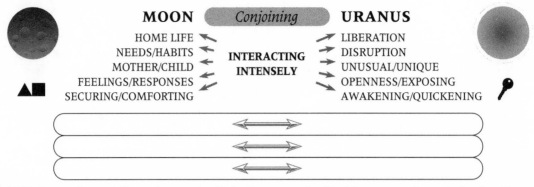

MOON *Conjoining* **URANUS**

HOME LIFE
NEEDS/HABITS
MOTHER/CHILD
FEELINGS/RESPONSES
SECURING/COMFORTING

INTERACTING
INTENSELY

LIBERATION
DISRUPTION
UNUSUAL/UNIQUE
OPENNESS/EXPOSING
AWAKENING/QUICKENING

⟺ This Interaction provides excitement but little, if any, security. The Moon person in particular should guard against expectations of comfort and predictability because they are not about to get them from Uranus. In fact, the very reason the Moon has been attracted to the Uranus individual is because their unconscious is trying to tell them, via Uranus, that it is time for them to review past attachments and outworn ideas of being settled. This Interaction also spells out for the Moon person the necessity of not being so attached to another human being (or anything else) for this smacks of their inner child running the show – or rather ruining it – with past agendas that now need seeing to. The Uranus person is a catalyst for this process, and as such can feel anything from uncomfortably distant to quite taken with being an agent of change in someone's life. There is a more subliminal effect that Uranus should be aware of, and this is that they should perhaps become less remote and emotionally distant, and the Moon person can show them how to be more 'feeling'. By way of exchange, the Moon person learns to cultivate a measure of emotional distance. This is not a stable Interaction for its dynamic is one of emotional change and reorientation. But because the experiencing of this is so important for both of you, you are strongly attracted to one another. For this reason, this Interaction can at times appear 'unfair' or 'impossible' as it seems not to offer anything that a conventional relationship expects of itself. You can expect surprise events that force you to change your respective emotional dispositions.

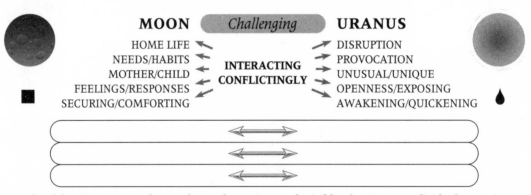

MOON *Challenging* **URANUS**

HOME LIFE
NEEDS/HABITS
MOTHER/CHILD
FEELINGS/RESPONSES
SECURING/COMFORTING

INTERACTING
CONFLICTINGLY

DISRUPTION
PROVOCATION
UNUSUAL/UNIQUE
OPENNESS/EXPOSING
AWAKENING/QUICKENING

The needs of the Moon person for comfort and security are denied by the Uranus individual's erratic nature and urge for freedom and independence. The Moon should view this Interaction, when not given its due, as having no place in a stable and enduring relationship. This is more of a home-breaker than a homemaker, and its agenda is that of breaking any outworn or mistaken attachments that the Moon has to mother, home or thoughts of matrimony. The same could also apply to Uranus, for social conditioning may even have caused them to go against their innate need for space to develop. So strong is this Interaction's power to break conventional moulds that it will disrupt the social and domestic lives of those around you as well. The unpredictable and unstable nature of this aspect can be very upsetting to the Moon person, and irritating to the Uranus person. Paradoxically though, such is the excitement caused by this coupling that it can go on, spasmodically, for quite some time. That is, until the Moon is somewhat freer from their claustrophobic ideas of emotional closeness, and Uranus recognizes that they are essentially just a catalyst for this process, or that they need to be more emotionally attuned or available.

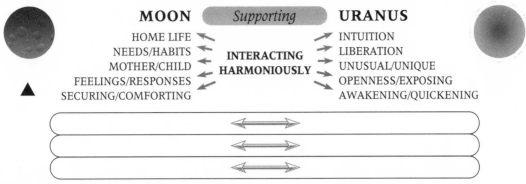

MOON *Supporting* **URANUS**

	INTERACTING HARMONIOUSLY	
HOME LIFE		INTUITION
NEEDS/HABITS		LIBERATION
MOTHER/CHILD		UNUSUAL/UNIQUE
FEELINGS/RESPONSES		OPENNESS/EXPOSING
SECURING/COMFORTING		AWAKENING/QUICKENING

Emotional liberation is the keynote of this Interaction. Notwithstanding the presence of any possessive or more passionate contacts between the two of you, both of you go to some lengths to help one another come to terms with past influences, and if necessary, cut the ties with them. This is also a relationship where a comfortable involvement with occult or esoteric subjects can take place. Practically speaking, unusual or alternative pursuits are accommodated by one or both of you. All of this makes you quite relaxed with each other in the face of making psychological inroads into yourselves or others. You both sort of stroke and poke at the same time, with the Moon being the 'stroker' or comforter and Uranus being the 'poker' or one who lays bare the truth of the matter. A slight danger with this essentially very positive Interaction is that you can become strangely detached from each other as your respective feelings become kind of academic, and you fail to see the emotional wood for the theoretical trees. Apart from that, you make a good team.

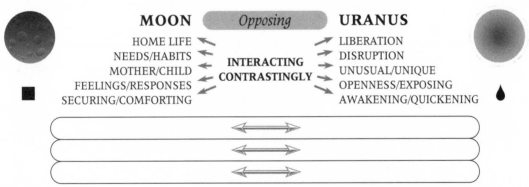

MOON *Opposing* **URANUS**

	INTERACTING CONTRASTINGLY	
HOME LIFE		LIBERATION
NEEDS/HABITS		DISRUPTION
MOTHER/CHILD		UNUSUAL/UNIQUE
FEELINGS/RESPONSES		OPENNESS/EXPOSING
SECURING/COMFORTING		AWAKENING/QUICKENING

As planets, the Moon and Uranus are antipathetic, so this is not an Interaction that anyone should invest in for the future, or at least, expect to have a conventional lifestyle with. The Moon needs security and comfort, family values and emotional receptivity. Uranus wants change and excitement, friendship values and mental freedom. So it is no surprise, or rather it is, when, after finding the Uranus individual such a turn-on, the Moon person discovers that they are also unpredictable and hard to keep to anything solid or routine. Furthermore, the Uranus person is liable to react in this way to an even greater extent when the Moon tries to mother them or be mothered by them. The sooner the Moon person realizes that they unconsciously became involved for reasons of freeing themselves from such blind and immature security needs, then the less likely they are to have such a hard time of it. Uranus, for their part, should endeavour to go a bit more gently on the Moon's feelings, and consider the possibility that their reason for allowing themselves to become involved are the opposite to the Moon's – that is, to recognize that their blows for freedom are more to do with a fear of emotional commitment, and to search for and explore something less cosy and more unusual in a relationship. Ultimately, you are in the relationship to show one another that the combining or confrontation of freedom and security takes a great deal of emotional honesty on both your parts. Without waking up to the 'emotional clearing' that this Interaction poses, you will find the extreme ups and downs that you experience very hard to endure or understand.

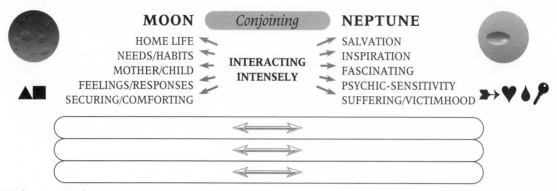

MOON *Conjoining* NEPTUNE

INTERACTING INTENSELY

MOON		NEPTUNE
HOME LIFE		SALVATION
NEEDS/HABITS		INSPIRATION
MOTHER/CHILD		FASCINATING
FEELINGS/RESPONSES		PSYCHIC-SENSITIVITY
SECURING/COMFORTING		SUFFERING/VICTIMHOOD

⟺ This is a highly sensitive connection which can create a wonderful emotional and spiritual rapport. However, there is also the danger of each partner losing themselves in the other. So it is important to establish and maintain individual identities and not live in each other's pockets. As Kahlil Gibran said, 'Let the winds of the Heavens dance between you.' Having achieved this, the psychic sensitivity of the one can nurture the inspirational nature of the other, while at the same time you delicately show one another your own individual emotional needs and state. This Interaction strongly favours any creative or spiritual pursuits of a joint nature. You are somewhat like twin radio receivers rather than one on its own, so you pick up more ideas and guidance than you would otherwise. So exquisite is the melding of your two personalities under the influence of this Interaction that it can, indeed has to, overcome any separative tendencies indicated elsewhere. Having said this though, you are also exceptionally able to accept whatever the river of life might bring you, even if it wishes you to go your separate ways. But then again, if there comes a point when your mystical link is made complete, probably through some acute emotional suffering, then no man can put asunder what God has joined together. Domestically or as a family, you emanate a subtle and gentle feel that is very special. In some respects this will need maintaining by being quite discriminating about what type of energies, physical or otherwise, you allow into your space – but without letting this become too precious. Basically, yours is a psychic bond and as such can pull in all manner of psychic phenomena, good, bad and indifferent. For the same reason, as a couple you are adept at creating a quite enchanting atmosphere which can be both healing and entertaining for those in its midst.

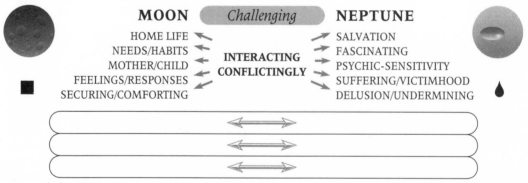

MOON *Challenging* NEPTUNE

INTERACTING CONFLICTINGLY

MOON		NEPTUNE
HOME LIFE		SALVATION
NEEDS/HABITS		FASCINATING
MOTHER/CHILD		PSYCHIC-SENSITIVITY
FEELINGS/RESPONSES		SUFFERING/VICTIMHOOD
SECURING/COMFORTING		DELUSION/UNDERMINING

⟺ One or both of you having personal boundaries that are defined too strongly or not strongly enough, is the issue here. Consequently, there are three possible scenarios. If you both have vague ideas of where you begin and end as individuals, you then accommodate each other only too well, in a rather indiscriminate fashion. This invites emotional confusion as you tend to drag one another down to the lowest common denominator of living standard. What allows this to happen is the fact that in the first place you kind of melt into each other, fostering the illusion that you are closer than you actually are or were. In this case, one or both of you has to find the strength or help to make a stand, possibly having to be quite ruthless in the process. The second case is when one of you is quite open emotionally, and the other is relatively closed. The open one gets under the closed one's skin, in spite of themselves, forcing them to be more emotionally forthcoming.

If a relationship is tired, bored or lost, pretend you have just met ...

Unfortunately, this is unlikely to be done consciously, but more in the way of being victim-like and needy, compromising the other 'stronger' person in the process. But the stronger person should read this as having to be more compassionate. The third case, when both of you are quite separate as people, would mean that something occurs or will occur that forces you to be more open about your individual vulnerability. Without dealing with whatever your scenario is in the constructive ways suggested here, your relationship could go from confusion to delusion, from misconception to rank deception.

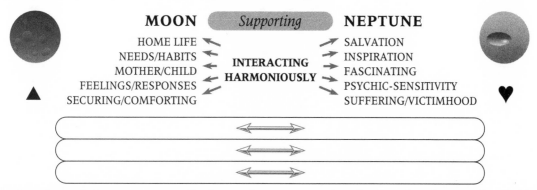

As a couple you feel as one at a very fundamental, even unconscious, level. And so there is what could be called a 'psychic familiarity' with each other – that feeling of having known each other before. All of this makes for a fine receptivity and sensitivity that not only enables you to sympathetically tune into each other's feelings, needs and weaknesses in a positively therapeutic fashion, but also allows other people (and animals too) to feel at home and at ease, even healed, in your presence. In addition, this psychic Interaction means that you can operate well together in any creative or spiritual endeavour. Such accord, other Interactions notwithstanding, can make for a particularly loving and caring relationship that can eventually spread to alleviating the suffering of certain areas of society as a whole.

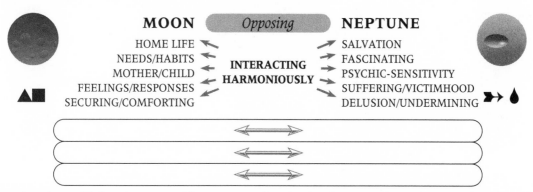

⟺ There is very likely to be a mutual fascination with each other, but one or both of you could wind up high and dry, where shortly before it seemed you were in a sea of heady emotions. This Interaction really sees love's illusions coming, whereas the two people concerned usually do not. This all has something to do with the Moon person longing for some kind of womb-like comfort and security that they did or did not get inside their mother, while the Neptune person is wistfully looking for their dream lover. So this Interaction has its psychological roots firmly placed in the unconscious – but not really anywhere else. This is why neither of you will see what is actually happening until the child in the Moon freaks out and/or the dream of Neptune fades. But all this may take a while because the Moon instinctively obliges in reflecting and giving emotional substance to Neptune's fantasies, while Neptune pretends to the point of being downright deceptive. However, because this Interaction is so unconsciously driven, mutual involvement with the mystical, musical or meditative can take you both to some genuinely blissful and enlightening places. But there is a sadness here which is only too much the tragic legacy of the human soul. As much as you reach for the soul-mate in each other, the image of it fades because it is more likely than not based on wishful thinking.

... and that each of you is still a mystery to the other

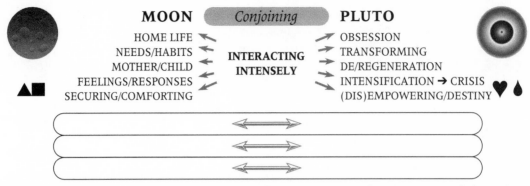

MOON   *Conjoining*   PLUTO

HOME LIFE | OBSESSION
NEEDS/HABITS | **INTERACTING** | TRANSFORMING
MOTHER/CHILD | **INTENSELY** | DE/REGENERATION
FEELINGS/RESPONSES | INTENSIFICATION → CRISIS
SECURING/COMFORTING | (DIS)EMPOWERING/DESTINY

⇔ This very intense Interaction will take you both down to some very deep emotions and churn them to the surface. In fact, you could go so far as to say that this is some form of emotional initiation, for it will transform the way you feel about yourselves, as individuals and as a couple. The sexual dimension, real or imagined, is a key area for it is the compulsions of desire and need that drive this Interaction, cementing you together or driving you apart, depending on how such intense feelings are managed. Sometimes you can feel overwhelmed with such intensity, causing the Moon person to withdraw from the onslaughts of the Pluto person – but it can also happen the other way around. But the emotional 'elastic' persists in bringing you back together again and again, no matter what. Such swinging back and forth between feelings of extreme closeness and painful distance (or painful closeness!) can be very trying, even despair-inducing. It is well to remember the old French adage 'A woman is like a man's shadow; go towards it and it will walk away from you, walk away from it and it will follow you'. No matter what the gender is though, this means that if the one of you can resist hungering after the other when the chips are down, they will come back – or it will be seen not to matter. Conversely, abandoning the other will only make them more persistent. Recognize that you do have a very deep bond – or that you are forging or letting go of one – and that you will have to confront inappropriate feelings and eliminate them. As a result, you will both be purged and therefore reunite with renewed and purer feelings of connectedness – or not. This process will go on inexorably until your respective emotional states are such that you either have an indestructible bond between the two of you, or you both agree that enough is enough. But until then neither of you will really have any choice in the matter other than how you handle such an intense Interaction.

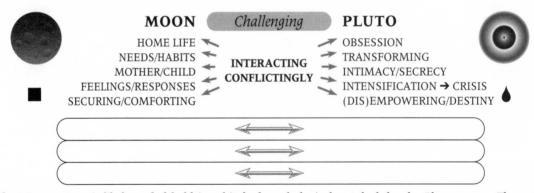

MOON   *Challenging*   PLUTO

HOME LIFE | OBSESSION
NEEDS/HABITS | **INTERACTING** | TRANSFORMING
MOTHER/CHILD | **CONFLICTINGLY** | INTIMACY/SECRECY
FEELINGS/RESPONSES | INTENSIFICATION → CRISIS
SECURING/COMFORTING | (DIS)EMPOWERING/DESTINY

The Moon person is likely to feel held in a kind of psychological arm-lock by the Pluto person. They will probably not let on, or even realize, that this is the case, and this makes it all the more incapacitating. The probable reason behind this is that the Pluto person's attitude to the Moon person can be one of disdain, because they see them as being weak or pathetic in some way. It is also likely that Pluto is projecting their own emotional vulnerability here, something which they deny. And so the Moon person will instinctively retaliate in an indirect or passive way. This reaction is usually determined by their Moon Sign itself. A Scorpio Moon would, for instance, get some hold over the Pluto person and threaten emotional blackmail. An Aries

Moon would be more direct and aggressive towards the Pluto person. But in all cases it would not be too obvious what was going on or why. Possessiveness and jealousy are also likely to raise their gnarled little heads, sooner or later. Again, suspicious looks and subtle sneers or jibes would, initially at least, be the only signs. This Interaction makes for a more or less constant erosion of whatever your emotional links are, but with a view to renewing them in the process. This obviously necessitates some pretty good mental and emotional rapport supplied from elsewhere. If this is so, then neither of you will allow the grass to grow under the feet of your relationship, and it will consequently last and last, yet probably with occasional 'black-outs' of communication. The alternative is, unfortunately, stagnation.

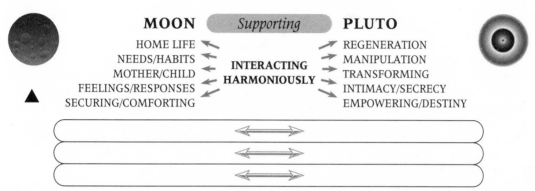

With this Interaction both of you should experience a degree of 'soul reconnection', which is rather like a garden hose that has come adrift from the tap being reconnected to it. So each of you in your own way can feel replenished and emotionally renewed by your involvement with one another. Such regeneration can also positively affect the domestic and/or family situation of one or both of you. However, it should be added that Plutonian Interactions often happen out of sight and over a longish period of time – a bit like an underground river. So don't expect to see all the results occurring that soon or that obviously. This Interaction, because it is regenerative at a very deep, even unconscious level, can greatly contribute to the durability of a partnership. Having said that though, positive results may even appear after the relationship itself is over. This is not to say that your relationship has to end for you to realize how good it was, but it gives an idea of the hidden and protracted way in which these Plutonian connections operate. Whatever the case, the material or personal assets of the Moon person are given a boost by the Pluto person, who in turn feels a sense of power and effectiveness coursing through them. This mutual effect can of course be profited from in areas outside of the relationship itself.

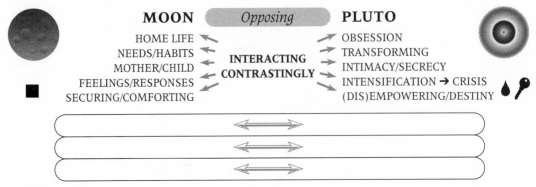

Here there is a great contrast between how the Moon person and the Pluto person experience this Interaction. Pluto is somehow emotionally 'feeding' off the Moon in order to satisfy – very unconsciously, initially at least – a deep craving to gain, or regain, a position of power. For some reason, most likely a feeling of being disempowered or denied something earlier in life, the Pluto individual wants to get their way – and will go through hell and high water to do so. Unfortunately this can be quite oppressive to the Moon whose feelings and security feel threatened by what they experience as Pluto's emotionally manipulative or merely neurotic onslaughts. How the Moon person deals with this very much depends upon the position of the Moon in their own Birthchart. As a general rule though, the Moon will feel rather like they did as a child when oppressed by their mother – and this means a sense of powerlessness that only has evasion or passivity, rebelliousness or contrariness, as a way of coping or resisting. Ultimately all of this leads to some sort of crisis which either tears the relationship apart or makes you closer and stronger as a couple. In turn, this process of going through the mill could also deeply involve the families, dependants and offspring of both of you. If you reflect for a moment, you will remember that there was always a sense of the inevitable about your coming together, like an appointment with Fate, that has been or will be in aid of putting you far more in touch with your respective emotional depths. However, because this Interaction does pose quite cataclysmic upheavals, you both may sense this and choose just to experience the chemistry between you as an almost irresistible tug with distinct sexual undertones – but if circumstances bring you together often enough it may prove fatal.

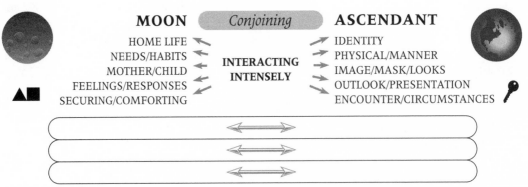

⟺ There is an instantaneous emotional link between the two of you. This means that you feel like 'family' to one another – and in fact you could actually be related. Whatever the case, you 'go way back', either literally or figuratively. And so the water-under-the-bridge issue can be an important one for you both, as memories of past experiences, be they shared or individual, form a great part of your lives and relationship together. On the positive side, you have an easy rapport as you share, instinctively or experientially, common emotional attitudes and habit patterns. Negatively though, it can be difficult for either one of you to break out of, or be seen to break out of, the mould in which each has cast the other. The making of a little distance, in time, space or both, can be very helpful in your both getting a clearer idea of who each of you are as distinct individuals rather than merely as jigsaw pieces, with no identity of their own, that fit into each other's puzzles.

The nature of all Interactions depends upon ...

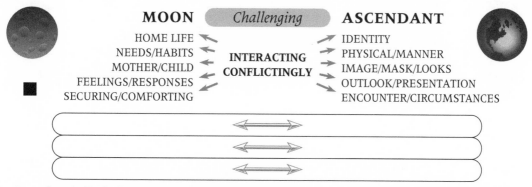

MOON *Challenging* **ASCENDANT**

MOON		ASCENDANT
HOME LIFE		IDENTITY
NEEDS/HABITS	**INTERACTING**	PHYSICAL/MANNER
MOTHER/CHILD	**CONFLICTINGLY**	IMAGE/MASK/LOOKS
FEELINGS/RESPONSES		OUTLOOK/PRESENTATION
SECURING/COMFORTING		ENCOUNTER/CIRCUMSTANCES

The Ascendant individual's manner of self-expression rubs up the wrong way the emotional sensibilities of the Moon person. In return, the Moon's reaction to this invites more of same. The Moon's habits and routines are also somewhat annoying to the Ascendant. This vicious circle needs to be broken by at least one of you to prevent such disharmony developing into an outright breakdown of any kind of positive Interaction. In other words, self-control and some compromises are called for in both of your behaviour patterns. Failure to do this can additionally preclude doing anything together that caters to others or the public. Neither is this Interaction that favourable for domestic co-existence.

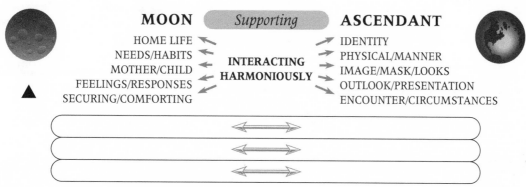

MOON *Supporting* **ASCENDANT**

MOON		ASCENDANT
HOME LIFE		IDENTITY
NEEDS/HABITS	**INTERACTING**	PHYSICAL/MANNER
MOTHER/CHILD	**HARMONIOUSLY**	IMAGE/MASK/LOOKS
FEELINGS/RESPONSES		OUTLOOK/PRESENTATION
SECURING/COMFORTING		ENCOUNTER/CIRCUMSTANCES

There is a comfortable feel between the two of you provided by this Interaction, but it is quite mild in its influence. So it will augment other harmonious links between you, but would do little to withstand or ameliorate deeper conflicts. Be that as it may, you do find that your feelings and attitudes fit well together. This would also mean that your timing was quite good, with you being in the right place at the right time for each other, and in relationship to circumstances around you.

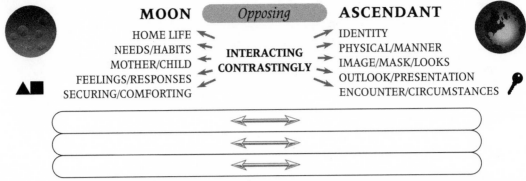

MOON *Opposing* **ASCENDANT**

HOME LIFE		IDENTITY
NEEDS/HABITS	**INTERACTING**	PHYSICAL/MANNER
MOTHER/CHILD	**CONTRASTINGLY**	IMAGE/MASK/LOOKS
FEELINGS/RESPONSES		OUTLOOK/PRESENTATION
SECURING/COMFORTING		ENCOUNTER/CIRCUMSTANCES

Here you really do have what is called an 'emotional relationship'. You have a mutual as well as natural need for one another, and endure and enjoy the ongoing highs and lows that are part and parcel of your being together. Even if this is not a marital, sexual or family relationship, you still interact in a quite intimate and familiar fashion. And where family is concerned, respective family members can be either a great mainstay or quite a burden to your own emotional harmony. This is a 'love me, love my family' sort of thing. The Moon person responds very well to the needs and expressions of the Ascendant person; so well in fact, that sometimes the Moon knows where the Ascendant is emotionally coming from way before they do. The down side to this, though, is that the Moon instinctively 'catches the Shadow' of the Ascendant person. This means that whatever the Ascendant person is unsure of in themselves, they can project on to the Moon and blame them for what is actually their 'stuff'. Yet at the same time, this is the price the Moon may have to pay for being so dependent on the Ascendant for displaying those positive qualities that they wish they had. Again, this can be seen in the family sense of one member taking care of a certain area of life, and another member taking care of something else. Traditionally, for instance, father brings home the bread, and mother makes the home and looks after the kids. So, in effect, yours is a symbiotic relationship, to one degree or another. As such it can work very well, and this Interaction, when accompanied by other favourable aspects, really can make one out of the two.

MERCURY

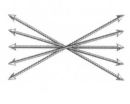

**INTERACTING
WITH**

MERCURY   URANUS
VENUS   NEPTUNE
MARS   PLUTO
JUPITER   ASCENDANT
SATURN

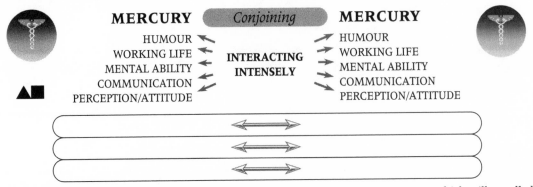

Your minds work very much the same way if you both have Mercury in the same Sign, which will usually be the case. In any event, you still connect well mentally – or sometimes too well. This latter point is owing to your sharing both the best and worst of the same kind of mentality. And so one of you can get irritated with the other if they are still stuck at a certain level of thinking or worrying, because it uncomfortably reminds them that they suffer, or used to, from the same complaint. You approach problems and work matters in a similar fashion too, and so can be efficient co-workers. However, the same issue can arise when one regards the other's methods as wanting or outmoded when really they are just reflecting back their own doubts or shortcomings. If both of you are pretty aware of the pluses and minuses of your intellectual state and attitude, then you can go from strength to strength as you develop your communication or work skills further and further. This is somewhat like how brothers and sisters learn to communicate through interacting with one another, and indeed, this Interaction can make for a brotherly/sisterly feel. Whether you are discussing some abstruse and complex issue or merely indulging in gossip, you do it brilliantly together.

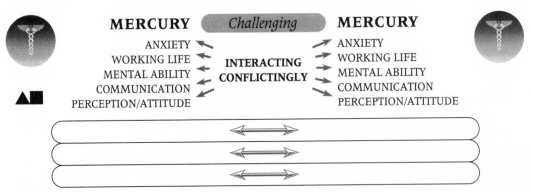

Here we have a battle of intellects and points of view. Consequently, the two of you do not communicate well at all, often getting the wrong end of the stick and not being able to trace where the misapprehensions occurred because more occur in the process. Also your day-to-day and work schedules do not mesh which can further sabotage communications. One, or preferably both, of you studying each of your individual Mercury Profiles (page 177) would help give some comprehension of the fact that you just have disharmonious mental processes, and are not necessarily wholly in conflict. Familiarizing yourselves with how the other's mind works would be an education in itself for it would simply mean that you'd come to know one another better. If yours is a more emotional/intuitive relationship, then this lack of mental rapport may not matter too much. Conversely, this Interaction could be interpreted as a device for getting you to relate more on an emotional/intuitive level – but getting to know how each other thinks should come first. In the process, the Mercurial joke is that you just might find that you are not as mentally different as you previously thought – and other Interactions may testify to this – for you discover something called 'intellectual integrity'.

No one Interaction makes or breaks a relationship

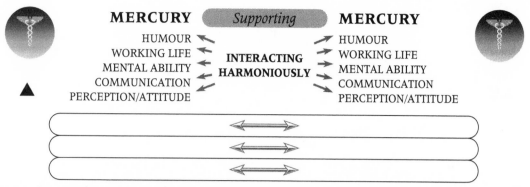

You get along much as siblings who have a healthy relationship would. The flow of ideas and their verbal expression come easily to you both. The actual nature of your easy discussions, though, depends upon other Interactions that you have between you. At one extreme, if yours is an intensely emotional relationship then your conversations will be rich and rewarding as you readily gain mental understanding of all that flows between you. At another extreme, where you do not quite hit it off emotionally or physically, conversation can be easy but does not seem to get anywhere in particular, for you are able to talk almost for its own sake. Possibly a working relationship is where most advantage can be drawn from your basically good communication.

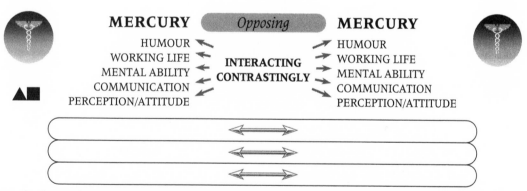

Not only do you literally have opposing types of perception, you also have completely different ways of interpreting those perceptions. For example, one of you may see life so sensitively and intuitively that they adopt a view that evades uncomfortable or seemingly threatening ideas. The other person, though, will see things more in black and white, 'for-me-or-against-me' mode, and so take the bull by the horns and analyse the hell out an issue until it is seen to be resolved. If the two of you could take the best out of each other's mental tool-kits, then you could be an exceptional team, tackling tasks with impressive skill and awareness. However, it would take an unusual amount of ego-surrendering for one or both of you to be able to filter out the 'static' of the other's opposing beam of communication or perception. Peculiarly enough though, it can be a sign that you're beginning unconsciously to appreciate that you each have one half of life's torn photograph when one of you starts using similar phrases to the other, or learns to listen to what the other is feeling rather than what they are saying. But until then, communicating or working together would be very uphill. Getting to know the qualities of each other's Mercury Sign would help considerably.

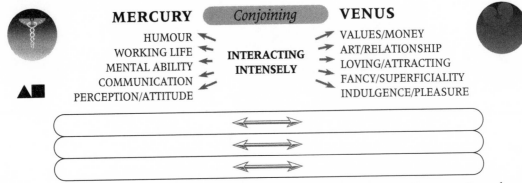

If the two of you do not enjoy talking together, then there must be something really wrong. Even then, you are drawn to discussing 'love problems' anyway, so on one level this Interaction is always getting what it wants. However, you do like your conversations to be pleasant and harmonious, and so may gloss over the nastier or more difficult issues that arise. On the other hand, it is your combined awareness of what looks and sounds right which is one of your stronger assets. So notwithstanding the tendency to gloss over, you can be an adept pair at finding a pleasing solution, one which is agreeable to most people concerned. As such, on a professional or merely social level, you excel at being diplomatic and discreet, and so should be welcome or in demand. You could also be creative together in some way – with Venus providing the appeal and aesthetics, and Mercury the interest and technical know-how.

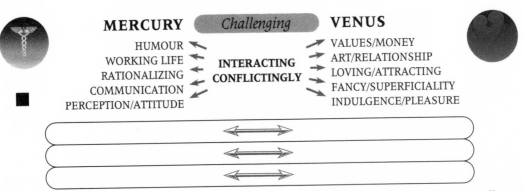

⟺ Here you have a work versus play, thinking versus feeling, conflict. Mercury approaches intellectually issues that Venus regards as either 'like' or 'don't like' situations, and no amount of explanation or argument is going to alter this. In the face of what they see as the Venus person's intransigence, Mercury can even go so far as laying down what love is or isn't, what is enjoyable or immoral. Venus can then react to this in a teasing or capricious manner that riles Mercury even more. This conflict is made more acute when, of the two of you, Mercury is the male and Venus the female. No amount of talk or theorizing can turn Venus on or off, whereas Venus's demand for sensation rather than reason is seen as aimless indulgence by Mercury. As a Challenging aspect, this demands that each of you be strong enough in your own convictions of reason and taste not to react to each other. Both of you should endeavour to meet the other half way: Mercury to listen and respond to Venus's emotional and body language; Venus to make some attempt to listen to the voice of reason.

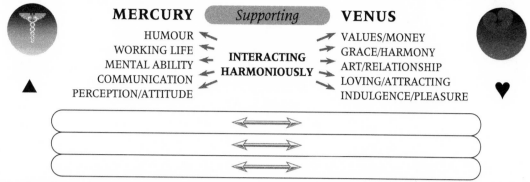

Both of you have a liking for the same people and pursuits, and have similar tastes. This goes a long way to ensuring a lasting interest and harmony between the two of you, and you are well able to have fun and be creative together. This Interaction especially favours any joint artistic endeavours, either as a pair or with one of you being in an advisory role. You are in tune with one another. Most significantly though, the emotional and intellectual accord of this Interaction enables you to see your way through to harmony and agreement even after the most severe conflicts. This is owing to your mutually creating an ongoing sense of what is good and decent about being human, and so co-operation leads to greater harmony, which in turn leads to more co-operation, and so on. You both profit from the simple activity of discussing your likes and dislikes, rather than either expecting to know them already, or assuming that they should be identical.

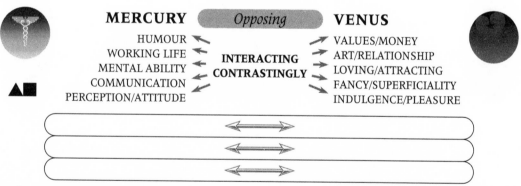

From the Mercury person's point of view, the Venus person's social and aesthetic values don't appeal to or connect with them. A similar experience occurs for Venus, with Mercury's intellectual or daily pursuits not being that attractive to them. So this is the kind of Interaction that happens when there is say, a sexual or security link between you, but not a lot in other departments like cultural and everyday interests. There is a lack of personal common ground that does not create conflict so much as dissatisfaction. It is as if you are on different wavelengths, at least in this area of your overall Interaction. It is unlikely there is a meeting of heart and mind here, and conversation will have a habit of hovering around the relatively trivial. If there are other strong Interactions between the two of you that provide some other kind of heart-mind link, then this not-so-powerful aspect will not matter. If not though, this Interaction's 'sin of omission' can prevent a relationship from getting past first base.

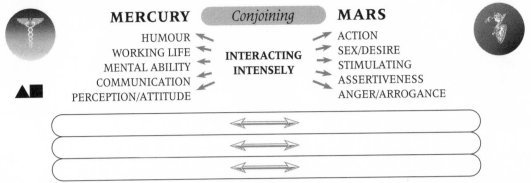

MERCURY *Conjoining* **MARS**

HUMOUR		ACTION
WORKING LIFE	**INTERACTING**	SEX/DESIRE
MENTAL ABILITY	**INTENSELY**	STIMULATING
COMMUNICATION		ASSERTIVENESS
PERCEPTION/ATTITUDE		ANGER/ARROGANCE

Ideas, attitudes and discussions are nearly always upfront with the two of you, and rarely left on the back-burner. This is because your thoughts and desires are like fuel to one another. Naturally enough, this can go in the direction of energetic and effective communication or outright disagreement or hot debate. A great deal depends here on what other Planets in either of your charts are interacting with Mercury and Mars (the Planets themselves), and in what way (see any other relevant Interactions given above or below). This, for the Mercury person, can make the difference between feeling pushed or stimulated by the Mars person; and for the Mars person, between feeling impatient with Mercury for being all talk and no action, or enjoying them as a source of information and a guide to their actions. On a sexual level, this can be a case of talking about or around it but never doing it, to being quite turned on by sexy ideas or sheer mental force.

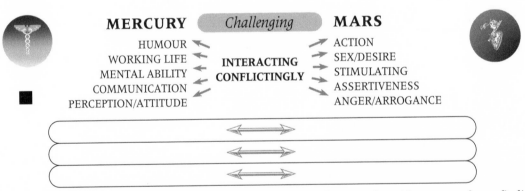

MERCURY *Challenging* **MARS**

HUMOUR		ACTION
WORKING LIFE	**INTERACTING**	SEX/DESIRE
MENTAL ABILITY	**CONFLICTINGLY**	STIMULATING
COMMUNICATION		ASSERTIVENESS
PERCEPTION/ATTITUDE		ANGER/ARROGANCE

This is an argumentative and disagreeable influence. Hardly a day goes by without one of you finding something which the other person says or does that you have to object to. You irritate each other far too easily for any kind of peace or harmony to exist for long. The reasons for such battles will have their origin in the other hard Interactions that you have. This aspect is not the source of conflict itself; it is simply a means (arguing) that you have of expressing discontent with yourselves, each other and life in general. It is almost as if you do not want to communicate properly in case you discover something that really needs seeing to. This mutual irritation and the bickering that it generates are not something others like to be around much – so do not expect many invitations to social occasions unless you both have dangerously convincing social masks, or have your heads stuck in the sand in the way just described. This Interaction is thought (Mercury) versus action (Mars). So Mars gets annoyed with Mercury as they see them as being permanently at the ideas or planning stage, while Mercury regards Mars as an impulsive fool. You probably both have a point here, but sheer annoyance prevents you both from seeing it.

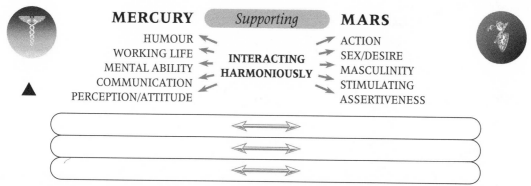

MERCURY *Supporting* **MARS**

MERCURY		MARS
HUMOUR		ACTION
WORKING LIFE	INTERACTING	SEX/DESIRE
MENTAL ABILITY	HARMONIOUSLY	MASCULINITY
COMMUNICATION		STIMULATING
PERCEPTION/ATTITUDE		ASSERTIVENESS

This is very much a 'get up and go' Interaction for it enables both of you to transform thoughts into deeds. Rather than leave something to go to seed, you are inclined to thrash out the best way of achieving an objective. You like locking horns in that mental competition comes naturally to you as a healthy means of keeping sharp and effective. If yours is a sexual relationship, you both appreciate the fact that the brain is the most erogenous zone of all, for sexual ideas and verbal interplay turn you both on. You make a clever team, and others are aware of this mental accord and instinctively steer clear of taking you on as a couple – or are best advised to. So this is a very dynamic Interaction, but with a minimum of friction (notwithstanding the challenging Interactions), which is based upon the Mars person being the ramrod, forcing ideas into action, while Mercury plots the best way of going about it.

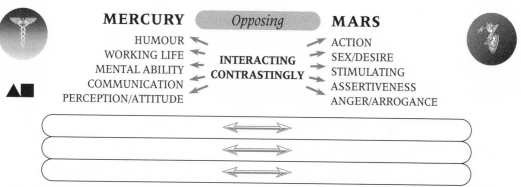

MERCURY *Opposing* **MARS**

MERCURY		MARS
HUMOUR		ACTION
WORKING LIFE	INTERACTING	SEX/DESIRE
MENTAL ABILITY	CONTRASTINGLY	STIMULATING
COMMUNICATION		ASSERTIVENESS
PERCEPTION/ATTITUDE		ANGER/ARROGANCE

The Mars person confronts the Mercury person's ideas, what they say, and how they say it. But as Mercury finds themself being more and more critical of what Mars does and wants, this Interaction can develop into an ongoing war of one person's thoughts versus the other's actions. In short, you argue a lot. If you can both look at this as 'worthy opponents' then you might benefit from having your respective points of view and manner of self-assertion sharpened and improved. Furthermore, such a way of handling the situation could mean that you as a couple become rather effective in putting across your ideas and also acting upon them.

Sometimes you'll find that one person's Planet is interchangeable with the other's

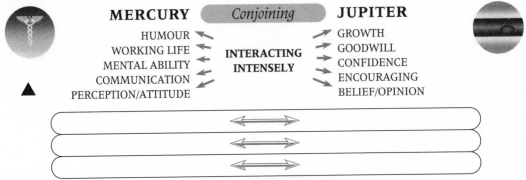

MERCURY *Conjoining* **JUPITER**

HUMOUR	GROWTH
WORKING LIFE	GOODWILL
MENTAL ABILITY	CONFIDENCE
COMMUNICATION	ENCOURAGING
PERCEPTION/ATTITUDE	BELIEF/OPINION

INTERACTING INTENSELY

⟺ You feed one another's minds and understanding to a great degree. Such an Interaction therefore favours any mental, educational or cultural pursuits that you might be involved in. One of you is more of an ideas and visions person, whereas the other helps put them into words or some other appreciable and practical form. These roles can also be interchangeable. Also, if one of you has a problem, the other can help alleviate or even solve it by helping them see it in a larger context, or by providing contacts or techniques to deal with it. Humour can also play a part in this, and may also be a central part of your relationship overall. Moreover, you make good travelling companions, and show one another where to go and how to get there – in more ways than one. There is a small danger of getting stuck in your heads with this Interaction, with perhaps one of you being too conceptual and the other being too pedantic, or of both of you blowing things out of proportion. But sooner or later you could make each other aware of that too, and actually use it to benefit further your communication and understanding.

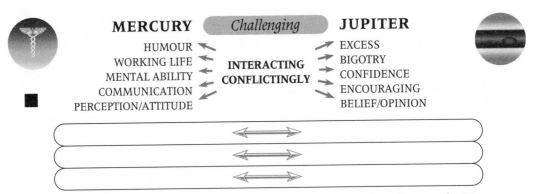

MERCURY *Challenging* **JUPITER**

HUMOUR	EXCESS
WORKING LIFE	BIGOTRY
MENTAL ABILITY	CONFIDENCE
COMMUNICATION	ENCOURAGING
PERCEPTION/ATTITUDE	BELIEF/OPINION

INTERACTING CONFLICTINGLY

⟺ There can be a lot of talk and not much achieved between the two of you because the Mercury person is concerned with details whereas the Jupiter person is more interested in an overall view of things. Jupiter's philosophical or religious concepts frustrate and annoy Mercury's more practical, logical approach. Jupiter's great plans confuse Mercury's work and everyday concerns, which to Jupiter seem piffling and short-sighted. If you could both appreciate that you are each seeing opposite sides of the same coin, then something useful, and inspiring too, could be the result. Jupiter could help Mercury to see the bigger picture and gain a better understanding of how their thoughts and ideas can fit into a greater whole, while Mercury can assist Jupiter in practically, technically and verbally expressing their grand ideas. Any Interactions that you have involving the Moon, Venus or Neptune could indicate whether or not you have the emotional harmony to come to this sort of mental agreement.

Remember that all Interactions are mutual in that each Planet is affecting the other

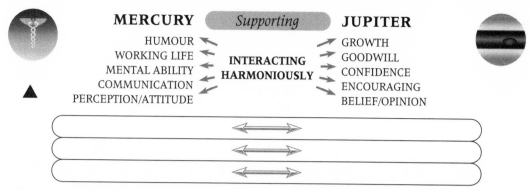

MERCURY *Supporting* **JUPITER**

HUMOUR ← → GROWTH
WORKING LIFE ← **INTERACTING** → GOODWILL
MENTAL ABILITY ← **HARMONIOUSLY** → CONFIDENCE
COMMUNICATION ← → ENCOURAGING
PERCEPTION/ATTITUDE → BELIEF/OPINION

⟺ You have an excellent mental rapport here because the Mercury individual can help the Jupiter individual to contact and express their visions and beliefs in a more effective way, while Jupiter enables Mercury to see how their ideas and attitudes fit into some broader, cultural perspective. Put more simply, you both support and further the minds of one another. As a result you can work together on projects where both the general and the particular need to be equally considered. You can also fruitfully discuss ethical matters and reach an understanding that oils the wheels of day-to-day, mundane matters. Literally or metaphorically speaking, this is rather like a positive relationship between writer (Mercury) and publisher (Jupiter).

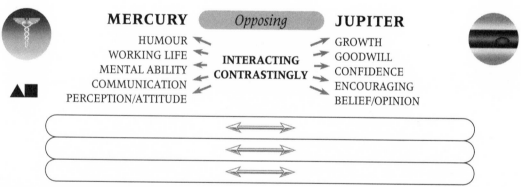

MERCURY *Opposing* **JUPITER**

HUMOUR ← → GROWTH
WORKING LIFE ← **INTERACTING** → GOODWILL
MENTAL ABILITY ← **CONTRASTINGLY** → CONFIDENCE
COMMUNICATION ← → ENCOURAGING
PERCEPTION/ATTITUDE → BELIEF/OPINION

⟺ With this Interaction it is ultimately a case of you both needing to agree to differ, otherwise interminable discussions that get nowhere will be your mental lot. Usually one of you, most likely Jupiter, will take a generalistic or 'visionary' viewpoint, while the other, probably Mercury, would just love to see the plan and feasibility study. Jupiter sees life in terms of the bigger picture, but to Mercury this is just armchair philosophizing. Jupiter will then regard Mercury as linear and short-sighted. Because of all this, a condescending attitude can develop toward one another – an 'I know best but I'll deign to listen to you' sort of thing. Owing to this, this Interaction would be more suited to a teacher/student relationship where one of you is supposed to know more. All the same, this Interaction can be a learning and mind-expanding experience, just so long as you appreciate that both of you have some valid points.

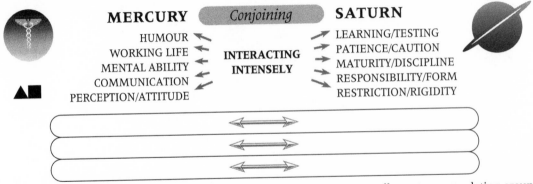

MERCURY *Conjoining* **SATURN**

MERCURY	INTERACTING INTENSELY	SATURN
HUMOUR		LEARNING/TESTING
WORKING LIFE		PATIENCE/CAUTION
MENTAL ABILITY		MATURITY/DISCIPLINE
COMMUNICATION		RESPONSIBILITY/FORM
PERCEPTION/ATTITUDE		RESTRICTION/RIGIDITY

You cannot escape a serious mental tone to your relationship; you may actually centre your relating around it. One of you is teaching the other something they need to know – it may well be mutual. At one level at least, you have a quite earnest or even erudite sense of what is worth talking about. However, a failure to communicate can arise through one or both of you trying to find a logical explanation for everything and thereby missing what is obvious on a more feeling level. Alternatively, a gap in your understanding of one another can occur when the Mercury person wants to dodge and weave around a given issue, while the Saturn person is more dutiful and methodical. Consequently, Mercury can come to regard Saturn as lugubrious, and Saturn judges Mercury to be flip and hasty. But if there is a worthwhile task to be done, you make an efficient team, and leave no stone unturned in your joint pursuit of getting a job well done. The solving of puzzles and the like can also be an absorbing pastime for the pair of you, as long as this too does not devolve into a rut of knowledge for knowledge's sake. This could wind up boring one or both of you, not to mention anyone in the same room. Apart from the dullish areas into which your intellectual assiduousness can get you, this Interaction makes for being a sober and reliable mainstay to any relationship.

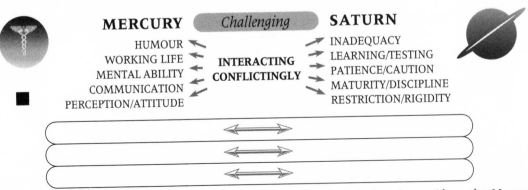

MERCURY *Challenging* **SATURN**

MERCURY	INTERACTING CONFLICTINGLY	SATURN
HUMOUR		INADEQUACY
WORKING LIFE		LEARNING/TESTING
MENTAL ABILITY		PATIENCE/CAUTION
COMMUNICATION		MATURITY/DISCIPLINE
PERCEPTION/ATTITUDE		RESTRICTION/RIGIDITY

You have here a communication block. Often, when putting forth their thoughts or ideas, the Mercury person seems to have to go through an examination under the Saturn person. Literally or metaphorically, this is a pupil/teacher relationship. In an emotional relationship of any kind, this can obviously give rise to an inferior/superior set-up, with the resentments and disdain that accompany it. If, however, the Mercury person can appreciate that their ideas probably do need to be made more practical, or put into practice, and that Saturn has a point, then this would make a potentially negative Interaction quite fruitful. Additionally or alternatively, Mercury may need to take on board the necessity of using their intellect less and their feelings more. Saturn, on the other hand, like any good teacher, has to find a way of saying what they have to say in a way that does not make Mercury feel stupid or inferior. Ironically, Mercury can see Saturn as being stupid because they appear dull and slow, unimaginative and overly conservative. Saturn should seriously consider (their forte, after all) whether Mercury has a point here, because one day Mercury might get so fed up with having their ideas squashed that they find a new teacher! If both of you can take these points on board, you can have an intellectually serious and mutual learning relationship, rather than a cold and dry one.

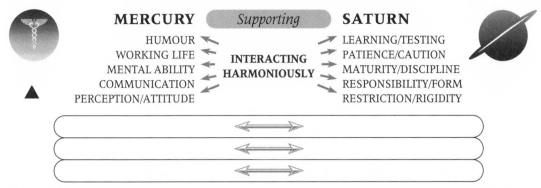

If a practical, working relationship is what you have in mind, then having this excellent Interaction of 'mental efficiency' will ensure that commercial details, information and accounts will be kept in excellent order. Also, relationships that necessitate one person (Saturn) being in authority over the other (Mercury), like teacher/student or parent/child, are favoured by this aspect. In a romantic relationship, your serious mental approach to things will ensure that problems are dealt with – as long as they are not too emotional or subtle. But day-to-day, mundane bumps are smoothed over and worked through efficiently and easily. Saturn will always make sure that Mercury keeps on the case in a practical way, whereas Mercury keeps Saturn informed with the latest 'down on the street'.

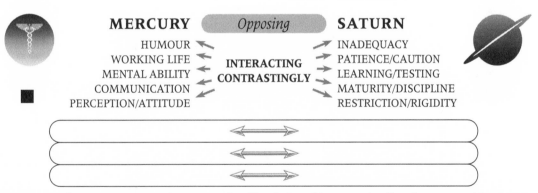

Mercury as a planetary energy is about mental agility, being able to spark off and connect with whatever presents itself, and when. Saturn, on the other hand, has a plan, structure or agenda that all things must somehow keep to. And so it can be seen that Mercury would be regarded by Saturn as shallow and flippant, flitting off in whatever direction interest took them. To Mercury, Saturn seems too serious by far, and in need of lightening up. Saturn will do their best to discipline and train Mercury to be more constructive in the area that Saturn deems necessary – and Mercury would do well to take some of this on board. But, by and large, Mercury will find this tiresome, especially if they already have their own work cut out for them by their own choice. Saturn, for their part, is learning in an oblique way that there is something about themselves that is just not easily understood. Overall then, this dry combination would find its most appropriate place in a relationship where Saturn is supposed to be the one in authority, and Mercury is supposed to be the one who is learning some dull but necessary lesson. Communication between the two of you is rather thin and one-dimensional, and at best merely functional.

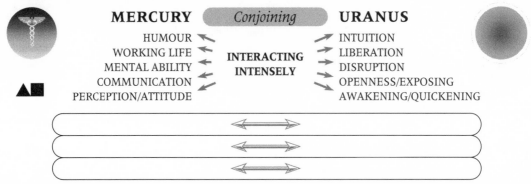

MERCURY *Conjoining* **URANUS**

HUMOUR → ← INTUITION
WORKING LIFE ← **INTERACTING** → LIBERATION
MENTAL ABILITY ← **INTENSELY** → DISRUPTION
COMMUNICATION ← → OPENNESS/EXPOSING
PERCEPTION/ATTITUDE ← ↘ AWAKENING/QUICKENING

⟺ As both Mercury and Uranus are Planets of the mind, you should have quite a strong and stimulating mental connection. Between the two of you, you can work through original ideas, give them verbal expression, and generally spark one another off. Metaphysical or technological subjects could be an area of interest – or one of you may introduce the other to such a pursuit. The Mercury person is usually more grounded in the everyday world. As such, they are able to help Uranus to get a practical handle on their inventiveness or apparently eccentric notions – but at times Mercury just will not be able to understand Uranus who seems to be too 'far out'. Uranus, on the other hand, can awaken Mercury to new attitudes of thought and perception – or simply blow them away. If there are several indications of rapport given elsewhere, then this can be a very innovative and mind-expanding Interaction.

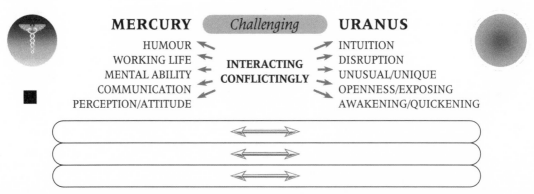

MERCURY *Challenging* **URANUS**

HUMOUR → ← INTUITION
WORKING LIFE ← **INTERACTING** → DISRUPTION
MENTAL ABILITY ← **CONFLICTINGLY** → UNUSUAL/UNIQUE
COMMUNICATION ← → OPENNESS/EXPOSING
PERCEPTION/ATTITUDE ← ↘ AWAKENING/QUICKENING

⟺ On first meeting the Uranus individual, the Mercury person is either impressed by their mental originality – or they see them as just a scatter-brained fool. Yet seeing that unpredictable thoughts, words and circumstances are the hallmark of this Interaction, Mercury is very likely to change their mind. In fact, looked at psychologically, the Uranus person is in Mercury's life to challenge and/or wake up the way they think. If Mercury has a strong mind, they will attempt to 'straighten out' Uranus's more hare-brained ideas, branding them as impractical and off-the-wall. Uranus may take this point on board if they are alive to the possibility that they do actually need to ground their thinking in the 'real world'. More usually though, Uranus will resort to being even more shocking and outlandish in protest against what they see as Mercury's limited viewpoint. So all in all, this Interaction can give rise to many a misunderstanding or crazy argument, scotching day-to-day plans and arrangements in the process. But occasionally, between the spark of Mercury's intellect and the flash of Uranus's intuition, a great idea or realization can be conjured into being.

The greatest act of love is to love the unlovable ...

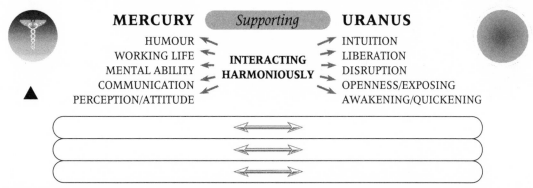

MERCURY **Supporting** URANUS

HUMOUR — INTUITION
WORKING LIFE — **INTERACTING** — LIBERATION
MENTAL ABILITY — **HARMONIOUSLY** — DISRUPTION
COMMUNICATION — OPENNESS/EXPOSING
PERCEPTION/ATTITUDE — AWAKENING/QUICKENING

⟺ Whatever else might be going on between you, this Interaction provides you with a combined mental awareness of new ways of seeing things, and consequently new ways of being and doing too. What's behind this mental awareness is a brilliant, almost telepathic, communication. It has been said that if we were telepathic as a race, then all our problems would cease to exist. The reason being that we would always know what someone really meant, and also when someone was lying. Such mental accord, of which you have some measure, can overcome or actually prevent disagreements and misunderstandings. One could call this Interaction 'The Problem Solver', as you free each other from whatever veils have obscured your perception of how things really are. You may even extend this mental tool to help others as well.

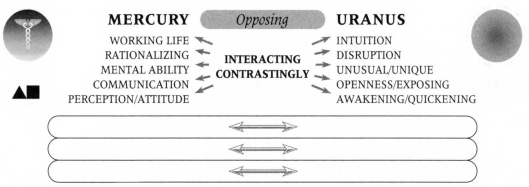

MERCURY **Opposing** URANUS

WORKING LIFE — INTUITION
RATIONALIZING — **INTERACTING** — DISRUPTION
MENTAL ABILITY — **CONTRASTINGLY** — UNUSUAL/UNIQUE
COMMUNICATION — OPENNESS/EXPOSING
PERCEPTION/ATTITUDE — AWAKENING/QUICKENING

⟺ Someone once said that when intuition works it is brilliant, and when it doesn't it is sheer stupidity. This Interaction embodies this statement because Mercury is stimulated and impressed by Uranus's brilliant insights and the new avenues of thought that they bring, but is frustrated and disdainful when any such ideas prove to have no practical substance. What is more, Uranus can in this way be disruptive to Mercury's day-to-day mental functioning – in their workplace, for instance, but possibly giving them a needed jolt in this area. From Uranus's point of view, Mercury can appear to be slow and pedantic as they seek to find a logical explanation for everything. But all this is really just the mental flak that is a necessary part of clearing out old, impractical or biased ideas in both of you. See past this flak, and your mental Interaction can produce quite enlightening and amusing, if sometimes crazy, material. You certainly spark one another off.

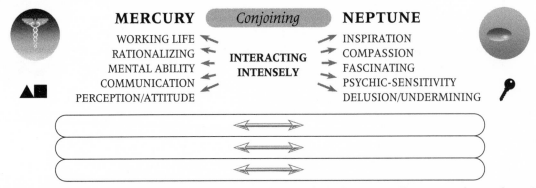

⬌ If both of you are fairly mature and have sorted your ideals from your illusions, and your fantasies from your visions, then this Interaction will enable you, individually and as a couple, to see a lot further and more clearly than many other people. If there are other intense or harmonious mental and emotional links between you, together you can tune into higher levels of intelligence. This amounts to 'channelling' or creative inspiration which may be used artistically, esoterically or therapeutically. One-to-one, the Neptune person is the psychic half who channels, inspires or visualizes, while the Mercury person gives it practical form and 'edits' what Neptune has received. It must be pointed out that these roles can at times be interchangeable. The difficult side to this potentially inspired and inspiring combination, is one of seeing only what you want to see, and reinforcing each other's illusions and wishful thinking. It should really be a case of you both checking out whether either of you are acting this way, or for that matter, being too rationalistic or cynical. And this could also go too far, with Mercury doubting and questioning the visions and impressions of Neptune, or just finding them vague and hard to understand, and Neptune regarding Mercury as being too critical, linear or lacking in imagination. In some respects this sifting process is an essential part of sorting the inspiring from the fanciful, for it is this that ensures that the gold of this mine of mystical information is real and not of the fool's variety. It would also guard against your day-to-day communications becoming garbled or misleading. In effect, you jointly possess a blend of imagination and the means of giving it some form of expression, and if you don't use it, it might well confuse you.

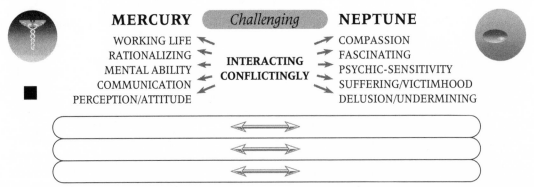

⬌ This can be a bit like trying to plug the telephone into the television. Both are wonderful transmitter/receivers, but without some radical rewiring (profound change in perception of how you view life and one another) they are not going to communicate very well with each other. The Mercury person's logical approach to things is annoyed or baffled by the Neptune person's more sensitive and holistic view of life. Mercury wants to see everything and everyone as separate, categorizable entities, whereas Neptune feels everything and everyone to be totally interconnected. What this does for your perception of one another is that Mercury holds Neptune to be an unrealistic dreamer – and therefore unreliable, possibly deceptive, even mentally unbalanced. Conversely, Neptune sees Mercury as not seeing the whole picture, over-simplifying what is complex but beautiful, and generally enchained by intellectual tyranny. Mercury's tunnel-vision of Neptune as a person is what can be really troublesome for Neptune, because they seem to be seen only as someone who does or does not fit into Mercury's linear landscape. Eventually, rather than argue the point, Neptune will, possibly unconsciously, go along with Mercury's idea of them, which ironically means that Neptune becomes the very shape-shifter that Mercury cannot handle. This is because Mercury is putting out myriad expectations that their rational perception overlooks. But all the while Mercury thinks they're the one with a firm grip on reality. The point is that they may well be, but they will have to prove it in the face of Neptune's possibly neurotic and evasive antics. But the reality is not that either of you is right or wrong, but that the telephone and the television are vaguely similar but quite different, and very unlikely ever to make lasting or meaningful contact – unless 'radical rewiring' is done. The reason why you experience this Interaction at all is so that you can hopefully appreciate the existence of both these modes of perception/communication, and not simply become alienated by getting stuck on the illusory fence between correct and incorrect, real and unreal. Incidentally, the crossed lines that this Interaction produces can also manifest as the two of you having some kind of breakdown of communication with others, like neighbours or colleagues. Overall, and basically, this Interaction causes a misconception of what one of you is to the other, and the glitches in communication that follow upon this.

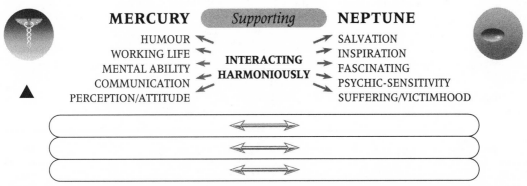

Because these two Planets represent the two sides of the brain – the psychic right and the logical left – when paired harmoniously as in this Interaction, the two of you can be expected to evolve progressively toward a greater and greater understanding of one another, and of life and people generally. What facilitates this process is a psychic rapport that you have, which means that you are consciously or unconsciously attuned to where each of you are mentally and emotionally. The old adage 'Do as you would be done by' is made real with you two as you deftly give each other space and avoid stepping on one another's toes. Not surprisingly, you are capable of working together on literary pursuits, with the Mercury individual editing and finding the right words or avenues of expression for the Neptune person's visions and ideas. In turn, Neptune shows Mercury that there are subtleties and incongruities to life that Mercury may overlook through being too 'scientific'. Art and music are an important part of your relationship together, either in terms of actually be creative or being simply appreciative. This Interaction is not dynamic in itself, which means it can recede into the background when more hot, forceful and negative Interactions come to the fore. It is therefore vital to give yourselves time after any such altercation, for this psychic connection will automatically right things in a quite mysterious way.

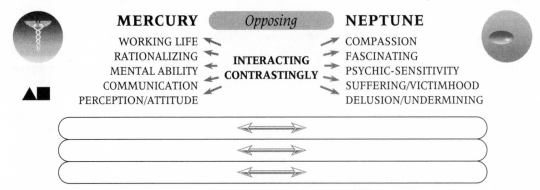

MERCURY *Opposing* **NEPTUNE**

WORKING LIFE		COMPASSION
RATIONALIZING	**INTERACTING**	FASCINATING
MENTAL ABILITY	**CONTRASTINGLY**	PSYCHIC-SENSITIVITY
COMMUNICATION		SUFFERING/VICTIMHOOD
PERCEPTION/ATTITUDE		DELUSION/UNDERMINING

⟺ The judgement of the Mercury individual can get confused by what they see as Neptune's vague or obscure behaviour. They may even see it as a subtlety that they cannot grasp. Most probably, Neptune is not clear about what they want or don't want from Mercury, and is putting out mixed or indistinct messages. One reason for this could be that Neptune is not sure of their own pitch, and the Mercury person puts them on the spot in some way. In any event, crossed lines are very likely, rather like what one would encounter when trying to get by in a country whose language you have little knowledge of. In some instances, Neptune can seem devious or mysterious or stupid, which may or may not be the case. And seeing as this is about mis-communication, Mercury could appear this way to Neptune. There may well be some external element like drugs or alcohol that is part and parcel of your interacting generally, and this Interaction really kicks your lack of mental accord into the stratosphere of total non-communication. Even if stone cold sober, there is still the likelihood that your failure to connect will result in confused arrangements and that kind of thing. Any emotional rapport or sympathy between you will do wonders to by-pass this poor channel of communication; maybe this Interaction occurs in order to force the development of empathy.

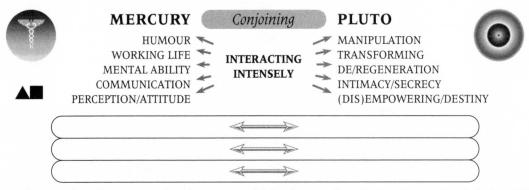

MERCURY *Conjoining* **PLUTO**

HUMOUR		MANIPULATION
WORKING LIFE	**INTERACTING**	TRANSFORMING
MENTAL ABILITY	**INTENSELY**	DE/REGENERATION
COMMUNICATION		INTIMACY/SECRECY
PERCEPTION/ATTITUDE		(DIS)EMPOWERING/DESTINY

⟺ What one of you has to say to the other, or even thinks about, makes a lasting impression. So be it positive or negative, expect it to eventually come back to you in some way. Also, the powerful effect of this combination has a great deal to do with the direction in which such power is expressed. For example, if both of you are involved in some sort of research or psychological work together, which is quite likely, then the mental power of it is seen to go outwards into the world and have some kind of effect which you can both monitor and work upon. If, on the other hand, that probing mentality is aimed at one another, a kind of psychological game of cat and mouse can ensue. Each or one of you can be intrigued by the insights the other has into your mind and make-up. But at a certain point this can feel like psychic invasion. So the issue that then arises is one of trust with each other's darkest secrets. Am I being helped or selfishly manipulated? Do I want to know more and get in deeper – or not? These could be the kind of questions that one or both of you might find that you're asking. This contact is rather like 'mind sex' because it is both mentally compelling and threatening; or a therapist/patient relationship where confidentiality and trust are vital. It is the Mercury person who is most likely to feel 'invaded', and by way of defence will try to dodge or trivialize Pluto's mind-probes. Pluto can find this reaction despicably superficial, but they should look to their motives for trying to rip away Mercury's apparent veil of pretence or cleverness. To a certain extent, or rather by its very nature, this mutual mind-probing will be unavoidable. When such an exercise is part and parcel of how you express yourselves to the world, individually or as a partnership, then you can wield a profound influence with great conviction and effect. In any event, this Interaction should make you both mentally or psychologically stronger. Black humour could also be on your mutual mental menu.

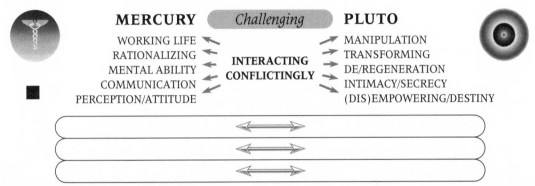

Usually the Mercury person's perception of life is the more practical and 'safe' in comparison to the Pluto person's probing or psychological way of looking at it. In the face of Pluto's X-ray gaze, Mercury finds that they have to dodge and weave and consequently appears even more superficial and 'reasonable'. On the other hand, Mercury may just refuse to budge from what they see as their more sensible standpoint, branding Pluto as being too obsessed with always wanting to get to the very bottom of things. Pluto's response to this will be to use every means at their disposal to influence Mercury's thinking with their propaganda of psychological or occult values. Not surprisingly, this is not an Interaction to inspire trust – on the contrary, it can lead to 'paranoia' on one or both of your parts. To resolve or prevent the breakdown in communication that this can create, Pluto should honestly look at the possibility that the reason they want Mercury to see things their way is that they are not entirely convinced of it themselves. Mercury, apart from getting Pluto to lighten up a bit, should meet Pluto half way and take a deeper look at themselves and the meaning of life. Who knows, they may then be able to give Pluto a spot of their own mental medicine.

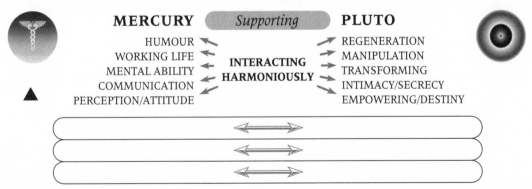

The Pluto individual can be very instrumental in regenerating or even transforming the Mercury person's career and/or everyday attitude. This may take some time to develop, but its effects upon Mercury are long-lasting – possibly beyond the span of the relationship itself, for this is no indicator of emotional durability, one way or the other. In return Pluto benefits from seeing their 'pupil' burgeon under their influence. This is not an ego-trip on their part, but just that it is gratifying for them to know that their deep and often invisible 'ray' is effective. On a more mutual level, your discussions are relatively quite profound, and probably include occult subjects, psychology, and anything dealing with the invisible or unknown. Because of this you are usually quite happy to be alone with each other's intellectual company.

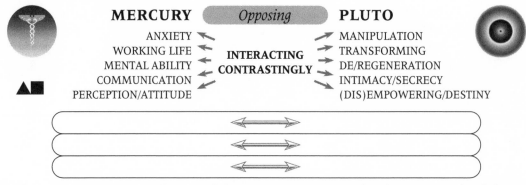

MERCURY *Opposing* **PLUTO**

ANXIETY		MANIPULATION
WORKING LIFE	INTERACTING	TRANSFORMING
MENTAL ABILITY	CONTRASTINGLY	DE/REGENERATION
COMMUNICATION		INTIMACY/SECRECY
PERCEPTION/ATTITUDE		(DIS)EMPOWERING/DESTINY

The Pluto person penetrates to the core of the Mercury person's mind and attempts to bend their way of thinking towards what they think is more valid and profound. Although Mercury can at first find this impressive and somehow compelling, they sooner or later experience such mental invasion as being nerve-wracking. So they then crave that erstwhile and relatively superficial attitude to life where probing and plumbing the depths is not regarded as essential mental activity. However, Pluto's hold on Mercury's mentality is as persistent as it is genuine in its profundity and psychological insight; if they have some point rooted in truth then Mercury will find it irresistible, despite their objections. If though, Pluto is simply out to suppress Mercury's own point of view, then Mercury will grow increasingly distrustful of Pluto's words and intentions – and ironically be intellectually more robust as a result. But as this is an Opposition aspect, it is important to remember that each of you is supposed to become more aware of your respective strengths and weaknesses, rather than simply resist or insist. This means that Mercury may gain some far more reliable insights into how life works, and get to the bottom of things rather than flitting around rather ineffectually. Pluto, on the other hand, can learn to take things more at face value and not be quite so interrogatory, letting Mercury (and themselves) take time out with a bit of brain candy every once in a while.

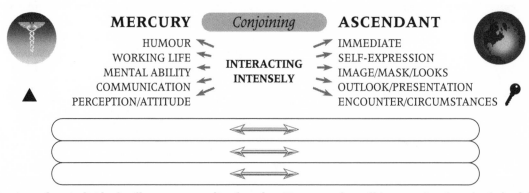

MERCURY *Conjoining* **ASCENDANT**

HUMOUR		IMMEDIATE
WORKING LIFE	INTERACTING	SELF-EXPRESSION
MENTAL ABILITY	INTENSELY	IMAGE/MASK/LOOKS
COMMUNICATION		OUTLOOK/PRESENTATION
PERCEPTION/ATTITUDE		ENCOUNTER/CIRCUMSTANCES

The Ascendant individual will act as a sounding board to Mercury, who will in turn give them back food for thought. In fact, 'food for thought' describes well what you both are to one another, in direct proportion, however, to your current states of mind as individuals. You put one another in touch with not only ideas and ways of translating the meaning of things, but also introduce one another to interesting people. You also stimulate each other's wits, and humour can be a strong component to your Interaction. Together you can bring alive the phrase 'body language' as you connect so well through word and physical expression. But this does not mean to say that what is communicated is always pleasant; you may even get on each other's nerves – a case of the media being good, but not necessarily the message.

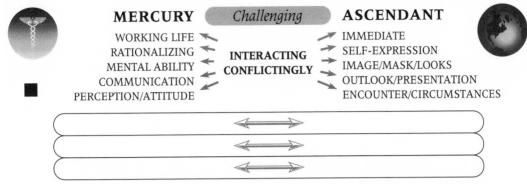

MERCURY — *Challenging* — **ASCENDANT**

MERCURY		ASCENDANT
WORKING LIFE	**INTERACTING CONFLICTINGLY**	IMMEDIATE
RATIONALIZING		SELF-EXPRESSION
MENTAL ABILITY		IMAGE/MASK/LOOKS
COMMUNICATION		OUTLOOK/PRESENTATION
PERCEPTION/ATTITUDE		ENCOUNTER/CIRCUMSTANCES

There is a mildly critical atmosphere that pervades your relationship. The perception of the one of you fails to appreciate the body language of the other, and this can lead to an irritation that infects other parts of your being together. Making decisions together could also present a problem in itself. If you can see your two different attitudes as a means of sorting things out in a good-humoured fashion, then this not-too-significant Interaction will have its 'irritant' value diminished, or even converted into something useful.

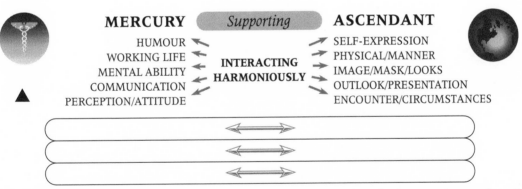

MERCURY — *Supporting* — **ASCENDANT**

MERCURY		ASCENDANT
HUMOUR	**INTERACTING HARMONIOUSLY**	SELF-EXPRESSION
WORKING LIFE		PHYSICAL/MANNER
MENTAL ABILITY		IMAGE/MASK/LOOKS
COMMUNICATION		OUTLOOK/PRESENTATION
PERCEPTION/ATTITUDE		ENCOUNTER/CIRCUMSTANCES

You have a fairly easy banter going on between you. You also make good working companions, and possibly even met in your place of work. The Mercury person gets along easily with the Ascendant in a day-to-day way, and connects with their personal style, while the Ascendant person finds the wit and agility of Mercury fun to be with and work alongside.

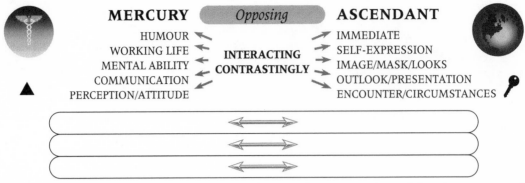

MERCURY *Opposing* **ASCENDANT**

HUMOUR		IMMEDIATE
WORKING LIFE	**INTERACTING**	SELF-EXPRESSION
MENTAL ABILITY	**CONTRASTINGLY**	IMAGE/MASK/LOOKS
COMMUNICATION		OUTLOOK/PRESENTATION
PERCEPTION/ATTITUDE		ENCOUNTER/CIRCUMSTANCES

Straightaway, something clicks on a mental level when you first meet. It is as if the Mercury person is a mental mirror to the Ascendant person. In fact, this contact is entirely cerebral and does not in itself suggest anything emotional or physical between the two of you. However, because of the excellent communication and intellectual rapport that it potentially bestows, any physical or emotional (or intellectual) issues that do arise can be thought through and talked out very efficiently between you. Notwithstanding any other Interactions you might have that are detrimental to communication, if there is a mental solution at all, you'll find it. Mercury is also of great help in accurately observing and helping to improve the Ascendant's manner of self-expression and outlook. In return, the Ascendant can aid Mercury in verbally expressing themselves with more effect and style, perhaps through putting them in contact with interesting and useful people. Note that this Interaction could also be called Mercury Conjoining Descendant, which would account for the intense verbal and intellectual interplay. If and when you have communication hitches, it is because one or both of you is failing to accept the other's ability to complement their thinking or point of view. The reason for this being that they think they have all the answers – when of course, they do not.

VENUS

INTERACTING
WITH

VENUS	URANUS
MARS	NEPTUNE
JUPITER	PLUTO
SATURN	ASCENDANT

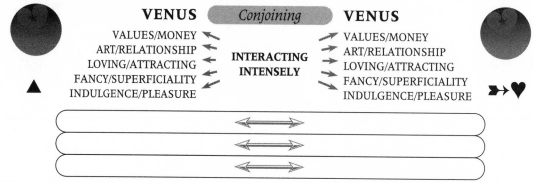

This Interaction could be called 'St Valentine's own' for it confers all the romantic and social graces upon your coming and being together. Your likes and dislikes are very similar, and you take great pleasure in each other's company. Others like to be around you too. Your style of relationship will fit very well with the respective requirements of your Venus Signs, which will usually be the same. Aesthetically and artistically, you also have a lot in common – and you resonate creatively with one another. The only pitfall to be wary of here is an inclination that you both have to base the relationship upon superficialities such as appearance and manners. Just tell yourselves that the inside of each of you is as good, if not better, than the outside. Then, hopefully, this will not only avert disappointment, but enable you both to attract more and more, both materially and spiritually, into your lives together.

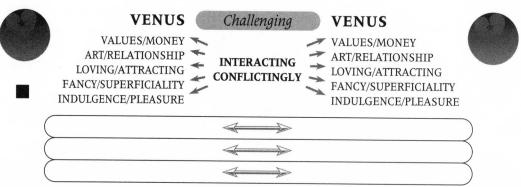

Your tastes and values clash in some areas. This may not be too great a problem unless you let it become so. Small things like disagreeing on what to buy, what film to see, what food to eat, etc, if allowed to become a priority, could undermine whatever sharing and harmony you have between you. More seriously though, an imbalance in terms of how much or what type of affection is shown could amount to a dissatisfaction that is hard to ignore. If such a thing can be regarded as not that important, then well and good. If not, however, dissatisfaction could lead to separation.

No one Interaction makes or breaks a relationship

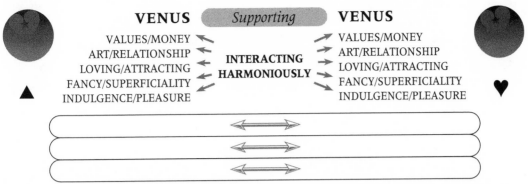

At one level at least, there is great harmony between you, making for mutual pleasure and complementary tastes and values. You are very much the 'couple' in the sense of being seen as a happy pair by others, and your social life could well be a central theme to your own relationship. If, however, you are loners by nature, you are happy in each other's company, playing and loving together on your own. Artistic pursuits and people are also something you can be involved with. Venus being Venus though, there is always the danger of there not being enough emotional depth, even, or especially, with the Supporting aspect. In fact, the possibility of there being too much ease or of encouraging each other's social or physical indulgences, can render your relationship a little meaningless. Appreciating the true value of the pleasantness that you have and feel as a couple can be a beautiful springboard for plunging into the deeper aspects of your being so much together.

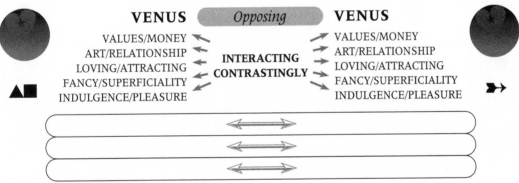

This is rather like two magnets coming together in that both pull together at once rather than just one attracting the other. So this is a classic mutual attraction, but after the initial clinching has occurred, both of you will find that you are a strange mixture of similar and dissimilar tastes and social standards. This can give rise to either being very happy doing the same thing together, or being annoyingly out of sync. What lies behind this is the need to become increasingly aware of what turns each other on – or off. Apart from simply observing this in one another, studying your respective Venus Sign positions would tell you a great deal about differences and similarities. In the process of doing this, both of you can become more aware of what appeals and doesn't appeal on a general level rather than just a personal one. This means that your combined sense of what is popular can give rise to a more commercial awareness – something about which your partnership may become quite astute. As hard aspects go, this isn't particularly 'hard' because Venus is about the pursuit of happiness and harmony and this is what you consistently drive one another towards. A very real danger is simply that you will overindulge in whatever it is that you both like. Conversely, one of you can be happy indulging in something when along comes the other and looks on disapprovingly, thereby spoiling their enjoyment. But probably the greatest hidden asset of this Interaction is that whatever happens between the two of you, those two magnets keep you together – sometimes whether you like it or not!

Not every Profile, or part of a Profile, is likely to apply all the time

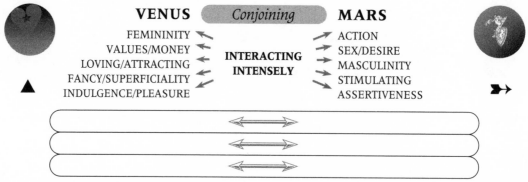

VENUS *Conjoining* **MARS**

FEMININITY
VALUES/MONEY
LOVING/ATTRACTING
FANCY/SUPERFICIALITY
INDULGENCE/PLEASURE

**INTERACTING
INTENSELY**

ACTION
SEX/DESIRE
MASCULINITY
STIMULATING
ASSERTIVENESS

Here Cupid scores a bull's eye! There is a natural and immediate sexual attraction between you. If this is not a sexual relationship – but it probably is – then this would certainly be a warm and tactile one. Not that this Interaction is troublesome – excepting that you may not be able to keep your hands off one another – but it is easier and more straightforward when Mars is a male and Venus a female. This is because natural or biological roles and drives find their right place, with the male initiating and the female gladly responding. When it's the other way around, the female's inclination to call the shots and do the chasing may find the male feeling slightly awkward, occasionally frustrated or even repulsed. If there are more difficult contacts between the two of you then such can be made more acute. Even so, the role-reversal can be a turn-on in itself! Generally, Venus can show Mars to be more sensual and responsive, whereas Mars is able to prompt Venus to go spontaneously and directly for what they desire.

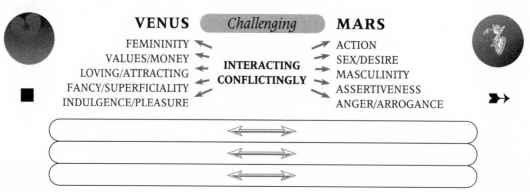

VENUS *Challenging* **MARS**

FEMININITY
VALUES/MONEY
LOVING/ATTRACTING
FANCY/SUPERFICIALITY
INDULGENCE/PLEASURE

**INTERACTING
CONFLICTINGLY**

ACTION
SEX/DESIRE
MASCULINITY
ASSERTIVENESS
ANGER/ARROGANCE

⟺ A quite immediate and very exciting feeling is evident from early on, even on first meeting. A thoroughly enlightened person would recognize such a sensation as one of Cupid's tricks, and steer clear. However, seeing as there are very few thoroughly enlightened beings around, and that there are probably other more valid agendas or Interactions between the two of you, you succumb. Yet the fact still remains that this aspect does create sexual attraction, but in itself, there is little else. One might say this has a 'one night stand' quality about it, for the sex may be gratifying on a physical level, but the lack or intrusion of finer feelings finds it very empty or crude. So what starts out as attracting can end up repelling. Usually it is the Mars person who loses interest first and looks elsewhere, but the Venus person may have felt uncomfortable beforehand but carried on succumbing in spite of such feelings. If there are indications elsewhere of the mutual understanding that this Interaction definitely doesn't provide, then you will both probably put such impulsive folly down to experience, or the lack of it. Mars could then learn to refine the expression of their desires, and Venus recover from any bruised sensitivity and teach them how to be more emotionally resilient.

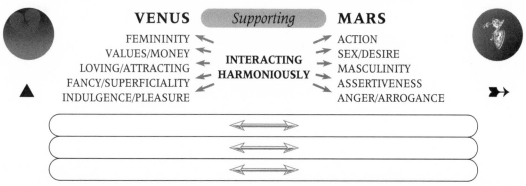

VENUS *Supporting* **MARS**

VENUS		MARS
FEMININITY		ACTION
VALUES/MONEY	**INTERACTING**	SEX/DESIRE
LOVING/ATTRACTING	**HARMONIOUSLY**	MASCULINITY
FANCY/SUPERFICIALITY		ASSERTIVENESS
INDULGENCE/PLEASURE		ANGER/ARROGANCE

This is an accurate but low-powered dart from Cupid. You are sexually or socially attracted to one another, but unless there are other more urgent Interactions, you are not going to plunge in on the strength of this one alone. A curious thing that comes into focus when studying relationships with astrology is that it is the 'noisy', jagged or sharp-edged feelings that so often propel us into relationship rather than the gentle, well-modulated kind like this one. The latter are what are (sometimes sorely) needed once a relationship is off the ground. So whatever the case, there is a pleasant spiciness to being in each other's company. This Interaction also contributes to any involvement you might have in the creative or performing arts. One to one, Venus can show Mars how to be more gracious and stylish in how they conduct themselves socially or go about getting what they want. Mars, on the other hand, can bring Venus out of their shell and get them to realize their worth or charm.

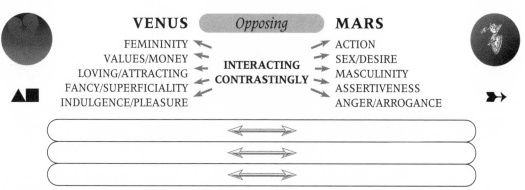

VENUS *Opposing* **MARS**

VENUS		MARS
FEMININITY		ACTION
VALUES/MONEY	**INTERACTING**	SEX/DESIRE
LOVING/ATTRACTING	**CONTRASTINGLY**	MASCULINITY
FANCY/SUPERFICIALITY		ASSERTIVENESS
INDULGENCE/PLEASURE		ANGER/ARROGANCE

This Interaction is a classic indication of mutual, and very possibly sexual, attraction. However, it is also a classic re-enactment of the basic differences between the sexes. This is particularly the case if Mars is a male and Venus is a female; his maleness is what turns her on, but at a later date this very thing becomes the forcefulness that she objects to. Conversely, what is initially experienced by the male as her female allure and mystique can later be seen to be inaccessibility or over-sensitivity. When the planets are reversed, the male Venus and the female Mars, there is confusion because the female is having to be the one that calls the shots while the male feels passive and submissive. If this is the case, then it can be managed as long as both of you can accept this role-reversal with grace, otherwise it will prove too uncomfortable to maintain. In either case, the awareness to aim for is a sharply increased sense of what it is to be male or female – quite possibly in contrast to what you previously felt or believed such to be. The male Mars/female Venus coupling is by far the simpler, especially if each of you can accept the traditional, even biological, roles of masculinity and femininity as being valid, comfortable and enjoyable. Failing this, your Interaction on this level could give rise to falling out over such typical issues as respective rights and property – not least of all the perceived owner-ship of each other. But mutual frustration would become the most damaging element, which is a shame considering that this aspect is there to remind you that men and women were made for one another.

Look at the Planet-Sign Profiles for the personal meaning of Planets in any Interaction

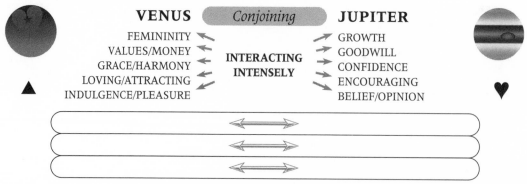

VENUS *Conjoining* JUPITER

VENUS		JUPITER
FEMININITY		GROWTH
VALUES/MONEY	**INTERACTING**	GOODWILL
GRACE/HARMONY	**INTENSELY**	CONFIDENCE
LOVING/ATTRACTING		ENCOURAGING
INDULGENCE/PLEASURE		BELIEF/OPINION

This is a particularly favourable Interaction because it ensures a benevolent and good-hearted feeling between the two of you. You tend to see the best in each other and this furthers positive development for both of you as individuals and as a couple. This can mean a number of things, from attracting wealth to helping you through hard or tense times together. There is an enthusiasm for life and each other which ultimately leads to quite a religious or spiritual understanding and expression of what your relationship means. Along the way, however, there can be quite a strong indulgent streak that best be curbed if your life together is to be more than just a feast of eating and drinking and social rounds. The Venus person can help give the Jupiter person a social direction and context to their visions of a better life, while Jupiter encourages Venus to make more of their talents. Through, or apart from, any storms that your relationship may have to endure, this Interaction will maintain a constant flow of joy and optimism.

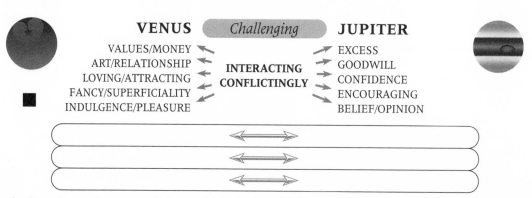

VENUS *Challenging* JUPITER

VENUS		JUPITER
VALUES/MONEY		EXCESS
ART/RELATIONSHIP	**INTERACTING**	GOODWILL
LOVING/ATTRACTING	**CONFLICTINGLY**	CONFIDENCE
FANCY/SUPERFICIALITY		ENCOURAGING
INDULGENCE/PLEASURE		BELIEF/OPINION

On the face of it you have, or could have, a high old time, for this makes for a pretty indulgent and hedonistic coupling. You encourage one another to seek pleasure and excitement which, although this may come under the heading of sowing some wild oats, does find you frittering away time, energy and/or money. Apart from someone having eventually to pay the piper, or watch their waistline, it can also be an imposition on others who have more serious things to do. There is also an easy-come-easy-go feel which can be quite upsetting to one of you if you have more earnest expectations of the relationship. Usually, it is Jupiter's urge for freedom and experience that can hurt and offend the sensibilities and desire for companionship of Venus. Moral issues come to be a major consideration, sooner or later.

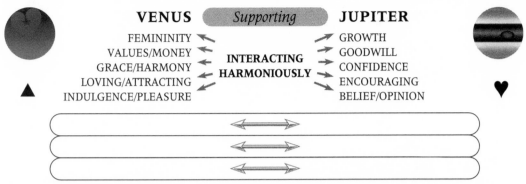

VENUS *Supporting* JUPITER

FEMININITY
VALUES/MONEY   **INTERACTING**
GRACE/HARMONY   **HARMONIOUSLY**
LOVING/ATTRACTING
INDULGENCE/PLEASURE

GROWTH
GOODWILL
CONFIDENCE
ENCOURAGING
BELIEF/OPINION

Your being together creates prosperity, or at least a promise of it. It should be said that this prosperity can take many forms – money, property, good living, access to luxuries, and most of all, burgeoning love. You are both good news to one another, in whatever way or context this applies. The crock of gold at the end of the rainbow – or simply a cup of water at the end of a dry and dusty road – is what this Interaction symbolizes. But wine will probably flow soon after – 'Good times here, better down the road'. There is one small snag with this combination, which is that it can blind you to or distract you from issues of more serious concern. All the same, this is an Interaction of joy and abundance.

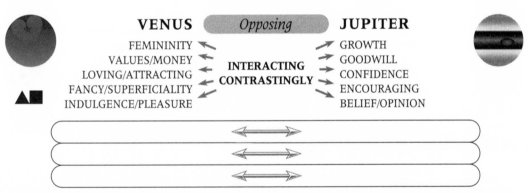

VENUS *Opposing* JUPITER

FEMININITY
VALUES/MONEY
LOVING/ATTRACTING   **INTERACTING**
FANCY/SUPERFICIALITY   **CONTRASTINGLY**
INDULGENCE/PLEASURE

GROWTH
GOODWILL
CONFIDENCE
ENCOURAGING
BELIEF/OPINION

As Planets, Venus and Jupiter are quite similar for they both relate to the pleasures and joys of life – so although this is an Opposing aspect, you will probably have plenty of fun together. The Venus person loves Jupiter's largesse and excessiveness, their cultural awareness and breadth of mind. Jupiter greatly values Venus's charm and social style, for it fits well into Jupiter's bigger picture. Because of this mutual enjoyment and admiration, many a flaw or sin of omission can be overlooked. But this is the danger of this Interaction: you can both be too busy being, or wanting to be, social successes or live wires to notice that you are not actually recognizing each other as individuals in your own right – only as social or cultural appliances. And of course another danger is indulgence in whatever your appetites include – food, drink, partying, social niceties, etc. So ironically, even though it is the value that you place or placed upon one another that draws you together, it is the failure to see each other's true value, warts and all, that can cause you to drift apart. But all the same, it is, or was, great fun!

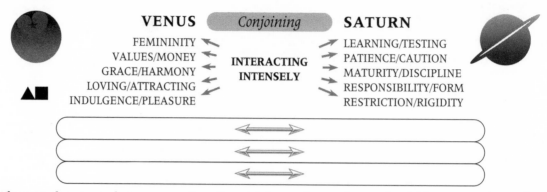

VENUS **Conjoining** SATURN

FEMININITY			LEARNING/TESTING
VALUES/MONEY	**INTERACTING**		PATIENCE/CAUTION
GRACE/HARMONY	**INTENSELY**		MATURITY/DISCIPLINE
LOVING/ATTRACTING			RESPONSIBILITY/FORM
INDULGENCE/PLEASURE			RESTRICTION/RIGIDITY

Whatever else goes on between you, there is certainly a serious and committed side to your relationship. Potentially, this has the makings of a classic marriage – given time. Ideally, you should be able to maintain a good balance between being playful and loving (the Venus person's department mainly) and order and duty (mostly the Saturn person's contribution). In order to do this, one of you should be progressively taking a page out of the other's book. If, however, a balance and exchange of this type is not created, then Saturn can seem to become a wet blanket or not be forthcoming at all, while Venus appears wanton and capricious – and the rot could set in. Alternatively, your relationship could be quite formal, or for reasons of convenience or money. If this is the case, it may only be a matter of time before one of you – Venus probably – craves a more romantic relationship, and Saturn has their expectation of 'love being for fools' confirmed. Whatever happens, unless there is some very negative event in your lives, such as an acrimonious parting, you will always give and receive from each other a sober kind of affection.

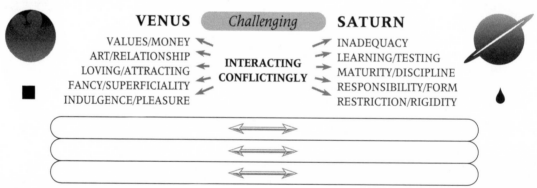

VENUS **Challenging** SATURN

VALUES/MONEY			INADEQUACY
ART/RELATIONSHIP	**INTERACTING**		LEARNING/TESTING
LOVING/ATTRACTING	**CONFLICTINGLY**		MATURITY/DISCIPLINE
FANCY/SUPERFICIALITY			RESPONSIBILITY/FORM
INDULGENCE/PLEASURE			RESTRICTION/RIGIDITY

There is a clash here because the Venus person will want to play and enjoy themselves while the Saturn individual is beset with duties and work. Or Saturn will try to instil discipline into how Venus goes about their aesthetic, social or other pursuits. So Saturn feels like the parent who is forever having to guide their child in the ways of the world, stressing that effort, economy and objectivity are necessary if one is to get on in life. Unfortunately, Venus will often regard this as being too serious and emotionally suppressive. Because Saturn is thus made to feel the killjoy or wet blanket, or simply socially or emotionally inadequate, it falls to them to realize that they are being forced to become more disciplined and responsible as well, but in the more refined sense of learning to draw the line yet at the same time not react to Venus's complaints, games or indulgences. Like the good teacher, Saturn should deliver the lessons with the firm inner assurance that sooner or later the pupil will have to learn – maybe the hard way, and in their own time – but without becoming embittered because they feel they are being misunderstood, like so many parents, real or metaphorical, so often do. Venus should tell themself that Saturn will ease off their pressure in proportion to how much they learn to become responsible and constructive with regard to their talents and moral behaviour. It is important, however, that Saturn does not overlook the sublime and childlike charm with which Venus can brighten up a dull day or even prevent Saturn from becoming dull or unloving. All in all, this makes for a serious relationship where each of you is learning to strike a balance between love and duty, pleasure and responsibility. Separation can occasionally threaten, or even become a reality, if the above 'writing on the wall' is not read and obeyed. But given time, it can go from strength to strength.

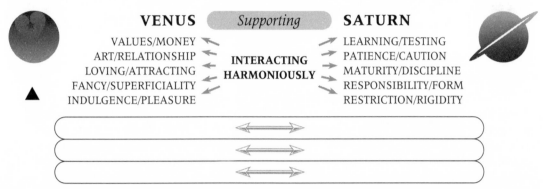

There is a definite layer of emotional responsibility and physical fidelity between the two of you. Any more flighty or indulgent elements in one or both of you will be prevented or at least brought to book by this sense of social propriety. Through highs and lows, this Interaction acts as a stabilizer, returning you to some kind of balance. The personal interchange behind this is the Saturn person validating the worth of the Venus person, but in a sober, understated way that is ultimately more substantial than a more sensational display of appreciation. Venus, in reciprocation, appreciates Saturn's quiet, less sensational side, thereby establishing a very personal bond. Although this Interaction is no more a guarantee of a sound and durable relationship than any other aspect, it is or could be the mainstay of a marriage, business or parent/child relationship.

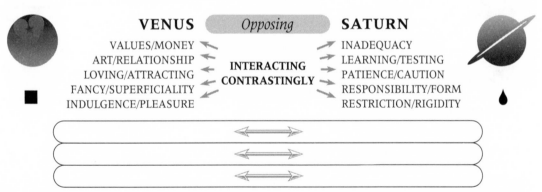

This can be very difficult to handle because as planetary energies Venus and Saturn are at odds with one another – Venus being love and play, Saturn being duty and work. And so this antipathetic theme can play itself out – or have to work itself out – through your relationship. The Venus person could appear frivolous or superficial to the Saturn person, whereas Saturn may seem inhibited or limited by their own feelings or responsibilities. Basically, Saturn is liable to feel unloved or be unloving, and Venus more socially flowing or even fancy-free. In the end it is a case of both of you being committed in your own individual ways. Venus will have to melt Saturn's wall, while Saturn should learn to be more trusting and not so stiff. Put more simply, Saturn is learning to love, and Venus should be a good example of love. But the danger is that Venus can resort to game-playing or capriciousness in the face of Saturn's apparent coldness. Needless to say, such behaviour would only increase Saturn's reserve. Possibly you may both have to look long and hard at what your real motivations are for being in this relationship. Without such serious reappraisal, a sizeable wedge could grow between you, leading to eventual separation. Bear in mind that time is a very important factor in the development and learning that this Interaction demands.

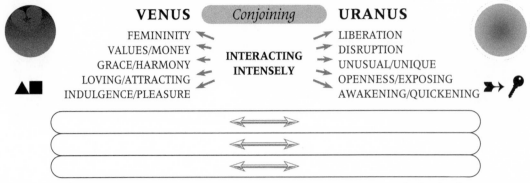

VENUS *Conjoining* **URANUS**

FEMININITY		LIBERATION
VALUES/MONEY	**INTERACTING**	DISRUPTION
GRACE/HARMONY	**INTENSELY**	UNUSUAL/UNIQUE
LOVING/ATTRACTING		OPENNESS/EXPOSING
INDULGENCE/PLEASURE		AWAKENING/QUICKENING

This is one of the most powerful mutually and instantly attracting Interactions in the book. The Venus person is swept off their feet by the extraordinary, possibly otherworldly, quality they perceive in the Uranus person. Uranus is drawn to the style and/or beauty of Venus. In fact the actual circumstances of your meeting could be otherworldly in some way, presaging the unusual nature and course of your relationship itself. If we take a brief look at the myth of Uranus it will give us some idea of why this is such an irresistible attraction. Uranus was the 'god of gods', Heaven, who lay across Gaia, the Earth, and Creation then came about. One of his sons, Saturn, strongly disapproved of his random way of ruling and deposed him by scything off his sexual organs and casting them into the sea. From the blood and foam of his severed genitals Aphrodite ('born of foam') or Venus was born. So you can see what a strong pull there would be between the man and his member! But the symbolism of this is that Uranus wants his power back and Venus wants the freedom to wield it. What all this adds up to is that each of you sees in the other an opening to make more of yourselves and life – although at the time of meeting the feelings are mainly sexual, not surprisingly. But then surprise is the element here, because the wind or tide of this Interaction sets you off on a course you wouldn't have accounted for – and quickly too. It is important to recognize and understand the process that is going on here – namely that Venus is being given a sharp awakening with regard to the nature of their social/aesthetic values and style, and Uranus is being made to see the reality of their own, possibly unconscious, desire for change, and of the unusual effect they can have upon others. Effectively then, this Interaction launches both of you into a very different orbit to the one you've been used to. But once the excitement and pyrotechnics of the launch are over there is that journey into the unknown to be reckoned with. What this is saying is that your relationship is only going to be as stable as your awareness of what it's really about and where it's going. Failing this, an 'abort mission' light may well start to flash as the intensity of the Interaction becomes too hard to handle. But this could simply be owing to your trying to repeat the thrill of the launch when you are already in flight. Once airborne, the force of this relationship could progressively take you somewhere new, refreshing itself as it goes. But whether or not you continue to experience this together depends greatly upon the presence of more long-lasting and stabilizing Interactions – otherwise it could just be a case of 'Wow! What happened there?'.

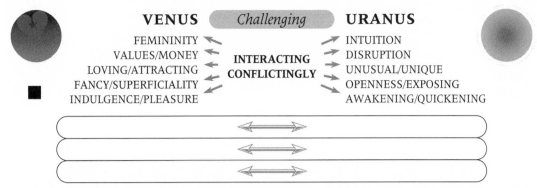

VENUS *Challenging* **URANUS**

FEMININITY	**INTERACTING CONFLICTINGLY**	INTUITION
VALUES/MONEY		DISRUPTION
LOVING/ATTRACTING		UNUSUAL/UNIQUE
FANCY/SUPERFICIALITY		OPENNESS/EXPOSING
INDULGENCE/PLEASURE		AWAKENING/QUICKENING

The Uranus individual gives the Venus person a sharp shock as to their real worth and attractiveness. Quite unceremoniously, Uranus will expose what is beautiful or ugly, talented or dull, about Venus. Venus finds all this quite irresistible, even though it gives them such mixed feelings about themselves and Uranus. It is almost as if Uranus is taking any feelings of alienation they have out on Venus. (If you read the myth of Uranus and Venus, given opposite under Venus Conjoining Uranus, you will see why this peculiar reaction exists with the Challenging aspect.) Uranus thinks 'If Venus is still around after so much fast and loose treatment, then they must love me.' Unfortunately, this does not work because all Uranus is getting from Venus is the measure of their lack of self-love, which perfectly reflects Uranus's own lack of self-love. All of this is important to understand, for it explains why you are so attracted to one another but fail to mesh in so many other areas of your respective lives. In the quirky way that is Uranus, you are both learning one of love's most important lessons: you can only truly love someone as much as you love yourself. If this relationship is handled right – which means not expecting it to be predictable – then you can both go some way towards loving more the unusual or outcast in yourselves and each other.

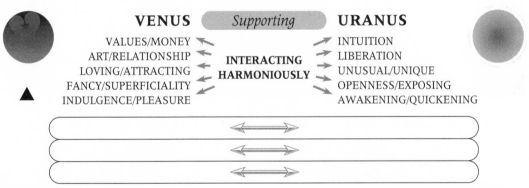

VENUS *Supporting* **URANUS**

VALUES/MONEY	**INTERACTING HARMONIOUSLY**	INTUITION
ART/RELATIONSHIP		LIBERATION
LOVING/ATTRACTING		UNUSUAL/UNIQUE
FANCY/SUPERFICIALITY		OPENNESS/EXPOSING
INDULGENCE/PLEASURE		AWAKENING/QUICKENING

Love and freedom coexist relatively easily, so this Interaction is non-possessive – or at least, it diffuses any other indications of jealousy. There is a friendliness between you if you are lovers, and you are loving if you are just friends. Venus really appreciates and is turned on by Uranus's unusualness, causing them to depart from their usual social or sensual style. This can actually cause fluctuations in Venus's affections, however, as they swing back and forth between their old and new values. To Uranus, Venus is the perfect playmate as they seem able to pick up on their odd or intuitive ideas – particularly in the sexual department – as well as being excitingly unpredictable. Not surprisingly, such an Interaction is a little too open or loose to ensure fidelity and durability, but it is extraordinarily pleasurable. If you are involved artistically in any way, this gives a zing of originality to whatever you create.

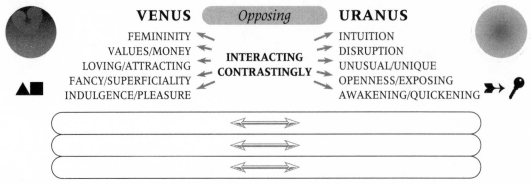

VENUS   *Opposing*   **URANUS**

FEMININITY		INTUITION
VALUES/MONEY	**INTERACTING**	DISRUPTION
LOVING/ATTRACTING	**CONTRASTINGLY**	UNUSUAL/UNIQUE
FANCY/SUPERFICIALITY		OPENNESS/EXPOSING
INDULGENCE/PLEASURE		AWAKENING/QUICKENING

As is often the case with hard Uranus Interactions, you are attracted to one another in a lightning-like, irresistible fashion. (You might be interested in reading the mythology of Venus and Uranus under Venus Conjoining Uranus, for this explains its psychological dynamic.) Because this is an Opposing aspect, though, there could be a certain sense of difference and distance at first meeting, something which may have taken place in an unusual place or circumstances. However, such is the electro-magnetism between the two of you that synchronicity conspires to bring you together again, seemingly by accident. The sexual dimension is strong between the two of you, but you may even try to resist this too. But again Venus/Uranus wins, and the whole subject of sex and what it implies becomes a major issue, with those Uranian qualities of coincidence, accident, unusualness, etc, streaking through it. But this is possibly all perennially resisted by one or both of you to a degree where the decidedly disruptive and unstable qualities of this Interaction seem to be strangely self-imposed. But then this is Uranus making the point that *everything* is self-imposed, consciously or unconsciously. And so indeed you are both on a sexual roller-coaster that'll lead you know not where. Socially too, Uranus will introduce Venus to new ideas and sensations. But the Planet Uranus's intention is to surprise and shock us out of our ruts and awaken us to whatever we need to know next about life and ourselves. And so Venus becomes more aware of what their values and pleasures really are by having them turned upside down by Uranus. Uranus will just re-throw the dice and hope for better luck next time. As you have probably guessed, this is not a relationship to grow old and grey together with, not unless there are other Interactions that bestow this, or unless you are both quite kinky or into openly sharing. On this last point, so-called 'open relationships' are more often than not just a reluctance to commit posing as 'liberation' – especially on Uranus's part.

The greatest act of love is to love the unlovable …

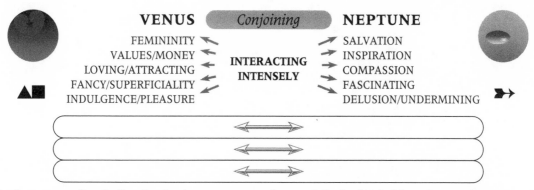

You have a very fine feeling flowing between you, and potentially the kind of love that survives many ups and downs. But 'transcends' might be a more accurate term than 'survives' because this Interaction does not necessarily make for durability in the sense of an everyday, steady but unsensational sort of bond. It is a highly romantic love, but it can also adjust itself to whatever else is going on around you – and that includes more or less everything. You are both inclined to go along with whatever happens to you as a couple; even if someone else should come along and woo one of you away, the other would be inclined to accept this. If there are any more possessive links between you, then such 'unconditional love' may have to rise to the occasion, identify any illusions, and walk its talk by bowing out gracefully. As with all Conjoining Interactions, a great deal depends upon what other Planets are aspecting these two. If there are easy aspects to the Venus of the one of you and/or the Neptune of the other, then it is unlikely that such a challenge to this spiritual bond is going to happen. A very pure and eternal, even platonic, relationship can be the fate of this Interaction. Whatever the case, this certainly has a quite uplifting influence upon both of you. Creative pursuits, such as music and dance, or simply artistic appreciation, could very much be a part of your time together.

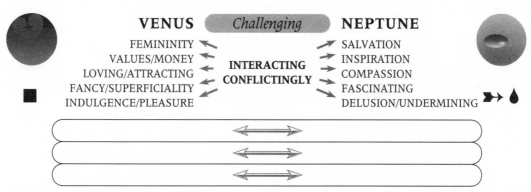

It could be that one of you is in love with their idea of the other rather than the person themselves – it could also be mutual. Depending on many factors such as having enough money to sustain illusions, or how much both of you wish to please one another by fitting their romantic ideal, this classic indication of 'love's illusions' can persist for quite some time. However, when something happens to bring you both down to earth – such as one of you being attracted to someone else, money problems, a loss, or one of you simply feeling that you are not being loved for yourself – then the real, human, fragile versions of yourselves begin to emerge. It is then when this Interaction challenges you to love unconditionally and spiritually. If you rise to this, then you will have put your relationship on a higher and nobler footing altogether. Failure, however, would amount to an uncomfortable and embarrassing separation, perhaps after trying to fake it for a bit longer. Be that as it may, it is also quite likely that you are involved creatively in some way – and this would greatly contribute to stabilizing this Interaction by giving imagination and fantasy a positive outlet.

... while not expecting love to be immediately returned

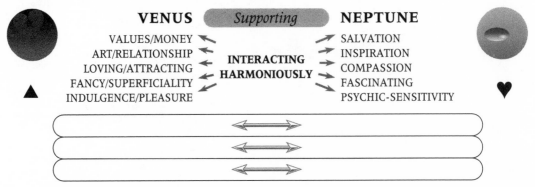

VENUS *Supporting* **NEPTUNE**

VALUES/MONEY → ← SALVATION
ART/RELATIONSHIP → **INTERACTING** → INSPIRATION
LOVING/ATTRACTING → **HARMONIOUSLY** → COMPASSION
FANCY/SUPERFICIALITY → → FASCINATING
INDULGENCE/PLEASURE → PSYCHIC-SENSITIVITY

Here you have a feeling between you that is so loving and harmonious that it is really quite fine and spiritual. You bring to one another the mysterious and the beautiful. Venus can take on the form of Neptune's imagination and longings, while Neptune inspires Venus socially and/or artistically. This is a wonderful Interaction for making music or being creative together in any way. There is a subtle attraction that gently persists, and could well exert a healing influence upon those around you too. This is not a 'robust' kind of Interaction and so does not in itself confer physical durability, but whatever the outcome of your relationship, there is always likely to be a wistful connection and sweetness between the two of you.

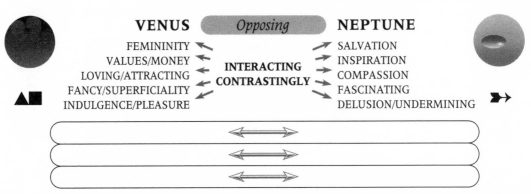

VENUS *Opposing* **NEPTUNE**

FEMININITY → ← SALVATION
VALUES/MONEY → **INTERACTING** → INSPIRATION
LOVING/ATTRACTING → **CONTRASTINGLY** → COMPASSION
FANCY/SUPERFICIALITY → → FASCINATING
INDULGENCE/PLEASURE → DELUSION/UNDERMINING

This is a real falling in love – with all the unreality that this engenders! The longings of one or both of you for the perfect match or soul-mate seems to be initially satisfied with this Interaction. But your respective illusions around such concepts are not far behind that original falling. Unless there is some very sound awareness concerning the pitfalls of romantic love, then hurt and deception (conscious or unconscious) is bound to descend upon the pair of you. But this is not to say that this is an entirely negative aspect – far from it. Its true intention is to lure both of you away from your respective illusions of a loving or satisfying relationship – but at first it does so by playing upon those very illusions. Either one of you may well feel that you have been taken for a ride at some point as the dream fades, but it is precisely at this juncture that you need to perceive what is really happening. For example, one of you (probably Neptune) has been playing at 'saviour' and then finds that it was far harder work than was first thought. It is just here that you have to tell yourself that such a 'saving' has very real spiritual reasons, but it means that you will have to face up to the fact that you need some saving too! As far as the other (probably Venus) is concerned, when the dream fades for Neptune you may well feel like used or damaged goods, and an unequal or unstable partnership can then seem your lot. But this is precisely the time when you must muster your self-worth and not merely allow Neptune to project first their ideal and then their disillusionment upon you. If this mutual realization takes place, then the two of you can enjoy a higher love and an ennobling kind of bond – but it will take time, effort, awareness, and most of all, sacrifice and acceptance. Apart from all of this, this Interaction can also make for a very creative coupling – especially with regard to music or the visual arts.

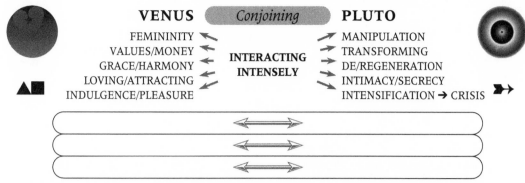

VENUS *Conjoining* **PLUTO**

FEMININITY		MANIPULATION
VALUES/MONEY	**INTERACTING**	TRANSFORMING
GRACE/HARMONY	**INTENSELY**	DE/REGENERATION
LOVING/ATTRACTING		INTIMACY/SECRECY
INDULGENCE/PLEASURE		INTENSIFICATION → CRISIS

This Interaction exercises a powerful pull towards each other, but to some degree it is unconscious. This means to say that the two of you would probably not realize how deeply involved you are with one another until later. Feelings of possessiveness or jealousy surfacing could be signs of this depth, especially on the part of the Pluto individual, who will also try to make the Venus person 'fit' their emotional requirements. From Pluto's intensely emotional and possibly isolated viewpoint, Venus seems to give off a take it or leave it attitude, which is not really the case, even though Venus would sometimes like to think so. Be that as it may, there is a quality to your relationship that keeps on bringing you through one crisis after another, and renewing yourselves and the relationship itself – sometimes in spite of yourselves. The sexual dimension to this Interaction is also deep and intense. Sexual feelings and activities go through significant changes as you are both inevitably, and sometimes painfully, made aware of what works for you – often through a process of occasionally getting stuck with what doesn't! Money can also be a very significant or even bargaining factor in your relationship. The fact that this bond is so powerful and deep is what makes you endure these deep changes and feelings. Unconsciously you are both aware that something won't let you go until it is satisfied, and then it won't matter. Till death us do part?

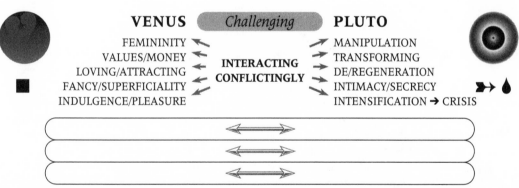

VENUS *Challenging* **PLUTO**

FEMININITY		MANIPULATION
VALUES/MONEY	**INTERACTING**	TRANSFORMING
LOVING/ATTRACTING	**CONFLICTINGLY**	DE/REGENERATION
FANCY/SUPERFICIALITY		INTIMACY/SECRECY
INDULGENCE/PLEASURE		INTENSIFICATION → CRISIS

There is a compulsive or oppressive quality to your relationship that is based upon a heavy need to be loved on the part of one of you (probably the Pluto person), and a need to deepen their sense of what love is on the part of the other (most likely the Venus person). And so possessiveness, jealousy or resentment are the unfortunate hues which colour this Interaction. Money too can come into the picture as an issue that makes matters worse, is used as leverage, or is actually the source of problems. One of you can feel coerced into being loving and affectionate by the other's desperate pleas, bribes and/or threats. Initially there may well be strong passionate feelings for one another, or at least one or both of you could be so swept off their feet as to mistake lust for love. Although this Interaction can bring a certain satisfaction, or at least a greater emotional understanding, the price can be very high in terms of soul-searching and deep hurt – or money.

... and that each of you is still a mystery to the other

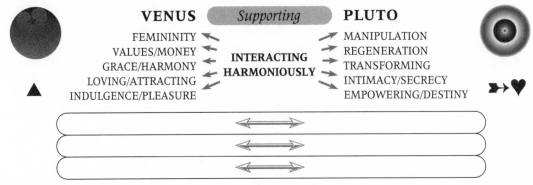

VENUS	*Supporting*	PLUTO
FEMININITY		MANIPULATION
VALUES/MONEY	INTERACTING	REGENERATION
GRACE/HARMONY	HARMONIOUSLY	TRANSFORMING
LOVING/ATTRACTING		INTIMACY/SECRECY
INDULGENCE/PLEASURE		EMPOWERING/DESTINY

There is a profound and deep bond between you that can heal rifts or take you through other difficulties. In fact, such is the strength of this bond it may insist that you endure and push on through any 'night' of emotional isolation and confusion. The Venus person can show the Pluto individual how to come out of their cave of despair or feelings of unlovableness. Pluto in return can lend more weight and authenticity to Venus's affections and emotional values. This Interaction is the kind that occurs when one or both people are 'about to believe in love again' after having endured painful experiences in the past. You must tell yourselves that this Interaction represents the underground river that can take you there!

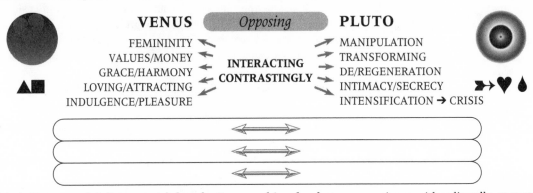

VENUS	*Opposing*	PLUTO
FEMININITY		MANIPULATION
VALUES/MONEY	INTERACTING	TRANSFORMING
GRACE/HARMONY	CONTRASTINGLY	DE/REGENERATION
LOVING/ATTRACTING		INTIMACY/SECRECY
INDULGENCE/PLEASURE		INTENSIFICATION → CRISIS

This is Romeo and Juliet material, but don't go reaching for daggers or poisons, either literally or metaphorically. It is just that you are powerfully attracted to one another, yet at the same time you encounter certain taboos in the process of getting or remaining as close as you want to. In the process, however, these 'taboos' won't be so obvious as coming from opposing families or backgrounds – although they might be. In fact, these taboos are more likely to be, or stem from, some internal taboo that may conveniently have an external manifestation, like for example, mixed race, same sex, big age gaps, incest, adultery, etc. Before going any further, it may be that one or both of you may sense all this difficulty and not enter into intimacy in the first place. The best way of expressing this is mythologically ... it is called the Rape of Persephone. Persephone was the daughter of Mother Earth and was closely protected by her for she was very ethereal, unworldly and innocent. Her polar opposite, Pluto, Lord of the Underworld, wanted her for his own, and forcibly took and dragged her down to his realm. After much pain and destruction (mostly on the part of Mother Earth who went on strike causing the world to go barren), a deal was struck after consulting Zeus, and Pluto was allowed to keep Persephone for four months of the year (which is how and when we get the barren winter), and her mother for the remainder. Pluto and Persephone went on to be one of the soundest relationships amongst the gods and goddesses. What all this means for you is that Venus has to go through a purging and steeping process as her superficial values and shallower feelings are eliminated and transformed. She then becomes a strong, emotional figure, capable of loving deeply, despite appearances and conventions – but she takes time out every so often. Pluto, for his part, simply has his loneliness put to an end – or at least, for some of the time, because Pluto's realm is about aloneness, after all. All of this is made possible by ultimately appealing to something higher for help. It has to be said, though, that this process can be so intense and gruelling as to finish off emotionally one or both of you. Apparent or real capriciousness on Venus's part can overwhelm Pluto with jealousy and despair, whereas Pluto's attempts to force Venus into the shape they think they desire can psychologically damage Venus, forcing them to escape (home to mother?). Handled right and the course seen through, this can find you in a deeply fulfilling relationship – like Beauty and the Beast.

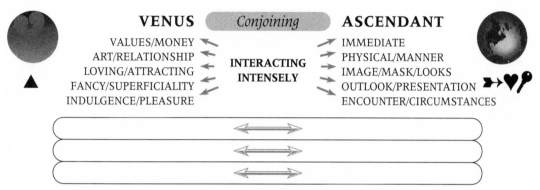

VENUS *Conjoining* **ASCENDANT**

VENUS		ASCENDANT
VALUES/MONEY		IMMEDIATE
ART/RELATIONSHIP	**INTERACTING**	PHYSICAL/MANNER
LOVING/ATTRACTING	**INTENSELY**	IMAGE/MASK/LOOKS
FANCY/SUPERFICIALITY		OUTLOOK/PRESENTATION
INDULGENCE/PLEASURE		ENCOUNTER/CIRCUMSTANCES

There is an immediate attraction towards one another, whether either of you admits it or not. This is an Interaction of 'style' for both of you focus your overall Interaction upon matters of love, art, pleasure, play, money, social pros and cons, etc. Whatever your sexes, there is an affection between you that is shown or not shown, depending on the personal inclinations of each of you. With a few natural exceptions, you tend to share the same likes and dislikes regarding people and things. If one of you is more socially or artistically aware they can help the other to improve greatly. Your great enemy is most probably boredom owing to a failure to amuse or be amused by each other or whatever social or aesthetic situation you find yourselves in. Having said this though, together you can possess a huge talent to entertain. This Interaction can be summed up with the word – affinity.

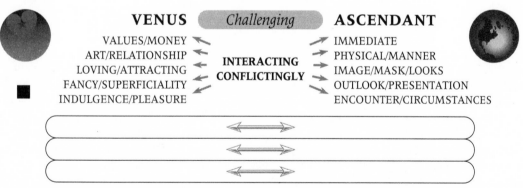

VENUS *Challenging* **ASCENDANT**

VENUS		ASCENDANT
VALUES/MONEY		IMMEDIATE
ART/RELATIONSHIP	**INTERACTING**	PHYSICAL/MANNER
LOVING/ATTRACTING	**CONFLICTINGLY**	IMAGE/MASK/LOOKS
FANCY/SUPERFICIALITY		OUTLOOK/PRESENTATION
INDULGENCE/PLEASURE		ENCOUNTER/CIRCUMSTANCES

The physical appearance and manner of the Ascendant person can seem unattractive or socially inept to the Venus person, or the Venus person may feel that way in comparison to the Ascendant. In return, the Ascendant finds Venus's standards here superficial. If there are more emotional and psychological attractions going on between the two of you, then this Interaction can seem peculiarly out of place – and indeed, superficial. In the end, or perhaps after it if this Interaction becomes really troublesome, it is up to the Venus person to scrutinize their possibly hollow and insincere feelings. Then again, and as ever, the Ascendant individual could make an effort to meet Venus half way by endeavouring to look as good as they can without becoming a slave to such an issue – or just play down the whole appearance thing. The looks thing could be an issue for one or both of you, something which this Interaction intensifies.

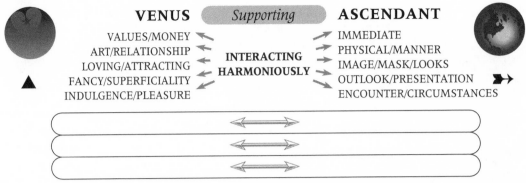

VENUS — *Supporting* — ASCENDANT

VALUES/MONEY	INTERACTING HARMONIOUSLY	IMMEDIATE
ART/RELATIONSHIP		PHYSICAL/MANNER
LOVING/ATTRACTING		IMAGE/MASK/LOOKS
FANCY/SUPERFICIALITY		OUTLOOK/PRESENTATION
INDULGENCE/PLEASURE		ENCOUNTER/CIRCUMSTANCES

The Venus person is quite simply attracted to the physical appearance and manner of the Ascendant person. This should be immediately obvious to the Ascendant who cannot but help feeling flattered by such a response to their image. But that is all it is, one person's image and another's liking of it, and as such this Interaction in itself could get a relationship started but little else – unless both of you were unbelievably vain or superficial! More profound and lasting Interactions should, and probably do, exist between the two of you.

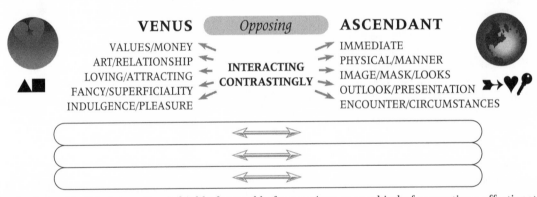

VENUS — *Opposing* — ASCENDANT

VALUES/MONEY	INTERACTING CONTRASTINGLY	IMMEDIATE
ART/RELATIONSHIP		PHYSICAL/MANNER
LOVING/ATTRACTING		IMAGE/MASK/LOOKS
FANCY/SUPERFICIALITY		OUTLOOK/PRESENTATION
INDULGENCE/PLEASURE		ENCOUNTER/CIRCUMSTANCES

On the face of it, this Interaction is highly favourable for marriage or any kind of romantic or affectionate relationship. The Ascendant person senses that the Venus person is the one who will make them happy and socially complete, while the Venus person responds accordingly. There is a double Venus connotation here, for here it is Conjoining the Descendant (because it is opposite the Ascendant) and both Venus and the Descendant have to do with relationship, marriage and social life. And so all these matters can be excellently starred – but with Venus there is always the danger of superficiality and/or social convention. This means to say that the 'idea' of marriage and living happily ever after, or simply being too 'social', can superimpose itself on the emotional reality of both of you. How long it takes before any cracks show is very dependent on what other Interactions you have between you. If there is plenty of harmony or depth elsewhere, then this Interaction will live up to its promise, and indeed contentment with one another will persist. If there are difficulties with the gilt fading, then the Ascendant person should bear in mind that the beauty, worth and lovability that they initially perceived in Venus was really their own unrecognized beauty, worth and lovability projected on to Venus. Venus, on the other hand, may need to learn not to please at the cost of losing sight of who they are in their own right.

The great key to relating is to understand what a relationship is telling you, then accept it

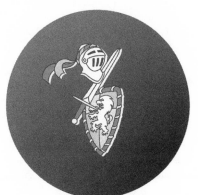

MARS

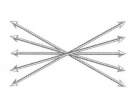

**INTERACTING
WITH**

MARS   NEPTUNE
JUPITER   PLUTO
SATURN   ASCENDANT
URANUS

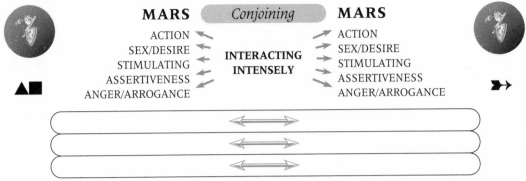

Hot! Hot! Hot! This Interaction had better be sexual, sporting or very active in some way. This is because it could otherwise degenerate into interminable battles as the raw or competitive energy created by the two of you being together finds nowhere positive to go. This is not to say that it ought to be sexual or physical in some way, but that it has a hard time expressing itself through other channels. One way or the other though, you do test each other's mettle quite frequently; a bit like a game of arm wrestling. If one or the other of you is not very assertive or sure of your act, this Interaction should teach you to be so – or you'll get knocked down or pushed around. You over-stimulate one another, which can give rise to the kitchen being too hot to stay in for long. This is more of a bout or match than it is a relationship – because you react rather than relate to one another. If you do both manage to harness this drive, this internal combustion engine of an Interaction, then you could achieve a great deal together.

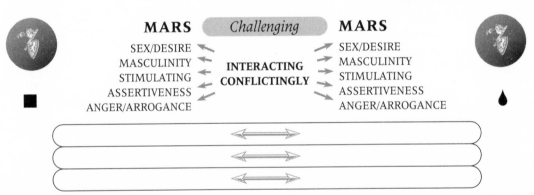

What each of you wants and the way that you both go about getting it is very different. Consequently, a lot of friction can develop between the two of you. In extreme cases, or if there is little or no indication of love and tenderness in other Interactions, such conflict can even get physically abusive. But this won't happen if both of you are of a reasonable and peaceful disposition. More subtly though, one of you has a different idea of manliness or courage to the other. For example, one of you might see courage as instinctively responding to someone attacking one's family or sense of security – but the other sees courage as holding back, thinking about it, and finding a more circumspect or diplomatic route. Usually one of you will have a 'hot' reaction, and the other a 'cool' reaction – but you might both be 'hot'! Either way, you can see how this could cause flare-ups or frustrations. Furthermore, such friction can build up to bursting point if there are more 'peaceful' areas to the relationship that you both try to keep to. A good battle or row once in a while is a healthy thing for it clears the air. However, with this difficult Interaction, these may be too frequent or not frequent enough. Ultimately, this Interaction could be saying that one or both of you are being challenged to fight, to one degree or another, for their own right to be what they essentially are.

No one Interaction makes or breaks a relationship

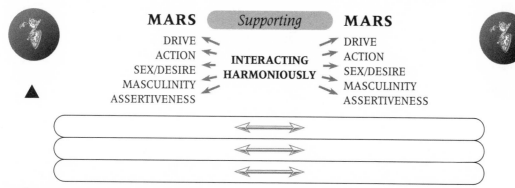

A combination of ease and activity makes you move or operate well together, be it on the dance floor or sports field, in the workplace or bedroom. There is also a youthful quality about you as a pair, as you have a physical and spontaneous approach to life. You spur one another on in a natural and unselfconscious way, making things easy that once were difficult, for this energy opens doors for both of you. The straightforwardness of this Interaction means that you usually press on through any difficulties without getting too bogged down. As time goes by, more fulfilling (or less exhausting) pursuits than these typically Martian or physical ones may be called for, something which this aspect in itself does not provide.

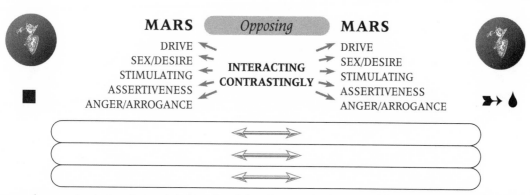

You can have a physical and sexual tie here, but left to its own devices it could well devolve into out-and-out conflict, even violence. A great deal initially depends upon how you both express, or are allowed to express, the sexual tension between you. If you are, for one reason or another, not able or willing to make the relationship physical, then that tension will just persist as ongoing frustration or stimulation. This is a case of what you never catch you never get tired of pursuing. If you do get together in any way, however, it will only be a matter of time before battle commences. If one of you allows themself to be easily subjugated then it will take longer. Unless there is a substantial amount of tenderness and mutual respect indicated by other Interactions, the shock of how harsh merely sexual or egotistical urges can be will become only too evident. Civilized veneers are inevitably worn away under this aspect. The reasons for being involved through such an Interaction are, for one of you, a case of being too submissive and having to become more assertive and independent. For the other, it is a case of exercising the 'right' that has hitherto always been assumed, only to find that your opposite number eventually fights back, or is vanquished. Such tough outcomes are probably only avoidable if neither of you need or choose to become thus involved in the first place.

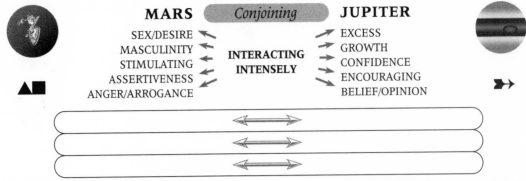

These are both fiery Planets so this is quite a 'hot' Interaction. This can launch you both to new heights of satisfaction and success in many areas of life, or simply result in burn-out if you merely indulge and behave as if you have more energy than sense. Positive activities together are the key here, and so being up and about the business of living through travel, sports and outdoor activities, are what get your wheels going round. This is an Interaction that needs you to have constructively employed the prodigious energy that it makes available to you as a couple. The Mars individual stimulates the Jupiter person to put their ideals and plans into action, thereby helping them to further themselves. Jupiter, on the other hand, encourages the Mars person to be more confident in themselves and their activities. And so this Interaction can positively escalate as one of you boosts the other who in turn is then able to boost the one, and so on. So much depends upon the direction of such self-propelling. You could merely romp around and exhaust or irritate each other, or launch yourselves anew. Other more passive or inertia-producing Interactions may stifle this one, or be overcome by it. This is a 'get it on' Interaction!

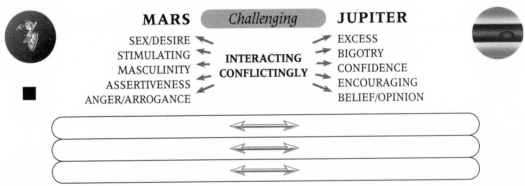

This is a swashbuckling kind of Interaction that attracts plenty of adventure and activity, but does not really lead anywhere. It could even get you into hot water or a brush with the law. Whatever more expansive or philosophical ideas the Jupiter person might have, the Mars person probably regards them as too academic or boring or just plain disagrees with them. Or Jupiter may encourage Mars to act unwisely and then not take responsibility for it. Hopefully there are indications to the contrary elsewhere, but this Interaction is rather lacking in the honour and ethics department. Conflicts of belief are a keynote for this combination, which may simply mean that one or both of you has yet to find a higher or more enterprising reason for living, and, by this relationship, is being forced eventually to do so. Essentially, Mars stimulates Jupiter's principles by attacking or offending them, thereby forcing them to be more aware of them and develop them. Jupiter subsequently comes down heavily on Mars for having so few principles! It could mean that Mars has to either rethink or leave.

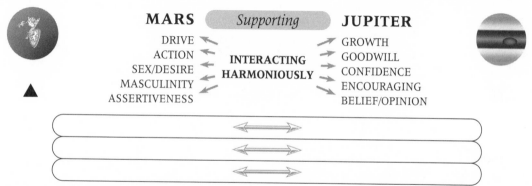

MARS *Supporting* **JUPITER**

DRIVE
ACTION
SEX/DESIRE
MASCULINITY
ASSERTIVENESS

**INTERACTING
HARMONIOUSLY**

GROWTH
GOODWILL
CONFIDENCE
ENCOURAGING
BELIEF/OPINION

There is a confident and loping quality to your being together that enables you to get a lot done with ease. It is as if the Mars person has the drive and the Jupiter person knows how to direct it – and then you feed each back to one another. You are probably quite keen on outdoor activities and sports, or failing this, get out and about a good deal and know how to enjoy yourselves in a pretty physical manner. As is often the case with 'healthy' Mars Interactions, they supply energy and decisiveness and therefore a minimum of complications. But a great deal depends upon how much meaning such activities have for you, and whether such ease ever forces you to look within. Hopefully, other more emotionally or psychologically significant Interactions will be present to supply this. When you do fix your sights upon some higher goal, the chances are that you'll not only achieve it, but show others how to as well.

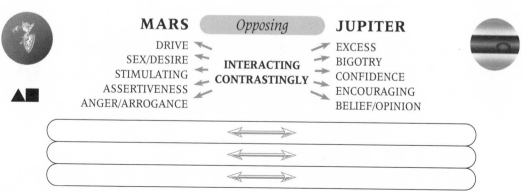

MARS *Opposing* **JUPITER**

DRIVE
SEX/DESIRE
STIMULATING
ASSERTIVENESS
ANGER/ARROGANCE

**INTERACTING
CONTRASTINGLY**

EXCESS
BIGOTRY
CONFIDENCE
ENCOURAGING
BELIEF/OPINION

As planets, Mars and Jupiter are similar in that they both have to do with 'energy' in the sense of getting or gaining something. So there can be quite a lot of activity, coming and going, and horsing around in your relationship. However, it may be a case of more energy than purpose as it eventually dawns on you that you are possibly espousing different causes, motivated by different objectives, or even fighting under opposing standards. But this 'dawning' will not happen until one day you realize that you both, literally or figuratively, share the same address but lead different lives. How uncomfortable this realization is depends upon the level of understanding you have between you that is indicated by other Interactions. For any number of reasons, you may choose to stay together while leading your own lives. If there are certain commitments, like family for instance, then this would be a sensible, if not totally desirable, expression of this Interaction. Failing this, a kind of *jihad* or holy war could be your ongoing lot. The freedom to roam is the keynote of this Interaction. Whatever you each make of the place of this in a relationship, one or both of you will inevitably go their own way – with or without the other's blessings. But this could actually be the elusive purpose of this Interaction: for one of you graciously to grant the other freedom, or at least help them to discover it.

Look at the Planet-Sign Profiles for the personal meaning of Planets in any Interaction   407

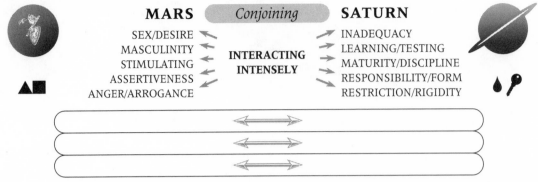

This is a Key Contact because the energies of Mars and Saturn are so different, and can be strangely attracted to one another because of this. Mars is hot, impulsive and boyish/childish; Saturn is cool, cautious and adult/mature. Because of these natural extremes, you are liable to bring them out in one another even further. The Mars individual will become more pushy and impatient, while the Saturn person can become cold and withdrawn. But really there is quite a positive dimension to this Interaction if we look at it in terms of 'blade' (Mars) and 'stone' (Saturn). The Mars person, rather than feeling confounded and frustrated by the Saturn person's doubts and inhibitions, could see this as an opportunity to sharpen their ability to show Saturn the exact nature of those doubts and how they might assert themselves more spontaneously. And Saturn, rather than feeling stiff and awkward, could teach Mars the value of planning and using time and non-action as instruments for getting what they want. Failing this, things can go from bad to worse. The key phrase for this Key Contact is Hard Work. If Mars works hard at controlling their energies and Saturn works hard at releasing them, with each other's help, then both of them will obviously gain. Otherwise it really will be 'hard work', a dead-end case of irresistible force meeting immovable object. Ultimately, all this could add up to a lesson in survival.

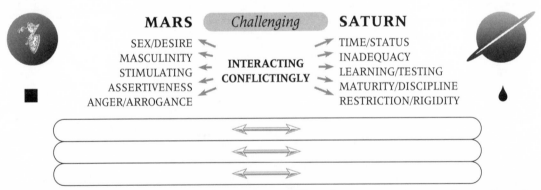

The Interaction that you have here is bound to give you trouble and stop you getting anywhere as a couple – unless Mars is prepared to take stock of how they actually go (or don't go) about getting what they want as an individual, and if Saturn is not too hard on Mars for not being as effective or mature as they deem Mars should be. But 'hard' is very much the keynote of this aspect, which means that hard feelings are bound to arise – that is unless you are both seeing the hardness as coming from some quarter external to the relationship itself. The reason behind such hardness is that Saturn is inclined to thwart and control Mars's urges in a way that reminds them of how this possibly happened to them in childhood. Consequently, Mars is bound to get angry or upset – which would offend Saturn's sense of propriety and order, causing them to suppress or belittle Mars even more. So the vicious circle of this Interaction is all too obvious. One could see your Interaction as a case of accelerator (Mars) and brakes (Saturn) being applied at the same time. As such, it will either never have got going at all, or it may not be long before your relationship breaks down altogether, and the question will arise as to whether it's a write-off or is simply in need of repair.

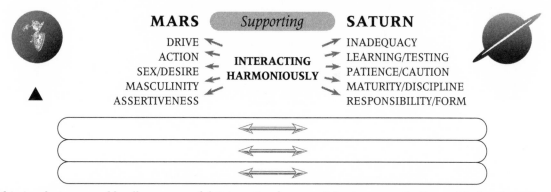

MARS   *Supporting*   SATURN

MARS		SATURN
DRIVE		INADEQUACY
ACTION	**INTERACTING**	LEARNING/TESTING
SEX/DESIRE	**HARMONIOUSLY**	PATIENCE/CAUTION
MASCULINITY		MATURITY/DISCIPLINE
ASSERTIVENESS		RESPONSIBILITY/FORM

This is what you could call a very useful Interaction because it bestows practicality and industriousness. Apart from favouring a business relationship, it also means that you are well able to assist one another in getting things done or off the ground. This feeling of 'things to be done' that exists between you is of inestimable value for it counteracts any woolly or overly romantic notions that are so common in many relationships. This is a no-nonsense aspect. The Mars person is very good at spurring the Saturn person to action, even or especially in the area where Saturn feels inertia and doubt. In return, Saturn shows Mars how to be more mature in their choice of activities, and how to be more responsible where they are possibly selfish or headstrong. Because together you link energy and control, you can become a very effective team.

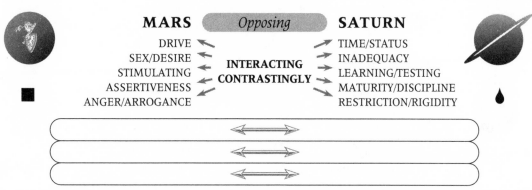

MARS   *Opposing*   SATURN

MARS		SATURN
DRIVE		TIME/STATUS
SEX/DESIRE	**INTERACTING**	INADEQUACY
STIMULATING	**CONTRASTINGLY**	LEARNING/TESTING
ASSERTIVENESS		MATURITY/DISCIPLINE
ANGER/ARROGANCE		RESTRICTION/RIGIDITY

This is one of those 'irresistible force meets immovable object' situations. When one of you says or wants 'go', the other says or wants 'stop'. So this can be a very wearying kind of Interaction if some ground rules are not established, like for instance 'I'll do what I want my way, but I won't expect you to do so as well or even approve of it' or 'I shan't judge you for the way you do what you do'. The trouble here is, of course, not seeing eye-to-eye in the first place, so sitting round the table may not exactly be on the cards. So one of you will have to be particularly sure of their act so as not to feel pushed or restricted by the other. In fact, this is probably what this Interaction is actually in aid of enforcing – becoming more independent, that is – not least of all because circumstances thwart your desires and simply do not allow you to have or be with one another in a usual or comfortable manner. If yours is a sexual relationship it will eventually pan out to be a hard learning experience in this respect. This could come as surprise because at first the 'irresistible force' and 'immovable object' see each other as a challenge and so feel attracted to one another. But before long your moods and desires will be felt to be very out of phase, with headaches and other excuses abounding. In any event, blocking each other's attempts at assertiveness, or attacking whatever position the other holds, will become a problem, To Mars, Saturn is too slow, withdrawn and cautious; to Saturn, Mars is too impulsive, coarse and unthinking. Ultimately, Saturn is learning to stand their ground, and Mars is learning to state their case. If this is done with integrity, then you can come to respect one another for what you each are in your own right, and for having taught one another to establish this very thing.

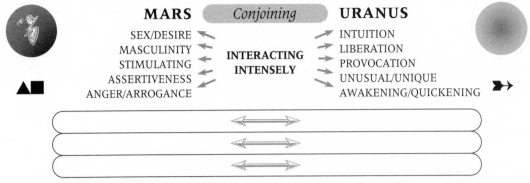

MARS *Conjoining* **URANUS**

SEX/DESIRE		INTUITION
MASCULINITY	**INTERACTING**	LIBERATION
STIMULATING	**INTENSELY**	PROVOCATION
ASSERTIVENESS		UNUSUAL/UNIQUE
ANGER/ARROGANCE		AWAKENING/QUICKENING

Here we have a mutual, and probably sexual, attraction that comes about in a very immediate manner which seems to overlook or bypass what could be regarded as more practical, or even moral, considerations. This is because the energy of this Interaction is in aid of freeing up both of your respective senses of who you each are as unique individuals, and as such, forces you uncompromisingly to exercise your right to assert your unique desires and feelings. This may, for example, involve unusual bursts of anger or sexual activity – or simply ongoing or periodic irritation. Of necessity, all this probably includes disrupting the status quo of one or both of you – and even those connected with you. So this is an Interaction that has a sort of electrifying urgency about it, for its dynamic is that of pushing each of you on towards the next step in your personal evolution. After the initial catalytic Interaction has taken place, there is no guarantee that the relationship will be long-lasting, but its effects certainly will be. However, if other Interactions indicate durability, as a couple you could, in an ongoing way, be involved in reforming or overthrowing certain existing norms, be they in your personal lives or in society as a whole. The presence of any other aspects to either Mars (from the Uranus individual's Planets) or to Uranus (from the Mars individual's Planets) will also help determine the relationship's overall stability, if such aspects are positive, or instability, if they are negative.

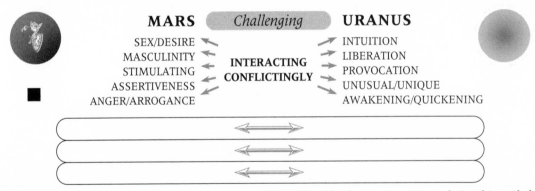

MARS *Challenging* **URANUS**

SEX/DESIRE		INTUITION
MASCULINITY	**INTERACTING**	LIBERATION
STIMULATING	**CONFLICTINGLY**	PROVOCATION
ASSERTIVENESS		UNUSUAL/UNIQUE
ANGER/ARROGANCE		AWAKENING/QUICKENING

This is an explosive Interaction that gives rise to instability and sudden happenings. Your relationship probably got started under the influence of this one – which could mean anything from taking exception to each other to winding up in bed together, or both. This is a very quick, unceremonious interchange and will continue to put you through changes and shocks right up until the end (and beyond) of the relationship. And no, this is not a pairing you can expect to grow old and grey together with – unless you are both members of some team whose express purpose is to shock, amaze or disrupt. The sexual dimension to your relationship, if there is one, is particularly fraught with ups and downs, unpredictability and experimentation. Each of you awakens the other to the true nature of your sexuality. It would seem that this Interaction has the express purpose of raising the nap on both of your respective ideas of life and yourselves. Highly stimulating and highly unstable. And as much as it suddenly or surprisingly brings you together, it could also explode you apart in a similar fashion. As a couple, you make an exciting mixture – a very effective cocktail, in fact! One glass and you're anybody's – or nobody's. Apart from the sexual aspect, this is the kind of aspect you would find between a parent and a 'difficult' child, where one or both individuals are being forced to be more open and direct.

Look for patterns or themes that emerge while reading all of your Profiles

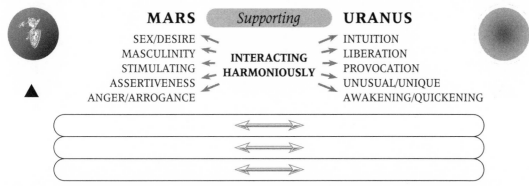

MARS *Supporting* **URANUS**

SEX/DESIRE		INTUITION
MASCULINITY	**INTERACTING**	LIBERATION
STIMULATING	**HARMONIOUSLY**	PROVOCATION
ASSERTIVENESS		UNUSUAL/UNIQUE
ANGER/ARROGANCE		AWAKENING/QUICKENING

Between the two of you much can be achieved that will make you feel more like individuals in your own right. So paradoxically this Interaction inclines towards a certain 'looseness' rather than closeness. A great deal depends upon other Interactions and your personal attitudes towards relationships, but ultimately this Interaction is saying that you can both follow your own stars and not jeopardize what you have between you. In truth, you actually make your feelings towards one another all the more positive – simply because it is evident that you trust those feelings. So there is a youthful and friendly flavour to your partnership that frees you from restrictions and the limiting ideas of life and love that created them in the first place. Very refreshing – and can be quite sexy in a breezy sort of way! Whatever the type of your relationship, you strike a blow for freedom, and maybe not just for yourselves.

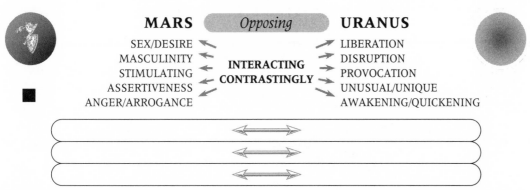

MARS *Opposing* **URANUS**

SEX/DESIRE		LIBERATION
MASCULINITY	**INTERACTING**	DISRUPTION
STIMULATING	**CONTRASTINGLY**	PROVOCATION
ASSERTIVENESS		UNUSUAL/UNIQUE
ANGER/ARROGANCE		AWAKENING/QUICKENING

This can be one the most disharmonious Interactions there is. It is as if you are both on a hair-trigger when it comes to one of you reacting to being told what to do by the other – or even if asked extremely nicely. In fact, there only has to be the merest suggestion of such a presumption. The energies of Mars and Uranus are similar for they both have to do with independence. But the Mars person's idea of this is much more bound up with their ego, so when it feels threatened by Uranus's air of independence – which is actually a radical viewpoint suspended in emotional detachment – then they get really mad! Uranus can respond to this with an even more abstract opinion or emotional aloofness, and so the firework display begins. At its most extreme, such a confrontation can become physically aggressive. This Interaction is a mutual cage-rattler and it has no part in a peaceful, live-in relationship. That is, not unless one of you feels decidedly inferior to the other and knuckles down in the first place. But the very nature of this Interaction is to bring about an increased awareness of each person's individual rights, so this arrangement wouldn't last very long. Such mutual provocation can amount to a feeling of sexual attraction, but this is really just a fuse to the bomb, so to speak. A sign of handling this Interaction correctly would be when one or both of you are able to control their urge to react or rebel, born of the realization that they do have their own mind, and are free to do and think as they please. Until then, you will continue to rile each other, simply because one or both of you is not yet sure of their own act.

The great key to relating is to understand what a relationship is telling you, then accept it

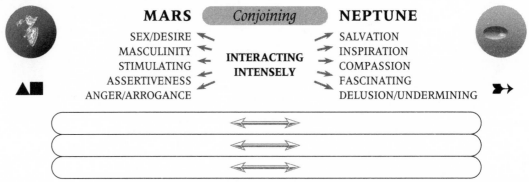

MARS *Conjoining* **NEPTUNE**

MARS		NEPTUNE
SEX/DESIRE		SALVATION
MASCULINITY	**INTERACTING**	INSPIRATION
STIMULATING	**INTENSELY**	COMPASSION
ASSERTIVENESS		FASCINATING
ANGER/ARROGANCE		DELUSION/UNDERMINING

⟺ All Interactions between Mars and Neptune, apart from the Supporting one, can lead you a merry dance – and sometimes not at all merry. In fact, 'dancing' makes a very apt metaphor for the Interaction between these two Planets. Firstly, who is leading whom? Owing to current gender confusions and the contemporary styles of dance that reflect them, very few people have a clear idea of this. And in families too, the hierarchy of leadership is often in disarray. But with this Interaction between you, some kind of rule had better be established or a lot of bruised shins and trodden-on toes will be the result. If yours is a sexual relationship, the range of shades and preferences is endless. Suffice to say that it can go from the extremely exotic to the peculiarly dissatisfying, from the intense to the infrequent or non-existent. Back to the dance – what music are you trying to dance to? In other words, what is the theme or philosophy, if any, of your intimate relations? Generally, it is about sexual refinement, which along the way finds Neptune's sensitivity and peculiarities reacting with disgust, evasion or confusion to Mars's hungry and hard pushing. Resort to artificial stimulants such as drugs or pornography can also enter the picture. Ideally, the pursuit of some spiritual-sexual discipline such as Tantrism or Taoism is recommended. As far as non-sexual relationships are concerned (or the parts that are not to do with sex), this Interaction makes for a subtle interplay between the two of you which can have many expressions, but probably the performing arts, healing and yoga are the major ones. In any event, finding a creative and positive way of channelling physical (Mars) and psychic (Neptune) energies together is the goal to aim for. Without aiming 'high' in this way, this Interaction can sink you quite low with deception, listlessness and frustration.

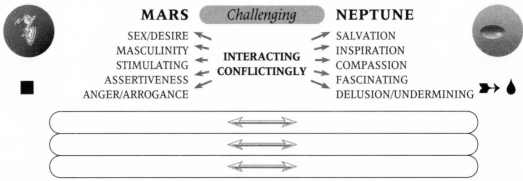

MARS *Challenging* **NEPTUNE**

MARS		NEPTUNE
SEX/DESIRE		SALVATION
MASCULINITY	**INTERACTING**	INSPIRATION
STIMULATING	**CONFLICTINGLY**	COMPASSION
ASSERTIVENESS		FASCINATING
ANGER/ARROGANCE		DELUSION/UNDERMINING

⟺ You both initially feel that there is something strange and wonderful about your coming together, or you feel drawn to one another but something seems to confound your getting closer – or then again, it could be a case of pursuer and evader. Whatever the case, it has to be said that this Interaction is very tricky and deceptive. The Mars person is most likely to make the moves, and the Neptune person either all too easily submits or tries to escape in some way. When and if you do actually get together, this pattern persists, which means that eventually it can devolve into a state of affairs that is highly frustrating, alienating or both. Mars keeps insisting on using the direct approach while Neptune becomes harder and harder to pin down, probably for subtle reasons that escape Mars's straightforwardness. And Mars's bluntness can be very wounding to

If a relationship is tired, bored or lost, pretend you have just met ...

Neptune's sensitivity, even though they have probably attracted it by being so hard to pin down. If yours is a sexual relationship, all this can make things impossible, with Mars charging in and overlooking a peculiarity or aversion of Neptune's, while Neptune can find sex gross or boring in comparison to the ideal they have in mind. This Interaction can start off in a highly sexual vein, only later to make do with abstinence born of confusion. So it can be seen here that you are both up against very different energies in each other which can cause you to be awkwardly out of step. This may even literally manifest as your being poor dancing partners. As ever, the only way of learning or gaining anything worthwhile is to take a leaf out of each other's book. Mars must learn to be more sensitive and circumspect, and be more aware of their ego's way of fouling things up. Neptune needs to be more direct, and manage their weak and sensitive spots better. Failing this, this can be a disastrous, even treacherous, Interaction.

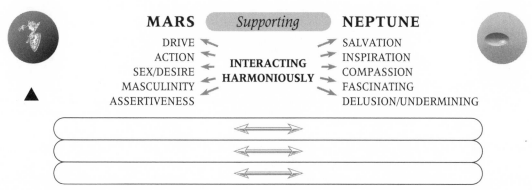

Because you instinctively and psychically pick up on each other's feelings and desires, it can mean anything from your becoming exquisitely intertwined emotionally and sexually – or that you avoid having much to do with each other at all. This is not as perplexing as it might seem. You really do sense what is best for each other, even despite your lesser thoughts and feelings. This is not to say that this fine sensibility cannot be over-ridden, but it will always be there, trying to make itself felt. Such a subtle Interaction is actually of the healing variety for it is this unerring ability to tune into areas of trouble and then lance or cleanse them that is the essence of it. If one or both of you are so inclined, this healing ray may be used very effectively upon others as well. In fact, there are many areas of endeavour, from dancing to business to film-making, that can draw from this sensitive interplay you have between body and psyche, muscle and the mystical.

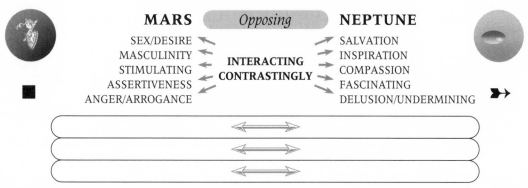

⟺ For you, trying to connect emotionally or sexually is sometimes like firing arrows under water – you think you're on target, but somehow it misses the mark. Usually it will be the Mars person who is doing the 'firing', but if the Neptune person is a male, he will try with equally confusing results. Owing to the frustration caused by these vain attempts to connect, the one who is making them will then possibly resort to cruder or blunter ways of satisfying their desires. This causes the other person to take evasive or elusive action, and so a vicious circle of frustration can ensue. Included in this could arise out-and-out deceptions on either of your parts, most likely taking the form of such things as feigned illness (possibly leading to the real thing), resorting to artificial or underhand means of getting what you want, or going off with someone else who appears to be more sensitive or more dynamic. There is the strong possibility that behind all of this confusion is the fact that you both got off on the wrong foot, or should not have got off together at all. Be that as it may, this Interaction is saying that one of you must review what they think they want, and how they go about *getting* it, and the other review what they think they want, and how they go about *attracting* it. 'Don't push the river' – meaning, don't let your desires or fantasies override the physical and emotional reality of the situation, because you will find yourselves floundering in physical and emotional confusion.

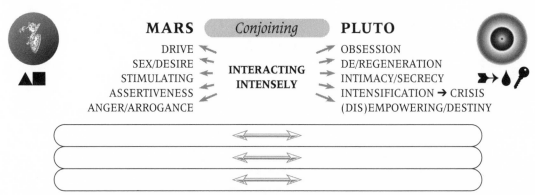

This is one of the most powerful Interactions there is, and as such, can corrupt or heal, transform or destroy. It is most likely that you are intensely and passionately involved in a sexual way, but such energy could also be used for any pursuit where a superior type of force is utilized, such as martial arts or some dynamic form of healing. In an emotional relationship, this Interaction reaches the parts other Interactions can't reach! This means to say that the intensity of your involvement brings all manner of feelings and desires to the surface, some wonderful, others hard to handle. A great deal depends upon what is motivating you both, and whether or not there is a higher goal you are aiming for. If you are simply getting off on the power and intensity merely for the sake of it, you are probably unwittingly sowing the wind only to find that you have a tornado on your hands. There is also a big brother/little brother, big sister/little sister, element in your relationship. The 'big' half is more liable to be the Pluto person, and the 'little' half the Mars person. If such is the case, Pluto may try to manipulate or dominate Mars who, in turn, may be tempted to use fair means or foul to get even. It is when such selfish interests creep into this relationship that the destructive element is set in motion, and can escalate horribly. Again, this stresses the importance of having an objective that is regenerative for one or both of you, or someone or something outside of your relationship. Something quite dark, and even dangerous, can, as I say, be brought to the surface by your coming together. If you are not aware of this and of some means of eliminating or transforming such crude emotions, then you could find yourselves in a sticky situation. Metaphorically, it is as if your relationship is an oil well that draws the black stuff to the surface, but it has to be processed and refined to render it manageable and useful.

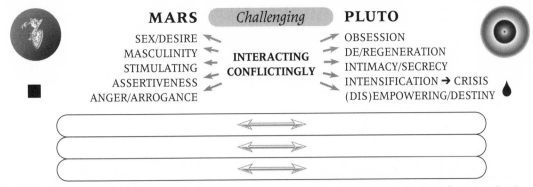

MARS *Challenging* **PLUTO**

SEX/DESIRE		OBSESSION
MASCULINITY	**INTERACTING**	DE/REGENERATION
STIMULATING	**CONFLICTINGLY**	INTIMACY/SECRECY
ASSERTIVENESS		INTENSIFICATION → CRISIS
ANGER/ARROGANCE		(DIS)EMPOWERING/DESTINY

There is an element of danger in your coming together. If there is something dark, brutal or negative in one or both of you, your relationship together could bring it to the surface. This does not mean to say you expose it for all to see, for there is a definite aura of secrecy in what you do together. This secrecy may involve certain taboos and/or emotional leverage. Pluto is more likely to have a stronger idea of the implications of Mars's actions – rather like a gangster to a punk! Because of this, Pluto will subtly or covertly set about curbing anything Mars is doing that they disapprove of. In return, or rather in retaliation, Mars will aggravate Pluto's innermost fears – especially those of losing self-concealment or any kind of power. Unless you become wise and cautious before the event, somewhere along the line, one or both of you will experience a crisis, small or large, that serves as a reminder from the unconscious of how dangerous playing with fire can be – the 'fire' most likely being base desire or deep rage. The sexual side of your relationship – actually more of a core element than merely a 'side' – can also be quite destructive or degrading, although initially very thrilling. But you are testing each other's power and survivability, so your relationship could be seen as a battleground where deep emotional truths are brought to the surface quite cathartically. The only really positive expression of this Interaction is one of refining the raw and basic energies that it evokes, and using them to heal, either each other or others generally. For this to be the case, a distinct spiritual maturity, either learned or already present, would be an absolute essential. All in all, what you have here could be called the 'Sexual Laser'.

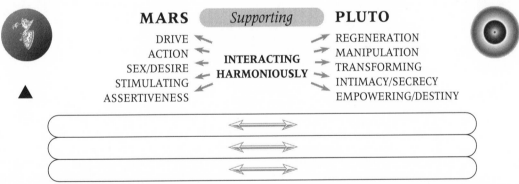

MARS *Supporting* **PLUTO**

DRIVE		REGENERATION
ACTION		MANIPULATION
SEX/DESIRE	**INTERACTING**	TRANSFORMING
STIMULATING	**HARMONIOUSLY**	INTIMACY/SECRECY
ASSERTIVENESS		EMPOWERING/DESTINY

There is a powerful and dynamic energy flowing between you which is basically sexual in nature. But, in itself, it is not an Interaction that will force itself upon you, or be forced upon one of you by the other. It is rather like a reservoir of physical and psychic energy that can be drawn upon if you both choose to or if you have to in time of need. In any event, it acts as a strong aid to survival, be it emotionally or physically. If your relationship is a sexual one, then this is the kind of Interaction that makes the earth move for both of you, especially if you are involved in some sort of sexual discipline like Tantrism or Taoism. Apart from such 'specialized' harnessing of this raw power, you are both instrumental in enabling one another to be more effective and independent in whatever fields you are involved in, to a lesser or greater degree. It is quite likely that in some way one or both of you are put back on your feet by the other, either through a prolonged process or simply through pushing one another in the right direction. Being able to eliminate some attachment that is holding one or both of you back could figure in this exercise. Taken some steps further, as a couple you could become effective in performing this service for others.

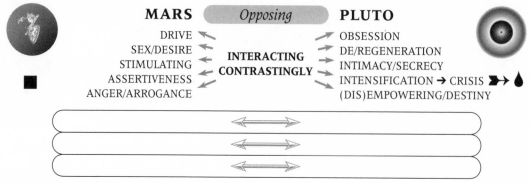

MARS *Opposing* **PLUTO**

DRIVE → OBSESSION
SEX/DESIRE → DE/REGENERATION
STIMULATING → **INTERACTING** → INTIMACY/SECRECY
ASSERTIVENESS → **CONTRASTINGLY** → INTENSIFICATION → CRISIS
ANGER/ARROGANCE → (DIS)EMPOWERING/DESTINY

There is a sense of something powerful pulling the two of you together, but if either one of you is sensitive enough, you would also be aware that something bigger than you can handle would be unleashed if you gave into this pull. More likely than not, this 'pull' will be sexual in nature. If you have given into this and have embarked upon an intimate relationship, you will be at some point along a line of increasing intensity of desire coupled with an equally strong sense in one or both of you that the other person is trying to take them over. Eventually, such a combination of desire and fight for survival can turn your relationship into a battleground, with sex and/or money being the stakes. Deep and negative psychological complexes in one or both of you can be forced to the surface under the influence of this Interaction. Softer and more tender feelings, and the expression of such feelings, become absent or even stamped upon. This Interaction amounts to 'basic training' in the awareness of your sexuality and sense of personal survival. Unless you have a quite profoundly loving relationship to contain the raw power of Mars and Pluto and express it in a positive way such as healing, then this Interaction must be regarded as unsuitable, or even unsafe, for a normal relationship.

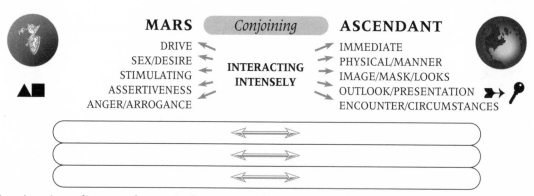

MARS *Conjoining* **ASCENDANT**

DRIVE → IMMEDIATE
SEX/DESIRE → PHYSICAL/MANNER
STIMULATING → **INTERACTING** → IMAGE/MASK/LOOKS
ASSERTIVENESS → **INTENSELY** → OUTLOOK/PRESENTATION
ANGER/ARROGANCE → ENCOUNTER/CIRCUMSTANCES

There is an immediate sexual attraction between you, but more particularly if the Ascendant person is female and the Mars person male. If this is the case, the Ascendant person sees Mars as masculinity incarnate, but it can work the other way around too with the female Mars person projecting her own maleness on to the Ascendant. In any event, you probably waste no time in getting physical in some way or other! Your 'body energies' really set each other off, causing you to be more direct and assertive than usual in making known your desires and individual identities. Such a quickening of each other's self-awareness can, however, lead to one or both of you being overly assertive, leaping before you look, or even to the point of being aggressive. The impulsive quality of this Interaction could be said to be in aid of precipitating you into a relationship when normally you may have held back. But once you are 'up and running' make sure you don't burn yourselves out, for eventually such intense energy as you generate together needs to find a direction that is worthy of it.

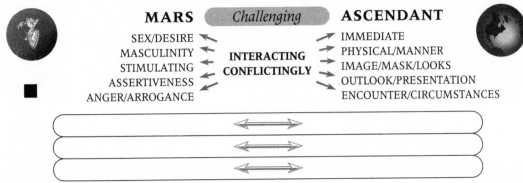

MARS *Challenging* **ASCENDANT**

MARS		ASCENDANT
SEX/DESIRE		IMMEDIATE
MASCULINITY	**INTERACTING**	PHYSICAL/MANNER
STIMULATING	**CONFLICTINGLY**	IMAGE/MASK/LOOKS
ASSERTIVENESS		OUTLOOK/PRESENTATION
ANGER/ARROGANCE		ENCOUNTER/CIRCUMSTANCES

The Mars person's manner of asserting themselves is sometimes offensive to the Ascendant person. Depending on what Sign the Ascendant is in (Rising Sign), they will react in such a way as possibly to make Mars's assertiveness turn to anger. It could also be said that something about the Ascendant's demeanour is what gets Mars going in the first place. The resolution for this possibly vicious circle is for Mars to temper their forcefulness or control their hot reactions, and the Ascendant to endeavour to be more assertive and less defensive. And patience needs to be exercised on both your parts.

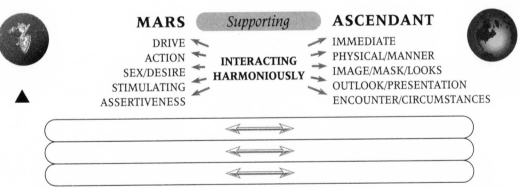

MARS *Supporting* **ASCENDANT**

MARS		ASCENDANT
DRIVE		IMMEDIATE
ACTION	**INTERACTING**	PHYSICAL/MANNER
SEX/DESIRE	**HARMONIOUSLY**	IMAGE/MASK/LOOKS
STIMULATING		OUTLOOK/PRESENTATION
ASSERTIVENESS		ENCOUNTER/CIRCUMSTANCES

This Interaction contributes to compatibility with regard to physical and sexual activity. You will find that there is a ready response to each other's desires and bodily movements, with a minimum of inhibition relative to any innate reserve on either of your parts. This is not a strong Interaction, but it can certainly oil the wheels of any endeavours you choose to pursue together.

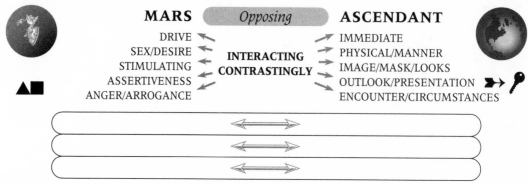

MARS	Opposing	ASCENDANT
DRIVE		IMMEDIATE
SEX/DESIRE	**INTERACTING**	PHYSICAL/MANNER
STIMULATING	**CONTRASTINGLY**	IMAGE/MASK/LOOKS
ASSERTIVENESS		OUTLOOK/PRESENTATION
ANGER/ARROGANCE		ENCOUNTER/CIRCUMSTANCES

Although this can bring about a quite immediate sexual reaction to one another – or simply a reaction – it can also lead to actual hostility. The Ascendant person has unconsciously attracted someone who will play out their own unexpressed assertive or aggressive qualities. If the Mars person is a male and the Ascendant the female, the above can run particularly true to form, even with the man becoming violent if the woman is notably passive or victim-like. At a less extreme level, the Ascendant person can simply introduce Mars to a new or different social scene, which Mars could react or respond to in any number of ways. Mars, for their part, can stimulate the Ascendant person in some way, either sexually or physically. This could lead to the Ascendant person becoming more aware of how they put themselves across. In fact, this is the important key to the aspect, because if the Ascendant person is good at asserting themselves, they get a positive reaction from the Mars person; but if they are weak or ineffectual, then they could get the negative reaction previously described. But it can also work the other way around – if the Mars person is not assertive enough and the Ascendant person is, then the Ascendant might give them a hard time. This mirroring effect is very important to recognize because it can make the difference between one or both people reacting hotly to the other, and simply being more aware of their right to be who they are, which in turn can result in them being more direct in stating their case.

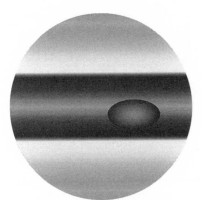

JUPITER

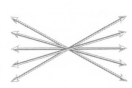

INTERACTING
WITH

JUPITER   NEPTUNE
SATURN   PLUTO
URANUS   ASCENDANT

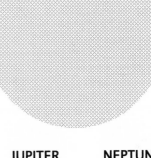

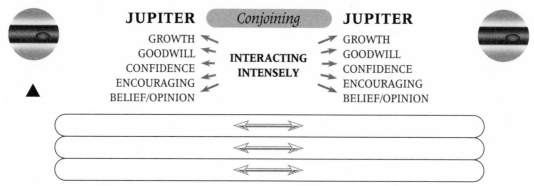

Your philosophies and cultural values are probably quite similar. This would allow you to function well together in educational or religious pursuits, or to enjoy travelling and exploring together. A good-heartedness exudes from your being together which is warming and consoling to both yourselves and others. You also share similar ideas on what is right or wrong, particularly in the moral sense. All of this means that you could go far together, but at the same time you are quite generous towards one another, and do not as a rule lay too much claim upon what each of you should do or where you should go individually. At times, however, you can try to manage each other and make out that you know what's best for the other. Another danger with this generally positive Interaction is that you can encourage each other's excesses. But, as a rule, your overall enthusiasm and goodwill tends to make these transgressions acceptable. You could even trim such excesses into something positive.

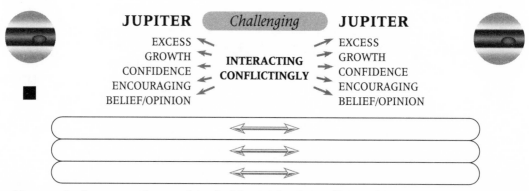

Trouble can arise from respective morals and ethics coming into collision. This can particularly centre upon issues of material values versus spiritual values. Interestingly, until you came to hotly disagree with one another over such principles, you possibly did not know just how strongly you felt about them. So, Jupiter, being the Planet of Expansion, causes you both to grow in many respects as this Interaction causes the friction that is necessary for growth. The difference of opinion, which is the essence of this Interaction, should therefore be seen as a good thing. However, it only needs one of you to think that they are completely in the right over any given issue, and that could drive a permanent wedge between you. Even then, if the other has the real faith to see things out in good grace, then it would only be a matter of time before such a fanatical belief was seen to be the hot air that it is. It could be quite a long wait though.

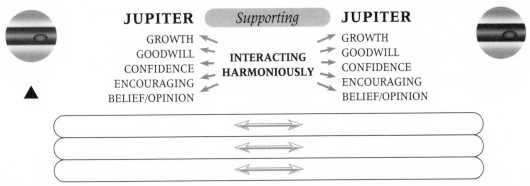

Philosophically and ethically you are in tune with one another. You also see worldly, political and religious issues and developments in more or less the same light. Anything to do with furtherance, you concur over. Because of all this harmony concerning the bigger picture or the higher mind, you sail along together quite nicely, encouraging each other to make more of yourselves and your lives. However, because this Interaction is really only concerned with these things, your more ordinary flesh-and-blood selves are not immune from the trials and tribulations of everyday existence. Indeed, such could well be grist for the excellent mill of your higher understanding. Whatever befalls you, your philanthropic attitude towards one another can or should overcome the relatively petty issues that can besiege other mortals.

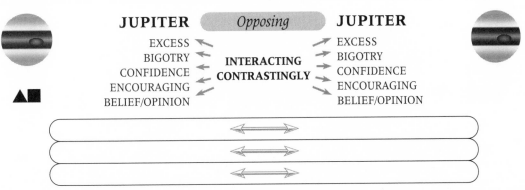

It is as if you are both looking at exactly the same thing but from totally opposite viewpoints. If you have some harmony and understanding between you indicated by other Interactions, then your opposing philosophies or belief systems can go to make up a complete whole. Such combined understanding would amount to a broadminded awareness of things that borders on the wise. If, or whenever, you have considerable disagreements between you though, your relationship becomes rather like 'believers versus infidels', with all the wars and fallings-out that can ensue from each side insisting that their world view is the right one. Yet another effect of all this could be that you make each other far more aware of what your respective beliefs and moral standards actually consist of.

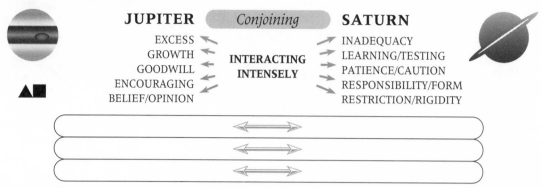

First it must be pointed out that this Interaction only forms a 'foundation' to a relationship, and needs more personal Interactions to give it a 'superstructure'. These two Planets are actually a pair in themselves (growth and limitation), and stand for the important principle that expansiveness must have order in it, and responsibility have joy in it. Be that as it may, if as a couple you can understand this balancing polarity and maintain its operation between the two of you, then your relationship will have a formidable quality about it, and will also probably get you somewhere in life. The establishing of something, mental or emotional, abstract or material, is what your relationship is all about. However, on a personal level the polar opposites that Jupiter and Saturn represent can give rise to conflict. For example, Jupiter can find Saturn's caution and discipline restrictive or oppressive, while Saturn sees Jupiter's big ideas or feelings as indulgence or mere flights of fancy. Positively though, Saturn can provide Jupiter with the material wherewithal to enable their projects, and Jupiter can bring hope and vision to Saturn when they are too earthbound and possibly depressed. So you have to find and maintain this balance between these two principles, inspired by the recognition that Fate brought you together to form these two halves of a meaningful whole. In any event, sooner or later, together or apart, it will be seen that your partnership does have some, even great, significance.

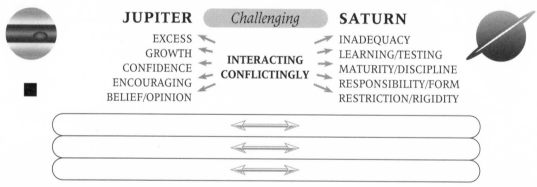

The Saturn individual sees the Jupiter person as impractical and over-indulgent, while Jupiter regards Saturn as purblind, too reliant upon status and rules, and possibly as a stick-in-the-mud. In truth though, this difficult Interaction is in aid of teaching both of you that creating a balance between these two sides of life – namely, growth and limitation – is highly important. As the Chinese philosopher Lao-Tzu said, 'If you wish to contract something, you must first let it fully expand.' This counsels Saturn to let Jupiter go off on their flights of fancy, possibly fall flat on their face, and come back the wiser. What can stop Saturn doing this is their own fear of taking chances or thinking big. So on the other hand, Saturn could learn a lesson or two from Jupiter by having more faith in life. Underlying all of this can be a fundamental difference in your respective socio-cultural backgrounds and values. Jupiter is more loose and fancy-free, while Saturn is structured and more formal. You both have something to offer one another, but deeply ingrained standards and opinions will be forced to the surface by the very conflict itself. In the process, hopefully both of you will consciously choose the best of each and discard whatever inherited beliefs or conditions are constricting, outmoded or useless.

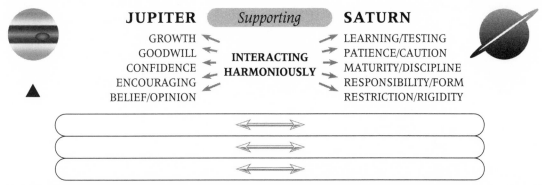

JUPITER *Supporting* **SATURN**

JUPITER		SATURN
GROWTH		LEARNING/TESTING
GOODWILL	**INTERACTING**	PATIENCE/CAUTION
CONFIDENCE	**HARMONIOUSLY**	MATURITY/DISCIPLINE
ENCOURAGING		RESPONSIBILITY/FORM
BELIEF/OPINION		RESTRICTION/RIGIDITY

If you have other Interactions that indicate emotional and personal harmony and stimulation, then you find that you also have an aspect to your relationship that is both enterprising and practical, confident and reliable. With Jupiter supplying the vision, and Saturn establishing the structure, you can build a relationship that in some way positively contributes to your society as a whole. On a personal level, Jupiter's expansiveness and optimism keep Saturn from getting too earthbound and downcast, while Saturn makes sure that Jupiter's ideas are grounded in common sense. This can be a relationship that goes from strength to strength if, as I say, there is more than just this mix of Jupiterian growth and Saturnian order. Otherwise, you'll be culturally, socially and religiously in tune, and on a business level too maybe, but without the interpersonal feelings of love and care it would be a bit like dough without the yeast or heat to make it into bread.

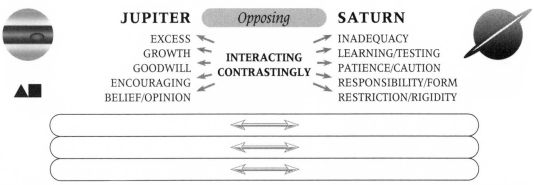

JUPITER *Opposing* **SATURN**

JUPITER		SATURN
EXCESS		INADEQUACY
GROWTH	**INTERACTING**	LEARNING/TESTING
GOODWILL	**CONTRASTINGLY**	PATIENCE/CAUTION
ENCOURAGING		RESPONSIBILITY/FORM
BELIEF/OPINION		RESTRICTION/RIGIDITY

The qualities of these two planets are naturally opposed in that Jupiter represents expansion and Saturn represents contraction. And so your basic values are at odds with one another; where the Jupiter person is liberal, adventurous and spiritually orientated, Saturn is conservative, cautious and materially orientated. And so you are inclined not to gel in the first place, often purely because circumstances do not seem to allow it, which can be frustrating if there is emotional/sexual attraction indicated elsewhere. If you are involved, then you run into difficulties while travelling or working out any kind of plan or programme, and disagree over matters of religion, education and how to live generally. In such an ongoing relationship it would be a good idea to recognize and accept that the Jupiter person is involved for reasons of learning from Saturn to be more practical and to exercise more restraint. The Saturn person is involved so that they might be given a glimpse, by Jupiter, that there is more to life than just what you can touch and see, or that tradition allows. If some kind of equilibrium can be found here, then you could make quite a healthy whole, giving and getting the best of both worlds (or Planets), but it would be rather like trying to merge two political parties.

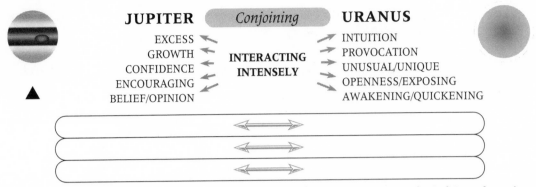

JUPITER *Conjoining* **URANUS**

EXCESS	**INTERACTING**	INTUITION
GROWTH	**INTENSELY**	PROVOCATION
CONFIDENCE		UNUSUAL/UNIQUE
ENCOURAGING		OPENNESS/EXPOSING
BELIEF/OPINION		AWAKENING/QUICKENING

This is primarily an Interaction that suits or indicates friendship and a 'marriage of minds' – at least, in one area of your relationship. As such it tends to bypass or rise above physical, sexual, or even emotional involvement. Yet because you tend to fire one another up with respect to subjects like metaphysics, religion, education, New Age thinking, etc, you could be forgiven for feeling that the fire is a bit lower down than it is! Any forays into the sensual are probably isolated incidents or are just titillating prospects that hover around. When such misconceptions of your interest in one another are put behind you, or if they never arose in the first place, this Interaction can enable you to discover together very unusual and encouraging insights into life, the Universe and everything. So what can start out as a very lively Interaction that promises all manner of exciting and unlikely things can evolve into something quite cerebral. However, there will probably always be that frisson of 'what if' whenever you are in each other's company. None of the above is to say that yours cannot be an ongoing relationship. If it is, then this Interaction would help to keep it refreshed, not least because your individual opinions cannot resist good-humouredly vying with one another, thereby upgrading your respective viewpoints and ideas of one another – and life itself.

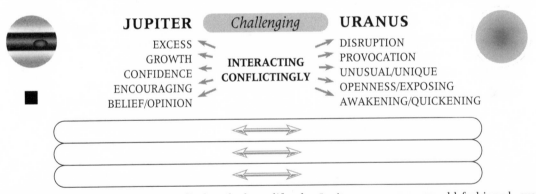

JUPITER *Challenging* **URANUS**

EXCESS	**INTERACTING**	DISRUPTION
GROWTH	**CONFLICTINGLY**	PROVOCATION
CONFIDENCE		UNUSUAL/UNIQUE
ENCOURAGING		OPENNESS/EXPOSING
BELIEF/OPINION		AWAKENING/QUICKENING

Compared to the Uranus person's radical outlook on life, the Jupiter person appears old-fashioned, even though they may not be in a general sense. And to Jupiter, Uranus seems exciting and unusual, but possibly unstable. But the dynamic of this Interaction is to shake or even shock Jupiter out of any stale beliefs or outmoded cultural values. Conversely, Uranus could learn some tolerance and generosity of spirit from Jupiter. However, the greater difficulty here is when you both 'agree' to charge around and do exactly as you want. This is liable to happen because both Planets are connected with freedom. And so it may not be long before you are more apart than together for reasons of each doing your own thing, chasing your personal rainbow, etc. At some point the question arises as to what takes precedence – your desire for freedom or your need to maintain a steady relationship. A great deal would depend here upon the amount of emotional compatibility shown elsewhere. If you trust one another then well and good. If you do not, you would wear one another out as you swung between, so to speak, a cosy home and the open road. This is the kind of Interaction that a film star couple might have. Through learning the price of freedom, you gain a clearer idea of what freedom actually is – or is not.

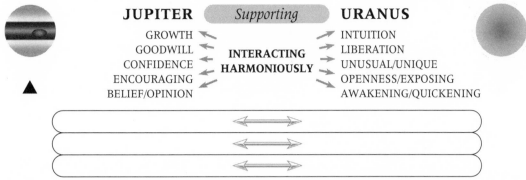

JUPITER *Supporting* URANUS

GROWTH — INTUITION
GOODWILL — LIBERATION
CONFIDENCE — **INTERACTING** UNUSUAL/UNIQUE
ENCOURAGING **HARMONIOUSLY** OPENNESS/EXPOSING
BELIEF/OPINION AWAKENING/QUICKENING

A healthy sense of freedom and equality is the keynote here, and it is linked to the fact that your individual philosophies of life, without necessarily being the same, are able to find common ground. Yours is a modern and future-orientated partnership, and you could both be actually involved with new realms of thought and religion. Without any conscious effort, this Interaction seems to foster the development of the innovative and unusual. This is not what you would call a dynamic Interaction, but it does provide an atmosphere of altruistic and platonic co-operation. This is a harmonious connecting of your higher minds – so to get the best out of this, quite a lot depends upon how consciously or deliberately you invest time and energy as a couple into mind-expanding pursuits. Potentially, you are able to further each other's higher or better interests, and this in turn would attract 'luck' into your life as a couple in the form of good timing and unexpected opportunities or windfalls, and possibly disappearing into the wild blue yonder every so often.

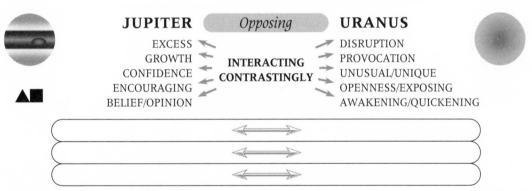

JUPITER *Opposing* URANUS

EXCESS — DISRUPTION
GROWTH — PROVOCATION
CONFIDENCE — **INTERACTING** UNUSUAL/UNIQUE
ENCOURAGING **CONTRASTINGLY** OPENNESS/EXPOSING
BELIEF/OPINION AWAKENING/QUICKENING

Because both Jupiter and Uranus as Planets symbolize qualities of the higher mind – like faith, intuition and collective codes of thought – you can at first seem to have a lot in common. But unless you also do so on a more personal level, it will become plain as time goes by that your ideas on how to live are distinctly at odds. For example, a theme of your relationship could be the seeking or practising of some unusual religious philosophy that progressively becomes a wedge between you as one of you becomes more and more convinced and the other more and more disenchanted. Apart from this kind of thing, there is a restlessness about you, or a chemistry between you, that can make things feel as if they are happening and on the move. But at a certain point, probably quite suddenly, you realize that you are on the same roundabout but turning off at different exits. If other more earthy and responsible ties exist between you, then this Interaction could provide stimulating differences of opinion that you combine into some meaningful whole. But even then, beware, for this is a pie-in-the-sky aspect.

… and that each of you is still a mystery to the other

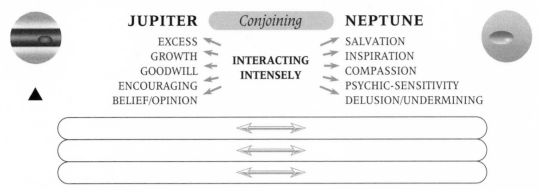

This is a subtle Interaction that can give you both a sense of connectedness that goes beyond the day-to-day circumstances and requirements of life. A mutual interest in the mystical or unseen realms is present, along with shared experiences in these areas. This can give your relationship a meaning and direction that puts the more mundane ups and downs into perspective, especially if metaphysical practices such as meditation, hypnosis, trance-work, or the investigation of such things as dreams and previous lives are embarked upon. On the other hand, this Interaction can make for fanciful and escapist ideas about yourselves as individuals and about your relationship itself. For example, one of you may encourage the weaker side of the other under the mistaken idea that you're being easygoing or compassionate. Or indulging in the idea that you as a pair are somehow more special than others. A great deal depends upon how down-to-earth you each are as individuals, for the ability of at least one of you to distinguish a vision from a mirage, or an ideal from an excuse, can make the difference between your having a gentle and spiritual bond, and merely living in cloud-cuckoo land until the bubble inevitably bursts. Whatever the case though, yours is a coupling that should sooner or later aspire to finding its higher reason for existing, simply because it has one.

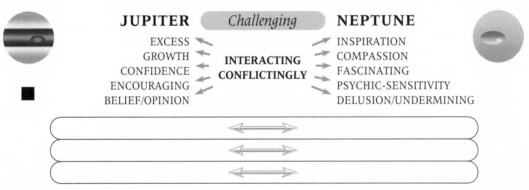

The Jupiter person encourages the Neptune person to lose their way in fantasies and great expectations, while Neptune confuses Jupiter's sense of right and wrong. There is a 'hippie' quality here which is fairly soft and harmless in the usual sense of the word, but it undermines any attempts to achieve anything more substantial. There is also a religious or spiritual feel about your being together, but this is possibly fanciful and notional. So unfortunately the cloud that you tend to float away on finds you resenting one another, being scorned by others, or at least feeling rather aimless. If this combination could be contained in some form of discipline, like meditating, performing, or doing some sort of charity work together, then it would have a positive outlet.

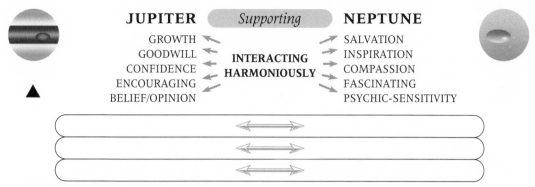

JUPITER *Supporting* **NEPTUNE**

GROWTH		SALVATION
GOODWILL	**INTERACTING**	INSPIRATION
CONFIDENCE	**HARMONIOUSLY**	COMPASSION
ENCOURAGING		FASCINATING
BELIEF/OPINION		PSYCHIC-SENSITIVITY

At a very basic level you have spiritual compatibility. This means that you treat each other as human beings in that you maintain a certain gentle tolerance and respect. Friends and associates will pick up on this harmonious vibration – possibly quite subliminally – and like to be around you, or even seek your help and sympathy in times of trouble. How much you make of this, or not, is the question. On the one hand, such passivity is developing towards something of its own peaceful accord. On the other, it can cause you just to coast along in a nice but somewhat ineffectual fashion. Ideally, if you are both evolved to some degree spiritually, then you can 'use' this spiritual energy to achieve greater good. Compassion and goodwill, are, after all, the basic ingredients of this compatibility.

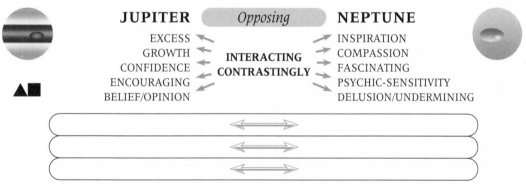

JUPITER *Opposing* **NEPTUNE**

EXCESS		INSPIRATION
GROWTH	**INTERACTING**	COMPASSION
CONFIDENCE	**CONTRASTINGLY**	FASCINATING
ENCOURAGING		PSYCHIC-SENSITIVITY
BELIEF/OPINION		DELUSION/UNDERMINING

This Interaction is likely to occur between two people when one of them, probably the Jupiter person, has reached a point when their beliefs or understanding of life need to become more inclusive, tolerant or even mystical. The other individual, probably the Neptune person, needs to adapt their ideals and visions to the cultural or social reality they find themselves in. This is, in effect, an interchange of one person's intellectually determined philosophy with the other's emotionally inspired one. However, before either of you accept this – that is if you ever do – you are going to become quite confused or indignant as the 'right versus wrong' attitude of the one of you collides with the 'live and let live' outlook of the other. You both have a point, so meeting somewhere in the middle is what you both should aim for. In the process, Neptune will have to accept Jupiter's inability to accept, and be tolerant of their intolerance. Curiously, Neptune may have to accept from Jupiter that in reality, as opposed to ideally, people fall into different and opposing camps, and that sometimes one is forced to take sides.

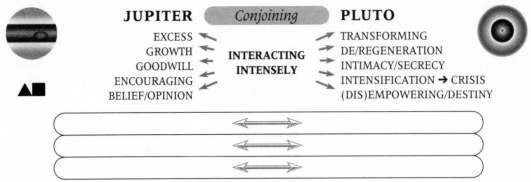

JUPITER *Conjoining* **PLUTO**

EXCESS		TRANSFORMING
GROWTH	**INTERACTING**	DE/REGENERATION
GOODWILL	**INTENSELY**	INTIMACY/SECRECY
ENCOURAGING		INTENSIFICATION ➔ CRISIS
BELIEF/OPINION		(DIS)EMPOWERING/DESTINY

The Jupiter person has their beliefs and opinions probed and questioned, influenced and possibly transformed in some way by the Pluto person. The Pluto person would be inclined to see the Jupiter person as impractical or lightweight in their philosophy of life until proven otherwise. Jupiter, on the other hand, can shine a ray of hope and goodness into what could be Pluto's dark and suspicious recesses. As ever with Conjoining aspects, a great deal depends on what other Interactions there are with Jupiter and Pluto in your Birthcharts, but overall this one has the potential of deepening and furthering whatever valid convictions either of you have. Jupiter can spiritually or professionally benefit from Pluto's insights and any powerful connections they may have. Pluto is made to feel less buried and alone by Jupiter's warmth and magnanimity. If other Interactions support or augment this one, you could make a formidable pair in converting the beliefs and ideas of the public at large.

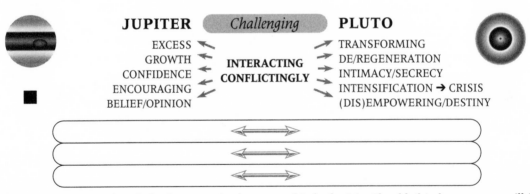

JUPITER *Challenging* **PLUTO**

EXCESS		TRANSFORMING
GROWTH	**INTERACTING**	DE/REGENERATION
CONFIDENCE	**CONFLICTINGLY**	INTIMACY/SECRECY
ENCOURAGING		INTENSIFICATION ➔ CRISIS
BELIEF/OPINION		(DIS)EMPOWERING/DESTINY

Any excesses or incautious behaviour may lead to some kind of crisis. Should this happen you will be confronted with some sort of moral dilemma. The Pluto person will attempt to steamroller the Jupiter person's thoughts or feelings on the matter, whereas the Jupiter person will resist this with ethical or religious justifications. But the fact is that both of you have been, or are in danger of being, remiss in some matter of judgement or conduct. So this Interaction is all about bringing to the surface some quite profound or taboo-ridden issue, possibly one that involves the law, be it made by man or God – or sex. Apart from being wise before the event, whatever that might be, the two of you should avoid bad feelings as much as possible by accepting that you are only human. But then the trouble with this aspect between two 'power' planets is that difficulties can arise simply because you forget that you really are just human. Accepting this, and that neither of you can really have the last word, is probably the only way of resolving the conflict. 'Vengeance is Mine, saith the Lord' or 'Judge not lest ye be judged'.

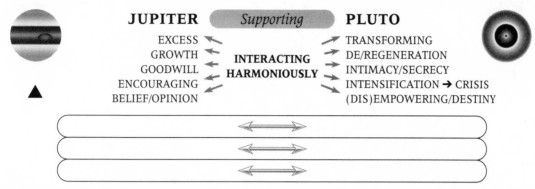

JUPITER *Supporting* **PLUTO**

EXCESS		TRANSFORMING
GROWTH	**INTERACTING**	DE/REGENERATION
GOODWILL	**HARMONIOUSLY**	INTIMACY/SECRECY
ENCOURAGING		INTENSIFICATION ➔ CRISIS
BELIEF/OPINION		(DIS)EMPOWERING/DESTINY

This Interaction is a bit like 'money for old rope' in that you are able to show each other that it is through getting rid of things you do not need that you acquire things that you do. Whatever is obstructing either one of you – be it an inappropriate belief, a sense of impotence, or a possession of some kind – the other is somehow able to help them let go of it. You make one another live up to the saying 'When one door closes, another one opens'. Great wealth, be it spiritual or material, can be gained through this simple 'give more to get more' philosophy that is the potential of your being together. Jupiter knows the way to get there; Pluto has the power to get there.

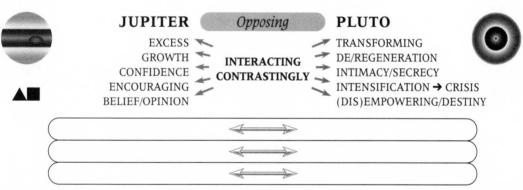

JUPITER *Opposing* **PLUTO**

EXCESS		TRANSFORMING
GROWTH	**INTERACTING**	DE/REGENERATION
CONFIDENCE	**CONTRASTINGLY**	INTIMACY/SECRECY
ENCOURAGING		INTENSIFICATION ➔ CRISIS
BELIEF/OPINION		(DIS)EMPOWERING/DESTINY

Moral principles are thrashed out through the sexual or other powerful forms of involvement that make up your relationship. This Interaction makes it clear that giving into your passions ultimately leads to some kind of reckoning, or that sooner or later ethical standards will have to prove themselves to be more than just opinions. The possibility of blame and recrimination is strong with this Interaction as the emotional urges or convictions of one of you clash with the beliefs of the other. The contrast between the two should serve to make you both more aware of where you stand with respect to these issues. Ultimately, what you are both after is some form of philosophy that goes deep enough to enable you both to understand what it is about human nature that draws us downwards and inwards, despite, or because of, our best intentions or sense of what is right and what is wrong.

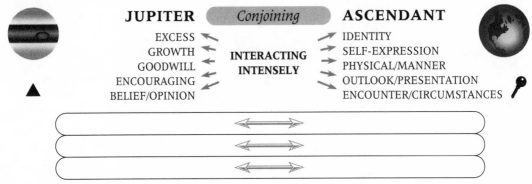

This is a very positive Interaction for an immediate sense of trust and goodwill is felt by both of you. Following upon this, the Ascendant person finds that Jupiter encourages them to express themself and opens up their horizons considerably, while the Ascendant acts as a touchstone for Jupiter's faith in life and themself. You both give each other a feeling that life and your relationship has meaning. The downside to Jupiter is always one of promising more than can be delivered, and to a degree this could become the case – and in return, the Ascendant person could also become a bit wayward. But the initial feelings of friendship and trust persist, within and without the relationship, together or apart. A philanthropic and mutually helpful flavour pervades your connection or dealings with one another. This is very much a Key Contact because it does offer one or both of you the key to a new and better life, or at least, to a means or way of getting there.

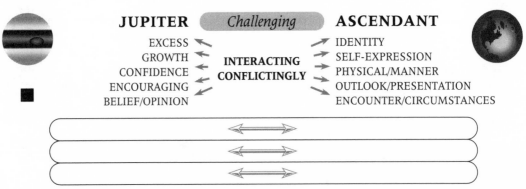

The Jupiter person is inclined to judge the Ascendant individual's moral or spiritual standing purely by their character and manner of expression. Understandably, the Ascendant person can be offended by this, seeing Jupiter as sanctimonious and hypocritical. More constructively, the Ascendant person can force the Jupiter person to 'walk their talk' if they wish to be taken seriously. However, what can follow upon this is that if Jupiter does walk their talk, then the Ascendant really will have to look to the ethical or spiritual dimension of their life.

The great key to relating is to understand what a relationship is telling you, then accept it

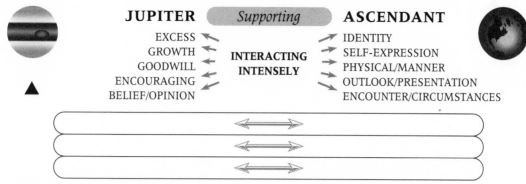

JUPITER	*Supporting*	ASCENDANT
EXCESS		IDENTITY
GROWTH	INTERACTING	SELF-EXPRESSION
GOODWILL	INTENSELY	PHYSICAL/MANNER
ENCOURAGING		OUTLOOK/PRESENTATION
BELIEF/OPINION		ENCOUNTER/CIRCUMSTANCES

You both blossom in the light and warmth of each other's attention. There may even be a 'master and protégé' quality about your relationship, rather as if one of you has the wisdom while the other has the image or looks to carry it off. Metaphorically, or perhaps even literally, Jupiter is the cultured and socially experienced person who grooms the naïve Ascendant youth. The creator and the created – the ultimate relationship made possible because you both have the grace to recognize each other's individual qualities.

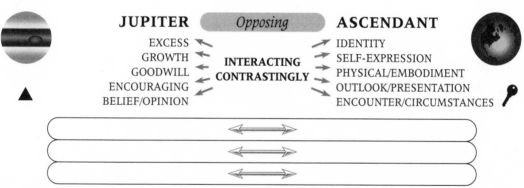

JUPITER	*Opposing*	ASCENDANT
EXCESS		IDENTITY
GROWTH	INTERACTING	SELF-EXPRESSION
GOODWILL	CONTRASTINGLY	PHYSICAL/EMBODIMENT
ENCOURAGING		OUTLOOK/PRESENTATION
BELIEF/OPINION		ENCOUNTER/CIRCUMSTANCES

The Jupiter individual can get the Ascendant person to accept and believe in the other side of their character, and thereby help them to relate more honestly and openly. This of course depends on how inclined they are to do so already, and what Jupiter is like in getting the best out of people generally – but one could say that Jupiter is 'good news' to the Ascendant. So, initially at least, the Ascendant person will feel they have struck gold with the Jupiter person, and feel irresistibly drawn to their expansiveness and philosophy. As time goes by, they may do a turnaround and find these qualities a bit wild and scatty, or even regard Jupiter as given over to trends and generalizations. But a feeling of being aware of and attracted to their better nature or higher mind persists, almost in spite of themselves. The Ascendant, in turn, makes Jupiter far more aware of what they do or don't believe in, as well as introducing them to new areas of religious or philosophical thought. All in all, this contact favours your relationship because it is somewhat impersonal, yet at the same time quite enjoyable. As long as the relationship doesn't become 'academic' through losing sight of any emotional substance, this Interaction can bring ethical steadiness and openly expressed goodwill to the relationship. Travelling near or far is also a strong aspect of your coming, or staying, together.

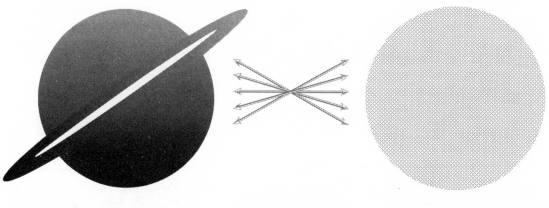

SATURN INTERACTING WITH

SATURN
URANUS
NEPTUNE

PLUTO
ASCENDANT

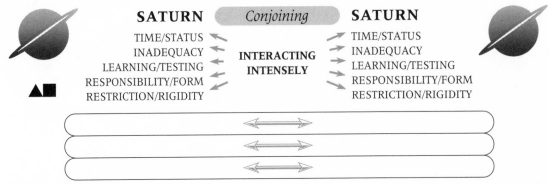

SATURN *Conjoining* **SATURN**

TIME/STATUS
INADEQUACY
LEARNING/TESTING
RESPONSIBILITY/FORM
RESTRICTION/RIGIDITY

INTERACTING INTENSELY

TIME/STATUS
INADEQUACY
LEARNING/TESTING
RESPONSIBILITY/FORM
RESTRICTION/RIGIDITY

This Interaction emphasizes the importance of making commitments and keeping to them, whether they be to one another or to someone or something else. On the positive side, you share similar ideas about what these things mean, along with status, politics, material stability, and the way of the world generally. However, if any of these issues are ill-founded, then you will reinforce them in each other. This in turn could result in your having difficulties with respect to them. So this Interaction is very much what you make it. It is as if you have been given a lump of clay which you can mould how you both see fit. A sense of constructiveness and order is therefore a prerequisite, while any inclination just to 'see how things turn out' or 'hope for the best' will be met with a diminishing sense of either one or both of you having any solid ground to stand upon. This Interaction is rather like knocking two houses together to make a bigger shared living space. This can work very nicely if it is well-planned and there is sufficient harmony indicated by other Interactions – but a sheer disaster if not.

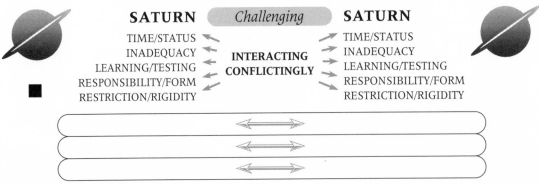

SATURN *Challenging* **SATURN**

TIME/STATUS
INADEQUACY
LEARNING/TESTING
RESPONSIBILITY/FORM
RESTRICTION/RIGIDITY

INTERACTING CONFLICTINGLY

TIME/STATUS
INADEQUACY
LEARNING/TESTING
RESPONSIBILITY/FORM
RESTRICTION/RIGIDITY

You tend to work at cross-purposes, yet at such a basic level that one or both of you may even overlook it until time together, or apart, makes this more obvious. Because of this, it would be wise for both of you to exercise considerable caution in making any kind of substantial commitment. Fortunately, this Interaction often implies that one of you won't be that keen on taking the plunge – but they will have their work cut out making this plain to the other, more eager, person. If one of you feels any doubt, it is imperative that you give expression to it, otherwise you could find yourselves in a highly inconvenient situation later on. Beneath it all, there are important differences between you with regard to what you take most seriously, what you define as appropriate behaviour, and your status or position in life. Having said all of this, if there are positive and harmonious connections elsewhere, this Interaction will still tend to slow things down and emphasize the duller side of life over the more uplifting. There is always the possibility that you are learning about the nature and necessity of your respective limitations and duties as a result of such a relationship, which may include having to learn which of those obligations are no longer necessary for you, and which you must break off from.

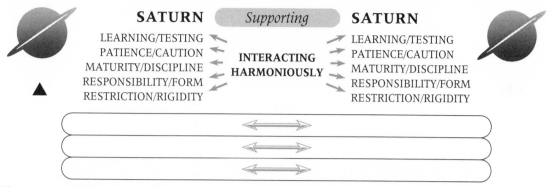

There is a stabilizing and industrious quality created by the two of you being together, but a mature or businesslike streak would have to be present in you as individuals in order to make anything of it. Even so, there is a basic sense of sobriety and mutual respect that will help you through more difficult times, or prevent you both from indulging too much in any feckless pursuits. This is not a powerful Interaction in itself, unless it is a Close One. To put it another way, it is like a good firm road going somewhere, but the vehicle for going down it needs to be supplied by other positive and constructive links and activities. If such is the case, then you are reliability itself, providing a firm base for anything from a family to a business. Another possibility is that you would attract someone or something that provides that firm base. What you do with it is another matter.

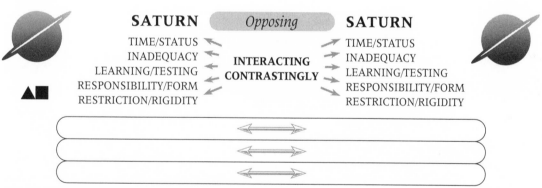

What is needed here is a kind of division of labour where each of you deals with your respective duties and objectives without falling into the mistake of insisting the other person have the same duties and objectives or ways of achieving them. Emotionally, we often have a need to feel 'together' with someone in more ways than is possible considering the different life circumstances of each individual, such as this Interaction indicates. Saturn as a planetary energy is not interested in such personal inclinations, and this Interaction makes that very clear. However, if it is not clear to both of you that you do have different paths and disciplines in certain areas, then this simple material difference can grow into what seems a great block to emotional harmony. Much of the difficulty may simply arise because one of you is 14 to 15 years older than the other, and their responsibilities are simply greater, their perspective more worldly-wise or world-weary. Ultimately, this Interaction could indeed spell out a difference between the two of you that does make untenable an ongoing relationship of any kind. It could be rather as if you pass one another by, test each other's standpoint and objective, and move on – hopefully leaving you both a little wiser as to what is hard but necessary in each of your lives, as opposed to what is easy and pleasurable.

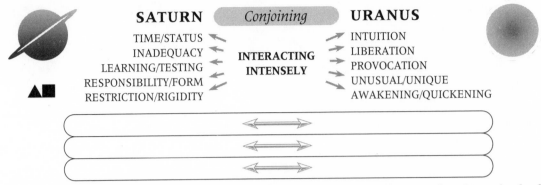

SATURN   *Conjoining*   **URANUS**

TIME/STATUS
INADEQUACY
LEARNING/TESTING
RESPONSIBILITY/FORM
RESTRICTION/RIGIDITY

**INTERACTING
INTENSELY**

INTUITION
LIBERATION
PROVOCATION
UNUSUAL/UNIQUE
AWAKENING/QUICKENING

Saturn and Uranus are very different as Planets, and the parts of you that come, or are forced, together by this Interaction are equally dissimilar. Uranus, being the proactive part, will help Saturn to come out of their shell and loosen their inhibitions. Uranus could do this intuitively or with shock tactics. Sometimes Uranus can appear icy-cold and detached in the way they do this. But Saturn can understand coldness and impersonality, and so can respond strangely well to Uranus's provocation – just because they are impersonal. Stranger still, Saturn's solid response to Uranus's off-the-wall behaviour gives Uranus permission to be the unique and maybe shocking or unusual person they feel themselves to be, but may not show others generally. However, with all this ice and cold around, it should come as no surprise that your relationship can go very cool sometimes. Again, this may be, or should be seen as being, all very well because there is a kind of impersonal, on-off process that goes on between you. In this way, you can remain friends until the end – with any romantic, sexual or warmer interludes being just oases along the dusty way. If your two charts are elsewhere seriously lacking in harmony and understanding, then indeed your relationship could go into an ice age and never come out. But even so, much as you might disapprove of one another, radical Uranus and conservative Saturn just cannot resist one another. (Perhaps to gain a deeper insight into this pairing and the enmity that is inherent in it, read the allusion to Saturn and Uranus in the myth described under the Interaction Venus Conjoining Uranus on page 394.)

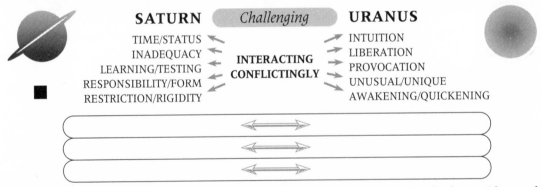

SATURN   *Challenging*   **URANUS**

TIME/STATUS
INADEQUACY
LEARNING/TESTING
RESPONSIBILITY/FORM
RESTRICTION/RIGIDITY

**INTERACTING
CONFLICTINGLY**

INTUITION
LIBERATION
PROVOCATION
UNUSUAL/UNIQUE
AWAKENING/QUICKENING

This Interaction definitely requires that some compromise be made between the both of you with regard to the Saturn partner who is inclined to being relatively conservative, and the Uranus partner who takes a more radical or liberal stance – at least, in relation to the Saturn person. So Saturn needs to loosen up a bit, change with the times and adopt new methods and approaches, and generally take a more alternative view of things. Uranus, on the other hand, should endeavour to toe the line, wait things out, and not get so hot and flustered and reactionary when things do not proceed at the speed and in the direction they desire. Looked at positively, which is the best way of dealing with Challenging Aspects, Saturn can benefit from Uranus's intuitive insights and innovative ideas, if they can be made to see a logical and practical reason for them – before it's too late. Conversely, Uranus can draw reassurance from Saturn's more solid, steady-as-she-goes, attitude – providing there is at least a token display of flexibility from them. Failing this, this Interaction can become quite separative or create a stalemate situation as Saturn regards Uranus as becoming unacceptably unstable and unpredictable, while Uranus sees Saturn as remaining impossibly stuck or stuffy and closed. This aspect can indicate a marked age difference, literally or psychologically, with Saturn being the 'older' person.

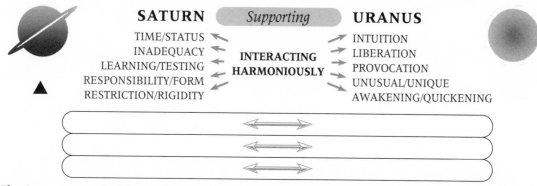

SATURN *Supporting* **URANUS**

TIME/STATUS		INTUITION
INADEQUACY	**INTERACTING**	LIBERATION
LEARNING/TESTING	**HARMONIOUSLY**	PROVOCATION
RESPONSIBILITY/FORM		UNUSUAL/UNIQUE
RESTRICTION/RIGIDITY		AWAKENING/QUICKENING

The Saturn person is able to affirm what is unique about the Uranus person, or at least make them constructively aware of how they should and could fit better into the status quo. Uranus, on the other hand, can show Saturn new ways of looking at life that clarify difficult issues and impartially point out where they are possibly being their own worst enemy. And so there is a mutual problem-solving element to this Interaction which is useful, to one degree or another. This is essentially a contact of sound and sincere friendship, or of working together on some specific project. If yours is an emotionally intimate relationship, you draw upon this resourcefulness and sense of 'unconditional comradeship' to get you through rocky patches. Taken further still, you could as a pair, or part of a team, be instrumental in helping others through difficulties.

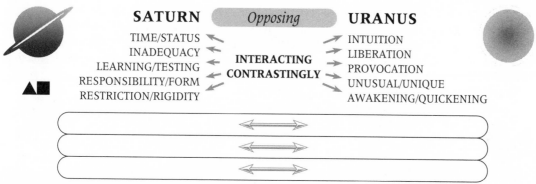

SATURN *Opposing* **URANUS**

TIME/STATUS		INTUITION
INADEQUACY		LIBERATION
LEARNING/TESTING	**INTERACTING**	PROVOCATION
RESPONSIBILITY/FORM	**CONTRASTINGLY**	UNUSUAL/UNIQUE
RESTRICTION/RIGIDITY		AWAKENING/QUICKENING

This Interaction is designated as both hard and easy, but for you as a partnership it is hard because it is fraught with tensions as Saturn doggedly sticks with the devil they know, while Uranus consciously or unconsciously endeavours to free Saturn from that very thing. Saturn's past involvements, especially those to which they still feel duty-bound, seem to get in the way of both the relationship and Saturn's own well-being. Uranus does not offer anything very solid – but has the allure of the wild blue yonder, all the same. And so an impasse can arise here as Saturn refuses to change but is tempted to, while Uranus maintains a fairly wide orbit, which is in itself provocative and unreliable. Saturn will also try to restrict or control Uranus's erratic and unpredictable behaviour. Not surprisingly, this relationship can appear impossible – mad even. But the simple truth is that Uranus is merely a catalyst, no more and no less, to shock or trick Saturn out of their rut. Once that mission is accomplished, they'll most likely be off for their own reasons. What they have got out of it will be something entirely different, like being shown how free they are compared to most people in general, and Saturn in particular. Or they may have learnt (or not) a lesson from Saturn that Uranus's original ideas are only as good as they are practical and appreciable by ordinary folk, and that for Uranus to believe they are unrecognized genius is misguided, to say the least. So that can be the 'easy' bit, that the pay-off is after the relationship is over – when Saturn has been liberated in some way and to some degree, and Uranus has a firmer or clearer idea of what is unique about them and what impact, if any, it can have upon others. Apart from this, in a more ongoing way, Uranus can make Saturn aware of their true standing in the world, a place from which Saturn may be able to help bestow the same upon Uranus. This Interaction is far better expressed and experienced in a friend relationship.

Look for patterns or themes that emerge while reading all of your Profiles

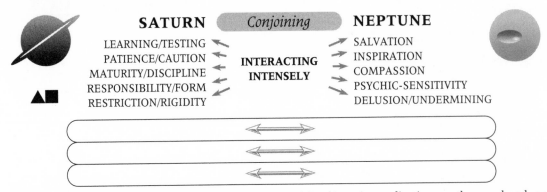

SATURN _Conjoining_ **NEPTUNE**

LEARNING/TESTING **INTERACTING** SALVATION
PATIENCE/CAUTION **INTENSELY** INSPIRATION
MATURITY/DISCIPLINE COMPASSION
RESPONSIBILITY/FORM PSYCHIC-SENSITIVITY
RESTRICTION/RIGIDITY DELUSION/UNDERMINING

This Interaction can amount to either enormous spiritual/creative realization on the one hand, or a boring and frustrating stalemate on the other. So much depends upon the preparedness of each of you to meet the other half way. This is because one of you is approaching matters from a pragmatic, materialistic and logical viewpoint, while the other is inspired by something idealistic, spiritual and mystical. This is rather as if one of you is the architect with this vision of something wonderful that could be built, while the other is the builder who has the wherewithal to make it a physical reality. However, if the builder thinks the architect is just dreaming of castles in the air they will look elsewhere for business, but possibly wind up erecting something dull and meaningless. And if the architect sees the builder as merely suppressive, limited or unimaginative, then they will look for someone who will give form to their dream, but find this an endless search. And yet, you both could have a valid point here, but just not be the 'architect' and 'builder' who are meant for one another – and you'll both have to keep on looking. If, however, your respective ideas and abilities gel, then your relationship will indeed be a monument to harmony, understanding and co-operation. It may even be your combined spiritual duty to make it work, by that meeting each other half way. This could be called a 'Jack Spratt and his wife' Interaction.

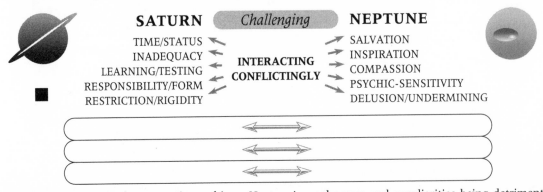

SATURN _Challenging_ **NEPTUNE**

TIME/STATUS SALVATION
INADEQUACY **INTERACTING** INSPIRATION
LEARNING/TESTING **CONFLICTINGLY** COMPASSION
RESPONSIBILITY/FORM PSYCHIC-SENSITIVITY
RESTRICTION/RIGIDITY DELUSION/UNDERMINING

The Saturn person tends to experience this as Neptune's weaknesses and peculiarities being detrimental to their stability and material well-being. Neptune, on the other hand, sees Saturn's ingrained fears and inhibitions as being frustrating and suppressive. So a lot of blame and guilt can be generated by this conflict of values and approach. Saturn finds themself in a position of having to hold the fort while Neptune is being feckless and irresponsible, at least from Saturn's point of view. But Neptune cannot stand playing by Saturn's rules, and regards them as the 'heavy father' who disapproves when they have a little fun. 'The Authoritarian and the Libertine' would be an apt title for this pairing. As far as adopting a more positive attitude, Saturn should endeavour to see that Neptune, consciously or unconsciously, is trying to get them to go with the flow more, to stop trying to control everything, and to confess their fears and thereby disperse them. Neptune should honestly admit to any need for self-control, more practicality and generally cleaning up their act. Ultimately, both of you are forced by this Interaction to listen to your consciences, rather than project them on to each other as blame and recrimination. Until this psychological impasse is dissolved, or at least recognized and admitted to, this is not a good aspect for the building of anything together.

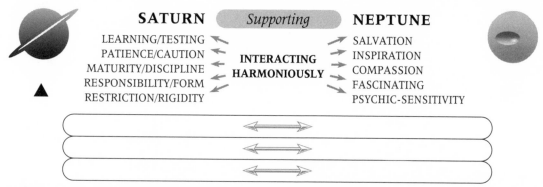

You have a great thing going for you both here because each of you takes care of and teaches the other just what they need to have or know at the time. This is because Saturn has a sound grip on reality just where Neptune does not, and Neptune is aware of another dimension of reality that can greatly relieve and enlighten Saturn. More precisely, Neptune gives Saturn a practical awareness of their psychic abilities and insights, and how they perhaps fulfil their duties in more or better ways than they have allowed themselves to think. Saturn gives substance to Neptune's vision and imagination – possibly furthering a creative endeavour – as well as allaying any unfounded anxieties. As a team, you would be very successful and effective where both a sense of form and imagination is required – like, for instance, film-making, speculation or psychotherapy.

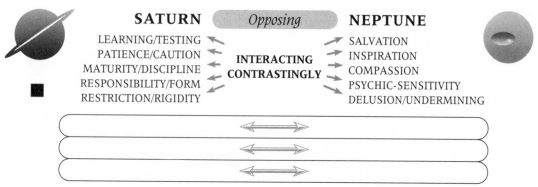

⟷ As Planets, Saturn and Neptune are in natural opposition, with the former representing material order and responsibility, and the latter symbolizing spiritual reality and obligation. And so one of you could see the other as being vague and afraid to make certain types of commitment, while the other sees their opposite number as dull, limited or suppressive. It could work the other way around as well because each Planet acts as the Shadow of the other and tends to catch their projection. So the Saturn person could conveniently load some of their material shortcomings on the Neptune person, and Neptune their emotional weaknesses on Saturn. Consequently, your relationship can often get caught in a muddy pool of not seeing one another at all clearly. On the face of it, you could learn a great deal about how you could be more balanced and stable if you owned up to this projection on to one another as something each of you finds hard to admit to having in themselves. Such self-honesty is best exercised early on, for in time that 'muddy pool' can turn into a veritable swamp. Try using The Mirror on page 485.

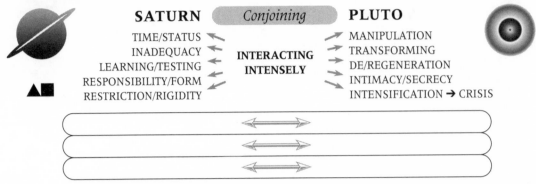

SATURN *Conjoining* **PLUTO**

TIME/STATUS
INADEQUACY
LEARNING/TESTING
RESPONSIBILITY/FORM
RESTRICTION/RIGIDITY

**INTERACTING
INTENSELY**

MANIPULATION
TRANSFORMING
DE/REGENERATION
INTIMACY/SECRECY
INTENSIFICATION ➔ CRISIS

⟺ This is essentially a businesslike contact – literally or figuratively. If other Interactions comply or contribute, you can further one another, individually or together, in your careers. The Saturn person will be the organizational side, and the Pluto person will provide the thrust and insight – but these delineations should not be taken too literally, for there should be some crossover of roles. Actually, the ability to interchange and trust, give and take power and position, is very important to your getting ahead and not running into a competition of control and manipulation. Together you can present a formidable front that would impress any group or individual. On the other hand, any power politics that go wrong will give off a decidedly nasty smell. So the good and enlightened management of your unmistakably powerful energy combination is vital. In fact, the clean and upright use of power may be the very thing you use, teach or espouse. On a more emotional level, which may or may not be that obvious with this aspect, Saturn acts as a limiting and disciplining influence over any degenerate or wasteful qualities in Pluto, while Pluto is able to penetrate to Saturn's secret weaknesses and show them the instability they can cause in their life structure. How successful you both are with such manipulation of your respective inner workings depends greatly on that trust-building and the debugging of any potentially suspicion-producing elements.

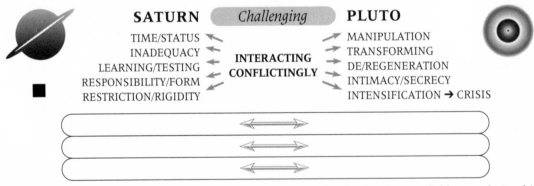

SATURN *Challenging* **PLUTO**

TIME/STATUS
INADEQUACY
LEARNING/TESTING
RESPONSIBILITY/FORM
RESTRICTION/RIGIDITY

**INTERACTING
CONFLICTINGLY**

MANIPULATION
TRANSFORMING
DE/REGENERATION
INTIMACY/SECRECY
INTENSIFICATION ➔ CRISIS

This is basically a struggle for power and authority, on whatever level or in whatever field your relationship is operating. Sex and money would be the main stakes here, but so too could be children or property or status. But the underlying matter here is an emotional rather than material one. One or both of you has had a hard time trusting long before this particular relationship began, and now you are experiencing the natural outcome of such distrust – that is, someone whom you feel is impossible *to* trust. And so you have to dig down and look at the roots of such distrust and the emotional control that developed in order to defend yourself (or yourselves) against it. It is as if one, but probably both, of you have made some rather rigid rules to life, and they have now become most unpleasantly restricting. The trouble is that you blame the other for it. Without coming to some personal reckoning in this way of self-honesty, your grievances will have to be settled by some external authority, such as a court of the law or the Hand of God.

... while not expecting love to be immediately returned

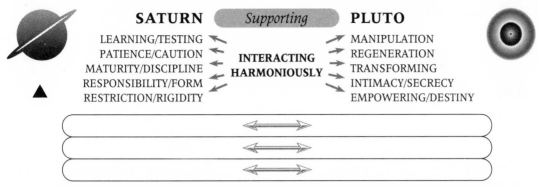

SATURN *Supporting* **PLUTO**

LEARNING/TESTING	↘		↗	MANIPULATION
PATIENCE/CAUTION	↖	**INTERACTING**	↗	REGENERATION
MATURITY/DISCIPLINE	←	**HARMONIOUSLY**	→	TRANSFORMING
RESPONSIBILITY/FORM	↙		↘	INTIMACY/SECRECY
RESTRICTION/RIGIDITY				EMPOWERING/DESTINY

This is an extremely down-to-earth Interaction, which isn't surprising when you consider that Saturn rules the material world and Pluto the Underworld. And so the Saturn person can help Pluto find their place in the world, and give stability to their insights or feelings of loneliness. Pluto's part of the 'deal' – for this is what this aspect of your relationship amounts to – is to confirm or intensify Saturn's sense of authority at a deep level. At the same time, Pluto will also eliminate Saturn's dead wood – sometimes quite ruthlessly. Saturn won't give in easily here, but this is what gives Pluto's persistence the Saturnian seal of approval. This no-nonsense element of your relationship is bound to profit both of you, no matter what else ever happens. You have the businesslike side of relating in hand, and as such this favours a business partnership.

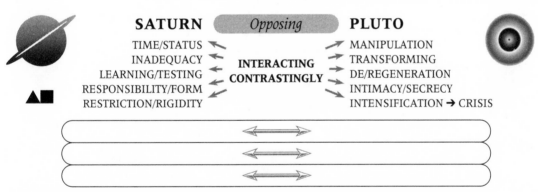

SATURN *Opposing* **PLUTO**

TIME/STATUS	↖		↗	MANIPULATION
INADEQUACY	↖	**INTERACTING**	↗	TRANSFORMING
LEARNING/TESTING	←	**CONTRASTINGLY**	→	DE/REGENERATION
RESPONSIBILITY/FORM	↙		↘	INTIMACY/SECRECY
RESTRICTION/RIGIDITY				INTENSIFICATION → CRISIS

As Planets, Saturn governs the material world, whereas Pluto rules over the Underworld. In ordinary terms, this is like the government of the day on the one hand, and the power base of secret services and multi-national corporations on the other. So, as a couple, you are vying for control and influence all of the time, or at least, some of the time. The wise way to handle this is to make concessions to one another as acts of trust and goodwill. Failing this, mutual 'paranoia' can set in, with the possibility of material and social collapse. But to a degree, this mistrusting of each other's motives can force each of you to study your own quite closely, and if they are suspect, to eliminate them. Again though, using a political analogy, you both have to be seen to 'disarm' at the same time and in equal proportions. Failure to do all this though – whether you are seen to or not – will inevitably sabotage the whole, which means that both of you would lose what you had spent so much time and energy building up. Trust or perish.

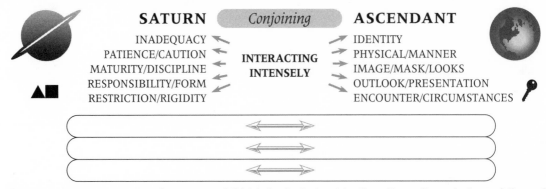

SATURN *Conjoining* **ASCENDANT**

INADEQUACY		IDENTITY
PATIENCE/CAUTION	**INTERACTING**	PHYSICAL/MANNER
MATURITY/DISCIPLINE	**INTENSELY**	IMAGE/MASK/LOOKS
RESPONSIBILITY/FORM		OUTLOOK/PRESENTATION
RESTRICTION/RIGIDITY		ENCOUNTER/CIRCUMSTANCES

This Key Contact is very much a parent/child kind of relationship, literally or figuratively. It falls to the Saturn person to be the teacher, guide and setter of limits with regard to the Ascendant person. This can be experienced by the Ascendant 'child' as the heavy 'father' who restricts their self-expression, moulds their character and way of doing things, and suppresses their very identity. On the other hand, it could be more a case of Saturn showing the Ascendant how to be more mature and methodical, objective and businesslike. How patient the teacher/Saturn is and how receptive the pupil/Ascendant is can therefore be the critical issue. What Saturn has to be careful of is to avoid projecting their own weaknesses and inadequacies on to the Ascendant and becoming the above-described brow-beater, chastising themselves through their partner. So this Interaction forces Saturn to be more mature, patient and responsible too, but with the difference that they are having to teach it all to themselves. If the Ascendant resists or rebels against Saturn even when they are being a just and level-headed teacher, then they can expect Saturn one day to leave them – temporarily or permanently – to their own devices. But Saturn has to learn to 'bear kindly with the fool' rather than dismiss the Ascendant as being hopelessly naïve, selfish and generally brat-like. The circumstances that you both find yourselves in may well be limiting in some way. This is because it is teaching you both to ascertain what is holding you back in life, get real and do something about it. By looking at the Sign position(s) of the Saturn and the Ascendant, it may be seen what issues this 'parent/child' type relationship revolves around, because they will tell you what you are both supposed to be learning about. It is unlikely that either of you will get out of this 'classroom' relationship until those lessons have been learned. This could take quite some time, and for this reason, if no other, your relationship is probably a long-lasting one.

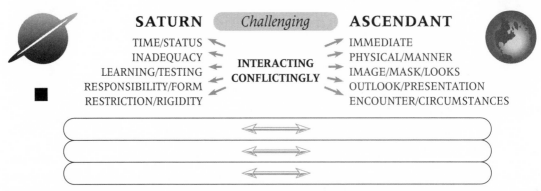

SATURN *Challenging* **ASCENDANT**

TIME/STATUS		IMMEDIATE
INADEQUACY	**INTERACTING**	PHYSICAL/MANNER
LEARNING/TESTING	**CONFLICTINGLY**	IMAGE/MASK/LOOKS
RESPONSIBILITY/FORM		OUTLOOK/PRESENTATION
RESTRICTION/RIGIDITY		ENCOUNTER/CIRCUMSTANCES

The Saturn person will find the personal manner of the Ascendant person offensive in some way – it'll be too childish, egocentric, showy, impulsive (depending on what Sign the Ascendant is in, ie their Rising Sign) or anything which Saturn feels is not good 'form'. Because of this, Saturn tries to discipline or belittle the Ascendant into behaving or expressing themselves in what they see as a more appropriate way. Naturally enough, the Ascendant finds this stifling, painful and/or boring, and will most probably step up the very behaviour that got Saturn going in the first place – either that or sulk. Needless to say, a good amount of love and understanding, hopefully provided by other Interactions, is needed to make each of you realize that the other has a point.

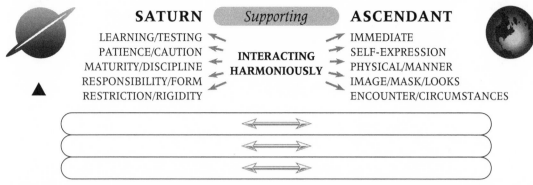

Something about the Ascendant person affects the Saturn individual in a way that causes them to feel in touch with something stable and accomplished inside of them. Consequently, the Ascendant person expects Saturn to live up to this feeling that they have evoked. Essentially then, a teacher/pupil type relationship develops, but it is not always clear which is which. All the same, this mutual feeling of respect for each other's weight and authority means that these very things are furthered by your coming and being together. This is quite a sober and serious connection that you have here, and other people sense it – and respond to it with whatever their own agendas might be. Cool composure can and should characterize you as a couple.

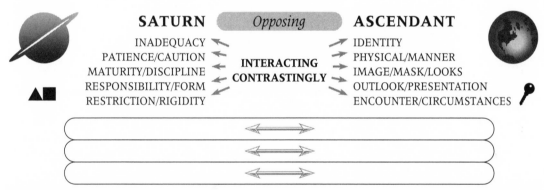

Your relationship imposes great responsibilities upon one another. These can be regarded as the essence of the relationship, with the enjoyment of the sense of purpose and stability that this confers, or your time together can seem like a long and meaningless haul up a steep and rocky road. A third alternative is that one or both of you is not ready for such responsibility and so the relationship never really gets off the ground in the first place, or it just limps along for a bit. This Interaction is the ultimate acid test of a relationship for it says 'Can you relate properly?'. The ultimate prize here is one of harmony and order combined, and it is your progressive working through all the trials and tribulations that earns you this. If you get to a point along this course and then wonder what it is all for, then you would need to take a less conventional look at the nature of relationships generally and your own in particular. On this score of 'conventional' relationship, there is a possibility that originally you got together entirely for reasons of status, convenience, tradition or money. If such is the case, you would be fortunate indeed if this need to review your relationship from a more emotionally valid standpoint never arises. Yet another possibility that extends from this is one of marrying someone who is beneath or above you. This can appear to preclude emotional difficulties as the 'lower' person is taken care of and can't complain, whereas the 'higher' person feels in charge and emotionally invulnerable. But this can backfire as one or both people feel less and less emotional satisfaction, and may look for it elsewhere. As Saturn and the Descendant (the point opposite the Ascendant and therefore Conjoining Saturn) are both symbolic of the 'Shadow', this Interaction demands that each of you own up to your respective Shadow, rather than being married to it in the form of someone who appears unlikeable to you! *(See pages 7, 246 and 263 concerning the nature of the Shadow.)*

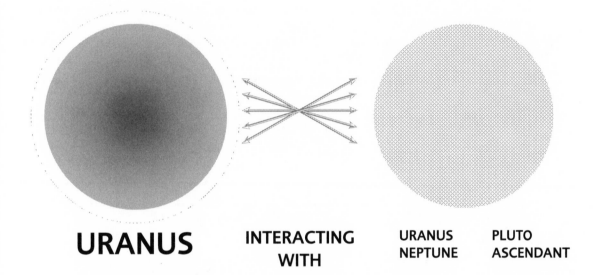

URANUS

**INTERACTING
WITH**

URANUS
NEPTUNE

PLUTO
ASCENDANT

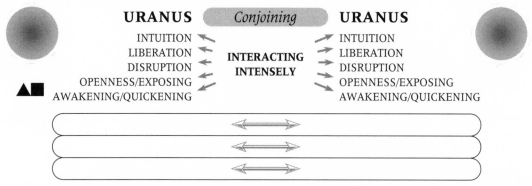

This Interaction is generational and so its significance for you as individuals depends upon what other Planets in each of your charts are interacting with Uranus. If there is a considerable amount of such Interaction, hard and/or easy, then this would mean that your relationship was a 'Uranian' one – that is, unconventional, exciting, unpredictable, open, liberating, etc. For more about the nature of Uranus and how it affects relationships, *see* page 11 in Planets of Love. On a purely generational level, you were both born and grew up in a time that saw the same technological advances and changes in social or political values.

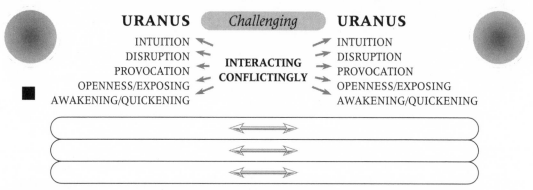

You probably excite or annoy one another, but it is unlikely that you have the makings of a smooth or predictable relationship – more likely a friendship. Your social values and approach to radical ideas is quite different. However, the fact that you differ here is what can be stimulating. It is as if you both give one another tacit permission to do your own thing, be outrageous and unpredictable, and discover or assert your most individualistic ideas or rebellious feelings. All of this could simply be down to the fact that your ages themselves differ by around 21 years, or even 63 years, but from an astrological viewpoint it has more to do with your soul-minds being different 'models', having different 'specifications'.

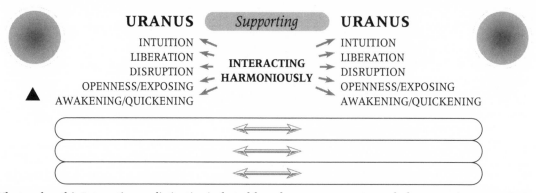

What makes this Interaction so distinctive is that although you are one or two whole generations apart in age, there is an intuitive understanding that seems to go beyond such normal considerations. The unusual quality of rapport that you enjoy is, however, something into which few others will be able to tune. You may even disturb others because of your unique connection. If there are constructive or creative Interactions between you, then you could be instrumental in making others aware of facets to life and human nature they never knew existed.

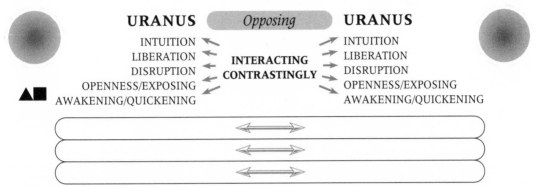

To have this Interaction, your ages would have to be around 40 years apart, and so it is unlikely, even for a parent/child relationship. Some other kind of family relationship or a friendship or business relationship is more likely. In any event though, this is not only an unusual Interaction but it would make for an unusual relationship – and not just because of the age gap. It is as if you keep waking one another up to something new you ought to know about, whether you think so or not. This may even be done unconsciously through one of you being disruptive or shocking in some way. The effects of this can range from being constantly stimulating to being like an ongoing crisis.

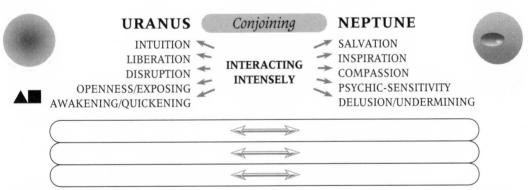

If one or both of you have not been interested in the metaphysical or mysterious side of life before, then this Interaction should herald experience and involvement with it, somehow or other. It may even have had something to do with the way you actually met. The Uranus individual is instrumental in making the Neptune person far more aware of their psychic or compassionate nature – and of their weaknesses and blind-spots too. Neptune, on the other hand, can suggest to Uranus a gentler and more collectively appealing way of giving expression to what is unusual, valuable or even brilliant about them. But Neptune will also show Uranus how hurtful and inappropriate they can be when insensitively, although truthfully, pointing out the frailties of anyone, especially Neptune. Although this Interaction can be quite far-reaching in its effect upon the lives and personalities of each of you – because it quickens your awareness of the more subtle side to being and relating – it can also be quite easily resisted and reasoned away if one or both of you is of a particularly conventional and scientific bent. If this is the case, then shocking and apparently unwarranted events could dog the relationship.

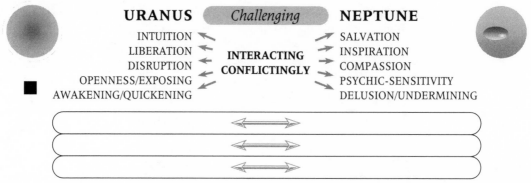

URANUS *Challenging* **NEPTUNE**

INTUITION		SALVATION
LIBERATION	**INTERACTING**	INSPIRATION
DISRUPTION	**CONFLICTINGLY**	COMPASSION
OPENNESS/EXPOSING		PSYCHIC-SENSITIVITY
AWAKENING/QUICKENING		DELUSION/UNDERMINING

You have a clash between intuition and compassion, which means that where Uranus takes a scientific, detached and impersonal view of things, Neptune is mystical, sentimental and subjective. And so Uranus can miss the subtle and sensitive messages that Neptune puts out, some of which are often complimentary to Uranus. Conversely, Neptune often suffers needlessly for want of seeing things impartially and as part of a greater process by tuning into Uranus's wavelength. This is an Interaction of misunderstanding rather than outright incompatibility. Furthermore, Uranus and/or Neptune would need to be contacting not just each other, but other Planets in each other's charts for it to have that much effect.

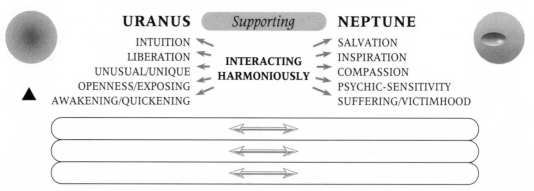

URANUS *Supporting* **NEPTUNE**

INTUITION		SALVATION
LIBERATION	**INTERACTING**	INSPIRATION
UNUSUAL/UNIQUE	**HARMONIOUSLY**	COMPASSION
OPENNESS/EXPOSING		PSYCHIC-SENSITIVITY
AWAKENING/QUICKENING		SUFFERING/VICTIMHOOD

If the two of you are interested or involved with metaphysical subjects or the frontiers of science and the understanding of human nature, then this Interaction will greatly contribute to your progress, individually or together. The Uranus person offers scientific explanations and formulas for Neptune's psychic impressions, while Neptune introduces a vision or myth to inspire Uranus's models or theories. However, the actual Planets Uranus and/or Neptune would need to be contacting not just each other, but other Planets in each other's charts for this Interaction to have that much effect. If, however, it is a Close One, the two of you can have a very creative and inventive rapport, almost like two imaginations working as one.

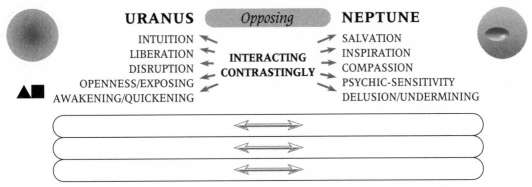

URANUS — *Opposing* — NEPTUNE

URANUS		NEPTUNE
INTUITION		SALVATION
LIBERATION	**INTERACTING**	INSPIRATION
DISRUPTION	**CONTRASTINGLY**	COMPASSION
OPENNESS/EXPOSING		PSYCHIC-SENSITIVITY
AWAKENING/QUICKENING		DELUSION/UNDERMINING

This not too common Interaction has a range of effects that can vary greatly, depending considerably upon the other Interactions that you have between you. The Uranus person can wake the Neptune person up to their psychic ability, creative imagination, or their sensitivity in general. On the other hand, the Neptune person may experience Uranus as someone who invades their psychic space and offends their sensibilities with radical outbursts and sudden changes. Likewise, Uranus can find Neptune a wistful, healing and soothing influence, or see them as weak, escapist and fanciful. When these energies are worked with positively, you can be of great help to one another, and even the world at large, in increasing your spiritual understanding of life.

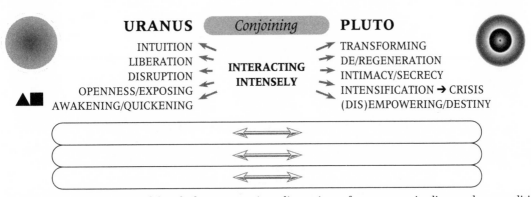

URANUS — *Conjoining* — PLUTO

URANUS		PLUTO
INTUITION		TRANSFORMING
LIBERATION	**INTERACTING**	DE/REGENERATION
DISRUPTION	**INTENSELY**	INTIMACY/SECRECY
OPENNESS/EXPOSING		INTENSIFICATION → CRISIS
AWAKENING/QUICKENING		(DIS)EMPOWERING/DESTINY

For better or worse, very powerful and often unconscious dimensions of your respective lives and personalities come to meet – or into collision – with this Interaction. An enormous amount depends on how much of a handle Uranus has upon their radical or rebellious nature – does it just want excitement and to shock, or is it more into creative and constructive change? Similarly, is Pluto's sense of power and insight expressed as compulsion or deep conviction? Because of these conditions, your effect upon one another can be anything from a positive transformation to an absolute disaster (which would eventually amount to a transformation of some sort anyway). If you are sexually involved, Uranus is likely to tune into Pluto's deepest desires and phobias concerning their sexuality, whereas Pluto zeroes in on Uranus's sexual quirks. With a good amount of harmony between you given elsewhere, your relationship can be extraordinarily satisfying, and healing too. Even so, these two Planets often indicate areas where and how we can be on the edge of, if not beyond, sexual 'acceptability'. So whatever the individual case for each of you, you should become a lot more aware of how you tick sexually. But as change and transformation is the dynamic of this Interaction, it will take one or both of you to a point where you have some kind of sexual reckoning, which may be quite difficult. Ideally, you should both establish and maintain an awareness of this powerful process that you are caught up in, and learn from it rather than get into judging one another. Another area in which this Interaction finds expression is through occult or esoteric study and involvement. Handled well, you could become far more aware of the forces of the Unconscious that govern your own and others' lives, and then somehow express such awareness.

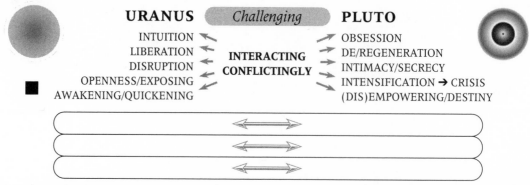

URANUS *Challenging* **PLUTO**

INTUITION		OBSESSION
LIBERATION	**INTERACTING**	DE/REGENERATION
DISRUPTION	**CONFLICTINGLY**	INTIMACY/SECRECY
OPENNESS/EXPOSING		INTENSIFICATION → CRISIS
AWAKENING/QUICKENING		(DIS)EMPOWERING/DESTINY

Your relationship has a dimension to it which resembles a state where there are those in power (the Pluto person) and those who are the revolutionary group (the Uranus person) who are against those in power. And so the Pluto person often sees the Uranus person as subversive, unruly and a threat to their security or deepest convictions – even if they do not know what they are. Uranus, on the other hand, regards Pluto as underhand, manipulative and possibly corrupt – or just unaware of their own depth. Far Right versus Far Left, in fact. What is required if your relationship is not to turn into a kind of 'civil war', is that both of you put your cards on the table and make it clear what you each actually want from the relationship. It is then highly likely that you'll find that you are working at cross-purposes in a number of areas. If you cannot find an amicable way of satisfying your individual needs and desires by respecting any differences, then an ongoing upheaval will be unavoidable. Eventually, a total breakdown in communication could then occur as you retreat to your own extremes. If yours is a sexual relationship, this power struggle will choose to play itself out in this area, with Pluto taunting Uranus or withholding what they want, and Uranus resorting to shock tactics such as going off with someone else or becoming, or pretending to become, disinterested.

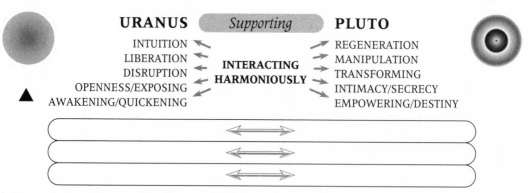

URANUS *Supporting* **PLUTO**

INTUITION		REGENERATION
LIBERATION	**INTERACTING**	MANIPULATION
DISRUPTION	**HARMONIOUSLY**	TRANSFORMING
OPENNESS/EXPOSING		INTIMACY/SECRECY
AWAKENING/QUICKENING		EMPOWERING/DESTINY

This Interaction sets a scene that allows each of you to become far more aware of your respective psychological make-up and how it fits in with society as a whole. So this favours your seeking truth and deeper understanding, either together or because of the other person's influence. But this Interaction is not, as a rule, a powerful one. It simply provides you both with the opportunity to take your investigations into the truths of life further than you could or would have done on your own. If you do happen to have a good handle on this aspect through other Planets in each of your charts being 'plugged' into it, then you may work together to help others to find what is original and powerful within themselves too.

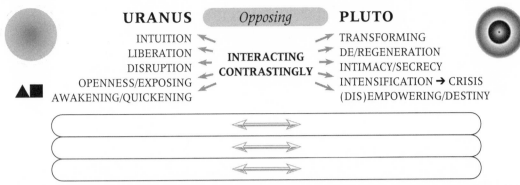

URANUS *Opposing* **PLUTO**

URANUS	INTERACTING	PLUTO
INTUITION		TRANSFORMING
LIBERATION	**INTERACTING**	DE/REGENERATION
DISRUPTION	**CONTRASTINGLY**	INTIMACY/SECRECY
OPENNESS/EXPOSING		INTENSIFICATION → CRISIS
AWAKENING/QUICKENING		(DIS)EMPOWERING/DESTINY

This Interaction will only occur between people who are some distance apart in age. On the face of it, the two of you are very different, and not just because of your ages. Uranus is brash or open, whereas Pluto is covert and manipulative. But you are both subversive – or rather you bring the subversive out in one another. So your relationship can be quite mischievous or irresponsible, in quite surprising or hidden ways. In no way does this Interaction have the makings of a stable, ongoing relationship. If you are together for any length of time, then you'd be the kind of odd couple they could make a film about!

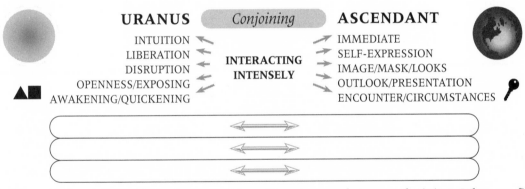

URANUS *Conjoining* **ASCENDANT**

URANUS	INTERACTING	ASCENDANT
INTUITION		IMMEDIATE
LIBERATION	**INTERACTING**	SELF-EXPRESSION
DISRUPTION	**INTENSELY**	IMAGE/MASK/LOOKS
OPENNESS/EXPOSING		OUTLOOK/PRESENTATION
AWAKENING/QUICKENING		ENCOUNTER/CIRCUMSTANCES

You have a unique relationship, and as such it is really up to you what you make it into. When you first met a light flashed on somewhere or a shock-wave went rippling through both of you. The great thing about this Interaction is that you should continuously surprise one another. Sometimes this can take the form of sudden breaks in your relationship which serve to remind you that you must not and cannot put either one of you, or the relationship itself, into some conventional category. You are there in each other's lives to be reminded that there is no-one like either of you in the whole Universe! What goes with this territory is that you force one another to evolve as individuals (especially Uranus to the Ascendant) and this will eventually amount to some form of spiritual development. Personal freedom is of paramount importance, and as such it is in some ways better if you are friends rather than lovers or members of the same family. Lovers and family tend to fix one another in some mould for the sake of security, in which case one of you would be forced to break away, rattling the other's cage in the process. Whatever the case, it would probably help to be alive to the fact that you are of the same family – the human one. As such you are born to be ever true to yourselves and not someone or something else. This Interaction, through a process of storms, unpredictable occurrences and amazing coincidences, keeps you both keenly aware of this cosmic fact. There is often the feeling that you should both amount to something extraordinary together. And it is through being true to your individual selves that you may well make this a reality.

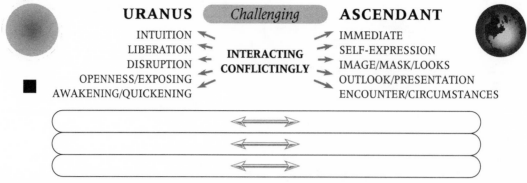

The Uranus individual will attempt to change the outlook of the Ascendant person in some way or other, but the Ascendant person may resist this. Uranus may do this unconsciously by being unpredictable or unreliable, or by actually causing them to move away from their previous environment, thereby forcing the Ascendant to adopt a more flexible attitude or simply become more aware that how they look at things is inappropriate and needs changing anyway. For example, Uranus would not take kindly to the Ascendant impinging on their freedom in any way, and so the Ascendant would have to adapt to this if they wanted to maintain the relationship. Alternatively, the Ascendant's behaviour could give Uranus a few shocks and bring about a few changes. All the same, it has to be said that this is not an Interaction that favours a stable and long-lasting bond. In fact, it is actually in aid of shaking off any idea that such a thing is possible with the current state of one or both of your personalities and abilities to relate. So in any event, this Interaction should find you somewhat the wiser with regard to appreciating the place and space that freedom of expression demands in a relationship.

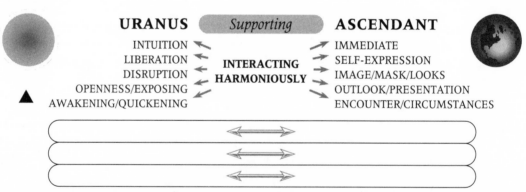

This is what you could call an extremely friendly Interaction because you allow one another the freedom and space to do what you each want to do in order to find and invent yourselves. Because of this, you continually find new and interesting things with which to fill your time. Some of these may include the Uranus person introducing the Ascendant person to new ways of looking at life and freeing up their personal means of expressing themselves. And because the Ascendant responds so well to this influence, it gives Uranus more confidence in their original ideas and helps them to accept and like quirky traits that hitherto may have been regarded as odd. Ultimately, you could collaborate in projects that help other people in these respects.

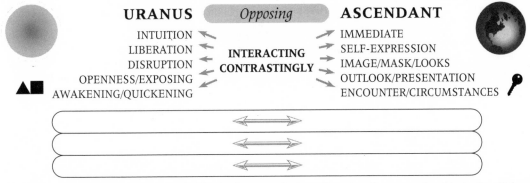

URANUS *Opposing* **ASCENDANT**

URANUS		ASCENDANT
INTUITION		IMMEDIATE
LIBERATION	**INTERACTING**	SELF-EXPRESSION
DISRUPTION	**CONTRASTINGLY**	IMAGE/MASK/LOOKS
OPENNESS/EXPOSING		OUTLOOK/PRESENTATION
AWAKENING/QUICKENING		ENCOUNTER/CIRCUMSTANCES

It could be said that this Interaction holds the key to relating. The esoteric reason for this is that Balance, which is what relating is essentially about, is really only found when both people have and allow each other the Freedom to find it. The point of Balance in a horoscope is the Descendant, the point always opposite to the Ascendant, and therefore the point which Uranus is conjoining when it is Opposing the Ascendant. And Uranus* is Freedom. But before you start opening the champagne and booking the reception, it has to be said that most people either do not know what Freedom actually is, or if they think they do and they are offered it, they feel quite threatened by it. For example, with this Interaction, Freedom can first show its face by not allowing you to plan or fix things as you'd like. It is as if Uranus tests our ability to be free by not letting us have what we expect, by not letting us feel too safe. But from a conventional standpoint, these are the very things that we want from a relationship. And so when either one of you feels shaky about the other being unreliable, think again, it is just Uranus rattling the cage of your conventional expectations. Another clue here is that Uranus governs friends and friendship. And so if this is a love or family relationship, attempt to see each other as friends do – that is, not making unnecessary, or least of all, possessive demands on one another. True friends don't. You may indeed find that you are quite easygoing with one another, and do not live in each other's pockets. This is a good sign that you are being true to one another – because you are feeling free to be yourselves, and allowing each other to be so too. However, if one or both of you is secretly hankering after something more cosy, and is just pretending to be 'modern' and laid-back, then expect the other person to start upping the Uranian dosage of unpredictability! Another very common manifestation of this Interaction is one that happens after two people have married and settled down – divorce. But this only happens because you got married for reasons of security and social convention – anathema to Uranus – even though you may have thought along the way that you were free and easygoing, and even open to experimentation. All the same, experimentation is what Uranus is about in a very pragmatic sense. In other words, with this Interaction you are both discovering something new, by trial and error, and possibly developing some new social values in the process. In any event, yours is not what others would class as a 'normal' relationship – whatever that is.

* When I use the word 'Uranus' on its own, I am referring to the Planet itself – but it may also imply the Uranus person.

The great key to relating is to understand what a relationship is telling you, then accept it

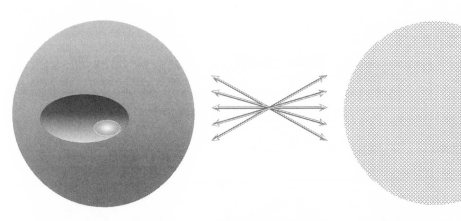

NEPTUNE   INTERACTING
                 WITH

NEPTUNE
PLUTO
ASCENDANT

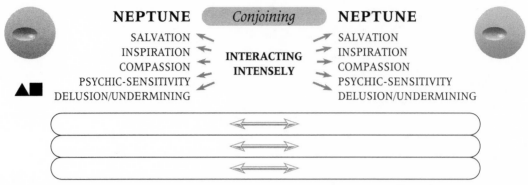

NEPTUNE — *Conjoining* — NEPTUNE

SALVATION
INSPIRATION
COMPASSION
PSYCHIC-SENSITIVITY
DELUSION/UNDERMINING

INTERACTING INTENSELY

SALVATION
INSPIRATION
COMPASSION
PSYCHIC-SENSITIVITY
DELUSION/UNDERMINING

This is a generational contact, meaning that you are more or less the same age and therefore have been subjected to similar cultural, spiritual and musical influences in your lives. Whether or not such similarities figure for you both in a personal way depends greatly on any other Interactions either of your Neptunes make with the other Planets in each other's charts.

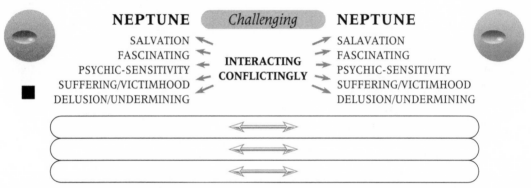

NEPTUNE — *Challenging* — NEPTUNE

SALVATION
FASCINATING
PSYCHIC-SENSITIVITY
SUFFERING/VICTIMHOOD
DELUSION/UNDERMINING

INTERACTING CONFLICTINGLY

SALAVATION
FASCINATING
PSYCHIC-SENSITIVITY
SUFFERING/VICTIMHOOD
DELUSION/UNDERMINING

This Interaction can only occur when there is an age gap of 40 or so years between you. In itself it would be of little influence other than occasionally getting your wires crossed. If, however, there are other Interactions that pose similar communication problems, then this one will scramble it further, laying confusion upon confusion. One of you at least would have to be very clear about themselves and the messages they put out, and how they interpret the other's messages, to overcome the conflicting impressions that you have, not just of one another, but of life in general.

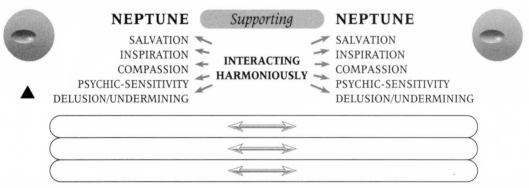

NEPTUNE — *Supporting* — NEPTUNE

SALVATION
INSPIRATION
COMPASSION
PSYCHIC-SENSITIVITY
DELUSION/UNDERMINING

INTERACTING HARMONIOUSLY

SALVATION
INSPIRATION
COMPASSION
PSYCHIC-SENSITIVITY
DELUSION/UNDERMINING

This Interaction will only occur between people of some 60 years age difference. So the most likely candidates for this are grandparents and grandchildren. The empathy and psychic rapport and attachment that so often occurs with these relationships is well borne out by the nature of this Interaction which is, quite simply, indicative of your having a subtle and sensitive feeling for one another. This Interaction, one way or the other, keeps or gets you in touch with the eternal verities.

No one Interaction makes or breaks a relationship

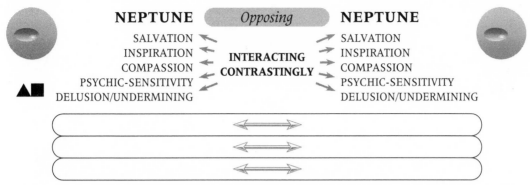

This Interaction would only occur between two people born 80 odd years apart and so there is little chance of there being much Interaction, other than that of a vague or poignant sense of something of emotional or spiritual significance.

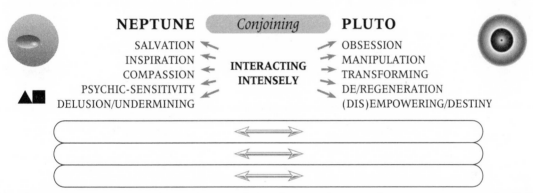

Superficially, this Interaction can just be regarded as being indicative of a generation gap, with all the classic symptoms which stem from having differing world views and values. Looked at more personally though, and dealt with more consciously and creatively, this contact can be quite profound. The Pluto person, either through their deep convictions or emotional compulsions, can arouse in the Neptune person a sense of the oneness of all creatures and things, and thereby cause them to develop the compassion which is a direct expression of this. Pluto may have to strip away Neptune's glamours or illusions in the process, however. Neptune, for their part, can show Pluto that their sense of power and psychological insight are nothing without the very things which Pluto has aroused, deliberately or accidentally, in Neptune: a sense of universality and compassion. So your relationship is deeply symbiotic, something which when viewed less spiritually would be merely seen as co-dependence.

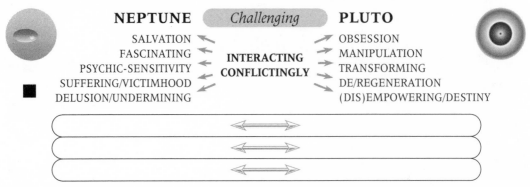

NEPTUNE *Challenging* **PLUTO**

NEPTUNE		PLUTO
SALVATION		OBSESSION
FASCINATING	**INTERACTING**	MANIPULATION
PSYCHIC-SENSITIVITY	**CONFLICTINGLY**	TRANSFORMING
SUFFERING/VICTIMHOOD		DE/REGENERATION
DELUSION/UNDERMINING		(DIS)EMPOWERING/DESTINY

The Pluto person, in their urge to impress or get what they desire, may overlook the subtleties and protective veils that the Neptune person has around their being. So what can happen is that in looking for strength in Neptune, Pluto finds what they see as weakness or evasiveness, overlooking the fact that their emotional missile was misguided at the outset. To make things more confusing, Neptune just might become quite addicted to these shows of power, yet at the same time try to avoid such invasions. If Neptune was given the chance, they could show Pluto how to go more gently into the night – that is, into the unknown of someone's emotional interior. However, unless this aspect is a Close One, it will probably just amount to a general conflict created by the differences in your respective world views as established by your formative years occurring at different times in social history.

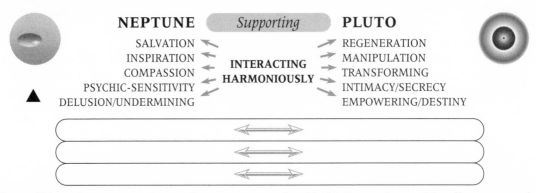

NEPTUNE *Supporting* **PLUTO**

NEPTUNE		PLUTO
SALVATION		REGENERATION
INSPIRATION	**INTERACTING**	MANIPULATION
COMPASSION	**HARMONIOUSLY**	TRANSFORMING
PSYCHIC-SENSITIVITY		INTIMACY/SECRECY
DELUSION/UNDERMINING		EMPOWERING/DESTINY

There will be at least a generation gap between two people with this Interaction, and its effects are not that noticeable anyway. It will give rise to mutual psychological support and guidance, but only if there are other Interactions to support this, or if one person is a professional trained in counselling or some kind of therapy.

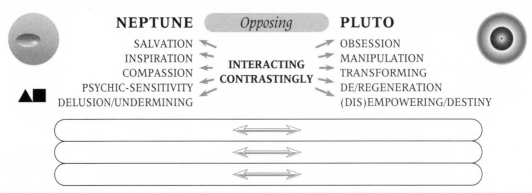

NEPTUNE *Opposing* **PLUTO**

NEPTUNE		PLUTO
SALVATION		OBSESSION
INSPIRATION	**INTERACTING**	MANIPULATION
COMPASSION	**CONTRASTINGLY**	TRANSFORMING
PSYCHIC-SENSITIVITY		DE/REGENERATION
DELUSION/UNDERMINING		(DIS)EMPOWERING/DESTINY

There is going to be two generations' gap between you both, which could be the problem in itself. Essentially though, the Neptune person experiences the Pluto person as being too invasive and ruthless emotionally, and lacking in finesse. Pluto sees Neptune as either just strange or overly sentimental and sensitive. Basically, this

Interaction is academic because two such people are just not about to encounter one another unless they are grandparents and grandchildren. In such a case, the understanding born of experience would be a crucial factor in the grandparent accepting the grandchild for what they are.

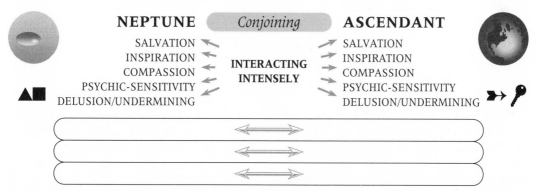

NEPTUNE	*Conjoining*	ASCENDANT
SALVATION		SALVATION
INSPIRATION	**INTERACTING**	INSPIRATION
COMPASSION	**INTENSELY**	COMPASSION
PSYCHIC-SENSITIVITY		PSYCHIC-SENSITIVITY
DELUSION/UNDERMINING		DELUSION/UNDERMINING

Because, on first meeting, this Interaction allows you both to see through each other's masks, defences or smoke-screens, the subsequent reaction of each of you can vary enormously. A great deal depends upon what it is that each of you senses within the other person. The chances are that whatever each of you sees will reflect or enhance some highly sensitive issue of your own. Your individual emotional reactions that follow upon this are what then characterize this Interaction, rather than what actually happened in the first place. There are usually two extremes here: one is where a glamorized image or another smoke-screen is quickly put up in order to protect yourself from the other person's psychic perception of your inner truth. The other extreme is that a great openness remains, allowing a wonderful psychic rapport to manifest between the two of you. This psychic rapport causes you to feel as one, to identify very closely with one another, and to detect at any distance the state of one another. However, it must be pointed out that it only takes one of you to adopt the first extreme in order, sadly, to preclude or at least greatly diminish the second one. And even when the second extreme has been maintained by one of you, the psychic defence screen erected by the other person could eventually become actually offensive, which would cause the 'open' person to close down defensively too. The outcome here is then a 'psychic war' of projected and imagined fears which can be quite sapping, physically and emotionally, to both of you. Generally speaking, because most people are not yet prepared to see clearly their inner truth as distinct from their outer display, the remedy to the negative expression of this Interaction is not very acceptable. All the same, here it is. If you are experiencing the negative expression, cast your minds back to when you first met, and visualize slowly and closely what actually transpired at that time. If you can do this, *without defensively reacting again*, you will gain a great insight into the truth of who you both are, as individuals and to one another. This Interaction reminds me of the Mayan greeting *In lak'ech* which means 'I am another (like) yourself'. One way or the other this Interaction will bring both of you an insight into spiritual reality or the mystery of being. How you respond to this determines whether you experience it as fascination or confusion, identification or alienation, love or hate – or a strange combination of some or all of these.

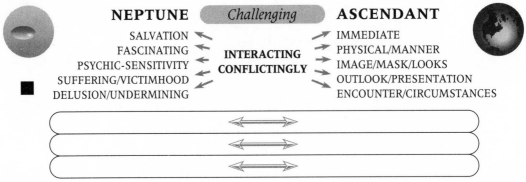

NEPTUNE	*Challenging*	ASCENDANT
SALVATION		IMMEDIATE
FASCINATING	**INTERACTING**	PHYSICAL/MANNER
PSYCHIC-SENSITIVITY	**CONFLICTINGLY**	IMAGE/MASK/LOOKS
SUFFERING/VICTIMHOOD		OUTLOOK/PRESENTATION
DELUSION/UNDERMINING		ENCOUNTER/CIRCUMSTANCES

The Neptune person has, initially at least, their own somewhat mistaken idea of who or what the Ascendant person is to them. Consequently, the Ascendant person can easily get the wrong idea of where Neptune is coming from, and even come to regard them as dubious or not entirely reliable. Your actual meeting was probably quite spellbinding in some way, but as time goes by, the spell, although quite real, is seen to have a different agenda to what it felt like at the time. If there are not some close and substantial Interactions between the two of you, this one can just produce disappointment. Whatever the case though, it is saying that first impressions can be deceptive, yet in retrospect can be seen to have had a subtle meaning all of their own. This is the kind of Interaction that will 'trick' you into an involvement for spiritual or karmic reasons that you would have otherwise avoided. The illusions of Neptune and the physical looks, manner and state of the Ascendant are what the 'trick' and the karma are based upon. If all this sounds confusing, that's because it is! But it is worth unravelling if one or both of you wish to become clearer about these particular issues so that you are no longer so vulnerable to them. Suffice to say that the fantasies of Neptune, which the appearance of the Ascendant seems to elicit, need to be transmuted into compassion for the Ascendant's circumstances.

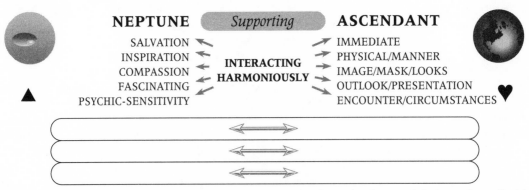

NEPTUNE	*Supporting*	ASCENDANT
SALVATION		IMMEDIATE
INSPIRATION		PHYSICAL/MANNER
COMPASSION	**INTERACTING**	IMAGE/MASK/LOOKS
FASCINATING	**HARMONIOUSLY**	OUTLOOK/PRESENTATION
PSYCHIC-SENSITIVITY		ENCOUNTER/CIRCUMSTANCES

There is a sensitive interplay here that enables you to understand one another's subtleties and peculiarities. This eventually can go quite some way towards healing any difficulties or complaints that you both may suffer from. The soul of the one is experienced through the physical senses of the other, and vice versa, making for a sweet and loving bond. However, this bond, by its very nature, is not robust or obvious, so it needs to be cherished for it to have the influence that it deserves upon each of you and upon the relationship itself. Enhancing such a gentle but positive Interaction in this way will increase the psychic and creative abilities of each of you. Literally or metaphorically, you can and should make music together.

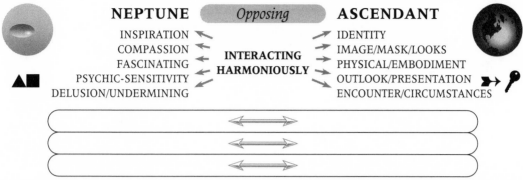

NEPTUNE *Opposing* **ASCENDANT**

NEPTUNE		ASCENDANT
INSPIRATION		IDENTITY
COMPASSION	**INTERACTING**	IMAGE/MASK/LOOKS
FASCINATING	**HARMONIOUSLY**	PHYSICAL/EMBODIMENT
PSYCHIC-SENSITIVITY		OUTLOOK/PRESENTATION
DELUSION/UNDERMINING		ENCOUNTER/CIRCUMSTANCES

The Ascendant person is fascinated by some quality in the Neptune person which they most likely will ascribe to something that may or may not prove to be the case at a later date. It is as if the Neptune person unconsciously picks up what the Ascendant finds irresistible and plays that card over and over again in an equally unconscious bid to be accepted or have some special quality in them recognized. But the Ascendant is all the while fitting Neptune's 'show' or mystique into whatever they fantasize as being their ideal partner. If there are also harmonious or Supporting Interactions from the Ascendant person's Planets to the Neptune, then both your respective 'ideals' are likely to coincide and a subtle, sensitive and exquisite bond would result. If, however, the Ascendant person's Planets make Challenging or Opposing aspects to the Neptune, then there will inevitably be the ghastly disappointment that is caused by such 'mistaken identities'.

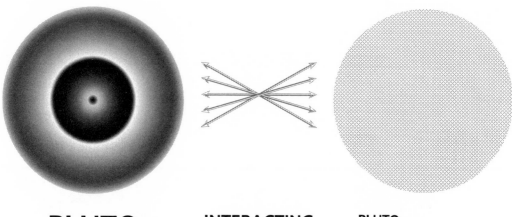

PLUTO INTERACTING
WITH PLUTO
ASCENDANT

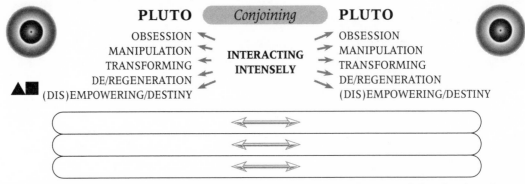

PLUTO *Conjoining* **PLUTO**

OBSESSION
MANIPULATION   **INTERACTING**
TRANSFORMING   **INTENSELY**
DE/REGENERATION
(DIS)EMPOWERING/DESTINY

OBSESSION
MANIPULATION
TRANSFORMING
DE/REGENERATION
(DIS)EMPOWERING/DESTINY

This is a generational contact, meaning that you are more or less the same age and therefore have been subjected to similar psychological, political and global changes in your lives. Whether or not such similarities figure for you both in a personal way depends greatly on any other Interactions either of your Plutos have with the other Planets in each other's charts.

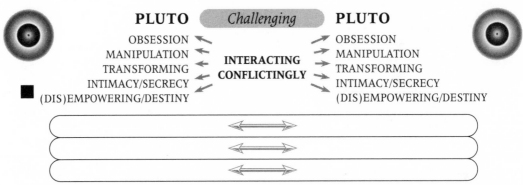

PLUTO *Challenging* **PLUTO**

OBSESSION
MANIPULATION   **INTERACTING**
TRANSFORMING   **CONFLICTINGLY**
INTIMACY/SECRECY
(DIS)EMPOWERING/DESTINY

OBSESSION
MANIPULATION
TRANSFORMING
INTIMACY/SECRECY
(DIS)EMPOWERING/DESTINY

There is liable to be a considerable age gap between the two of you. Apart from there being a certain conflict of wills and psychological or political dispositions, this Interaction will not amount to much unless there are other Interactions between you that involve one or both of your Plutos. If such is the case, the power and influence wielded by one or both of you will be a determining factor in the fate of your relationship.

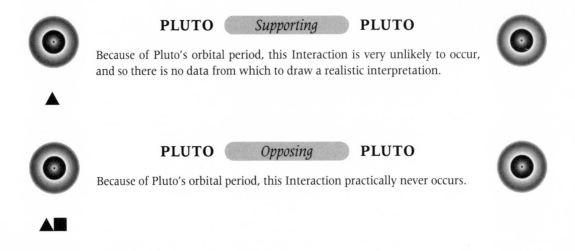

PLUTO *Supporting* **PLUTO**

Because of Pluto's orbital period, this Interaction is very unlikely to occur, and so there is no data from which to draw a realistic interpretation.

PLUTO *Opposing* **PLUTO**

Because of Pluto's orbital period, this Interaction practically never occurs.

   No one Interaction makes or breaks a relationship

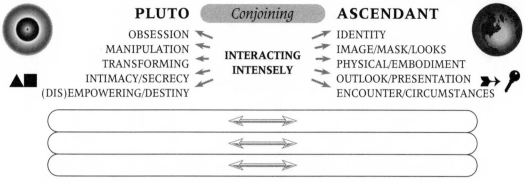

PLUTO *Conjoining* **ASCENDANT**

OBSESSION	IDENTITY
MANIPULATION	IMAGE/MASK/LOOKS
TRANSFORMING	PHYSICAL/EMBODIMENT
INTIMACY/SECRECY	OUTLOOK/PRESENTATION
(DIS)EMPOWERING/DESTINY	ENCOUNTER/CIRCUMSTANCES

INTERACTING INTENSELY

One of you, most likely the Ascendant individual, is strongly inclined to feel under the influence of the other person, probably the Pluto individual – but it can sometimes seem the other way around. At first, the feeling of being 'under the influence' could amount simply to being impressed. Later on, however, this can come to be a feeling of empowerment or disempowerment as the person *with* the influence feels disposed towards either attacking or supporting the one who is *under* their influence. In either case, this influence is taken in quite compulsively because the 'influenced' feels very dependent upon the 'influencer' in some way. If the influencing is entirely positive, then you can either instil or confirm a sense of effectiveness and worth in each other. The Ascendant individual benefits particularly from having their image bolstered or their appearance transformed in some way. The Pluto individual gets to feel more influential as a person. If, or when, the negative holds sway, then one or both of you will have to look at why your need to gain approval for yourself has degenerated to the point of receiving abuse instead – maybe in the hope of getting a few crumbs of praise. But merely to resist the 'influencer' would not turn things around. Whichever of you is needing such affirmation of their existence – and it could well be both of you – would be far better off seeking something that would do this more consciously and without an emotional agenda. Verbal affirmations (like 'I am that I am' or something more personal), psychotherapy or some course of self-improvement are a few suggestions. If you are both confident enough in yourselves, none of the above should be that much of an issue, one way or the other. Instead, you could both be deeply involved together in a programme of self-transformation or some other kind of psycho-spiritual project. Or you may simply enjoy a very deep emotional and physical intimacy.

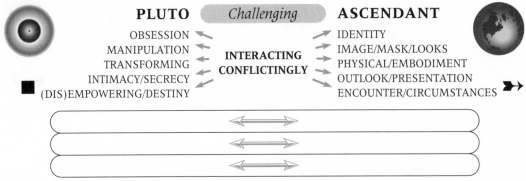

PLUTO *Challenging* **ASCENDANT**

PLUTO	INTERACTING CONFLICTINGLY	ASCENDANT
OBSESSION		IDENTITY
MANIPULATION		IMAGE/MASK/LOOKS
TRANSFORMING		PHYSICAL/EMBODIMENT
INTIMACY/SECRECY		OUTLOOK/PRESENTATION
(DIS)EMPOWERING/DESTINY		ENCOUNTER/CIRCUMSTANCES

Initially, and maybe for quite some time, your relationship (or a part of it) has to go on in secret, with few or noone knowing about it. As such, this imposes the pressure and the excitement of forbidden fruit upon your coming together at any time. When and if you are able to 'come out' and show your face to the world there may still be a deal of trouble stemming from conflicting or awkward circumstances, and possibly from someone else who is involved with one or both of you in such a way that is not easily got out of. So although this compulsive sort of Interaction is the type that actually forms a relationship in the first place, it does tend to get you off on the wrong foot with convolutions and machinations being apparently unavoidable. Yet the best way to deal with all of this intrigue is to be as open and honest as possible, which would entail the Ascendant dropping their façade and eventually coming clean, and Pluto eliminating whatever is getting in the way of what they want before getting in too deep. In any event, what is behind this Interaction, and what is probably a perennial difficulty, is preventing concealed or hard to pinpoint issues getting in the way of any genuine connection that you have between you. This is in aid of eliminating any possibility that all there is to the relationship is compulsion and intrigue.

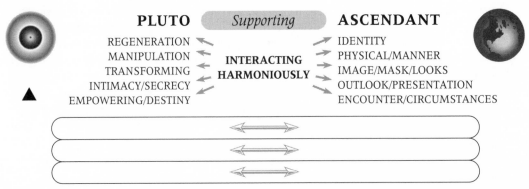

PLUTO *Supporting* **ASCENDANT**

PLUTO	INTERACTING HARMONIOUSLY	ASCENDANT
REGENERATION		IDENTITY
MANIPULATION		PHYSICAL/MANNER
TRANSFORMING		IMAGE/MASK/LOOKS
INTIMACY/SECRECY		OUTLOOK/PRESENTATION
EMPOWERING/DESTINY		ENCOUNTER/CIRCUMSTANCES

The Pluto person makes the Ascendant person more deeply aware of how they express themselves physically, how they appear, etc. However, because Pluto's effect is deep, this may not be immediately noticeable, but the feeling that the Ascendant experiences upon first meeting the Pluto person is felt to be significant in that something 'moves' inside of them. How they continue to respond to such a movement will depend greatly on other Interactions between the two of you. If the Pluto person is aware that they do have this influence, then they can help the Ascendant to become more aware of the hidden side that lies behind the outer façade, not just of themselves but of appearances generally. Pluto, in return, can feel pleasantly conscious of how they are able to penetrate to the core with both ease and intensity.

Along with Key Contacts, Close Ones form the core of a relationship

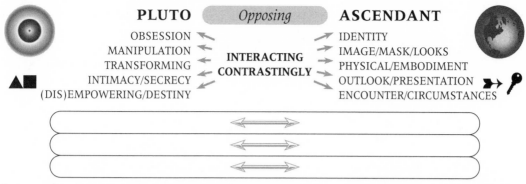

PLUTO *Opposing* ASCENDANT

PLUTO		ASCENDANT
OBSESSION		IDENTITY
MANIPULATION	**INTERACTING**	IMAGE/MASK/LOOKS
TRANSFORMING	**CONTRASTINGLY**	PHYSICAL/EMBODIMENT
INTIMACY/SECRECY		OUTLOOK/PRESENTATION
(DIS)EMPOWERING/DESTINY		ENCOUNTER/CIRCUMSTANCES

If the Ascendant person is rather unconscious of their Shadow side or alter ego, the Pluto person will play this out for them in a manner that makes both people deeply dependent upon one another, or even obsessed with one another. In effect, consciously or unconsciously, the Pluto person can exert an enormous influence over the Ascendant individual. But as they do so through playing out the Ascendant's darker and more dynamic side – or at least the part they cannot seem to express easily – they too become dependent upon the Ascendant person, because of the power this seems to invest in them. All of this sounds rather vampiristic – and it can be, with intense passion and possessiveness also being on the menu. However, if the Ascendant can take back or repossess some of the personal power that is theirs, then Pluto will have to come out of the shadows and show their darker side too, with a view to being positively transformed in the process. What can make this difficult is that the Ascendant has grown used to depending on others for a show of power (because then they needn't take the flak that expressing their own power would attract), and this Interaction marks some sort of reckoning. But Pluto can also be the 'patsy' here for allowing themselves to be set up as the 'power-player', when really they are playing along with the Ascendant person's (unconscious) ruse to manipulate a partner into being what they want them to be – that is, their Shadow. It can be the case that both of you are happy with this arrangement, which could, for example, take the form of the Pluto person being well-off materially and the Ascendant person being dependent upon them for their power to earn, while Pluto is dependent upon the Ascendant's physical charms and emotional support. Whatever, the 'deal' that this Interaction translates into, your relationship will attract and go through many changes, some quite cathartic. This is because the Plutonian influence (of the Planet and maybe the person too) is geared to creating deeper and deeper levels of involvement, with usually money and/or sex as the lever. It may appear to one or other of you that at times you have to use your own particular 'lever' to get what you want, but this only invites a game of psychological poker as the other person is then forced to use their 'lever'. A more honest and psychologically aware approach to relating on the part of one, but ultimately both, of you could make this Interaction into a deep, lasting and emotionally satisfying bond.

When you have finished reading a set of Profiles, use the Final Focus which follows them

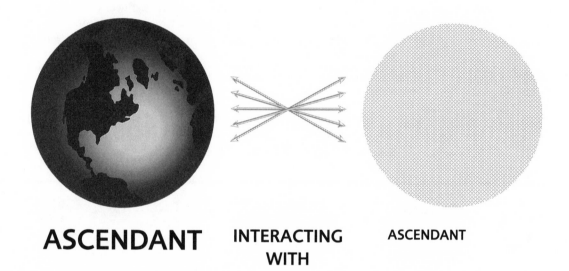

ASCENDANT   INTERACTING WITH   ASCENDANT

Be sure that both your birth times are
accurate to within five minutes for these
interactions to be reliable!

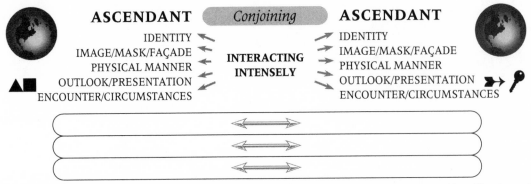

There is an immediate and mutual physical attraction between you, as well as a strong identification with one another. However, the quality of it and how such an attraction develops greatly depends on the Signs which you both have rising, which will usually be the same. Certain Signs are destined to get on together better and longer, like Sagittarius or Taurus, whereas others can fall foul of a doubling up of inherent weakness. For example, Libra can fall in love with love only to find a mirage is all that they're left with; Gemini can amuse and interest each other but never get that involved; Cancer can cling together tightly and securely, but suffer claustrophobia later. Aries or Leo would be exciting but competitive; Virgo just right or just not quite right. Scorpio is a pairing that can definitely merge and stay that way, come hell or high water; but Capricorn would get too dull if it ever got off the ground at all. Aquarius could be a very easy, friendly pairing as long as neither wanted anything more emotionally profound. Finally, Pisces could be blissful if they managed to stay entwined long enough to find out. This Interaction is one to get you going in the first place, but the course of your relationship will depend upon the other Interactions between you.

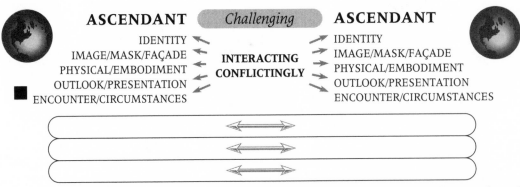

There can be a strong physical attraction and identification with each other initially, but at a later date you can find yourselves at cross-purposes, with circumstances preventing you from being together as much as you'd like – or as much as you think you ought to be together. It is as if what was so important initially eventually becomes secondary at most. If there is a pronounced mutual attraction and harmony between you indicated elsewhere with planetary Interactions, then this denial of each other's physical presence and attention can be steered round and compensated for. You would also be able to see, or maybe have to see, that physical appearance and image are relatively unimportant. Without such compatibility though, your relationship could be dogged by physical disappointment, inappropriate circumstances and a simple lack of opportunity.

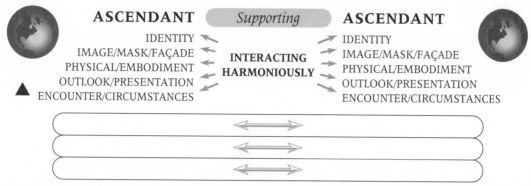

ASCENDANT *Supporting* **ASCENDANT**

IDENTITY | IDENTITY
IMAGE/MASK/FAÇADE | **INTERACTING** | IMAGE/MASK/FAÇADE
PHYSICAL/EMBODIMENT | **HARMONIOUSLY** | PHYSICAL/EMBODIMENT
OUTLOOK/PRESENTATION | OUTLOOK/PRESENTATION
ENCOUNTER/CIRCUMSTANCES | ENCOUNTER/CIRCUMSTANCES

You see eye-to-eye and are physically at ease with each other. As is the case with all Ascendant to Ascendant contacts, however, this effect may only last long enough to get you interested in one another. You may hit it off on the dance floor or in bed; or there are simply plenty of times when your paths cross, giving rise to opportunity. Physical compatibility is what this aspect is all about. So much so, that even if you go for long periods apart when the initial intimacy has worn off, you still feel that immediacy of physical connectedness. Looked at another way, even if there are storms on emotional or mental levels, this physical accord keeps you on intimate terms or gives you the feeling that you had when you first met.

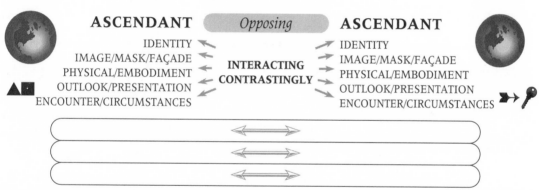

ASCENDANT *Opposing* **ASCENDANT**

IDENTITY | IDENTITY
IMAGE/MASK/FAÇADE | **INTERACTING** | IMAGE/MASK/FAÇADE
PHYSICAL/EMBODIMENT | **CONTRASTINGLY** | PHYSICAL/EMBODIMENT
OUTLOOK/PRESENTATION | OUTLOOK/PRESENTATION
ENCOUNTER/CIRCUMSTANCES | ENCOUNTER/CIRCUMSTANCES

This is a curious 'head-to-toe' kind of contact. Remembering that the Descendant, the 'erogenous zone' of your chart, is always opposite to the Ascendant, this Interaction could also be described as Ascendant Conjoining Descendant and Descendant Conjoining Ascendant. The image here is that of the snake eating its own tail. What all this means in plain English is that you strongly identify with the part of yourself that you cannot understand or accept *through being attracted to it in Other*, while Other experiences exactly the same thing with you. If there are many harmonious or positive connections supplied by planetary Interaction between you, then this aspect can eventually make you as one. More often though, this Interaction seems to occur when both of you need to have a good look at what it is about each of you that is dragging its feet. This will have a lot to do with your Rising and Setting Signs, and so you should study both yours and Other's in the section that begins on page 243. Here you should be able to see how what is called the 'Shadow process' operates, enabling you to see that your relationship with Other is an opportunity to become a more complete person.

Now you have finished reading a set of Profiles, use the Final Focus which follows

THE FINAL FOCUS

THE FINAL FOCUS

Now that we have acquired and used the CROSS-ASPECTS, we can look at what Planets in each person's Birthchart are focalized by the Interaction between them, meaning what parts of each person's life and personality are the *most affected or turned on* by it, be it overall, or in terms of being particularly stressed/challenging or capable/supporting. Having established this, we can then refer once more to the relevant individual PLANET-SIGN PROFILES (Chapter Two) and the general Planet meanings in the context of relationships in PLANETS OF LOVE (Chapter One), and review those PLANET-TO-PLANET PROFILES (Chapter Three) that involve these Focal Planets, thereby giving you a firm handle on and a sharp perception of the Interaction between a pair of people.

JUST SEVEN LAST STEPS ...

1 Using the FINAL FOCUS CHART FOR PERSON A opposite (also at the back of book to photocopy), we enter, for each of their Planets and their ASCendant, ONE POINT SCORES apiece for EASY or for HARD Aspects. These we extract from the QUALITY OF ASPECT column of the CROSS-ASPECTS (*see example on page 305*) but NOT YET from the CLOSE ONES given at the end of the CROSS-ASPECTS list. Starting with the SUN, simply add all the 'Easy' aspects together and then all the 'Hard' aspects and enter them in the appropriate column of the FINAL FOCUS CHART FOR PERSON A. Wherever it says 'Hard and Easy' (under Quality of Aspect), enter one Hard point and one Easy point. Hard Teardrop means one point for Hard; Easy Heart means one point for Easy, etc. Continue in the same way through all the rest of A's Planets, MOOn through to ASCendant.
NOTE: If either A or B does not have a reliably accurate birth time (within ten minutes) then DO NOT include their ASCendant in your assessment for the FINAL FOCUS.

2 Now do the same again for Person A's Planets and their ASCendant, but this time using the CLOSE ONES list, entering single point scores in the column headed 'Close and Easy' or 'Close and Hard'.

3 Add up all the points for 'Easy' and 'Close and Easy' for each Planet and the ASCendant, and enter the totals in the 'Total Easy' column, then do the same for the 'Hard' and 'Close and Hard' points and enter them in the 'Total Hard' column. Then just add the sum of both for each Planet and enter it in the 'Total Easy plus Total Hard' column. The highest score in this column denotes the Person A's MOST FOCAL PLANET (or Planets if there are equal scores).

4 In the last column, 'Total Hard Minus Total Easy', we enter the difference between 'Total Easy' and 'Total Hard' for each Planet by subtracting the lower score from the higher. If the 'Total Easy' is the higher, then we mark the result with an 'E'; if the 'Total Hard' is the higher, we mark the result with an 'H'. So if the 'Total Easy' was 8, and the 'Total Hard' was 7, then the result would be 1 E (8 – 7=1, with Easy being the higher score). If there is no difference between the two, then just enter 0.

Yet again, the best way of demonstrating this is through our example of Jack and Jill. Starting with Jack, his FINAL FOCUS CHART so far would look like the one on page 476.

PLANET-TO-PLANET INTERACTION – *FINAL FOCUS CHART FOR PERSON A*

PERSON A's ⬚ PLANETS and ASCENDANT	EASY	HARD	CLOSE AND EASY	CLOSE AND HARD	TOTAL EASY	TOTAL HARD	TOTAL EASY PLUS TOTAL HARD	TOTAL EASY MINUS TOTAL HARD
SUN								
MOOn								
MERcury								
VENus								
MARs								
JUPiter								
SATurn								
URAnus								
NEPtune								
PLUto								
ASCendant								
TOTALS								

PERSON A'S FOCAL PLANETS or   *Star Players*

A's MOST FOCAL PLANET(S) (Highest Hard plus Easy)	
A's MOST CHALLENGED/ING PLANET(S) (Highest Hard)	
A's MOST SUPPORTED/ING PLANET(S) (Highest Easy)	

? EVEN SCORES ? – If you get three or more even scores for any of the Focal Planets, favour the Sun, Moon, Ascendant, Ruling Planet or Setting Ruler as that Focal Planet. If after doing this you still have more than one particular Focal Planet, then use them both/all.

NOTE!! – IF THERE SHOULD BE ANY INTERACTIONS BETWEEN PERSON A's AND PERSON B's FOCAL PLANETS, THEN THESE WOULD BE HIGHLY SIGNIFICANT.

PLANET-TO-PLANET INTERACTION – *FINAL FOCUS CHART FOR PERSON A*

PERSON A's JACK PLANETS and ASCENDANT	EASY	HARD	CLOSE AND EASY	CLOSE AND HARD	TOTAL EASY	TOTAL HARD	TOTAL EASY PLUS TOTAL HARD	TOTAL EASY MINUS TOTAL HARD
SUN	2	2	–	–	2	2	4	0
MOOn	3	2	3	1	6	3	9	3 E
MERcury	2	2	–	–	2	2	4	0
VENus	–	2	–	2	–	4	4	4 H
MARs	2	1	1	1	3	2	5	1 E
JUPiter	1	2	–	–	1	2	4	1 H
SATurn	1	2	–	–	1	2	3	1 H
URAnus	–	2	–	–	–	2	2	2 H
NEPtune	1	2	–	–	1	2	3	1 H
PLUto	3	1	–	–	3	1	4	2 E
ASCendant	–	1	–	1	–	2	2	2 H
TOTALS	15	19	4	5	19	24	43	5H

5 Finally, we sum it all up by determining A's MOST FOCAL PLANET as being the one with the highest 'Total Hard Plus Total Easy'; A's MOST CHALLENGED/ING PLANET as being the one with highest 'Difference Between Total Easy and Total Hard' in favour of Hard (the scores marked with an'H'); and A'S MOST SUPPORTED/ING PLANET as being the one with highest 'Difference Between Total Easy and Total Hard' in favour of Easy (the scores marked with an 'E'). If you get three or more even scores, favour the Sun, Moon, Ascendant, Ruling Planet or Setting Ruler as that Focal Planet.

NOTE: You can do column totals (as shown above) which gives you an idea of the overall hardness or ease of the Interaction. But I would strongly advise against drawing categorical conclusions from them. Apart from this, they can be used to cross-check your entries – if you have a book-keeping disposition!

In our example this final summing up for Person A (Jack) would look like this:

PERSON A'S FOCAL PLANETS or **JACK'S**   *Star Players*

A's MOST FOCAL PLANET(S) (Highest Hard plus Easy)	MOOn (9)
A's MOST CHALLENGED/ING PLANET(S) (Highest Hard)	VENus (4H)
A's MOST SUPPORTED/ING PLANET(S) (Highest Easy)	MOOn (3E)

6 We can now interpret this vital information by looking up what each of these Planets means, firstly for the individual, and secondly for the Interaction between both people. In the first case we can initially use the FOCAL PLANET READY-RECKONER overleaf, or PLANETS OF LOVE in Chapter One. Then, to gain an even more personal insight we can also look at each Focal Planet's Sign Position in the PLANET-SIGN PROFILES in Chapter Two (although you will not find Uranus, Neptune or Pluto there). In the second case, by reviewing the PLANET-TO-PLANET PROFILES that involve these Planets, we can see what Interaction or chemistry between the two people carries the most weight for Person A. Note that with unavoidably equal scores there would be two or more Planets for each category.

7 And last but by no means least, and of course if you wish to, repeat the above six steps to acquire the FINAL FOCUS from Other's or Person B's perspective. This time we'd use the FINAL FOCUS CHART FOR PERSON B on page 479 (also at the back to be photocopied), and extract the Hard and Easy point scores as before from the CROSS-ASPECTS given from B's perspective (*see* page 480). The exercise is exactly the same as it was for Person A.

In our Jack and Jill example then, Person B's or Jill's FINAL FOCUS CHART would be as shown on page 481.

FOCAL PLANET READY-RECKONER

This table allows you to look up each of the Focal Planets and see what areas of life and personality are affected by them – and in what way. The Most Focal Planet will be the 'manager'* of the relationship in question, and determine the area of most concern and attention, at least from that person's own point of view and experience. The Most Challenged/ing Planet will indicate the area where one is most pressured and called upon to grow stronger and more aware, to deliver the goods, and not be let off the hook; and the Most Supported/ing Planet will show what is one's position of strength and/or ease, thereby making it possible to oil the wheels and further the relationship and fortunes of one or both people.

WHEN THE FOCAL PLANET IS	THE AREA OF LIFE AND PERSONALITY AFFECTED IS
The SUN	Willpower, Creative Expression, Confidence, Fatherhood, Ego, Pride, Dominance
The MOOn	Unconscious Conditioning, Feelings, Motherhood, Security, Family and Domestic Matters
MERcury	Communication, Work, Intellectual Matters, Education, Mental Attitude, Anxiety
VENus	Social and Aesthetic Values and Pleasures, Finances, Sense of Harmony, Art and Grace
MARs	Physical Energy, Activity and Survival, Self-assertion, Sexual Desires, Anger, Independence
JUPiter	Ethics, Beliefs, Philosophy, Law, Opinions, Growth, Vision, Travel and Foreign Matters
SATurn	Responsibility, Age and Maturity, Karma, Status, Fears, Life's Lessons, Material Stability
URAnus	Change, Freedom, Rebellion and Fighting for Rights, Awakening to Truths of Self and Life
NEPtune	Compassion, Acceptance, Fantasies, Music, Non-physical Issues, Delusions, Sensitivities
PLUto	Deep, Inevitable Feelings, Crises, Fate, Obsessions, Power, Transformation, Manipulation
The ASCendant	Immediate Impressions, Personal Circumstances, Physical Presence, Looks and Expression

* As distinct from the 'general manager' of relationships, the Setting Ruler described in Chapter Two – The Individual.

With our example then, Jack, with his MOOn being both his Most Focal Planet and his Most Supported/ing Planet, unconscious conditioning, feelings, motherhood, security, family and domestic matters will all be centrally important factors in the relationship and particularly concerning his part in it and experience of it. And with his MOOn in PISces, his ability to make sacrifices for others and show great sensitivity toward them will be an issue that brings both great emotional reward and some acute emotional suffering. With VENus as his Most Challenged/ing Planet, the issues resulting from the relationship will confront and bear down upon his social and aesthetic values and pleasures, finances, sense of harmony, art and grace.

Finally, further reading of all the Aspects that Jack's MOOn makes to five of Jill's Planets will shed a quite focused light upon the issues between them that these Aspects describe, particularly as they apply to him. Similarly, the Aspects that his VENus makes to Jill's Planets, especially the two Hard Cupid Aspects to her MOOn and NEPtune, should be regarded as areas of great importance. Any of these Aspects which are also Close Ones would indicate the real nub of the relationship in Jack's experience.

PLANET-TO-PLANET INTERACTION – *FINAL FOCUS CHART FOR PERSON B*

PERSON B's ⬭ PLANETS and ASCENDANT	EASY	HARD	CLOSE AND EASY	CLOSE AND HARD	TOTAL EASY	TOTAL HARD	TOTAL EASY PLUS TOTAL HARD	TOTAL EASY MINUS TOTAL HARD
SUN								
MOOn								
MERcury								
VENus								
MARs								
JUPiter								
SATurn								
URAnus								
NEPtune								
PLUto								
ASCendant								
TOTALS								

PERSON B'S FOCAL PLANETS or   *Star Players*

B's MOST FOCAL PLANET(S) (Highest Hard plus Easy)	
B's MOST CHALLENGED/ING PLANET(S) (Highest Hard)	
B's MOST SUPPORTED/ING PLANET(S) (Highest Easy)	

? EVEN SCORES ? – If you get three or more even scores for any of the Focal Planets, favour the Sun, Moon, Ascendant, Ruling Planet or Setting Ruler as that Focal Planet. If after doing this you still have more than one particular Focal Planet, then use them both/all.

NOTE!! – IF THERE SHOULD BE ANY INTERACTIONS BETWEEN PERSON A's AND PERSON B's FOCAL PLANETS, THEN THESE WOULD BE HIGHLY SIGNIFICANT.

CROSS-ASPECTS

From the perspective of Jill (Person B) to Jack (Person A):

INTERACTION	QUALITY OF ASPECT*	PAGE
B's MOOn SUPporting A's MOOn	*EASY – Heart*	*345*
B's MOOn CHAllenging A's VENus	*HARD*	*348*
B's MOOn CHAllenging A's JUPiter	*HARD*	*352*
B's MOOn CHAllenging A's URAnus	*HARD – Teardrop*	*356*
B's MOOn CONjoining A's NEPtune	*HARD AND EASY – Cupid, Heart, Teardrop, Key*	*358*
B's MERcury SUPporting A's MOOn	*EASY*	*347*
B's VENus CHAllenging A's MOOn	*HARD*	*348*
B's MARs SUPporting A's SUN	*EASY*	*327*
B's MARs SUPporting A's MERcury	*EASY*	*371*
B's MARs SUPporting A's MARs	*EASY*	*405*
B's MARs OPPosing A's NEPtune	*HARD – Cupid*	*413*
B's MARs SUPporting A's PLUto	*EASY*	*415*
B's JUPiter SUPporting A's PLUto	*EASY*	*429*
B's URAnus CONjoining A's SUN	*HARD AND EASY*	*332*
B's URAnus CONjoining A's MERcury	*HARD AND EASY*	*376*
B's URAnus CONjoining A's MARs	*HARD AND EASY – Cupid*	*410*
B's URAnus CONjoining A's JUPiter	*EASY*	*424*
B's URAnus CHAllenging A's SATurn	*HARD*	*436*
B's NEPtune CHAllenging A's SUN	*HARD – Teardrop*	*336*
B's NEPtune SUPporting A's MOOn	*EASY – Heart*	*359*
B's NEPtune CHAllenging A's MERcury	*HARD*	*378*
B's NEPtune CHAllenging A's VENus	*HARD – Cupid, Teardrop*	*397*
B's NEPtune CHAllenging A's JUPiter	*HARD*	*426*
B's NEPtune CONjoining A's SATurn	*HARD AND EASY*	*438*
B's NEPtune CHAllenging A's URAnus	*HARD*	*448*
B's PLUto OPPosing A's MOOn	*HARD – Teardrop, Key*	*362*
B's PLUto CONjoining A's PLUto	*HARD AND EASY*	*464*
B's PLUto CHAllenging A's ASCendant	*HARD – Cupid*	*466*

*
EASY = usually SUPporting (*see* page 303 for meaning).
HARD = usually CHAllenging (*see* page 303 for meaning).
HARD AND EASY = usually CONjoining or OPPosing (*see* page 303 for meaning).
Cupid = precipitating, mutually attracting, falling in love/lust, necessary for relationship to happen.
Heart = positive and lasting, marriage/partnership material.
Teardrop = involving suffering, acutely/profoundly emotional.
Key (Contact) = highly significant interactions.

Of the above, the following are **CLOSE ONES:**

INTERACTION	QUALITY OF ASPECT*	PAGE
B's MOOn SUPporting A's MOOn	*EASY – Heart*	*345*
B's MOOn CHAllenging A's VENus	*HARD*	*348*
B's MERcury SUPporting A's MOOn	*EASY*	*347*
B's URAnus CONjoining A's MARs	*HARD AND EASY – Cupid*	*410*
B's NEPtune SUPporting A's MOOn	*EASY – Heart*	*359*
B's NEPtune CHAllenging A's VENus	*HARD – Cupid, Teardrop*	*397*
B's PLUto OPPosing A's MOOn	*HARD – Teardrop, Key*	*362*
B's PLUto CHAllenging A's ASCendant	*HARD – Cupid*	*466*

PLANET-TO-PLANET INTERACTION – *FINAL FOCUS CHART FOR PERSON B*

PERSON A's JILL PLANETS and ASCENDANT	EASY	HARD	CLOSE AND EASY	CLOSE AND HARD	TOTAL EASY	TOTAL HARD	TOTAL EASY PLUS TOTAL HARD	TOTAL EASY MINUS TOTAL HARD
SUN	–	–	–	–	–	–	–	–
MOOn	2	4	1	1	3	5	8	2 H
MERcury	1	–	1	–	2	–	2	2 E
VENus	–	1	–	–	–	1	1	1 H
MARs	4	1	–	–	4	1	5	3 E
JUPiter	1	–	–	–	1	–	1	1 E
SATurn	–	–	–	–	–	–	–	–
URAnus	4	4	1	1	5	5	10	0
NEPtune	2	6	1	1	3	7	10	4 H
PLUto	1	3	–	2	1	5	6	4 H
ASCendant	–	–	–	–	–	–	–	–
TOTALS	15	19	4	5	19	24	43	5 H

PERSON B'S FOCAL PLANETS or *JILL'S*   *Star Players*

B's MOST FOCAL PLANET(S) (Highest Hard plus Easy)	*NEPtune /URA*
B's MOST CHALLENGED/ING PLANET(S) (Highest Hard)	*PLUto & NEP*
B's MOST SUPPORTED/ING PLANET(S) (Highest Easy)	*MARs*

So, using the READY-RECKONER, Jill, with NEPtune being her Most Focal Planet (rather than Uranus, because Neptune is also her SETTING RULER and one of her Most Challenged/ing Planets), then compassion, acceptance, fantasies, music, non-physical (or metaphysical) issues, escapism and sensitivities will be centrally important and ultimately unavoidable factors to come to terms with in the relationship, and particularly concerning her part in it. Further reading about NEPtune in PLANETS OF LOVE (Chapter One) would indicate the experiencing of the mysterious and unexplainable as part of the relationship. Note the Uranus effects as well, but they would be very secondary to Neptune.

With PLUto also as one of her Most Challenged/ing Planets, the issues resulting from the relationship will confront and bear down upon her in terms of deep, inevitable feelings, crises, fate, obsessions, power, transformation and manipulation. We would also read about Pluto in PLANETS OF LOVE for further insights.

With MARs as her Most Supported/ing Planet, these heavy demands would be met by physical energy, activity and survival, self-assertion, sexual desires, anger and competition. Also, by looking up her MARs Sign in the PLANET-SIGN PROFILES, we see that her MARs in ARIes is, fortunately, strong in itself. Moreover, as Mars is so often symbolic of the man in a woman's life, this would indicate that Jack is a strong and positive male influence in her life. Yet again, further understanding of Mars itself can be gained from PLANETS OF LOVE.

Finally, further reading of all the Aspects that Jill's NEPtune, PLUto and MARs make to Jack's Planets will shed quite a focused light upon these issues between them that these Aspects describe, particularly as they apply to her.

AND IF THERE SHOULD BE ANY INTERACTIONS BETWEEN PERSON A's AND PERSON B's FOCAL PLANETS, THEN THESE WOULD BE HIGHLY SIGNIFICANT.

These would reflect the central and most important reasons for the relationship – and the fact that there *are* these reasons for two people being involved with each other. Making use of, or paying heed to, such Interactions would therefore do much to further and maintain the relationship through an increased and precise understanding of it and the two individuals that are making it.

In Jack and Jill's case it would be: his MOOn SUPporting her NEPtune; his MOOn OPPosing her PLUto; his VENus CHAllenging her NEPtune. This could be summed up by saying that as a result of emotional crisis/crises the couple gain a deeper and highly attuned sense of one another's natures and needs, thereby taking their love past romantic illusions and through to a particularly high expression of love. Or such crises would try them to the point that their illusions of love outweighed their sensitive perception of each other's real selves (something which a romantic view is blind to) and disillusionment and estrangement would follow. So, in Jack and Jill's relationship, it can be seen that a great deal depends upon that sensitive attunement provided by his MOOn SUPporting her NEPtune, and vice versa.

NOTE: You may discover that the significance of Person A's Focal Planets also applies to Person B, and vice versa. This is simply because it *is* a relationship, and the two people will usually feel, in their own way, what the other is experiencing. *In the example of Jack and Jill, the Moon issues that Jack experiences are definitely experienced by Jill too, not least of all because it concerns motherhood. And the sensitivities of Jill's NEPtune would be picked up by Jack's MOOn in PISces with total empathy. (Note that Neptune rules Pisces.)*

KEYWORD CORNER

The use of Keywords in astrology is probably the easiest way to make full use of astrological symbolism. Simply to read interpretations that have been made by an astrologer – such as the ones I have made for each Interaction in the PLANET-TO-PLANET PROFILES – limits you to whatever that particular interpretation happens to focus upon, accurate though it may be. The beauty of symbols, however, is that they represent an almost unlimited supply of information from which you can draw meanings that are highly specific to you personally – and in the context of this book, to how you and Other interact.

Hopefully you will already have gathered important and enlightening information from the PLANET-TO-PLANET PROFILES. Now I will show you how to make key phrases and key sentences out of the Keywords for a particular Interaction or Aspect, and for each of the two Planets involved in that Interaction, in order that you can glean further, more customized interpretations that refer to the chemistry between one person and another, and to the circumstances and prospects that such an Interaction attracts. I have used Keywords throughout this book, especially in Planets of Love (in italics), but here is a good selection of ...

PLANET KEYWORDS

SUN	MOON	MERCURY	VENUS
WILL	HOME LIFE	ANXIETY	FEMININITY
FATHER	INSECURITY	HUMOUR	VALUES/MONEY
CONCEIT	IMMATURITY	WORKING LIFE	LOVE/AFFECTION
EGOTISM	NEEDS/HABITS	RATIONALIZING	GRACE/HARMONY
IMPORTANCE	MOTHER/CHILD	MENTAL ABILITY	ART/RELATIONSHIP
ILLUMINATING	FEELINGS/RESPONSES	COMMUNICATION	FANCY/SUPERFICIALITY
STRENGTH/VITALITY	SECURITY/COMFORTING	PERCEPTION/ATTITUDE	SENSUALITY/PLEASURE

MARS	JUPITER	SATURN	URANUS
DRIVE	EXCESS	TIME/FATE	INTUITION
ACTION	BIGOTRY	STATUS/INADEQUACY	LIBERATION
SEX/DESIRE	OPINION	LEARNING/TESTING	DISRUPTION
MASCULINITY	GROWTH	PATIENCE/CAUTION	PROVOCATION
STIMULATING	GOODWILL	MATURITY/DISCIPLINE	UNUSUAL/UNIQUE
ASSERTIVENESS	CONFIDENCE	RESPONSIBILITY/FORM	OPENNESS/EXPOSING
ANGER/ARROGANCE	ENCOURAGING	RESTRICTION/RIGIDITY	AWAKENING/QUICKENING

NEPTUNE	PLUTO	ASCENDANT	SOME LINKWORDS
SALVATION	OBSESSION	IDENTITY	TO • FROM • AND
INSPIRATION	REGENERATION	IMMEDIATE	OR • WITH • ABOUT
COMPASSION	MANIPULATION	SELF-EXPRESSION	HIS/HIM • MY • HER/S
FASCINATING	TRANSFORMING	IMAGE/MASK/LOOKS	OF • THROUGH • IN
SUPER-SENSITIVITY	INTIMACY/SECRECY	ENCOUNTER/CIRCUMSTANCES	• IN A WAY THAT IS •
SUFFERING/VICTIMHOOD	INTENSIFICATION→CRISIS	OUTLOOK/PRESENTATION	• FEELINGS OF •
DELUSION/UNDERMINING	(DIS)EMPOWERING/DESTINY	PHYSICAL/EMBODIMENT	• AS A RESULT OF •

INTERACTION OR CROSS-ASPECT KEYWORDS

CONjoining	INTENSIFYING/INTENSELY • UNITING • BINDING • ENERGIZING
CHAllenging	CONFLICTING/CONFLICTINGLY • STRENGTH-DEMANDING OR STRENGTH-PRODUCING
SUPporting	HARMONIZING/HARMONIOUSLY • CO-OPERATIVE • MUTUALLY HELPFUL and REWARDING
OPPosing	CONTRASTING/CONTRASTINGLY • SEPARATIVE • AWARENESS-PRODUCING OR AWARENESS-DEMANDING

And now, with the aid of the LINKWORDS and a generous helping of play-power, imagination and flexibility (ONCE YOU START YOU'LL FIND IT JUST COMES TO YOU!), is how to attain ...

• CONFIRMATION OF THE INDIVIDUAL MEANING AND QUALITY OF AN INTERACTION – For example, supposing a mother and child have MOOn SUPorting MOOn as one of their Interactions. As the Keywords suggest MOTHER SUPPORTING CHILD HARMONIOUSLY in a way that is MUTUALLY HELPFUL and REWARDING, it is a clear indication to the mother (and eventually the child too) that this is a basically positive parent/offspring relationship.

• A POSITIVE ATTITUDE OR THEME TO A DIFFICULT INTERACTION – Take an Interaction like SATurn CHAllenging URAnus, that is occurring, say, between the SATurn of a man and the URAnus of a woman who is considerably younger than him. This could typically imply issues where she DISRUPTS his RIGID TIMETABLE or the FORM that his lifestyle has taken, or PROVOKES his feelings of INADEQUACY which he is quite likely to feel at times. But we could turn this all around by positifying the expression of the Planets involved. How about, she LIBERATES him from RESTRICTIONS, PROVOKING him to LEARN to take RESPONSIBILITY, all as a result of her INTUITION AWAKENING him in a CHALLENGING way to a sense of FATE being at work as their relationship takes the FORM of an UNUSUAL RESPONSIBILITY as he TESTS her INTUITION and gives MATURITY and FORM to her UNIQUENESS, and DISCIPLINES her DISRUPTIVENESS. You will find plenty of positive insights in this way, thereby helping you to overwhelm the negatives. Also look at the Signs involved; if his SATurn was in CANcer then some or all the qualities of this Planet-Sign position (as given in the Planet-Sign Profiles, like learning to nurture, establishing roots, etc) would be AWAKENED and/or DISRUPTED by her.

• DEEPENING AND SEEING ANOTHER SIDE TO AN INTERACTION – Her URAnus is CONjoining his NEPtune, which is initially felt as AWAKENING his COMPASSION and him being FASCINATED by her UNIQUENESS. Later on however, he experiences SUFFERING as the VICTIM in him is EXPOSED by her OPENNESS and INTUITION. Where he might well be her SALVATION, the 'awakening of his compassion' would also come to include a QUICKENING of his DELUSIONS (of invulnerability).

• AWARENESS OF THE MEANING OF A RELATIONSHIP – There is always some meaning to any relationship, providing we are prepared to identify and put aside inappropriate feelings and habits, ideas and values. The OPPOSITION Aspect is especially effective in PRODUCING or DEMANDING AWARENESS of certain traits of character that are biased and therefore inhibit healthy relating. Take, say, VENus OPPosing VENus, which brings about CONTRASTING VALUES and FINANCIAL (MONEY) circumstances. Initially, such a CONTRAST would make each person very AWARE of the PLEASURE and SENSUALITY between them, and the one with more money is happy to help out the one with less, LOVE being in the air. However, when the real differences become uncomfortable and threaten SEPARATION, it would be wise to temper the extremes and correct the faults indicated by their respective VENus Profiles. For example, if the Opposition took place between ARIes and LIBra, then the former would be advised to be less headstrong and more socially aware, and the latter less socially fastidious and more emotionally honest and forthright (see Planet-Sign Profiles).

• THE FREEDOM AND ABILITY TO CREATE YOUR OWN KEYWORDS – The above, as you will have seen, 'turns' the Keywords to make them fit the context of the Interaction, thereby 'unlocking' the meaning or answer that you are after. In the process, you may well find that another, more appropriate, Keyword comes to mind. Providing that you are not leaping wildly in order to make it fit your fears or wishes, and are using other Keywords as well, then go for it. For instance, you may find you want to use the word AUTHORITY rather than DISCIPLINE as a Keyword for SATurn when Other's URAnus is DISRUPTING it. Leaving it at that would be self-righteous, so it would be fair to say that Other is also QUICKENING your INADEQUACIES, and that assumption of AUTHORITY could be a cover-up for this. You will find that, as in relating itself, when using Keywords ...

♥ HONESTY IS THE POLICY ♥

THE MIRROR

The surest way to resolve any relationship difficulty is to identify what it is in Other that appears to be giving you the trouble, and then recognize that it is reflecting something about you. Upon this 'reflection' you find that you feel less or no longer perturbed by Other – you may even feel greatly relieved and empowered because you have taken back a part of yourself. Or you may simply discover an answer.

You have to *work at it*, and you have to *be honest*. While doing this for yourself, look at the Mirror overleaf and jot down your Reflections and Projections as you do so on the Chart on page 487 (copy this or the one given at the back of this book). Here is an example list of Reflections and Projections to help you.

REFLECTION What Other appears as (to me) that concerns, confuses, obsesses or irritates	PROJECTION What I, upon reflection, see that I am 'sending' to Other and so getting back as the Reflection, or realize is true, fair or a simple solution
Being unreasonable	Basing things too much on reason. The times *I* have been unreasonable.
Not listening to me	Me not listening to my own feelings or better judgement, or to Other. A historical problem with my older brother and sister not listening to little me.
Being lazy	The times when I was lazy owing to a lack of confidence, indecisiveness or a lack of motivation.
Being obsessed with looks	I too am obsessed with looks – and how do *I* look?
Emotionally reacting	I do so too at times, or the fact that at other times I uncomfortably suppress my feelings.
Thinking life should fit some theory	I do, or have done, exactly that myself.
Not liking certain pieces of music which I love	Music has emotional associations and so I feel my feelings are not being appreciated. Another childhood issue.
Being a pain/embarrassment in company	My internal distress which I think is under control when really I have merely suppressed/internalized it.
Being inadequate, a victim	The times I too have suffered from this, and how I still do in that I still feel victimized by certain people. That I'm able to protect Other when they feel weak.
Not respecting my time and space and feelings	That I do not feel entitled to my own time, space and feelings – so I have a right to defend and assert them gently but firmly.
Being childish	Let he who is without childishness not throw a tantrum! That I need to be more mature myself.
Being disinclined sexually to give me what I want or when I want it	Sex is not enjoyable when I don't want it so why should it be for Other. What is it about me sexually that I should look at, change, discuss with Other.
Not closing doors, turning lights off, or replacing lids and caps	Where Other fails to get the message, in the long run it's easier to do it myself, and teach by example.

NOTE: You can also project back and forward in time. For example, something Other is doing now might be something you *used* to do, or you could be expecting Other to be, say, aggressive and they turn out not to be so. Also, and this is very important, Other's Reflection may be a COMPENSATION for what you are (sending). For example, you could see Other as being only ever concerned with themselves, reflecting that you are too much concerned with Other(s) and not nearly enough with yourself.
There can be many versions and reasons for Compensation.

The truth, psychology and efficacy of the Mirror is borne out by astrology – *see* page 246.

THE MIRROR

INSTRUCTIONS FOR USE

1 Close your eyes and take time to concentrate upon the Image, that is, what is concerning, confusing, obsessing or irritating you about Other, until you have it clearly in focus.

2 Open your eyes and gaze into the Mirror until you realize that the Image is actually a Reflection of a facet of your own personality that you have Projected on to Other. Jot down these Reflections and Projections on the Chart opposite. Again, take your time.

3 Having successfully accomplished this, appreciate how you now no longer feel (so) concerned, confused, obsessed or irritated – because you have now reclaimed possession of a part of your Self, or found a simple answer.

Please see **the previous page for more about the Mirror.**

THE MIRROR CHART

REFLECTION What Other appears as (to me) that concerns, confuses, obsesses or irritates	PROJECTION What I, upon reflection, see that I am 'sending' to Other and so getting back as the Reflection, or realize is true, fair or a simple solution

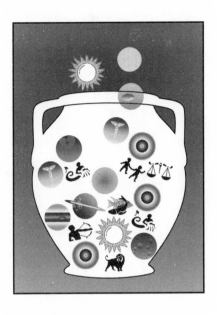

Chapter Four

THE RELATIONSHIP

You and I one day will plunge into
A wave of rich remembering
That sucks us soft deep down into
A sapphire world on turquoise wings.
You and I one day with Soul's caress
Shall surrender to our great Oneness …

from *NEPTUNE – Planet of Unification, Redemption and Unconditional Love*

THE THIRD ENTITY

The Individual and Other create a third entity which has a life, character and influence of its own – the Relationship itself. This can be appreciated when we think about how we refer to various relationships between One and an Other.

We say we are going around to 'Jack and Jill's place' where the atmosphere is very much a blend of both of them; we talk about 'Mrs So-and-so and her Dog' because they are inseparable; we cannot think about 'Jim' without also thinking of his wife who is everything to him. And probably more significantly, it is often the case that if a relationship is going through a bad patch, people do not mind being in the company of one half of it, but not both. In other words, a relationship is something that those outside of it also have to relate to in a certain way.

With astrology we can determine the nature of the relationship – its purpose and nature. The most traditional way is the working out of a Composite Chart, but the complex calculation of this is way outside the scope of this book. What we can do quite easily is establish the THEME of a relationship by discovering its predominant quality in terms of Zodiacal Signs. This is rather like looking at the most influential Signs in an individual, which are usually their Sun Sign, Moon Sign and Rising Sign. But as most people do not know exactly when a particular relationship was 'born', we cannot really do this in the same way as for an individual. What the THEME actually does is act as the route and direction of the relationship, and as a bridge or common ground between the two people by compensating for extremes and dissimilarities, while emphasizing similarities – which often include personal conflicts and difficulties. This is Fate, Nature or the Unconscious doing their best to bring about that Reunion we referred to in the beginning.

Having worked out this THEME in terms of Signs, which I tell you how to do overleaf, we can then look at how these Signs give us the relationship's LAWS which guide and support it, as well as warn us of its inherent weaknesses. After this, we can then investigate how these Themes interact, much as we did with the Sign-to-Sign Interaction in Chapter Three. This Interaction, though, would spell out the DYNAMIC of a relationship, telling us its plot in the form of its strengths and challenges. By focusing upon all of this, we can become aware of the road we are both supposed to be heading down, and how hard or easy it is. We could say that the relationship is a manifesto that life has laid upon us to live by and up to.

**BE TRUE TO THE RELATIONSHIP
AND THE RELATIONSHIP WILL BE TRUE TO YOU.**

SIGN-TO-SIGN INTERACTION (AND RELATIONSHIP THEME) CHART
E X A M P L E

PERSON A: *Jack*   **PERSON B:** *Jill*

SIGN	PERSON A's PLANETS (incl. ASC and DES)		+	PERSON B's PLANETS (incl. ASC and DES)	+	THEME Double the lower or equal point scores
ARIes				MAR 3	3	0
TAUrus						0
GEMini	DES 4		4	SUN 4 / VEN 3	(7)	8
CANcer	URA 1		1	MER 3	3	2
LEO	SUN 4 / MER 3 / VEN 3	MAR 3 / JUP 2 / PLU 1	(16)	URA 1	1	2
VIRgo				ASC 4 / PLU 1	(5)	0
LIBra	NEP 1		1			0
SCOrpio	SAT 2		2	MOO 4 / NEP 1	(5)	4
SAGittarius	ASC 4		4			0
CAPricorn				JUP 2 / SAT 2	4	0
AQUarius						0
PISces	MOO 4		4	DES 4	4	8

POINT SCORES: SUN, MOOn, ASCendant, DEScendant=4 each. MERcury, VENus, MARs=3 each. JUPiter, SATurn=2 each. URAnus, NEPtune, PLUto=1 each.

THE RELATIONSHIP THEME

WORKING IT OUT – Three Steps to Find Out Where It Wants to Go

1 Go to the SIGN-TO-SIGN INTERACTION CHART that you filled in earlier at the beginning of Chapter Three – The Interaction (*see* page 283). This is the chart where you entered both Person A's and Person B's Planets according to their Sign positions, giving each Planet a point score as you did so. Now you will notice that this chart is also called the RELATIONSHIP THEME CHART, and that the last column is headed 'THEME – Double the lower or equal point scores'. What we enter here is all that is needed to establish both the THEME and the DYNAMIC of the relationship in question.

Simply look at the total Planet point score (Planet-Sign score) for ARIes of *each* person under the + sign, and *double* the *lower* of these two scores. If the scores are *equal,* then just double one of the scores. Enter this doubled amount, the Theme Score for ARIes, in the THEME column of the ARIes row. *With our ongoing example of Jack and Jill, we see that Jack has no Planets at all in ARIes, whereas Jill has MARs which gives her a total Planet-Sign score of three points. So doubling the lower score, Jack's, which is zero, gives a Theme Score, for ARIes, of zero.*

Now carry on in the same way for each Planet-Sign score for each person. *With our example, the Theme Score for TAUrus is again zero, but the Theme Score for GEMini is eight, because Jack has the lower score of four. Opposite, you will see the completed chart for Jack and Jill.*

In case you are wondering, the logic behind this calculation is that first we add together the total point scores for each Sign and each person, for this sum mathematically represents the combining of A's and B's energies. Then we subtract the difference between those scores from the sum of them as this represents the way in which the Relationship Theme tries to compensate for extremes and dissimilarities, while emphasizing similarities. However this whole calculation can be achieved in just one stroke by simply doubling the lower or equal point score.

2 Having completed your own chart for Theme Scores, enter those scores on your CHARTWHEEL in the ring shaded ▨▨▨, in the appropriate segments for each Sign. *You will see how this is done for our example on the CHARTWHEEL – EXAMPLE 3, on page 495.*

3 Now we look for UP TO FOUR of the most emphasized Signs – which will actually be the RELATION-SHIP THEME itself – according to which ones have the Highest Theme Scores. In other words, THE NUMBER OF THEMES WITH THE HIGHEST SCORES MUST BE BETWEEN ONE AND FOUR.

So in our example, we see that Jack and Jill's Highest Theme Scores are GEMini eight , SCOrpio four and PISces eight. So this is their RELATIONSHIP THEME. Note how we do not use the two scores of two because that would have given us an 'illegal' five Highest Theme Scores (and by reason of rule (b) below).

4 Usually it is fairly obvious what these one to four Highest Theme Scores are, but in a few cases it may not be quite clear – or there could be a yawning gap between the highest and lowest of your Highest Theme Scores – so you will need rules for determining them. The rules you'll occasionally have to apply are as follows:

a) SCORES OF FOUR – Only use a Theme Score of four as one of your Highest Theme Scores when there are fewer than three Theme Scores higher than four, *and* there are no other Theme Scores of four (eg,

Jack and Jill can use their four score for Scorpio, but if they had, say, four for Leo too, then they would only be allowed to use the two scores of eight for Gemini and Pisces). *However,* if only one or no Theme Score is higher than four, then you may use up to three or four Scores of four (eg, if Jack and Jill had zero for Pisces rather than eight, and four for Leo, then they would have as their Relationship Theme: Gemini eight, Leo four and Scorpio four).

b) SCORES OF TWO – Only use Theme Scores of two as one of your Highest Theme Scores when there are no Theme Scores higher than two.

c) OUTRIGHT HIGHEST SCORE – If you have only one Theme Score which is clearly the highest (that is, just one Sign has a higher score than all the rest which are the same score, or all twos and zeros), then that Sign is your RELATIONSHIP THEME. (This is rarely the case.)

d) TIE-BREAKER – Having applied the above rules, if you still are stuck with a choice between equal scores, select in favour of the Sign/s that include the Sun, Moon, Ascendant or Descendant.

5 Finally, take the one to four Signs that comprise the RELATIONSHIP THEME and enter them on to the CHARTWHEEL by shading in the appropriate segments surrounding the Earth at the centre of the Wheel. See how this has been done for our example on the CHARTWHEEL – EXAMPLE 3 opposite. This is a symbolic depiction of the RELATIONSHIP THEME – and of the RELATIONSHIP DYNAMIC, which we look at on page 511.

NOW WE ARE READY TO TURN THE PAGE AND STUDY LAW, ZODIACAL STYLE ...

In the case of our Example of Jack and Jill we would read the Zodiacal Laws for Gemini, Scorpio and Pisces, reading the most into the Gemini and Pisces Themes because they have the higher scores and are therefore predominant in the relationship.

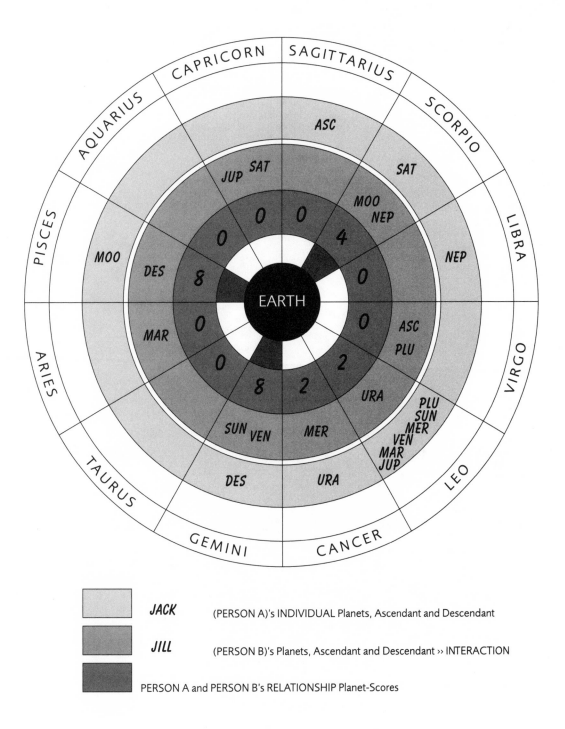

JACK (PERSON A)'s INDIVIDUAL Planets, Ascendant and Descendant

JILL (PERSON B)'s Planets, Ascendant and Descendant ›› INTERACTION

PERSON A and PERSON B's RELATIONSHIP Planet-Scores

Chartwheel – Example 3

THE 12 LAWS OR THEMES
OF THE ZODIAC

Now that we have our RELATIONSHIP THEME worked out, we can look at
what it means. This is done by reading the 'Laws', which begin overleaf,
for those one to four Signs that comprise the Theme. Start with any Sign/s with
the highest score/s for their LAWS will possibly, but not definitely,
predominate as that RELATIONSHIP THEME.

TIP – You will find that reading all the Laws will be a great help in
relating and living generally.

A R I E S

Leanings

INDEPENDENCE – Much as you are a couple, it is vitally important that both of you feel free to do your own thing by following your individual impulses, seeking each other's approval first of all purely as a formality. However, this should not preclude relying upon one another for support.

ARTLESSNESS – As a couple you are childlike and without agenda or guile. This could make for a 'Babes in the Wood' scenario where your naïveté is a liability, but this ingenuousness can, if it hasn't already, evolve into an innocent and straightforward nature that others find refreshing to be around.

ACTIVITY – Leading an active and physical lifestyle is important to you as a couple – that is, you need to be *doing* things together like sports, walking, dancing, etc. You do not like to stand still, so some competitiveness acts as a healthy fillip to making all-important advances.

Advantages

COURAGE – If there is a battle to be fought or some challenge to be met, you have the guts and push to face the music. Significantly, this includes being prepared to take an honest look at the reason for difficult circumstances you may be in together and act upon them as a couple.

LEADERSHIP – In some respect or other, as a pair you lead the way for others. Your relationship is a pioneering one in that you could be exploring untried methods of being together, discovering the rules of the game or inventing your own as you go along. You are your own couple.

SPONTANEITY – At a moment's notice, you are quite capable of changing your tack or dropping everything and taking off in another direction. As a couple you like to travel light, not be weighed down by unnecessary ties. You can turn the unexpected into an exciting surprise.

Weaknesses

IMPETUOSITY – Together you leap into things before you have had a proper look at what you might be getting yourselves into. Very likely this applied to your actually getting involved as a couple in the first place. It could also be how you quickly leap out of it (and into another relationship)!

COMBATIVENESS – You can have quite fierce battles. If the above qualities, like Independence and Activity, are not exercised then this could continue to be the case, with destructive consequences. You have to appreciate the difference between a 'good' fight and a 'bad' one.

UNSOCIABILITY – Because you often tend to be into your own thing and ways of doing things, or in conflict, involving other people in your life as a couple can be deemed compromising, frustrating or awkward. But this can find you uninvited, bored and lonely at a later date.

TAURUS

Leanings

SUBSTANCE – A firm grip and appreciation of the actual facts and possibilities of your being together holds sway. This means that if your relationship works it proves itself simply by enduring and producing something of worth. Conversely, if your relationship lacks a sense of reality, it will fail to exist to any substantial degree.

POSSESSION – It is important that each of you feels that you belong to one another and that you have something material, like property, to call your own too. It is as if the proof of and testament to your relationship lies in this 'having and holding' of one another – for better or worse.

TERRITORY – This is inextricably linked with possession in that you have to have some physical area to call your own. It also means that you need to have clear, uncomplicated boundaries regarding 'right and wrong', and what parts each of you are playing in, and contributing to, the relationship.

Advantages

STABILITY – You provide a good base for creating and maintaining anything – particularly a family. There is also a relaxing, unhurried atmosphere about you as a couple, and others see you as something permanent which endures amidst the storms of life in general.

SENSUALITY – Without a strong sense and appreciation of the physical and aesthetic pleasures of life, you would never have come together in the first place. And so you continue to be quite sensual with one another, despite any decline that might arise in other areas of relating.

PRODUCTIVITY – Ultimately, the whole point to your being together is to create something more than what you are as individuals. As well as this meaning the likelihood of raising a family, you probably actively pursue arts or crafts together or individually, and pass it on to your kin.

Weaknesses

OBSTINACY – You are slow or resistant to any kind of change or anything 'newfangled' or suggestive of transformation. This could be regarded as the necessary downside to being so stable and enduring, but if taken too far such stubbornness can lead to a stagnation within your relationship itself.

JEALOUSY – Because you invest a great deal of yourselves into each other in order to create that all-important dependability, you are understandably sensitive to any third party upsetting the apple cart. But should this occur it would be owing to your resisting change on other levels – that is, the third party would be merely an agent of change.

GULLIBILITY – Wholesome and uncomplicated as your relationship might be, at least on the outside, such can give rise to a psychologically rather unsophisticated attitude – a bit like the farmer and his wife. This can find you precariously uninformed and open to being taken advantage of.

GEMINI

Leanings

INTEREST – As a couple you depend upon a constant stream of various interests to stimulate you. It is as if you are a pair of lungs that has to breathe in order to live, taking in all sorts of ideas and experiences. Such curiosity also makes for being an interesting couple, in one way or another.

COMMUNICATION – Having plenty to talk about, both to each other and to people outside your relationship, is very likely and quite essential. In fact, without this intellectual stimulation, your relationship could flag. Consequently, you will endeavour to ensure that a supply of contacts and information is always forthcoming – even if it irritates at times.

LIGHTNESS – You do not as a rule like to get too heavy or bogged down through looking too deeply into the whys and wherefores of your being together – not unless you really have to. You like to tread lightly across the surface of things and not look under every emotional stone.

Advantages

EASY-GOING – The laid-back and friendly quality that is the product of that Lightness is pleasant and refreshing for others to be around. As a couple you are therefore popular, although possibly very few would really know you. Be that as it may, such affability is priceless.

YOUTHFULNESS – You are quite young in the way you behave together. Unless there is a big problem, you usually have a skip in your step, and can put one into others' as well. You are able to tune into the latest fashions and possibly use your creative wits to contribute to and profit from such.

HUMOUR – You see the funny side of life together and probably have a good laugh together. In company you will bring out the wit and brilliance of others, making for highly stimulating gatherings. At your best, you can see your own joke, but not take yourselves too lightly either.

Weaknesses

FLIPPANCY – This, the Shadow of your Lightness, may not become a problem – but it could attract a situation that forces you to dig deeper into your feelings, or to understand why you are together. You may be able to coast along unperturbed for quite some time – but not indefinitely.

FRIVOLITY – This would be an excess of the Lightness mentioned above, and as such can degenerate into a dangerous disrespect for your own and each other's feelings. Ironically, this breeziness may have been initially what you found attractive in being together, like light relief.

DISTRACTION – Another irony is that the inherent inclination of this Theme to seek variety and avoid difficult emotions means that you get into a rut of never being with one another long enough. Something or someone is always getting the attention of one or the other of you. For the same reason, flirtatiousness can also be a weakening influence.

CANCER

Leanings

SECURITY – The outright ruling need of this Theme is to feel safe and comfortable with one another in the sense of your being a couple who together feel protected from the hard cold world outside. Needless to say, a home or place of retreat is your primary material requirement.

FAMILIARITY – You form yourselves into a private, family-oriented unit quite instinctively, with all the pluses and minuses of such a state. You also like a definite measure of routine and predictability in your relationship, for this maintains a feeling of certainty and natural rhythm.

DREAMINESS – As a pair you live quite close to the Unconscious. This can mean anything from being driven by conditioned needs or fears, to being pleasantly wistful and vague, to being actively concerned with the whole realm of dream-life and the workings of the unconscious mind.

Advantages

SENTIMENTALITY – You have a childlike, romantic way of being together. Nostalgia and the value of the past play an important part in your manner of relating. People who have associated with you from the beginning of your relationship have a special place in your joint heart.

PROTECTION – This has primarily to do with your natural ability to raise a happy family – or at least, a family that has a strong family feel to it. This is founded upon a sympathy and concern that you have for one another's welfare. This may, or should, persist despite any falling out.

TENACITY – You are able to stay together through decidedly tough circumstances. This will be mainly because of the need to keep family together, or simply to continue what you are both so accustomed to. You are probably tied to one other by bonds stronger than you may appreciate – which is why you could keep testing them, or having them tested.

Weaknesses

HABIT – Your need for the Familiar and predictable can insidiously amount to doing things together purely because you have got into the habit of doing so. These things may actually become negative or stress-producing. Make a conscious effort to identify and break such habits for there is an ultimate danger of the relationship itself becoming one.

BLACKMAIL – Owing to the strong needs for Security and Protection, there is unfortunately an inclination on one or both of your parts to use guilt and/or indispensability to keep the other where you want them. Indeed, this is a cancer that could be the death of your relationship – root it out.

MOODINESS – Being so feeling- and needs-oriented, it is not surprising that your being together can create an emotional swell that has you both lurching from high to low, from desperate to hopeful – and reacting to one another to perpetuate this. You both should contact the inner child in yourselves and one another and heal its hurts – or you'll 'drown'.

L E O

Leanings

PLAYFULNESS – A sense of drama and of the game of life is vital to this Theme. Playing in the way that children do (make-believe, costumes, characterization, pet names, etc) creates a sense of life being fun and romantic, and not just a lack-lustre, day-to-day business. Parties, passions and highs and lows are what this Theme thrives upon.

CREATIVITY – Art or some other form of self-expression, individually or together, gives and maintains the sense of personal uniqueness and self-esteem that creates the all-important mutual respect essential to this Theme. Having and bringing up children is also regarded as Creativity.

HIERARCHY – Who's in charge of what is a serious issue, so this relationship must consciously and deliberately devise and agree upon individual duties, positions and rights – or else chaos can reign. Having a sense of respect for one another – and respect from others – is important.

Advantages

STYLE – This Theme usually attracts a comparatively up-market lifestyle, even if it is slightly down-at-heel in itself – paupers in a stately home kind of thing. Others find this relationship exciting or eventful to be around for this Theme exudes a sense of occasion which is part of the creativity.

WARMTH – There is a good-heartedness within the relationship which also radiates out to friends and family. There is also an enthusiastic appreciation and recognition of talent or class in others. Hospitality is granted to those that are gracious, and always graciously received.

DIGNITY – This Theme demands that high standards of behaviour be set and maintained. Consequently, shady or shoddy goings-on are not tolerated. Respect for others' time and situation is strongly linked to the respect shown to this couple's own time and situation.

Weaknesses

PRIDE – This is really an over-sensitivity towards having dirty laundry aired in public. This relationship does not like the world to see any cracks in it. But ironically, what are regarded as shortcomings by this couple are probably regarded as quite normal by ordinary, lesser mortals.

MELODRAMA – This is a case of making a crisis out of what could have been simply passed over as an everyday emotional hiccup. Such a reaction stems from this Theme's sense that life should always be larger than it actually or usually is. Such a crisis can turn into a real disaster.

ELITISM – There is a sense of specialness to this relationship that can unfortunately devolve into an exclusiveness that allows very few people into it. This can eventually result in a somewhat incestuous affair that drowns in an excess of itself, and suffocates for lack of external input.

VIRGO

Leanings

PURITY – This is a much misunderstood concept which you can fall foul of because it is central to this Theme. The Latin *virgo* refers to something which is nothing but itself – that is, not sullied by anything or missing anything. So your relationship has a distinct quality and purpose that must be identified so that it may be worked upon, improved, and kept intact.

HEALTH – The promotion and maintenance of health – be it mental, physical, emotional or spiritual – is an issue that should concern you. Such health, and a helpfulness which characterizes it, may be extended to the human, animal, vegetable, mineral or abstract realms.

ORDER – Legendary Virgoan tidiness is one of the issues here. This relationship likes to have a sense of order about it, so both of you maintaining domestic and personal tidiness and hygiene is important, as too is being precise in what you say and do together.

Advantages

SOBRIETY – This may sound like a rather dull asset but it does in fact go a long way towards keeping your relationship on an even keel. And should there be an indulgent streak in you too, you are aware of it and keep it within healthy bounds.

IDIOSYNCRASY – There is a quality to your relationship that is both complex and unique. Others may find it difficult to see what you have going for you in some respects, but that is because you have this link which is exquisitely personal. An aspect of love you could call the 'glass slipper'.

HARDWORKING – Industriousness is an integral part of the fabric of your relationship. You do not mind time apart spent working, and you work together quite happily too. Moreover, you are a service to others, and you (should) also work at improving your relationship itself.

Weaknesses

FUSSINESS – Avoid a neurotic need for Order, for this would be counter-productive. This is most likely to manifest in being over-critical of one another, or of those around you. Underlying such a corrosive inclination as this is a lack of acceptance of something within yourselves as individuals.

INHIBITION – You may not notice it, but lurking somewhere within your relationship is a fear of doing or saying something. This may well be sexual in nature. It is as if you are afraid to expose or plunge into some issue – but failing to do this could cause this very thing to go critical.

PARSIMONY – Together you should have a natural sense of economy. Unfortunately, this can devolve into a stinginess with yourselves and others you have dealings with. Really, this is emotional in nature for it smacks of being afraid or reluctant to give something of yourselves away. You probably think there is something about you that is too personal or would be censored – but you would be wrong in thinking this.

Leanings

HARMONY – 'Don't let the Sun go down on your wrath' could be a very apt motto for you as a couple. Striving for a pleasant and peaceful atmosphere is vital to your well-being as a relationship. As such, this Theme is the most effective for maintaining a positive partnership.

JUSTICE – Having a sound sense of what is right and wrong with regard to one person's behaviour towards another is of paramount importance to you both. It is as if you are innately aware that there is such a thing as 'establishing right relations' and you strive morally to achieve this.

ART – Life without Art is for you two a life which is not worth living. So in your daily lives together it is imperative that you have beauty and elegance around you for most of the time, especially where you live. If you don't already, pursue some form of artistic practice or appreciation.

Advantages

CONSIDERATION – You take time out to weigh the pros and cons, the best way of going about relating to one another. You also have the sensibility to take into Consideration the emotional and social positions of those around you with a view to alleviating or improving their situation.

AESTHETICS – You have an awareness of how to please others as well as each other. The look, taste, smell, sound and feel of things is something which you deem highly desirable and significant. You use music and fine food to good effect, to entertain or simply live amidst.

SOCIABILITY – You should be quite popular as a couple for you grace your social environment to one degree or another. Most significantly, it is the fact that you are, or at least appear to be, an item in the accepted sense of the term. A harmonious couple creates Harmony around it.

Weaknesses

INDECISIVENESS – Being merely a social response to your social environment finds you lacking in the direction and principles needed to determine what you want to do or be as a couple in its own right. Choosing an objective and progressively striving toward it is the answer.

TIMIDITY – Because of your joint need to be liked, appreciated, understood or approved of, you can lack the identity as a pair that is spirited and sure enough of its own integrity not to be manipulated or compromised by one or more other people. Forge your own strengths.

SUPERFICIALITY – If you find your lives together getting meaningless, or that you are a couple in name only, then it is because you have settled for a semblance of compatibility, for being in a relationship for fear of being alone. Dig beneath each other's surface for the gold.

SCORPIO

Leanings

INTENSITY – With this Theme there is no danger of your relationship being insipid. You were drawn together initially by powerful urges such as sexual desire or emotional hunger. It is also likely that you will at some time have these feelings re-intensified by some factor, like a third party.

INVOLVEMENT – The chemistry between you is such that you become automatically and progressively more involved. This is an all-or-nothing kind of thing, and you will make your bond increasingly inextricable through the establishing of joint finances, shared investments and, more to the point, unconscious ties that are kept intact by certain taboos.

CRISIS – This Theme does not make for a smooth, uneventful partnership, however much you may want or pretend to have such a thing. In fact, pretence and compromise would quicken the process whereby you are plunged into profound emotional experiences, from grief to great intimacy.

Advantages

INSIGHT – The more you are together, the greater your sense of what lies beneath the surface of not just each other but anyone that spends any time with you. As a couple you can develop a penetrating Insight into the inner truths of life. This could, in some cases, lead to an interest in the occult.

GENUINENESS – You can be trusted to express yourselves in a manner that is unalloyed by formality. Such emotional authenticity can act like a magnet to certain others outside your relationship, as well as giving any children you might have a deep sense of the worth of (their own) feelings.

COMMITMENT – The dynamics of this Theme guarantee, through one means or another, that your relationship has emotional substance and a lasting psychological bond. Where priorities are concerned, sentiment, romantic love and social niceties fall way behind your 'urge to merge'.

Weaknesses

MANIPULATION – Much as, or rather because, you want to be involved body and soul, there is also the temptation to use underhand means to achieve this objective. Using each other's desires and fears to keep them where you want them can do this, but the price you pay is being in bondage rather than having a loving bond.

SECRETIVENESS – A feature of Manipulation is enabled by having the 'dope' on each other. But this means that you will then keep certain things to yourself which effectively undermines the relationship because such Secretiveness is denying Other a part of your Self. A cold war, in fact.

DESTRUCTIVENESS – This is the 'nothing' part of the above-described 'all or nothing' quality of this Theme. If, along with Manipulation and Secretiveness, the negative aspects of distrust and suspicion – the hazards of intimacy – are allowed to get out of control, this relationship dies a death. And because of an inherent lack of forgiveness it might be a lingering one.

SAGITTARIUS

Leanings

IDEALISM – Together you feel and know that there is something that you are seeking. This could be finding the meaning of a sound and healthy partnership, raising a wholesome family, or even striving toward some religious objective. Whatever it might be, you have a sense of there being something you have to make or discover that is higher and better.

FURTHERANCE – This springs from the Idealism. Because you have this expansive sense of life and of yourselves as a couple going somewhere, you pursue various projects or programmes that are in aid of educating, promoting and furthering you and yours – or you just travel/explore a lot together.

ETHICS – You share a sense of there being a right and a wrong way of relating. Possibly you devise a set of 'laws' for your relationship to steer itself by. Or your relationship itself may raise some moral issue that you have to contend with, which in turn determines its success or failure.

Advantages

CONFIDENCE – There is an innate sense of sureness within and about you as a couple. Whatever the status of your relationship or the feelings between you, there exists a certain positivity, or at least an absence of neurosis. Consequently, you go about things with an enthusiasm and optimism that breeds success. You can be enterprising too.

ADVENTUROUSNESS – You are an outgoing couple, which means that you can be active in the field of sports, outdoor pursuits, travel, partying or anything that takes you out of yourselves. You do not get cooped up and gloomy. You see the world as your oyster and make the most of it.

CONTEMPORARY – You are in tune with the culture in which you live, and therefore make an advantage out of it; you both know who or what is 'in'. So you are also 'in flow' with the times, giving you a sense of where things are bound politically, morally, religiously, educationally, etc.

Weaknesses

SMUGNESS – This is the downside of being so positive and with-it. You can get carried away on the wave of your own sense of enjoyment or of being right. Like a hot-air balloon, you get so 'high' that you do not notice you have left reality and other people way behind. So eventually you disappear into nothing or come crashing down to Earth.

NONCHALANCE – Negatively, your essentially broad and expansive nature as a couple can reach a point where you lose sight of each other as ordinary emotional people with their 'little' problems and concerns. Realize this and you will restore your feelings for one another.

TRENDINESS – There is a danger of mistaking what most people appear to be doing as being right merely because that is the general trend. Being 'in the know' is another possible pitfall. You may even flip this over and be disdainful of what's in vogue. In either case, you can lose sight of the importance of having your own values – and ultimately of each other.

CAPRICORN

Leanings

RESPONSIBILITY – Without a serious purpose to your relationship which must be observed and adhered to, it would not exist at all. This can mean that the relationship has responsibility as an inherent part of it, or that that is precisely what is imposed upon you in order that you may learn from it.

TRADITION – You are inclined as a couple to follow a quite conventional route in your relationship – namely marriage, officially or unofficially. But whether you remain together because you want to or have to is another matter, as too is how it appears on the outside not necessarily concurring with how you are in private.

REGULATION – An order and pattern to your life together is something that seems to get installed one way or another. Possibly you are in a business together which dictates this. Whether it is that, or running home and family, you make it into a businesslike affair with routines, economy, etc.

Advantages

DUTIFULNESS – Because you conduct your relationship in such a responsible manner, you come to rely upon one another more and more as time goes by. And with time comes trust and the learning of valuable lessons which enable you to build your relationship into something lasting.

OBJECTIVITY – You are not a pair to let emotions get the better of you to a point where you overlook the practical realities of your relationship and the context in which it exists. Whether it is a family, a business or anything else you are jointly responsible for, you both see what has to be done, and do it.

CONSTRUCTIVITY – Being practical and aware of material issues – or at least when the relationship has made you so – you set about ensuring that you and yours amount to something in the world at large. Professional plans and activities (should) come high up on your list of priorities.

Weaknesses

COLDNESS – Not surprisingly, a disadvantage of the above-described practicality and Objectivity is that your respective inner feelings get overlooked or suppressed. In time, this could find you seriously out of touch with the very feelings that endeared you to one another in the first place.

RIGIDITY – Whatever pattern or order you have devised, possibly over years, to create stability and security, could devolve into tramlines that you have to keep to day-in-day-out. If this has made your relationship stale and turned it into a meaningless drudge, then consciously introduce some change and flexibility.

AUSTERITY – Economy is one thing, but denial is another. An almost Dickensian set of values can creep up on you both, causing you, either emotionally or materially, to be mean with yourselves, and possibly others too. This would reflect the degree to which the love and soul had drained from your relationship owing to that Coldness and a need to control.

Leanings

LIBERATION – Through your relationship you look for the true reason for being in a relationship at all. It is essential that you have an openness with each other as only this can grant you the freedom to find out why you are together as a unique couple of two unique human beings. Ultimately it is about finding the right amount of freedom; neither too much nor too little.

UNUSUALNESS – This goes hand in hand with Liberation because without being unusual in some way, as a pair you'd conform to some stereotype which stifles freedom and Originality. Relatively at least, you should be involved as a couple in some out-of-the-ordinary or awakening pursuits.

EQUALITY – The presence of any kind of discrimination between you is an abomination for it goes against the basic fabric of your relationship, whether you know it or not. Any thought of one of you being better or less than the other would automatically destabilize the whole relationship.

Advantages

ORIGINALITY – Like a distinct individual, yours is a relationship that follows its own star, is true to itself. This will also be evidenced in the actual circumstances of your being together having a unique and unprecedented quality. You can inspire other couples to be this way too.

BROAD-MINDEDNESS – There is an openness and spirit of experimentation about your being together. You not only tolerate odd people and things, but may even venture into unusual and ground-breaking ways of discovering your sexual and emotional parameters.

FRIENDLINESS – This part of this Theme is highly valuable in a relationship because it is actually more reliable than passion or what passes for love. This is because Friendliness is non-possessive and non-judgemental, and you apply it to each other and those involved with you.

Weaknesses

INDIFFERENCE – Because your relationship inclines toward cool impartiality rather than fiery passion, there is an incipient tendency to 'de-emotionalize' your interaction with each other so that gradually an absence of motivation or meaning can beset you as a couple.

ALIENATION – Your relationship stands in danger of cutting itself off from the society or culture in which it lives. When your qualities of Unusualness and Originality are not recognized or positively expressed, you tacitly or actively turn yourselves as a couple into misfits or outcasts.

REBELLIOUSNESS – This is really the Shadow of your specialness and uniqueness as a couple. Rather than living and expressing your sense of freedom and Originality, you attract the 'petty tyrant', that is, someone who suppresses you, causing one or both of you merely to rebel or be bolshy. Then again, rebellion may be your only way to free yourselves.

P I S C E S

Leanings

IMAGINATION – Your relationship, whether you are aware of it or not, is largely determined by what you imagine it to be. As you both feed one another's imaginations, you progressively make it into what you hope or fear it to be. If you have a positive vision of it, then that is what it shall develop into. If vague, negative or unconscious – then chaos could descend.

SACRIFICE – There is something about the energy of your relationship that attracts, sooner or later, a need to make a Sacrifice. This could occur willingly or unwillingly, and be accompanied by great suffering. When this is consciously surrendered to, a great sense of peace or bliss envelopes you.

SENSITIVITY – This, arguably the definitive human quality, runs through your relationship like a river through a valley, bringing it life and beauty. Great care must therefore be taken that it never dries up through denying, suppressing or over-rationalizing it. Being ever-sensitive to one another, without being hysterical, will elevate and refine your relationship.

Advantages

COMPASSION – This, the ultimate product of Sensitivity, is something you extend not just to each other but to all around and about you. You may even be actively involved in some charitable organization. Somehow the relationship may cause one or both of you to pursue some 'good work'.

ARTISTRY – It is quite possible that one or both of you is involved in some form of artistic expression. If not, the way that you relate and live could be an art-form in itself. One way or another, the creative flow and process is, or should be, central to your relationship, for this vitalizes it.

PSYCHISM – You are highly attuned to each other's thoughts and feelings. At its most evolved, this can find you living and acting as one. The experiencing together of psychic phenomena – be it discarnate entities, significant coincidences or whatever – should and could give your relationship guidance and spiritual meaning.

Weaknesses

FANTASY – Owing to the influence of so much Sensitivity and Imagination, there is a danger of your relationship pretending to be something that it is not. This may even include believing you have a viable relationship when you don't. The only remedy is to determine the truth of what your being together actually is – and gracefully accept it.

EVASIVENESS – Again, owing to your innate Sensitivity, there can be a reluctance to take a good look at what is actually happening in your relationship. Trust that by following and being true to that river of feelings, you will both find a way through to the 'ocean' of peace and healing.

ADDICTION – If one or both of you is any way addicted to a substance or a distracted or compulsive way of being, or to the other or another person, then Fantasy and Evasiveness have done their worst. Here, the best, and maybe only way, is one of seeking spiritual help and redemption.

THE RELATIONSHIP
DYNAMIC

THE RELATIONSHIP DYNAMIC

The last thing we look at in this book is probably the last thing that would occur to most people in any kind of relationship – that is that their relationship is a force in itself. So we will not go into too much depth or detail here, but treat this area of relating as a kind of postscript.

A dynamic is a pattern of growth and change; so a Relationship Dynamic is the package of energy within your relationship that forces it to go somewhere and do something – or not, if one or both of you are resisting it. First, however, you must become acquainted with …

THE THREE LAWS OF RELATIONSHIP DYNAMICS

1 A HIGHLY SIGNIFICANT POINT THAT SEEMS TO EMERGE AS YOU STUDY DYNAMICS IS THAT THEY BEST BE A BLEND OF DIFFICULTY AND EASE FOR A RELATIONSHIP TO HAPPEN OR EXIST AT ALL.

2 This flies in the face of romantic notions of love and relating. Because of this, it may come as a surprise that when you find a Dynamic that is full of mental, emotional and physical harmony, it is abortive, disappointing or doesn't take off at all. Or it only works in a limited way – like an affair.

3 Conversely, ones that are full of only challenge and confrontation *can* happen, and indeed persist over the years – hard though this may be. This will be because some difficult and important lessons are having to be learnt by both people.

Now go back to the SIGN-TO-SIGN PROFILES that begin on page 289, and see how each Sign in your Relationship Theme interacts with the others – for the combined effect of this one- to four-way Interaction *is* the DYNAMIC, and the areas you shaded in on the CHARTWHEEL give it a graphic, gear-like image. In fact, you will find that the image reflects the nature of the dynamic; when it has a symmetry or some kind of balance or inner composition, then so does that relation. Now imagine that the court characters that are used in the Profiles to illustrate each Sign/Theme's influence (Monarchs, Jesters, Priests, etc) comprise your Dynamic, and you will get an idea of the forces in play. It may seem to you that one person or the other matches these characters, but really it is the relationship's embodiment of the blending of the two of you. As such, it has a life and personality of its own, as I have stated above. In other words, the relationship itself influences both of you in its own way, in addition to the direct personal influences that you each have upon one another.

As well as using the SIGN-TO-SIGN PROFILES in order to understand the Dynamic, also use THE 12 LAWS OR THEMES OF THE ZODIAC with regard to the relevant Signs that you have read about previously so that you may gain a fuller idea of what part each Sign plays within the Dynamic, and how they assist or challenge one another.

In the case of Jack and Jill's Relationship Dynamic, GEMini–SCOrpio–PISces, we first go to page 292, which is headed THE SIGN OF GEMINI INTERACTS WITH. We see that Gemini interacting with Scorpio is done ABRASIVELY because it is THE JESTER AND THE SPY – and the text tells us about that. Gemini interacting with Pisces is done ADAPTIVELY as it is THE JESTER AND THE MESSIAH – and again the text elaborates on why.

So far it looks as if their Relationship Dynamic is pretty demanding – but then the third and final part of the Dynamic is Scorpio interacting with Pisces. This we find on page 297 headed THE SIGN OF SCORPIO INTERACTS WITH, and we see that with Pisces it is INTUITIVELY – THE SPY AND THE MESSIAH. This third Interaction of the Dynamic is obviously vital to the relationship for it points to what is a powerful subtlety of the relationship that is able to make and accept the compromises, and overcome the challenges represented by the other two Interactions.

Applying THE 12 LAWS to Jack and Jill's Relationship Dynamic we notice that again the Pisces and Scorpio themes blend well because they are both emotionally oriented, but that the Gemini Theme of Lightness, Humour and Frivolity would conflict with the Scorpio theme of Intensity, Genuineness and Secretiveness, and be made even more slippery by the Pisces theme of Imagination, Psychism and Evasiveness! On the other hand, the Gemini theme could be used to Lighten up the Intensity of Scorpio and communicate the Imagination of Pisces.

Because it is important that you appreciate that a Relationship Dynamic is, by definition, a set of Interactions rather than just a single quality or attribute, let's look at a few more examples.

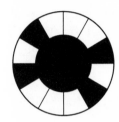

First let's look at a four-way Theme and Dynamic, for they have even more permutations. Take a couple who have the Dynamic ARIes–LEO–LIBra–AQUarius. This is as though there were an Aries LEADER in there, trying to get both people to go ahead and break new ground, but the CONFRONTATIONAL Interaction with the Libra DIPLOMAT inhibits this with all kinds of social and emotional considerations. (NOTE how it is best to look at the OPPOSING and CHALLENGING interactions first if they are there, because the Dynamic is, remember, based on them.) But the Aries Leader is interacting HEROICALLY with the Leo MONARCH, so, in spite of the Diplomat, much will be achieved when these two team up. But then we see that the Leo Monarch is interacting REACTIVELY with the Aquarian REFORMIST, which creates a tension between somewhat self-centredly getting on with it (Leo) and the low-profile and democratic nature of Aquarius. The plot thickens even further when we see that the Aquarian REFORMIST interacts THOUGHTFULLY with the Libran DIPLOMAT, for they handle difficult situations philosophically together, if they have to – and they do! So all in all, this Dynamic is self-sustaining as long as it avoids stalemates. Also, we see that in addition there is that PROGRESSIVE Interaction between Aries and Aquarius, and the GRACIOUS one between Leo and Libra – further cementing the concerted quality of such a dynamic. Confrontation is benefited from because of a sense of heroism and graciousness. A reactionary element in the relationship is channelled thoughtfully towards something more progressive.

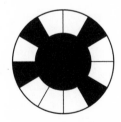

Another example, this time an unusual relationship between a man and a woman who are just friends, with complications caused by the man having feelings that are not reciprocated by the woman. Their Dynamic is similar to the previous example, except for one fatal difference: it is ARIes–LEO–*SCOrpio*–AQUarius. The Leo/Aquarius REACTION and possible impasse is sorted out by the Arian honesty and straightforwardness in a way which compares with the above dynamic, but the whole dynamic is vastly compromised by that Scorpio part. The SPY is paranoid and full of veiled feelings, intrigues and subterfuges which foil the saving grace of the Aries part – and DANGEROUSLY blocks the Playfulness of Leo and FRUSTRATES the Openness of Aquarius. In practical terms, unless the Arian Directness is boldly given almost too much rein, the Scorpionic undercurrent could bring the relationship to grief. Looked at positively, the Scorpio part represents deep and dark emotions that can and should be brought consciously to the surface.

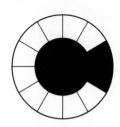

Finally, let us look at the Dynamic of a parent-child relationship. This time we have a two-way Dynamic of VIRgo–LIBra, which is described as PEDANTIC. It is also often the case that a child will emphasize or oppose the nature of a parent. In this example, the mother and child are both strongly Virgoan individuals, with distinct Libran overtones – so this is a case of emphasis rather than opposition. In other words, the Virgo ADVISOR is hard put to satisfy the Libra DIPLOMAT's need for grace and harmony. Conversely, the Diplomat has to strive to cater to the Advisor's exacting demands. All in all, such a Dynamic pushes to the limits the acceptability of such extreme Virgo–Libra values and displays, calling for a more relaxed and trusting attitude towards life in general, yet at the same time testing the abilities of these Signs to measure up to their own criteria of Perfection and Harmony.

Relationship Dynamics are not easy to understand. This is firstly because we are not culturally given any awareness of their existence, and secondly because the astrology of them is somewhat complex. But gaining even a small insight into the power of them will help you make far more out a relationship – simply because you have acknowledged its own existence and made an inroad into the actual nature of it.

THE MORE YOU USE ASTROLOGY AND THIS BOOK TO INVESTIGATE RELATIONSHIPS, THE MORE YOU WILL BE ABLE TO UNDERSTAND AND APPRECIATE RELATIONSHIP DYNAMICS.

APPENDIX

GLOSSARY

THIS INCLUDES ASTROLOGICAL AND PSYCHOLOGICAL TERMS AND CONCEPTS,
AS WELL AS SOME ORIGINAL ONES THAT APPLY ESPECIALLY TO THE CONTEXT OF THIS BOOK.
CROSS-REFERENCES APPEAR IN *CAPITAL ITALICS*. REFERRING TO MY PREVIOUS BOOK *DO IT YOURSELF ASTROLOGY* (ELEMENT BOOKS) WILL INFORM YOU OF MORE ASTROLOGICAL AND PSYCHOLOGICAL CONCEPTS.

AGE OF AQUARIUS – The *ASTROLOGICAL AGE* we are just entering which is concerned with an awakening to the truth, especially regarding humanity and human nature, and which is necessarily disruptive.

ASCENDANT – The Eastern point on the Horizon of a *BIRTHCHART* where the *PLANETS* and *SIGNS* are seen to rise. The sign on the Ascendant at any given time is called the *RISING SIGN*.

ASPECTS – Certain angular relationships between one *PLANET* or point (like the *ASCENDANT*) and another that indicate the tension and flow within an individual, or between one person and another (*CROSS-ASPECTS*).

ASTROLOGICAL AGE – A 2160-year period of time which is governed by a certain *SIGN*, the quality of which determines the character of this evolutionary era.

BIRTHCHART – A map of where the *PLANETS, SIGNS* and *HOUSES* are positioned at the time of birth.

CHALLENGING – One of the *CROSS-ASPECTS* or *PLANET-TO-PLANET INTERACTIONS* where one *PLANET* is at right angles to another across the *CHARTWHEEL*. Technically called a *SQUARE*.

CHARTWHEEL – A version of the *BIRTHCHART* that has been specially adapted for use in Relationship Astrology.

CLOSE ONES – *CROSS-ASPECTS* that are within three degrees of exact and are deemed to form the central core of the chemistry between two people. Provided in the Cross-Aspects obtained from me.

COMPENSATION – What astrologer Liz Greene called the commonest human psychological trait, it describes how we respond to characteristics in ourselves or *OTHER* by going to the opposite extreme. For example, one is told one talks too much, so one then says nothing at all, or says 'I'll never say anything again!' – or being attracted to/involved with an Other who has the absolute opposite of one or more of one's own traits.

CONJOINING – One of the *CROSS-ASPECTS* or *PLANET-TO-PLANET INTERACTIONS* where one *PLANET* is in more or less the same position on the *CHARTWHEEL*. Also called a Conjunction.

CROSS-ASPECTS – *ASPECTS* between the *PLANETS* in one person's *BIRTHCHART* and the Planets in another's. The actual meanings of Cross-Aspects are given in the *PLANET-TO-PLANET PROFILES*. Also a list of the *CROSS-ASPECTS* between a pair of people, ordered from me or someone else.

CUPID ASPECTS – *CROSS-ASPECTS* that initially and irresistibly attract one person to another. Denoted by the symbol ➤➤ in the *PLANET-TO-PLANET PROFILES*.

CUPID'S TRICKS – How *CUPID ASPECTS* get one involved with another for reasons entirely different to what you first thought.

DAYLIGHT SAVING TIME (DST) – A *TIME STANDARD* that many countries adopt during the summer months to give more daylight at the end of the day by putting the clocks forward an hour. This always needs to be taken into consideration for the accurate calculation of a *BIRTHCHART*. Because this can vary from year to year, from place to place, this can be quite disconcerting and has been called the 'astrologer's bane' (at least, before we used modern computer software).

DESCENDANT – The Western point on the Horizon of a *BIRTHCHART* where the *PLANETS* and *SIGNS* are seen to set. The sign on the Descendant at any given time is called the *SETTING SIGN* and is always exactly opposite the *ASCENDANT* or *RISING SIGN*.

DISPOSITION – A chain of command created by the *PLANET-SIGN POSITIONS* and the *RULING PLANETS* that affects the influence of those Planet-Sign Positions.

DIVINE ELLIPSE – An *ESOTERIC* concept concerning the gulf of misunderstandings and the battle of the sexes that afflict humanity.

DOUBLE WHAMMIES – When you get the same *CROSS-ASPECT* going both ways, for example, when *PERSON A's* Venus is *CONJOINING PERSON B's* Mars, and vice versa (ie PERSON B's Venus is conjoining PERSON A's Mars), this is a Double Whammy. This makes the meaning of this Cross-Aspect especially significant and powerful in that relationship.

DYNAMICS – The Dynamics of Relationship are forces or the interaction of *THEMES* within a particular relationship (arrived at through assessing the combined *PLANET-SIGN POSITIONS* of both *BIRTHCHARTS*) which are like a third entity that has a will of its own, affecting both people involved.

EASY ASPECTS – *CROSS-ASPECTS* which bring harmony and compatibility to a relationship. Denoted by the symbol ▲ in the *PLANET-TO-PLANET PROFILES*.

EGO – In the context of this book I have mainly used the word Ego to mean that vain, childish, over-sensitive and self-important part of the *SELF* that is inherently inept at relating in a healthy or objective way. As such, it is a false or incomplete sense of *SELF*. However, it is important to state that Ego, in the sense of having a strong sense of the *SELF's* significance, is essential, especially when growing up in the world or when up against someone with an Ego of the negative variety here described.

ELEMENTS – The four basic qualities of life – see *Do It Yourself Astrology* (Element Books).

ESOTERIC – Teachings and information about life that are reserved for people who have reached a certain level of awareness. The word literally means 'inside the temple'. The esoteric word is that more people than ever have now reached that 'certain level of awareness'.

FINAL FOCUS – The means by which this book enables you to determine precisely what a relationship between two people is really all about, and what it means for each individual involved.

FINAL FOCUS CHART – Chart used to work out the *FINAL FOCUS*.

FOCAL PLANETS – The *PLANETS* which comprise the *FINAL FOCUS*, which includes the Most Focal Planet, the Most Challenged/ing Planet, and the Most Supported/ing Planet.

HARD ASPECTS – *CROSS-ASPECTS* which bring conflict, challenge and confrontation to a relationship. Denoted by the symbol ■ in the *PLANET-TO-PLANET PROFILES*.

HARD AND EASY ASPECTS – *CROSS-ASPECTS* which are a combination of both *HARD* and *EASY ASPECTS*. Denoted by the symbol ▲■ in the *PLANET-TO-PLANET PROFILES*.

HEART ASPECTS – *CROSS-ASPECTS* which bring love and sweet accord to a relationship. Denoted by the symbol ♥ in the *PLANET-TO-PLANET PROFILES*.

HOUSES – Twelve segments of space which represent the various experiences of life. Each House begins with a House Cusp. The First House Cusp is the *ASCENDANT* and the Seventh House Cusp is the *DESCENDANT*. Because Houses requires complex calculation and tables, they are not comprehensively included in this book.

INTERACTION – The chemistry between one person and another as determined by the effects of the *PLANETS* and *SIGNS* of each of the two *BIRTHCHARTS* upon each other.

INTERCHANGEABLE – A *CROSS-ASPECT* where the effect of *PERSON A's PLANET* is Interchangeable with the effect of *PERSON B's* Planet. Denoted by the symbol ⟺ in the *PLANET-TO-PLANET PROFILES*.

KEY CONTACTS – *CROSS-ASPECTS* which are highly significant to a relationship. Denoted by the symbol ⚷ in the *PLANET-TO-PLANET PROFILES*. The existence of one or more of a certain type of

Key Contact has been regarded by some astrologers as essential for a relationship to have any real significance at all. These particular types of Key Contact are *CONJOINING* or *OPPOSING* Cross-Aspects between the *ASCENDANT* in one person's *BIRTHCHART* and a *PLANET* in another's.

KEYWORDS – Specially chosen words that focus the meaning of a particular *PLANET, SIGN* or *ASPECT*.

KEYWORD CORNER – A section of this book which gives a selection of *KEYWORDS* and tells you how to use them so that you can customize and get more out of your *PLANET-TO-PLANET PROFILES*.

LAWS OF THE ZODIAC – The dynamics of the *SIGNS* seen as a set of precepts for relationship *THEMES*.

LOWER MIDHEAVEN – The important, and lowest, point on a *BIRTHCHART*, which is the cusp of the Fourth *HOUSE*, the House of background, home life, etc. It is not used in this book because, although it does have some indirect bearing on relationships, it needs another complex means of calculation. It is abbreviated as the IC.

MIDHEAVEN – The important, and highest, point on a *BIRTHCHART*, which is the cusp of the Tenth *HOUSE*, the House of profession, status, etc. It is not used in this book because, although it does have some indirect bearing on relationships, it needs another complex means of calculation. It is situated exactly opposite the *LOWER MIDHEAVEN* and is abbreviated as the MC.

MIRROR – The Mirror is the means by which you can identify and take back your *PROJECTIONS*, thereby sorting out relationship difficulties at source, and empowering yourself at the same time. Its origins go way back to the Mayan and North American Indian cultures. The Mirror that is a sacred symbol in the Mayan Sacred Calendar actually means 'Sword of Truth'.

MODES – The three basic Modes of life, astrologically speaking. See *Do It Yourself Astrology* (Element Books).

MUTUALITY – The fact that *CROSS-ASPECTS* go both ways. For example, if *PERSON A* had their Mercury *SUPPORTING PERSON B's* Neptune, then Person B's Neptune would also be Supporting Person A's Mercury.

OPPOSING – One of the *CROSS-ASPECTS* or *PLANET-TO-PLANET INTERACTIONS* where one *PLANET* is directly opposite another across the *CHARTWHEEL*. Also called an Opposition.

OTHER – The term used in this book to describe anyone (or anything) *other* than your *SELF*. This word has the advantage of therefore referring to whoever or whatever you want it to refer to, rather than being limited to 'partner', 'spouse', 'girlfriend', 'boyfriend', 'friend', 'colleague', 'mother', 'father', 'child', 'the world', 'the public', 'someone you've just met', 'someone you fancy', 'a stranger', 'other people generally', 'a pet', 'your car', etc.

PERSON A AND PERSON B – The general terms used to identify the two people involved in a relationship. *(Jack and Jill in the ongoing example used throughout the book.)*

PERSONAL UNCONSCIOUS – *See THE UNCONSCIOUS.*

PLANETS – The Sun, Moon and all the Planets of our Solar System which symbolize, along with the SIGNS, the various energies or influences operating in a *BIRTHCHART*. The term often includes the ASCENDANT as well. The *PLANETS* themselves are divided into the *inner* Planets: the Sun, the Moon, Mercury, Venus, Mars, Jupiter and Saturn, which represent personal or cultural influences – and the *outer* Planets: Uranus, Neptune and Pluto, which represent transformational or evolutionary influences.

PLANETS OF LOVE – The part of this book which describes the meanings of all the *PLANETS* (including the Earth, that is the *ASCENDANT* and *DESCENDANT*).

PLANET-SIGN POSITIONS – The *SIGN* positions for all the *PLANETS* for any particular time, day and year.

PLANET-SIGN PROFILES – The actual meaning, in terms of personal traits, what you attract and manner of relating, of all the *INNER PLANETS* through all the *SIGNS* of the Zodiac.

PLANET-SIGN PROFILES INDEX – The index for looking up the page numbers for the relevant *PLANET-SIGN PROFILES*.

PLANET-SIGN TABLES – Easy-to-use tables for determining the *PLANET-SIGN POSITIONS* for any date between 1 January 1900 to 31 December 2012.

PLANET-TO-PLANET INTERACTION – *INTERACTION* that is determined by *PLANETS*.

PLANET-TO-PLANET PROFILES – The actual interpretations of the meaning of every individual *CROSS-ASPECT* or *PLANET-TO-PLANET INTERACTION*.

POINT SCORES – The numerical values or 'weights' given to each *PLANET* for determining *SIGN-TO-SIGN INTERACTION* and *THEMES*. These are given at the foot of the *SIGN-TO-SIGN INTERACTION (AND RELATIONSHIP THEME) CHART*.

PROJECTED SELF – The part of the *SELF* that is the *PROJECTION* you make upon *OTHER* – so much so that *OTHER* actually becomes a part of the *SELF*.

PROJECTION – The psychological phenomenon of seeing in *OTHER* what is actually or also a trait of one's own. This is done because that trait is regarded as either too bad or too good to belong to oneself. This is an unconscious function – until of course you become aware of it. This book is, to quite a degree, aimed at making you aware of it, simply because most relationship difficulties stem from Projection.

QUALITY OF ASPECT – The classification given to any *TYPE OF (CROSS-)ASPECT*, namely *HARD, EASY, CUPID, HEART, TEARDROP, KEY CONTACT*.

REUNION – The esoteric teaching that we will all become one again, one day – and that this process has begun in earnest with the dawning of the *AGE OF AQUARIUS*.

RISING SIGN – The *SIGN* rising in the East, on the *ASCENDANT*, at any given time. This symbolizes your image, the manner in which you present yourself to the world around you.

RISING SIGN PROFILES – The actual meanings, in terms of personal traits, what you attract, and manner of relating, of all the *RISING SIGNS* and *SETTING SIGNS*.

RISING SIGN TABLES – Easy-to-use tables for determining the *RISING SIGN*.

RULING PLANETS – How certain PLANETS correspond to certain SIGNS in terms of quality and character, and are therefore said to rule them. Also the Ruling Planet that rules your chart/personality as a whole.

SELF – The totality of your being, conscious and unconscious. Also used as a term which distinguishes it from its opposite, *OTHER*. Paradoxically though, *OTHER* can be seen as a part of the Self (*see PROJECTED SELF*).

SETTING RULER – The *RULING PLANET* of your *SETTING SIGN*.

SETTING SIGN – The *SIGN* setting in the West at any given time. This symbolizes the kind of *OTHER* you attract or are attracted to, and also, to a degree, your *PROJECTED SELF* and *SHADOW*.

SHADOW – The part of your *SELF* that you usually do not like to admit to having because it goes against the image you have of yourself. The crucial point here is that your Shadow also contains, in crude form, the part that you need in order to make yourself more complete and effective, both in terms of self-expression and of relating to *OTHER*. For instance, a common Shadow is power, because having and using power means that you may have to be someone whom others do not like or approve of, and that power is something that only the government, state, church, boss, *OTHER*, etc, has (over you, and it's bad) – in other words, you are disempowered. The Shadow, in the unconscious state, always takes the form of a *PROJECTION*.

SIGNS – The 12 segments of space comprising a gigantic band encircling the Earth. This is called the Zodiac of Signs (not to be confused with the Constellations of Signs which are the actual fixed stars with the same zodiacal names) and can be seen as the 12 seasons of the Sun. From our Earthly point of view, the influences of the *PLANETS* vary as they appear to orbit us, each one travelling through the Signs at their own individual rate. One scientific explanation for the influence of the Signs is that the

Solar Wind varies in quality, depending where it is in relation to the Sun. As we orbit the Sun and go through those various areas of space which are the Signs of the Zodiac, the Solar Wind will have different influences according to the time of year. The fact is that the Solar Wind is known to directly affect DNA, the basic building block of all life, and so therefore would also affect human personality.

SIGN-TO-SIGN INTERACTION – *INTERACTION* that is determined by *SIGNS*.

SIGN-TO-SIGN INTERACTION (AND RELATIONSHIP THEME) CHART – The chart you use to determine *SIGN-TO-SIGN INTERACTION* and the *THEMES* of a particular relationship.

SIGN-TO-SIGN PROFILES – The actual interpretations of the meaning of every individual *SIGN-TO-SIGN INTERACTION*.

SQUARE – The technical term for the *CHALLENGING ASPECT*.

STAR PLAYERS – The *FOCAL PLANETS* for an individual.

SUPPORTING – One of the *CROSS-ASPECTS* or *PLANET-TO-PLANET INTERACTIONS* where one *PLANET* is more or less 120 degrees apart from another across the *CHARTWHEEL*. Technically called the *TRINE*.

TEARDROP ASPECTS – *CROSS-ASPECTS* which bring acute conflict and emotional suffering to a relationship. Denoted by the symbol ◖ in the *PLANET-TO-PLANET PROFILES*.

THE UNCONSCIOUS – If human beings are seen as pieces in some gigantic cosmic game, then the Unconscious is what is actually playing that game. Your *PERSONAL UNCONSCIOUS* is your particular connection with the Unconscious, and therefore partly determines, along with your conscious will and senses, your Fate. Astrology is a map and mapper of the Unconscious, which is why it is able to predict or provide an insight into what is determining your Fate in terms of *PLANETS* and *SIGNS*. Relationships are particularly favoured by the Unconscious as a means of influencing us because they *MIRROR* and intensify an individual's Personal Unconscious. They also reflect, or maybe perpetuate the illusion, that the cosmic game is between one side and another. One can also view the Unconscious as a great sea upon which the little boat of your personality (a mixture of consciousness and unconsciousness) is floating or travelling, as it negotiates and navigates the currents (planetary influences).

THEMES – Relationship Themes are the *SIGN* qualities which comprise the *LAWS* and *DYNAMICS* of a particular relationship, as determined by combining the *PLANET-SIGN POSITIONS* of both people, with the aid of the *SIGN-TO-SIGN INTERACTION (AND RELATIONSHIP THEME) CHART*.

TIME STANDARD – The time 'convention' that is used for any particular place on Earth which is a certain number of hours or minutes ahead of (when East) or behind (when West) Greenwich Mean Time. GMT is the 'base line' for all Time Standards because it is placed on the Zero Meridian of the globe.

TRINE – The technical term for the *SUPPORTING ASPECT*.

TYPE OF ASPECT – One of the four major *ASPECTS* or *CROSS-ASPECTS* used in this book, namely *CONJOINING*, *CHALLENGING*, *SUPPORTING* and *OPPOSING*.

UNCONSCIOUS – Describing anything that lies in *THE UNCONSCIOUS*.

UNKNOWN BIRTH TIME – If your birth time is not known it means that you will not be able to determine your *RISING SIGN, SETTING SIGN,* or any other *HOUSE* cusps or positions. It may also give you a choice of two Moon Signs on days when the Moon changes *SIGNS*. However, by reading the interpretations for all Rising/Setting Signs and possibly two Moon Signs, you could come to some idea of birth time by working it backwards – or getting an astrologer to do it for you.

VALE OF SORROW – A more poetic term for the *DIVINE ELLIPSE*.

VENOUS BLOOD SYNDROME – A metaphor whereby it can be seen that it is healthy to expose, express or bring to the surface stale, repressed or unregenerate parts of the personality – parts which may be wholly or partly *UNCONSCIOUS*.

BLANK CHARTS

(be sure to photocopy!)

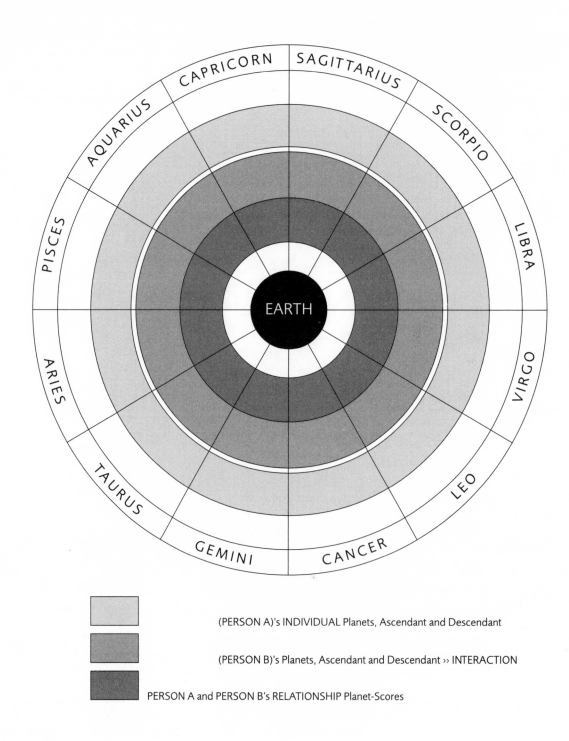

	(PERSON A)'s INDIVIDUAL Planets, Ascendant and Descendant
	(PERSON B)'s Planets, Ascendant and Descendant ›› INTERACTION
	PERSON A and PERSON B's RELATIONSHIP Planet-Scores

The Chartwheel

SIGN-TO-SIGN INTERACTION (AND RELATIONSHIP THEME) CHART

PERSON A: **PERSON B:**

S I G N	PERSON A's PLANETS (incl. ASC and DES)	+	PERSON B's PLANETS (incl. ASC and DES)	+	THEME Double the lower or equal point scores
ARIes					
TAUrus					
GEMini					
CANcer					
LEO					
VIRgo					
LIBra					
SCOrpio					
SAGittarius					
CAPricorn					
AQUarius					
PISces					

POINT SCORES: SUN, MOOn, ASCendant, DEScendant=4 each. MERcury, VENus, MARs=3 each. JUPiter, SATurn=2 each. URAnus, NEPtune, PLUto=1 each.

CROSS-ASPECTS – TO ORDER FROM LYN

<u>*SEND*</u> (postage is included) **UK** £5.00 cash, PO or UK cheque; **USA** US$10 cash or US$ cheque; **CANADA** CAN$15 cash or CAN$ cheque; **AUSTRALIA** A$15 cash only; **NEW ZEALAND** NZ$15 cash or NZ$ cheque; **EIRE** I£10 cash only; **INDIA** £5 Sterling PO only; **SOUTH AFRICA** 60 rand or £5 PO; **ABOVE AND ALL OTHER COUNTRIES** £5 Sterling cash or UK cheque.

<u>*TO:*</u> **LYN BIRKBECK, P2P, c/o ELEMENT BOOKS LTD, BELL STREET, SHAFTESBURY, DORSET SP7 8BP, UK** with the following information, and please write clearly in BLOCK CAPITALS. NOTE: The CROSS-ASPECTS will be given first from Person A's perspective, and then from Person B's, in order to facilitate extracting further information for the FINAL FOCUS.

✄ ....

Please send me the CROSS-ASPECTS between:

PERSON A

FULL NAME:	TIME OF BIRTH:*
DATE OF BIRTH:	PLACE OF BIRTH (if very small, give nearest town):

and

PERSON B

FULL NAME:	TIME OF BIRTH:*
DATE OF BIRTH:	PLACE OF BIRTH (if very small, give nearest town):

*give time on the clock, and if it was at midnight make it clear whether at the start or end of that day

NAME AND ADDRESS TO SEND TO:	
POST/ZIP CODE:	DAYTIME PHONE No.

I enclose £5.00 or equivalent *(see above)*

	SIGNED:

✄ ....

Please send me the CROSS-ASPECTS between:

PERSON A

FULL NAME:	TIME OF BIRTH:*
DATE OF BIRTH:	PLACE OF BIRTH (if very small, give nearest town):

and

PERSON B

FULL NAME:	TIME OF BIRTH:*
DATE OF BIRTH:	PLACE OF BIRTH (if very small, give nearest town):

*give time on the clock, and if it was at midnight make it clear whether at the start or end of that day

NAME AND ADDRESS TO SEND TO:	
POST/ZIP CODE:	DAYTIME PHONE No.

I enclose £5.00 or equivalent *(see above)*

	SIGNED:

PLANET-TO-PLANET INTERACTION – *FINAL FOCUS CHART FOR PERSON A*

PERSON A's [____] PLANETS and ASCENDANT	EASY	HARD	CLOSE AND EASY	CLOSE AND HARD	TOTAL EASY	TOTAL HARD	TOTAL EASY PLUS TOTAL HARD	TOTAL EASY MINUS TOTAL HARD
SUN								
MOOn								
MERcury								
VENus								
MARs								
JUPiter								
SATurn								
URAnus								
NEPtune								
PLUto								
ASCendant								
TOTALS								

PERSON A'S FOCAL PLANETS or   *Star Players*

A's MOST FOCAL PLANET(S) (Highest Hard plus Easy)	
A's MOST CHALLENGED/ING PLANET(S) (Highest Hard)	
A's MOST SUPPORTED/ING PLANET(S) (Highest Easy)	

? EVEN SCORES ? – If you get three or more even scores for any of the Focal Planets, favour the Sun, Moon, Ascendant, Ruling Planet or Setting Ruler as that Focal Planet. If after doing this you still have more than one particular Focal Planet, then use them both/all.

NOW interpret this vital information by looking up what each of these Planets mean, firstly for the individual, and secondly for the relationship and for both people. In the first case we can initially look up the relevant Planets in the FOCAL PLANET READY-RECKONER on page 478, or in PLANETS OF LOVE on page 11. Then, to gain an even more personal insight we can look at each Focal Planets' Sign Position in the PLANET-SIGN PROFILES from page 147 (but you will not find Uranus, Neptune or Pluto there). In the second case, by reviewing the PLANET-TO-PLANET PROFILES (from page 317) that involve these Planets we can see what Interaction or chemistry between the two people carries the most weight for Person A. Note that with equal scores there would be two or more Planets for each category.

NOTE: IF THERE SHOULD BE ANY INTERACTIONS BETWEEN PERSON A's AND PERSON B's FOCAL PLANETS, THEN THESE WOULD BE HIGHLY SIGNIFICANT.

PLANET-TO-PLANET INTERACTION – *FINAL FOCUS CHART FOR PERSON B*

PERSON B's ⬚ PLANETS and ASCENDANT	EASY	HARD	CLOSE AND EASY	CLOSE AND HARD	TOTAL EASY	TOTAL HARD	TOTAL EASY PLUS TOTAL HARD	TOTAL EASY MINUS TOTAL HARD
SUN								
MOOn								
MERcury								
VENus								
MARs								
JUPiter								
SATurn								
URAnus								
NEPtune								
PLUto								
ASCendant								
TOTALS								

PERSON B'S FOCAL PLANETS or *Star Players*

B's MOST FOCAL PLANET(S) (Highest Hard plus Easy)	
B's MOST CHALLENGED/ING PLANET(S) (Highest Hard)	
B's MOST SUPPORTED/ING PLANET(S) (Highest Easy)	

? EVEN SCORES ? – If you get three or more even scores for any of the Focal Planets, favour the Sun, Moon, Ascendant, Ruling Planet or Setting Ruler as that Focal Planet. If after doing this you still have more than one particular Focal Planet, then use them both/all.

NOW interpret this vital information by looking up what each of these Planets mean, firstly for the individual, and secondly for the relationship and for both people. In the first case we can initially look up the relevant Planets in the FOCAL PLANET READY-RECKONER on page 478, or in PLANETS OF LOVE on page 11. Then, to gain an even more personal insight we can look at each Focal Planets' Sign Position in the PLANET-SIGN PROFILES from page 147 (but you will not find Uranus, Neptune or Pluto there). In the second case, by reviewing the PLANET-TO-PLANET PROFILES (from page 317) that involve these Planets we can see what Interaction or chemistry between the two people carries the most weight for Person A. Note that with equal scores there would be two or more Planets for each category.

NOTE: IF THERE SHOULD BE ANY INTERACTIONS BETWEEN PERSON A's AND PERSON B's FOCAL PLANETS, THEN THESE WOULD BE HIGHLY SIGNIFICANT.

THE MIRROR CHART

REFLECTION What Other appears as (to me) that concerns, confuses, obsesses or irritates	PROJECTION What I, upon reflection, see that I am 'sending' to Other and so getting back as the Reflection, or realize is true, fair or a simple solution

RESOURCES

If you wish to take your interest in astrology further, I recommend that you contact:

AUSTRALIA
Federation of Australian Astrologers
Lynda Hill
20 Harley Road
Avalon NSW 2107
Tel: +61-2-918-9539

CANADA
Association Canadiennes des Astrologues Francophones
Denise Chrzanwska
CP 1715
Succ 'B'
Montreal HSB 3LB
Tel: +1-514-831-4153
Fax: +1-514-521-1502

Astrolinguistics Institute
Anne Black
2182 Cubbon Drive
Victoria
British Columbia V8R 1R5
Tel: +1-604-370-1874
Fax: +1-604-370-1891
e-mail: ablack@islandnet.com

NEW ZEALAND
Astrological Society of New Zealand
Joy Dowler
5266 Wellesley Street
Auckland 1003

Astrological Foundation Inc.
Hamish Saunders
41 New North Road
Eden Terrace
Auckland 1003
Tel/Fax: +64-9-373-5304

SOUTH AFRICA
Astrological Society of South Africa
Cynthia Thorburn
PO BOX 2968
Rivonia 2128
Tel +27-11-864-1436

UNITED KINGDOM
The Astrological Association
396 Caledonian Road
London N1 1DN
+171-700-6479

USA
American Federation of Astrologers
Robert Cooper
PO Box 22040
Tempe
AZ 85285-2040
Tel: +602-838-1751
Fax: +602-838-8293

Association for Astrological Networking
8306 Wilshire Blvd
Suite 537
Beverley Hills
CA 90211

If you require your CROSS-ASPECTS, use the Order Form a few pages back.

Any other queries or correspondence for Lyn Birkbeck to be sent (enclose SAE if from UK) to:

Lyn Birkbeck (RA)
c/o Element Books Ltd, The Old School House, The Courtyard,
Bell Street, SHAFTESBURY, Dorset SP7 8BP, England